The Jefferson Papers
of the
University of Virginia

The letters of a person, especially of one whose business has been chiefly transacted by letters, form the only full and genuine journal of his life; and few can let them go out of their own hands while they live. A life written after these hoards become opened to investigation must supercede any previous one.

Thomas Jefferson to Robert Walsh, 5 April 1823.

The Jefferson Papers
of the
University of Virginia

PART I

A CALENDAR COMPILED BY CONSTANCE E. THURLOW AND
FRANCIS L. BERKELEY, JR., OF MANUSCRIPTS ACQUIRED
THROUGH 1950

PART II

A SUPPLEMENTARY CALENDAR COMPILED BY JOHN CASTEEN AND
ANNE FREUDENBERG OF MANUSCRIPTS ACQUIRED
1950–1970

WITH A COMBINED INDEX

Published for
The University of Virginia Library

———

The University Press of Virginia
Charlottesville

THE UNIVERSITY PRESS OF VIRGINIA
Copyright © 1973 by the Rector and Visitors
of the University of Virginia

Published 1973

Part I appeared in 1950
and is reproduced by photo-offset.

ISBN: 0–8139–0414–5
Library of Congress Catalog Card Number: 72–91896
Printed in the United States of America

Contents

Key to Published Works Cited by Symbols

ADAMS — Herbert Baxter Adams, *Thomas Jefferson and the University of Virginia*, Washington, 1888.

B OF R — *Bulletin of the Bureau of Rolls and Library of the Department of State*, No. 6 (Calendar of letters from Jefferson) and No. 8 (Calendar of letters to Jefferson), published by the 57th Congress, Washington, 1894–1896.

BETTS, *GARDEN BOOK* — Edwin Morris Betts, ed., *Thomas Jefferson's Garden Book*, Philadelphia, 1944.

BETTS, *FARM BOOK* — Edwin Morris Betts, ed., *Thomas Jefferson's Farm Book*, Princeton, 1953.

BETTS and BEAR — Edwin Morris Betts and James Adam Bear, Jr., *The Family Letters of Thomas Jefferson*, Columbia, Mo., 1966.

BOYD — Julian P. Boyd, ed., *The Papers of Thomas Jefferson*, Princeton, 1950–

As of 1973 and the republication of Part I of the Calendar, eighteen volumes (through Jan. 24, 1791) of Julian P. Boyd's *The Papers of Thomas Jefferson* have appeared. These printed texts are not cited in Part I because it was printed from the 1950 edition by offset.

BULLOCK — Helen D. Bullock, *My Head and My Heart, a Little History of Thomas Jefferson and Maria Cosway*, New York, 1945.

CABELL — Nathaniel Francis Cabell, *Early History of the University of Virginia, as Contained in the Letters of Thomas Jefferson and Joseph C. Cabell . . .*, Richmond, 1856.

DAB — *Dictionary of American Biography*, New York, 1928–1937.

DORSEY — John M. Dorsey, *The Jefferson-Dunglison Letters*, Charlottesville, 1960.

FORD — Paul Leicester Ford, *The Writings of Thomas Jefferson*, New York, 1892–1899.

FORD-BIXBY — Worthington C. Ford, ed., *Thomas Jefferson Correspondence, Printed from the Originals in the Collections of William K. Bixby . . .*, Boston, 1916.

JENKINS
Charles F. Jenkins, *Jefferson's Germantown Letters . . .*, Philadelphia, 1906.

L & B
Andrew A. Lipscomb and Albert E. Bergh, eds., *The Writings of Thomas Jefferson . . .*, Washington, 1903–1904.

MD. HIST. MAG.
Maryland Historical Magazine, Baltimore, 1906– .

MHS COLL
Massachusetts Historical Society Collections, Cambridge, 1792– .

MAYO
Bernard Mayo, *Thomas Jefferson and his unknown brother Randolph . . .*, Charlottesville, 1942.

NICHOLS
Frederick Doveton Nichols, *Thomas Jefferson's Architectural Drawings*, Boston, 1961 [third edition].

OFFICIAL LETTERS
Official Letters of the Governors of the State of Virginia, Vol. II, Richmond, 1926.

RANDALL
Henry S. Randall, *The Life of Thomas Jefferson*, New York, 1858.

SNR
Sarah Nicholas Randolph, *The Domestic Life of Thomas Jefferson*, New York, 1871.

TJR
Thomas Jefferson Randolph, ed., *Memoir, Correspondence, and Miscellanies, from the Papers of Thomas Jefferson*, Charlottesville, 1829.

TUCKER
George Tucker, *The Life of Thomas Jefferson*, London, 1837.

VA. MAG. HIST.
The Virginia Magazine of History and Biography . . ., Virginia Historical Society, Richmond, 1893– .

W(1) and W(2)
William and Mary College Quarterly Historical Magazine, first and second series, Williamsburg, 1892–1919, and 1921–1943.

WASHINGTON
H. A. Washington, ed., *The Writings of Thomas Jefferson . . .*, Washington, 1853–1855.

WOODS
Edgar Woods, *Albemarle County in Virginia*, Bridgewater, Va., 1932.

Key to Other Symbols

AD	Autograph document
ADS	Autograph document, signed
AL	Autograph letter
ALS	Autograph letter, signed
AMS	Autograph manuscript
AN	Autograph note
ANS	Autograph note, signed
CSmH	Henry E. Huntington Library, San Marino, California
D	Document
DLC	Library of Congress, Washington, D.C.
DS	Document, signed
L	Letter
LS	Letter, signed
MdHi	Maryland Historical Society, Baltimore, Maryland
MHi	Massachusetts Historical Society, Boston, Massachusetts
MoHi	Missouri Historical Society, St. Louis, Missouri
MS	Manuscript
MSS	Manuscripts
NcD	Duke University, Durham, North Carolina
NjP	Princeton University, Princeton, New Jersey
NNP	Pierpont Morgan Library, New York City
NS	Note, signed
PPHi	Historical Society of Pennsylvania, Philadelphia, Pennsylvania
VHi	Virginia Historical Society, Richmond, Virginia
VWW	College of William and Mary, Williamsburg, Virginia

PART I

A Calendar of Manuscripts
Acquired through 1950

Editor's note: Asterisks refer the reader to Errata, page 497.

INTRODUCTION

IN preparing this calendar of the University's Jefferson manuscripts, Mrs. Thurlow and I have freely made use of many people's work. Daily reference has been made to our Jefferson Checklist, a chronological card-file of some sixty thousand of Jefferson's manuscripts, and letters to and from him, now known to be extant in public and private libraries, in manuscript and in print. This Checklist was begun by John Cook Wyllie more than fifteen years ago, and has been expanded by many hands, particularly by a former staff member, Mrs. Helen D. Bullock. The Checklist is now being duplicated, expanded, and improved by Julian P. Boyd and the editors associated with him in the Princeton University publication project. Copies of the Checklist in its final form may later be made available at the Library of Congress as well as at the University of Virginia, and I venture to express here the hope that it may be printed for the use of students elsewhere. For it will contain much of value which must doubtless be omitted from publication in the *Papers*.

The typescript calendar of our Jefferson Papers, prepared by Mrs. Bullock in 1941, has been very useful here and at the Library of Congress, and particularly helpful in preparing the present calendar for publication. Printing costs and other factors have made necessary a more condensed form of entry in the present calendar. Since the preparation of Mrs. Bullock's calendar, which included photostats in our collections, our holdings of original manuscripts have nearly doubled. Photographic copies (more than 50,000 now being available in our reading room) have here been excluded except in a few instances of manuscripts in private hands and county court houses, which in a number of cases are the only known texts.

Researchers are warned that the length of an entry does not necessarily indicate our judgment of the importance of the item. We have attempted to include all names of persons and places. As a result, entries for certain legal documents are disproportionately long. We have tried to mention all major subjects discussed in each letter, but the reader who wants full details will be obliged to consult the original manuscript or order a photographic copy.

Each entry contains two paragraphs, the second of which is a condensed summary of the text of the manuscript, followed by a bracketed number for purposes of indexing. The first paragraph contains all "bibliographical data" about the manuscript and all other texts of it which are known to us from the data recorded and filed in our Jefferson Checklist. Following the date in a typical entry is the name of the writer, the place from which he writes, the name of the recipient, and the place to which the letter is directed. Then follows a symbol (see list below) which tells whether the manuscript is signed and whether or not it is written in the hand of the signer, with a statement of the number of pages in the manuscript. If another text of the manuscript is known to us, this information is then given as explicit as possible. In some cases we can only say "another manuscript in DLC" (Library of Congress; see list of abbreviations below); often, however, we are able to state that the other manuscript is the recipient's copy, a polygraph copy, a letter-press copy, a file draft, or an extract or copy by another hand, either contemporary or later.

The final statement in each heading concerns known printed versions of the manuscript as recorded in our Jefferson Checklist. Many of the published texts are inaccurate or incomplete, as we indicate when known. All frequently cited publications are referred to by symbols (as listed in the table below), and punctuation is simplified for convenience in printing.

Special attention is invited to the case of "printing" which we indicate by the following oft-recurring expression: "Printed: B of R VI 372 (MS. in DLC)". This means that an abstract of *another text* of our manuscript (the other text usually being Jefferson's file copy) is to be found in the "Calendar of Letters from Jefferson", in the *Bulletin of the Bureau of Rolls and Library of the Department of State,* No. 6, Washington, 1894-1896, page 372, and that the manuscript so calendared is now in the Library of Congress. Virtually none of the Jefferson manuscripts in the Bureau of Rolls (all of which are now in the Library of Congress) were *printed in full* in the "Calendar" which appeared in volumes 6 (letters from Jefferson) and 8 (letters to Jefferson) of the *Bulletin.* It is hoped that no student will be misled by this type-saving method of entry. All other printings indicated are assumed to be complete unless otherwise stated.

Docketings, and other brief endorsements on letters are indicated simply by the word "endorsed" unless they appear to require special comment. "Endorsed by T. J." indicates that such an endorsement is in Jefferson's autograph. Spelling has normally been corrected outside of direct quotations, and we have never hesitated to expand "Mr. Randolph" to "Thomas Mann Randolph" when the identity is certain. Square brackets have, therefore, been rather sparingly used to supply missing names, facts, and dates in the headings which could be supplied with reasonable certainty. In summarizing the texts of letters and other items, the main object has been brevity rather than any attempt to reproduce the original language. Parentheses have been freely used in the summaries for the provision of explanatory comment.

All manuscripts not otherwise designated are in our general collection of Jefferson Papers. Others are listed in the heading of the entry as being in the McGregor Library (which is the most important of the special libraries constituting the Division of Rare Books and Manuscripts) or in any of our various collections of manuscripts which happen to contain papers of Jefferson, such as the following: the Berkeley Manuscripts, the Cabell Papers, the Carr-Cary Papers, the Cocke Papers, the Edgehill-Randolph Papers, and the Page-Walker Papers. Some of these special collections are not owned by the University, but are on deposit for safekeeping and historical reference. Other privately owned individual manuscripts on deposit are listed with the owner's name. Photographic copies can be provided in most cases, but a few are subject to restrictions stipulated by the owner.

It will be noted that we have included certain manuscripts of Jefferson's father which have some relevancy to the career of the son. In addition to a few special photostats already mentioned, a number of older transcripts of Jefferson's papers have also been included. The most important of these are the copies and extracts made by Martha Jefferson, Randolph and her daughters and by Nicholas P. Trist during the decade following Jefferson's death. These and other copies have been identified in the headings. In a considerable number of cases, however, chiefly of copies which appear to have been made by or for members of the family, we have had to fall back on the expression, "nineteenth century copy".

Omitted from this calendar are a number of papers in this library which were once in Jefferson's possession, or closely associated with him, but which were not composed, drafted, or endorsed by him. Such, for example, are the groups of legal papers, 1740-1759, which Robert Carter Nicholas turned over to him as attorney in 1771; a correspondence of the Associates of the late Doctor Bray, 1757-1773, concerning the Negro school at Williamsburg, sponsored by the Society for the Propagation of the Gospel; correspondence of Robley Dunglison with Jefferson's biographer, Henry S. Randall; and great numbers of letters by Jefferson's executor and by members of his immediate family which are to be found in the University archives and such of our collections as the Carr-Cary Papers, the Edgehill-Randolph Papers, and the Francis Walker Gilmer Manuscripts. Typical of other materials omitted are an eighteen-page manuscript pedigree of the Jefferson family, compiled by Paul Berghaus, and kept with our Jefferson Papers for the convenience of researchers; memorial addresses following Jefferson's death in 1826; and letters of condolence to his family. A revealing item of Jeffersoniana, omitted here, but shortly to be published by the library as a separate volume, is the manuscript of the recollections of Isaac Jefferson, a household servant at Monticello, as dictated in old age to the historian, Charles Campbell.

One conspicuous omission which we hope will not be attributed to ingratitude has been that of the names of donors. From 1825 to 1949 we have received from Jefferson himself, from every generation of his descendants, and from a host of admirers of Jefferson and friends of the University, gifts of Jeffersoniana or funds for their acquisition. The addition of donors' names to already elaborate calendar headings, particularly in the group entries covering numerous separate gifts, might, we feel, confuse the student. In our published annual reports we attempt at least to record from year to year the names of the benefactors on whom we rely so heavily for the growth of the collections.

To the Research Council of the Richmond Area University Center we are indebted for the grant-in-aid which has made possible this publication. The courtesy and patience of the Administrator and of the members of the Council in connection with our unavoidable delays in printing are particularly appreciated.

If this work had a dedication, it would be to Harry Clemons, who brought the Manuscript Division into being, whose faith has a way of moving mountains, and to whom all of the daily tasks of our staff are truly dedicated by our admiration and affection.

University of Virginia

1 October 1949   F. L. B.

(preliminary draft?) of this boundary line, with an almost identical legend but in a different hand, is owned by the U. S. Coast and Geodetic Survey, Washington, D. C. (E. G. Swem, *Maps Relating to Virginia . . .* p. 58).   [6]

1751 Mar. 30 *et seq.* POPLAR FOREST SURVEYS AND PLATS. 3 items (one a T. J. AD and one endorsed by T. J.) McGregor Library.

Two plats of same date for 11,777 and 1,790 acres of land on branches of Black Water, and on Tomahawk and Rock Castle creeks, respectively, of Black Water, a tributary of the Fluvanna (James) River in Albemarle (later Bedford) County, Va. Both surveyed for Thomas Ballow, William Dawson, Joshua Fry, Peter Jefferson, Charles Lynch, and Thomas Turpin. Indicate lands owned by Blankenship, Chetwood, Samuel Cobbs, Jr., Nicholas Davies, John Dawson, Francis Galloway, James, Hardwick, Benjamin Johnson, Thomas Meriwether, Rev. Mr. Stith, Richard Tullos, G. Walton, and John Wayles. First plat attested by Daniel Smith, Albemarle County Surveyor; second amended by T. J. with notes on sequence of titles.

Undated plat by T. J. of Poplar Forest tract shows boundaries, roads, existing and proposed buildings; floor plan of house on verso, rooms designated in Anglo-Saxon.   [7]

1751 June 6. PLAT OF THE TOWN OF BEVERLEY, Henrico County, surveyed by Peter Jefferson. D. 1 p. Endorsed by T. J. Edgehill-Randolph Papers.

Indicates lots belonging to T. J.   [8]

1751 Nov. 25. PETER JEFFERSON to the CLERK OF THE COURT OF GOOCHLAND COUNTY. ALS. 1 p.

Consent for the marriage of Daniel Scott to Anna Randolph, daughter of Isham Randolph. Peter Jefferson was her nearest male relative. Witnessed by Richard Amis, Elizabeth LeVillian, and John Woodson.   [9]

1757 July 13. PETER JEFFERSON'S WILL. Typescript copy, 7 pp. Original in Albemarle County Court House. Probated 13 Oct. 1757, John Nicholas, Clerk.

Provides for division of his home property and farms in Albemarle County (on the Rivanna and Hardware rivers), land on the Mississippi River, slaves, and money among his wife, Jane; his daughters, Jane, Elizabeth, Martha, and Lucy; and his sons, Thomas and Randolph. Thomas is to receive a portion of the slaves, his choice of the lands, and the residue of the estate. Executors named are Peter Randolph, Thomas Turpin, John Nicholas, Dr. Thomas Walker, and John Harvie.   [10]

1758 Apr. 13. PETER JEFFERSON'S INVENTORY. Typescript copy. 12 pp. Original in Albemarle County Court House. Recorded by John Nicholas, Clerk.

Lists books, furniture, personal effects, plantation equipment, slaves, and livestock, valued at more than £2400, on Peter Jefferson's property lying on the Rivanna River and its branches; appraisal made by Charles Lewis, Jr., John Henderson, and Thomas Smith.   [11]

1759 May 12. FRANCIS FAUQUIER. LAND GRANT TO FRANCIS CALLAWAY. DS. 1 p. Endorsed. McGregor Library.

Royal grant, issued by the Lieutenant Governor of Virginia, of 380 acres in

1732-1825. LAND TITLE PAPERS. 25 items. Edgehill-Randolph Papers.

Deeds, plats, patents, and other legal papers concerning lands in Albemarle, Fluvanna, Goochland, Henrico, and Powhatan Counties, several of which establish the chain of title to Edgehill. Deeds for land owned by the Randolph Family (Richard Randolph, Jr., Thomas Mann Randolph, Thomas Jefferson Randolph), the Eppes Family (Francis Eppes, Richard Eppes, and William Eppes), and the Nicholas Family (John Nicholas, George Nicholas, and Robert Carter Nicholas.) Jefferson items are more fully calendared under dates 6 June 1751 and 29 March 1762. [1]

1735 Sept. 16. PETER JEFFERSON to WILLIAM RANDOLPH, JR. D. 1 p. Typescript. Original in Goochland County Court House. Copy attested by Margaret K. Miller, Clerk.

Power of attorney, acknowledged before Henry Wood, Clerk. [2]

1736 May 18. PETER JEFFERSON to WILLIAM RANDOLPH, JR. D. 2 pp. Typescript copy of original in Goochland County Court House, attested by Margaret K. Miller, Clerk.

Deed for 3 acres of land in Goochland County. This deed was executed on the same day as one from Randolph to Jefferson, the payment in the latter being "Henry Wetherburn's biggest bowl of Arrack punch". [3]

1739 Oct. 3 PETER JEFFERSON'S MARRIAGE BOND. DS. 1 p. Photostat. Original in Goochland County Court House.

Marriage bond for £50 signed by Peter Jefferson and countersigned by Arthur Hopkins, void if there be lawful cause to obstruct Jefferson's marriage with Jane Randolph. [4]

1745 May 23. PETER JEFFERSON. SURVEY. ADS. 3 pp. Endorsed.

Map of 2470 acres of land in Goochland County, surveyed by Peter Jefferson for the Rev. William Stith. [5]

1749. PETER JEFFERSON. MAP OF VIRGINIA-NORTH CAROLINA BOUNDARY. ADS. Measurements: 6' 2½" x 11"; scale of miles 1": 5 mi.

Original map of the Virginia-North Carolina boundary to show the extension of William Byrd's survey of 1728 from Peter's Creek to Steep Rock Creek, as surveyed in 1749 by Joshua Fry and Peter Jefferson.

The legend, and presumably the entire drawing, is in the hand of Peter Jefferson. No other original map of the line of 1749 is known, but a "tracing"

Albemarle County (later Bedford) on the branches of Tomahawk Creek and Blackwater, adjoining the Rev. Mr. Stith's land. [12]

1760 Sept. 11. ESTATE OF PETER JEFFERSON in account with JOHN HARVIE, Executor. Typescript copy. 7 pp. Original in Albemarle County Court House. Recorded by John Nicholas, Clerk.

John Harvie's accounts for family and planation expenses totaling £1489, account for tobacco crops, and an account with the Surveyor's Office of Albemarle County totaling £351. [13]

[ca. 1760?]. T. J. GERMAN SONGS. AD. 2 pp. Printed: Randall I 25 (partial).

Words and translation of "Ohne Lieb und ohne Wein" and "Falle doch auf Doris Augenlieder", music by Mr. Fleischer of Brunswick. A painfully literal translation, probably a student exercise at James Maury's or William and Mary. [14]

1762 Mar. 29. THOMAS LEWIS. SURVEY OF THOMAS BRYAN MARTIN'S LAND. D. 1 p. Endorsed by T. J. Edgehill-Randolph Papers.

Survey of the Manor of Greenway Court, a tract of 8840 acres in Frederick County granted to Martin by Thomas Lord Fairfax, made in connection with the lawsuit of Thomas B. Martin vs. Peter Wolf, defendant in an ejection suit. (Perhaps used after 1762 in an early case, not listed in T. J.'s Case Book.) [15]

1762 Dec. 25. T. J., Fairfield, to JOHN PAGE, [Rosewell]. ALS. 4 pp. Photostat. Original privately owned. Printed: Tucker I 24; L & B IV 1-6; Ford I 341-316. I 341-346.

Lists his misfortunes: his pocketbook, silk garters and new minuets eaten by rats; his watch and Rebecca Burwell's picture ruined by water. Her image prevents his getting to old Coke. Asks news of deaths, courtships, marriages. Greetings to Alice Corbin, Rebecca Burwell, and "Sukey" Potter. Is now near Shadwell. [16]

1763 Mar. 30. FRANCIS FAUQUIER. LAND GRANT TO T. J. DS. 1 p. Photostat. Original at Monticello.

Royal grant, issued by the Lieutenant Governor of Virginia, of 950 acres in Albemarle County in the fork of the Rivanna River. Mentions Cunningham's tract, John Webb, Richard Perkins. [17]

1764 Mar. 27. FRANCIS CALLAWAY. SURVEY FOR JOHN ROBERTSON. D. 1 p. Copy attested by J. Steptoe, Clerk of Bedford County. Endorsed by T. J. McGregor Library.

Copy of surveyor's courses in deed for 380-acre tract in Albemarle (later Bedford) County. [18]

1769 Apr. 19. T. J., Williamsburg, to [ALEXANDER WHITE]. ALS. 1 p. Endorsed.

Advice, in a case shared with John Blair, on land surveys, patents, and claims. Mentions Mr. Benson, Mr. Green, Mr. Harrison, Mr. Sevear (Sevier?), Mr. and Mrs. James Wood, and Colonel Wood. [19]

1769 Nov. INDENTURE BETWEEN BENJAMIN HARRISON, Charles City County, and ISAAC COLES, Halifax County. DS (T. J. AD). 2 pp. Endorsed. Recorded 5 May 1770 by Ben Waller, Clerk. Witnessed by Robert Carter Nicholas, Edmund Pendleton, and James Mercer. Bruce Family Manuscripts.

Deed, Harrison to Coles, conveying 1020 acres of land on the Dan River (the Berry Hill tract), formerly the property of William Byrd and sold to Richard Bland 16 April 1751. Drafted by Jefferson. [20]

1770 [Apr.] 14. MARY LEWIS, Albemarle County, to T. J. ALS. 1 p. Endorsed by T. J. Edgehill-Randolph Papers.

Letter from agent's wife regarding conditions at Bedford County (Poplar Forest) and Shadwell. Mr. Lewis' illness, measles among the slaves at Bedford, prices of wheat and tobacco. Mentions Mr. Clark and Mr. Meriwether. Sends ham, venison, and bacon. [21]

1771 Aug. 3. T. J., Monticello, to ROBERT SHIPWITH [SKIPWITH]. ALS. 3 pp. Printed: L & B IV 237-240; Ford I 396-399; B of R VI 429 (MS. in DLC).

Advice on choice of books; defense of fiction. Sends greetings to Wintipock. [22]

1771 Dec. 6. T. J., Monticello, to [THOMAS BURKE]. ALS. 1 p. McGregor Library.

Request for further information on the case of Matthew MacVee vs. James Wilson and William Orange (case 508). Refers to drawing of bill in case of Henry Brown vs. William Tucker *et al.*, for money due Brown for slave hired by Tucker, for which Tucker's vessel was attached (case 548). [23]

1772 Sept. 3. T. J., Monticello, to [WILLIAM CABELL]. ALS. 1 p. Cabell Family Manuscripts.

Incloses copy of Dickie's bill against Cabell. Requests Cabell's statement regarding the boundary dispute. [24]

1773 Oct. 27. John Doe, Lessee of WILLIAM FARRAR, vs. THOMAS MANN RANDOLPH, SR. D. 4 pp. Endorsed by T. J. McGregor Library.

Verdict of the special jury in a dispute regarding land on the James River. Signed by Ben. Waller, Clerk of the General Court. References to John Farrar, Thomas Farrar, John Sutton Farrar, Thomas Lygon, and Mr. Turpin. [25]

[1775 Oct. 10.] T. J., Philadelphia, to FRANCIS EPPES. AL. 1 p. Printed: L & B IV 245-247; Ford I 485-487; Randall III 568-569.

News from England of British strategy. References to Sir Jeffery Amherst, Guy Carleton, Lord Dunmore, General Gage, Commodore Molyneux Shuldham, and William Tryon. [26]

1775 Nov. 21. T. J., Philadelphia, to [FRANCIS EPPES]. ALS. 1 p. Photostat. Original owned by Mrs. Irene Hallam. Printed: Randall III 570; L & B IV 251; Ford I 490-491.

Hopes Arnold is in possession of Quebec, since intercepted letters indicate a large British army will soon be sent. Has written to Patty to keep at a distance from the alarms of Lord Dunmore. [27]

[1776-1778]. T. J. INDEX TO ACCOUNT BOOK. AD. 16 pp. Deposited by
C. S. Hutter, Jr.

List of names appearing in Jefferson's account books for the years [1776-1778].
The account book itself (original in the Massachusetts Historical Society, micro-
film in the Alderman Library) was written on blank pages of the Virginia
Almanac for 1776-1778. [28]

1776-1779. BILLS PREPARED FOR THE REVISION OF THE LAWS OF
VIRGINIA. MS. D. 205 pp. Index: AD by T. J. 4 pp.

A committee of five, consisting of Jefferson, Thomas Ludwell Lee, George
Mason, Edmund Pendleton, and George Wythe, were appointed by the Virginia
Convention of 1776 to draft a revision of the Virginia laws—the genesis of Jefferson's epochal work for religious and intellectual freedom. Lee died, Mason
resigned, and the work was divided among the other three. Jefferson prepared
the sections on common law and statutes to 4 James I; Wythe prepared the
British statutes from that date to 1776; Pendleton worked on laws passed in
Virginia. The index is in Jefferson's hand, the ordinances in several other hands,
probably of clerks of the committee. Jefferson indexes 126 bills, 66 of which are
included in this draft. The bills were printed by Dixon and Holt, Richmond,
1784. [29]

1777 Nov. 21. T. J., Williamsburg. OPINION ON THE WILL OF CARTER
BURWELL. D. 2 pp. Copy by Francis L. Berkeley, 1925. Berkeley Manuscripts.

Legal opinion on a much disputed will. Bequests of Neck of Land, Bull Run,
and Shenandoah to Nathaniel Burwell, Carter B. Fontaine, Mr. Griffin, and
daughter. [30]

1778 Sept. 21-Nov. 2. HENRY and ANNE SKIPWITH, Cumberland County, Va.,
to T. J. DS (T. J. AD). 2 pp. Recorded by Valentine Wood, Clerk of Goochland
County, 15 February 1779. Photostat. Endorsed. Original owned by Miss Amanda
Pitts.

Deed for Elk Hill, a tract of land in Goochland County. Certification by
Beverley Randolph and John Woodson that Anne Skipwith freely relinquishes
her right of dower in this tract, November 1778. Witnessed by Henry Cox,
Thomas Young, Henry Tuggle. [31]

1779 June 12. T. J., Richmond, to CAPT. [CHARLES] DE KLAUMAN. ADS.
1 p.

Authorization to inspect and state the quantity and condition of all military
stores in Virginia. [32]

1779 Nov. 8. T. J., Richmond, to BENJAMIN HARRISON, Speaker of the
House of Delegates. ALS. 1 p. Endorsed. Enclosure: 2 Nov. 1779, Alexander
Dick. ADS. 2 pp. Endorsed.

Transmitting a petition from Alexander Dick to the Governor and Council
of Virginia requesting a commission as major in the Marines. [33]

1779-1782. T. J. INDEX TO ACCOUNT BOOK. AD. 20 pp. McGregor Library.
Alphabetical index to his Account Book for 1779-1782, which is owned by the
Library of Congress.   [34]

[1780] Jan. [Incorrectly dated 1779]. T. J., Williamsburg, to GEORGE ROGERS
CLARK. AL. 1 p. File draft. Photostat. Endorsed by T. J. Original owned by
Miss Ellen Bagby.
Summer operations in the West. Clark has a choice between an expedition
against Detroit or a war against the Indians. The Shawnees, Mingoes, Munnies,
and Wyandottes should be exterminated or moved beyond the lakes or the
Illinois River. Major Slaughter's men will complete Clark's battalion. Pro-
posed chain of posts on the Ohio at the mouth of the Fishinger, the Little
Kanawha, Great Kanawha, Great Salt Cut, Scioto, and Kentucky, which will connect Pittsburgh and the falls of the Ohio, or possibly the mouth of the Ohio.
                                                                       [35]

1780 Jan. 2. T. J., Williamsburg, to RICHARD HENRY LEE. ALS. 1 p. Endorsed. Lee Papers.
Forwards letter from France. Asks instructions regarding sending of *Parliamentary Register* containing correspondence of Sir William Howe and John
Burgoyne. Pensacola and St. Augustine taken by the Spaniards. Enemy attack
not imminent.   [36]

1780 Jan. 31. JOHN JAMES, JR. MARRIAGE BOND. DS. 1 p. In the hand of
C. H. Moseley, Jr.
John James, Jr., and Adam Lovitt's bond to Thomas Jefferson, Chief Magistrate
of the Commonwealth of Virginia, void if due cause is found why James cannot
marry Seabrook Woodhouse.   [37]

1780 July 20. T. J. to THOMAS WALKER. DS. 1 p. Endorsed. Page-Walker
Papers.
Grant for 400 acres of land in Louisa and Albemarle counties; land forfeited
by Nicholas Oliver on failure to pay quitrents on said land.   [38]

1780 July 27. T. J., Richmond, to SAMUEL HUNTINGTON. L. 3 pp. Extract.
Endorsed. Lee Papers. Another MS. in DLC. Printed: Ford II 322-328; *Official
Letters* II 142-145.
Regarding requisitions of money, supplies, and troops from Virginia by the
Continental Congress.   [39]

1780 July 28. T. J., Richmond, to THEODORICK BLAND, Prince George.
LS. 1 p. Endorsed. Deposited by Mrs. Kirkland Ruffin.
Requesting certificates for the number of arms carried by his regiment at the
time it entered the Continental service. Certificate needed for settling of accounts
between Virginia and Congress.   [40]

1780 Sept. 1. T. J. to MARTIN WETSELL. DS. 1 p. Photostat. Original owned
by Mrs. Alfred R. Berkeley, Jr.
Patent for 1773 acres in Augusta County.   [41]

1780 Oct. 2. T. J. to WILLIAM LATANÉ. DS. 1 p. Seal.

Commission, appointing Latané a lieutenant in the Essex County militia.
[42]

[1780 Dec.]. T. J., [Richmond], to [GEN. JOHN P. G. MUHLENBERG?]. L. 2 pp. Extract in a Virginia Militia Order Book.

Transmitting his official thanks to the militia and their officers. [43]

[ca. 1780]. T. J. MEMORANDUM ON PAPER MONEY. AD. 1 p.

Concerning taxes necessary for the support of paper currency issues (in Virginia?) for the years 1778-1784. [44]

1781 Apr. 16. T. J., Richmond, to RICHARD HENRY LEE, Westmoreland County, Va. ALS. 2 pp. Endorsed. Lee Papers. Printed: L & B XIX 340-341; Official Letters II 478.

Stores wanted for the militia of Westmoreland. News of Lord Cornwallis, General Greene, and General Phillips. [45]

1781 May 26. T. J., Charlottesville. COMMISSION to FRANCIS WALKER, of Albemarle County. DS. 1 p. Seal. Page-Walker Papers.

Appointing him ensign in the Virginia militia. [46]

1781 May 29. T. J. COMMISSION to JUSTICES of the Peace. D. 1 p. Copy. Original owned by Mrs. W. S. Morton. Printed: L & B XIX 353-354.

Joint commission of Joseph Moore, Charles Allen, Richard Foster, Joseph Parks, William Wooton, and Richard Winn, as justices of the peace for Prince Edward County. [47]

1781 May 29. T. J., Charlottesville, to [RICHARD HENRY LEE], Westmoreland. LS. 1 p. Lee Papers.

Apprehension of French deserters for the Marquis de Lafayette. [48]

1781 Oct. 5. T. J., Virginia, to [BENJAMIN FRANKLIN, Paris.] ALS. 1 p. Photostat. Original owned by Stuart Jackson.

Introducing Col. James Monroe, who is resuming his studies in Europe. Prospects for capturing Cornwallis, recovering Georgia and South Carolina. Mentions Princeton, N. J., and Charleston, S. C. [49]

[ca. 1781?] T. J. EXTRACTS FROM JOURNALS OF VIRGINIA HOUSE OF BURGESSES, 1651-1652. AD. 6 pp. McGregor Library.

These notes, copied from manuscript journals no longer in existence, begin with the articles of agreement of Governor Sir William Berkeley and his Council with the Commissioners of the Commonwealth of England, 12 March 1651. They end abruptly six pages later, the remainder of the leather-bound volume being blank. It is presumed that they were made in connection with Query XIII (on Virginia's Constitution) of the *Notes on the State of Virginia*. It is possible, however, that the extracts date from 1774; precedents from the Commonwealth period are cited in *A Summary View of the Rights of British America*. [50]

1782 Jan. 21. EDWARD AND SALLY SMITH, Goochland County, to T. J. AD
by T. J. 5 pp. Photostat. Original owned by Miss Amanda Pitts.

Deed for 120 acres of land in Goochland County. Commission, signed by G.
Payne, to John Hopkins, William Holman, and Nathaniel Mason, Justices of the
Peace, to determine whether Sally Smith freely relinquishes her dower rights in
said land, 12 March, and the report by John Hopkins and William Holman, 12
April, 1782. Witnessed by Robert Lewis, Henry Macklim, and Charles Smith.
[51]

* 17[83] Feb. 15. T. J., Baltimore, to JOHN WAYLES EPPES. ALS. 2 pp. Endorsed.
McGregor Library.

Possibility of forming a company with Gov. [Abner] Nash to speculate in
land between the Cherokee and Mississippi Rivers. If Jefferson goes to France,
the responsibility would fall on Mr. Lewis and on Eppes. Determined to keep
clear of anything that might make private interests interfere with public duties.
[52]

1783 May 19, JUDITH AND REUBEN SMITH to T. J. AD by T. J. 2 pp. Photostat. Endorsed by T. J. Original owned by Miss Amanda Pitts.

Deed for 50 acres of land in Goochland County. Witnesses: Charles Kerr, Nancy
Scott Jefferson, Peter Carr. Recorded 19 May 1783 by G. Payne, Clerk of Goochland County.   [53]

* 1783 Dec. 11. T. J., Annapolis, to PETER CARR. ALS. 2 pp. McGregor Library.
Advice concerning his education and conduct. Respect due to Mr. and Mrs.
[James] Maury. Recommends he make the acquaintance of James Madison.
[54]

* 1783 Dec. 22. FRANCIS EPPES, Eppington, to T. J. ALS. 3 pp. Endorsed by
T. J. Edgehill-Randolph Papers.

News of Patsy (Martha) and Polly (Maria) Jefferson and Elizabeth Eppes.
Price of tobacco. Richard Randolph's account with Mr. Wayles' estate. [James]
Maury has removed his school from Orange to Williamsburg. Mentions Peter
Carr and John Wayles Eppes.   [55]

[ca. 1783-1787]. T. J. CIPHER CODES USED FOR SECRET DIPLOMATIC
CORRESPONDENCE. 16 items. 24 pp. Printed and manuscript, 13 partly in
Jefferson's hand or endorsed by him.

Nine codes are included. Most of these are simple substitution ciphers, numerals
being substituted for words or syllables. Two are more complicated; one is
developed from a column arrangement of the Lord's Prayer; another is a dictionary cipher involving the use of a French-English pocket dictionary. One of
the number codes in Jefferson's hand has a note, "frequently throw in numbers
higher than 1545, which meaning nothing will serve to perplex." Some codes are
endorsed with names of users, Robert R. Livingston, J. M. [James Madison?],
Thomas Jefferson, Edmund Randolph, Edmund Pendleton.   [56]

[ca. 1783-1784. JOHN DAVIDSON?], Annapolis, Md. D. 4 pp.
Wine ledger sheet and "list of sundry memorandoms", itemizing the sale of
table cloths and loaf sugar to T. J.   [57]

1783-1794. T. J. in account with THOMAS WALKER. D. 1 p. Page-Walker Papers.
Settlement of T. J.'s bond (to Walker?) by an order on Alexander McDonald of Richmond. [58]

1784 Jan. 18. T. J., Annapolis, to EDMUND PENDLETON, Caroline County, Va. ALS. 3 pp. Photostat. Endorsed by Pendleton. Original owned by Nathaniel Pendleton.
Ratification of French treaty. Difficulties involved in gaining the necessary vote of nine states on important business. Russo-Turkish relations. Possibility of new attack on the U. S. by Great Britain. [59]

1784 Feb. 29. T. J., Annapolis, to EDMUND PENDLETON. ALS. 2 pp. Fragment. Photostat. Original owned by Nathaniel W. Pendleton.
Russo-Turkish relations. Cool reception of John Adams and John Jay in London. [60]

1784 Oct. 13. ELIZABETH EPPES, Eppington, to T. J. ALS. 2 pp. Edgehill-Randolph Papers. Printed: SNR 102n.
Death of Lucy Jefferson and Lucy Eppes, both from whooping cough. Polly Jefferson and Bolling Eppes both ill. Regards to Patsy. [61]

[1784]. T. J. to MARQUIS DE LAFAYETTE. AD. 1 p.
Autograph inscription in presentation copy of Notes on the State of Virginia, Paris, 1784-85. Warns against publication. [62]

[1784]. T. J. to [THOMAS?] BARCLAY. Autograph inscription. 1 p. Photostat. Original owned by Herman H. Diers.
Inscription in a presentation copy of the Notes on Virginia (French edition). Asks that he guard against its publication. [63]

[1784]. T. J., to DR. [RICHARD] PRICE. Autograph inscription. 1 p. Photostat. Original owned by Herman H. Diers.
Inscription in a presentation copy of the Notes on Virginia (French edition). Asks that he guard against its publication. [64]

[1784-1789]. PETER COMPTANT LESJOURGNOT, Paris, to T. J., Paris. D. 1 p. Endorsed by T. J. McGregor Library.
Bill for clothing for Jefferson and his daughters. [65]

1785 Apr. 20. PETER CARR, Williamsburg, to T. J. ALS. 2 pp. Endorsed by T. J. Carr-Cary Papers.
Report on his education with Matthew Maury and his brother Dabney's education with Smith at Prince Edward Academy. References to [Bishop] James Madison and the College of William and Mary. [66]

1785 Aug. 28. T. J., Paris, to JAMES MONROE. ALS. 4 pp. Endorsed. Partly in code. Printed: Ford IV 84-87; L & B V 96-100; Washington I 405-408; TJR I 293-295; B of R VI 328 (MS. in DLC).
The Emperor hurt by German Confederation. Need to reestablish trade with

England. Recommends Mr. Barclay be sent to treat with the Barbary States. Necessity for minister to Portugal. Appointment of William Short as his private secretary. Pleasure with Land Ordinance of 1785. Adoption of the dollar as the U. S. monetary unit. Importance of a favorable reception for Benjamin Franklin in the U. S. Reference to John Adams and Colonel Humphreys.   [67]

1786 Jan. 24. T. J. to M. DE MEUSNIER. D. 5 pp. Extract by N. P. Trist, *ca.* 1830. Printed: Ford IV 138-158; B of R XVIII 3090 and 3162 (MS. in DLC).
Replies to questions propounded by the editor of the Encyclopédie Politique. Degree to which Congress or the state legislatures regulate foreign commerce. Reasons why Rhode Island opposes federal regulation, and possible solutions of the problem. Economic character of Connecticut and Rhode Island. Right of the Union to compel one state to obedience. Coercion by naval force less dangerous. Comparison of American government with European forms.   [68]

1786 Mar. 14, Apr. 1 and 24. ROBERT CANNON, [London], to T. J. D. 3 pp. Endorsed by T. J. Edgehill-Randolph Papers.
Three bills for clothing.   [69]

1786 Apr. 3. P. & T. DOLLOND, London, to T. J. D. 1 p. Endorsed by T. J. Edgehill-Randolph Papers.
Bill for scientific apparatus and mathematics instruments.   [70]

[1786] Apr. 17. H. PORTER, [London] to T. J. D. 1 p. Endorsed by T. J. Edgehill-Randolph Papers.
Bill for repairing ivory chessmen.   [71]

1786 Oct. 23. FRANCIS EPPES, Eppington, to T. J. ALS. 3 pp. Endorsed by T. J. Edgehill-Randolph Papers.
Claims against the John Wayles estate by Farrell & Jones, Mr. Cary, Mrs. Nick, Kippen & Co., and T. J. himself. Regrets Polly was not sent to him. Thanks for gift of anchovies and claret. Mentions Martha Jefferson and Elizabeth Eppes.
            [72]

17[86] Nov. 19. T. J., Paris, to MARIA COSWAY. AL. 1 p. Letterpress copy. McGregor Library. Recipient's copy in NcD. Printed: Bullock 55-56.
Cramp in hand prevents a long letter. He has cleared up her misunderstanding with Madame de Corny. Greetings to her husband.   [73]

1786 Nov. 29. T. J., Paris, to MARIA COSWAY. AL. 2 pp. Letterpress copy. McGregor Library. Recipient's copy in NcD. Printed: Bullock 58-59.
His letters too full of pure affection to go by the public post. Hopes to see her again. Must trust this to the post-office, but will disguise his seal and super-scription.   [74]

1786 Dec. 24. T. J., Paris, to MARIA COSWAY. AL. 2 pp. Letterpress copy. McGregor Library. Recipient's copy in NcD. Printed: Bullock 60-61.
Reason she has not received his letters. Wishes he were with her. Hopes she is coming to Paris. Possibility of her drawing Natural Bridge and the Peaks of Otter. Thanks for a gift of songs she has composed.   [75]

1786 Dec. 30. PETER CARR, Williamsburg, to T. J., Paris. ALS. 3 pp. Endorsed by T. J. Carr-Cary Papers.

Course of study under George Wythe and others. News of his brothers Dabney and Samuel. References to Charles Bellini, Maria Jefferson, and [Bishop] James Madison.   [76]

[ca. 1786?] T. J. GARDEN MEMORANDA. AD. 2 pp. Endorsed by T. J. Edgehill-Randolph Papers. Printed: *Garden Book* 634.

List of vegetables and flowers with proper times for sowing, in French with English translations.   [77]

1787 Mar. 19. JAMES MADISON, New York, to T. J., Paris. L. 2 pp. Extract by N. P. Trist, ca. 1830. Printed: Burnett VIII 560.

Appointment of members to the Constitutional Convention. Growth of monarchist strength. Recommends a federal government with supreme power. Change in the principle of representation.   [78]

1787 Mar. 30. FRANCIS EPPES, Eppington, to T. J., [Paris]. ALS. 2 pp. Endorsed by T. J. Edgehill-Randolph Papers.

Shipment of cones, holly, cedar berries, and myrtle berries. Tobacco at Monticello and Bedford. Colonel Lewis has the whole management of Jefferson's affairs. Polly will go to France with the French consul and his wife. Claret has arrived. Mentions Mr. Beall of Williamsburg and Mr. Bondfield.   [79]

1787 Apr. 7. T. J., Toulon, to MARTHA JEFFERSON, [Paris]. ALS. 2 pp. Letterpress copy. Edgehill-Randolph Papers. Printed: SNR 118-119; Ford IV 375-376.

Instructions regarding her responsibilities for her sister Maria.   [80]

1787 Apr. 18. PETER CARR, Williamsburg, to T. J., Paris. ALS. 3 pp. Endorsed by T. J. Carr-Cary Papers.

Maria Jefferson about to sail to France. Report on his studies at William and Mary under George Wythe; Wythe's religious views. Samuel and Dabney Carr's education. Wishes to "get the polish of Europe". Mentions Martha Jefferson and Matthew Maury.   [81]

1787 July 1. T. J., Paris, to MARIA COSWAY. ALS. 2 pp. Letterpress copy. McGregor Library. Recipient's copy in NcD. Printed: Bullock 68-69.

Description of trip to Italy, mentioning Turin, Milan, Genoa, Nice, Col de Tende, Chateau de Saorgis. Wishes she would come to Paris.   [82]

1787 July 9. MARIA COSWAY, London, to T. J., Paris. ALS. 4 pp. Endorsed by T. J. McGregor Library. Another text in NcD. Partly printed: Bullock 71-72.

He does not deserve a long letter. Discusses his trip through Italy, mentioning Turin, Genoa, Milan. She has finally met Madame de Corny. Letters and a parcel for the Duchess of Kingston.   [83]

1787 July 25. T. J., Paris, to MARTHA CARR. ALS. 2 pp. Photostat. Original owned by Mrs. John White.

Dabney Carr estate unpaid for Bernard Moore's purchase of Dabney Carr's books. Favorable accounts of her sons, Peter, Samuel, and Dabney Carr, received from George Wythe and [Bishop] James Madison. References to Nicholas Lewis, Martha Jefferson, Maria Jefferson, Lucy Carr, and Nancy Carr.   [84]

[1787 Aug. 10]. T. J., Paris, to PETER CARR, Williamsburg. ALS. 2 pp. Fragment. Carr-Cary Papers. Printed: L & B VI 256-262; Ford IV 427-434; TJR II 215-219; Randall I 26 (excerpt); B of R VI 70 (MS. in DLC).

Advice on religion and on travel in Europe.   [85]

1787 Aug. 13. T. J., Paris, to JOHN BLAIR. L. 1 p. Extract by N. P. Trist ca. 1830. Printed: L & B VI 272-273; B of R VI 38 (MS. in DLC).

Need for powerful federal government in foreign affairs.   [86]

1787 Aug. 15. T. J., Paris, to the COUNT DEL VERMI. L. 1 p. Extract by N. P. Trist, ca. 1830. MS. in DLC. Printed: L & B VI 282-284.

Concerning the Constitutional Convention. Predicts federal sovereignty in foreign affairs and in matters relative to all the states, means of enforcement for the national government, separation of powers.   [87]

1787 Oct. 22. T. J. EXTRACT OF A LETTER FROM PROFESSOR[MARC AUGUSTE] PICTET, Geneva, to ——— Wedgewood. AD. 1 p.

Describes education system in use in his academy.   [88]

1787 Oct. 24. JAMES MADISON, New York, to T. J., Paris. L. 19 pp. Extract by N. P. Trist, ca. 1830, Virginia J. Trist, Cornelia J. Randolph, and Martha J. Randolph assisting. Printed: Burnett VIII 662.

Observations on the Constitutional Convention. Federal government to operate on individuals not on the states. Division of power between executive and legislative branches, and between Federal and State governments. Adjustment of interests of large and small states. Sectional interests. Extensive discussion of precedents and questions involved in these matters. Reasons why only three Virginia names are subscribed to the Constitution. Discussion of public opinion of the Constitution, state by state. References to Samuel Chase, Patrick Henry, James Innes, Arthur Lee, Richard Henry Lee, James McClurg, John Marshall, George Mason, James Mercer, William Paca, Mann Page, Edmund Pendleton, George Washington, and George Wythe.   [89]

1787 Dec. 10. PETER CARR, Spring Forest, Va., to T. J., Paris. ALS. 2 pp. Endorsed by T. J. Carr-Cary Papers.

Education at William and Mary interrupted by lack of funds. Need for Spanish dictionary. Requests advice on matters of importance in his life. News of Sam and Dabney Carr. References to Mr. Elder, Martha and Maria Jefferson, [Bishop] James Madison, and George Wythe.   [90]

[ca. 1787 Dec. MARIA COSWAY, Paris, to T. J., Paris.] AL. 2 pp. Endorsed by T. J. McGregor Library. Another text in DLC. Printed: Bullock 80-81.

Dinner invitations for Messrs. d'Hancarville, St. André, Niemscevicz, and Count Btocki. Wishes she had seen more of Jefferson while in Paris.   [91]

1787. T. J. NOTES ON THE STATE OF VIRGINIA . . . London, Printed for John Stockdale, 1787. McGregor Library.

Copy used by Jefferson, containing his manuscript additions, revisions, maps, and plates. Bound into this book are eleven letters of Edward D. Ingraham of Philadelphia and John Spear Smith, 1845-1847, dealing with a proposed publication of the *Notes* from this copy, then owned by Smith. No edition of the *Notes* having appeared between 1847 and 1853, it can be assumed that Smith's work was either not published or was published by J. W. Randolph in 1853 without mention of Smith's editorial work. [92]

1788 Jan. 6. ELIZABETH EPPES, Eppington, to T. J. ALS. 1 p. Edgehill-Randolph Papers.

Thanks for news of Polly Jefferson. Mentions Martha Jefferson, Martha Jefferson Carr, and Anna Jefferson Marks. [93]

[1788] Jan. [14]. T. J., Paris, to MARIA COSWAY, [London]. AL. 1 p. Letterpress copy. McGregor Library. Printed: Bullock 84-85.

Pain of parting. Illness of M. de Corny. Arrival of Mrs. Church. Wishes she had fewer friends and servants so he might have more time alone with her. [94]

[1788 *ca.* Jan. 31]. T. J., Paris, to MARIA COSWAY, [London]. AL. 1 p. Letterpress copy. McGregor Library. Recipient's copy in NcD. Printed: Bullock 86-87.

Has not written because he could find no private conveyance. Choice of a tea vase in which Mrs. Church and Mr. Turnbull have helped. Compliments to Mr. Cosway. [95]

1788 Feb. 2. T. J., Paris, to [JOHN] RUTLEDGE, [JR.], London. ALS. 2 pp. McGregor Library. Printed: Ford V 3-5; L & B VI 417-419; T J R II 288-289; B of R VI 401 (MS. in DLC).

Warren Hastings' trial. Ratification of the Constitution. Lack of religious toleration for Protestants in France. (The printed copies address the letter to William Edward Rutledge; however, Jefferson's "Epistolary Record" refers to the letter as to John Rutledge, Jr.) [96]

1788 Feb. 6. T. J., Paris, to JAMES MADISON. L. 1 p. Extract by N. P. Trist *ca.* 1830. Printed: Ford V 5-6; B of R VI 288 (MS. in DLC).

Hopes for ratification of Constitution with amendment of its defects. [97]

1788 Feb. 12. T. J., Paris, to [C. W. F.] DUMAS. L. 1 p. Extract by N. P. Trist *ca.* 1830. Printed: L & B VI 429-430; B of R VI 132 (MS. in DLC).

Virginia's opposition to ratification of the Constitution will produce beneficial amendments. Bill of Rights. [98]

1788 Mar. 18. PETER CARR, Williamsburg, to T. J., Paris. ALS. 2 pp. Endorsed by T. J. Carr-Cary Papers.

Course of study at William and Mary. Books received from John Paradise, but not from T. J. Mentions George Wythe. [99]

1788 Apr. 24. T. J., Paris, to MARIA COSWAY, London. ALS. 3 pp. Letterpress copy. McGregor Library. Recipient's copy in NcD. Printed: Bullock 90-92.

Reasons he has not written. Prefers the paintings of Van der Werff and Carlo Dolce to Rubens. Trip to Dusseldorff, Heidelberg, and Strasbourg. Mentions Laurence Sterne, Princess Lubomirski, and M. de Simoulin.   [100]

[1788] Apr. 29. MARIA COSWAY, London, to T. J., Paris. ALS. 3 pp. Endorsed by T. J. McGregor Library. Another text in NcD. Printed: Bullock 92-94.

Angry that he does not write more often. Suggests he come to England. Mentions John Trumbull, William Short, Mme. Palivae de Corny, Luigi Marchesi, Richard Cosway.   [101]

1788 May 27. T. J., Paris, to [EDWARD] CARRINGTON. L. 2 pp. Extract by N. P. Trist, ca. 1830. Printed: Ford V 19-22; B of R VI 72 (MS. in DLC); L & B VII 36-39.

The Constitution should be ratified with two amendments: a bill of rights and a law preventing re-election of the president. Confidence in Washington. What shall be done about Rhode Island?   [102]

1788 June 3. T. J., Paris, to [WILLIAM] CARMICHAEL. L. 1 p. Extract by N. P. Trist ca. 1830. Printed: Ford V 22-27; Shepperson, *John Paradise and Lucy Ludwell* 304-305; B of R VI 67 (MS. in DLC).

Massachusetts' ratification of the Constitution. Two amendments needed: bill of rights and expunging the principle of necessary rotation in office. States should ratify first and amend later.   [103]

[1788] June 23. MARIA COSWAY, London, to T. J., Paris. ALS. 1 p. Endorsed by T. J. McGregor Library. Another text in NcD. Printed: Bullock 95.

Writes note to him only because Mr. Trumbull knows a person who is going to see T. J.; charges that T. J. neglects her.   [104]

1788 July 8. T. J., Paris, to JOHN B. CUTTING, London, L. 1 p. Extract by N. P. Trist ca. 1830. Letterpress copy in DLC.

Ratification of the Constitution by Massachusetts, South Carolina. Benjamin Barton has arrived. Mentions Colonel Smith.   [105]

1788 July 13. T. J., Paris, to BARON DE GEISMER. L. 1 p. Extract by N. P. Trist ca. 1830. Printed: B of R VI 175 (letterpress copy in DLC).

Ratification of the Constitution. New York is doubtful and Rhode Island against it.   [106]

1788 July 15. MARIA COSWAY, London, to T. J., Paris. ALS. 1 p. Endorsed by T. J. McGregor Library. Another text in NcD. Printed: Bullock 95-96.

Begging a letter from him. M. St. André has asked for a letter for T. J.   [107]

1788 July 18. T. J., Paris, to EDWARD RUTLEDGE. L. 1 p. Extract by N. P. Trist ca. 1830. Printed: L & B VII 79-82; Ford V 41-42; TJR II 339-340; B of R VI 401 (MS. in DLC).

Congratulations on South Carolina's ratification of the Constitution. A bill of rights is necessary. Regrets abandonment of principle of rotation in office for the president and senators.   [108]

1788 July 27. T. J., Paris, to MARIA COSWAY, London. ALS. 2 pp. Letterpress copy. McGregor Library. Recipient's copy in NcD. Printed: Bullock 96-97.
   Public triumph of her engraving of the "Hours." Request for a design for his visiting cards.   [109]

1788 July 30. T. J., Paris, to MARIA COSWAY, London. ALS. 1 p. Letterpress copy. Endorsed by T. J. McGregor Library. Recipient's copy in NcD. Printed: Bullock 98.
   "Cease to chide me . . . I am incapable of forgetting or neglecting you."
                                                                        [110]

1788 July 30-Sept. 1. T. J., Paris, to the COMTE DE MONTMARIN, C.W.F. DUMAS, and N. VAN STAPHORST. N. P. Trist's extracts of four letters, ca. 1830. Printed: B of R VI 132, 339 (MS. in DLC); L & B XIX 46-47.
   Concerning the ratification of the Constitution by New Hampshire and New York.   [111]

1788 Aug. 6. T. J., Paris, to PETER CARR, Williamsburg. ALS. 1 p. Carr-Cary Papers. Printed: B of R VI 71 (MS. in DLC).
   Advises that he learn Spanish. Advice on learning, health, and virtue. Mentions George Wythe.   [112]

1788 Aug. 9. T. J., Paris, to JAMES MONROE. L. 1 p. Extract by N. P. Trist ca. 1830. Printed: L & B VII 112-113; TJR II 349-350.
   Ratification of the Constitution; the Bill of Rights; abandonment of the principle of rotation in the Senate and presidency.   [113]

1788 Aug. 19. MARIA COSWAY, Down Place, England, to T. J., Paris. AL. 2 pp. Endorsed by T. J. McGregor Library. Another MS. in NcD. Printed: Bullock 100-101.
   Thanks for his compliments for her "Hours". She will work on his visiting card when she can. Jefferson's return to America. Plans trip to Italy. She now has a picture of T. J. Mentions Angelica Church, John Trumbull, Richard Cosway.   [114]

1788 Sept. 26. T. J., Paris, to MARIA COSWAY, London. ALS. 2 pp. Letterpress copy. Endorsed by T. J. McGregor Library Recipient's copy in NcD. Printed: Bullock 102-103.
   Design for his visiting card. Jefferson goes to America; she to Italy. Suggests she go by way of Col de Tende and see the castle of Saorgio. Would prefer her to come to U. S. with Mrs. Church and John Trumbull, to sketch Natural Bridge and Niagara Falls.   [115]

1788 Oct. 22. SPANISH AMBASSADOR at PARIS to T. J., Paris. AL. 1 p. Endorsed by T. J.
   Announcing the death of Charles III of Spain. T. J.'s draft of his condolences on the same sheet.   [116]

1788 Dec. 21. T. J., Paris, to FRANCIS HOPKINSON. L. 1 p. Extract by N. P. Trist *ca.* 1830. Printed: B of R VI 219 (letterpress copy in DLC) ; L & B XIX 48-52.

Ratification of Constitution; Bill of Rights; re-eligibility of the president. [117]

[1788] Dec. 23. MARIA COSWAY, London, to T. J., Paris. ALS. 2 pp. Endorsed by T. J. McGregor Library. Another text at NcD. Printed: Bullock 103.

Presenting Mrs. Hannah Cowley, the first female dramatic author in England. [118]

1789 Jan. 8. T. J., Paris, to Dr. [RICHARD] PRICE. L. 1 p. Extract by N. P. Trist *ca.* 1830. Printed: L & B VII 252-259; B of R VI 377 (letterpress copy in DLC).

Ratification of Constitution a proof that whenever the people are well-informed, they can be trusted with their government. [119]

1789 Jan. 14. T. J., Paris, to MARIA COSWAY, London. ALS. 2 pp. Letterpress copy. Endorsed by T. J. McGregor Library. Recipient's copy at NcD. Printed: Bullock 108-110.

Comments on severe winter. News of Princess Lubomirski, M. D'Hancarville, Mrs. Church, Mr. Trumbull, and Mr. Short. Mme. de Brehan disappointed with America's lack of simplicity. [120]

[1789] Feb. 6. MARIA COSWAY, London, to T. J., Paris. ALS. 3 pp. Endorsed by T. J. McGregor Library. Another text at NcD. Printed: Bullock 112.

Mrs. Church's trip to America. Requests true account of French Revolution since English newspapers are all biased. Hopes he has seen Mrs. Cowley. [121]

1789 May 21. T. J., Paris, to MARIA COSWAY, London. AL. 1 p. Letterpress copy. Endorsed by T. J. McGregor Library. Recipient's copy at NcD. Printed: Bullock 114-115.

Leaves for America for six months. France a scene of tumult. Wishes she would join Mrs. Church in America. Discourse on the nature of their friendship. [122]

1789 June 29. PETER CARR, New York, to T. J., Paris. ALS. 3 pp. Endorsed by T. J. Carr-Cary Papers.

Recent illness. Reading and attending congressional debates in N. Y. George Wythe's educational methods. Study of modern languages more useful than that of ancient ones. Spanish. Books in his father's library. References to Samuel and Dabney Carr, James Madison, and Thomas Mann Randolph, Jr. [123]

1789 July 25. T. J., Paris., to MARIA COSWAY, London. ALS. 2 pp. Letterpress copy. Endorsed by T. J. McGregor Library. Recipient's copy at NcD. Printed: Bullock 115-116.

Violence in the French Revolution. Introduces Gouverneur Morris. [124]

[1789] Aug. 9. MARIA COSWAY, London, to T. J., Paris. ALS. 1 p. Endorsed by T. J. McGregor Library. Another MS. at NcD. Printed: Bullock 116-117.

Acknowledges letter sent by Gouverneur Morris. Sends note by John Trumbull. [125]

[1789] Aug. 19. MARIA COSWAY, London, to T. J., Paris. ALS. 4 pp. Endorsed by T. J. McGregor Library. Another MS. at NcD. Printed: Bullock 117-118.

Conspiracy against George III. Finds Mr. Morris very enjoyable. Asks about affairs in France. Introduces her brother. Mentions Mr. Trumbull. [126]

1789 Aug. 30. T. J., Paris, to N[ATHANIEL] CUTTING, le Havre. ALS. 2 pp. Photostat. Original: N. Y., private collection.

Requests information on ships sailing from le Havre to the United States. [127]

1789 Sept. 11. T. J., Paris, to MARIA COSWAY, [London]. AL. 2 pp. Letterpress copy. Endorsed by T. J. McGregor Library. Another MS. in NcD. Printed: Bullock 120.

Reasons why he did not see more of her brother. Departure for America. [128]

1789 Sept. 15. T. J., Paris, to [NATHANIEL] CUTTING, le Havre. ALS. 2 pp. Photostat. Original: N. Y., private collection.

Passage to the United States. Books for Dr. Franklin to go in Captain Stotesbury's vessel. [129]

1789 Oct. 13. GEORGE WASHINGTON, New York, to T. J. L. 1 p. 19th century copy. Edgehill-Randolph Papers. Printed: Randall I 554-555; B of R VIII 563 (MS. in DLC).

Offering T. J. the post of Secretary of State. Suggests Roger Alden as Assistant Secretary. Papers in the care of John Jay and Henry Remsen. [130]

1789 Oct. 14. T. J., Cowes, to MARIA COSWAY, London. AL. 1 p. Letterpress copy. Endorsed by T. J. McGregor Library. Another copy in NcD. Printed: Bullock 125.

Leaves soon for America. Hopes to see her in Paris in April if matters are "tranquilized". [131]

1789 Nov. 30. GEORGE WASHINGTON, New York, to T. J. L. 1 p. 19th century copy. Edgehill-Randolph Papers. Printed: B of R VIII 564 (MS. in DLC).

Requesting an answer, when convenient, to his offer of the post of Secretary of State to T. J. [132]

1789 Dec. 15. T. J., Chesterfield, to GEORGE WASHINGTON, [New York]. L. 2 pp. 19th century copy. Edgehill-Randolph Papers. Printed: Ford V 140-141; SNR 170-171; TJR III 45-46; L & B VIII 1-3.

Will accept the post of Secretary of State if Washington thinks best, but feels most suited to his present post as Minister to France. Possible commercial treaties with France. [133]

1790 Jan. 3. T. J., Monticello, to AUGUSTINE DAVIES. L. 1 p. 19th century copy. Edgehill-Randolph Papers.

Requests forwarding of letters to Colonel Lewis. James Brown will pay postage. [134]

1790 Jan. 3. T. J., Monticello, to NICHOLAS B. SEABROOK. L. 1 p. 19th century copy. Edgehill-Randolph Papers.

Tobacco owed to the late Mr. M————. Mentions Nicholas Lewis, Mr. Coleman, and Mr. Ross.   [135]

1790 Jan. 6. T. J., Monticello, to ANDERSON BRYAN. L. 2 pp. 19th century copy. Edgehill-Randolph Papers.

Protests survey by James Marks of the boundary between Randolph's Edgehill and John Harvie's property.   [136]

1790 Jan. 8. T. J., Monticello, to [MATTHEW MAURY]. L. 2 pp. 19th century copy. Edgehill-Randolph Papers.

Asking that he accept Dabney Carr as a student in his school. Prescribes course of study. Nicholas Lewis will pay expenses. Asks information regarding an edition of "septuagist" (Septuagint?). Respects to Mrs. Maury.   [137]

1790 Jan. 9. T. J., Monticello, to ————. L. 1 p. 19th century copy. Edgehill-Randolph Papers. Another copy in MHi.

Enclosing a letter.   [138]

1790 Jan. 10. T. J., Monticello, to MARY LEWIS. L. 1 p. 19th century copy. Edgehill-Randolph Papers. Another copy in MHi.

Refusing her offer of a bed. Future plans; visit to Buck Island.   [139]

1790 Jan. 10. T. J., Monticello, to THOMAS WALKER. L. 5 pp. 19th century copy. Edgehill-Randolph Papers.

Details of the settlement of Peter Jefferson's estate, mentioning accounts of Kippen & Co., Dabney Carr, Sr., Alexander McCaul; expenses while a student at William and Mary and under George Wythe; payment of his sisters' portions; expenses of maintaining the family charged to the estate; division between Randolph and Thomas. John Harvie and John Nicholas, Sr., the other executors.
                                                                          [140]

1790 Jan. 11. T. J., Monticello, to JOHN HARVIE. L and map. 4 pp. 19th century copy. Edgehill-Randolph Papers. ALS, 4 February 1790, to T. M. Randolph, Sr., on verso last page. Map: 3 additional copies, original and 2 letterpress copies.

Boundary dispute regarding land bought by Harvie from James Marks, bordering on property of Thomas Mann Randolph, Sr., James Hickman, Martin Key, and William Watson. Anderson Bryan, the official surveyor. Map of the land in dispute.   [141]

[1790] Jan. 11 [incorrectly dated 1791]. T. J., Monticello, to NICHOLAS LEWIS. L. 1 p. 19th century copy. Edgehill-Randolph Papers.

Encloses a letter to be read and posted.   [142]

1790 Jan. 20. T. J., Monticello, to JOHN NICHOLAS, [SR.]. L. 2 pp. 19th century copy. Edgehill-Randolph Papers.

Encloses copy of his letter of 10 January to Dr. Thomas Walker concerning Peter Jefferson's estate. Confusion regarding board and clothing of his sisters, charged to the estate.   [143]

1790 Jan. 21. GEORGE WASHINGTON, New York, to T. J. L. 2 pp. 19th century copy. Edgehill-Randolph Papers. Printed: Randall I 557-558; B of R VIII 564 (MS. in DLC).

Arrival of Mr. Madison. Confidence in Jefferson's ability to carry out important duties of Secretary of State. Public satisfaction with Jefferson's French ministry. No alteration likely in the commission from the United States to the Court of France.   [144]

1790 Feb. 4. T. J., Monticello, to THOMAS MANN RANDOLPH, SR. ALS. 1 p. Apparently a contemporary accidental offset impression. Also a portion of 19th century copy. Edgehill-Randolph Papers.

Marriage of Martha Jefferson and Thomas Mann Randolph, Jr. Property settlements. Wedding plans.   [145]

1790 Feb. 5. T. J., Monticello, to JAMES LYLE. L. 1 p. 19th century copy. Apparently a contemporary accidently offset impression.
Edgehill-Randolph Papers.

Settlement of account of Kippen & Co. against Peter Jefferson's estate. Mentions Thomas Walker, an executor, and Alexander McCaul.   [146]

1790 Feb. 21. T. J. DEED to MARTHA JEFFERSON. ADS. 2 pp. Edgehill-Randolph Papers. Printed: B of R VIII 564 (MS. in DLC).

Conveying 1,000 acres of land in Bedford County, a portion of Poplar Forest, together with all its appurtenances, slaves (27 in all), and livestock, given to Martha upon her marriage to Thomas Mann Randolph, Jr. Includes Jefferson's map of Poplar Forest. Mentions a similar conveyance of property in Henrico County, called Varina, from Thomas Mann Randolph, Sr., to Thomas Mann Randolph, Jr.   [147]

1790 Mar. 5. PETER CARR, Spring Forest, Va., to T. J. ALS. 1 p. Carr-Cary Papers.

Unable to find any books, papers throwing light on Dabney Carr's transactions with Thomas Walker. Difficulties in procuring Coke on *Littleton*. References to Martha and Maria Jefferson and to James Minor.   [148]

1790 Mar. 7. T. J. to JAMES LYLE. L. 1 p 19th century copy. Edgehill-Randolph Papers.

Settlement of Peter Jefferson's estate. Mentions accounts and payments of R. (John?) Harvie, A. Donald and Alexander McCaul.   [149]

1790 Mar. 11. T. J., [Alexandria], Va., to [FRANCIS] COFFIN, Dunkerque. L. 1 p. 19th century copy. Edgehill-Randolph Papers. Printed: B of R VI 90 (MS. in DLC).

Box of plants for the Comtesse de Tessé, for which William Short, U. S. Chargé at Paris, will pay charges.   [150]

1790 Mar. 11. T. J., Alexandria, Va., to ALEXANDER DONALD, Richmond. L. 1 p. 19th century copy. Edgehill-Randolph Papers.

Ship box of plants for the Comtesse de Tessé to M. Lamotte at le Havre or Mr. Coffin at Dunkerque.   [151]

1790 Mar. 11. T. J., Alexandria, Va., to [WILLIAM] FITZHUGH. L. 1 p. 19th century copy. Edgehill-Randolph Papers.

Purchase of a horse. Will go to New York by stage because of deep snow. Offers any services he can render in New York.   [152]

1790 Mar. 11. T. J., Virginia, to M. [DE LA] MOTTE, le Havre. L. 1 p. 19th century copy. Edgehill-Randolph Papers. Printed: B of R VI 257 (MS. in DLC).

Box of plants for Mme. la Comtesse de Tessé. Charge expenses to William Short, U. S. Chargé d'Affaires at Paris.   [153]

1790 Mar. 28. T. J., New York, to PETER CARR. L. 2 pp. 19th century copy. Edgehill-Randolph Papers. Printed: B of R VI 71 (MS. in DLC).

Proof of payment to Dabney Carr's estate rests with Dr. Thomas Walker. List of law readings. References to Coke on *Littleton,* to James Monroe, and to Dabney Carr, Jr.   [154]

1790 Apr. 1. T. J., New York, to [EDWARD] DOWSE, Boston. L. 1 p. 19th century copy. Edgehill-Randolph Papers. Printed: B of R VI 126 (MS. in DLC).

Ordering set of porcelain from the Indies.   [155]

1790 Apr. 2. T. J., New York, to the MARQUIS DE LAFAYETTE. L. 1 p. Extract by N. P. Trist *ca.* 1830. Printed: Ford V 151-153; L & B VIII 11-13; B of R VI 254 (letterpress copy in DLC).

Opposition to the Constitution has disappeared with the amendments; the "vaut-rien" Rhode Island will soon come over.   [156]

[1790 Apr. 4]. T. J. to DR. GEM. L. 1 p. Fragment. 19th century copy. Edgehill-Randolph Papers.

Martha's marriage to Thomas Mann Randolph, Jr.   [157]

1790 Apr. 4. T. J., New York, to MARTHA JEFFERSON RANDOLPH. ALS. 2 pp. Deposited from Monticello. 19th century copy in Edgehill-Randolph Papers. Printed: SNR 180-181; Randall I 622 (extract).

News of Mrs. Trist, Miss Rittenhouse, Mrs. Buchanan, and Miss Holliday. Difficulty in procuring a house in New York. Misses Martha and Maria. Admonishes her to cherish her husband.   [158]

1790 Apr. 6. T. J., New York, to WILLIAM SHORT, Paris. LS. 3 pp. Endorsed. Deposited by C. S. Hutter, Esq. Printed: W (2) XII 294-296.

Official notification of his recall to be transmitted to the King and to M. de Montmarin. U. S. will repay its foreign debts, although the act of Congress may be too late to save the French court. Parts missing from officer's fusils. Negotiation for captives in the line. Requests authentic data to supplement information in *Leyden Gazette* and lies in the British press. Mentions Jacques Necker.   [159]

1790 Apr. 11. T. J., New York, to MARIA JEFFERSON. ALS. 1 p. Photostat of original lent by Mrs. William S. Gooch. Printed: Randall I 622; SNR 181.

Requesting a letter. Fatherly advice. Greetings to Mr. Randolph, Martha, and to her aunt and uncle.   [160]

1790 Apr. 24. T. J., New York, to the MARQUIS DE LAFAYETTE. L. 1 p. 19th
century copy. Edgehill-Randolph Papers. Printed: L & B VIII 25-27; TJR III
55-56; B of R VI 254 (MS. in DLC).
Introducing Mr. Horry, a nephew of General Pinckney. [161]

1790 Apr. 24. T. J., New York, to WILLIAM SHORT, Paris. L. 1 p. 19th
century copy. Edgehill-Randolph Papers.
Introducing Mr. Horry. [162]

1790 Apr. 25. MARY [i.e. MARIA] JEFFERSON, Richmond, to T. J. L. 1 p.
Typescript. Gift of Miss Olivia Taylor.
Trip to Richmond. Report on her reading and music. Reference to Thomas
Mann Randolph, Jr. [163]

1790 Apr. 26. T. J., New York, to MARTHA JEFFERSON RANDOLPH,
[Richmond]. L. 2 pp. 19th century copy. Edgehill-Randolph Papers. Another
MS. in MHi. Printed: Randall I 623; SNR 181-182.
T. M. Randolph, Jr., Martha, and Maria are not good correspondents. Encloses
Fenno's *Gazette* which will henceforth copy news from the *Leyden Gazette*.
Hopes the Randolphs will settle at Edgehill. [164]

1790 Apr. 30. PETER CARR, Spring Forest, Va., to T. J., New York. ALS.
Endorsed by T. J. Another copy: ALS. 3 pp. File draft. Endorsed by Carr. Carr-
Cary Papers.
Discussion of reading of Blackstone and Coke. Debates in the House of
Representatives. References to Maria Jefferson, James Madison, James Monroe,
Thomas Mann Randolph, Jr., and Martha Randolph. [165]

1790 May 3. T. J. MEMORANDUM ON GEORGIA-INDIAN QUESTION. D. 2
pp. Copy by N. P. Trist, *ca.* 1830. Another MS. in DLC. Printed: Ford V 165-167.
Opinion, given as member of Washington's cabinet, on Georgia's right to
grant lands to which the Indian claims have not yet been extinguished. [166]

1790 May 23. ELIZABETH EPPES, Eppington, to T. J., New York. ALS. 1 p.
Endorsed by T. J. Edgehill-Randolph Papers. Another MS. in MHi.
News of Martha and Maria. [167]

1790 May 23. MARIA JEFFERSON, Eppington, to T. J., [New York]. ALS. 2 pp.
Endorsed by T. J. Deposited by Gen. Jefferson Randolph Kean.
An account of her day. [168]

1790 May 25. THOMAS MANN RANDOLPH, JR., Richmond, to T. J. ALS.
3 pp. Endorsed by T. J. Edgehill-Randolph Papers.
Plans to settle at Varina, and to buy small farm near Monticello. Illness due
to sun stroke. Superiority of New England farmers to Virginia overseers. [169]

1790 May 30. FRANCIS EPPES, Eppington, to T. J., [New York]. ALS. 1 p.
Endorsed by T. J. Edgehill-Randolph Papers.
Accounts with Daniel Ross & Co. Has been served with a writ on account of
the *Prince of Wayles* (sic) cargo. [170]

1790 June 6. T. J., New York, to MARTHA JEFFERSON RANDOLPH. L. 2 pp.
19th century copy. Edgehill-Randolph Papers. Another MS. in MHi.

Is glad she is going to settle in Albemarle. Possibility of moving the government to Philadelphia. Recurrent headaches. Sailing party with the President.
Mentions Maria Jefferson and Thomas Mann Randolph, Jr.   [171]

1790 June 11. T. J., New York, to GARLAND JEFFERSON. L. 4 pp. 19th
century copy. Carr-Cary Papers. Printed: Ford V 179-182; B of R VI 239 (MS.
in DLC).

No clerkship available. Advises study of law in Albemarle where he can share
the use of T. J.'s library with Peter Carr. Outline of course of reading.
[172]

1790 June 11. T. J., New York, to NICHOLAS LEWIS, Albemarle County.
L. 1 p. 19th century copy. Edgehill-Randolph Papers. Printed: B of R VI 270
(MS. in DLC).

Introducing his relative, Garland Jefferson, for whom Jefferson is providing
board, room, and the use of his law books.   [173]

1790 June 13. T. J., New York, to PETER CARR, Albemarle County. L.
L. 1 p. 19th century copy. Edgehill-Randolph Papers. Printed: B of R VI 329
(MS. in DLC).

Introducing Garland Jefferson, his relative.   [174]

1790 June 13. T. J., New York, to PETER CARR, Albemarle County. L.
2 pp. 19th century copy. Edgehill-Randolph Papers. Printed: B of R VI 71
(MS. in DLC).

Recurrent headaches. Introducing Garland Jefferson, who will share with him
the use of Jefferson's books. Recommendations for his study of law. Possibility
of Congress' moving to Baltimore. Money paid to Dr. Walker, on account of
[Dabney Carr's?] estate.   [175]

1790 June 13. T. J., New York, to NICHOLAS LEWIS, Albemarle County.
L. 2 pp. 19th century copy. Edgehill-Randolph Papers. Printed: B of R VI 270
(MS. in DLC).

Receipt of Mrs. Lewis' letter. Recurrent headaches. Enclosed grains of high-
land rice. Advises concentration on wheat rather than tobacco. Price of tobacco.
Congress may remove to Baltimore or Philadelphia. Hams sent by Mrs. Lewis.
[176]

1790 June 13. T. J., New York, to GEORGE MASON. L. 1 p. Extract by N. P.
Trist ca. 1830. Printed: L & B VIII 35-36; Ford V 183-184; B of R VI 316
(letterpress copy in DLC).

Amendments to the Constitution.   [177]

1790 June 13. T. J., New York, to RICHARD PETERS, Philadelphia. L. 1 p.
19th century copy. Edgehill-Randolph Papers. Printed: B of R VI 369 (MS. in
DLC). Another MS. in PPHi.

Apology to the Society of St. Patrick for not accepting their invitation. Possible
sojourn in Philadelphia.   [178]

1790 June 13. T. J., New York, to THOMAS RUSSELL. L. 1 p. 19th century copy. Edgehill-Randolph Papers. Printed: B of R VI 401 (MS. in DLC). Another MS. in PPHi.

Returning a letter (of introduction?) for which he expresses thanks.

[179]

1790 June 25. T. J., New York, to GEORGE CLINTON. LS. 1 p. McGregor Library.

Enclosing, to the Governor of New York, a copy of the enabling act for establishing U. S. courts in the State of Rhode Island. [180]

1790 July 6. PETER CARR, Spring Forest, Va., to T. J., New York. ALS. 2 pp. Endorsed by T. J. Another copy: ALS. 2 pp. File draft. Endorsed by Carr. Carr-Cary Papers.

Reports on reading for law. Dabney has all needed books. Thomas Mann Randolph, Jr., and Patsy at Eppington. His mother ill. [181]

1790 July 7. JOHN GARLAND JEFFERSON, Hanover, Va., to T. J., New York. ALS. 2 pp. Endorsed by T. J. Carr-Cary Papers.

Thanks for T. J.'s patronage. Will soon leave Washington Henry Academy for law study in Albemarle. [182]

1790 July 9. T. J., New York, to GEORGE CLINTON. LS. 1 p. Endorsed.

Sending the New York Governor copies of the U. S. Census Act, the act respecting Rhode Island, and the act for the purchase of the District of Columbia.

[183]

1790 July 17. T. J., New York, to MARTHA J. RANDOLPH. L. 3 pp. 19th century copy. Edgehill-Randolph Papers. Another MS. in MHi. Printed: Randall I 625-626; SNR 187-188.

Advice on her attitude toward Gabriella Harvie, in the event that T. M. Randolph, Sr., should marry Gabriella. Prospect of buying land near Edgehill from Mr. [John?] H[arvie?], with Colonel Monroe as intermediary. [184]

1790 July 25. T. J., New York, to WILLIAM TEMPLE FRANKLIN, Philadelphia. ALS. 3 pp. Deposited by Edward R. Stettinius, Jr. Also a 19th century copy in the Edgehill-Randolph Papers.

Specifications for quarters for the State Department, to be rented from Mr. Leiper. [185]

[1790 ca. July]. T. J., [New York], to FRANCIS EPPES. L. 1 p. Fragment. 19th century copy. Edgehill-Randolph Papers.

Good price for wheat. French Revolution. French West Indies open for trade. Removal of government to Philadelphia. [186]

1790 Aug. 3. T. J., New York, to THOMAS MANN RANDOLPH, JR. L. 2 pp. 19th century copy, and a letterpress copy of the last page. Edgehill-Randolph Papers.

Randolph's recommendation of Mr. Thompson for consulship in the Canary Islands. T. J.'s attitude toward personal recommendations of this type. English

undecided as to peace or war. Report on measures, weights, and coins. Declines membership in the Society of Edinburgh. Model of T. J.'s mouldboard plow.
[187]

1790 Aug. 7. T. J., New York, to [LOUIS] DE PINTO. L. 1 p. Extract by N. P. Trist, *ca.* 1830. Printed: L & B VIII 73-76; TJR III 64-66.
Superiority of the Constitution to the Articles of Confederation.   [188]

1790 Aug. 8. T. J., New York, to MARTHA J. RANDOLPH. AL. 1 p. Letterpress copy and 19th century copy (both incomplete). Edgehill-Randolph Papers.
Plans for return to Monticello in September. Arrangements for residence in Philadelphia. Model of mouldboard plow. Mentions David Randolph, Thomas Mann Randolph, Jr., Martin (servant), Mr. Fitzhugh, [James] Brown, Maria Jefferson.   [189]

1790 Aug. 12. T. J., New York, to WILLIAM SHORT, Paris. L. 1 p. 19th century copy. Edgehill-Randolph Papers. Original MS. in VWW. Printed: W (2) XII 300-301.
Commission to Short, U. S. Chargé at Paris, to purchase forty bottles of champagne from M. Dorsey of Aij [Aix?], Champagne. Mentions a M. Cousin.
[190]

1790 Aug. 22. T. J., New York, to CAPT. NATHANIEL COLLY. L. 2 pp. 19th century copy. Edgehill-Randolph Papers.
Memorandum for the purchase of mahogany tables. Martha's marriage to Thomas Mann Randolph, Jr.   [191]

1790 Aug. 22. T. J., New York, to MARTHA J. RANDOLPH. L. 1 p. 19th century copy. Edgehill-Randolph Papers. Another MS. in MHi.
Visit to Rhode Island with President Washington. Plans for return to Monticello. Harness from France. Marriage of Lady Caroline Tufton. War between England and Spain. Mentions Mr. Rutledge and Maria Jefferson.   [192]

1790 Aug. 24. T. J., New York, to WILLIAM FITZHUGH. L. 1 p. 19th century copy. Edgehill-Randolph Papers.
Return to Monticello *via* Alexandria, Newgate, or Fredericksburg with James Madison. Directs servant Bob to go to Monticello. Order for a carriage horse.
[193]

1790 Aug. 28 [date received]. MARIA JEFFERSON to T. J., New York. ALS. 2 pp. Endorsed by T. J. Edgehill-Randolph Papers.
Singing lessons. Dates for arrival of peas, strawberries, marlin swallows, and whippoorwills.   [194]

1790 Sept. 20. T. J., Philadelphia, to JAMES BROWN, Philadelphia. L. 1 p. 19th century copy. Edgehill-Randolph Papers.
Order for table cloths, blankets, teakettle, sugar, cheese, and chocolate for Monticello.   [195]

1790 Sept. 20. T. J., Monticello, to JAMES MADISON. L. 1 p. 19th century copy. Edgehill-Randolph Papers.
Purchase of a horse from Madison. Mentions Thomas Mann Randolph, Jr.
[196]

1790 Sept. 20. T. J., Monticello, to WILLIAM RONALD. L. 1 p. 19th century copy. Edgehill-Randolph Papers.

Sale of lands on the James River opposite Elk Island to pay his part of Mr. Wayles' debt to Farrell & Jones. [197]

1790 Sept. 23. T. J., Monticello, to JAMES MADISON. L. 1 p. 19th century copy. Edgehill-Randolph Papers.

Terms for purchase of a horse. Mentions Thomas Mann Randolph, Jr. [198]

1790 Oct. 1. T. J., Monticello, to HENRY REMSEN, New York. ALS. 1 p. Endorsed. Printed: B of R VI 387.

To the Chief Clerk of the Secretary of the State's Office concerning recognition of Mr. McDonogh by the U. S. Government. Renting of T. J.'s house. Enclosure for William Short. Reference to Mr. Bruce. [199]

1790 Oct. 8. T. J., Monticello, to [FRANCIS EPPES, Eppington]. ALS. 3 pp. Letterpress copy. Edgehill-Randolph Papers.

Purchase of Edgehill for Thomas Mann Randolph, Jr. Possibilities for educating John Wayles Eppes at Princeton, the Philadelphia College, reading law at Eppington or Monticello, or working in the State Dept. with T. J. Mentions Mr. and Mrs. Skipworth [Henry Skipwith?], and Elizabeth Eppes. [200]

1790 Oct. 8. T. J., Monticello, to JOHN KEY. L. 1 p. 19th century copy. Edgehill-Randolph Papers.

Mr. Inis has not credited his tobacco at just prices. [201]

1790 Oct. 22. T. J., Monticello, to DR. JAMES CURRIE. L. 1 p. 19th century copy. Edgehill-Randolph Papers.

Has mentioned the subject (a government post?) Dr. Currie desired to the gentleman who was to call on him. [202]

1790 Oct. 22. T. J., Monticello, to THOMAS MANN RANDOLPH, JR. L. 1 p. 19th century copy. Edgehill-Randolph Papers.

Col. T. M. Randolph's objections to the purchase of Edgehill for Martha and T. M. R., Jr. Little prospect of buying from Mr. [Edward] Carter. [203]

1790 Oct. 22. T. J., Monticello, to THOMAS MANN RANDOLPH, SR. L. 4 pp. 19th century copy. Edgehill-Randolph Papers. Another MS. in CSmH.

Offers to compromise points at issue in the purchase of Edgehill for T. M. Randolph, Jr.: price, slaves, land included. [204]

1790 Oct. 29. T. J., Monticello, to [WILLIAM] FITZHUGH. L. 1 p. 19th century copy. Edgehill-Randolph Papers.

Purchase of a horse; Mr. Vernon's horse too expensive. [205]

1790 Nov. 2. T. J., Monticello, to JOHN HARVIE. L. 4 pp. 19th century copy. Edgehill-Randolph Papers.

Land purchased by Harvie from James Marks, to which Jefferson had a prior claim. [206]

1790 Nov. 2. T. J., Monticello, to MERIWETHER SMITH. L. 1 p. 19th century copy. Edgehill-Randolph Papers.
Concerning a letter forwarded to Mr. William Short. Recurrent headaches.
[207]

1790 Nov. 3. T. J., Monticello, to GARLAND CARR. L. 1 p. 19th century copy. Edgehill-Randolph Papers. Another MS. in CSmH.
Papers on the matter in dispute with Mr. and Mrs. Reddick to be given to a lawyer, possibly Colonel Monroe, who will defend Sam Carr in the aid of Mr. Ronald. The attorney should decide on the advisability of a separate suit for waste.
[208]

1790 Nov. 3. T. J., Monticello, to [FRANCIS] WALKER. L. 2 pp. 19th century copy. Edgehill-Randolph Papers.
Concerning Alexander McCaul's account [against Peter Jefferson's estate], mentioning two executors, Thomas Walker and John Harvie. Account against Mr. Carr's estate has been turned over to Peter Carr.
[209]

1790 Nov. 7. T. J., Monticello, to MARTHA JEFFERSON CARR. L. 2 pp. 19th century copy. Edgehill-Randolph Papers. Another MS. in CSmH.
Scurrilous piece written against the inhabitants of Charlottesville by a Mr. Rind, which has been attributed to Peter Carr and Garland Jefferson. Need for Garland to leave Charlottesville. Mr. Lewis will pay Dr. Walker's account against Dabney Carr, Sr., since T. J. still owes the Carr estate.
[210]

1790 Nov. 7. T. J., Monticello, to ANDREW DONALD, at Osborne's. L. 1 p. 19th century copy. Edgehill-Randolph Papers. Other MSS. in CSmH and MHi.
Nicholas Lewis will pay balance owed to Donald by T. J.
[211]

1790 Nov. 7. T. J., Monticello, to DR. [GEORGE] GILMER. L. 1 p. 19th century copy. Edgehill-Randolph Papers.
Delays his opinion on the case of Mr. Harmer's will until his papers arrive from Paris. Mentions James Madison.
[212]

1790 Nov. 7. T. J., Monticello, to JOHN HANSON. L. 1 p. 19th century copy. Edgehill-Randolph Papers. Another MS. in MHi.
Wheat crop has cleared all debts except those to [William] Jones and Kippen & Co., which will be paid from the tobacco crop.
[213]

1790 Nov. 11. THOMAS M. RANDOLPH, JR., Richmond, to T. J. ALS. 2 pp. Endorsed by T. J. Edgehill-Randolph Papers.
Anderson's account of the Hebrides mislaid. Will give up purchase of Edgehill from his father. Possible sale of glebe at Varina. Considering purchase of Mazzei's place, plus 300 acres from Colonel Carter.
[214]

1790 Nov. 12. JOHN GARLAND JEFFERSON, Goochland, Va., to T. J., Philadelphia. ALS. 3 pp. Endorsed by T. J. Carr-Cary Papers.
Boarding with Hilton. Determined on Jefferson's and Carr's advice to break off with the unfortunate Rind.
[215]

[1790 Nov. 24]. T. J. to JOHN CHURCHMAN. L. 1 p. 19th century copy. Edgehill-Randolph Papers. Printed: B of R VI 82 (letterpress copy in DLC).

Thanks for pamphlet and chart. M. Le Roy will distribute pamphlets in Paris.   [216]

1790 Nov. 24. T. J., Philadelphia, to M. LEROY, Paris. L. 1 p. 19th century copy. Edgehill-Randolph Papers. Printed: B of R VI 267 (MS. in DLC).

Distribution of John Churchman's variation charts and pamphlets.   [217]

1790 Nov. NICHOLAS LEWIS. Account with [PETER] JEFFERSON ESTATE. AD. 2 pp. Endorsed by T. J. Edgehill-Randolph Papers.

Estimate of sums owed to, and charges against, the estate of Peter Jefferson. Includes state and county taxes, cost of Dabney Carr's education, value of crops of corn, wheat, and tobacco.   [218]

1790 Dec. 1. T. J., Philadelphia, to MARTHA J. RANDOLPH. L. 1 p. 19th century copy. Edgehill-Randolph Papers. Another MS. in MHi. Printed: Randall II 14; SNR 190-191.

Plan for regular family correspondence. Messages from Mrs. Waters (née Rittenhouse) and Mrs. Trist. Arrival of furniture from Paris. France is emitting great sums of paper money. Possibility of war. Price of wheat. Mentions Maria Jefferson and Thomas Mann Randolph, Jr.   [219]

1790 Dec. 16. T. J., Philadelphia, to JAMES BROWN. L. 1 p. 19th century copy. Edgehill-Randolph Papers.

Furniture to be forwarded from Norfolk to Monticello.   [220]

1790 Dec. 16. T. J., Philadelphia, to THOMAS MANN RANDOLPH, JR. L. 1 p. 19th century copy. Edgehill-Randolph Papers.

Mr. Mazzei authorizes sale of Colle. Possibilities of purchasing [Edward] Carter's land adjoining. Instructions for planting sugar maple and paccan (pecan) nut trees. Official account of the western expedition. Wheat prices. Mentions [Nicholas] Lewis.   [221]

1790 Dec. 23. T. J., Philadelphia, to THOMAS McKEAN. L. 1 p. 19th century copy. Edgehill-Randolph Papers.

Opinion of the Attorney General on Philip Wilson's application.   [222]

1790 Dec. 23. T. J., Philadelphia, to MARTHA J. RANDOLPH. L. 1 p. 19th century copy. Edgehill-Randolph Papers. Printed: Randall II 15 (extract); SNR 191-192.

A scolding letter requesting that she write. Furniture delayed. Mentions Maria Jefferson and Thomas Mann Randolph, Jr.   [223]

[ca. 1790]. T. J. to A[LEXANDER] DONALD. L. 1 p. Fragment. 19th century copy. Edgehill-Randolph Papers.

Sending of a Minister to England.   [224]

[*ca.* 1790]. T. J. LIST OF LAND HOLDINGS. AD. 2 pp.

Lists more than 5000 acres in Monticello, Shadwell, and his other tracts in Albemarle County, plus 474 acres deeded to Philip Mazzei *et al.* for the purpose of maturing wine. Also listed are 157 acres including Natural Bridge in Rockbridge County, and a lot in Richmond. Details all patents and conveyances from the original patent until the land was deeded to Peter or Thomas Jefferson. Portions of his lands had passed through the following hands: Nelson Anderson, William Byrd, Edward Carter, John Carter, Jonathan Clarke, ———— Crawford, Thomas Garth, Thomas Graves, John Harvie, Edwin Hickman, James Hickman, Thomas Hickman, William Hickman, James Marks, Walter Monsley, William Randolph, Robert Sharpe, John Smith, Joseph Smith, Philip Smith, and Thomas Smith. Mentions Lord Dunmore.   [225]

[1790?]. T. J., [Monticello?], to [NICHOLAS LEWIS]. L. 1 p. Fragment. 19th century copy. Edgehill-Randolph Papers.

Hopes Lewis' health better. Mentions Mrs. Lewis.   [226]

[*ca.* 1790]. T. J., Philadelphia, to THOMAS MANN RANDOLPH, JR., L. 1 p. Fragment. 19th century copy. Edgehill-Randolph Papers.

News of Mrs. Trist and Miss Rittenhouse for Martha and Maria.   [227]

[1791] Jan. 5 [incorrectly dated 1790]. T. J., Philadelphia, to MARIA JEFFERSON, Monticello. ALS. 1 p. McGregor Library. Printed: Randall II 15; SNR 192.

Angry that she has not written.   [228]

1791 Jan. 20. T. J., Philadelphia, to MARTHA JEFFERSON RANDOLPH. L. 1 p. Two 19th century copies, one by Cornelia J. Randolph. Edgehill-Randolph Papers. Another MS. in MHi.

News from William Short in France: sale of church lands, riot in Paris which destroyed M. de Castrie's furniture. Copy of the Encyclopédie and of Buffon's works for Mr. Randolph. Needs warm stockings. Letter for a neighbor from Paris. Mentions Maria Jefferson.   [229]

1791 Jan. 29. T. J., Philadelphia, to DAVID STUART. L. 1 p. Typescript. Original owned by A. Gordon Stephenson. Printed: B of R VI 444 (MS. in DLC).

Mr. Carrol[l] will not act as one of the commissioners for the federal seat. President thinks Major L'Enfant qualified to make a survey of the ground.
                                                                             [230]

1791 Feb. 4. T. J., Philadelphia, to GEORGE MASON. L. 2 pp. Copied for N. P. Trist *ca.* 1830. Printed: L & B VIII 123-125; Ford V 274-276; B of R VI 316 (letterpress copy in DLC).

Importance of the French Revolution in preventing our falling back to the halfway house, the English Constitution. Fears effect of fiscal arrangements by our government. Need to augment numbers in the House of Representatives to give more representation to farmers. Madison's esteem for Mason. Is endeavoring to get distinction for the French, our useful customers. Sends copy of a report.
                                                                             [231]

1791 Feb. 13. MARIA JEFFERSON to T. J., Philadelphia. ALS. 2 pp. Endorsed by T. J. Edgehill-Randolph Papers. Printed: SNR 193-194.
   News of Martha and her daughter, Anne. [232]

1791 Feb. 16. T. J., Philadelphia, to MARIA JEFFERSON, Monticello. ALS. 1 p. Another MS. in MHi. Printed: SNR 193; Randall II 16.
   Congratulations on her new niece. Book for Martha. Reference to Thomas Mann Randolph, Jr. [233]

1791 Feb. 26. JOHN GARLAND JEFFERSON to T. J., Philadelphia. ALS. 3 pp. Endorsed by T. J. Carr-Cary Papers.
   Progress in his reading. Birth of Anne Cary Randolph. Rage of the people of Albemarle against him (Garland) has abated. Sam Carr's contract with John Carr for Mrs. Reddick's dower. Peter Carr at Monticello. Request for a watch. [234]

1791 Mar. 1. T. J., Philadelphia, to DANIEL S. HYLTON. L .1 p. 19th century copy. Edgehill-Randolph Papers.
   Requests information on shipment of the vis-a-vis. Possibility of marketing tobacco in Philadelphia. [235]

[1791] Mar. 2. T. J., Philadelphia, to MARTHA J. RANDOLPH. L. 1 p. 19th century copy. Edgehill-Randolph Papers.
   Mrs. Trist and Mrs. Waters have inquired for Martha. Hopes she and baby are well. Mentions Maria and Thomas Mann Randolph, Jr. Letter for Justin P. P. Derieux. [236]

1791 Mar. 6. MARIA JEFFERSON to T. J., [Philadelphia]. ALS. 2 pp. Endorsed by T. J. Edgehill-Randolph Papers. Printed: SNR 195-196.
   Furniture has arrived. Naming of the Thomas M. Randolphs' daughter. Mentions Jenny and Mrs. Fleming. [237]

1791 Mar. 9. T. J., Philadelphia, to MARIA JEFFERSON, Monticello. ALS. 1 p. Letterpress copy. Edgehill-Randolph Papers.
   Requests that she list appearance of everything animal and vegetable so as to compare climates of Monticello and Philadelphia. Mentions Thomas Mann Randolph, Jr., Miss Jenny [Randolph?], Martha Randolph, and Anne Randolph. [238]

1791 Mar. 13. T. J., Philadelphia, to ANDREW DONALD. L. 1 p. 19th century copy. Edgehill-Randolph Papers.
   Concerning his portion of the debts of estate of John Wayles, his father-in-law. Refers Donald to Francis Eppes as executor. [239]

1791 Mar. 17. T. J., Philadelphia, to WILLIAM BROWN. L. 2 pp. 19th century copy. Edgehill-Randolph Papers.
   Disagreement as to price of tobacco listed in an account with Thomas Adamson for 1771. Price of tobacco in Richmond and in London. Mentions Messrs. Adams, Perkins, Buchanan, and Brown. [240]

1791 Mar. 17. T. J., Philadelphia, to JOHN LAMB, New York. L. 1 p. 19th century copy. Edgehill-Randolph Papers.

To the Collector for the Port of New York concerning dutiable articles, including newspapers and pamphlets. Mentions Captain Bayley. [241]

1791 Mar. 17. T. J., Philadelphia, to ADAM LINDSAY. L. 1 p. 19th century copy. Edgehill-Randolph Papers.

Thanks for forwarding books for public use from W. Nelson. Order for moulded myrtle wax candles. [242]

[1791] Mar. 17. T. J., Philadelphia, to THOMAS MANN RANDOLPH, JR. L. 1 p. 19th century copy. Edgehill-Randolph Papers.

Suggests name of Anne for his granddaughter. Plans to sell his tobacco in Philadelphia. President's trip to Richmond, Va., Charleston, S. C., Savannah and Augusta, Ga. Mentions Martha Randolph. [243]

1791 Mar. 20. MARIA JEFFERSON to T. J., Philadelphia. ALS. 2 pp. Endorsed by T. J. Edgehill-Randolph Papers.

All await his naming of the grandchild. Gift of a habit from Mrs. Lewis. [244]

1791 Mar. 20. T. J., Philadelphia, to JAMES MAXWELL. L. 1 p. 19th century copy. Edgehill-Randolph Papers.

Order for Hughes [Hewes] crab cider. Furniture forwarded to James Brown at Richmond. [245]

1791 Mar. 24. T. J., Philadelphia, to [JAMES CURRIE]. L. 1 p. Fragment. 19th century copy. Edgehill-Randolph Papers.

Reason for Mr. Potter's inability to pay two notes. [246]

1791 Mar. 24. T. J., Philadelphia, to JOSEPH FENWICK, [Bordeaux]. L. 3 pp. 19th century copy. Edgehill-Randolph Papers.

Requesting Fenwick's aid in presenting the case of Justin P. P. de Rieux, to de Rieux's uncle, M. Le Roy of Bordeaux. Despite de Rieux's worth and hard work, he is in straitened circumstances and needs help. [247]

[1791] Mar. 26. MARY [i.e., MARIA] JEFFERSON to T. J. L. 1 p. Typescript. Original owned by Miss Olivia Taylor.

Awaits the naming of Martha's child. Mrs. Lewis' gift. [248]

1791 Apr. 4. T. J., Philadelphia, to CHARLES CARROLL. L. 2 pp. 19th century copy. Edgehill-Randolph Papers.

Settlement of balance with Mr. Brown. Duty must be laid on grain exported in British bottoms to equalize chances of our vessels. [249]

1791 Apr. 4. T. J., Philadelphia, to NICHOLAS LEWIS. L. 3 pp. 19th century copy. Edgehill-Randolph Papers. MS. in CSmH.

Has sold Albemarle and Bedford tobacco in Philadelphia. Sale of the fired tobacco in Richmond by Daniel Hylton. Payment to Lyle and Hanson. Payments due from Wilson. Debts of the John Wayles estate to Dr. Currie and Dobson. Francis Eppes, executor. White clover is the best improver of lands. [250]

1791 Apr. 5. T. J., Philadelphia, to JOHN HANSON. L. 2 pp. 19th century copy. Edgehill-Randolph Papers.
Payments to Hanson and to Kippen & Co. will be met from sale of tobacco. Asks that he accept as payment of debt Mr. Ronald's mortgage bonds on Cumberland lands sold to Ronald by T. J. [251]

1791 Apr. 5. T. J., Philadelphia, to DANIEL L. HYLTON, Richmond. L. 2 pp. 19th century copy. Edgehill-Randolph Papers.
Bill of lading for the vis-a-vis (carriage). T. J. has sold his tobaco crop in Philadelphia; asks that Hylton forward it and charge expenses to him. [252]

1791 Apr. 5. T. J., Philadelphia, to WAREHOUSE INSPECTORS, Richmond. L. 1 p. 19th century copy. Edgehill-Randolph Papers.
Order to deliver his tobacco to Daniel Hylton, excepting that which was fired and that belonging to Nicholas Lewis and B [owling] Clarke for overseers' shares. [253]

1791 Apr. 6. ELIZABETH EPPES, Eppington, to T. J., Philadelphia. ALS. 2 pp. Endorsed by T. J. Edgehill-Randolph Papers.
Congratulations on his granddaughter. Will be glad to have Polly stay with her. Is delighted with his plans for John Wayles Eppes. [254]

1791 Apr. 22. T. J., Philadelphia, to BENJAMIN FRANKLIN BACHE. L. 1 p. Typescript. Original owned by Franklin Bache.
Desires Bache to make his paper (the *General Advertiser*), a purely Republican vehicle of news with general distribution. [255]

1791 Apr. 27. FRANCIS EPPES, Bermuda Hundred, to T. J., Philadelphia. ALS. 1 p. Endorsed by T. J. Edgehill-Randolph Papers.
The John Wayles estate will be responsible for the Prince of "Wayles" cargo. Choice of profession for John Wayles Eppes. [256]

1791 May 1. PETER CARR, Monticello, to T. J., Philadelphia. ALS. 2 pp. Endorsed by T. J. Carr-Cary Papers.
Course of reading. Asks advice on practical side of law. Debts in Williamsburg unpaid. Draft on Nicholas Lewis. Garland Jefferson a "close student". References to Dabney Carr, [Matthew] Maury, and James Monroe. [257]

1791 May 1. T. J., Philadelphia, to JAMES McCLURG. L. 1 p. 19th century copy. Edgehill-Randolph Papers. Printed: B of R VI 284 (MS. in DLC).
Introducing Mr. Cassinove, of the banking firm of Van Staphorst in Amsterdam, who is visiting Norfolk and Richmond. [258]

1791 May 1. T. J., Philadelphia, to JAMES MAURY. L. 1 p. 19th century copy. Edgehill-Randolph Papers. Another text in MHi.
Introducing Tench Coxe, Assistant Secretary of the Treasury, who has interested himself in Mr. Parkinson. [259]

1791 May 1. T. J., Philadelphia, to BEVERLEY RANDOLPH. L. 1 p. 19th century copy. Edgehill-Randolph Papers. Printed: B of R VI 380 (MS. in DLC).
Introducing Mr. Cassinove of Amsterdam. Asks that he show Tuckahoe to him. [260]

1791 May 8. T. J., Philadelphia, to PETER CARR. ALS. 2 pp. Carr-Cary Papers. Another MS. in MHi.
Advice on reading and practice of law. Dabney Carr's progress. Delay in payment of Carr's debts at Williamsburg. Payment of Mr. Wayles' debts has crippled his funds. References to Nicholas Lewis and Dr. Thomas Walker. [261]

1791 May 8. T. J., Philadelphia, to MARTHA JEFFERSON RANDOLPH. L. 2 pp. 19th century copy. Edgehill-Randolph Papers. MS. in MHi. Printed: Randall II 9 (extract); SNR 199 (extract).
Importance of good relations with her neighbors. Loss of his vis-a-vis (carriage) in shipment; possible loss of tobacco and John Eppes' books and baggage on Captain Stratton's ship. List of books and furniture to be sent to Monticello. Petit has agreed to come from France as T. J.'s housekeeper. Mentions Thomas Mann Randolph. [262]

1791 May 8. T. J., Philadelphia, to GEORGE WASHINGTON. L. 3 pp. Copied for N. P. Trist ca. 1830. Printed: Ford V 328-330; L & B VIII 192-195.
Indiscretion of J. B. Smith's brother in printing T. J.'s note in approbation of Tom Paine's Rights of Man has caused a split with John Adams. Accounts in Fenno's papers. Discourse on Davila. Plan to replace public records of Virginia burned by the British. Asks permission to copy his letters to Washington written while governor of Virginia. [263]

1791 May 10. T. J., Philadelphia, to THOMAS LIEPER. L. 1 p. 19th century copy. Edgehill-Randolph Papers.
Requests payment for Bedford tobacco arrived on Captain Stratton's ship. Painters should start work Monday. [264]

1791 May 11. T. J., Philadelphia, to JAMES LYLE. L. 1 p. 19th century copy. Edgehill-Randolph Papers.
Offers bonds backed by mortgages on land sold to Mr. Ronald in payment for his debts to Lyle, to Kippen & Co. and to Farrell & Jones. Mentions [Alexander] McCaul. [265]

1791 May 11. T. J., Philadelphia, to BENJAMIN VAUGHAN. L. 3 pp. Copy and an abstract by N. P. Trist ca 1830. Letterpress copy in DLC. Printed: Ford V 332-334.
Experiments with mountain rice from Africa and Timor. Thanks for Sacontalá and for Smeaton's book. Astonishment at Burke's "Reflections on the French Revolution". Paine's answer. Satisfaction with the new Constitution. Greetings to Lord Wycombe and Dr. Price. Mentions Dr. Priestley. [266]

1791 May 13. T. J., Philadelphia, to JAMES MAURY. L. 1 p. Extract by N. P. Trist ca. 1830. Printed: B of R VI 318 (MS. in DLC).
Prosperity of the Union. [267]

1791 May 23. MARTHA RANDOLPH, Monticello, to T. J. ALS. 1 p. Endorsed by T. J. Edgehill-Randolph Papers.

Farming notes from Monticello: strawberries, cherries, beans, inoculation of trees by Anthony. Irregularity of the postal service. [268]

1791 May 29. MARIA JEFFERSON, Monticello, to T. J., Philadelphia. AL. 2 pp. Edgehill-Randolph Papers.

Thanks for a veil he sent. Study of botany and arithmetic. Her mare is pretty. Abundance of fruit. Mentions Thomas Mann Randolph, Jr., and Anne Randolph. [269]

1791 May 31. T. J., Lake Champlain, to MARTHA JEFFERSON RANDOLPH. L. 2 pp. 19th century copy. Edgehill-Randolph Papers. Printed: Ford V 337-338; SNR 201-202.

Beauty of Lake George; Lake Champlain less attractive. Trip through New England and New York to Philadelphia. Superior climate of Virginia. Good wishes to Anne. [270]

1791 June 23. T. J., Philadelphia, to MARTHA JEFFERSON RANDOLPH. L. 2 pp. 19th century copy. Edgehill-Randolph Papers. Printed: Randall II 21-22; SNR 203-204.

Headaches gone. Uncertain when he will return to Monticello. Duke of Dorset's daughter complains that Martha has not written. Mentions Fulwar Skipwith, Mrs. Trist, and Mrs. Waters. Asks that tobacco be sent so that he may make payment to John Hanson. Mirabeau and Duke de Richelieu are dead and Duke de Fronsac is head of the family. Mentions Thomas Mann Randolph, Jr., Maria Jefferson, and Anne Randolph. [271]

1791 June 26. T. J., Philadelphia, to MARIA JEFFERSON, Monticello. ALS. 1 p. Draft in MHi. Printed: Randall II 22; SNR 204.

Geography of Lake George. Receipt of news of his tobacco from Nicholas Lewis and Daniel Hylton. [272]

1791 July 4. T. J., Philadelphia, to JOHN DOBSON. L. 2 pp. 19th century copy. Edgehill-Randolph Papers. MS. in CSmH.

T. J.'s tobacco will not produce the expected payment on bonds assigned to Dobson by John Hanson, T. J.'s portion of the John Wayles estate debt to Farrell & Jones. [273]

1791 July 10. T. J., Philadelphia, to MARTHA JEFFERSON RANDOLPH, [Monticello]. L. 1 p. 19th century copy. Edgehill-Randolph Papers. MS. in MHi.

Postal route from Richmond to Staunton via Tuckahoe, Goochland Courthouse, Columbia, and Charlottesville. Stores for Monticello sent by Captain Stratton. Messages for Maria Jefferson, Anne Randolph, and Thomas Mann Randolph, Jr. [274]

1791 July 17. T. J., Philadelphia, to [THOMAS MANN RANDOLPH, JR., Monticello.] L. 1 p. Fragment. 19th century copy. Edgehill-Randolph Papers.

Sugar maple trees from Prince on Long Island. Conversion from tobacco to

wheat. Sale of tobacco crop. Stores for Monticello sent by Captain Stratton. Delay
in return to Monticello.   [275]

1791 July 24. T. J., Philadelphia, to JOHN DOBSON. L. 1 p. Edgehill-Randolph
Papers.
   Deficiency in payment of his debts from proceeds of his tobacco crop will be
made up by the wheat crop.   [276]

1791 July 24. T. J., Philadelphia, to MARTHA JEFFERSON RANDOLPH,
[Monticello]. L. 1 p. 19th century copy. Edgehill-Randolph Papers. MS. in MHi.
   Arrival of Petit from France. News of the Convent of Panthemont which
Martha attended. Stores for Monticello sent by Captain Stratton. President is ill.
News of Mme. de Taubenheim, Botitorer, and William Short.   [277]

1791 July 24. T. J., Philadelphia, to THOMAS MANN RANDOLPH, JR.,
[Monticello]. L. 1 p. 19th century copy. Edgehill-Randolph Papers. MS. in
CSmH.
   Proposes to build and rent a mill to Mr. Divers and others. Letters for P.
Marks and [Justin P. P.] de Rieux. Mentions Mr. Henderson.   [278]

1791 July 31. T. J., Philadelphia, to NATHANIEL COLLEY. L. 1 p. 19th century copy. Edgehill-Randolph Papers.
   Receipt of tables.   [279]

1791 July 31. T. J., Philadelphia, to MARIA JEFFERSON, [Monticello]. ALS. 1
p. McGregor Library. Printed: Randall II 22; SNR 204-205.
   Shipment of furniture. Asks where his ivory chessmen are.   [280]

1791 Aug. 1. T. J., Philadelphia, to NATHANIEL BURWELL. L. 1 p. 19th
century copy. Edgehill-Randolph Papers.
   Requests information on the public certificates owned by [John?] Paradise
which can be used to pay off his debts.   [281]

*1791 Aug. 2. T. J., Philadelphia, to [PHILIP MAZZEI]. L. 3 pp. 19th century
copy. Edgehill-Randolph Papers.
   Dohrman's, Blair's, Bowdoin's, and George Nicholas' debts to Mazzei. Encloses
copies of papers given to T. J. when he departed to Paris. Advises that he turn
Virginia certificates into U. S. paper, and consult Edward Randolph about it.
Disapproves of the assumption of state paper at discount. Sale of Colle. Value of
Mazzei's land in Richmond. Will take books in payment of Barrois' debt. Glad
Mazzei is under the wings of the Diet and King. Distaste for his office. News of
Maria Jefferson and Martha Randolph. Greetings to Duchess of Danville and
Duke and Duchess de la Rochefoucault. Mentions Foster Debbs and Mr. Garth.
                                                                           [282]

1791 Aug. 7. T. J., Philadelphia, to THOMAS MANN RANDOLPH, JR., [Monti-
cello]. ALS. 2 pp. Photostat. Original owned by Harold Jefferson Coolidge.
   Aug. Davies' proposed postal route from Richmond through Columbia and
Charlottesville to Staunton. Washington's illness. Need for replacing a carriage

horse. England's preparation for war. Revolution in Santo Domingo. Estimates census will total 3,800,000 in habitants.   [283]

1791 Aug. 14. T. J., Philadelphia, to CHRISTIAN BAEHR. L. 1 p. 19th century copy. Edgehill-Randolph Papers.
    Order for coat and breeches.   [284]

1791 Aug. 14. T. J., Philadelphia, to COLONEL FORREST, [Georgetown]. L. 1 p. 19th century copy. Edgehill-Randolph Papers.
    Introducing Tench Coxe.   [285]

1791 Aug. 14. T. J., Philadelphia, to MARTHA JEFFERSON RANDOLPH, [Monticello]. L. 1 p. 19th century copy. Edgehill-Randolph Papers.
    Return to Monticello in September. Stores sent by Captain Stratton. Mentions Thomas Mann Randolph, Jr., Maria Jefferson, and Anne Randolph.   [286]

1791 Aug. 14. T. J., Philadelphia, to [BENJAMIN] STODDERT. L. 1 p. 19th century copy. Edgehill-Randolph Papers.
    Introducing Tench Coxe.   [287]

1791 Aug. 21. T. J., Philadelphia, to MARIA JEFFERSON, Monticello. ALS. 1 p. Printed: Randall II 23; SNR 205-206.
    Date for return to Monticello. Purchase of horse for T. J. by Thomas Mann Randolph, Jr. Reference to James Madison.   [288]

1791 Aug 22. THOMAS MANN RANDOLPH, JR., Tuckahoe, to T. J. ALS. 2 pp. Endorsed by T. J. Edgehill-Randolph Papers.
    Visit to Tuckahoe to vote for his father for a seat in the Virginia Senate. Purchase of Edgehill. Papers relating to the legacy left to M. de Rieux. Stoves at Mr. Brown's. T. J.'s return to Monticello. Mentions Martha Randolph. [289]

1791 Aug. 28. T. J., Philadelphia, to THOMAS MANN RANDOLPH, JR. L. 1 p. 19th century copy. Edgehill-Randolph Papers. MS. in MHi.
    [Justin P. P.] de Rieux's letters and power-of-attorney. Will meet Commissioners of Public Buildings in Georgetown; then to Orange with James Madison. Requests two wagon horses to meet him. King of France attempts to escape.   [290]

1791 Aug. 29. T. J. Philadelphia, to CHRISTIAN BAEHR. L. 1 p. 19th century copy. Edgehill-Randolph Papers.
    Order for gilet and breeches.   [291]

1791 Aug 29. T. J., Philadelphia, to JAMES BROWN, Richmond. L. 1 p. 19th century copy. Edgehill-Randolph Papers. MS. in MHi.
    Shipment of putty for Monticello by the Sloop *Polly*.   [292]

1791 Aug. 30. T. J., Philadelphia, to [JAMES] CURRIE. L. 1 p. 19th century copy. Edgehill-Randolph Papers.
    Mr. Morris' bonds are to serve as security for his debt to Dr. Currie after Dr. Griffin has been satisfied.   [293]

1791 Aug. 30. T. J., Philadelphia, to JAMES MAURY, Liverpool, England. ALS. 1 p. Endorsed. Deposited by Mrs. Anne F. Maury. Printed: B of R VI 318 (MS. in DLC).

Acknowledges receipt of copy of the Corn Law. Refusal of ship masters to render accounts. Crop of wheat is fine, but corn and tobacco have been hurt by a drought.   [294]

1791 Aug. 31. T. J., Philadelphia, to THOMAS LIEPER. L. 1 p. 19th century copy. Edgehill-Randolph Papers.

Requests note for fifty or one hundred dollars. Shipment of tobacco expected on Captain Stratton's ship.   [295]

1791 Sept. 2. FRANCIS EPPES, Richmond, to T. J., Philadelphia. ALS. 2 pp. Endorsed by T. J. Edgehill-Randolph Papers.

Mazzei's claims against Captain Hylton's estate will be referred to Ralph Hylton. Betsy [Elizabeth Eppes?] has another girl. Invitation to T. J., the Randolphs, and Maria Jefferson to come to Eppington. Education of John Wayles Eppes.   [296]

1791 Sept. 15. T. J., Monticello, to ANDREW ELLICOT. L. 2 pp. 19th century copy. Edgehill-Randolph Papers.

Offer to hire Mr. Shuter's houseboy, Billy.   [297]

1791 Sept. 15. T. J., Monticello, to ADAM LINDSAY. L. 1 p. 19th century copy. Edgehill-Randolph Papers.

Order for myrtle wax candles and Hughes [Hewes] crab cider.   [298]

1791 Sept. 15. T. J., Monticello, to JAMES LYLE. L. 1 p. 19th century copy. Edgehill-Randolph Papers. MS. in CSmH.

Requests account of Peter Jefferson's estate, necessary for settlement of Dr. Walker's account. Will make payment upon the sale of his tobacco. Mentions John Nicholas.   [299]

1791 Sept. 21. T. J., Monticello, to JAMES WILSON. L. 1 p. 19th century copy. Edgehill-Randolph Papers.

Requesting that he come to Monticello to make a settlement with T. J. Mentions Nicholas Lewis.   [300]

1791 Sept. 27. T. J., Monticello, to JAMES BROWN, Richmond. L. 1 p. 19th century copy. Edgehill-Randolph Papers.

Requests list of tobacco sold to Mr. Donald. Order for muslin, dimity, and shoes for Maria Jefferson, and cash for his return to Philadelphia. Discusses various methods of payment.   [301]

1791 Oct. 5. T. J., Monticello, to HENRY SKIPWITH. L. 2 pp. 19th century copy. Edgehill-Randolph Papers. MS. in CSmH.

Hopes for an accommodation in the action by Bevins' executor against them. T. J.'s opinion of the paper signed by Skipwith and John Hanson (concerning the Wayles estate). Will not assume responsibility if John Wayles was security for a debt of Benjamin Harrison to Coles. Mentions Eppington, Hors du Monde, Mrs. Skipwith, and Mr. and Mrs. Francis Eppes.   [302]

1791 Oct. 6. T. J., Monticello, to JAMES WILSON. L. 2 pp. 19th century copy. Edgehill-Randolph Papers.

Wilson's account with T. J., covering the bonds of Richardson & Scruggs, Austin, James, Carter, and Randolph. Will send an order on Wilson to [John] Dobson for the balance due. Wilson will handle other bonds in the future for T. J.   [303]

1791 Oct. 7. T. J., [Monticello], to NATHANIEL POPE. L. 1 p. 19th century copy. Edgehill-Randolph Papers.

Order on Pope in favor of Andrew Donald for William and James Donald & Co. to be paid from money collected from Robert Lewis and Samuel Woodson.
          [304]

1791 Oct. 7. T. J., [Monticello], to NATHANIEL POPE. L. 1 p. 19th century copy. Edgehill-Randolph Papers.

Order on Pope in favor of James Strange for Donald Scott & Co., to be paid from collections from Robert Lewis and Samuel Woodson.   [305]

1791 Oct. 7. T. J., Monticello, to NATHANIEL POPE. L. 1 p. 19th century copy. Edgehill-Randolph Papers.

Nicholas Lewis has given up the management of T. J.'s affairs. Directions for collection and payment of his debts. Money due from Robert Lewis and Samuel Woodson. Payment due James Strange of Richmond for Donald Scott & Co., to Andrew Donald for William and James Donald & Co., and to [John] Dobson. Stop the suit against Lewis and Ware.   [306]

1791 Oct. 11. T. J., Monticello, to NICHOLAS LEWIS. L. 1 p. 19th century copy. Edgehill-Randolph Papers.

Payments to [James] Currie, John Dobson, and John Hanson. Loss of tobacco shipped for Tom Cobbs to Mr. Ballow by T. J.'s servant, Phill.   [307]

[1791] Oct. 18. T. J. to MARIA JEFFERSON. ALS. 1 p. McGregor Library.

Instructions regarding her trip to Baltimore and Philadelphia. Mentions Mr. Giles.   [308]

1791 Oct. 24. FRANCIS EPPES, Eppington, to T. J., Monticello. ALS. 1 p. Endorsed by T. J. Edgehill-Randolph Papers.

Elizabeth Eppes' illness. Purchase of donkey from Mrs. Bolling. John Wayles Eppes' expenses. [Henry?] Skipwith's sale [of tobacco?] a good one. Fall in tobacco price. Mentions Nicholas Lewis.   [309]

1791 Oct. 25. T. J., Philadelphia, to the REV. MATTHEW MAURY. L. 1 p. 19th century copy. Edgehill-Randolph Papers.

Payment to Maury through his brother at Fredericksburg.   [310]

1791 Oct. 25. T. J., Philadelphia, to THOMAS MANN RANDOLPH, JR., [Monticello]. L. 1 p. 19th century copy. Edgehill-Randolph Papers. Printed: SNR 207.

Difficult trip to Philadelphia. Mrs. Washington's kindness to Maria. Maria's education at Mrs. Pine's. Washington's speech on land law, militia law, post office, weights and measures, navigation, and commerce. Arrival of Mr. Hammond, British Minister. New legislature now sitting in France. Peace throughout Europe. Mentions Nelly Custis, Martha Randolph, and Anne Randolph. [311]

1791 Oct. 31. FRANCIS EPPES, Richmond, to T. J., [Philadelphia]. ALS. 1 p. Edgehill-Randolph Papers.

Betsy in better health. Mentions John Wayles Eppes and Maria Jefferson. [312]

1791 Nov. 13. T. J., Philadelphia, to MARTHA J. RANDOLPH, [Monticello]. ALS. 1 p. Letterpress copy. Deposit of Robert H. Kean. Also 19th century copy, Edgehill-Randolph Papers.

Comparison of the newspapers of Freneau and Bache. Desperate state of the French West Indies. Shipment of clothing for house servants by Captain Stratton. Maria, at Mrs. Pine's has received calls from Mesdames Adams, Randolph, Rittenhouse, Sarjeant, Waters, and Davies. Greetings to Thomas M. and Anne Randolph. [313]

1791 Nov. 25. T. J., Philadelphia, to WILLIAM SHORT, Philadelphia. L. 3 pp. 19th century copy. Edgehill-Randolph Papers. MS. in VWW. Printed: *The Southern Bivouac* II 433; W (2) XIII 107-109.

T. J.'s account with Short. Order for thirty bottles of champagne from M. D'Orsay for the President, using money in his, M. Grand's, or M. Van Staphorst's hands. Request for his traveling expense account to lay before Congress. Seeds and maple sugar for the Duchess of Danville. Peach grafts for the Duke de la Rochefoucault. Possibility of exporting maple sugar. Death of Mr. Edmunds, Eliza Edmunds, a son of Peyton Short, and Sally Short. Eliza and Jenny Short have gone to Kentucky. Greetings to M. and Mme. de Lafayette. [314]

1791 Nov. 27. T. J., Philadelphia, to THOMAS MANN RANDOLPH, JR., [Monticello]. L. 1 p. 19th century copy. Edgehill-Randolph Papers.

Trees from Mr. Prince for Monticello sent to Mr. Brown in Richmond. Mr. Davies says post started on the 15th. Clothes for the house servants sent by Captain Stratton. Cold weather. [David] Rittenhouse will furnish Freneau with meteorological observations. Love to Martha Randolph. [315]

1791 Dec. 4. T. J., Philadelphia, to [JOHN DOBSON]. L. 2 pp. Fragment. 19th century copy. Edgehill-Randolph Papers. MS. in MHi.

Payment of his debts to Dobson, consisting of bond to Farrell & Jones, assigned to Dobson, and a bill of exchange from Tabb. Partial payment by orders on James Wilson and Nathaniel Pope (money received in a suit against Woodson and Lewis), by money from his 1790 and 1791 tobacco crop, and by the sale of forty slaves. Mentions Nicholas Lewis. [316]

1791 Dec. 5. T. J., Philadelphia, to MARTHA JEFFERSON RANDOLPH, [Monticello]. L. 1 p. 19th century copy. Edgehill-Randolph Papers.

News of Maria Jefferson. Clothes for the housemaids. Books for Martha on

cooking, and for Thomas Mann Randolph on agriculture by Ginani and Duha-
mel. Possible sale of wheat in Philadelphia.   [317]

1791 Dec. 11. T. J., Philadelphia, to THOMAS MANN RANDOLPH, JR., [Mon-
ticello]. L. 1 p. 19th century copy. Edgehill-Randolph Papers
  Captain Stratton left with servants' clothes. Trees received by James Brown.
Defeat of St. Clair in Indian battle on Wabash near Fort Wayne. Preference
for militia over regulars. Affairs in France happily terminated. Greetings to
Martha and Anne Randolph.   [318]

1791 Dec. 18. T. J., Philadelphia, to THOMAS MANN RANDOLPH, JR., [Monti-
cello]. L. 3 pp. 19th century copy. Edgehill-Randolph Papers.
  Thomas Walker's account against Peter Jefferson's estate. Confusion concerning payment to Kippen & Co. for the estate, made by John Harvie to Mr. McCaul.
Mentions Richard Randolph, David Randolph, Martha Jefferson Randolph. [319]

1791 Dec. 23. T. J., Philadelphia, to ARCHIBALD STUART. L. 1 p. Extract by
N. P. Trist *ca.* 1830. Printed: Ford V 408-411; L & B VIII 275-278; B of R VI
443 (MS. in DLC).
  Importance of strengthening state governments to prevent encroachment by
the federal government. Specific means for strengthening the executive, legislative, and judicial branches of the state governments.   [320]

1791 Dec. 24. T. J., Philadelphia, to HENRY MULLINS. L. 1 p. 19th century
copy. Edgehill-Randolph Papers.
  Payment Mullins failed to make to Richard Anderson was to be turned over
to James Strange of Richmond for Donald Scott & Co.   [321]

1791 Dec. 25. T. J., Philadelphia, to MARTHA JEFFERSON RANDOLPH,
[Monticello]. L. 1 p. 19th century copy. Edgehill-Randolph Papers. MS. in
CSmH.
  Illness of Mrs. Gilmer, Colonel Lewis, and Anne Randolph. Postal route
through Columbia, Charlottesville, and Staunton. Greetings to Thomas Mann
Randolph, Jr.   [322]

*1792 Jan. 1. T. J., Philadelphia, to THOMAS MANN RANDOLPH, JR., Mon-
ticello. ALS. 2 pp. Photostat. Deposited from Monticello. Printed: Ford V 415-417;
B of R VI 384 (MS. in DLC).
  Postal route from Richmond through Columbia, Charlottesville, Staunton, and
into Kentucky. The representation bill might have been saved by Richard H.
Lee. Measures for defense of the West. Experiment with peach trees for firewood.
Weariness with public office.   [323]

1792 Jan. 8. T. J., Philadelphia, to FRANCIS EPPES. L. 1 p. 19th century copy.
Edgehill-Randolph Papers. MS. in CSmH.
  Expenses for education of John Wayles Eppes. Intemperate letter from John
Dobson in regard to T. J.'s account. No report from Nicholas Lewis concerning
the sale of slaves at Bedford. Mentions Maria Jefferson, Elizabeth Eppes, and
[Daniel] Hylton.   [324]

1792 Jan. 8. T. J., Philadelphia, to THOMAS MANN RANDOLPH, JR., [Monticello]. L. 1 p. 19th century copy. Edgehill-Randolph Papers. MS at MHi.

Will not lease Edgehill (i. e. Elk Hill?) to Mr. Forster, owing to probability of its sale to pay part of John Wayles estate debt to Farrell & Jones. Anxious to receive Nicholas Lewis' account of sale of Negroes at Bedford. Reference to [Daniel] Hylton. [325]

1792 Jan. 15. T. J., Philadelphia, to MARTHA JEFFERSON RANDOLPH, [Monticello]. L. 1 p. 19th century copy. Edgehill-Randolph Papers. Printed: Ford V 422-423; SNR 208.

Desire to leave public office and return to Monticello with Martha, Anne, and Thomas Mann Randolph, Jr. [326]

1792 Jan. 22. T. J., Philadelphia, to THOMAS MANN RANDOLPH, JR., [Monticello] L. 1 p. 19th century copy. Edgehill-Randolph Papers.

Rates for Freneau's newspaper on the postal route from Richmond through Columbia, Charlottesville, and Staunton, Va. Wants to hear results of his sale [of slaves]. Requests that [Bowling] Clarke or the manager send his tobacco for sale in Richmond after its inspection at Lynchburg. Terms for sale of Bedford tobacco. Clarkson is managing T. J.'s affairs in Albemarle. [327]

1792 Feb. 1. THOMAS MANN RANDOLPH, JR., Bizarre, to T. J. ALS. 1 p. Endorsed by T. J. Edgehill-Randolph Papers.

Letters from T. J. and Maria. Information from David Randolph concerning Colonel Dicke. Return to Monticello. [328]

1792 Feb. 5. T. J., Philadelphia, to MARTHA J. RANDOLPH. L. 1 p. 19th century copy. Edgehill-Randolph Papers.

Recent illness. Maria Jefferson's refusal to write. Requests information on wheat, payment of debts, and Negroes, since Clarkson cannot write. [329]

[1792] Feb. 6. T. J., Monticello, to THOMAS MANN RANDOLPH, JR. ALS. 1 p. Letterpress copy. Endorsed by T. J. Edgehill-Randolph Papers.

Requests certified copy of a deed. Mentions Martha and Thomas Jefferson Randolph. [330]

1792 Feb. 17. THOMAS MANN RANDOLPH, JR., Monticello, to T. J. ALS. 4 pp. Endorsed by T. J. Edgehill-Randolph Papers.

Heavy snow and ice along James River. Hopes snow will prevent multiplication of the weevil. Mentions Mr. Clarkson and Colonel Carter. [331]

1792 Feb. 20. MARTHA J. RANDOLPH, Monticello, to T. J., Philadelphia. ALS. 2 pp. Endorsed by T. J. Edgehill-Randolph Papers.

Dismal journey from Dick Randolph's. Purchase of Edgehill and its slaves completed. Wants him to return to Monticello. Mrs. Gilsner is recovered from her insanity. News of Anne Randolph. Greetings to Maria Jefferson. [332]

1792 Feb. 26. T. J., Philadelphia, to JAMES CURRIE. L. 1 p. 19th century copy. Edgehill-Randolph Papers. Another MS. in MHi.

A judgment has been obtained for Currie against Dr. Griffin, but that against the garnishees will take time. [333]

1792 Feb. 26. T. J., Philadelphia, to MARTHA JEFFERSON RANDOLPH, Monticello. L. 1 p. 19th century copy. Edgehill-Randolph Papers. Another MS. in MHi. Printed: Randall II 76; SNR 208-209.

Homesickness for Monticello. News of Maria Jefferson, Mrs. Trist, and Mrs. Waters. *Leyden Gazette* says British were beaten by Tippoo Saib, and were saved by the arrival of the Mahrattas, suing for peace for Cornwallis. Mentions Mr. Randolph. [334]

*1792 Mar. 14. T. J., Philadelphia, to THOMAS MANN RANDOLPH, JR., Monticello. L. 1 p. 19th century copy. Edgehill-Randolph Papers.

Glad that Randolph has obtained Edgehill. Books for Maria Jefferson sent by Captain Stratton. Greetings to Martha Randolph. [335]

1792 Mar. 16. T. J., Philadelphia, to THOMAS MANN RANDOLPH, JR., Monticello. L. 1 p. 19th century copy. Edgehill-Randolph Papers. Printed: Ford V 455-456; B of R VI 384 (MS. in DLC).

Severe winter. Fate of the country based on gambling scoundrels, the stock sellers. Fate of the representation bill. The emperor will not meddle in France's rearming. Postal time between Richmond and Philadelphia. Mr. Clark to ship T. J.'s tobacco to Philadelphia. [336]

1792 Mar. 30. T. J., Philadelphia, to THOMAS MANN RANDOLPH, JR., Monticello. L. 1 p. 19th century copy. Edgehill-Randolph Papers. Another MS. in MHi.

Instructions for planting Acacia Farnesiana. Gooseberry, lilac, and weeping willow are leafing. Martins have appeared. References to Elizabeth Eppes, Maria Jefferson, Martha Randolph, and Anne Randolph. [337]

1792 Apr. 6. T. J., Philadelphia, to MARTHA JEFFERSON RANDOLPH, Monticello. L. 1 p. 19th century copy. Edgehill-Randolph Papers. Printed: B of R X 17 (MS. in DLC).

Letter for Great Britain and commission to Dr. Barton taken care of for Thomas Mann Randolph, Jr. Shackleford should manure the gardens at Monticello. Copies of Fenno's *Gazette* forwarded. [338]

1792 Apr. 7. T. J., Philadelphia, to ADAM LINDSAY. L. 1 p. 19th century copy. Edgehill-Randolph Papers.

Payment for candles. Bill for apportioning representatives to each state vetoed by Washington. [339]

1792 Apr. 12. T. J., Philadelphia, to THOMAS MANN RANDOLPH, JR. L. 1 p. 19th century copy. Edgehill-Randolph Papers. Another MS. in CSmH.

Request as to Doctor Barton complied with. Requests that Mr. Lewis deliver bonds taken at his sale [of slaves?] to Mr. Eppes, who will use them to pay Mr. Hanson. Urges that Clarke hurry T. J.'s Bedford tobacco. Randolph's researches into the opossum. Colonel Monroe leaves soon. Mentions T. Shackleford. [340]

1792 Apr. 14. T. J., Philadelphia, to HENRY REMSEN. ALS. 2 pp. Endorsed.
McGregor Library. Printed: B of R VI 388 (MS. in DLC).

Receipt of pamphlet attacking him; author unmistakable (John Fenno?).
Criminality of paper money system. Report of rioting around William Duer's
place of confinement.   [341]

1792 May 7. THOMAS MANN RANDOLPH, JR., Richmond, to T. J. ALS. 1 p.
Endorsed by T. J. Edgehill-Randolph Papers.

Sends a bill instead of damaged tobacco to repay money T. J. paid for him.
Requests copy of Lavater's *Moral Aphorisms* for Martha Randolph. Bonds for
Mr. Eppes.   [342]

1792 May 23. T. J., Philadelphia, to GEORGE WASHINGTON. L. 7 pp. Copied
by Cornelia J. Randolph for N. P. Trist, *ca.* 1830. Letterpress copy in DLC.
Printed: Ford VI 1-6; Tucker I 427-434; L & B VIII 341-349; *Penn. Mag. of
Hist. and Biog.* XX 342.

Cites reasons why Washington should continue as President: a public debt so
large that it strains the impost; draining of specie abroad by payments on the
foreign debt; large amount of paper money that encourages speculation, corrupts
the legislature, and menaces the republican form of government. Only hope of
safety lies in numerous representation. Possibility of a split North and South if
the paper money, monarchical interest remains dominant. Negotiations with
England and Spain are at a delicate point.   [343]

1792 May 27. T. J., Philadelphia, to MARTHA JEFFERSON RANDOLPH,
Monticello. ALS. 1 p. Photostat. Original owned by Harold Jefferson Coolidge.

To send Ferris' papers to Mr. Madison. The President's arrival. Colonel and
Mrs. Monroe's visit at Monticello. Attempted murder of King of Sweden; pros-
perity of French affairs, and rising value of assignats. Probable defeat of John
Jay in New York. Shipment of bacon and tobacco.   [344]

1792 May 27. MARTHA RANDOLPH, Monticello, to T. J., Philadelphia. L. 2
pp. 19th century copy. Edgehill-Randolph Papers.

Nicholas Lewis, Jr., returned from Williamsburg with his lady. Airs that the
Lewises have taken of late. Effect of drought on sugar maples, acacias, and the
crops. Illness of Joseph Monroe.   [345]

1792 May 28. PETER CARR, Monticello, to T. J., Philadelphia. ALS. 2 pp.
Endorsed by T. J. Carr-Cary Papers.

Hears news of him from Thomas Mann Randolph, Jr., and Patsy. Discusses law
reading, lawyer's prospects. Encloses opinion on the law of waste. (see 22 June
1792 and 18 Feb. 1793). Reference to Mr. Steward (Archibald Stuart?) of
Staunton.   [346]

1792 June 1. T. J., Philadelphia, to THOMAS MANN RANDOLPH, JR., Monticello. L. 1 p. 19th century copy. Edgehill-Randolph Papers.

Copies of Fenno's and Freneau's newspapers. Possibility that Maria will enter
Miss Brodeaux's school. Instructions to [Bowling] Clarke necessitated by miser-
able condition of his tobacco.   [347]

1792 June 3. T. J., Philadelphia, to DOCTOR WITHERSPOON. L. 1 p. 19th century copy. Edgehill-Randolph Papers. Another MS. in MHi.
Mr. Baker's explanation regarding a tutor for Mr. Robinson. [348]

1792 June 4. THOMAS M. RANDOLPH, JR., Monticello, to T. J. ALS. 3 pp. Endorsed by T. J. Edgehill-Randolph Papers.
Wheat and corn crop at Monticello and Shadwell. Importance of abolishing tobacco and Indian corn to protect soil; the area peculiarly favorable to wheat. [349]

1792 June 6. JOHN GARLAND JEFFERSON, Goochland County, to T. J., Philadelphia. ALS. 2 pp. Endorsed by T. J. Carr-Cary Papers.
Attended Charlottesville District Court. Plans for law study. [350]

1792 June 9. T. J., Philadelphia, to BROWSE TRIST. ALS. 2 pp. Letterpress copy. Edgehill-Randolph Papers.
Urges him to exercise his legal rights in property entailed to him in England, with aid from Thomas Pinckney. [351]

1792 June 15. T. J., Philadelphia, to SAMUEL MACKAY. AL. Fragment. 1 p. Letterpress copy. Edgehill-Randolph Papers. Printed: B of R VI 369 (MS. in DLC).
Possibility of Mackay's making a living as a French tutor in Philadelphia, Baltimore, or Richmond. [352]

1792 June 22. T. J., Philadelphia, to PETER CARR. ALS. 2 pp. Carr-Cary Papers. Printed: Ford VI 91-92; L & B VIII 383-385; B of R VI 71 (MS. in DLC).
Opinion on the law of waste. [353]

1792 June 29. T. J., Philadelphia, to THOMAS MANN RANDOLPH, JR., Monticello. L. 1 p. 19th century copy. Edgehill-Randolph Papers. Other MSS. in CSmH and MHi.
Goods for Monticello sent to James Brown in Richmond via the Schooner Relief. Mentions George Washington. [354]

1792 July 3. T. J., Philadelphia, to MARTHA J. RANDOLPH, Monticello. L. 2 pp. 19th century copy. Edgehill-Randolph Papers.
Stores for Monticello. Plans for return to Monticello via James Madison's home and John Jones' tavern. Mentions Mr. Claxton, Mr. Petit, Mr. Williams, Thomas Mann Randolph, Jr., and George Washington. [355]

1792 July 13. T. J., Philadelphia, to MARTHA J. RANDOLPH, Monticello. L. 1 p. 19th century copy. Edgehill-Randolph Papers. Another MS. in NNP.
Horses for his return to Monticello. Greetings to Mr. Randolph. [356]

1792 July 21. T. J., Philadelphia, to PIERRE GUIDE. L. 1 p. 19th century copy. Edgehill-Randolph Papers.
Receipt of raisins and wine ordered from Guide. [357]

1792 Aug. 14. JOHN GARLAND JEFFERSON, Goochland County, to T. J., Monticello. ALS. 1 p. Endorsed by T. J. Carr-Cary Papers.

Glad T. J. is at Monticello. Asks for horse in order to attend Court. Regards to Thomas M. and Mrs. Randolph.   [358]

1792 Sept. 9. JOHN GARLAND JEFFERSON, Goochland County, to T. J., Monticello. ALS. 1 p. Endorsed by T. J. Carr-Cary Papers.

Illness of Martha J. Carr, Lucy Carr, and himself. Jefferson's plans to reside in Virginia. Asks instructions about returning books. Samuel Carr's education at Williamsburg.   [359]

1792 Sept. 9. T. J., Monticello, to GEORGE WASHINGTON, Mount Vernon. L. 12 pp. Copy made for N. P. Trist, *ca.* 1830. Letterpress copy in DLC. Printed: Ford VI 101-109; L & B VIII 394-408.

Negotiations by William Short and William Carmichael with England and Spain regarding their interference with the Indians. Dissention among the executive departments. Disapproval of Hamilton: his policies, his undue influencing of the legislature, his interference in negotiations with England and France. Differences of opinion between Hamilton and T. J. regarding the Constitution and public debt. Justification of Philip Freneau. Asserts that he has never dictated Freneau's policies except to advise use of information in the *Leyden Gazette.* Rivalry between Freneau and Fenno. Importance of a free press. Anonymous slanders by Hamilton, which he will answer after his retirement. Mentions writings of Publicola and Discourses on Davila.   [360]

1792 Sept. 15. T. J. to [EDMUND RANDOLPH]. AD. 1 p. Edgehill-Randolph Papers.

Memorandum relative to William Short's letter of 15 September 1792.   [361]

1792 Sept. 23. T. J. MEMORANDUM OF ACCOUNTS. AD. 1 p. Endorsed by T. J. McGregor Library.

Brief memorandum of accounts with the following people: Albemarle County Sheriff, Thomas Bell, James Brown, Benjamin Calvard, Manoah Clarkson, Hierom Gaines, Henry Guy, John Henderson's executors, John Garland Jefferson, Nicholas Lewis, Joseph Mansfield, Peter Marks, Thomas Massey, Matthew Maury, John Quarles, Thomas Mann Randolph, Jr., and David Wood.   [362]

1792 Oct. 10. WILSON MILES CARY, Ceeleys, Va., to T. J. ALS. 1 p. Endorsed by T. J. Carr-Cary Papers.

His son and family have scarlet fever. Concerned about education of grandsons. Solicits appointment to lighthouse at Cape Henry for Maj. George Wray.
                                                                              [363]

1792 Oct. 10. T. J., Philadelphia, to M. DE LA MOTTE, [le Havre]. L. 1 p. 19th century copy. Edgehill-Randolph Papers. Another MS. in MHi.

Request that M. Frouille, Libraire Quai des Augustin[s], Paris, forward the Encyclopedie. Order for macaroni. Goods to be shipped to James Brown in Richmond. Draft on Donald & Barton, London.   [364]

1792 Oct. 10. T. J., Philadelphia, to VAN STAPHORST & HUBBARD, Amsterdam. L. 1 p. 19th century copy. Edgehill-Randolph Papers.

Concerning a balance against T. J. in favor of Van Staphorst & Hubbard, resulting from public accounts while T. J. was minister to France. Mentions John Dobson.   [365]

1792 Oct. 12. T. J., Philadelphia, to THOMAS MANN RANDOLPH, JR., Monticello. L. 2 pp. 19th century copy. Edgehill-Randolph Papers.

Orders to sell Negroes in Bedford and Albemarle. Flooring for the stables. Turnip crop. Maria lives with a Mrs. Fullerton. Greetings to Martha Randolph and to Miss Jane (Randolph?). Forwards Freneau's and Fenno's newspapers *via* Mr. Madison. Mentions servants Dinah and Caesar.   [366]

1792 Oct. 13. T. J., Philadelphia, to [DANIEL CARROLL]. L. 1 p. 19th century copy. Edgehill-Randolph Papers. Printed: B of R VIII 97 (MS. in DLC). Another MS. in MHi.

Poverty of Etienne Hallet, architect at Georgetown.   [367]

1792 Oct. 13. T. J., Philadelphia, to JOSIAH PARKER. L. 1 p. 19th century copy. Edgehill-Randolph Papers. Another MS. in MHi.

Letter for Messrs. Blow and Milhaddo.   [368]

1792 Oct. 13. T. J., Philadelphia, to THOMAS MANN RANDOLPH, JR. L. 1 p. 19th century copy. Edgehill-Randolph Papers.

Anne Randolph's illness. President Washington's scheme of crop rotation. [369]

1792 Oct. 21. JOHN GARLAND JEFFERSON, Monticello, to T. J., Philadelphia. ALS. 1 p. Endorsed by T. J. Carr-Cary Papers.

Will board with John Shelton, Goochland. Asks for money for winter clothes and for board. Course of reading. Direct letter care George Jefferson, Richmond.
                                                               [370]

1792 Nov. 4. T. J., Philadelphia, to JOSEPH FRY. L. 1 p. 19th century copy. Edgehill-Randolph Papers. Printed: B of R VI 147 (MS. in DLC).

Receipt of sugar maple seeds for the President, Mr. Madison, and T. J. Congress in session.   [371]

1792 Nov. 4. T. J., Philadelphia, to ADAM LINDSAY. L. 1 p. 19th century copy. Edgehill-Randolph Papers. Another MS. in MHi.

Order for myrtle-wax candles. Application from the Mayor of Marseilles that U. S. merchants be encouraged to send wheat and flour in great quantities. [372]

1792 Nov. 4. T. J., Philadelphia, to [JOHN F. MERCER]. L. 1 p. 19th century copy. Edgehill-Randolph Papers. Printed: B of R VI 322 (MS. in DLC).

Mr. Otis' note. Senate without a head since the Vice-president is away and R. H. Lee resigned. Mr. and Mrs. Monroe's arrival.   [373]

*1972 Nov. 4. T. J., Philadelphia, to GEORGE REEVELY. L. 1 p. 19th century copy. Edgehill-Randolph Papers. Another MS. in MHi.

Bonds payable to T. J. turned over to John Hanson. References to William Mickle, Reuben Smith, David Ross, and Robert Wilson.   [374]

1792 Nov. 5. T. J., Philadelphia, to JOSEPH G. CHAMBERS, Mercersburg, Pa.
L. 1 p. 19th century copy. Edgehill-Randolph Papers. Printed: B of R VI 78
(MS. in DLC).
Advising that he consult the French minister concerning the weapon he has
developed, or that he apply for a patent.   [375]

1792 Nov. 5. T. J., Philadelphia, to WILLIAM COBBETT. L. 1 p. 19th century
copy. Edgehill-Randolph Papers. Printed: B of R VI 89 (MS. in DLC).
No government post available, despite William Short's assurances of Cobbett's
merit.   [376]

1792 Nov. 6. JOHN GARLAND JEFFERSON, Richmond, to T. J., Philadelphia.
ALS. 1 p. Endorsed by T. J. Carr-Cary Papers.
Arrived Richmond with Peter and Samuel Carr. Needs money urgently. [377]

1792 Nov. 6. T. J., Philadelphia, to VAN STAPHORST & HUBBARD, Amsterdam. L. 1 p. 19th century copy. Edgehill-Randolph Papers.
Covering a letter for William Short.   [378]

1792 Nov. 7. T. J., Philadelphia, to [GOUVERNEUR] MORRIS, Paris. L. 2
pp. 19th century copy. Edgehill-Randolph Papers. Printed: B of R VI 343 (MS.
in DLC).
Information concerning Mme. de la Mariniere and a servant Henri. Determination to retire. (Jefferson wrote twice to Gouverneur Morris on this date.)
                                                                       [379]

1792 Nov. 8. T. J., Philadelphia, to THOMAS PINCKNEY, London. L. 1 p. 19th
century copy. Edgehill-Randolph Papers. Printed: Ford VI 132-133; B of R VI
373 (MS. in DLC).
Plan to retire. Request for purchase of threshing machine. Peace concluded
with Wabash and Illinois Indians.   [380]

1792 Nov. 13. T. J., Philadelphia, to THOMAS PINCKNEY, London. ALS. 1 p.
Endorsed. Printed: B of R 373 (MS. in DLC).
Denies that Mr. [Stephen?] Sayre has any claim against the U. S. Treasury.
Indian prospects improved. Delay of [Thomas?] Barclay's mission.   [381]

1792 Nov. 14. T. J., Philadelphia, to CHRISTIAN BAEHR, New York. ALS.
1 p. Letterpress copy. Edgehill-Randolph Papers.
Order for waistcoat and breeches.   [382]

1792 Nov. 18. JOHN GARLAND JEFFERSON, Goochland County, to T. J.,
Philadelphia. ALS. 2 pp. Endorsed by T. J. Carr-Cary Papers.
Receipt of money. Discourse on good conduct.   [383]

1792 Nov. 18. MARTHA RANDOLPH, Bizarre, to T. J., Philadelphia. ALS. 2 pp.
Endorsed by T. J. Edgehill-Randolph Papers.
Anne Randolph's illness. Mr. Randolph's absence. Mentions Maria and Thomas
Jefferson Randolph.   [384]

1792 Nov. 19. T. J., Philadelphia, to MANN PAGE. L. 1 p. 19th century copy. Edgehill-Randolph Papers. Printed: B of R VI 361 (MS. in DLC).

Request that he secure Mazzei's gun from Mr. Hunter and place it with Joseph Jones of Fredericksburg. Rejection by Congress of proposal that executive heads meet with Congress. [385]

1792 Nov. 30. T. J., Philadelphia, to THOMAS MANN RANDOLPH, JR., [Monticello]. L. 1 p. 19th century copy. Edgehill-Randolph Papers. Printed: B of R VI 384 (MS. in DLC).

Forwards agricultural pamphlet. Instructions regarding books, hams, and a stalactite in Richmond. Reported surrender of Dumourier to the Duke of Brunswick. Mentions Philadelphia's Peale Museum, Brussels and Ostend, Belgium. [386]

1792 Dec. 6. T. J., Philadelphia, to MARTHA J. RANDOLPH. L. 1 p. 19th century copy. Edgehill-Randolph Papers.

Urges that she avoid use of medicine for Anne Randolph. Mentions Maria Jefferson, Thomas Jefferson Randolph, and Thomas Mann Randolph, Jr. [387]

1792 Dec. 7. FRANCIS EPPES, Eppington, to T. J., Philadelphia. ALS. 1 p. Edgehill-Randolph Papers.

[Archibald] Cary's executors promise payment to the Wayles estate. Purchase of donkeys. [388]

1792 Dec. 15. MARTHA J. CARR, Spring Forest, Va., to T. J., Philadelphia. ALS. 1 p. Endoresd by T. J. Carr-Cary Papers.

Request for money to pay debts to [M. & J.] Myers, incurred in marriage of her daughter. Pure air of Monticello cured fever. [389]

1792 Dec. 20. T. J., Philadelphia, to JAMES BROWN, Richmond. L. 1 p. 19th century copy. Edgehill-Randolph Papers. Another MS. in MHi.

Lower French duty on U. S. tobacco; drafts on Brown for Clow & Co., J. G. Jefferson, [Matthew] Maury; payment due from Cary estate. [390]

1792 Dec. 31. T. J., Philadelphia, to DANIEL HYLTON. L. 1 p. 19th century copy. Edgehill-Randolph Papers.

On the renting of Elkhill. [391]

1792 Dec. 31. T. J., Philadelphia, to MARTHA J. RANDOLPH. L. 1 p. 19th century copy. Edgehill-Randolph Papers. Another MS. in MHi. Printed: L & B XIII 191-192; MHi Collections I 46-47.

Anne Randolph's return to health. Postal information. Visit of an Indian of the Peoria Nation. Blanchard's balloon ascent. French affairs. Renting of Elkhill. Mentions Thomas Mann Randolph, Jr. [392]

1792 Dec. 31. T. J., Philadelphia, to THOMAS MANN RANDOLPH, JR. L. 1 p. 19th century copy. Edgehill-Randolph Papers. Another MS. in CSmH.

Renting of Elkhill to John Ashlin on share-crop basis. Mentions H. Mullins. [393]

1793 Jan. 2. FRANCIS EPPES, Eppington, to T J., Philadelphia. ALS. 2 pp.
Endorsed by T. J. Deposited by Robert H. Kean.
    Payment from [Archibald] Cary's estate to John Wayles' estate. Defeat of the
Duke of Brunswick. Price of wheat. Mentions Burgoyne, Cornwallis, John Wayles
Eppes, and Maria Jefferson.   [394]

1793 Jan. 4. T. J., Philadelphia, to PETER DERIEUX. L. 1 p. 19th century copy.
Edgehill-Randolph Papers. Printed: B of R VI 389 (M.S. in DLC).
    Letter from Mr. Fenirch (i.e. Fenwick?) concerning Derieux's legacy. French
victories. Letters for Mr. Vaughan and Mr. Fenirch.   [395]

1793 Jan. 8. T. J., Philadelphia, to FREDERICK GAYER. L. 1 p. 19th century
copy. Edgehill-Randolph Papers. Printed: B of R VI 174 (MS. in DLC) .
    Regrets that he cannot lend Gayer $600 to set up a type-founder business. [396]

1793 Jan. 14. T. J., Philadelphia, to MARTHA J. RANDOLPH. L. 1 p. 19th
century copy. Edgehill-Randolph Papers. Another MS. in MHi. Printed: Randall
II 191.
    Anne Randolph's health; servants' clothes; Mr. Blanchard's balloon ascent.
Mentions Maria Jefferson, Mr. Randolph.   [397]

1793 Jan. 16. MARTHA RANDOLPH, Monticello, to T. J., Philadelphia. ALS.
2 pp. Endorsed by T. J. Edgehill-Randolph Papers.
    News of Anne and Thomas Jefferson Randolph. Delay in receiving letters
concerning the books and stalactite. Mentions Thomas Mann Randolph, Jr. [398]

1793 Jan. 17. FRANCIS EPPES, Eppington, to T. J., Philadelphia. ALS. 2 pp.
Endorsed by T. J. Edgehill-Randolph Papers.
    Permission for John Wayles Eppes to accompany the commissioners to the
Council of Indians. Edmund Randolph's bonds available to pay John's expenses.
Mentions Elizabeth Eppes and Maria Jefferson.   [399]

1793 Jan. 17. T. J., Philadelphia, to [RICHARD GAMBLE]. L. 1 p. 19th
century copy. Edgehill-Randolph Papers.
    Concerning payment due from Colonel Bell.   [400]

1793 Jan. 20. T. J., Philadelphia, to [PETER] DERIEUX, [JR.]. L. 1 p. 19th
century copy. Edgehill-Randolph Papers. Printed: B of R VI 389 (MS. in DLC).
    Regarding Mr. Fenwick's bill, and funds sent through Richard Gamble. [401]

1793 Jan. 20. T. J., Philadelphia, to RICHARD HANSON. L. 1 p. 19th century
copy. Edgehill-Randolph Papers. Another MS. in MHi.
    Daniel Hylton's letter on the sale of Elkhill to Dr. Taylor and Banks; payment
in bonds backed with Greenbriar land. Debt to Farrell & Jones.   [402]

[1793] Jan. 20 [incorrectly dated 1788]. T. J., Philadelphia, to DANIEL L.
HYLTON, L. 1 p. 19th century copy. Edgehill-Randolph Papers. Another MS. in
MHi.
    Regarding sale of Elkhill. Deliver bonds to Thomas Mann Randolph, Jr. [403]

1793 Jan. 21. T. J., Philadelphia, to THOMAS MANN RANDOLPH, JR., Monticello. L. 1 p. 19th century copy. Edgehill-Randolph Papers. Other MSS. in CSmH and MHi.

Acknowledgment of letters. Information from Hylton concerning the sale of Elkhill. Asks about sale at Bedford. Instructions regarding building at Monticello (stables?) . [404]

1793 Jan. 24. T. J., Philadelphia, to J. W. KITTERA. L. 1 p. 19th century copy. Edgehill-Randolph Papers. Printed: B of R VI 250 (MS. in DLC).

Instructions regarding Mr. Chambers' invention. [405]

1793 Jan. 26. T. J., Philadelphia, to MARTHA JEFFERSON RANDOLPH, Monticello. L. 2 pp. 19th century copy Edgehill-Randolph Papers. Printed: Ford VI 163-165; SNR 214-215; L & B IX 15-17.

Uncertainly as to his retirement from office. Building of his canal in Albemarle. Mentions Anne Randolph, Samuel Clarkson, Mr. George, Thomas Mann Randolph, Jr., and George Washington. [406]

1793 Feb. 2. MARTHA CARR. Draft on T. J. See 1793 Dec. 2.

[407]

1793 Feb. 2. T. J., Philadelphia, to SAMUEL CLARKSON. L. 1 p. 19th century copy. Edgehill-Randolph Papers. Printed: B of R VI 86 (M.S. in DLC).

Sale of a horse. [408]

1793 Feb. 11. T. J., Philadelphia, to MARTHA J. RANDOLPH, Monticello. L. 1 p. 19th century copy. Edgehill-Randolph Papers.

Acknowledging receipt of Mr. Randolph's letter. [409]

1793 Feb. 13. THOMAS MANN RANDOLPH, SR., Tuckahoe, to [T. M. RANDOLPH, JR.], Monticello. ALS. 1 p. Endorsed. Edgehill-Randolph Papers.

Prospective visit to Tuckahoe. Deep snow. Account between T. M. R., Sr. and T. M. R., Jr. Mentions Anne and Martha Randolph, also seeds, grape cuttings, fruit trees, and calacanthus roots. [410]

1793 Feb. 18. T. J., Philadelphia, to MARTHA J. CARR, Spring Forest. L. 1 p. Contemporary copy. Carr-Cary Papers. Another MS. in CSmH.

Reasons for delay in sending money to pay her debt to [M. & J.] Myers and T. J.'s bond to Dabney Carr's estate. Greetings to Mr. and Mrs. Terrell, his newly married niece. (Attached is Peter Carr's opinion on waste which belongs with Carr's letter of 28 May 1792.) [411]

1793 Feb. 18. T. J., Philadelphia, to [JACOB HOLLINGSWORTH]. L. 1 p. 19th century copy. Edgehill-Randolph Papers. Printed: B of R VI 248 (MS. in DLC).

Procedures in the case of lost loan office certificates. Renting of 2,000 acres of land. Mentions [Samuel] Biddle. [412]

1793 Feb. 24. T. J., Philadelphia, to MARTHA RANDOLPH. ALS. 1 p. Letter-press copy, and a 19th century copy. Edgehill-Randolph Papers. Printed: Randall II 191.

Adjournment of Congress. Servants' clothes sent to Richmond on Schooner *Mary,* Captain Swaile. Mentions James Monroe, Anne Randolph, Thomas Jefferson Randolph, Thomas Mann Randolph, Jr., and servant Bob.   [413]

1793 Feb. 24. T. J., Philadelphia. to PEYTON SHORT L. 1 p. 19th century copy. Edgehill-Randolph Papers. Printed: B of R VI 420 (MS. in DLC).

Kentucky Constitution. Letter from William Short.   [414]

1793 Feb. 26. T. J., Philadelphia, to ELBRIDGE GERRY. L. 1 p. 19th century copy. Edgehill-Randolph Papers. Printed: B of R VI 181 (MS. in DLC). Another MS. in NNP.

Sauterne wine. Feeding of horses. Mentions Joseph Fenwick, U. S. Consul at Bordeaux.   [415]

1793 Feb. 26. T. J., Philadelphia, to JOHN PENDLETON. L. 1 p. 19th century copy. Edgehill-Randolph Papers.

Concerns a request for something lodged at Monticello.   [416]

1793 Mar. 3. T. J., Philadelphia, to JACOB HOLLINGSWORTH. L. 1 p. 19th century copy. Edgehill-Randolph Papers.

Renting of his lands near Shadwell. Mentions trip to Brandywine and Elkton, Va., to secure tenant for his mill. References to Samuel Biddle and Thomas Mann Randolph, Jr.   [417]

1793 Mar. 3. T. J., Philadelphia, to THOMAS MANN RANDOLPH, JR. L. 2 pp. 19th century copy. Edgehill-Randolph Papers. Printed: Ford VI 194-196; B of R VI 384 (MS. in DLC).

Letters received. Plan to rent lands on the Shadwell side of the river. Inquiries in the House of Representatives regarding actions of the Secretary of the Treasury. Control of Congress by stockjobbers and bankers. Republican victory in the new Congress.   [418]

1793 Mar. 3. T. J., Philadelphia, to STEPHEN WILLIS, L. 1 p. 19th century copy. Edgehill-Randolph Papers.

Delay in returning to Monticello. Directions for construction at Monticello. Procurement of workmen in Philadelphia.   [419]

1793 Mar. 5. T. J., Philadelphia, to ALEXANDER DONALD. L. 2 pp. 19th century copy. Edgehill-Randolph Papers. Printed: B of R VI 125 (M.S. in DLC).

Receipt of letters. Bill in favor of William B. Giles. Marketing of Bedford tobacco. Scarcity of cash and depression in public paper. Views of the Republican and fiscal parties concerning payment of the debt. Constitutionality of the Bank. Desire for peace.   [420]

1793 Mar. 6. FRANCIS EPPES, Richmond, to T. J., Philadelphia. ALS. 1 p. Endorsed by T. J. Edgehill-Randolph Papers .

Money for John Wayles Eppes. Payments from the Cary estate.   [421]

1793 Mar. 7. T. J., Philadelphia, to MOSES COX. L. 1 p. 19th century copy.
Edgehill-Randolph Papers.

Proposal to rent Cox's house. [422]

1793 Mar. 10. T. J., Philadelphia, to MARTHA J. RANDOLPH, Monticello. L.
1 p. 19th century copy. Edgehill-Randolph Papers. Another MS. in MHi.

Urging that Mr. Randolph use the servants for his convenience in the garden.
Has rented a house in the country. Plan to return to Monticello. Mentions
Maria Jefferson, Thomas J. Randolph, and Anne Randolph. [423]

1793 Mar. 12. T. J., Philadelphia, to MOSES COX. L. 1 p. 19th century copy.
Edgehill-Randolph Papers.

Renting of Cox's house. [424]

1793 Mar. 24. T. J., Philadelphia, to MARTHA J. RANDOLPH, Monticello. L.
1 p. 19th century copy. Edgehill-Randolph Papers. Another MS. in MHi.

Trees, grass, and garden at Monticello. Fenno's newspapers sent by Mr.
Madison. Mentions Mr. Hawkins, Colonel Monroe, and Thomas Mann Randolph,
Jr. [425]

1793 Mar. 28. PETER CARR, Monticello, to T. J., Philadelphia. ALS. 2 pp.
Endoresd by T. J. Carr-Cary Papers.

Asks opinion on recovery of slaves under grandfather's will. Intends to begin
law practice in summer, location undecided. [426]

1793 Mar. 31. T. J. to NATHANIEL CUTTING. AL. 1 p. Endorsed. McGregor
Library. MS. in PPHi.

Recommends trip to England by American vessel rather than by packet, because of prospects of war. [427]

1793 Mar. 31. JOHN GARLAND JEFFERSON, Goochland County, to T. J.,
Philadelphia. ALS. 2 pp. Endorsed by T. J. Carr-Cary Papers.

Reports on reading. Return of T. J.'s books. Request for money. References
to Peter and Samuel Carr. [428]

1793 Apr. 1. T. J., Philadelphia, to TIMOTHY PICKERING. L. 1 p. 19th
century copy. Edgehill-Randolph Papers. Printed: B of R VI 371 (MS. in DLC).

Complaint to the Postmaster General concerning lack of punctuality of the
post rider from Richmond to Charlottesville. [429]

1793 Apr. 7. T. J., Philadelphia, to JAMES BROWN, Richmond. L. 1 p. 19th
century copy. Edgehill-Randolph Papers. Printed: B of R VI 52 (MS. in DLC).

Books from Dublin and from Alexander Donald in London. Shipment of Bedford tobacco to France. War between England and France. Furniture sent aboard
the Sloop *Union*, Captain Bradford, to Richmond. Special instructions regarding
looking glasses. [430]

1793 Apr. 8. T. J., Philadelphia, to MARTHA J. RANDOLPH, Monticello. L.
1 p. 19th century copy. Edgehill-Randolph Papers.
Maria's illness. Mr. Boulding sent by Jacob Hollingsworth as prospective
tenant for lands near Shadwell. Furniture sent to James Brown in Richmond.
War between France, England, and Holland. John Eppes at William and Mary
College. Letter from Mr. Carr. Mentions Thomas Mann Randolph, Jr.   [431]

1793 Apr. 9. T. J., Philadelphia, to ALEXANDER HAMILTON. L. 1 p. 19th
century copy. Edgehill-Randolph Papers. Printed: B of R VI 199 (MS. in DLC).
Disposal of William Short's property in the public funds. Mentions James
Brown.   [432]

1793 Apr. 14. T. J., Philadelphia, to [THOMAS] BELL, [Albemarle County].
L. 1 p. 19th century copy. Edgehill-Randolph Papers. Another MS. in MHi.
Valuation of Mary (slave). Request that he supply J. Garland Jefferson with
necessities. Mr. Derieux's affairs. Dearth of money in Philadelphia. Mentions
Nicholas Lewis and Dr. Gilmer.   [433]

1793 Apr. 14. T. J., Philadelphia, to [PETER CARR, Monticello]. ALS. 2 pp.
Carr-Cary Papers. Printed: B of R VI 71 (MS. in DLC).
Advises Dabney Carr to begin study of law. Unable to advise Peter as to best
site for law practice in Virginia. He is free to revive the question of his claim
to slaves. Pamphlets for Thomas Mann Randolph, Jr., including articles signed
"Timon".   [434]

1793 Apr. 14. T. J., Philadelphia, to JOHN GARLAND JEFFERSON. L. 1 p.
19th century copy. Carr-Cary Papers. Printed: L & B XIX 103-105; B of R VI
239 (MS. in DLC).
Courses of reading for Jefferson and Dabney Carr. Suggests he stand at the
bar in the fall. Refers him to Thomas Bell in Charlottesville for funds.   [435]

1793 Apr. 15. JAMES BROWN, Richmond, to T. J., Philadelphia. L. 1 p. 19th
century extract. Edgehill-Randolph Papers. Printed: B of R VIII 75 (MS. in
DLC).
William Short's certificates.   [436]

1793 Apr. 27. JOHN GARLAND JEFFERSON, Goochland County, to T. J.,
Philadelphia. ALS. 2 pp. Endorsed by T. J. Carr-Cary Papers.
Considering living between Petersburg and Richmond, to practice in the dis-
trict courts of Brunswick and Lunenburg Counties. Prefers to get clothes from
John Shelton rather than from Thomas Bell. Need for money.   [437]

1793 Apr. 28. T. J. REPORT to GEORGE WASHINGTON. D. 12 pp. Copied
for N. P. Trist by Martha Randolph, ca. 1830. (Also a partial copy in another
hand, 3 pp.). Printed: Ford VI 219-231; Tucker I 464-473.
Opinion on the right of the U. S. to renounce their treaties with France,
citing Grotius, Puffendorf, Vattel, and Wolf as authorities.   [438]

1793 May 1. JOHN WAYLES EPPES, Eppington, to T. J., Philadelphia. ALS. 2 pp. Endorsed by T. J. Edgehill-Randolph Papers.

Discharging of Gordon's account. Decree with regard to [Archibald] Cary's estate. [Anne Cary] Randolph and Richard Randolph have been absolved in court. Mentions Mr. Campbell and Mr. Marshall. [439]

1793 May 19. T. J., Philadelphia, to JOHN GARLAND JEFFERSON, Goochland County. L. 1 p. 19th century copy. Carr-Cary Papers. Printed: B of R VI 239 (MS. in DLC).

Financial difficulties make it necessary that Garland get his clothes from Thomas Bell. Approves Garland's district for law practice. [440]

1793 May 22. THOMAS MANN RANDOLPH, JR., Monticello, to T. J., Philadelphia. ALS. 3 pp. Endorsed by T. J. Edgehill-Randolph Papers.

Bonds deposited by Bowling Clarke. Bonds taken by Mr. Hylton for Elkhill not yet arrived. Damage to grain by the weevil. Barley, wheat, rye, clover, and mocking birds at Monticello. Loan of two pamphlets, one on "popery laws" in Ireland. Mentions Martha Randolph and the children. [441]

1793 May 24. DANIEL L. HYLTON, Richmond, to T. J., Philadelphia. ALS. 2 pp. Endorsed by T. J. Carr-Cary Papers.

Purchase of Wilson Miles Cary's estate, Rich Neck, by Miles King, Dr. William Foushee, William Hylton, and Daniel Hylton. Sends sample of their lumber for Edmund Genet. [442]

1793 June 6. JOHN GARLAND JEFFERSON, Goochland County, to T. J. Philadelphia. ALS. 1 p. Endorsed by T. J. Carr-Cary Papers.

Explanation why he bought from Shelton and Harris rather than Thomas Bell. Borrowing books from Monticello. Reference to William Pope. [443]

1793 June 11. T. J., Philadelphia, to JOHN MIXON. L. 1 p. 19th century copy. Edgehill-Randolph Papers. Printed: B of R VI 355 (MS. in DLC).

Letter covering Mr. Curuger's papers. [444]

1793 July 7. T. J., Philadelphia, to MARTHA J. RANDOLPH, Monticello. L. 1 p. 19th century copy. Edgehill-Randolph Papers. Printed: Randall II 191-192; SNR 221-222; B of R VI 386 (MS. in DLC).

Enjoyment of the trees at his house. Provision for celery and endive for the winter. Mentions Maria Jefferson and Thomas Mann Randolph, Jr. [445]

1793 July 21. FRANCIS EPPES, Eppington, to T. J., Philadelphia. ALS. 1 p. Endorsed by T. J. Edgehill-Randolph Papers.

Payment for A[rchibald] Cary's estate. Polly's letter to her aunt. [446]

1793 July 21. T. J., Philadelphia, to MARTHA J. RANDOLPH, Monticello. L. 1 p. 19th century copy. Edgehill-Randolph Papers. Another MS. in MHi. Printed: Randall II 192; SNR 222.

Date of arival of peaches and corn; peas at Monticello. Need for enriching the soil at Monticello with manure. Possibility of peace between England and France.   [447]

1793 July 27. T. J., Philadelphia, to JOSEPH FENWICK. L. 1 p. 19th century copy. Edgehill-Randolph Papers. Printed: B of R VI 148 (MS. in DLC).
   Introducing [Edward?] Livingston.   [448]

1793 July 27. T. J., Philadelphia, to M. LA MOTTE. L. 1 p. 19th century copy. Edgehill-Randolph Papers.
   Introducing [Edward?] Livingston.   [449]

1793 July 28. T. J., Philadelphia, to JAMES MADISON. L. 1 p. 19th century copy. Edgehill-Randolph Papers. Printed: B of R VI 292.
   Anxious regarding failure to acknowledge his letters. Death of Roger Sherman. Mentions [John?] Blair and [Matthew?] Maury.   [450]

*1793 Aug. 3. T. J., Philadelphia, to MR. SHUTER, Georgetown. L. 1 p. 19th century copy. Edgehill-Randolph Papers. Printed: B of R VI 428 (MS. in DLC.)
   Will pay expenses of servants who will meet at Shuter's tavern to exchange horses.   [451]

1793 Aug. 18. T. J., Philadelphia, to PETER DERIEUX. L. 1 p. 19th century copy. Edgehill-Randolph Papers. Printed: B of R VI 389 (MS. in DLC).
   Sum due Derieux from Mr. Vaughan.   [452]

1793 Aug. [18. Incorrectly dated Aug. 8]. T. J., Philadelphia, to ROBERT GAM-BLE, Richmond. L. 1 p. 19th century copy. Edgehill-Randolph Papers. Printed: B of R VI 171 (MS. in DLC).
   Forwarding of claret and stores to Monticello. Mentions Archibald Campbell of Baltimore.   [453]

1793 Aug. 18. T. J., Philadelphia, to MARTHA J. RANDOLPH, Monticello. L. 1 p. 19th century copy. Edgehill-Randolph Papers. Another MS. in MHi. Printed: Randall II 192; SNR 222.
   News of D. Randolph. Arrangement for exchanging Tarquin for another horse. Wine, stores, and clothing for the servants at Monticello. Mentions Jupiter, Tom Shackleford, and Thomas Mann Randolph, Jr.   [454]

1793 Aug. [20]. T. J., Philadelphia, to THOMAS PINCKNEY. L. 1 p. 19th century copy. Edgehill-Randolph Papers.
   Letter for Mr. Domal. Requests information about threshing machine. Delay in his departure.   [455]

1793 Aug. 22. T. J., Philadelphia, to [ALEXANDER DONALD, London]. L. 1 p. 19th century copy. Edgehill-Randolph Papers. Printed: B of R VI 125 (MS. in DLC).
   Promises shipment of tobacco to aid Donald in the calamity (bankruptcy) that has befallen him. Plans to return to Monticello. Books received. Mentions James Brown and Mr. Marshall.   [456]

1793 Aug. 22. T. J., Philadelphia, to JOSEPH FENWICK. L. 1 p. 19th century copy. Edgehill-Randolph Papers. Printed: B of R VI 148 (MS. in DLC).
Payment for wine. Mentions draft on Donald & Burton. [457]

1793 Aug. 22. T. J., Philadelphia, to M. LA MOTTE. L. 1 p. 19th century copy. Edgehill-Randolph Papers. Printed: B of R VI 258 (MS. in DLC).
Payment for the Encyclopédie. Failure of Donald & Burton. [458]

1793 Aug. 22. T. J., Philadelphia, to McHENRY, GILMER, & STERRETT. L. 1 p. 19th century copy. Edgehill-Randolph Papers. Printed: B of R VI 283 (MS. in DLC).
George Hammond's refusal to give passports to French passengers. [459]

1793 Aug. 25. T. J., Philadelphia, to THOMAS MANN RANDOLPH, JR., Monticello. L. 1 p. 19th century copy. Edgehill-Randolph Papers. Another MS. in MHi.
Exchanging Tarquin for another horse. Washington's trip to Mt. Vernon. Plan to send off the rest of his furniture, in preparation for his return to Monticello. [460]

1793 Aug. 26. T. J., Philadelphia, to JAMES H. McHENRY. L. 1 p. 19th century copy. Edgehill-Randolph Papers. Printed: B of R VI 283 (MS. in DLC).
Misfortunes of M. Lenblhon, a fugitive from Santo Domingo awaiting passage to France. [461]

1793 Aug. 26. T. J., Philadelphia, to THAYER, BARTLET & CO., Charleston. L. 1 p. 19th century copy. Edgehill-Randolph Papers.
Concerning two boxes of china sent by [Edward?] Dowse. [462]

1793 Aug. 29. THOMAS MANN RANDOLPH, JR., Monticello, to T. J., Philadelphia. ALS. 2 pp. Endorsed by T. J. Edgehill-Randolph Papers.
Mail from Philadelphia. News of James Madison, Colonel, Mrs., and Eliza Monroe. Effect of weevil on wheat crop. Mentions Mr. Clarkson, Martha Randolph, and Maria Jefferson. [463]

1793 Aug. 30. T. J., Philadelphia, to RICHARD DOBSON. L. 1 p. 19th century copy. Edgehill-Randolph Papers. Printed: B of R VI 124 (MS. in DLC).
Payments on T. J.'s bond and bill of exchange. [464]

1793 Aug. 30. T. J., Philadelphia, to MONTGOMERY & HENRY. L. 1 p. 19th century copy. Edgehill-Randolph Papers. Printed: B of R VI 339. (MS. in DLC).
T. J.'s debt to Montgomery & Henry. Mentions Nicholas Lewis. [465]

1793 Sept. 1. T. J., Philadelphia, to PETER DERIEUX. L. 1 p. 19th century copy. Edgehill-Randolph Papers. Printed: B of R VI 389 (MS. in DLC).
Forwards letter from Ballanger. John Vaughan's account. [466]

1793 Sept. 1. T. J., Philadelphia, to DAVID MEADE RANDOLPH. L. 1 p. 19th century copy. Edgehill-Randolph Papers. Printed: B of R VI 380 (MS. in DLC).
Reasons why Mr. Gregoire is not appointed consul at Dunkerque. Consular

service at Bordeaux, Nantes, and le Havre. Mentions Mr. Barksdale, Francis Coffin, and Benjamin Franklin.   [467]

1793 Sept. 1. T. J., Philadelphia, to GEORGE TAYLOR. L. 1 p. 19th century copy. Edgehill-Randolph Papers. Printed: B of R VI 449 (MS. in DLC).
Letters for George Hammond, Mr. Van Berckel, Mr. Viar, and Mr. Jaudenes regarding passports and letters requested by the Charitable Committee of Baltimore.   [468]

1793. Sept. 1 T. J., Philadelphia, to GEORGE WYTHE. L. 1 p. 19th century copy. Edgehill-Randolph Papers.
Wythe's address delivered to President Washington.   [469]

1793 Sept. 3. T. J., Philadelphia, to THE REV. SAMUEL MILLER. L. 1 p. 19th century copy. Edgehill-Randolph Papers. Printed: B of R VI 325 (MS. in DLC). Another MS. in NJP.
Independence Day Sermon.   [470]

1793 Sept. 7. T. J., Philadelphia, to D. GRIFFITH. L. 1 p. 19th century copy. Edgehill-Randolph Papers. Printed: B of R VI 193 (MS. in DLC).
Exact location of the Maryland-Virginia boundary as given in his *Notes on Virginia;* [Jacques?] Cassini's method of computing latitude compared with Mason and Dixon's; George Mason's papers.   [471]

1793 Sept. 10. T. J., Philadelphia, to TENCH COXE. L. 1 p. 19th century copy. Edgehill-Randolph Papers. Printed: L & B IX 236.
It is not permitted to place consuls in the British Islands (West Indies?).
                                                                               [472]

1793 Sept. 10. T. J., Philadelphia, to ADAM LINDSAY. L. 1 p. 19th century copy. Edgehill-Randolph Papers. Printed: B of R VI 275 (MS. in DLC).
Plague in Philadelphia. Colonel Hamilton ill. Washington has left for Mt. Vernon. T. J. to go to Monticello.   [473]

1793 Sept. 10. T. J., Philadelphia, to DAVID MEADE RANDOLPH. L. 1 p. 19th century copy. Edgehill-Randolph Papers. Printed: B of R VI 380 (MS. in DLC).
Duty on package at the Custom House in Bermuda. Yellow fever in Philadelphia. References to Robert Gamble, Alexander Hamilton, George Washington, and Henry Knox.   [474]

1793 Sept. 11. T. J., Philadelphia, to BENJAMIN BANKSON. L. 1 p. 19th century copy. Edgehill-Randolph Papers. Printed: B of R VI 23 (MS. in DLC).
Instructions regarding letters for Gouverneur Morris.   [475]

1793 Sept. 11. T. J., Philadelphia, to BENJAMIN BANKSON. L. 1 p. 19th century copy. Edgehill-Randolph Papers. Printed: B of R VI 23 (MS. in DLC).
Return of a Senator for Delaware to be sent to the Secretary of the Senate.
                                                                               [476]

1793 Sept. 11. T. J., Philadelphia, to GEORGE HAMMOND. L. 1 p. 19th century copy. Edgehill-Randolph Papers. Printed: B of R VI 203 (MS. in DLC).
Requesting passports for 430 passengers to France from Baltimore. Mentions Samuel Sterrett of Baltimore, Captain Ardouin of the *Marianne* and Captain Dupouy of the *Nouvelle Rosalie*. [477]

1793 Sept. 11. T. J., Philadelphia, to HENRY REMSEN. L. 1 p. 19th century copy. Edgehill-Randolph Papers. Printed: B of R VI 388 (MS. in DLC).
Receipt of an ink pot. Letter for Thomas Pinckney covering a bill of exchange. Owing to epidemic of yellow fever in Philadelphia, Hamilton, Washington, and Knox have left. [478]

1793 Sept. 11. T. J., Schuylkill, Pa., to SAMUEL STERRETT, Baltimore. L. 1 p. 19th century copy. Edgehill-Randolph Papers.
Passports from Mr. Hammond for those seeking passage to France. [479]

1793 Sept. 13. T. J., Schuylkill, Pa., to BENJAMIN BANKSON. L. 1 p. 19th century copy. Edgehill-Randolph Papers.
Order to pay money due John Ross. [480]

1793 Sept. 13. T. J., Philadelphia, to THOMAS S. LEE. L. 1 p. 19th century copy. Edgehill-Randolph Papers. Printed: B of R VI 262 (MS. in DLC). Original MS. in MoHi.
To the Governor of Maryland, concerning the improper actions in Baltimore of French agents (A. C. Duplaine? Genet?). [481]

1793 Sept. 13. T. J., Philadelphia, to THOMAS G. PEACHY. L. 1 p. 19th century copy. Edgehill-Randolph Papers. Printed: B of R VI 366 (MS. in DLC).
Acknowledging receipt of resolutions of the inhabitants of Petersburg commending the President's conduct in pursuit of peace. [482]

1793 Sept. 13. T. J., Schuylkill, Pa., to JOHN ROSS. L. 1 p. 19th century copy. Edgehill-Randolph Papers. Printed: Ford VI 427-428; Jenkins 102-103n; B of R VI 397 (MS. in DLC). Another MS. in PPHi.
Request for a loan of $100, the amount of an order on Benjamin Bankson. [483]

1793 Sept. 15. T. J., Schuylkill, Pa., to PETER DERIEUX. L. 1 p. 19th century copy. Edgehill-Randolph Papers. Another MS. in DLC.
Balance due from John Vaughan. Yellow fever in Philadelphia. [484]

1793 Sept. 15. T. J., Schuylkill, Pa., to MR. KER. L. 1 p. 19th century copy. Edgehill-Randolph Papers. Printed: B of R VI 247 (MS. in DLC).
Payment of money due Ker made through Mr. Bankson. Mentions note of J. Bringhurst. [485]

1793 Sept. 15. T. J., Schuylkill, Pa., to THOMAS MANN RANDOLPH, JR. L. 1 p. 19th century copy. Edgehill-Randolph Papers. Printed: B of R VI 385 (MS. in DLC).
Plans to return to Monticello because of the yellow fever epidemic in Philadelphia. [486]

1793 Sept. 15. T. J., Philadelphia, to JOHN VAUGHAN. L. 1 p. 19th century copy. Edgehill-Randolph Papers. Another MS. in MHi.
  Value of lands beyond the mountains. Balance due Peter Derieux.   [487]

1793 Sept. 16. T. J., Schuylkill, Pa., to MRS. VALERIE FULLARTON. L. 1 p. 19th century copy. Edgehill-Randolph Papers. Printed: B of R VI 153 (MS. in DLC).
  Money due her left in the hands of Mr. Bankson.   [488]

1793 Sept. 26. T. J., Monticello, to ROBERT GAMBLE. L. 1 p. 19th century copy. Edgehill-Randolph Papers. Printed: B of R VI 171 (MS. in DLC).
  Books and wine shipped to T. J. *via* Gamble in Baltimore. Mentions Sloop *Polly,* James Tibbitt, master.   [489]

1793 Oct. 3. T. J., Monticello, to BENJAMIN BANKSON. L. 1 p. 19th century copy. Edgehill-Randolph Papers. Printed: B of R VI 24 (MS. in DLC).
  Urges Bankson to get out of Philadelphia during the epidemic. Mentions Mr. Crosby and Mr. Grey.   [490]

1793 Oct. 3. T. J., Monticello, to BENJAMIN BANKSON. L. 1 p. 19th century copy. Edgehill--Randolph Papers. Printed: B of R VI 24 (MS. in DLC).
  Covering letter for a group of letters and documents including letters patent revoking the Exequatur of A. C. Duplaine, Vice Consul at Boston, letters to A. C. Duplaine, Mr. Genet, and [Gouverneur] Morris. Letters patent to be published in Fenno's and Freneau's papers.   [491]

1793 Oct. 3. T. J., Monticello, to BENJAMIN BANKSON. L. 1 p. 19th century copy. Edgehill-Randolph Papers. Printed: B or R VI 24 (MS. in DLC).
  Covers a commission for Mr. Dannery as Consul of France at Boston and a letter for Mr. Genet.   [492]

1793 Oct. 3. T. J., Monticello, to TENCH COXE. L. 1 p. 19th century copy. Edgehill-Randolph Papers.
  Returning Mr. Frank's letter discussing damage to our commerce in the West Indies.   [493]

1793 Oct. 3. T. J., Monticello, to GEORGE WASHINGTON. L. 1 p. 19th century copy. Edgehill-Randolph Papers. Printed: B of R VI 496 (MS. in DLC).
  Commission for Mr. Dannery as French Consul in Boston; letters to Mr. Genet and Mr. Bankson.   [494]

1793 Oct. 3. T. J., Monticello, to GEORGE WASHINGTON. L. 1 p. 19th century copy. Edgehill-Randolph Papers. Printed: B of R VI 496 (MS. in DLC).
  Answer to Bournonville's letter sent for the President's approval. Mentions Benjamin Bankson and Mr. Dandridge.   [495]

1793 Oct. 3. T. J., Monticello, to GEORGE WASHINGTON. L. 1 p. 19th century copy. Edgehill-Randolph Papers. Printed: B of R VI 497 (MS. in DLC).
  Note to Tench Coxe.   [496]

1793 Oct. 9. T. J., Monticello, to GEORGE WASHINGTON. ALS. 1 p. 19th century copy. Edgehill-Randolph Papers.

Messrs. King, Pratt, *et al.,* owners of ship *Andrew,* should apply to France for indemnification for cargo of rice seized at Lorient and detention of the vessel. U. S. Minister, Gouverneur Morris, will exert pressure for the owners.   [497]

1793 Oct. 10. MARTHA CARR, DRAFT ON T. J. See 2 Dec. 1793.   [498]

1793 Oct. 10. T. J., Monticello, to JOHN HOPKINS. L. 1 p. 19th century copy. Edgehill-Randolph Papers. Printed: B of R VI 218 (MS. in DLC).

To the Commissioner of Loans regarding William Short's loan office certificates. Mentions James Brown.   [499]

1793 Oct. 18. T. J., Monticello, to RICHARD HANSON. L. 1 p. 19th century copy. Edgehill-Randolph Papers. Printed: B of R VI 205 (MS. in DLC).

Bonds from the sale of Negroes, from Mr. Ronald for Cumberland lands, and for the Elkhill lands should discharge T. J.'s bonds to William Jones. Mentions Daniel Hylton.   [500]

1793 Oct. 18. T. J., Monticello, to DANIEL HYLTON. L. 1 p. 19th century copy. Edgehill-Randolph Papers. Printed: B of R VI 227 (MS. in DLC).

Order to deliver bonds on Elkhill lands, from Banks & Taylor, to Richard Hanson, to discharge T. J.'s bonds to William Jones of Farrell & Jones.   [501]

1793 Oct. 19. T. J., Monticello, to MARTHA JEFFERSON CARR. L. 1 p. 19th century copy. Edgehill-Randolph Papers.

Letter of credit for Anna Scott Marks. Estate of John Wayles. Mentions Mr. Myers and Francis Eppes.   [502]

1793 Oct. 19, T. J. LETTER OF CREDIT. D. 1 p. 19th century copy. Edgehill-Randolph Papers.

Letter of credit for Anna Scott Marks or Martha Carr.   [503]

1793 Oct. 19 T. J., Monticello, to ANNA SCOTT MARKS. L. 1 p. 19th century copy. Edgehill-Randolph Papers. Printed: B of R VI 315 (MS. in DLC).

Notifying his sister that a letter of credit for her use has been sent to Martha Carr.   [504]

1793 Oct. 24. PETER CARR, Spring Forest, to T. J., Monticello. ALS. 1 p. Endorsed by T. J. Carr-Cary Papers.

Requests funds for his mother.   [505]

1793 Oct. 31. T. M.. RANDOLPH, JR., Monticello, to T. J., Philadelphia. T. J.'s extract made for enclosure to Herman LeRoy in letter of 11 November 1793. T. J. AD. 2 pp. Letterpress copy (and a 19th century copy, incorrectly dated 31 December). Edgehill-Randolph Papers. Another MS. in MHi.

Payment to Herman LeRoy (of mortgage bond secured by Henrico County land given to T. M. R., Jr., by his father) to be made by the wheat crop at Varina, now ready for market. Refers to David Ross and Alexander Donald.   [506]

1793 Nov. 3 T. J., Germantown, to RICHARD DOBSON. L. 1 p. 19th century copy. Edgehill-Randolph Papers. Printed: B of R VI 124 (MS. in DLC); Jenkins 33.
   Payments made on T. J.'s bill of exchange and bond.   [507]

1793 Nov. 5. T. J., Philadelphia, to WALTER BOYD, Paris. L. 1 p. 19th century copy. Edgehill-Randolph Papers. Printed: B of R VI 45 (MS. in DLC).
   Letter of introduction for Tobias Lear. Mentions Boyd's brother in Bladens-burgh.   [508]

1793 Nov. 5. T. J., Philadelphia, to U. S. CONSULS, C. W. F. Dumas, Joseph Fenwick, Mr. La Motte, and Stephen Cathalan. L. 1 p. 19th century copy. Circular. Edgehill-Randolph Papers. Printed: B of R VI 133 (MS. in DLC).
   Introducing Tobias Lear, formerly President Washington's secretary, who proposes to establish in commerce in the city of Washington.   [509]

1793 Nov. 5. T. J., Philadelphia, to FERDINAND GRAND. L. 1 p. 19th century copy. Edgehill-Randolph Papers. Printed: B of R VI 189 (MS. in DLC).
   Letter of introduction for Tobias Lear.   [510]

1793 Nov. 5. T. J., Germantown, to TOBIAS LEAR. L. 1 p. 19th century copy. Edgehill-Randolph Papers. Printed: Jenkins 37; B of R VI 262 (MS. in DLC). Original MS. owned by Francis R. Stoddard.
   Letters of introduction. References to C. W. F. Dumas in Amsterdam, Van Staphorst & Hubbard, and to Mr. Greenlief. The Revolution has turned adrift many of his French friends.   [511]

1793 Nov. 7. THOMAS MANN RANDOLPH, JR., Monticello, to T. J., Philadelphia. ALS. 2 pp. Endorsed by T. J. Edgehill-Randolph Papers.
   Forwarding of books, letters, and papers. Wheat crop prospects. Illness of a servant. Mentions Samuel Biddle, Watson, Dr. Gilmer, Martha Randolph, and Maria Jefferson.   [512]

1793 Nov. 10. T. J., Germantown, to PETER CARR, Spring Forest. ALS. 1 p. Carr-Cary Papers. Printed: Jenkins 54-55; B of R VI 71 (MS. in DLC).
   Will pay Martha Carr the money from the execution of Wayles' representatives against Archibald Cary's estate. Account of Carr's debut in Albemarle Courts is flattering. References to Francis Eppes and Carter Page.   [513]

1793 Nov. 11. T. J., Germantown, to HERMAN LEROY, Philadelphia. ALS. 2 pp. Letterpress copy. Edgehill-Randolph Papers.
   Terms of repayment of mortgage on Varina, land owned by Thomas Mann Randolph, Jr., son of Colonel Randolph of Tuckahoe.   [514]

1793 Nov. 13. T. J., Germantown, to CHARLES HOMASSEL. L. 1 p. 19th century copy. Edgehill-Randolph Papers. Printed: Jenkins 67; B of R VI 218 (MS. in DLC).
   Sale of goods shipped from France for Peter Derieux. Mentions John Vaughan.
                                                                         [515]

1793 Nov. 13. T. J., Germantown, to JOHN HOPKINS, Richmond. L. 1 p. 19th century copy. Edgehill-Randolph Papers. Printed: B of R VI 218 (MS. in DLC); Jenkins 66.
Transferral of William Short's government stock from Richmond and New York to Philadelphia. [516]

1793 Nov. 13. T. J., Germantown, to PATRICK KENNON, New York. L. 1 p. 19th century copy. Edgehill-Randolph Papers. Printed: Jenkins 64-65; B of R VI 245 (MS. in DLC).
Transferral of William Short's government stock (U. S. loan office certificates) from New York and Richmond to Philadelphia. [517]

1793 Nov. 14. T. J., Germantown, to ROBERT GAMBLE. L. 1 p. 19th century copy. Edgehill-Randolph Papers. Printed: B of R VI 171 (MS. in DLC); Jenkins 71-73.
Letter for Mr. Mewbern of Richmond. Yellow fever epidemic in Philadelphia is over. Return of Congress and President Washington. [518]

1793 Nov. 14. T. J., Germantown, to PATRICK HART. L. 1 p. 19th century copy. Edgehill-Randolph Papers. Printed: Jenkins 74; B of R VI 208 (MS. in DLC).
Thanks for forwarding his orrery (astronomical instrument). Mentions David Randolph and Thomas Mann Randolph, Jr. [519]

1793 Nov. 14. T. J., Germantown, to MR. MEWBERN, Richmond. L. 1 p. 19th century copy. Edgehill-Randolph Papers. Printed: Jenkins 72; B of R VI 324 (MS. in DLC).
Request that he deliver T. J.'s telescope to T. M. Randolph, Jr. [520]

1793 Nov. 14. THOMAS MANN RANDOLPH, JR., Monticello, to T. J., Philadelphia. ALS. 2 pp. Endorsed by T. J. Edgehill-Randolph Papers.
Inquiries as to T. J.'s health. Illness of Thomas Mann Randolph, Sr. Removal of T. J.'s furniture to Belvedere. Health of the "colored part of the family." Purchase of T. J.'s horse, Tarquin. Mentions Maria Jefferson. [521]

1793 Nov. 16. T. J., Germantown, to JOHN KEAN. L. 1 p. 19th century copy. Edgehill-Randolph Papers. Printed: Ford VI 449; Jenkins 93; B of R VI 246 (MS. in DLC).
Requesting his salary for the quarter. Mentions possible removal of Congress to Lancaster, Pa., because of the yellow fever. [522]

1793 Nov. 16. T. J., Germantown, to ELI WHITNEY, New Haven. L. 1 p. 19th century copy. Edgehill-Randolph Papers. Printed: Ford VI 448; Jenkins 90-91.
Patenting of the cotton gin. Its practicability. Mentions advertisement by Pearce of the Patterson Manufacory. [523]

1793 Nov. 16-18. T. J., Germantown, to GEORGE TAYLOR, Philadelphia. L. 1 p. 19th century copy. Edgehill-Randolph Papers. Printed: Jenkins 99-101; B of R VI 449 and X 18 (MSS. in DLC).
Requesting that Taylor endorse a note for him and send it to John Kean. [George?] Wythe's money received. [524]

1793 Nov. 17. T. J., Germantown, to HERMAN LEROY, Philadelphia. L. 1 p. 19th century copy. Edgehill-Randolph Papers. Another MS. in PPHi. Printed: Jenkins 94-95.

Wishes both Dover and Varina to stand as security for debt of Thomas Mann Randolph, Jr., to Mr. LeRoy. Mentions Mr. Bayard.   [525]

1793 Nov. 19. T. J., Germantown, to JOHN ROSS. L. 1 p. 19th century copy. Edgehill-Randolph Papers. Printed: Jenkins 102-103; B of R VI 397 (MS. in DLC).

Payment of $100. Congratulations on his resurrection (death reported in newspapers).   [526]

1793 Nov. 20. T. J., Philadelphia, to JOHN MASON. L. 1 p. 19th century copy. Edgehill-Randolph Papers. Printed: B of R VI 317 (MS. in DLC).

Payment of his debts and of Joseph Fenwick's draft.   [527]

1793 Nov. 21. T. J., Germantown, to JACOB HOLLINGSWORTH. L. 1 p. 19th century copy. Edgehill-Randolph Papers.

Order for red clover seed for Elk Hill. Terms for the new overseer [at Elk Hill] the same as for Samuel Biddle.   [528]

1793 Nov. 24. T. J., Germantown, to M. & J. MYERS. L. 1 p. 19th century copy. Edgehill-Randolph Papers. Printed: B of R VI 346 (MS. in DLC); Jenkins 119.

Money to be passed to the credit of Mrs. Carr.   [529]

1793 Nov. 24. T. J., Germantown, to THOMAS MANN RANDOLPH, JR., Montincello. L. 1 p. 19th century copy. Edgehill-Randolph Papers. Printed: Jenkins 118-119; B of R VI 385 (MS. in DLC).

Gift of the horse Tarquin. Letter to Archibald Stuart. Instructions for Samuel Biddle to get sheep from Stuart. Questions advisability of acting as his father's executor. Greetings to Martha and Maria.   [530]

1793 Nov. 24. T. J., Germantown, to ARCHIBALD STUART. L. 1 p. 19th century copy. Edgehill-Randolph Papers. Printed: Ford VI 453-454; Jenkins 115-116; B of R VI 443 (MS. in DLC).

Purchase of sheep at Staunton, to be sent to T. M. Randolph, Jr., or to Samuel Biddle, overseer at Monticello. Stuart's offer of potatoes. France triumphant in the North.   [531]

1793 Nov. 28. T. J., Germantown, to JOHN NANCARROW. L. 1 p. 19th century copy. Edgehill-Randolph Papers. Printed: Jenkins 124-125; B of R VI 346 (MS. in DLC).

Refusing his offer of quarters.   [532]

1793 Nov. 30. THOMAS MANN RANDOLPH, JR., Richmond, to T. J., Philadelphia. ALS. 2 pp. Endorsed by T. J. Edgehill-Randolph Papers.

Death of Thomas Mann Randolph, Sr. Dissatisfaction with terms of his will, drawn by John Harvie. Failure of Daniel Hylton to move T. J.'s furniture. Bond to Mr. LeRoy. Mentions James Brown, Martha Randolph, and Maria Jefferson.   [533]

1793 Dec. 1. T. J., Philadelphia, to MARTHA J. RANDOLPH. L. 1 p. 19th century copy. Edgehill-Randolph Papers.

Return to Philadelphia of George Washington, Dr. and Mrs. Waters, and Mr. Trist. French triumphant. Revolution in Santo Domingo. Freneau's and Fenno's papers have been discontinued. Mentions Edmund Randolph, the Duke of Brunswick, Thomas Mann Randolph, Jr., and Maria Jefferson.   [534]

1793 Dec. 2. M. & J. MYERS, Goochland County, to T. J. ALS. 1 p. 2 enclosures. Endorsed by T. J. Carr-Cary Papers.

Receipt of money for acceptance of Martha Carr's drafts on T. J. (Enclosures: her drafts of 2 Feb. and of 10 Oct. 1793, in favor of William Austin and Mr. Myers, respectively.)   [535]

1793 Dec. 4. T. J., Philadelphia, to JACOB HOLLINGSWORTH. L. 1 p. 19th century copy. Edgehill-Randolph Papers. Printed: B of R VI 216 (MS. in DLC).

Appointment of Eli Alexander as overseer of Shadwell. Suggests he go *via* Richmond. Purchase of red clover seed. Mentions Thomas Mann Randolph, Jr. and Samuel Biddle.   [536]

1793 Dec. 8. T. J., Philadelphia, to JAMES BROWN, Richmond. L. 1 p. 19th century copy. Edgehill-Randolph Papers. Printed: B of R VI 52 (MS. in DLC).

William Short's loan office certificates. Furniture for Monticello. Mentions Mr. Hague, John Hopkins, and Thomas Mann Randolph, Jr.   [537]

1793 Dec. 8. T. J., Philadelphia, to ROBERT GAMBLE, Richmond. L. 1 p. 19th century copy. Edgehill-Randolph Papers. Printed: B of R VI 171 (MS. in DLC).

Shipment of threshing machine by the *Ellica*, Captain Waymouth.   [538]

1793 Dec. 8. T. J., Philadelphia, to JOHN HOPKINS, Richmond. L. 1 p. 19th century copy. Edgehill-Randolph Papers. Printed: B of R VI 218 (MS. in DLC).

William Short's loan office certificates.   [539]

1793 Dec. 8. T. J., Philadelphia, to PATRICK KENNON, New York. L. 1 19th century copy. Edgehill-Randolph Papers. Printed: B of R VI 246 (MS. in DLC).

William Short's loan office certificates.   [540]

1793 Dec. 8. T. J., Philadelphia, to THOMAS MANN RANDOLPH, JR., Monticello. L. 2 pp. 19th century copy. Edgehill-Randolph Papers. Printed: B of R VI 385 (MS. in DLC). Another MS. in CSmH.

Randolph's debts to Herman LeRoy. Horses for T. J.'s return to Monticello. Arrangements for Eli Alexander, overseer on east side of the Rivanna. Discontinuation of Freneau's and Fenno's newspapers. Important victories of the French. Toulon in enemy hands. Death of T. M. Randolph, Sr. Mentions Maria, Samuel Biddle, Mr. Fitch, [Byrd] Rogers, Dabney Carr, Fredericksburg.   [541]

1793 Dec. 12. T. J., Philadelphia, to ROBERT LESLIE [London]. L. 2 pp. 19th century copy. Edgehill-Randolph Papers. Printed: B of R VI 267 (MS. in DLC).

Directions for the making and repairing of watches and clocks.   [542]

1793 Dec. 12. T. J., Philadelphia, to THOMAS PINCKNEY, [London]. L. 1 p.
19th century copy. Edgehill-Randolph Papers. Printed: B of R VI 375 (MS. in
DLC).

Payment for the threshing machine. Truce established by Algiers, Portugal,
and Holland. Letters to Messrs. Van Staphorst, Mr. Church, and Robert Leslie.
Mentions ship *George Barclay*.   [543]

1793 Dec. 15. T. J., Philadelphia, to BENJAMIN BLANCHARD. L. 1 p. 19th
century copy. Edgehill-Randolph Papers. Printed: B of R VI 38 (MS. in DLC).

Refusing to lend him money or to refer the solicitation to the President. [544]

1793 Dec. 15. T. J., Philadelphia, to MARIA JEFFERSON, Monticello. L. 1 p.
19th century copy. Edgehill-Randolph Papers. Printed: Randall II 220; SNR
225-226.

Writing desk to be made by Mr. Watson. News of Mrs. Fullerton, Sally
Cropper, and Maria's maid. Horses for his return to Monticello. Information
regarding Eli Alexander, who is to take charge of Shadwell farm under Byrd
Rogers. Mentions Thomas Mann Randolph, Jr., and Martha Randolph.   [545]

1793 Dec. 17. T. J., Philadelphia, to JACOB HOLLINGSWORTH, Elkton. L. 1 p.
19th century copy. Edgehill-Randolph Papers. Printed: B of R VI 216 (MS. in
DLC).

Red clover seed. Eli Alexander's departure.   [546]

1793 Dec. 18. T. J., Philadelphia, to CALEB LOWNES. L. 1 p. 19th century
copy. Edgehill-Randolph Papers. Printed: B of R VI 280 (MS. in DLC).

Shipment of books and furniture to Robert Gamble in Richmond. Order for a
ton of nailrod.   [547]

1793 Dec. 21. T. J., Philadelphia, to BENJAMIN WALLER. L. 1 p. 19th century
copy. Edgehill-Randolph Papers.

Debt of the John Wayles estate to Mr. Welsh. Mentions Francis Eppes, an
executor, and Farrell & Jones, creditors of the estate.   [548]

1793 Dec. 22. T. J., Philadelphia, to MARTHA J. RANDOLPH, Monticello. L.
1 p. 19th century copy. Edgehill-Randolph Papers. Printed: Ford VI 488-489.

Horses for return to Monticello. Retirement from office is definite. Shipment
of books and furniture. Printed copy of correspondence with Genet and Hammond to be sent soon. Relations with England and Spain. England has let loose
the Algerians on us. Mentions Thomas Mann Randolph, Jr., and Maria Jefferson.
                                                                  [549]

1793 Dec. [23-31]. LIST OF CERTIFICATES received by T. J. for WILLIAM
SHORT. D. 1 p. 19th century copy. Edgehill-Randolph Papers. Original MS. of
letter of transmittal, Dec. 23, in VWW. Printed: B of R VI 426 (MS. in DLC).

Listing items received from John Hopkins, James Brown, and Patrick Kennon.
Postscript memorandum to Short reports resignation as Secretary of State; to
be succeeded by Edmund Randolph.   [550]

1793 Dec. 30. T. J., Philadelphia, to THOMAS MANN RANDOLPH, JR., Monticello. L. 1 p. 19th century copy. Edgehill-Randolph Papers. Printed: B of R VI 385 (MS. in DLC).

Delay in shipment of furniture. Gift of horse "Tarquin." Edmund Randolph succeeds T. J. Arrangements for meeting horses at Fredericksburg. Mentions Mann Page and Peter Carr. [551]

1793 Dec. [31]. T. J., Philadelphia, to JOSEPH YZNARDI. L. 1 p. Incorrectly dated Dec. 3. 19th century copy. Edgehill-Randolph Papers.

Order for wine to be sent to Richmond. [552]

[1793]. T. J. to JAMES MONROE. L. 1 p. 19th century copy. Edgehill-Randolph Papers.

Distribution of money which may be obtained from suits against Lewis and Woodson to Donald Scott & Co., William and James Donald, and James Monroe. References to Nathaniel Pope, Nicholas Lewis, and John Dobson. [553]

[1793?] T. J., to [THOMAS M. RANDOLPH, JR.]. AL. 1 p. Letterpress copy. Fragment. Edgehill-Randolph Papers.

Case concerning Thomas Mann Randolph, Sr.'s mortgage on Varina, payable after his death by his son, T. M. R., Jr. Deed for Poplar Forest to Martha Jefferson. Mentions David Ross. [554]

[1793]. T. J., [Philadelphia], to [WILLIAM SHORT?]. L. 1 p. 19th century copy. Fragment. Edgehill-Randolph Papers.

Shorts public bonds. New Secretary of State yet unnamed. Letter from Peyton Short. [555]

1794 Apr. 28. T. J., Monticello, to WILLIAM NELSON, Richmond. ALS. 2 pp. Photostat. Endorsed. Original owned by Edward O. McCague. Printed: B of R VI 349 (MS. in DLC).

Patents dependent on Virginia-Kentucky and Virginia-North Carolina boundary disputes. Mentions Walker-Henderson Line. [556]

1794 Apr. LIST OF LIVESTOCK AT POPLAR FOREST. D. 1 p. Edgehill-Randolph Papers.

T. J.'s overseer lists 139 cattle and 203 hogs. [557]

1794 Sept. 24. T. J., Monticello, to DABNEY CARR. ALS. 1 p. Letterpress copy. Carr-Cary Papers.

Advises study of French with Martha Radolph. Plans sale of his law books. Martha Carr, Maria Jefferson, and Miss Cary mentioned. [558]

1794 Oct. 9. T. J., Monticello, to [JOHN] BARNES, Philadelphia. ALS. 1 p. Letterpress copy. Edgehill-Randolph Papers.

Order for tea. Reference to [Joseph] Mussi. [559]

1794 Nov. 20. T. J., Monticello, to JOHN BARNES, Philadelphia. ALS. 1 p. Letterpress copy. Edgehill-Randolph Papers.

Bill of exchange for Messrs. Van Staphorst includes money for Philip Mazzei. Request for prices of German and British osnaburg, cotton cloth, striped blankets, and plaid hose for Negroes. Mentions Mr. Blair. [560]

1794 Dec. 17. T. J., Monticello, to WILLIAM B. GILES. L. 1 p. Extract by N. P. Trist *ca.* 1830. Printed: B of R VI 183 (MS. in DLC); Ford VI 515-516.

Conference concerning attacks on freedom of speech. [561]

1794 Dec. 26. T. J., Monticello, to [THOMAS MANN RANDOLPH, JR.] AL. 1 p. Letterpress copy. Fragment. Edgehill-Randolph Papers.

Delay in returning T. M. R.'s wagon. Shipment of nailrod from Richmond. Asparagus for Martha. Mentions [Thomas] Bell and servants Billy and Zachary. [562]

[1794] Dec. 27. T. J., Monticello, to [THOMAS MANN RANDOLPH, JR.] AL. 1 p. Letterpress copy. Fragment. Edgehill-Randolph Papers.

Arrival of Billy. Difference of opinion between George Wythe and Edmund Pendleton on division of Dabney Carr's property and servants after death of Barbara O. Carr. Portion due Peter Carr. Shipment of nailrod. Payment to John Taylor for drill-plow. References to Mr. Stras, John Harvie. [563]

1795 Jan. 22. T. J., Monticello, to MARTHA RANDOLPH, Varina. ALS. 2 pp. Letterpress copy. Endorsed by T. J. Edgehill-Randolph Papers.

The Dover sale. Request that Thomas Mann Randolph, Jr., remit Mr. Stras' money to [Joseph] Mussi in Philadelphia. Shipment of nailrod, a drill-plow, and clover. Wheels for T. J.'s chariot. Wheat crop improved by cold weather. News of Anne and Thomas Jefferson Randolph, Mrs. Peter Marks, Dr. [George] Gilmer. Mentions Mr. Snelson and Maria Jefferson. [564]

1795 Feb. 5. T. J., Monticello, to MARTHA RANDOLPH, Varina. ALS. 1 p. Letterpress copy. Endorsed by T. J. Edgehill-Randolph Papers.

News of Thomas Jefferson Randolph. Cold weather. Hughes, overseer at Varina, should relieve Thomas Mann Randolph at Varina. [Bowling] Clarke reports short tobacco crop and loss of a horse. [565]

1795 Feb. 12. T. J., Monticello, to THOMAS MANN RANDOLPH, JR. ALS. 1 p. Letterpress copy. Endorsed by T. J. Edgehill-Randolph Papers.

Clover seed. Cold weather. Arrival of a mule. Col. [Thomas] Bell's illness. Mentions Martha Randolph. Partly illegible. [566]

[1795 Feb. 26]. T. J., to THOMAS MANN RANDOLPH, JR. ALS. 1 p. Letterpress copy. Edgehill-Randolph Papers.

Crisis regarding mortgage on Varina. References to Herman LeRoy and Dover plantation. [567]

1795 May 17. T. J., Monticello, to ARCHIBALD STUART, Staunton. ALS. 1 p. McGregor Library. Printed: B of R VI 443 (MS. in DLC).

Introducing Mr. Strickland. [568]

1795 May 23. T. J., Monticello, to ARCHIBALD STUART, Staunton. ALS. 2 pp. McGregor Library. Partly printed: W(2) V 292-293.

List of law books to be forwarded to Stuart at Staunton by Col. [Thomas] Bell. Requests Staunton clockmender for work on Monticello clocks. Mentions Dabney Carr. (List of books previously unpublished.) [569]

1795 Sept. 16. T. J., Monticello, to JOSIAH DONATH, Philadelphia. ALS. 1 p. Photostat. Original owned by Robert G. Hopkins.

Order for panes of glass for Monticello. [570]

1795 Dec. 5. LAND OFFICE TREASURY WARRANT No. 1724 to T. J. D. 2 pp. Contemporary Copy. Endorsed by T. J. McGregor Library.

Warrant for 100 acres of land in Campbell County. Surveyed by Richard Smith (i.e., Stith). [571]

*1895 Dec. 23. RICHARD STITH. SURVEY. D. 1 p. Endorsed. Copy attested by William P. Martin. McGregor Library.

Copy of plat and surveyor's courses for 100 acres of land surveyed for T. J. in Campbell County. [572]

1795 Dec. 23. T. J. LAND PATENT, Poplar Forest. D. 2 items. Endorsed. Mc-Gregor Library.

Patent for 800 acres in Bedford County, a part of the Poplar Forest tract, surveyed for John Wayles by Richard Stith, 20 March 1770, and patented in the name of T. J., 1795. Plat shows adjoining lands belonging to Richard Callaway, William Callaway, and Mr. Moseby. [573]

1796 Jan. 1. MARTHA RANDOLPH, Dungeness, to T. J., Monticello. ALS. 1 p. Endorsed by T. J. Edgehill-Randolph Papers.

List of articles needed at Varina. Greetings to Maria and the children. [574]

1796 Jan. 3. T. J., Monticello, to PETER DERIEUX. ALS. 1 p. Photostat. Original owned by Dr. Dabney Lancaster.

Mr. Payne's foreclosure of mortgage on Derieux's tenement leased from Wood. [575]

1796 Jan. 25. T. J., Monticello, to MARTHA RANDOLPH. ALS. 1 p. Letterpress copy. Endorsed by T. J. Edgehill-Randolph Papers.

Mr. Randolph's wagon. News of Thomas Jefferson Randolph. Depositions of the Shocko inspectors. Cold weather. Peter Carr at Philadelphia. References to Maria Jefferson and Anne Randolph. [576]

1796 Feb. 5. T. J. DEED to SERVANT, JAMES HEMINGS. ADS. 2 pp. Photostat. Original, Albemarle County Court House. Recorded by John Nicholas, Clerk, April Court, 1796.

Deed of manumission, witnessed by John Carr and Francis Anderson. [577]

1796 Feb. 7. T. J., Monticello, to THOMAS MANN RANDOLPH, JR. ALS. 2
pp. Letterpress copy. Photostat. Endorsed by T. J. Deposited from Monticello.

Cold weather; Randolph's affairs at Edgehill; scarcity of corn; payment of Mr.
Divers; land grants in Bedford and Campbell Counties. Action regarding tobacco
passed by Cobb (tobacco inspector) around 1786. Mr. Faris to pick up machine
from Mr. Britton. Construction work (at Monticello?). References to Peter Carr,
[Robert?] Gamble, and to Shadwell.   [578]

1796 Feb. 29. T. J., Monticello, to THOMAS MANN RANDOLPH, JR. ALS. 1 p.
Letterpress copy. Endorsed by T. J. Edgehill-Randolph Papers.

Marriage of Captain Allcock to Mrs. [Mildred] Walker. Plowing at Monticello
and Edgehill. Peas, clover, groceries at Monticello. References to [Thomas] Bell,
Adrien Petit, Mr. Page, and Mr. Robertson.   [579]

1796 Apr. 17. RANDOLPH JEFFERSON. DEED TO T. J. D. Attested copy.
2 pp. Endorsed by T. J. Witnessed by John Nicholas, John Carr, and Alexander
Garrett. Proved April 1796. Copy attested by Alexander Garrett, Clerk. Carr-
Cary Papers.

Conveying 400 acres of land on Hardware River in Albemarle County inherited
from Peter Jefferson.   [580]

*1796 May 5. ALBEMARLE COUNTY COURT to ELIZABETH HENDERSON.
D. 3 pp. Endorsed by T. J. Recorded June 1796, and this copy attested by John
Nicholas, Clerk.

Assignment to Mrs. Henderson by special Commissioners (William Clark,
Robert Snelson, John Watson) of her dower in the estate of her husband,
Bennett Henderson, deceased: profits of mill and warehouse, buildings and land,
town lots at Milton. References to her son, John Henderson.   [581]

1796 June 20. RICHARD STITH, Campbell County, to T. J., Monticello. ALS.
1 p. Endorsed by T. J. McGregor Library.

Surveyor's difficulty in keeping up with legislative changes.   [582]

1796 Aug. 19 T. J., Monticello, to WILSON CARY NICHOLAS. ALS. 1 p. Wilson Cary Nicholas Papers.

Enclosing draft of Nicholas' house plans. Needs good overseer.   [583]

1796 Sept. 21. JOHN GARLAND JEFFERSON, Petersburg, to T. J., [Monticello].
ALS. 2 pp. Endorsed by T. J. Carr-Cary Papers.

No conveyance by Peter Jefferson recorded in Lunenburg County 1750 to
1757. Will search in Bedford and Halifax Counties. Pleased that Washington
will not serve another term.   [584]

1796 Oct. 2. T. J., Monticello, to JOSIAH DONATH, Philadelphia. ALS. 1 p.
Endorsed. McGregor Library.

Order for window glass, paid for by draft on John Barnes.   [585]

1796 Oct. 25. JAMES LYLE, Manchester, England, to T. J. ALS. 2 pp. Edgehill-
Randolph Papers.

Covering letter for an account with Henderson, McCaul & Co. Records receipts
from James Brown, Christopher Clark, and T. M. Randolph, Jr.   [586]

1796 Dec. 4. T. J., Monticello, to JOSIAH DONATH, Philadelphia. ALS. 1 p. Endorsed. McGregor Library.

Payment for window glass by draft on John Barnes. [587]

1797 Mar. 11. T. J., Philadelphia, to MARIA JEFFERSON, Varina. AL. 1 p.
News of her friends, Miss Geddis and Miss McKain. Unable to provide Miss Bruni a place in his carriage. Permission to remain at Varina. [588]

1797 Mar. 27. T. J., Monticello, to MARTHA RANDOLPH. AL. 1 p. Letterpress copy. Endorsed by T. J. Edgehill-Randolph Papers. Printed: Randall II 338; SNR 242-243.

Spring earlier at Monticello than at Fredericksburg. Loneliness for Maria and Martha. Healthfulness of Monticello compared with Varina. References to T. M. Randolph, Jr., and Billy Wood. [589]

1797 Apr. 9. T. J., Monticello, to THOMAS MANN RANDOLPH, JR. AL. 1 p. Endorsed by T. J. Edgehill-Randolph Papers.

Apologies to the militia captains for T. M. R.'s absence. Clover, mules, price of wheat. [590]

1797 May 19. T. J., [Monticello], to THOMAS MANN RANDOLPH, JR. ALS. 1 p. Letterpress copy. Endorsed by T. J. Edgehill-Randolph Papers.

Illegible copy dealing with tobacco. [591]

*1797 May 22. JAMES WOOD. LAND GRANT TO T. J. DS. 1 p. Printed on parchment. Endorsed. Certified by William Price, Register, Virginia Land Office.

Patent for 100 acres on Ivy Creek in Campbell County, adjoining Wilkerson, Johnson, Tullos. [592]

1797 July 26. JOHN BARNES, Philadelphia, to T. J., Monticello. ALS. 1 p. Endorsed by T. J. Edgehill-Randolph Papers.

Is repacking the enormous (fossil) tooth. Incloses invoice for sash doors and his account. Draft in favor of C. Johnson; W. and S. Keith's notes. Tobacco prices. [593]

1797 Aug. 10. JOHN BARNES, Philadelphia, to T. J., Monticello. ALS. 1 p. Endorsed by T. J. Edgehill-Randolph Papers.

Account of Mr. Lote. [594]

*[1797] Aug. 20 [date received]. JOHN GARLAND JEFFERSON to T. J. ALS. 2 pp. Endorsed by T. J. Carr-Cary Papers.

Report on law reading. Requests permission to return to Albemarle where he can get books more easily and counteract bad opinion of him there. Reference to his uncle John Garland. [595]

1797 Sept. 14. JOHN BARNES, Philadelphia, to T. J., Monticello. ALS. 1 p. Endorsed by T. J. Edgehill-Randolph Papers.

Draft on William Short's account. Yellow fever epidemic has emptied the city. [596]

1797 Oct. 19. JOHN BARNES, Philadelphia, to T. J., Monticello. ALS. 1 p. Endorsed by T. J. Edgehill-Randolph Papers.

T. J.'s power of attorney confirmed. James Monroe's draft. Yellow fever epidemic. Letter to [James Thomson?] Callender.   [597]

[1797 Nov.] JOHN WAYLES EPPES to T. J., Monticello. ALS. 2 pp. Endorsed by T. J. Edgehill-Randolph Papers.

News of Maria's health. Greetings to Martha and Thomas Mann Randolph, Jr.
                                                                                      [598]

1798 Jan. 30. THOMAS MANN RANDOLPH, JR., Belmont, Va., to T. J., Philadelphia. ALS. 2 pp. Endorsed by T. J. Edgehill-Randolph Papers.

Jupiter reports theft at Monticello; York (servant) suspected. References to [Richard] Richardson, overseer at Monticello, and George (servant). Order for window glass and for the last edition of Linnaeus' *Genera Plantarum*.
                                                                                      [599]

1798 Feb. 21. T. J., Philadelphia, to HORATIO GATES, New York. ALS. 2 pp. Endorsed. Printed: Ford VII 203-206; L & B IX 441-443; TJR III 374-375 (in part); B of R VI 174 (MS. in DLC).

Letter delivered to General Kosciuszko. Possible war with France, whose attitude, like England's, threatens U. S. commerce. Kosciuszko disappointed at France's peace with Austria; had hoped his country would rise again.   [600]

1798 Feb. 23. T. J., Philadelphia, to PEREGRINE FITZHUGH. L. 1 p. Extract by N. P. Trist *ca.* 1830. Printed: Ford VII 208-211; L & B X 104; B of R VI 149 (letterpress copy in DLC).

Importance of proper adjustment of both federal and state governments. Differences in Congress respecting comparative influence of the two.   [601]

1798 Feb. 26. THOMAS MANN RANDOLPH, JR., Belmont, Va., to T. J., Philadelphia. ALS. 1 p. Endorsed by T. J. Edgehill-Randolph Papers.

Need for nailrod at Monticello's nail manufactory. Need for a journeyman blacksmith. Tobacco crop. References to servants George, James, and Page.
                                                                                      [602]

1798 Mar. 12. THOMAS MANN RANDOLPH, JR., Belmont, Va., to T. J. ALS. 1 p. Endorsed by T. J. Deposited by Robert H. Kean.

Purchase of horses and mules. Mr. Hore [Browse] Trist unlikely to purchase [Nicholas?] Lewis' farm, since he prefers the country near Frederick County, Va., or Berkeley County, [W.] Va.   [603]

1798 Apr. 11. T. J., Philadelphia, to JOHN WAYLES EPPES. AL. 2 pp. Printed: Randall II 383-384.

Discussion of the XYZ Affair; Charles Talleyrand.   [604]

1798 Apr. 22. THOMAS MANN RANDOLPH, JR., Belmont, Va., to T. J., Philadelphia. ALS. 1 p. Fragment. Endorsed by T. J. Edgehill-Randolph Papers.

Work done by George at Monticello. XYZ Affair. Suspects Talleyrand's honesty. Tobacco prices. References to Wilson Cary Nicholas and Thomas Walker. T. J.'s return to Monticello.   [605]

1798 Apr. 29. THOMAS MANN RANDOLPH, JR., Belmont, Va., to T. J., Philadelphia. ALS. 3 pp. Endorsed by T. J. Edgehill-Randolph Papers.

Shipment of trees and a harpsichord. Supply of lumber for work at Monticello. Tobacco and corn crops. Purchase of horses. Books by Lescarbot and Champlain. Accident to his horse Darlington. References to Davenport, George (servant), and to [Richard?] Richardson.   [606]

1798 May 5. TADEUSZ KOSCIUSZKO. WILL. D. 1 p. Copy. Original in Albemarle County Will Book I 42.

Bequeaths property to T. J. to purchase Negroes and give them liberty. T. J.'s refusal to execute will, 12 May 1819, attested by John Carr, Clerk of Albemarle County.   [607]

1798 May 6. T. J., Philadelphia, to JOHN WAYLES EPPES. [Eppington]. AL. 2 pp. Another MS. in MHi. Printed: Randall II 384-385.

XYZ Affair. Possibility of war. Cannot visit Eppington. Hopes J. W. E. and Maria can go to Monticello.   [608]

1798 May 27. MARIA EPPES, Eppington, to T. J., Philadelphia. ALS. 2 pp. Endorsed by T. J. Edgehill-Randolph Papers.

Proposed trip to Monticello. Trip to Petersburg and Shirley. Smallpox vaccination. Harpsichord at Monticello. Mentions Polly Archer, Mary J. Bolling, Martha J. Carr, Thomas Mann Randolph, Jr., Bolling Walker, John Walker, and Tabby Walker.   [609]

1798 June 3. THOMAS MANN RANDOLPH, JR., Belmont, Va., to T. J., Philadelphia. ALS. 2 pp. Endorsed by T. J. Edgehill-Randolph Papers.

Acknowledges receipt of various letters. Forwards book by Lescarbot. Tobacco crop at Shadwell. George's difficulties in handling the servants. People suspicious of Federal law empowering recruitment of army.   [610]

1798 June 6. T. J., Philadelphia, to MARIA EPPES, Eppington. ALS. 1 p. Mutilated. Printed: Randall II 408.

Hopes to see Maria at Monticello. Maria's harpsichord in good condition. Reports from Charles C. Pinckney, John Marshall, and Elbridge Gerry on relations with France. Greetings to Mr. and Mrs. Francis Eppes and John Wayles Eppes.   [611]

1798 June 10. THOMAS MANN RANDOLPH, JR., Belmont, Va., to T. J., Philadelphia. ALS. 1 p. Endorsed by T. J. Edgehill-Randolph Papers.

Detestable triumph of principles (Alien and Sedition Acts etc.) repugnant to T. J. Note for Mr. [Hore Browse?] Trist. Things are well at Belmont, Dunlora, and Carrsbrook. Medicines required.   [612]

1798 Oct. 30. T. J., Monticello, to HERBERT CROFT, London. ALS. 2 pp. File draft. Endorsed by T. J. Printed: L & B XVIII 361-364.

Expresses pleasure at Croft's letter on the German and English languages. Criticism of Johnson and Skinner as etymologists. Proposals for simplifying the study of Anglo-Saxon. Approves Croft's idea of a dictionary as a general index to literature.   [613]

1798 Nov. 17. T. J., Monticello, to JAMES MADISON. L. 1 p. Extract by N. P. Trist *ca.* 1830. Printed: Ford VII 288; L & B X 62-63; B of R VI 295 (letterpress copy in DLC).
Affirmation of principles of the Kentucky Resolutions.   [614]

1798 Nov. 29. T. J. to WILSON CARY NICHOLAS. L. 1 p. Copy by N. P. Trist *ca.* 1830. Printed: Ford VII 312-313; B of R VI 352 (letterpress copy in DLC).
Phraseology of a paper concurring with the Kentucky Resolutions.   [615]

1798 Dec. 8. T. J., Monticello, to MARIA JEFFERSON EPPES, Eppington. AL. 1 p. Fragment. McGregor Library. Another MS. in CSmH.
Lucy has increased her family. Plans to set out for Philadelphia. News of John Wayles Eppes, Francis Eppes, Thomas Mann Randolph, Jr., and Ellen Randolph.   [616]

1798 Dec. 27. T. J., Philadelphia, to MARTHA J. RANDOLPH. AL. 1 p. Letterpress copy. Endorsed by T. J. Edgehill-Randolph Papers.
Illness resulting from trip to Philadelphia *via* Fredericksburg. Republican Party advances in the public mind. Greetings to Thomas Mann Randolph and the children.   [617]

1799 Jan. 1. T. J., Philadelphia, to MARIA J. EPPES. ALS. 2 pp. Printed: Randall II 480-481; SNR 254-255.
Recent illness. Plans for Monticello in the spring.   [618]

1799 Jan. 19. THOMAS MANN RANDOLPH, JR., Belmont, Va., to T. J., Philadelphia. ALS. 1 p. Endorsed by T. J. Edgehill-Randolph Papers.
Christmas festivities. All well at Monticello. Visit to George Dineer. Mentions Martha, Virginia, Nancy, and Ellen Randolph.   [619]

1799 Jan. 20. JOHN WAYLES EPPES, Eppington, to T. J., Philadelphia. ALS. 1 p. Endorsed by T. J. Edgehill-Randolph Papers.
Sale of lands at Bermuda Hundred and Martin's Swamp. Receipt from Mr. Page. Maria Eppes' health improving.   [620]

1799 Jan. 24. JOHN WAYLES EPPES to T. J., Philadelphia. ALS. 2 pp. Endorsed by T. J. Edgehill-Randolph Papers.
Possible renting of his land at Bermuda Hundred. Advantages of the property. Poor quality tenants in that area. References to Monticello, Mont Blanco, Maria Eppes, and the Randolphs.   [621]

1799 Jan. 30 T. J. to NICHOLAS LEWIS. L. 1 p. Copy by N. P. Trist *ca.* 1830. Letterpress copy in DLC. Printed: L & B X 89-92.
Advising reason not rashness (regarding the Alien and Sedition laws).
                [622]

1799 Jan. 30. T. J. to JAMES MADISON. L. 1 p. Extract by N. P. Trist *ca.* 1830. Printed: B of R VI 296 (letterpress copy in DLC).
Measures against the Alien and Sedition laws.   [623]

1799 Feb. 7. T. J., Philadelphia, to JOHN WAYLES EPPES. ALS. 1 p. Another MS. in MHi.

Sale of Eppes' lands, and hiring of his Negroes by T. M. Randolph, Jr. Recruiting army for French war. Bill to retaliate on French citizens if French injure inpressed seamen. Copy of [John?] Nicholas' pamphlet. [624]

1799 Feb. 13. T. J. to ARCHIBALD STUART. L. 1 p. Extract by N. P. Trist *ca.* 1830. Printed: Ford VII 350-355; L & B X 100-104; B of R VI 444 (letterpress copy in DLC). Another MS. in VHi.

Petitions from Pennsylvania, New Jersey, and New York against standing armies and the Alien and Sedition Acts. [625]

1799 Mar. 8. [T. J.], Monticello, to MARIA EPPES, Mont Blanco, Va. AL[S clipped]. 1 p. McGregor Library.Printed: Randall II 506-507; SNR 257.

Martha Randolph has arrived from Belmont. Attempts to make Monticello habitable. Hopes for visit from Maria. Mentions John Wayles Eppes. [626]

1799 Mar. 10. JOHN BARNES, Philadelphia, to T. J., Monticello. ALS. 2 pp. Endorsed by T. J. Edgehill-Randolph Papers.

Subscriptions to U. S. Government loan of five millions. William Short's certificates. Good for Monticello, including linseed oil, sweet oil, figs and raisins, sash doors, cloverseed, groceries, and books, shipped aboard the Sloop *Little Jim.* [627]

1799 Apr. 2. JOHN BARNES, Philadelphia. to T. J., Monticello. ALS. 2 pp. Endorsed by T. J. Edgehill-Randolph Papers.

Myers' account of his travels in France not available in Philadelphia. Payment of drafts for T. J. and William Short. Scrip is down. Goods and bill of exchange sent to General Kosciuszko in care of Messrs. Nicholas and Jacob Van Staphorst and Hubbard *via* the ship *Stadt Hamburgh,* Capt. Heer Sjoerds. Planes, saws, plants, coffee, and rice ready for Sloop *Sally,* Capt. E. Potter. [628]

1799 Apr. 6. JOHN BARNES, Philadelphia, to T. J., Monticello. ALS. 2 pp. Endorsed by T. J. Edgehill-Randolph Papers.

Invoices enclosed. Plants for Monticello. Letter for [Benjamin F.] Bache. Payment to Joseph Roberts. Reference to Mr. Bartram. [629]

1799 Apr. 6. JOHN BARNES, Philadelphia, to T. J., Monticello. ALS. 2 pp. Endorsed by T. J. Edgehill-Randolph Papers.

Goods, bills of exchange, and letters for General Kosciuszko shipped aboard the *Stadt Hamburgh,* to Van Staphorst & Hubbard. Mentions [William?] Adamson. [630]

1799 Apr. 13. T. J., Monticello, to MARIA EPPES, [Eppington]. ALS. 1 p. Printed: Randall II 507.

Doubts he can visit Eppington. Work done by Page on J. W. Eppes' land. News of Peter Carr, Samuel Carr, Dr. and Mrs. [Benjamin F.] Bache, Champe Carter, Dupont de Nemours, and Ellen Randolph. [631]

1799 May 1. JOHN BARNES, Philadelphia, to T. J., Monticello. ALS. 2 pp. Endorsed by T. J. Edgehill-Randolph Papers.

Certificates for William Short. Chimney piece in charge of Mr. Dorsey. Letter enclosed from [Tench] Coxe. [632]

1799 May 26. JOHN BARNES, Philadelphia, to T. J., Monticello. ALS. 4 pp. Endorsed by T. J. Edgehill-Randolph Papers.

Account with T. J. Payment to Joseph Roberts. Tobacco prices falling. Recommends barter of tobacco for clothes. Great risks involved in shipments to Europe. Scarcity of money. [633]

1799 June 7. T. J., Monticello, to JOHN WAYLES EPPES, Chesterfield. ALS. 1 p.

Crop prospects poor. Has given Page corn for Eppes' servants and horses until harvest. Urges early visit to Monticello. [634]

1799 June 20. JOHN BARNES, Philadelphia, to T. J., Monticello. ALS. 1 p. Endorsed by T. J. Edgehill-Randolph Papers.

Mr. Brand's patent for 1,000 acres of land. Doors made for T. J. by Mr. Trump. Nailrod from Joseph Roberts. [635]

1799 Aug. 5. T.J. DEED to THOMAS AUGUSTUS TAYLOR, Chesterfield County. ADS. 2 pp. Endorsed. Photostat. Original owned by Miss Amanda Pitts. Witnessed by David Bullock, Elisha Leak, Lilburne Lewis, Randolph Lewis, and James Martin. Recorded by W. Miller, Clerk of Goochland County.

Conveying 669 acres of land in Goochland County, including Elkhill, which T. J. had purchased from Henry and Anne Skipwith. [636]

1799 Aug. 23. T. J., Monticello, to JAMES MADISON. L. 2 pp. Extract by N. P. Trist, *ca.* 1830, with memorandum in the hand of James Madison. Partly printed: Ford VII 387-388; B of R VI 296 (MS. in DLC).

Recommends meeting of Madison, Wilson Cary Nicholas, and himself to consider action to be taken on the principles already advanced by Virginia and Kentucky. Brief outlined suggested for "declaration or Resolution by their Legislatures." Madison notes that the meeting took the place of an answer to this letter. [637]

1799 Oct. 1. T. J. LEASE OF SHADWELL to CRAVEN PEYTON. ADS. 2 pp. Endorsed. Letterpress copy. Original MS. owned by C. S. Hutter, Jr. Witnessed by Robert Bolling, James Densmore, and Richard Richardson.

Lease for a part of Shadwell for five years, the rent to be paid in gold or silver money. No field to be sown in corn more than one year; each field to lie fallow or be sown in peas or clover for two years. [638]

1799 Oct. 27. T. J., Monticello, to STEPHEN T. MASON. L. 1 p. Extract by N. P. Trist, *ca.* 1830. Printed: Ford VII 379-399.

Congratulations on [Thomas] McKean's election [as Governor of Pennsylvania]. Republican party in Pennsylvania. Reformation of Congress at least two years away. Protagonists of England and France in Congress. [639]

1799 Oct. 29. T. J., Monticello, to CHARLES PINCKNEY. L. 1 p. Extract by N. P. Trist, *ca.* 1830. Printed: Ford VII 379-399; B of R VI 371 (MS. in DLC).
Oliver Ellsworth and James Iredell working toward a monarchy through common law doctrine. Washington's attitude. French misfortunes and British aggressions. [640]

1799 Dec. 13. JOHN BRECKINRIDGE, Frankfort, Ky., to T. J., Monticello. L. 1 p. Extract for N. P. Trist, *ca.* 1830. Printed: B of R VIII 68 (MS. in DLC).
Kentucky Resolutions. Popular opposition to the Alien and Sedition laws. [641]

1799 Dec. 21. T. J., Monticello, to JOHN WAYLES EPPES. ALS. 1 p.
[William] Woods defeated Peter Carr in election. [Wilson C.?] Nicholas and T. J. delayed by snow. News of Eppes' Negroes. Agrees to engage Powell (as overseer?). Reference to Mr. and Mrs. Francis Eppes. [642]

* 1799 Dec. 28. JAMES L. HENDERSON. DEED to TUCKER M. WOODSON. D. 4 pp. Endorsed by T. J. and others.
Conveying his share of Bennett Henderson's estate, excepting his interest in a mill and a lot and house in Milton. Witnessed by Marbell Camden, William Gambill, and Bennett [H.] Henderson. John Henderson's bond for James Henderson's performance of contract, 28 December 1799, witnessed by Thomas Concord and John Agg. Woodson's assignment of his title to Craxen Peyton, 25 April 1801, witnessed by Samuel H. Woodson and Bred. Gaines. (See letter from Jefferson to Peyton regarding purchase of Woodson's share 15 January 1801). [643]

Post 1799. T. J. MATHEMATICS PROBLEM. AD. 2 pp.
Solution of a geometrical problem from Jonathan Williams' *Thermometrical Navigation.* [644]

1800 Jan. 1. JOHN WAYLES EPPES, Eppnigton, to T. J. ALS. 1 p. Endorsed by T. J. Edgehill-Randolph Papers.
Birth of Maria's daughter. [645]

1800 Jan. 25. HENRY REMSEN, New York, to T. J., Philadelphia. ALS. 3 pp. Endorsed by T. J. Edgehill-Randolph Papers.
Factors involved in low tobacco prices. Possibilities of peace in Europe. Subscription to newspapers and to prices current. Yellow fever epidemics. Gouverneur Morris' oration on the death of George Washington. [646]

1800 Jan. 29. T. J., Philadelphia, to JOHN BRECKINRIDGE, Frankfort, Ky. L. 1 p. Extract by N. P. Trist *ca.* 1830. Printed: Ford VI 416-419; L & B X 149-150; B of R VI 47 (letterpress copy in DLC).
Kentucky Resolutions. Judiciary district for the West. Fear for republicanism in France. References to Napoleon Bonaparte and the Directory. [647]

1800 Jan. 31. T. J., Philadelphia, to BISHOP JAMES MADISON. L. 2 pp. Type-script copy. Original owned by St. George Tucker Grinnan. Printed: B of R VI 287 (MS. in DLC).

Sends book by Joseph Priestley. Discussion of Augustin Barruel's *Antisocial Conspiracy*. Religious and philosophical doctrines of Wishaupt, Godwin, and Morse.   [648]

1800 Feb. 2. T. J., Philadelphia, to [WILLIAM] BACHE. L. 1 p. Extract by N. P. Trist *ca.* 1830. Printed: B of R VI 20 (MS. in DLC).

Importance of minority rights with majority rule. Danger of a military force. Bonaparte's overthrow of the French Constitution.   [649]

[1800 Feb. 4. T. J. to THOMAS MANN RANDOLPH, JR.]. AL. 1 p. Fragment. Photostat. Original owned by Harold Jefferson Coolidge; probably the last page of a letter in possession of MHi.

Death of his coachman, Jupiter, at Fredericksburg. Orders for bottling cider. Mentions [Richard] Richardson.   [650]

1800 Feb. 7. JOHN WAYLES EPPES, Eppington, to T. J. ALS. 1 p. Endorsed by T. J. Edgehill-Randolph Papers.

Maria's illness; attended by Dr. Turpin.   [651]

1800 Feb. 12. T. J., Philadelphia, to MARIA EPPES, Eppington. ALS. 2 pp. Printed: Randall II 535-536; SNR 263-264.

Death of Maria's child. Failure of the mails. Plans to visit her on the way to Monticello. Inquiries about her health. References to Thomas Mann Randolph, Jr., and John Wayles Eppes.   [652]

1800 Feb. 16. JOHN WAYLES EPPES, Eppington, to T. J., Philadelphia. ALS. 1 p. Endorsed by T. J. Edgehill-Randolph Papers.

Maria's illness.   [653]

1800 Mar. 23. THOMAS CARR. RECEIPT TO T. J. D. 1 p. Edgehill-Randolph Papers.

For nails received from [Richard] Richardson by Carr and Thomas Bell. [654]

1800 Mar. 26. T. J., Philadelphia, to JAMES MONROE. L. 1 p. Extract by N. P. Trist, *ca.* 1830. Printed: B of R VI 332 and II 111 (letterpress copy in DLC).

Aversion to ceremony and wish to avoid newspaper publicity. Visit to Epping-ton. Progress of good sense and Republicanism.   [655]

1800 Mar. 31. T. J., Philadelphia, to RICHARD RICHARDSON, Monticello. ALS. 1 p. Photostat. Deposited from Monticello.

Sent box of plants and plaster of Paris. Instructions for construction at Mon-ticello. Horses to meet him at Eppington. References to Davy Bowles, Nicholas Lewis, Reuben Perry, and Mr. Short.   [656]

1800 Apr. 6. T. J., Philadelphia, to MARIA EPPES, Mont Blanco. AL[S clipped]. 1 p. Printed: Randall II 536-537; SNR 264-265. Pencil note: "Signature cut by permission of Mrs. Francis Eppes. Chas. W. Ward."

Plans for trip to Monticello via Eppington or Mont Blanco. References to John Wayles Eppes, Francis Eppes, Martha Randolph, and Thomas Mann Randolph, Jr.   [657]

1800 Apr. 22. JOHN WAYLES EPPES, Mont Blanco, to T. J., Philadelphia. ALS. 2 pp. Endorsed by T. J. Edgehill-Randolph Papers.

Maria's health restored. T. J.'s trip to Mont Blanco. Mr. Powell has agreed to go to Monticello (as overseer?). Reference to Miss Church. Death of [John?] Bolling.   [658]

[1800] Apr. 25 [date received]. THOMAS MANN RANDOLPH, JR., to T. J. ALS. 3 pp. Endorsed by T. J. Edgehill-Randolph Papers.

Suit against D. Mossis, involving James Ross, Mr. Skitt, P. Cours, and Colonel Morrir. Lilly's efficiency as overseer. Wheat crop, fruit, and sheep in good condition. [Richard] Richardson's work on T. J.'s apartment. Ursula's illness due to poisons of the Buckingham Negro conjuror. Forwards sheeting samples. [659]

1800 May 24. JOHN BARNES, Philadelphia, to T. J., Monticello. ALS. 3 pp. Endorsed by T. J. McGregor Library.

Covering an account. Packages in the hands of Mr. Sheaff. Shipment of goods includng china and oil. Eight per cent stock looking up. Purchase of government stock for William Short, Tadeusz Kosciuszko, and T. J. Medicine from Dr. Jackson. References to Mr. Stewart (Gilbert Stuart?) and G. Simpson.   [660]

1800 May 26. T. J., Eppington, to JAMES MONROE. L. 1 p. Extract by N. P. Trist ca. 1830. Printed: Ford VII 447-449; B of R II 111 and VI 332 (MS. in DLC).

Disapproves of Union dinner. Disregard of Chase's accusations of atheism. Callender should be defended. Arrival of treaty from France. Reference to Dupont.   [661]

1800 June 1. T. J. IN ACCOUNT WITH HENDERSON, McCAUL & CO., Manchester, England. D. 1 p. Endorsed by T. J. Edgehill-Randolph Papers.

Company's account, signed by James Lyle, covering T. J.'s payments from 4 March 1790 to 12 November 1798 on his bond.   [662]

1800 July 4. T. J., Monticello, to MARIA EPPES, Mont Blanco, Va. ALS. 1 p. McGregor Library. Printed: Randall II 565; SNR 268.

Dr. and Mrs. [William] Bache, and Mrs. Monroe are in the neighborhood. The "Forte piano" has arrived. Murder of Birch [Samuel Burch] by George Carter. Heavy wheat crop. Hopes for visit from Maria and John Eppes.   [663]

1800 July 26. JOHN BARNES, Georgetown, to T. J., Monticello. ALS. 2 pp. Endorsed by T. J. Edgehill-Randolph Papers.

Bill of exchange for Van Staphorst & Hubbard. T. J.'s chairs misdirected to

[James?] Brown for Col. [Samuel J.?] Cabell. References to Mrs. Ratcliffe and [J.] Letchworth.   [664]

1800 Aug. 4. JOHN WAYLES EPPES, Eppington, to T. J., Monticello. ALS. 2 pp. Endorsed by T. J. Edgehill-Randolph Papers.
Francis Eppes' accident. Money required by Francis Eppes as security for Daniel Hylton. Maria Eppes mentioned.   [665]

*1800 Aug. 23. JOHN BARNES, Georgetown, to T. J., Monticello. ALS. 2 pp. Edgehill-Randolph Papers.
Forwarding an account. Discounts at the Bank of Pennsylvania. Bill of exchange to Van Staphorst & Hubbard for the credit of "P. M." Has acquired new house and store. Government stock for Tadeusz Kosciuszko, William Short, and J. B. Reference to Mrs. Ratcliffe, [John] Richards, S. T. Mason.   [666]

1800 Nov. 20. JOHN BARNES, Georgetown, to T. J., Monticello. ALS. 2 pp. Endorsed by T. J. Edgehill-Randolph Papers.
T. J.'s accommodations at Mr. Conrade's. *Nautical Almanacs* ordered. Pamphlet regarding C. C. P[inckney]. References to Messrs. Langdon, Baldwin, and Brown.   [667]

1800 Dec. 5. JOHN BARNES, Georgetown, to T. J. ALS. 1 p. Endorsed by T. J. Edgehill-Randolph Papers.
Price of handkerchiefs. Reference to Mr. Munn.   [668]

1800 Dec. 8. THOMAS MANN RANDOLPH, JR., Richmond, to T. J., Washington. ALS. 1 p. Endorsed by T. J. Edgehill-Randolph Papers.
Requests that Samuel Woodson replace Nathaniel Perkins as postmaster at Goochland Court House.   [669]

1800. T. J. IN ACCOUNT WITH JOHN BARNES. DS. 5 items. Edgehill-Randolph Papers.
Accounts for the year 1800 with John Barnes, his commission agent and financial manager.   [670]

1800. T. J. [Monticello], to CRAVEN PEYTON. AD. 1 p. Edgehill-Randolph Papers.
Plan for crop rotation—wheat, corn, and rye—for the years 1800-1804. [671]

1801 Jan. 3. THOMAS MANN RANDOLPH, JR., Edgehill, to T. J., Washington. ALS. 3 pp. Endorsed by T. J.
Family's health good. Lilly's difficulties in hiring workers. Arrival of [John] Craven, new overseer. Work done at Monticello in clearing fields and in the nailery. Problems of handling the Negroes. Mentions Mr. Powell and [Richard] Richardson, overseers.   [672]

[1801] Jan. 4 [incorrectly dated 1800]. T. J., Washington, to MARIA EPPES, Bermuda Hundred. AL. 1 p. Printed: Ford VII 477-479; Randall II 594; SNR 271-272.
Visit to Mount Vernon. Enquiries about Maria from Martha Washington and

Mrs. Lewis. Election of 1800. Colonel Burr's conduct honorable. Family meetings at Monticello and in Washington planned. [673]

1801 Jan. 7. JOHN BARNES, Georgetown, to T. J., Washington. ALS. 1 p. Endorsed by T. J. Edgehill-Randolph Papers.
  Money for T. J. in check and cash. Reference to John Richards. [674]

1801 Jan. 10. THOMAS MANN RANDOLPH, JR., to T. J., Washington. ALS. 3 pp. Endorsed by T. J. Edgehill-Randolph Papers.
  Martha's illness. Lilly making up a gang. Clover, peas, turnips for the garden. Turnips required to feed sheep. Election to be decided in the House of Representatives. Reference to Cornelia Randolph. [675]

1801 Jan. 15. JOHN BARNES, Georgetown, to T. J., Washington. ALS. 1 p. Endorsed by T. J. McGregor Library.
  Remittance to Gibson & Jefferson. Credit to William Short's account. [676]

1801 Jan. 15. T. J., Washington, to CRAVEN PEYTON. ALS. 1 p. Letterpress copy. Endorsed by T. J. McGregor Library.
  Requests Peyton to purchase shares of Henderson estate for T. J. in Peyton's name. Survey of line between T. J.'s land and the Henderson land. Equal vote for Republican candidates in the election of 1800. References to Colle, [John] Watson, and [Robert] Snelson. [677]

1801 Jan. 17. JOHN GARLAND JEFFERSON, Amelia, Va., to T. J., Washington. ALS. 3 pp. Endorsed by T. J. Carr-Cary Papers.
  Apologizes for long delay in writing. Offers to purchase his land near Lynchburg. Report that T. J. cast deciding vote in nomination of bankrupt son-in-law of Adams, Joshua Johnston, as postmaster. [678]

1801 Jan. 21. JOHN BARNES, Georgetown, to T. J., Washington. ALS. 1 p. Endorsed by T. J. Edgehill-Randolph Papers.
  William Short's account. [679]

1801 Jan. 24. JOHN BARNES, Georgetown, to T. J., Washington. ALS. 1 p. Endorsed by T. J. Edgehill-Randolph Papers.
  Sends two pairs of black silk stockings. References to Mr. Pickford and Mr. Latimore. [680]

1801 Feb. 1. T. J., Washington, to JOHN GARLAND JEFFERSON, Amelia, Va. ALS. 2 pp. Letterpress copy. Endorsed by T. J. Carr-Cary Papers.
  Refuses to sell Poplar Forest. Justifies his vote for Joshua Johnston. References to John Adams and George Washington. [681]

*1801 Feb. 5. T. J., Washington, to MARTHA J. RANDOLPH. ALS. 2 pp. Endorsed by T. J. Edgehill-Randolph Papers.
  Martha's illness. Anne Jefferson's disposition. Election thrown into the House of Representatives. Comments on visitors who refuse to confine themselves to visiting hours. [682]

1801 Feb. 9. JOHN BARNES, Georgetown, to [T. J.]. AL. 2 pp. Edgehill-Randolph Papers.

Salary payments when he changes position on March 4. Urges that T. J. draw on him if necessary. Accounts with William Short and Tadeusz Kosciuszko. [683]

1801 Feb. 15. T. J., Washington, to MARIA EPPES, Bermuda Hundred. ALS. 1 p. Printed: Randall II 599-600.

Election still deadlocked. Denies personal ambition, but wishes to bring government back to republican principles. Plans for trip to Monticello.   [684]

1801 Feb. 18. T. J., Washington, to CRAVEN PEYTON. ALS. 1 p. Letterpress copy. Endorsed by T. J. McGregor Library.

Purchase of John R. Kerr's and Tucker Woodson's shares of the Bennett Henderson estate. Election concluded.   [685]

1801 Mar. 1. JOHN GARLAND JEFFERSON, Amelia, Va., to T. J., Washington. ALS. 2 pp. Endorsed by T. J. Carr-Cary Papers.

Glad of his explanation of Joshua Johnston's appointment. Congratulations on his election to presidency. Asks for appointment to office.   [686]

1801 Mar. 4. T. J. FIRST INAUGURAL ADDRESS. AD. 4 pp. Photostat. Original owned by Herman H. Diers. Printed: Ford VIII 1-6; Tucker II 87-92.

Stressing harmony and unity, the value of Republican principles, need for wise and frugal, but not too powerful, government. Outlines the essential principles of our government.   [687]

1801 Mar. 13. T. J., Washington, to SAMUEL SMITH. ALS. 1 p. Endorsed. Printed: B of R VI 435 (MS. in DLC).

Measures relative to the Navy. Postpones answer to Smith's letter regarding a consulship for William Buchanan. References to James Madison, Albert Gallatin.   [688]

1801 Mar. 17. ISHAM HENDERSON. DEED to JAMES L. HENDERSON, Albemarle County. DS. 5 pp. Endorsed by T. J. McGregor Library.

Conveying Isham Henderson's share of Bennett Henderson's estate to James L. Henderson, and from him to Craven Peyton. Witnesses: Dan Richarson, Abraham Grove, John McLean, and William Clark. Confirmation of deed by Isham upon his coming of age, 6 June 1804. Certification by Matthew Flournoy and Thomas Given, Justices of the Peace of Shelby County, Ky., by James Craig, Clerk of Shelby County, Ky., and by Isaac Ellis, Presiding Justice of the Peace of Shelby County.   [689]

1801 Mar. 21. T. J., Washington, to JAMES WARREN. L. 1 p. Extract by N. P. Trist ca. 1830. Letterpress copy in DLC. Printed: L & B X 231-232.

Rejoicing over the victory of the Republican Party.   [690]

1801 Mar. 23. T. J., Washington, to BENJAMIN WARING, Columbia, S. C. L. 1 p. Extract by N. P. Trist ca. 1830. Letterpress copy in DLC. Printed: L & B X 235-236.

The will of the people is the only legitimate foundation of government.   [691]

1801 Mar. 24. T. J., Washington, to SAMUEL SMITH, Baltimore. ALS. 1 p. Endorsed. Printed: B of R VI 435 (MS. in DLC); Ford VIII 28-29.

Suggesting temporary acceptance of the post of Secretary of the Navy. Factors involved in the appointments of [William] Kilty, [Wilson Cary] Nicholas, and James Wilkinson. Importance of civilian control of the military. References to [Gabriel] Duval.   [692]

1801 Mar. 26. T. J., Washington, to SAMUEL SMITH, Baltimore. ALS. 1 p. Endorsed. Printed: B of R VI 435 (MS. in DLC); Randall III 630.

Consultation regarding the Navy Department.   [693]

1801 Mar. 27. T. J., Washington, to Messrs. Eddy, [Jonathan Russell], [Thurber], [Seth?] [Wheaton], and [Smith], Providence, R. I. L. 1 p. Extract by N. P. Trist ca. 1830. Printed: L & B X 248-249; B of R VI 139 (letterpress copy in DLC).

Constitution will be administered according to the will of the founders. [694]

1801 Mar. 27. T. J., Washington, to JOHN WAYLES EPPES, Bermuda Hundred. ALS. 2 pp. Photostat. Original owned by Francis Shine.

Trip to Monticello. Purchase of horses from Dr. Walker, [Thomas] Bell, Mr. Haxall, or Dr. Shore. Draft on Gibson & Jefferson. [John] Dawson's mission to France. Robert R. Livingston appointed minister to France. Adams' midnight appointments. Policy with respect to removal of incumbents from office.   [695]

1801 Mar. 28. JOHN BARNES, Georgetown, to T. J. ALS. 1 p. Endorsed by T. J. McGregor Library.

Information regarding T. J.'s accounts with Gibson & Jefferson, Rapin & Co., Mr. Carpenter, S. H. Smith, and [James?] Stewart. References to Joseph Dougherty and the Bank of Columbia.   [696]

1801 Mar. 29. JOHN GARLAND JEFFERSON, Amelia, to T. J., Washington. ALS. 3 pp. Endorsed by T. J. Carr-Cary Papers.

Defends himself against brother's charge of lack of delicacy in requesting an appointment to office.   [697]

1801 Apr. 8. T. J., Monticello, to JOHN WAYLES EPPES, Bermuda Hundred. ALS. 1 p. Photostat. Original owned by Luther Ely Smith.

Family at Edgehill well. Nancy Jefferson's marriage to Charles Lewis. Purchase of horses. New British Admiralty Courts in Jamaica and the Windward Islands will relieve U. S. of British spoliation. References to Martha Randolph and Maria Eppes.   [698]

1801 Apr. 16. JOHN BARNES, Georgetown, to T. J., Monticello. ALS. 2 pp. Endorsed by T. J. McGregor Library.

Will send the copper sheeting for Monticello roof. James Madison may rent Mr. [John?] Marshall's dwelling. Mentions [John] Richards, Gibson & Jefferson.
                                                                              [699]

1801 Apr. 17. T. J., Monticello, to SAMUEL SMITH. ALS. 2 pp. Endorsed. Photostat. Original owned by Mrs. Laird U. Park. Printed: B of R VI 435 (MS. in DLC).

Navy Department matters. Appointments. Letters from St. George Tucker regarding Captain Cowper. Letter from [Stephen] Sayre regarding a purchase on Long Island. Letter from General [Alexander] Spotswood. Necessity of silence regarding appointments. Mentions John Adams and Benjamin Stoddert.　　[700]

1801 Apr. 25. T. J., Monticello, to JOHN WAYLES EPPES, Eppington. ALS. 1 p.

Breaking in of horses bought for T. J. Plans for the summer at Monticello. References to Thomas Mann Randolph, Jr., Martha Randolph, Maria Eppes, Frances Eppes I, the Trist family, Martin (servant), and Davy (servant). [701]

*1801 May 1. T. J., Washington, to SAMUEL CARR. ALS. 1 p. Letterpress copy. Endorsed by T. J.

Election of Peter Carr. Purchase of fish. Birth of Samuel Carr's son. References to Overton Carr and Dolly Madison.　　　　　　　　[702]

1801 May 6. JOHN BARNES, Georgetown, to T. J., Washington. ALS. 1 p. Endorsed by T. J. McGregor Library.

Payments to Mr. Peale, Colonel Hoomes, and Mr. Rapin.　　[703]

801 May 11. JOHN BARNES, Georgetown, to T. J., Washington. ALS. 1 p. Endorsed by T. J. Edgehill-Randolph Papers.

Check for and address of James Stewart, Philadelphia.　　　[704]

1801 May 15. JOHN BARNES, Georgetown, to T. J., Washington. ALS 1 p. Endorsed by T. J. Edgehill-Randolph Papers.

Concerning T. J.'s account with Barnes.　　　　　　[705]

1801 May 26. T. J. to the GENERAL ASSEMBLY OF RHODE ISLAND. L. 1 p. Extract by N. P. Trist ca. 1830. Printed: L & B X 262-263; B of R VI 388 (MS. in DLC).

Returning thanks for their congratulations on his election. Safety rests with preservation of union, with powers divided between state and federal governments.　　　　　　　　[706]

1801 May 28. T. J., Washington, to MARIA J. EPPES, Bermuda Hundred. ALS. 1 p. Photostat. Original owned by Mrs. William S. Gooch. Printed: Randall II 664.

Pleasant society in Washington. Visit by Mr. and Mrs. Madison. Meeting of the Eppes, Randolphs, and T. J. at Monticello.　　　　[707]

1801 May 29. T. J., Washington, to JAMES MONROE. L. 1 p. Extract by N. P. Trist ca. 1830. Printed: Ford VIII 58-60; B of R VI 332 (letterpress copy in DLC).

Favors simple etiquette in correspondence between the President and governors.
[708]

1801 June 6. T. J. SHIP'S PAPERS. DS. 1 p. Photostat. Original owned by I. Witkins.

Clearance papers for the Ship *Venus,* Capt. Samuel Bunce, bound for Liverpool, countersigned by James Madison. [709]

1801 June 10. T. J. SHIP'S PAPERS. DS. 1 p. Deposited by C. S. Hutter, Jr.

Clearance papers for Schooner *Maria,* Joseph Storey, captain, bound for St. Sebastians, countersigned by James Madison. [710]

1801 June 13. THOMAS MANN RANDOLPH, JR.. to T. J., Washington. ALS. 1 p. Endorsed by T. J. Edgehill-Randolph Papers.

Martha and the children. George Jefferson's account of work at Bermuda Hundred. Lilly has begun work on the canal. Request by a Mr. Dillon to collect pine knots on T. J.'s land on the Hardware River. Reference to [John] Craven and Christopher Hudson. [711]

1801 June 17. T. J., Washington, to JOHN WAYLES EPPES, Bermuda Hundred. ALS. 1 p.

Directions for safe journey to Monticello for Maria. Satisfaction with horses purchased from Dr. [John] Shore and Mr. Haxall. [712]

1801 June 24. T. J., Washington, to SAMUEL SMITH. ALS. 1 p. Endorsed. Printed: B of R VI 435 (MS. in DLC).

Appointment of Mr. Buchanan as consul to the isles of France and Bourbon. Midnight appointments. Navy Department offered to John Langdon. News of arrival of the ships *General Greene* and *John Adams.* References to appointments of Messrs. [John M.?] Forbes, [William?] Lewis, and Stacey. [713]

1801 June 25. T. J., Washington, to MARTHA J. RANDOLPH. ALS. 1 p. Letterpress copy. Endorsed by T. J. Edgehill-Randolph Papers.

Mr. Eppes and Mr. Randolph's harvest; wheat prices; threshing machine; storm in Albemarle. Messages for Anne and Ellen Randolph. Cucumbers and raspberries not yet on the market. References to Maria Eppes. [714]

1801 July 10. M. W. JONES, Richmond, to JAMES MADISON. ALS. 1 p. Endorsed. Signed annotation by T. J.

Requesting appointment of Dr. John K. Read of Norfolk to supply medicine to marines or army. Note by T. J.: " . . . not a man . . .deserves countenance less than Dr. Reade . . . " [715]

1801 July 10. CRAVEN PEYTON, Shadwell, to T. J., Washington. ALS. 1 p. Endorsed by T. J. McGregor Library.

Request for funds to be sent *via* Thomas Walker. Division of the Henderson estate delayed until T. J. arrives. [716]

1801 July 11. T. J., Washington, to SAMUEL SMITH, Baltimore. ALS. 1 p. Endorsed. Printed: B of R VI 435 (MS. in DLC).

Controversy regarding dismantling of the *Berceau.* References to Colonel Habersham and Benjamin Stoddert. [717]

1801 July 14. T. J., Washington, to CRAVEN PEYTON, Shadwell. ALS. 1 p.
Letterpress copy. Endorsed by T. J. McGregor Library.
Sends money by Thomas Walker. Expects to be home soon. Sorry J[ohn?] Henderson did not sell his shares. [718]

1801 July 16. T. J., Washington, to MARTHA J. RANDOLPH. ALS. 1 p. Letterpress copy. Endorsed by T. J. Edgehill-Randolph Papers.
Visit by the Eppes and Randolphs to Monticello. Smallpox vaccination. Sends some music. [719]

1801 July 21. T. J., Washington, to EDMUND JENINGS. ALS. 1 p. Letterpress copy. Endorsed by T. J. Carr-Cary Papers.
Death of Mrs. Ariana Jenings Randolph. Unable to spare the time to act as guardian to the grandchildren. References to [Philip Ludwell?] Grymes, John Randolph (1727-1784) , and [Robert?] Gourslay. [720]

1801 Aug. 3. JOHN BARNES, Georgetown, to T. J., Monticello. ALS. 3 pp. Endorsed by T. J. Edgehill-Randolph Papers.
T. J.'s groceries and plaster of Paris aboard the sloop *Abigail and Rebecca*. Payment by John Richards on T. J.'s account to Dr. Jackson and Mr. Mercire for syrup of punch. Purchase of figs, raisins, almonds, looking glasses. References to Mr. Rapin and Mr. Conrad. [721]

1801 Aug. 3. JOHN BARNES, Georgetown, to TADEUSZ KOSCIUSZKO, Paris. ALS. 1 p. Draft sent to T. J. Edgehill-Randolph Papers.
Interest and dividend on government stock. [722]

1801 Aug. 3. JOHN BARNES, Georgetown, to WILLIAM SHORT, Paris. ALS. Draft. 2 pp. Enclosure: ADS. 1 p. Edgehill-Randolph Papers.
Letter covering his account; purchase of public stock; letter for Peyton Short. Enclosure: Account recording debit and credit entries from 15 May to 31 July 1801. [723]

1801 Aug. 10. JOHN BARNES, Georgetown, to T. J., Monticello. ALS. 3 pp. Endorsed by T. J. Edgehill-Randolph Papers.
Plasterers for Monticello. Letter from Mr. Rapin regarding "old LaMair" (Etienne LeMaire) . [724]

1801 Aug. 16. JAMES MADISON, [Washington], to T. J., Monticello. ALS. 1 p. Endorsed by T. J.
Transmitting official papers *via* a tourist, Mrs. Tudor of Boston. [725]

1801 Aug. 17. JOHN BARNES, Georgetown, to T. J., Monticello. ALS. 4 pp. Endorsed by T. J. Edgehill-Randolph Papers.
Vicissitudes of the plasterers for Monticello: Mr. King in jail for debt; Mr. Martin Wairscher unable to collect an account and with a new wife. Books, dry fruits, almonds, glass tumblers, plaster of Paris for T. J. Eyeglasses for Mrs. Conrad. Visit from [David] Higginbotham. References to John Richards and Mr. Rapin. [726]

1801 Aug. 24. JOHN BARNES, Georgetown, to T. J., Monticello. ALS. 3 pp. Endorsed by T. J. Edgehill-Randolph Papers.

Goods for T. J. Receipt from the James River Canal Co. for William Short. Purchase of government stocks for Short. Advises that Jefferson buy stock. References to Gibson & Jefferson, Mr. Andrews, [Joseph] Dougherty, [John?] Hanson, Etienne LeMaire, Mr. Rapin, and Martin Wairscher.   [727]

1801 Aug. 31. JOHN BARNES, Georgetown, to T. J., Monticello. ALS. 2 pp. Endorsed by T. J. Edgehill-Randolph Papers.

Experiment regarding cowpox. Payment of the servants (at the Executive Mansion?) by Mr. Rapin. Marriage of Frederick and Molly (servants). Receipt of T. J.'s salary, portions of which are assigned to Mr. M. and to the Bank of Columbia. Reference to [Etienne] LeMaire.   [728]

1801 Sept. 7. JOHN BARNES, Georgetown, to T. J., Monticello. ALS. 4 pp. Endorsed by T. J. Edgehill-Randolph Papers.

Suggests that [Joseph] Dougherty bring T. J.'s new chariot and harness, made by Conrad Hanse, from Philadelphia to Washington. Information given to Dr. Edwards respecting Mr. Stewart's (i.e. Gilbert Stuart) portrait. Failure of John Richards to ship window glass or sheeting. Receipt of T. J.'s salary from the Treasury. References to Mr. Donath, [Etienne] LeMaire, Mr. Rapin, and Mr. Taylor.   [729]

1801 Sept. 10. T. J. to JOHN DRAYTON. L. 1 p. Extract by N. P. Trist *ca.* 1830.

Will give strength to rights of states reserved to them and will keep powers of the executive within a safe line.   [730]

1801 Sept. 14. JOHN BARNES, Georgetown, to T. J., Monticello. ALS. 2 pp. Endorsed by T. J. Edgehill-Randolph Papers.

Payments to Mr. Carpenter and Mr. Gilpin by Mr. Rapin. Payment to Conrad Hanse for harness and chariot and to Gilbert Stuart for the portrait of T. J. Accounts with Messrs. Robert and Jones. Drafts on the Bank of the U. S. [731]

* 1801 Sept. 15. BERIAH NORTON, Edgartown, Mass., to T. J., Washington. ALS. 1 p. Endorsed by T. J. Printed: Ford-Bixby 91-92.

Requesting a pardon for his son-in-law, Mr. Dotton. References to Judge William Paterson and Aaron Ogden.   [732]

1801 Sept. 21. JOHN BARNES, Georgetown, to T. J., Monticello. ALS. and a second autograph draft signed. 3 pp. Endorsed by T. J. Edgehill-Randolph Papers.

[Joseph] Dougherty's trip to Philadelphia to get T. J.'s chariot from Conrad Hanse. Payments to Conrad Hanse by Brown, Rives & Co.'s draft on Walker & Kennedy of Philadelphia. Payments to Roberts & Jones, and Mr. Carpenter. Account with Mr. Sheaff. Dr. Edwards' information regarding Mr. Stuart. [733]

1801 Sept. 25. CRAVEN PEYTON to T. J. DS. (AD by T. J.). 1 p. Endorsed by T. J. Seal. Also the letterpress copy. McGregor Library.

Declaration by Peyton that he holds in trust for T. J. the lands purchased from John R. and Sarah Kerr, James L. Henderson, Isham Henderson, and Charles Henderson, their shares in the estate of Bennett Henderson.   [734]

[*ca.* 1801 Sept.]. JOHN BARNES, Georgetown, to [T. J.]. AL. 2 pp. Edgehill-Randolph Papers.

Covering a statement of payments to be made to Bank of Columbia, Mr. Harris, Mr. Rapin, J. Roberts, William Sheaff, and Mr. Taylor.   [735]

* 1801 Oct. 1. ALBEMARLE COUNTY COURT. Partition of the estate of Bennett Henderson. D. 2 pp. Copy. Endorsed by T. J.

Lands divided among Eliza, Isham, Lucy, Charles, Bennett H., James L., Frances, John, Sarah, and Nancy Henderson. Returned to the Albemarle County Court by David Anderson, David Higingbotham (i.e. Higginbotham), and John Lewis, Commissioners.   [736]

1801 Oct. 7. JOHN BARNES, Georgetown, to T. J. ALS. 1 p. Endorsed by T. J. McGregor Library.

Remittance of Craven Peyton's post notes, which are passed conveniently. Mentions John Watson, David Higginbotham, Mr. Heath, and Mr. Davison. [737]

1801 Oct. 8. T. J., Washington, to CRAVEN PEYTON. ALS. 4 pp. Endorsed by T. J. McGregor Library.

Payment for the Bennett Henderson estate land. Requests exact statement of all shares and a plat of the property. Instructions regarding future purchasers. Descriptions and forms for the deeds of James L. Henderson, Isham Henderson, Charles Henderson, and John R. Kerr.   [738]

1801 Oct. 9. JOHN BARNES, Washington, to T. J. AD. 1 p. Endorsed by T. J. McGregor Library.

Memorandum regarding T. J.'s accounts, with references to Mr. Rapin, Mr. Andrews, Dr. Edward, and [Gilbert?] Stuart.   [739]

1801 Oct. 13. T. J. SHIP'S PAPERS. DS. 1 p. Deposited from Monticello.

Clearance papers for the Brig *James,* William Fairchild master, sailing from New Haven, Conn., to Dominica.   [740]

1801 Oct. 16. CRAVEN PEYTON, Shadwell, to T. J., Washington. ALS. 2 pp. Endorsed by T. J. McGregor Library.

Purchase of shares in the Bennett Henderson estate. Instructions about Shadwell. References to John R. Kerr, J[ohn?] Henderson, James L. Henderson, [Dabney] Carr, and [William] Woods.   [741]

1801 Oct. 19. CONRAD HANSE. RECEIPT TO JOHN BARNES. ADS. 1 p. Endorsed by T. J. McGregor Library.

Receipt for $206 for T. J.'s chariot and harness.   [742]

[1801 Oct. 19]. T. J. LAND GRANT to VALENTINE PEYTON. D. 1 p. Copy by Valentine Peyton. McDowell Papers.

Patent for 2,000 acres of land between the Little Miami and the Scioto Rivers, to Peyton, assignee of William Washington. Grant given in consideration of Washington's military service in the Revolution, a part of Military Warrant No. 2263. Countersigned by James Madison.   [743]

1801 Oct. 19. T. J. LAND GRANT to BAILY WASHINGTON, Jr., D. 1 p. Copy by Baily Washington, Jr. McDowell Papers.

Patent for 2,000 acres of land between the Little Miami and Scioto Rivers, to Washington, assignee of William Washington. Grant given in consideration of William Washington's military service in the Revolution, a part of Military Warrant No. 2263. Countersigned by James Madson.   [744]

1801 Oct. 25. JOHN WAYLES EPPES, Monticello, to T. J., Washington. ALS. 3 pp. Endorsed by T. J. Edgehill-Randolph Papers.

Declines T. J.'s offer of money to clear Bedford County lands. Plans to build at Pantops where he has sown bearded wheat. Work on pecan trees by Gabriel Lilly. Health of Maria and her son.   [745]

1801 Oct. 25. T. J., Washington, to CRAVEN PEYTON, Shadwell. ALS. 1 p. Letterpress copy. Endorsed by T. J. McGregor Library.

Instructions to rent Shadwell. References to Thomas Mann Randolph, Jr., and to Thomas Eston Randolph.   [746]

1801 Oct. 26. T. J., Washington, to MARIA EPPES, Monticello. ALS. 1 p. Printed: Randall II 675: SNR 280-281.

Inquiries about her health and the little boy's. Recommends Mrs. Suddarth as a nurse. Proposal to Mr. Eppes regarding Pantops and Poplar Forest. Hopes they will stay at Monticello.   [747]

1801 Nov. 1. T. J., Washington, to CRAVEN PEYTON. ALS. 1 p. Letterpress copy. Endorsed by T. J. McGregor Library.

Disposal of notes of Bank of Columbia which is in serious crisis. Reference to Col. C. L. Lewis.   [748]

1801 Nov. 10. MARTHA J. RANDOLPH to T. J., Washington. ALS. 1 p. Endorsed by T. J. Edgehill-Randolph Papers.

Illness of Ellen, Cornelia, and Virginia Randolph, and Francis Eppes.   [749]

* 1801 Nov. 11. CRAVEN PEYTON, Shadwell, to T. J., Washington. ALS. 1 p. Endorsed by T. J. McGregor Library.

Bank of Columbia notes. Renting of Shadwell. Plat of the Henderson lands made by William Wood. Contracting to supply Miltonians with firewood. Reference to Thomas Eston Randolph and William Davenport.   [750]

1801 Nov. 13. BOWLING CLARKE, Poplar Forest, to T. J., Washington. ALS. 3 pp. Endorsed by T. J. Edgehill-Randolph Papers.

Report from T. J.'s overseer: division of Poplar Forest with John W. Eppes and Thomas Mann Randolph, Jr.; corn, wheat, and tobacco crops; beef and hogs killed; Thomas Whittinton's and Bowling Clarke's share of the profits. Reference to Brown & Co.   [751]

1801 Nov. 29. JAMES L. and ELIZABETH HENDERSON, Albemarle County, to CRAVEN PEYTON, Albemarle County. DS. 2 pp. Endorsed by T. J. Witnessed by George W. Catlett, John L. Cosby, and Joel Shiflett. Recorded 4 August 1802, John Nicholas, Clerk. McGregor Library.
    Deeding their share in the Bennett Henderson estate (with certain exceptions).   [752]

[1801 Nov.]. WILLIAM WOODS. PLAT OF HENDERSON ESTATE. D. 2 pp. Endorsed by T. J. McGregor Library.
    Plat of the land in Milton or elsewhere in Albemarle County. The shares of the heirs labelled by T. J.   [753]

1801 Dec. 3. T. J., Washington, to CRAVEN PEYTON, Shadwell. ALS. 1 p. Letterpress copy. Endorsed by T. J., McGregor Library.
    Leasing of Shadwell to William Davenport. Purchase of John, Bennett H., and Nancy Henderson's shares of the Bennett Henderson estate.   [754]

1801 Dec. 25. OVERTON CARR to T. J. ALS. 2 pp. Endorsed by T. J. Carr-Cary Papers.
    Gift of a ham. Quotes Jonathan Swift on gifts.   [755]

1801. JOHN BARNES, Georgetown. ACCOUNTS AGAINST T. J., Washington. 26 ADS. Some endorsed by T. J. McGregor Library and Edgehill-Randolph Papers.
    Accounts submitted by Barnes, who acted as T. J.'s fiscal agent and commission merchant during the year 1801.   [756]

[1801-1808?]. T. J. MEMORANDUM ON U. S. CONSTITUTION. D. 2 pp. [Copy by N. P. Trist?] McGregor Library.
    Controlling authority, recognized by the compact, is that of three-fourths of the states. President's duty with regard to the rights of the states.   [757]

1801-108. T. J. PERSONAL ACCOUNTS. 15 items. Some endorsed by T. J. Edgehill-Randolph Papers.
    Bills rendered to T. J., or to Joseph Dougherty, Etienne LeMaire, and Mr. Rapin for T. J., by Middleton Bett, W. A. Burford, Francis Clark, Benjamin Jones, W. Markey, Peter Miller, John Moffitt, Jacob Munsell, Susanna Orr, and Joseph Wheaton, principally for food and dry goods.   [758]

[1801 et seq. T. J.] SCRAPBOOK OF SONGS AND POEMS. 204 pp. Many pasted on sheets made from letters addressed to T. J.
    Clippings from contemporary newspapers and journals: political and patriotic poems; satirical poems, parodies and songs lampooning Jefferson and other public men; sentimental songs, humorous songs, and ballads.   [759]

1802 Jan. 1. T. J., Washington, to DANIEL BROWN et al, Cheshire, Mass. L. 1 p. Extract by N. P. Trist ca. 1830. Printed: B of R VI 52 (letterpress copy in DLC).
    Value of the Constitution. Acknowledges address of the citizens of Cheshire.   [760]

1802 Jan. 1. T. J. to NEHEMIAH DODGE *et al.*, Conn. L. 1 p. Extract by N. P. Trist *ca.* 1830. Printed: L & B XVI 181-182; B of R VI 124 (letterpress copy in DLC). Original MS. in Baptist Historical Society, Richmond.
Opposition to established religion. [761]

1802 Jan. 1. T. J., Washington, to JOHN WAYLES EPPES. ALS. 2 pp.
Extremely busy. Sending rather than reading the State of the Union message contributes to harmony. Strength of Federalists and Republicans in the Congress. French expedition against Santo Domingo. Arrival of mammoth cheese. Prospect of New England's return to Republican principles. Importance of laying off counties into hundreds or captaincies. Method of waterproofing clothes. [762]

1802 Jan. 15. T. J., Washington, to the GEORGIA LEGISLATURE. L. 1 p. Extract by N. P. Trist *ca.* 1830. Printed: B of R VI 181 (letterpress copy in DLC).
States' rights essential to our political fabric. [763]

1802 Feb. 6. THOMAS MANN RANDOLPH, JR., Edgehill, to T. J., Washington. ALS. 2 pp. Endorsed by T. J. Edgehill-Randolph Papers.
John Perrie's (Perry?) mistake in letter informing T. J. of purchases for Monticello. Conduct of T. J.'s foreman, Gabriel Lilly, [John] Craven, and Burgess Griffin. References to N. Allen, Martha Randolph, Virginia Randolph, and Dr. Wardlaw. [764]

1802 Feb. 26. ANNE CARY RANDOLPH, Edgehill, to T. J., Washington. ALS. 2 pp. Endorsed by T. J. Edgehill-Randolph Papers.
Whooping cough better. Translation of Justin's ancient history. [765]

1802 Mar. 3. T. J., Washington, to JOHN WAYLES EPPES, Bermuda Hundred. ALS. 1 p.
Encloses letter for Maria. House of Representatives repealed judiciary bill. Needs another horse. All well at Edgehill. Mr. and Mrs. [Hore Browse?] Trist here. [766]

1802 Mar. 11. JOHN WAYLES EPPES, Bermuda Hundred, to T. J. ALS. 2 pp. Endorsed by T. J. Edgehill-Randolph Papers.
Purchase of horse to match Castor. Maria and their son in good health. [767]

1802 Mar. 29. T. J., Washington, to MARIA EPPES, Bermuda Hundred. ALS. 1 p. Printed: Randall III 4-5.
Thomas Mann Randolph, Jr. has decided to purchase land in Georgia rather than in Mississippi. Hopes Maria and John Wayles Eppes will visit Monticello. Best route to Monticello. Gift of medals taken from the Houdon bust of Jefferson. [768]

1802 Apr. 20. T. J. to C. F. C. DE VOLNEY. L. 1 p. Extract by N. P. Trist *ca.* 1830. Letterpress copy in DLC.
Faith in the will of the people as exercised in their elective franchise. Comments on election of 1800. [769]

1802 Apr. 29. T. J., Washington, to JOHN WAYLES EPPES. AL[S clipped]. 1 p.
Plans for meeting the Eppes. Amendment for means of designating president and vice-president.   [770]

1802 May 1. T. J., Washington, to MARIA EPPES, Eppington. ALS. 1 p. McGregor Library. Printed: Randall III 5.
To leave for Monticello when Congress adjourns. Books for Maria. Spectacles for [Elizabeth] Eppes. Proposed visit by Maria to Monticello. Mentions Dr. Walker and John Wayles Eppes.   [771]

1802 May 10. JOHN BARNES, Georgetown, to T. J., Monticello. ALS. 2 pp. Endorsed by T. J. Edgehill-Randolph Papers.
Payment of T. J.'s accounts due. Failure of the Bank of Columbia to pay a note because of scarcity of bank paper. Purchase of government stock for William Short through C. Ludlow. Budget for T. J.'s salary.   [772]

1802 May 21. JOHN BARNES, Georgetown, to T. J., Monticello. ALS. 2 pp. Endorsed by T. J. Edgehill-Randolph Papers.
Failure of a discount at the Bank of Columbia. Purchase of government stock for William Short through C. Ludlow in New York. Payment of T. J.'s accounts. Bills of exchange for General Kosciuszko. Need for regulation of lower class. References to Gibson & Jefferson, Mr. Hooper, Etienne LeMaire.   [773]

1802 May 30. CRAVEN PEYTON, Stump Island, Va., to T. J., Washington. ALS. 1 p. Endorsed by T. J. McGregor Library.
Business regarding the Bennett Henderson estate. References to John R. Kerr and James L. Henderson.   [774]

1802 June 8. T. J., Washington, to CRAVEN PEYTON. ALS. 1 p. Letterpress copy. Endorsed by T. J. McGregor Library.
Payment through George Jefferson, Richmond, for work done in regard to Henderson lands.   [775]

1802 June 8. T. J., Washington, to CRAVEN PEYTON. ALS. 1 p. Letterpress copy. McGregor Library.
Request for delay in paying for further shares in Henderson tract. Henderson mill useless.   [776]

1802 June 12. JOHN BARNES, Georgetown, to T. J. ALS. 1 p. Endorsed by T. J. Edgehill-Randolph Papers.
Courtesy offer of general services.   [777]

* 1802 June 21. MARIA EPPES, Eppington, to T. J. ALS. 2 pp. Endorsed by T. J. Edgehill-Randolph Papers.
She and Francis Eppes have been ill. Is keeping Francis' nurse, Crity (i.e. Critta). Trip to Monticello. John Wayles Eppes finishing his harvest. References to Martha Randolph and Elizabeth Eppes.   [778]

1802 June 22. T. J., Washington, to JAMES DINSMORE, Monticello. ALS. 1 p. Photostat. Original owned by James B. Twyman.

Work to be done to the house and buildings at Monticello. Work on balusters for Mr. Fitch.   [779]

1802 June 25. JOHN WAYLES EPPES, Bermuda Hundred, to T. J., Washington. ALS. 2 pp. Endorsed by T. J.

Maria is unwell at Eppington. Cannot accept T. J.'s offer of residence at Monticello because he is candidate for House of Representatives. Wheat crop. [780]

1802 July 2. T. J., Washington, to MARIA EPPES, Eppington. ALS. 1 p. Printed: Randall III 14; SNR 285-286.

Measles in the Randolph family. Reference to servants, Bet, Sally, and Critta. Spectacles for Elizabeth Eppes.   [781]

1802 July 10. MARTHA RANDOLPH, Edgehill, to T. J., Washington. ALS. 3 pp. Endorsed by T. J. Edgehill-Randolph Papers.

Measles escaped. References to the health of Anne and Cornelia Randolph, and Peter Hemming. Measles in Mr. Walton's family and at Monticello. Need for sheets, towels, counterpane, and tea china.   [782]

1802 July 14. JOHN WAYLES EPPES, Bermuda Hundred, to T. J., Washington. ALS. 2 pp. Endorsed by T. J. Edgehill-Randolph Papers.

Maria's miscarriage. Trip to Monticello postponed because of Francis Eppes' bad health.   [783]

1802 July 17. ISHAM and BENNETT H. HENDERSON to JOHN HENDERSON. D. 2 pp. Endorsed by T. J. Witnessed by Richard Anderson, [Martin] Dawson, and John Peyton. Recorded December 1802 and attested by John Nicholas, Clerk of Albemarle County. McGregor Library.

Deed to lot no. 15 in Milton, Va., and to tobacco warehouses on the Rivanna River.   [784]

1802 July 17. JOHN and ANNE B. HENDERSON, Albemarle County, to RICHARD SEABROOK, Baltimore. D. 2 pp. Endorsed by T. J. Witnessed by Richard Anderson, Martin Dawson, and John Peyton. Recorded 6 September 1802 and attested by John Nicholas, Clerk. (Mrs. Henderson's signature: Nancy Henderson.) McGregor Library.

Deed to three tenths of warehouse, one half of lot no. 15 and all of lot no. 57 in Milton, Va.   [785]

1802 July 28. CHILES TERRELL in account with T. J. AD. 1 p. Endorsed. Watson Papers.

Bill for nails, receipt of which is acknowledged by James Dinsmore.   [786]

1802 July 30. JOHN BARNES, Georgetown, to T. J., Monticello. ALS. 3 pp. Endorsed by T. J. Edgehill-Randolph Papers.

Receipt by Gibson & Jefferson of money on accounts of William Short and the James River Canal Co. Dr. Wardlaw's payment to Mrs. Jackson. Window blinds, books, and claret awaiting a conveyance. Comments on the latest Federalist *Brutus*.   [787]

1802 Aug. 3. JOHN BARNES, Georgetown, to T. J., Monticello. ALS. 2 pp. Endorsed by T. J. Edgehill-Randolph Papers.
   Payment in bank notes by Mr. Smith, will void T. J.'s draft on Smith paid to Mr. Pennington. Gibson & Jefferson's account. Account with T. J. for July. [788]

1802 Aug. 10. JOHN BARNES, Georgetown, to T. J., Monticello. ALS. 2 pp. Endorsed by T. J. Edgehill-Randolph Papers.
   William Short's account. China and liquor in the possession of Etienne LeMaire await shipment.   [789]

1802 Aug. 16. JOHN BARNES, Georgetown, to T. J., Monticello. ALS. 2 pp. Endorsed by T. J. Edgehill-Randolph Papers.
   Visit by William Short. Mail service to Charlottesville. Payment to Etienne LeMaire.   [790]

1802 Aug. 20. JOHN BARNES, Georgetown, to T. J., Monticello. ALS. 2 pp. Endorsed by T. J. Edgehill-Randolph Papers.
   William Short's journey. T. J.'s financial resources. Report by Etienne LeMaire regarding pump at President's House needing repair.   [791]

1802 Aug. 20. DAVID HIGGINBOTHAM, Milton, to T. J., Monticello. ALS. 1 p. Endorsed by T. J. McGregor Library.
   Introducing Isham Henderson who wishes to borrow law books. Endorsement: "lent him 4th Blackstone / Ruffhead: Jacob's L. Dict / June 7.08. wrote to C. Peyton to recover it."   [792]

1802 Aug. 31. JOHN BARNES, Georgetown, to T. J., Monticello. ALS. 2 pp. Endorsed by T. J. Edgehill-Randolph Papers.
   Slanderous publications regarding T. J. William Short expected at Monticello. T. J.'s account with Barnes.   [793]

1802 Sept. 6. T. J., Monticello, to ROBERT SMITH, [Washington]. AL. 1 p. Fragment. Photostat. Original owned by Harold Jefferson Coolidge. Printed: B of R VI 432 (MS. in DLC).
   Proposes delay in orders for the frigate *John Adams*, until the conditions in Tunis and the Mediterranean area are stabilized. Mentions Tripoli, Emperor of Morocco, Governor of Tangiers, Mr. Simpson, Dale.   [794]

1802 Sept. 7. JOHN BARNES, Georgetown, to T. J., Monticello. ALS. 2 pp. Endorsed by T. J. Edgehill-Randolph Papers.
   Letters for William and Peyton Short. Payments to Etienne LeMaire and Joseph Dougherty. Carriage tax. Warrant for T. J.'s salary to take up his bank debt.   [795]

1802 Sept. 14. JOHN BARNES, Georgetown, to T. J., Monticello. ALS. 2 pp. Endorsed by T. J. Edgehill-Randolph Papers.

Account with Brown & Relf paid by John Richards. T. J.'s present balance. Offers to loan T. J. money to pay Gibson & Jefferson in Richmond. [796]

1802 Sept. 18. ELIZABETH HENDERSON. CONTRACT WITH CRAVEN PEYTON. D. 1 p. 2 copies (one T. J. AD). Endorsed by T. J. Witnesses: James L. and Charles Henderson. McGregor Library.

Agreement on rent of house in Milton sold to Peyton, which John Henderson has rented from Elizabeth Henderson. [797]

1802 Sept. 18. ELIZABETH HENDERSON, Kentucky. DEED to CRAVEN PEYTON, Virginia. D. 2 pp. Attested copy. Endorsed by T. J. McGregor Library.

Conveying all dower rights in estate of husband, Bennett Henderson, except mill, warehouse, improved lots in town of Milton. Witnesses: James L. Henderson, Charles Anderson, Eliza Henderson, Isham Henderson, John Gentry. Acknowledgment of deed in Shelby County, Ky., before Matthew Flournoy and Thomas I. Givin, Justices, by Isham Henderson and John L. Henderson, 6 June 1804. Certified by James Craig, Clerk of Shelby County Court, same date. Craig's certificate certified by Isaac Ellis, Presiding Justice, Shelby County Court. Deed recorded Albemarle County, July 1804. Attested by John Nicholas, Clerk. [798]

1802 Sept. 18. JAMES L. HENDERSON, Shelby County, Ky. DEED to CRAVEN PEYTON. DS. 4 pp. Endorsed by T. J. Seals. Original and 2 copies (one attested by William Wertenbaker, one T. J. AD). McGregor Library.

Deed from James L. Henderson for legatees of Bennett Henderson, deceased (Bennett H., Eliza, Frances, Lucy, and Nancy Henderson) to all lands in Albemarle County except a mill, warehouse, and storehouse in Milton, Va. Witnesses: Charles Henderson, G. Tennill (?), James Barlow. Acknowledged before Matthew Flournoy, Thomas Givin, Justices of the Peace of Shelby County, 6 June 1804. Certification that Flournoy and Givin are Justices of the Peace by James Craig, Clerk of Shelby County Court, 6 June 1804. Certification by Isaac Ellis, Presiding Justice of the Peace, that James Craig's certificate is in due form, 6 June 1804. Recorded by John Nicholas, Clerk of Albemarle County Court, July 1804. [799]

1802 Sept. 20. T. J., Monticello, to ROBERT SMITH, Washington. ALS. 1 p. Photostat. Original owned by Harold Jefferson Coolidge. Printed: B of R VI 432 (MS. in DLC).

Approval for the sailing of Navy's frigate *John Adams,* in order to withdraw from Morocco and Tunis forces not needed against Tripoli. Commends speed with which the *New York* was fitted out. Mentions James Madison, Albert Gallatin. [800]

1802 Sept. 21. JOHN BARNES, Georgetown, to T. J., Monticello. ALS. 2 pp. Endorsed by T. J. Edgehill-Randolph Papers.

Payments to Mr Claxton and to Gibson & Jefferson. Etienne LeMaire's illness. Letters for William Short. [801]

1802 Sept. 24. JOHN BARNES, Georgetown, to T. J., Monticello. ALS. 2 pp. Endorsed by T. J. Edgehill-Randolph Papers.

Etienne LeMaire improving. Uprising of Negroes in Washington has subsided. [802]

1802 Sept. 28. JOHN BARNES, Georgetown, to T. J., Monticello. ALS. 2 pp. Endorsed by T. J. Edgehill-Randolph Papers.

Suit against E. Lanham on account of [James?] Oldham's note. Etienne LeMaire recovered. References to Mr. Morse, William Short, and Dr. Gant. [803]

1802 Oct. 7. T. J., Washington, to MARIA EPPES. ALS. 1 p. McGregor Library. Printed: Randall III 22; SNR 288.

Ill upon arrival. Details of Maria's proposed visit to Washington. John Wayles Eppes' bridle is delivered to Davy Bowles. Mentions [George] Jefferson. [804]

1802 Oct. [8?]. T. J. MEMORANDUM to JAMES MADISON. ADS. 1 p. Mutilated. McGregor Library.

Instructions to name the following as Commissioners of Bankruptcy: Samuel Prentiss, Darius Chipman, Richard Skinner, Mark Richards, Reuben Atwater, James Elliot, and Oliver Gallop, all of Vermont; and to issue to Robert Kran, a commission as Marshall of South Carolina in place of Charles B. Cockran, resigned. [805]

1802 Oct. 15. JOHN BARNES, Georgetown, to T. J., Washington. ALS. 1 p. Endorsed by T. J. Edgehill-Randolph Papers.

T. J.'s account; payment of bills. [806]

1802 Oct. 16. JOHN BARNES, Georgetown, to T. J., Washington. ALS. 1 p. Endorsed by T. J. Edgehill-Randolph Papers.

Refusal to handle General M.'s [John P. G. Muhlenberg?] business. [807]

1802 Oct. 16. JOHN BARNES, Georgetown, to T. J., Washington. ALS. 2 pp. Endorsed by T. J. Edgehill-Randolph Papers.

Concerning General M's business. (Second letter of 16 October on this subject.) [808]

1802 Oct. 27. CRAVEN PEYTON, Stump Island, to T. J. ALS. 1 p. Endorsed by T. J. McGregor Library.

Purchase of lands of Bennett Henderson, deceased, from his widow, Elizabeth Henderson. Conveyance of land in Boone County, [Ky.?] from [James L.?] Henderson. [809]

1802 Oct. 29. MARTHA RANDOLPH to T. J., Washington. ALS. 1 p. Endorsed. Edgehill-Randolph Papers.

Trip to Washington to visit T. J. Requests an order of wigs from Mme. de Pick of Philadelphia. Mentions Mrs. Madison. [810]

1802 Oct. JOHN BARNES, Georgetown, to T. J., Washington. ALS. 4 pp. Endorsed by T. J. Edgehill-Randolph Papers.

Transmitting T. J.'s account covering the month of October 1802. Urging him not to resort to bank credit. [811]

1802 Nov. 2. T. J., Washington, to CRAVEN PEYTON, Stump Island. ALS. 1 p. Letterpress copy. Endorsed by T. J. McGregor Library.

Must delay payment for lands of the Henderson estate, because of payments due to Messrs. Overton, Brown, and Wells. References to Bennett H., Eliza, Frances, Lucy, and Nancy Henderson. [812]

1802 Nov. 2. T. J., Washington, to MARTHA RANDOLPH, Edgehill. ALS. 1 p. Edgehill-Randolph Papers. (Accidental offset on letter of 29 October 1802 to T. J. from M. J. R.)

Wigs from Philadelphia ordered by Mrs. Madison. Plans for Maria and Martha's trip to Washington. [813]

1802 Nov. 5. MARIA EPPES to T. J., Washington. ALS. 1 p. Endorsed by T. J. Edgehill-Randolph Papers.

Plans for trip to Washington. References to T. M. Randolph, Jr., Martha Randolph, Mr. [Nicholas?] Lewis, and John Wayles Eppes. Lock of hair to be matched by the wigs. [814]

1802 Nov. 13. CRAVEN PEYTON, Stump Island, to T. J., Washington. ALS. 1 p. Endorsed by T. J. McGregor Library.

Delay in payment will be satisfactory. Asks for authority to act to put someone on Henderson lands. John Henderson's unwillingness to sell. Purchase of the Kerr share. [815]

1802 Nov. 20. T. J., Washington, to CRAVEN PEYTON. ALS. 1 p. Letterpress copy. Endorsed by T. J. McGregor Library.

Payment for Henderson estate lands. Prefers action in Peyton's name. Purchase of the Kerr share. [816]

1802 Dec. 16. CRAVEN PEYTON, Stump Island, to T. J., Washington. ALS. 1 p. Endorsed by T. J. McGregor Library.

Draft on T. J. given to D[abney] Carr. Part payment for Henderson estate lands. [817]

[ca. 1802]. T. J., Washington. MEMORANDA to JAMES MADISON. 2 items (AD and ADS). McGregor Library.

Regarding appointment of William Bellinger Bullock, Joseph Welscher, Edward Stebbins, and John Postel Williamson, as Commissioners of Bankruptcy for Georgia. Commission to George Gilpin, as Judge of Orphan's Court, Alexandria, Va. [818]

1803 Jan. 4. JOHN WAYLES EPPES, Richmond, to T. J., Washington. ALS. 1 p. Endorsed by T. J. Edgehill-Randolph Papers.

James T. Callender's dismissal by the County Court of Henrico. [819]

1803 Jan. 19. JOHN WAYLES EPPES, Richmond, to T. J., Washington. ALS. 1 p. Endorsed by T. J. Edgehill-Randolph Papers.

Recommending Lewis Harvey as secretary to James Monroe's embassy. [820]

1803 Feb. 6. T. J., Washington, to JOHN BARNES, Georgetown. AD. 1 p. Edge-hill-Randolph Papers.

Order for sugar, tea, rice, barley, crackers, and porter to be sent to Monticello.
[821]

1803 Feb. 8. T. J., Washington, to CRAVEN PEYTON. ALS. 1 p. Letterpress copy. Endorsed by T. J. McGregor Library.

Difficulty in making payment for Henderson estate. Draft in favor of [Dabney] Carr.   [822]

1803 Feb. 10. JOHN BARNES, Georgetown, to T. J. ALS. 2 pp. Endorsed by T. J. McGregor Library.

Purchase of coffee, sugar, barley, rice, raisins, olives, spices, crackers, and por-ter for T. J.   [823]

1803 Feb. 10. JOHN WAYLES EPPES, Eppington, to T. J., Washington. ALS. 2 pp. Endorsed by T. J. Edgehill-Randolph Papers.

Health of Maria and Francis. Gabriel Lilly unable to hire hands to work at Pantops because of fear of Mr. Page. Trip to Monticello in March. No competi-tor in the election in his district. Report on debt due from the Commonwealth of Virginia. References to Thomas M. Randolph, Jr., City Point, and Edgehill. [824]

1803 Feb. 19. CRAVEN PEYTON, Stump Island, to T. J., Washington. ALS. 1 p. Endorsed by T. J. McGregor Library.

Requests draft on George Jefferson in payment for Henderson estate. [825]

1803 Feb. 21. BILL OF LADING. D. 1 p. Endorsed by T. J. McGregor Library.

For 2 pipes of wine from Haarlem, Netherlands, consigned to John Barnes, signed by Francis O'Meara, master of the Sloop *Maria*.   [826]

1803 Feb. 23. T. J., Washington, to CRAVEN PEYTON. ALS. 1 p. Letterpress copy. Endorsed by T. J. McGregor Library.

Gives him order on Gibson & Jefferson, Richmond, with the help of John Barnes of Georgetown. Copy of draft.   [827]

1803 Feb. GEORGE ANDREWS to T. J. D. 2 pp. (1 p. a memorandum by T. J.).

Bill for ornaments, friezes, and mouldings (for the Executive Mansion?). Memorandum, dated March 1803 in T. J.'s hand, gives description and speci-fications.   [828]

1803 Mar. 1. T. J., Washington, to JAMES MADISON. ALS. 1 p. McGregor Library.

Memorandum regarding issuing of Commissions of Bankruptcy to John Mussey at Portland; Simeon Thomas at New London, Conn.; John Stephen at Baltimore, Md.; Cowles Meade, Robert Walker, and George Watkins at Augusta, Ga.; and Thomas Collier at Louisville, Ga.   [829]

1803 Mar. 3. CRAVEN PEYTON, Richmond, to T. J., Washington. ALS. 1 p. Endorsed by T. J. McGregor Library.

Financing of Henderson estate purchase; draft on Gibson & Jeff:erson; pay-ment to Robert Burtin.   [830]

1803 Mar. 6. T. J., Washington, to BENJAMIN H. LATROBE. AL [S clipped].
1 p. Photostat. Original owned by Mrs. Gamble Latrobe, Jr.
Offering him the post of Surveyor of Public Buildings. References to Mr.
Monroe, Superintendent of Public Buildings, and Col. D. C. Brent.   [831]

1803 Mar. 6. T. J., Washington, to BENJAMIN H. LATROBE. ALS. 1 p. Photostat. Original owned by Mrs. Gamble Latrobe, Jr.
Details regarding post of Surveyor of Public Buildings. Work on the Capitol,
President's House, and a drydock. References to Mr. Monroe, Superintendent
of Public Buildings. (Second letter of this date to Latrobe).   [832]

1803 Apr. 14. JOHN WAYLES EPPES, Bermuda Hundred, to T. J., Washington.
ALS. 2 pp. Endorsed by T. J. Edgehill-Randolph Papers.
Shrub forwarded by Mr. Hancocke. [William H.?] Cabell's anger at Eppes'
opposition in the Albemarle election. Payment of $400 to Eppes. Maria and
Francis well. Election in Chesterfield.   [833]

1803 Apr. 21. T. J., [Washington] to BENJAMIN RUSH. L. 13 pp. 19th century
copy. Edgehill-Randolph Papers. Printed: TJR III 514-515; L & B 379-385; B
of R VI 398 (MS. in DLC).
Letter detailing T. J.'s religious views, to which is appended his syllabus on
the comparative merits of Christianity. Right of religious liberty. References to
Priestley's *Socrates and Jesus Compared.* Outer sheet contains a quotation describing the death of Emperor Julian.   [834]

1803 Apr. 25. T. J., Washington, to MARIA EPPES, Eppington. ALS. 1 p.
Photostat. Original owned by Mrs. Irene Hallam. Printed: SNR 292-293; Randall
III 45.
Views on Christianity, agreeing with Joseph Priestley's *History of the Cor-
ruptions of Christianity.* References to Francis and John Wayles Eppes, Martha
Randolph, Peter and Nelly Carr.   [835]

1803 Apr. 29. CRAVEN PEYTON, Milton, Va., to T. J., Washington. ALS. 1 p.
Endorsed by T. J. McGregor Library.
Actions of Isaac Miller and John Henderson regarding the Henderson estate
mill seat. Election of Thomas Mann Randolph, Jr. Reference to [William]
Meriwether.   [836]

1803 Apr. 29. THOMAS MANN RANDOLPH, JR., Monticello, to T. J., Washington. ALS. 2 pp. Endorsed by T. J. Edgehill-Randolph Papers.
Election contest between T. M. R. and [William H.?] Cabell. Capt. [Christo-
pher?] Hudson's price of wood. $5 note mistaken for a $50 note. Bowling Clarke's
success as overseer of Poplar Forest. Martha's trip to Washington. Negroes to be
sold in Georgia. References to John Craven, John Perrie, and Gabriel Lilly. [837]

1803 Apr. 30. JOHN and ANN[E] B. HENDERSON, Albemarle County, to
CRAVEN PEYTON, Albemarle County. DS. 2 pp. Endorsed by T. J. Witnesses:
Richard Anderson, Richard Johnson, David Anderson, Will. Clarkson. Proved

and recorded, February, 1804, attested John Nicholas. Mrs. Henderson's signature: "Nancy Henderson". McGregor Library.

Deed to share in estate of Bennett Henderson, including lots in Milton, land. [838]

1803 May 2. T. J., Washington, to CRAVEN PEYTON. ALS. 1 p. Letterpress copy. Endorsed by T. J. McGregor Library.

Instructions on preventing John Henderson from building a mill. T. J.'s plan for a mill of his own. References to Isaac Miller, [William] Meriwether, and [Dabney] Carr. [839]

1803 May 12. T. J., Washington, to JOHN WAYLES EPPES. ALS. 1 p. Photostat. Original owned by Mrs. Irene Hallam.

Syrup of punch from Mr. Hancocke. Proposition for exchanging lands at Bedford for Lego not satisfactory to T. J. References to Mr. Petty [Adrien Petit?], Garland Jefferson, Maria Eppes, and Thomas Mann Randolph, Jr. [840]

1803 May 27. JOHN BARNES, Georgetown, to T. J. Washington. ADS. 1 p. Endorsed. McGregor Library.

Memorandum with estimate of T. J.'s monthly statements and balances from 31 March 1801 to 8 June 1803. [841]

1803 May 30. THOMAS MANN RANDOLPH, JR., Edgehill, to T. J., Washington. ALS. 4 pp. Endorsed by T. J. Edgehill-Randolph Papers.

Trepanning operation necessary after Cary hit Brown on the skull with a piece of nailrod. Martha's pregnancy. Consultation with Craven Peyton concerning John Henderson's claim to ground where T. J.'s mill is to be built. Meriwether and Miller's offer to purchase whole or half of T. M. R.'s mill seat. [842]

1803 June 7. JOHN R. and SARAH KERR. DEED to CRAVEN PEYTON. DS. 2 pp. Endorsed by T. J. Recorded June 1803 by John Nicholas, Clerk of Albemarle County. McGregor Library.

Conveying a share of Bennett Henderson's estate with certain exceptions. References to Elizabeth and William Henderson. [843]

1803 June 8. CRAVEN PEYTON, Stump Island, to T. J., Washington. ALS. 1 p. Endorsed by T. J. McGregor Library.

Court action on John Henderson's mill. References to [Dabney] Carr, Mr. Barbour, Mr. Nelson, Isaac Miller, and [William] Meriwether. [844]

1803 June 14. JOHN WAYLES EPPES, Bermuda Hundred, to T. J., Washington. ALS. 3 pp. Endorsed by T. J. Edgehill-Randolph Papers.

Visit to Eppes' sister, Mrs. Walker. Offering to buy a part of Lego. Damage to wheat by Hessian fly. [845]

1803 June 14. T. J., Washington, to CRAVEN PEYTON. ALS. 1 p. Letterpress copy. Endorsed by T. J. McGregor Library.

Consultation with Thomas Mann Randolph, Jr., regarding the mill right of John Henderson. [846]

1803 June 19. T. J., Washington, to JOHN WAYLES EPPES. ALS. 1 p. McGregor Library.
Would prefer the Eppes come to Monticello rather than to stay at Bermuda Hundred. Advice on a plague of Hessian flies. Payment to Mr. Hancocke for syrup of punch. All well at Edgehill.   [847]

1803 Aug. 7. ELIZABETH HENDERSON to JOHN HENDERSON. D. 1 p. Copy by T. J. Endorsed by T. J. McGregor Library.
Declaration regarding John Henderson's rights to a house and mill race. Reference to Craven Peyton.   [848]

1803 Aug. 24. CRAVEN PEYTON, Stump Island, to T. J. ALS. 1 p. Endorsed by T. J. McGregor Library.
Information regardng T. J.'s tenants, Mr. Johnson and Mr. Shickle. Wheat and corn crops. Requests remittance.   [849]

1803 Sept. 7. T. J., Monticello, to CRAVEN PEYTON. ALS. 1 p. Letterpress copy. McGregor Library.
Instructions for [John] Fentress, who is going to Kentucky to have Elizabeth Henderson acknowledge her deed to Peyton. Mentions D[abney] Carr. [850]

1803 Sept. 7. CRAVEN PEYTON, Stump Island, to T. J. ALS. 1 p. Endorsed by T. J. McGregor Library.
Fentress to set out for Kentucky to have Elizabeth Henderson's deed acknowledged and to purchase Henderson family shares in the mill.   [851]

1803 Sept. 8. T. J., Monticello, to CRAVEN PEYTON. ALS. 1 p. Letterpress copy. Endorsed by T. J. McGregor Library.
Purchase of shares in the Henderson family mill.   [852]

1803 Sept. 9. JAMES IDDINGS, Duck Creek County, Del., to T. J. ALS. 2 pp. Endorsed by T. J. McGregor Library. Printed: Ford-Bixby 103-104.
Concerning a manuscript he propose to publish. Reference to the Quakers.
                                                                       [853]

1803 Sept. 20. CRAVEN PEYTON, Stump Island, to T. J. ALS. 1 p. Endorsed and annotated by T. J. McGregor Library.
Requests draft on Gibson & Jefferson. Difficulty in buying mill shares because John Henderson has deepened the mill race.   [854]

1803 Sept. [28]. T. J., Monticello, to CRAVEN PEYTON. ALS. 1 p. Letterpress copy. Endorsed by T. J. McGregor Library.
Remittance sent in payment for Henderson lands. Copy of draft on Gibson & Jefferson.   [855]

1803 Oct. DAVID GELSTON, COLLECTOR, PORT OF NEW YORK, to T. J. D. 2 items. Endorsed. McGregor Library.
Freight bill and customs account for 10 cases of wine, receipted by J. Speyer.
                                                                       [856]

1803 Nov. 12. SAMUEL CARR, Dunlora, to T. J. ALS. 1 p. Endorsed by T. J. Carr-Cary Papers.

Dr. Baker's terms for sale of a slave. References to Nelly Carr, Carrsbrook, and Edgehill.   [857]

1803 Nov. 27. T. J., Washington, to CRAVEN PEYTON, Stump Island, Va. ALS. 1 p. Original and letterpress copy. Letterpress copy endorsed by T. J. McGregor Library. Original deposited by J. Lynn Cochran.

Requests postponement and payment by installments of money due Peyton. (This is the letter reproduced in facsimile and widely distributed by the Morris Plan Banks. The excellent facsimiles are frequently mistaken for the original.)
[858]

1803 Dec. 8. CRAVEN PEYTON, Stump Island, to T. J., Washington. ALS. 1 p. Endorsed by T. J. McGregor Library.

Financial matters. John Henderson has completed an excellent canal, which was stopped by a court bill. References to [James] Barbour, Mr. Gamble, Mr. Kenny, [Nicholas] Lewis, and Sheriff Yancy.   [859]

1803 Dec. 24. T. M. RANDOLPH, JR., Edgehill, to T. J., Washington. ALS. 3 pp. Endorsed by T. J. Edgehill-Randolph Papers.

Workings of T. J.'s mill and canal. New Orleans news. Mentions Gabriel Lilly and John Wayles Eppes.   [860]

1803 Dec. 26. SURVEY. LAND OF EDMUND TATE. D. 1 p. Endorsed. McGregor Library.

Survey of 54¾ acres of land adjoining that of Mr. Wilkerson, Samuel Scott, Mr. Johnson, and Mr. Tillis (i.e., Richard Tullos). Land later transferred to Samuel Scott.   [861]

1803 Dec. 31. T. J. to GEORGE CLINTON, N. Y. L. 1 p. Extract by N. P. Trist *ca.* 1834. Printed: L & B X 439-441; B of R VI 88 (MS. in DLC).

Bringing back of Republicans into the fold.   [862]

1803. JOHN BARNES, Georgetown, to T. J., Washington. ADS. 4 items. McGregor Library.

Bills and accounts rendered to T. J. by Barnes as his fiscal and purchasing agent.   [863]

1804 Jan. 9. T. J., Washington, to ANNE C. RANDOLPH, Edgehill. ALS. 1 p. Letterpress copy. Endorsed by T. J. Edgehill-Randolph Papers.

Anne, Ellen, and Thomas Jefferson Randolph's education. Pair of fowls. Requests Davy Bowles to bring his chair for return trip to Monticello. References to Jane Randolph, Maria Eppes, and Martha Randolph.   [864]

1804 Jan. 14. MARTHA RANDOLPH, Edgehill, to T. J., Washington. ALS. 3 pp. Endorsed by T. J. Edgehill-Randolph Papers.

Davy Bowles to go to Washington. Sale of slave, Kit. Attachment of Mr. Stewart's goods. Francis Eppes' epileptic fits. Maria disturbed by John Wayles

Eppes' absence. Jane Randolph now a neighbor. References to Gabriel Lilly
and [David] Higginbotham. [865]

1804 Jan. 15. T. J. EXAMINATION INTO THE BOUNDARIES OF LOUISI-
ANA; and a chronological series of facts relative to Louisiana. AD. 2 items. 20 pp.
Printed: *Documents Relating to the Purchase and Exploration of Louisiana* 7-45.
Letter to John Wayles Eppes (see 5 January 1811) explains purpose of its
compilation. Of the appendix he says ". . . a chronological table [1673-1803]
of all the facts relating to the discovery & history of Louisiana which I compiled
from all the authors I possess or could obtain, who have written on Louisiana,
with a reference to the authority for every fact." [866]

1804 Jan. 16. T. J., Washington, to CRAVEN PEYTON. ALS. 1 p. Letterpress
copy. Endorsed by T. J. McGregor Library.
Asks explanation of draft on himself received from [David] Higginbotham.
Thought the Henderson estate transaction was closed. [867]

1804 Jan. 23. CRAVEN PEYTON, Stump Island, to T. J., Washington. ALS. 1 p.
Endorsed by T. J. McGregor Library.
Draft in favor of [David] Higginbotham was for corn. [868]

1804 Jan. 30. T. J., Washington, to CRAVEN PEYTON. ALS. 1 p. Letterpress
copy. Endorsed by T. J. McGregor Library.
Has accepted draft in favor of [David] Higginbotham in payment for corn.
[869]

1804 Jan. 31. CHARLES HENDERSON, Albemarle County, to CRAVEN PEY-
TON. D. 2 pp. Endorsed by T. J. Recorded 2 July 1804 and this copy attested
by John Nicholas, Clerk. McGregor Library.
Being of lawful age, confirms previous deeds to his share in the Henderson
estate, with reserved portions: to James L. Henderson, 18 March 1801, and from
James L. Henderson to Craven Peyton, 19 March 1801. Witnesses: Bennett H.
Henderson, Isham Henderson, John Peyton, John McLean, Davi[d] Richardson,
John L. Thomas, Ma. Camden, and David Anderson. [870]

1804 Feb. 6. ELIZABETH HENDERSON, by Charles Henderson, attorney, to
JOHN HENDERSON. D. 2 pp. Endorsed by T. J. Recorded March 1804 and
this copy attested by John Nicholas, Clerk of Albemarle County. McGregor
Library.
Conveys land necessary for digging a mill-race. [871]

1804 Feb. 9. JOHN BARNES, Georgetown, to T. J., Washington. ALS. 2 pp.
Endorsed by T. J. Edgehill-Randolph Papers.
Plans for removal to Philadelphia. [872]

1804 Feb. 14. CRAVEN PEYTON, Stump Island, to T. J., Washington. ALS. 2 pp.
Endorsed by T. J. McGregor Library.
Purchase of John Henderson's mill seat proposed. Peyton offers to share in
purchase. Requests draft on Gibson & Jefferson. References to [David] Higginbotham and Isaac Miller. [873]

1804 Feb. 14. ANNE C. RANDOLPH, Edgehill, to T. J., Washington. ALS. 1 p.
Endorsed by T. J. Edgehill-Randolph Papers.
News of the family, T. J. Randolph, Martha Randolph, and Francis Eppes.
[874]

*1804 Feb. 22. ANNE CARY RANDOLPH, Edgehill, to T. J., Washington. ALS. 1
p. Endorsed by T. J. Edgehill-Randolph Papers.
Plans to change her name to Anastasia.   [875]

1804 Feb. 25. T. J., Washington, to CRAVEN PEYTON, Stump Island. ALS. 1 p.
File draft. Endorsed by T. J. McGregor Library.
Prefers to have the Henderson mill question settled in courts rather than to
pay more than his previous offer. Payment for corn. References to [James]
Barbour and [Dabney] Carr.   [876]

1804 Mar. 9. JOHN WAYLES EPPES, Edgehill, to T. J., Washington. ALS. 2 pp.
Endorsed by T. J. Edgehill-Randolph Papers.
Health of Maria and her child. Difficult trip from Washington *via* Elk Run.
Request for oats.   [877]

*1804 Mar. 10. JOHN WAYLES EPPES, Monticello, to T. J., Washington. ALS.
1 p. Endorsed by T. J. Edgehill-Randolph Papers.
Weakness of Maria and the child.   [878]

1804 Mar. 19. JOHN WAYLES EPPES, Edgehill, to T. J., Washington. ALS. 1
p. Endorsed by T. J. Edgehill-Randolph Papers.
Maria's condition bad.   [879]

1804 Mar. 23. JOHN WAYLES EPPES, Edgehill, to T. J., Washington. ALS.
1 p. Endorsed by T. J. Edgehill-Randolph Papers.
Improvement in Maria's health. Mrs. [Nicholas?] Lewis' kindness.   [880]

1804 Mar. 26. JOHN WAYLES EPPES, Edgehill, to T. J., Washington. ALS.
1 p. Endorsed by T. J. Edgehill-Randolph Papers.
Maria's health the same.   [881]

1804 Mar. 29. CRAVEN PEYTON, Stump Island, to T. J., Washington. ALS.
1 p. Endorsed by T. J. McGregor Library.
Chancellor [George Wythe?] stopped all proceedings upon Peyton's entering
into bond. Requests acceptance of draft in favor of George Jefferson for corn
contract.   [882]

1804 Apr. 9. JOHN BARNES, Georgetown, to T. J., Monticello. ALS. 2 pp.
Endorsed by T. J. Edgehill-Randolph Papers.
Warns of the low state of his (Barnes') resources. Includes an account with
T. J. Mentions William Short and Etienne LeMaire.   [883]

1804 Apr. 20. JOHN BARNES, Georgetown, to T. J., Monticello. ALS. 2 pp.
Endorsed by T. J. Edgehill-Randolph Papers.
Receipt of money from Gibson & Jefferson in Richmond. Payment for cider.

Maria Eppes' illness. Packages from New York, Philadelphia, and Baltimore.
Reference to Etienne LeMaire.   [884]

1804 Apr. 30. T. J., Monticello, to CRAVEN PEYTON, Stump Island. ALS. 1 p.
Letterpress copy. Endorsed by T. J. McGregor Library.
The mill dispute with John Henderson should be thrown into a single bill
in chancery. Reference to Dabney Carr.   [885]

1804 May 2. JOHN BARNES, Georgetown, to T. J., Monticello. ALS. 2 pp.
Endorsed by T. J. Edgehill-Randolph Papers.
T. J.'s receipts from tobacco sale in the hands of Gibson & Jefferson. Claims
of William Short and Etienne LeMaire. Condolences on Maria's death. [886]

[1804 May 2]. WILSON CARY NICHOLAS, Warren, to T. J. ALS. 3 pp. Frag-
ment. Endorsed by T. J. Deposited by Robert H. Kean.
Death of Maria. Appointment of W. C. Nicholas Collector for Norfolk after
Mr. Davis resigns. Reference to Albert Gallatin.   [887]

1804 May 4. CRAVEN PEYTON, Albemarle County. DEED to T. J. DS (AD by
T. J.). 1 p. Endorsed by T. J. Witnesses: James Dinsmore, James Oldham, John
Perry, William Stewart. McGregor Library.
Deed of trust to all shares of estate of Bennett Henderson on the Rivanna
River near Milton, purchased on T. J.'s account and paid for by him.   [888]

1804 May 8. T. J., Monticello, to CRAVEN PEYTON, Stump Island. ALS. 1 p.
Letterpress copy. Endorsed by T. J. McGregor Library.
Sends draft on Gibson & Jefferson. Mrs. Kerr's title to Henderson warehouses.
Reference to Gabriel Lilly.   [889]

1804 May 8 [date received]. CRAVEN PEYTON, Stump Island, to T. J. ALS. 1
p. Endorsed by T. J. McGregor Library.
Sends copy of partition of Henderson estate. Requests payment on corn
contract.   [890]

1804 May 15. [T. J.] to JOHN BARNES. D. 1 p. Copy in John Barnes' hand.
Endorsed by T. J. Edgehill-Randolph Papers.
Note for $1000 payable in 60 days negotiable at the Bank of Columbia. [891]

1804 May 15. T. J., Washington, to WILSON CARY NICHOLAS, Norfolk. ALS.
1 p. Edgehill-Randolph Papers. Printed: B of R X 13 (MS. in DLC).
Commission as Collector (at the Port of Norfolk) has been forwarded. Mentions Albert Gallatin, James Madison, Mr. Newton, Jr., and Mr. Bedinger. [892]

1804 May 21. T. J., Washington, to HENRY FRY, Culpeper. ALS. 1 p. McGregor
Library. Printed: B of R VI 153 (MS. in DLC); Philip Slaughter, *Memoir of
Joshua Fry* 108.
Gift of Joseph Priestley's *Corruptions of Christianity*. Reference to [Fontaine?]
Maury.   [893]

1804 May 24. T. J., Washington, to JAMES DINSMORE, Monticello. ALS. 1 p.
Payment for Mr. Wairscher, Mr. Duncan, and Alexander Perry for work at
Monticello. Requests water be drawn from icehouse. References to J[ohn M.]
Perry and [William?] Stewart.   [894]

1804 May 31. MARTHA RANDOLPH, Edgehill, to T. J., Washington. ALS. 2
pp. Endorsed by T. J. Deposited by Robert H. Kean.
     T. J.'s tedious journey from Monticello. Declares her affection. Anne Ran-
dolph's visit to Elizabeth Eppes. Her recent illness. References to Thomas Mann
Randolph, Jr.   [895]

1804 June 17. T. J., Washington, to HENRY FRY, Culpeper. ALS. 1 p. Mc-
Gregor Library. Printed: B of R VI 153 (MS. in DLC); Philip Slaughter,
Memoir of Joshua Fry 109-110.
     Priestley's *Corruptions of Christianity.* T. J.'s religious views. Recommends
his own method of riding a trotting horse to strengthen his bowels. References
to Dr. [William?] Eustis of Boston and Dr. Sydenham.   [896]

1804 June 28. BENNETT H. HENDERSON, Shelby County, Ky. DEED to
CRAVEN PEYTON, Albemarle County. DS. 4 pp. Seal. Endorsed by T. J.
McGregor Library.
     Deed to his share of the estate of Bennett Henderson, except mill, warehouse,
storehouse, and lot in Milton, Va. Acknowledged before Willam Taylor and
David Demaree, Justices of Shelby County, 9 July 1804; their commissions certified
by James Craig, Clerk of Shelby County Court, 6 August 1804. Certification by
Robert Jeffries, Presiding Justice of Shelby County, that James Craig's certificate
is in order, 16 January 1805. Recorded by John Nicholas, Clerk of Albemarle
County Court, 1 July 1805.   [897]

1804 July 5. CRAVEN PEYTON, Stump Island, to T. J. ALS. 1 p. Endorsed
by T. J. McGregor Library.
     Recording of deeds to the Bennett Henderson estate. Army commission for
Robert Peyton held probable by Thomas Mann Randolph, Jr.   [898]

1804 July 16. JOHN WAYLES EPPES, Eppington, to T. J. ALS. 2 pp. Endorsed
by T. J. Edgehill-Randolph Papers.
     Exchange of Bedford County lands for Lego (land adjoining Pantops). Health
of Francis and the baby. Purchase of horse suitable for T. J. T. J.'s donkey sent
back with Martin (servant). Proposed marriage between Eppes' servant Melinda
and T. J.'s John.   [899]

1804 July 20. T. J., Washington, to JAMES MAURY, Liverpool, England. ALS.
1 p. Endorsed. Deposited by Mrs. Anne F. Maury. Printed: B of R VI 318 (MS. in
DLC).
     Bills of exchange on Maury in favor of Joseph Yznardi, Cadiz; Thomas Apple-
ton, Leghorn; and William Jarvis, Lisbon. Assurances of his friendship. News of
Rev. [Matthew] Maury, his brother. Anxiety concerning affairs between France
and England.   [900]

1804 Aug. 8. T. J., Monticello, to WILSON CARY NICHOLAS. ALS. 1 p. Photostat. Original owned by Harold J. Coolidge.

Asks recommendation of successor for Mr. Chisman, Collector of Hampton. Death of Gen. William Irvine. References to Mr. Booker, Robert Armistead. [901]

1804 Aug. 21. JOHN BARNES, Georgetown, to T. J., Monticello. ALS. 3 pp. Endorsed by T. J. Edgehill-Randolph Papers.

T. J.'s accounts for the months of July and August. Expected trip to Monticello *via* Fredericksburg and Orange. [902]

1804 Sept. 16. JOHN WAYLES EPPES, Eppington, to T. J. ALS. 1 p. Endorsed by T. J. Edgehill-Randolph Papers.

Trip to Monticello. Reference to Mr. Baker's accident and to Elizabeth Eppes. [903]

1804 Oct. 12. T. J., Washington, to JAMES MADISON. ALS. 1 p. McGregor Library.

Memorandum for appointment of Nathaniel Ewing of Pennsylvania to be Receiver of Public Monies at Vincennes. [904]

1804 Nov. 30. MARTHA RANDOLPH, Edgehill, to T. J., Washington. ALS. 3 pp. Endorsed by T. J. Edgehill-Randolph Papers.

Lilly unwilling to sell corn needed at Monticello. Difficulties with servant John who incites the hands. Thomas Jefferson Randolph's education. References to Messrs. Anderson, Moran, and Irving. [905]

1804 Dec. 19. T. J., Washington, to WILSON C. NICHOLAS. AL[S clipped]. 1 p. Endorsed. Edgehill-Randolph Papers. Printed: B of R X 13 (MS. in DLC).

Regarding Nicholas' resignation. Reference to Colonel Newton. [906]

1804-1812. CRAVEN PEYTON vs. JOHN HENDERSON. COURT RECORD. D. 50 pp. Copy attested by John Nicholas, Clerk of Albemarle, and H. Dance, Clerk of Va. Court of Appeals. McGregor Library.

Complete record of legal action arising from Peyton's purchase of the estate of Bennett Henderson. Suit over matter of rights reserved by Mrs. Elizabeth Henderson for her son, John, to permit him to convey water through her land from the Rivanna River to his mill. Peyton stopped him with injunction from Albemarle County Court, which was dissolved on appeal. Complete record of trial in county court at which Peyton attempted to prove document reserving this right was fraudulent. Deposition of witnesses, exhibits of certified copies of documents. Case decided in favor of Henderson. Peyton appealed to High Court of Chancery. Appeal refused. After inquest of jurors, Henderson established mill. Petition of appeal to George Wythe, Judge of District Chancery Court, from Peyton allowed. At Court of Appeals held at Capitol in Richmond, 7 January 1812, action of lower court affirmed.

Names appearing in the record: William Alcock, James Barbour, Christopher W. Barker, James W. Bramham, N. Bramham, G. Carr, John Carr, Peter Carr, Kemp Catlett, Charlottesville, Va., Henry Chiles, Mr. Connard, James Craig, H. Dance, Martin Dawson, Isaac Ellis, Triplett T. Estis, John Fentress, Thomas C.

Fletcher, Matthew Flournoy, Thomas L. Givin, Bennett Henderson, Bennett H. Henderson, Charles Henderson, Eliza Henderson, Elizabeth Henderson, Frances Henderson, Isham Henderson, Helman Henderson, James L. Henderson, John Henderson, Lucy Henderson, Matthew Henderson, Nancy Henderson, Richard Henderson, Sarah Henderson, William Henderson, Henderson & Connard, Elijah Hogg, John R. Kerr, Sarah Henderson Kerr, John Key, Walter Key, Charles Lewis, James Lewis, J. W. Lewis, Reuben Lewis, William McKim, Isaac Miller, Milton, Va., Dabney Minor, William D. Meriwether, Edward Moore, John Nicholas, James Old, Richard Overton, George Poindexter, Richard Price, Thomas Mann Randolph, Jr., Aaron Ray, Richmond, Va., Rivanna River, John Rogers, Shelby County, Ky., G. Termille, Mr. Thorp, Peter Tinsley, John Watson, Christian Wertenbaker (Wertinbaker), Christopher Wingfield. William Wingfield, W. Wood, Tucker Woodson, George Wythe, Charles Yancey. [907]

[1804-1816]. T. J. AND CRAVEN PEYTON. Documents for chancery suit against ESTATE OF BENNETT HENDERSON. 14 items T. J. AD, 2 items Craven Peyton AD. McGregor Library.

Craven Peyton's bill in the case of Peyton *vs.* Henderson, presented to George Wythe, judge of the High Court of Chancery; chronology of sales by various heirs to the estate; notes on rent claims in the case of the Henderson lands; 2 copies of deed, John Wood and Lucy Henderson Wood to T. J.; 3 copies of an agreement between John Wood and T. J. regarding his share of the Henderson estate; statement of the real property belonging to the legatees; and miscellaneous notes on pertinent information. Names mentioned: Richard Anderson, N. Bramham, Eliza Bullock, Kemp Catlett, George Hay, Bennett H. Henderson, Charles Henderson, Eliza Henderson, Elizabeth Henderson, Isham Henderson, James Lewis Henderson, John Henderson, Matthew Henderson, Nancy Crawford Henderson, Sarah Henderson, and William Henderson; Henderson & Connard, David Higginbotham, Elijah Hogg, Mr. Johnson, John R. Kerr, Sarah Henderson Kerr, Walte Key, Isaac Miller, E. Moore, Matthew Nelson, Nancy Crawford Henderson Nelson, Craven Peyton, Richard Price, Thomas Eston Randolph, Richard Seabrook, Watson & Snelson, John Wood, Lucy Henderson Wood, and Tucker M. Woodson.   [908]

[1804-1818]. BENNETT HENDERSON ESTATE. Surveys and other documents dealing with the rights to lands. 24 items, 33 pp. Some in T. J.'s hand, others endorsed by T. J. McGregor Library.

Includes tabular view of rights in lands of Bennett Henderson, showing portions of widow (Elizabeth Henderson), John Henderson, Sarah Henderson Kerr, James Lewis Henderson, Charles Henderson, Isham Henderson, Bennett Hillsboro Henderson, Eliza Henderson, Frances Henderson, Lucy Henderson, Nancy Crawford Henderson, with notations of conveyances to T. J., Craven Peyton, Mr. Bramham, Tucker M. Woodson, James L. Henderson, Richard Seabrook, and John Henderson. A statement of the real property of Bennett Henderson, deceased. Courses of deed and plat of land sold to Martin Dawson by T. J. Estimate of the property of Bennett Henderson in which dower was assigned. Estimate of Bennett Henderson's estate for assigning dower. Estimate of Henderson's lands by Messrs. Watson & [Snelson?]. List of Henderson's lands purchased by T. J. The rights of T. J. to the warehouses. List of deeds for the Henderson lands. References to Watson E. Alexander, David Anderson, Eliza Bullock, John H. Bullock, Mr. Fitch, David Higginbotham, John R. Kerr, William D. Meriwether, David Mickie, Thomas E. Randolph, and Mr. Suttle.

[909]

1805 Jan. 3. CRAVEN PEYTON, Stump Island, to T. J., Washington. ALS. 1 p. Endorsed by T. J. McGregor Library.

Price for shares in warehouse of the Henderson estate.   [910]

1805 Jan. 5. [JOSEPH DOUGHERTY] to T. J. AD. 1 p. Endorsed by T. J. McGregor Library.

Stable bill for the year 1804.   [911]

1805 Jan. 5. T. J., Washington, to LITTLETON WALLER TAZEWELL. ALS. 4 pp.

Establishment of a state university in Virginia. Detailed advice regarding the charter, purpose, endowment, board of visitors, professorships, and buildings. Will leave his library to the university if it should be set up.   [912]

1805 Feb. 4. T. J., Washington, to CRAVEN PEYTON. ALS. 1 p. Endorsed by T. J. McGregor Library.

Information from Thomas Mann Randolph, Jr., on a commission for Robert Peyton. Purchase of shares in Henderson's warehouse difficult in present circumstances.   [913]

1805 Feb. 25. FRANCES, LUCY, AND NANCY HENDERSON, Shelby County, Ky., to CRAVEN PEYTON, Albemarle County, Va. DS. 2 pp. Seal. Endorsed by T. J. McGregor Library.

Deed to their shares in Henderson's warehouse in Milton, Va., witnessed by John H. Bullock, James Davis, and John Fentress. Sworn before Matthew Flournoy and Abraham Owen, Justices of the Peace of Shelby County, Ky. Flournoy's and Owen's commissions certified by James Craig, Clerk of Shelby County. James L. Henderson and Elizabeth Henderson's guarantee of the deed (grantors being under age), 25 February 1805. Recorded by John Nicholas, Clerk of Albemarle County Court, 7 October 1805.   [914]

1805 Feb. 26. JOHN H. BULLOCK and ELIZA, his wife, Shelby County, Ky., to CRAVEN PEYTON, Albemarle County, Va. DS. 2 pp. Seal. Endorsed by T. J. McGregor Library.

Deeds to share of lands, warehouses, storehouses, mills, lots, etc., inherited by Eliza Bullock from her father, Bennett Henderson. Acknowledged before Matthew Flournoy and Abraham Owen, Justices, Shelby County, 28 February 1805, whose commissions are certified by James Craig, Clerk of Court. Foregoing certificates attested in good form by Robert Jeffries, Presiding Justice of Peace, 15 March 1805. Recorded, Albemarle County Court, October 1805, John Nicholas, Clerk.   [915]

1805 Feb. 28. MARTHA RANDOLPH, Edgehill, to T. J., Washington. ALS. 1 p. Endorsed by T. J. Edgehill-Randolph Papers.
Martha's illness. References to Dr. [Charles] Everett and Mr. Terry.   [916]

1805 Mar. 9. T. J. SHIP'S PAPERS. DS. 1 p. Endorsed. Deposited by Thomas Jefferson Unitarian Church.
Clearance papers for Schooner *Mercury*, Caleb Smith master, bound for Barbados.   [917]

1805 Mar. 10. T. J., Washington, to WILLIAM C. C. CLAIBORNE. AL. Fragment. 1 p. File draft. Endorsed by T. J.
Informing the Louisina Governor that Mr. Briggs is to survey lands between New Orleans and the Bayou St. Jean, preparatory to the issuance of a grant to Lafayette. Requesting information as to the advantages of different pieces of land.   [918]

1805 Mar. 10. T. J., Washington, to the MARQUIS DE LAFAYETTE. ALS. 1 p. Photostat. Original owned by St. Paul's School. Another MS. in CSmH.
Land to be granted to Lafayette near New Orleans.   [919]

1805 Mar. 11. T. J., Washington, to JAMES OLDHAM. ALS. 1 p. McGregor Library.
Work (at Monticello?) can be done in Mr. Andrews' absence if moulds are available.   [920]

1805 Mar. 13. T. J. SHIP'S PAPERS. DS. 1 p. Seal. Endorsed.
Clearance papers for Schooner *Fair Trader*, John Simpson master, bound for Jamaica. Countersigned by James Madison.   [921]

1805 Mar. 22. ANNE CARY RANDOLPH, Edgehill, to T. J., Washington. ALS. 1 p. Endorsed by T. J. Edgehill-Randolph Papers.
Family news. Martha's illness.   [922]

1805 Mar. 26. JOHN BARNES, Georgetown, to T. J., Monticello. ALS. 1 p. Enclosure: AD. 1 p. Both endorsed by T. J. Edgehill-Randolph Papers.
Painter setting out for Monticello. Reference to Joseph Dougherty. Enclosure: bill for coffee, sugar, chocolate, barley, rice, and spices.   [923]

1805 Apr. 6. T. J., Monticello, to THOMAS CARR. ALS. 2 pp. Endorsed by T. J. Carr-Cary Papers.
Regarding his account with [Thomas] Bell. Reference to Reuben Perry and to George Washington.   [924]

1805 Apr. 19. MARTHA RANDOLPH, Monticello, to T. J., Washington. ALS. 1 p. Endorsed by T. J. Edgehill-Randolph Papers.
Thomas Mann Randolph, Jr.'s election seems certain.   [925]

1805 Apr. 25. CRAVEN PEYTON, Stump Island, to T. J. ALS. 2 pp. Endorsed by T. J. McGregor Library.
Deeds received from James L. Henderson, Eliza Henderson Bullock, and other

members of the family for their shares in Bennett Henderson's estate. [Richard] Anderson's doubtful title secured. Draft on T. J. in favor of George Jefferson.

[926]

1805 Apr. 27. THOMAS MANN RANDOLPH, JR., Edgehill, to T. J., Washington. ALS. 1 p. Endorsed by T. J. Deposited by Robert H. Kean.

Martha's health. Election results.   [927]

1805 May 2. T. J., Washington, to JAMES OLDHAM, Richmond. ALS. 1 p. Photostat. Original owned by Dr. Mary Parmenter. Printed: B of R VI 356 (MS. in DLC).

Letter to Judge Gantt of Bladensburg, Md., regarding Oldham's concerns in the Jackson estate. Ornaments for Corinthian frieze. Mentions Mr. Andrews.

[928]

1805 May 27. T. J., Washington, to JOHN WAYLES EPPES. ALS. 1 p. Printed: Randall III 136.

Payment for a horse. Plans to lay off portion of Poplar Forest (for Eppes?) with aid of [Charles] Clay and [Bowling] Clarke. Invitation to Monticello. Misleading letter of [James?] Elliot printed in the paper.   [929]

[1805 May 31]. T. J. to JUSTIN PIERRE P. DE RIEUX. ALS. 1 p. Fragment. Printed: B of R VI 390 (MS. in DLC).

Failure of solid-stemmed wheat.   [930]

1805 June 3. JOHN BARNES, Georgetown, to T. J., Washington. ALS. 2 pp. Endorsed by T. J. Edgehill-Randolph Papers.

Accounts with Mr. Cheetham, Mr. Erwin, Mrs. Radcliffe, Colonel Colfax settled by John Richards and Mr. Ludlow.   [931]

1805 June 3. JOHN BARNES, Georgetown, to T. J., Washington. ALS. 1 p. Endorsed by T. J. Edgehill-Randolph Papers.

Accounts with T. J. and General Kosciuszko. Reference to Van Staphorst & Hubbard.   [932]

1805 June 9. ROBERT BRENT to T. J., Monticello. ALS. 1 p. McGregor Library.

Accepts dinner invitation.   [933]

1805 June 9. CRAVEN PEYTON to T. J., Washington. ALS. 2 pp. Endorsed by T. J. McGregor Library.

[John] Henderson's interference in the collections for firewood. Deeds, depositions regarding the Henderson estate forwarded to George Hay. Requests remittance through George Jefferson. Mentions [Richard] Anderson.   [934]

1805 June 13. T. J., Washington, to CRAVEN PEYTON. ALS. 4 pp. File draft. Endorsed by T. J. McGregor Library.

Arrangements for remittance through George Jefferson. Requests particulars of purchase from Eliza Bullock and a note of the quantity of tobacco received at the Henderson warehouses for the past years. Statement of the rights in the warehouses of the Henderson heirs, Elizabeth, John, James L., Charles, Isham, Bennett H., Frances, Lucy, and Nancy C. Henderson, Eliza Henderson Bullock, and Sarah Kerr. Mentions Richard Anderson, [James W.?] Bramham, Richard Seabrook, and Tucker M. Woodson.   [935]

1805 June 16. T. M. RANDOLPH, JR., to T. J., Washington. ALS. 3 pp. Endorsed by T. J. Edgehill-Randolph Papers.
Lilly's plan to leave Monticello to supervise work of clearing the Rivanna River. Suggestion that Lilly might be retained by being allowed to oversee a farm as well as the nailery. Damage done to crops by the Hessian fly. Health of Martha, Anne, Ellen, Cornelia, Virginia, and Thomas Jefferson Randolph. Mentions Mrs. [Nicholas?] Lewis and [John] Craven.   [936]

1805 June 25 [date received]. CRAVEN PEYTON to T. J. ALS. 1 p. Endorsed by T. J. McGregor Library.
Payment for Bennett Henderson estate shares. Decline in Henderson's warehouse business can be remedied by cash commission, which would restore tobacco business now going to Columbia, Va.   [937]

1805 June 28. T. J., Washington, to CRAVEN PEYTON. ALS. 1 p. File draft. Endorsed by T. J. McGregor Library.
Payments to George Jefferson. Deeds to Bennett Henderson estate. Reference to John Bullock.   [938]

[1805 June]. T. J. MEMORANDUM ON HENDERSON ESTATE. AD. 1 p. McGregor Library.
Memorandum of the rights in the tobacco warehouses of the Henderson estate. (See entry, T. J. to Craven Peyton, 13 June 1805, for details.)   [939]

1805 July 3. JOHN BARNES, Georgetown, to T. J., Washington. ALS. 3 pp. Endorsed by T. J. Edgehill-Randolph Papers.
Barnes' resources insufficient to handle T. J.'s business.   [940]

1805 July 15. JOHN BARNES, Georgetown, to T. J., Monticello. ALS. 1 p. Endorsed by T. J. Edgehill-Randolph Papers.
Thanks for T. J.'s gift of Commodore Preble's marsalla and sherry wines. [941]

1805 July 25. JOHN BARNES, Georgetown, to T. J., Monticello. ALS. 1 p. Endorsed by T. J. Edgehill-Randolph Papers.
Perilous thunderstorm. Letter from Etienne LeMaire. References to Mr. Burwell, Mr. and Mrs. Carey.   [942]

1805 Aug. 4. BOWLING CLARK[E], Hillscreek, to T. J., Monticello. ALS. 1 p. Endorsed by T. J. Edgehill-Randolph Papers.
Value of T. J.'s lands at the time Clarke left Poplar Forest. References to Messrs. Callaway and Robertson.   [943]

1805 Aug. 15. JOHN BARNES, Georgetown, to T. J., Monticello. ALS. 2 pp. Endorsed by T. J. Edgehill-Randolph Papers.
Payments for T. J. to the Rev. Mr. Pryce and to Mr. Corkle. Barnes' account with T. J. enclosed. T. J.'s visit to Bedford County.   [944]

1805 Aug. 15. T. J., Monticello, to CRAVEN PEYTON. ALS. 1 p. File draft. Endorsed by T. J. McGregor Library.

Asks consultation to inform George Hay whether he should enter an appeal in the Henderson case.   [945]

1805 Aug. 15 [date received]. GEORGE WHITE, Spread Eagle, Penna., to T. J. ALS. 2 pp. Endorsed by T. J. McGregor Library. Printed: Ford-Bixby 116-117.

Asks patronage for a straw hat factory. Mentions Mr. Emery, American Consul in England.   [946]

1805 Aug. 28. JOHN BARNES, Georgetown, to T. J., Monticello. ALS. 2 pp. Endorsed by T. J. Edgehill-Randolph Papers.

James Madison's draft on T. J. will be honored. Payment to Mr. LeMaire for servants' wages. Plentiful crops. References to Joseph Dougherty and Mr. Andrews.   [947]

1805 Aug. PETER CARR in ACCOUNT WITH T. J. D. 1 p. Endorsed by T. J. Carr-Cary Papers.

Account for nails, brads, spikes rendered by Gabriel Lilly for T. J., to Peter Carr for the years 1804-1805.   [948]

1805 Sept. 2. JOHN BARNES, Georgetown, to T. J., Monticello. ALS. 2 pp. Endorsed by T. J. Edgehill-Randolph Papers.

Payments to James Madison, Etienne LeMaire, the Rev. Mr. Pryce, and Mr. Corkle. Arrival of wine, brandy, spermacetti and tallow candles, soap, and loaf sugar. Competition from new stores in Georgetown.   [949]

1805 Sept. 5 [date received]. CRAVEN PEYTON to T. J. ALS. 1 p. Endorsed by T. J. McGregor Library.

List of shares in the tobacco warehouse of the Henderson estate purchased by T. J. [George] Hay has taken the appeal in the Henderson case.   [950]

1805 Sept. 11. JOHN BARNES, Georgetown, to T. J., Monticello. ALS. 1 p. Endorsed by T. J. Enclosure: ADS. 1 p. Edgehill-Randolph Papers.

T. J.'s accounts. Yellow fever in New York and Philadelphia. Enclosure: account from 12 July to 9 September.   [951]

1805 Dec. 20. T. J., Washington, to JOHN MINOR. ALS. 1 p. Photostat. Original owned by Dr. L. M. Blackford. Printed: B of R VI 327 (MS. in DLC).

Asks Minor's opinion on whether the Virginia legislature would do anything for Tom Paine.   [952]

1806 Jan. 28. BENNETT H. HENDERSON, Shelbyville, Ky., to CRAVEN PEYTON, Milton, Va. ALS. 1 p. McGregor Library.

Will sign papers when he receives balance due. Mentions James Craig, John Henderson, and James L. Henderson.   [953]

1806 Jan. 29. JAMES CRAIG, Shelbyville, Ky., to CRAVEN PEYTON, Milton, Va. ALS. 2 pp. Endorsed by T. J. McGregor Library.

Answer delayed by death of younger son. Henderson deeds. Acknowledgment of Hilsman (i.e. Bennett H.) Henderson delayed until he is of age.   [954]

1806 Feb. 7. T. J., Washington, to [JOHN HOLMES FREEMAN], Monticello. ALS. 2 pp. McGregor Library.

Instructions to the overseer. Brown (a servant) to go to Mr. Jordan at Lexington. Purchase of molasses, fish, and other provisions from [George] Jefferson and [John] Craven. Road repair. Trees to be planted. Payment of debts to James Walker, Cleviers (?) Duke, Thomas Eston Randolph. Essential to get nail factory under way to meet debts. Planting of oats, clover, peas. Mentions [Martin] Dawson, [David] Higginbotham, Gabriel Lilly, Martha Randolph, Jerry and Fanny (servants). [955]

1806 Apr. 11. T. J. ADDRESS TO CHIEFS OF INDIAN TRIBES: Osages, Kansas, Ottos, Panis, Ayowais, Sioux, Potawatamies, Foxes, Sacs, and Missouri. D. 3 pp. Contemporary copy. Printed: B of R VI 357 (MS. in DLC).

Urging them to live at peace and cultivate the land. [956]

1806 Apr. 27. T. J., Washington, to DR. [EDWARD] MILLER. AL. 1 p. File draft. Endorsed by T. J.

Thanks for pamphlet on yellow fever. Copies sent to diplomatic agents to counteract the disastrous effects on commerce produced by other views. [957]

1806 May 8. JOHN BARNES, Georgetown, to T. J., Monticello. ALS. 1 p. Endorsed by T. J. Edgehill-Randolph Papers.

Acceptance of appointment of Collector of the District of Georgetown. [958]

1806 May 26. LUCY LEWIS, Monteagle, to T. J., Washington. ALS. 1 p. Edgehill-Randolph Papers.

Parcel from Charles Lewis (her son). Greetings from [Charles L.] Lewis (her husband). [959]

1806 June 23. T. J., Washington, to THOMAS MANN RANDOLPH, JR. ALS. 3 pp. File draft. Endorsed by T. J. Edgehill-Randolph Papers.

Urging that there be no duel to settle the quarrel between T. M. Randolph, Jr. and John Randolph, but that he seek advice from Peter Carr, [George?] Divers, and [Wilson Cary] Nicholas. Notices of the matter in the *National Intelligencer* and the *Enquirer*. [960]

1806 June 25. JOHN BARNES, Georgetown, to T. J., Washington. AL. 1 p. Endorsed by T. J. Edgehill-Randolph Papers.

T. J.'s accounts. [961]

1806 July 4. ANNE CARY RANDOLPH, Edgehill, to T. J., Washington. ALS. 1 p. Endorsed by T. J. Edgehill-Randolph Papers.

Barbecue and an oration in Charlottesville for the Fourth of July. News of Aunt Jane [Randolph], Aunt Lucy [Lewis], Aunt Harriet [Randolph], and Aunt [Martha] Carr. Miss Nicholson reports [Albert] Gallatin may not visit Monticello. [962]

1806 July 9 [date received]. JOHN BARNES, Georgetown, to T. J., Monticello. AL. 1 p. Endorsed by T. J. Edgehill-Randolph Papers.

Receipt of four barrels of white sugar on Schooner *Brothers*. [963]

1806 Aug. 8. JOHN BARNES, Georgetown, to T. J., Monticello. ALS. 2 pp. Endorsed by T. J. Edgehill-Randolph Papers.

T. J.'s accounts. Payments to S. H. Smith, Mr. Peal (Rubens Peale?), Mr. Cheetham and the Washington Academy. Drought in Washington has raised price of wheat. Package arrived in the Sloop *Harmony*.   [964]

1806 Aug. 12. T. J., Monticello, to CRAVEN PEYTON. ALS. 1 p. File draft. Endorsed by T. J. McGregor Library.

Cannot remit money. Valuation of the Henderson mill.   [965]

1806 Aug. 22. JOHN BARNES, Georgetown, to T. J., Monticello. ALS. 1 p. Endorsed by T. J. Edgehill-Randolph Papers.

Payment of T. J.'s note.   [966]

1806 Sept. 5. JOHN BARNES, Georgetown, to T. J., Monticello. ALS. 2 pp. Endorsed by T. J. Edgehill-Randolph Papers.

T. J.'s accounts. Payment to James Brand. Receipt of wine. References to Thomas Carpenter, Etienne LeMaire, and William Short.   [967]

1806 Sept. 8. JOHN BARNES, Georgetown, to T. J., Monticello. ALS. 1 p. Endorsed by T. J. Edgehill-Randolph Papers.

Payments to James Brand, Oliver Evans, Jones & Howell, and Thomas Carpenter.   [968]

1806 Oct. 4. T. M. RANDOLPH, JR., Edgehill, to T. J., Washington. ALS. 3 pp. Endorsed by T. J. Edgehill-Randolph Papers.

Martha Randolph and John (servant?) ill. Theft of money intended for Colonel Van Ness. Tobacco crop safe. References to Mr. Estis, J. Speir, and [Ralph?] Wormeley.   [969]

1806 Oct. 9. JOHN HENDERSON, Albemarle County. DEED TO MATTHEW HENDERSON AND JAMES LEWIS. D. 5 pp. Endorsed by T. J. Witnesses: Henry Medearis, Flemg. Goolsby, John H. Martin, and Edward Stone. Copy attested by John Nicholas, Clerk. McGregor Library.

Deed to tract of land on the Hardware River in Albemarle County, property in the town of Milton, a mill seat, property occupied by Thomas Eston Randolph, land in Kentucky. James Lewis and Matthew Henderson are to pay certain debts to David Higginbotham, John George, Brown, Rives & Co., Thomas Norvell & Co., Dr. Charles Everette and others. References to Hill Carter, Shelton Connard, Martha Henderson, Elizabeth Henderson, James and Richard Smith, and Thomas Wells, Jr.   [970]

1806 Oct. 9. CRAVEN PEYTON, Lancaster, Penna., to T. J., Washington. ALS. 1 p. Endorsed by T. J. McGregor Library.

Col. [Nicholas?] Lewis' daughters and Peyton attacked by fever. Death of Betsy Lewis. Details of Henderson estate to be settled in case of his death. Attended by Doctors Coon and Freemon.   [971]

1806 Oct. 14. MARTHA RANDOLPH, Monticello, to T. J., Washington. ALS.
1 p. Endorsed by T. J. Edgehill-Randolph Papers.
    Work delayed on the Randolph house. John's illness.   [972]

1806 Oct. 15. T. J., Washington, to SAMUEL SMITH, Baltimore. ALS. 1 p.
Endorsed. Printed: B of R VI 436 (MS. in DLC).
    Appointment of a successor to Robert Purviance. Discord among American
officers in St. Louis. Enquiry for a box sent by Brig *Lucy*, Capt. Peckham, to
Mr. Patterson, Consul at Nantes. Relations with the Spanish in West Florida
and Louisiana. References to Natchitoches and Bayou Pierre, La.   [973]

1806 Oct. 18. T. J., Washington, to MICAJAH CARR. ALS. 1 p. McGregor
Library.
    Mr. Strange not the agent of Donald & Burton, London. Sends letter to Mr.
Brown, plaintiff's attorney, to prevent steps prejudicial to Carr.   [974]

1806 Oct. 20. T. J., Washington, to SAMUEL SMITH, Baltimore. AL[S clipped].
1 p. Endorsed. Printed: B of R VI 436 (MS. in DLC).
    Condolences for his loss. Mr. Buchanan's enquiry for package sent by Brig
Lucy.   [975]

1806 Dec. 12. ANNE C. RANDOLPH, Edgehill, to T. J., Washington. ALS. 1 p.
Endorsed by T. J. Edgehill-Randolph Papers.
    Thanks for grass, fowls, and flowers. References to Mr. Shoemaker, [Craven]
Peyton, and Martha Randolph.   [976]

1806 Dec. 25. JOHN HENDERSON. PROPERTY SCHEDULE. D. 1 p.
Attested by John Nicholas, Clerk. Endorsed by T. J. McGregor Library.
    Schedule of the property of John Henderson, deeds, and papers in trust for
purpose of securing certain moneys to James Lewis and Matthew Henderson.
                                                                    [977]

[1806?]. T. J. to JUSTIN P. P. DERIEUX. ALS. 1 p. Fragment. Photostat.
Original owned by Dabney Lancaster.
    His gift of bed ticks, sheets, and blankets now at [Thomas] Bell's. Thanks
for eggplants.   [978]

1807 Jan. 6. JOHN PERRY to T. J. ADS. 1 p. Endorsed. Carr-Cary Papers.
    Order on T. J. in favor of Dabney Carr.   [979]

1807 Jan. 13. JOHN BARNES, Georgetown, to T. J., Washington. ALS. 1 p.
Endorsed by T. J. Edgehill-Randolph Papers.
    State of T. J.'s finances for the ensuing months.   [980]

1807 Jan. 16. DABNEY CARR, Charlottesville, to T. J. ALS. 1 p. Endorsed by
T. J. Carr-Cary Papers.
    Enclosing a draft on T. J. by John Perry, which pays Mrs. Carter for hire
of Negroes. Martha Carr mentioned.   [981]

[1807 Jan. 20]. WILSON CARY NICHOLAS to T. J. ALS. 5 pp. Fragment. Edgehill-Randolph Papers. Printed: B of R VIII 427 (MS. in DLC).

Urges that T. J. run for another term. Notes accomplishments of T. J.'s administration. Incompetency of Henry Dearborn as Secretary of War. Suggests Dearborn be made Collector of Boston. Burr Conspiracy. Defenselessness of New Orleans. References to James Wilkinson. [982]

1807 Jan. 22. JOHN DICKINSON, Wilmington, to T. J., Washington. ALS. 5 pp. Endorsed by T. J. McGregor Library.

Recommends civil reforms and legislative action to prevent lawsuits and protect the citizen; policy on territories. Country loves Jefferson despite hatred of Federalists. [983]

1807 Jan. 26. T. J., Washington, to DABNEY CARR. ALS. 1 p. File draft. Endorsed by T. J. Carr-Cary Papers.

Payment of John Perry's draft on T. J. [984]

1807 Jan. 28. T. J., Washington, to CRAVEN PEYTON. ALS. 1 p. File draft. Endorsed by T. J. McGregor Library.

Wants William Wirt to assist George Hay in suit against John Henderson. [985]

1807 Feb. 6. DABNEY CARR, Charlottesville, to T. J., Washington. ALS. 1 p. Endorsed by T. J. Carr-Cary Papers.

Encloses draft from John Perry, payable in monthly installments. [986]

1807 Feb. 19. T. J., Washington, to T. M. RANDOLPH, JR., Edgehill. ALS. 1 p. File draft. Endorsed by T. J. Edgehill-Randolph Papers.

Declaring his affection and respect. Assurances that he does not think T. M. R. has joined the Federalists. References to Colonel Heath. [987]

1807 Mar. 14. MARTHA RANDOLPH, Edgehill, to T. J., Washington. ALS. 1 p. Endorsed by T. J. Edgehill-Randolph Papers.

Thomas Mann Randolph's illness. Arrival of Mr. Burwell. [988]

1807 Mar. 18. T. J. Washington, to JOSEPH C. CABELL. ALS. 1 p. Endorsed.

Appreciates receipt of [James] Workman's pamphlet; disapproves his use of office as judge to liberate accomplices. Fault in our Constitution in irresponsible power of the judiciary. [989]

1807 Mar. 21. T. J., Washington, to JOHN WAYLES EPPES. ALS. 1 p.

Suggests sending mare to Eppes, so as not to endanger her foal. Thomas Mann Randolph, Jr.'s illness. T. J.'s headache. [990]

1807 Apr. 20. RANDOLPH LEWIS, Byrd, Va., to T. J., Washington. ALS. 2 pp. Endorsed by T. J. Edgehill-Randolph Papers.

Offering to sell his servant who is the wife of T. J.'s Moses, since Lewis is moving to Kentucky. [991]

1807 Apr. 28. T. J., Monticello, to JOHN CARR. ALS. 2 pp. File draft. Endorsed by T. J. Carr-Cary Papers.

Recommends course of study for Carr's son, Lewis Carr, preparatory to entrance at William and Mary.   [992]

1807 May 25. T. J., Washington, to DABNEY CARR. ALS. 1 p. File draft. Endorsed by T. J. Carr-Cary Papers.

Delays payment of John Perry's draft in favor of Carr because of heavy bills for wine. Remittance to James Walker as bail for Stewart in return for year's hire of Melinda (servant?).   [993]

1807 May 28. T. J., Washington, to JOHN WAYLES EPPES, Eppington. ALS. 1 p. Printed: Ford IX 67-68; B of R VI 142 (MS. in DLC).

Health of Francis Eppes II. John Wayles Eppes' mare in good travelling order. Friendly letter from Bey of Tunis. Despite high opinion of Marshall's integrity, finds jury in Aaron Burr's trial unfairly weighted with two Federalists, four Quids, and ten Repubicans. Mentions Eppes' servant, Martin.   [994]

1807 June 9. T. J. PATENT to WILLIAM PHOEBUS. DS. 2 pp. Photostat. Original owned by John D. Murphy.

Countersigned by James Madison. For a salivating device. Description of device by Phoebus.   [995]

1807 July 1. T. J. LAND GRANT to EDWARD S. HALL, Baltimore County, Md. DS. 1 p. Seal. James Manuscripts.

Patent for lot in Range Eight, Section Three of the Northwest Territory.   [996]

1807 July 9. RANDOLPH JEFFERSON, to T. J., Monticello. ALS. 1 p. Endorsed by T. J. Carr-Cary Papers. Printed: Mayo 13.

Terms for sale of clover and grass seed. Reference to Thomas Mann Randolph, Jr.   [997]

1807 July 11. MARTHA J. RANDOLPH, Edgehill, to T. J., Washington. ALS. 1 p. Endorsed by T. J.

Request for a comb. Heel of shoe needs changing. News of *Chesapeake* affair. Fresh meat supply for the summer. Mentions Edmund Bacon.   [998]

1807 July 22. JOHN DICKINSON, Wilmington, to CAESAR A. RODNEY, Washington. ALS. 3 pp. Endorsed by T. J. McGregor Library.

Interdiction of British ships-of-war should be strictly enforced. Hopes T. J. will accept another term; approval of T. J.'s late proclamation and of his defeat of the Burr Conspiracy.   [999]

1807 Aug. 6. JOHN BARNES, Georgetown, to T. J., [Monticello]. ALS. 1 p. Endorsed by T. J. Edgehill-Randolph Papers.

Payments to William Pennock of Norfolk and to Jones & Howell of Philadelphia.   [1000]

1807 Aug. 10. T. J., Monticello, to CRAVEN PEYTON. ALS. 1 p. File draft. Endorsed by T. J. McGregor Library.

Cannot undertake the settlement between Col. [Nicholas?] Lewis and Peyton because of unusual press of public affairs brought on by *Chesapeake* affair.

[1001]

1807 Aug. 12. T. J., Monticello, to RANDOLPH JEFFERSON. ALS. 1 p. File draft. Endorsed by T. J. Carr-Cary Papers. Printed: Mayo 14.

Payment for clover and greensward seed. Clover to be sent to Burgess Griffin at Poplar Forest. Mentions Mr. Crouch, Mr. Brown, and Anna Scott Marks.

[1002]

1807 Aug. 19. JOHN BARNES, Georgetown, to T. J., Monticello. ALS. 2 pp. Endorsed by T. J. Enclosure: D. 2 pp. Edgehill-Randolph Papers.

James Davidson's explanation of enclosed bill of exchange. Damage from storms near Monticello. Offers draft or a remittance. Enclosure: bill of exchange drawn by Stephen Cathalan, Jr., on T. J. in favor of Capt. William Hazard.

[1003]

1807 Sept. 3. JOHN BARNES, Georgetown, to T. J., Monticello. ALS. 2 pp. Endorsed by T. J. Edgehill-Randolph Papers.

Financial matters. T. J.'s fatiguing visit to Bedford County. Order on Jonathan Smith, of the Bank of Pennsylvania, for Tadeusz Kosciuszko's account.

[1004]

1807 Sept. 18. T. J., Monticello, to WILLIAM H. CABELL. ALS. 1 p. Endorsed. McGregor Library. Printed: L & B XI 369-370; B of R VI 61 (MS. in DLC).

To the Governor of Virginia, concerning Lowrie's correspondence. Approves Cabell's instructions to Major Newton. Provisions for troops. Report from Mr. Belscher of Gloucester regarding contraventions of the proclamation denying British vessels the hospitality of American waters. [1005]

1807 Sept. 26. T. J., Monticello, to JOHN WAYLES EPPES. ALS. 1 p. Printed: B of R VI 143 (MS. in DLC).

Purchase of horse. Shipment of harpsichord, table, copying press, and a bust to Mr. George Jefferson at Richmond. Asks instructions about presses. Acquisition of Floridas and peace with England very uncertain. Mentions Mr. Coles. Francis Eppes II, and Mr. and Mrs. Francis Eppes I. [1006]

1807 Sept. 26. T. J., Monticello, to JAMES MADISON. L. 1 p. Typescript copy. Original owned by Samuel H. McVitty.

Plans for meeting Madison at Montpellier. Mentions Dolly Madison. [1007]

*1807 Oct. 3. CRAVEN PEYTON, Shadwell, to T. J. ALS. 1 p. Endorsed by T. J. McGregor Library.

T. J. fortunate in balloting for lots in Bennett Henderson estate. James L. Henderson who got the mill seat can be bought out. Disposition of houses occupied by [Marcy?] Thorp and Faris. [1008]

1807 Oct. 16. CRAVEN PEYTON, Stump Island, to T. J. ALS. 2 pp. Endorsed by T. J. McGregor Library.

Offers to sell Colle to T. J. and to trade other tracts with Mr. Carr. T. J.'s tenant at Milton, [Richard?] Johnson, has corn and wheat which Edmund Bacon should call for. Warehouse money all drawn. Firewood cutting prohibited at Milton. [1009]

1807 Oct. 25. T. J., Washington, to CRAVEN PEYTON. ALS. 1 p. File draft. Endorsed by T. J. McGregor Library.

Debts will not permit him to buy Colle. Instructions regarding corn and wheat to be delivered to Edmund Bacon. Purchase of the right of James Lewis and Matthew Henderson in the Bennett Henderson estate. Joseph C. Cabell might buy Peyton's land. [1010]

1807 Nov. 5. T. J. SHIP'S PAPERS. DS. 1 p. Deposited by C. S. Hutter, Jr.

Clearance papers for Brig *Alexander,* William Miller Captain, bound for Guadeloupe. Countersigned by James Madison. [1011]

1807 Nov. 11. CRAVEN PEYTON to WILLIAM C. BRADBOURN, Jacob Cooper, William D. Fitch, David Higginbotham, C. T. Wertenbaker, Richard Johnson, Thomas Wells, Paul Weyate, David Anderson, Mary Thorp, Reuben Grady, and John Burks. ADS. 2 pp. McGregor Library.

Terms for cutting firewood on Jefferson's land near Milton. [1012]

1807 Nov. 17. JOHN HENDERSON. DEED to CRAVEN PEYTON. DS. 2 pp. Endorsed by T. J. McGregor Library.

Conveying shares of Frances L., Lucy L., and Nancy Henderson in the estate of their father, Bennett Henderson, signed by John Henderson as guardian. Witnesses: Fleming Turner, M[artin] Dawson, James Bullock. Receipt from Henderson for money paid by Peyton on the above. Witness: Fleming Turner. [1013]

1807 Nov. 19. LUCY LEWIS, Monteagle, to T. J., Washington. ALS. 1 p. Endorsed by T. J. Edgehill-Randolph Papers.

Letter of farewell upon leaving for mouth of Cumberland River. Mr. Peyton's goodness to her. [1014]

1808 Jan. 2. MARTHA RANDOLPH, Edgehill, to T. J., Washington. ALS. 2 pp. Endorsed by T. J. Edgehill-Randolph Papers.

T. J.'s health. David and William Randolph in bankruptcy. Thomas Mann Randolph's responsibilities. [1015]

1808 Jan. 2. ROS[WEL]L SALTONSTALL, New York, to T. J., Washington. ALS. 3 pp. Endorsed by T. J. Printed: Ford-Bixby 155-156.

Letter from a loyal but crackpot Republican. Advises annexation of the Floridas, but Canada and Nova Scotia "a dred to our union" if taken. Evils of the Quakers and Methodists in attacks on T. J. Mentions General Lyman, James Madison, William Thornton, William B. Giles, and [John] Pope. [1016]

1808 Jan. 3. T. J., Washington, to BENJAMIN RUSH, Philadelphia. ALS. 1 p. Photostat. Original owned by Dr. Josiah C. Treat. Printed: L & B XI 412-413; B of R VI 399 (MS. in DLC).

Appointment of Benjamin Waterhouse, who introduced vaccination in this country, to the Marine Hospital of Boston. T. J. Randolph's prospective trip to Philadelphia. Mr. Rose's mission. Embargo.   [1017]

1808 Jan. 22. ANNE CARY RANDOLPH, Edgehill, to T. J., Washington. ALS. 2 pp. Endorsed by T. J. Edgehill-Randolph Papers.

Ellen's and her own education. Flowers, trees, and vines at Edgehill: cypress vine, prickly ash trees, mignonette, marigold. Lucy Lewis has gone to Kentucky. References to Virginia and Mary Randolph, Mrs. [Nicholas?] Lewis, and Aunt Jane [Randolph].   [1018]

*[1808 Feb. 1?]. CORNELIA J. RANDOLPH to T. J. L. 1 p. Typescript copy. Gift of Miss Olivia Taylor.

"the first letter I ever wrote." Family news.   [1019]

1808 Feb. 19. ANNE CARY RANDOLPH, Edgehill, to T. J., Washington. ALS. 1 p. Endorsed by T. J. Edgehill-Randolph Papers.

Peas, roses, and amaryllis in her gardens. Reported engagement of Evalina Bolling to Mr. Garett (Alexander Garrett?) of Charlottesville.   [1020]

1808 Feb. 20. MARTHA RANDOLPH, Edgehill, to T. J., Washington. ALS. 1 p. Endorsed by T. J. Edgehill-Randolph Papers.

Introducing Beverley Randolph, who is living in young Nourse's place. Broken seal and watch key. Mentions Dolly Madison.   [1021]

1808 Mar. 15. T. J., Washington, to THOMAS MANN RANDOLPH, JR. ALS. 1 p. Photostat. Original owned by Harold J. Coolidge. Another MS. in DLC.

Compromise between Republicans and Quids in Lancaster, Pa., caucus for electors. Madison's chances in Pennsylvania, Connecticut, and Delaware. References to George Clinton, James Madison, James Monroe, and Simon Snyder.   [1022]

1808 Mar. 20. T. J., Washingon, to the DEMOCRATIC CITIZENS OF ADAMS COUNTY, Penna. L. 1 p. Extract by N. P. Trist *ca.* 1830. Printed: L & B XII 17-18; B of R VI 2 (MS. in DLC).

First principle of our government: the will of the majority.   [1023]

1808 May 14. HENDERSON, McCAUL & CO. ACCOUNT AGAINST T. J. D. 2 pp. Edgehill-Randolph Papers.

For November 1798 through July 1806, signed by James Lyle. Records payments from Gibson & Jefferson and C. Clarke. Mentions bonds for Mrs. Jane Jefferson and bond to Richard Harvie.   [1024]

1808 May 27. RANDOLPH JEFFERSON. WILL. T. J. AD. 1 p. File draft. Endorsed by T. J. Second copy: R. J. AD. 1 p. Carr-Cary Papers.

The will of T. J.'s brother. Land and slaves to be divided equally among five sons, Thomas, Robert Lewis, Field, [Isham] Randolph, and [James] Lilburne Jefferson. Executors named: Harding Perkins, Robert Craig, Robert Lewis Jefferson, and T. J.   [1025]

1808 June 28. T. J., Washington, to JAMES MADISON. ALS. 1 p. McGregor Library.
    Appoints Robert H. Jones of Warrenton, [N. C.], District Attorney for North Carolina.   [1026]

1808 Aug. 9. T. J., Monticello, to HENRY DEARBORN. L. 1 p. Extract by N. P. Trist *ca.* 1830. Printed: Ford IX 201-202; L & B XII 119-120; B of R VI 116 (MS. in DLC). Another MS. in PPHi.
    Threat of insurrection by Boston Tories if importation of flour from southern states is stopped. Instructions to Dearborn for War Department action.   [1027]

1808 Aug. 9. T. J., Monticello, to ROBERT SMITH. L. 1 p. Extract by N. P. Trist *ca.* 1830. Printed: L & B XII 121; B of R VI 348 (MS. in DLC).
    Boston opposition to stoppage of importation of flour.   [1028]

1808 Aug. 11. T. J., Monticello, to ALBERT GALLATIN. L. 1 p. Extract by N. P. Trist *ca.* 1830. Printed: Ford IX 202-203; L & B XII 121-128; B of R VI 167 (MS. in DLC).
    Difficulties in execution of the Embargo Act. References to Orders in Council and to the Napoleonic Decrees.   [1029]

1808 Aug. 12. T. J., Monticello, to JAMES SULLIVAN. L. 1 p. Extract by N. P. Trist *ca.* 1830. Printed B of R VI 447 (MS. in DLC).
    To the Governor of Massachusetts, concerning enforcement of the Embargo.
                                                                        [1030]

1808 Sept. 5. JOHN WAYLES EPPES, Richmond, to T. J., Monticello. ALS. 3 pp. Endorsed by T. J. Edgehill-Randolph Papers.
    Arrival of boxes. Purchase of a horse for T. J. from Richard Thweatt. References to [Thomas] Bell, Mr. Eggleston, Francis Eppes, and Thomas Mann Randolph, Jr.   [1031]

1808 Sept. 5. T. J., Monticello, to ALBERT GALLATIN. L. 1 p. Extract by N. P. Trist *ca.* 1830. Printed: B of R VI 167 (MS. in DLC).
    Regarding a breach of duty by one of the U. S. Collectors.   [1032]

1808 Sept. 6. T. J., Monticello, to JOHN PAGE, Richmond. ALS. 1 p. Endorsed. Another MS. in DLC.
    Offers to transfer Page's office of Commissioner of Loans for Virginia to his son, Francis, because of Page's ill health. Page's endorsement: "Most generous & consolatory to me! !"   [1033]

1808 Sept. 20. T. J., Monticello, to JOHN WAYLES EPPES. ALS. 1 p. Printed: Randall III 264.
    Purchase of horse. Marriage of Anne Randolph and Charles L. Bankhead.

Action regarding the Embargo, Orders-in-Council, and Napoleon's decrees. Resistance to Napoleon in Spain. Reference to George Canning. [1034]

1808 Sept. 21. JOHN WAYLES EPPES, Eppington, to T. J., Monticello. ALS. 1 p. Endorsed by T. J. Edgehill-Randolph Papers.

Horse purchased for T. J., paid by draft on Gibson & Jefferson, and forwarded by Martin, together with a petrified snake. References to Mr. Williams and Martha Randolph. [1035]

1808 Sept. 30. T. J., Montpelier, to MARTHA RANDOLPH, Edgehill. ALS. 1 p. Tracing. Endorsed by T. J. Edgehill-Randolph Papers.

Gravy spoons to be converted into dessert spoons. Difficulties with his new horse. References to J. Peyton, Mr. Shoemaker, [Edmund] Bacon, James Madison, and Thomas Mann Randolph, Jr. [1036]

1808 Oct. 14. THOMAS MANN RANDOLPH, JR., Monticello, to T. J., Washington. ALS. 1 p. Endorsed by T. J. Edgehill-Randolph Papers.

T. J.'s papers. Construction of his mouldboard plow. Pleased to hear of the dynamometer. References to [William?] Meriwether and Nicholas Lewis. [1037]

1808 Oct. 27. MARTHA RANDOLPH, Edgehill, to T. J., Washington. ALS. 1 p. Endorsed by T. J. Edgehill-Randolph Papers.

Spoons and books for Thomas J. Randolph forwarded. Wine bottling. Remedies for T. J.'s rheumatism. [1038]

1808 Nov. 8. JAMES and LUCY LEWIS. DEED to CRAVEN PEYTON, Albemarle County. DS. 2 pp. Endorsed by T. J. Witnessed by Charles D. Thomas, N. K. Thomas, Joel Shiflett, and Whittiker Carter. Recorded 4 April 1809 by John Nicholas, Clerk of Albemarle County Court. McGregor Library.

Conveying the mill site of the Bennett Henderson estate. Mentions John Henderson and Matthew Henderson. [1039]

1808 Nov. 11. THOMAS J. RANDOLPH, Museum, Philadelphia, to T. J., Washington. ALS. 1 p. Endorsed by T. J. Edgehill-Randolph Papers.

Progress in Medical School. References to Philip S. Physick, James Woodhouse, Caspar Wistar, and Benjamin Say. Purchase of Bell's *Anatomy*. [1040]

1808 Dec. 7. T. J., Washington, to THOMAS J. RANDOLPH, Philadelphia. ALS. 2 pp. File draft. Endorsed by T. J. Deposited by Robert H. Kean.

Requesting that he make payments to Mr. McAlister and Mr. Pemberton. Shipment of a polygraph to [Rubens?] Peale. Advice on notetaking, with Sallust and Tacitus as models. Counsels reserve on political subjects. [1041]

1808 Dec. 19. CORNELIA RANDOLPH, Edgehill, to T. J., Washington. ALS. 3 pp. Endorsed by T. J. Edgehill-Randolph Papers.

Is reading *Dramatic Dialogues*, a gift from Mrs. Smith to Ellen. [1042]

1808 Dec. 20. C. L. BANKHEAD, Port Royal, to T. J., Washington. ALS. 3 pp. Endorsed by T. J. Edgehill-Randolph Papers.

Will keep a watchful eye on T. J. Randolph. Evil of polemical debate. References to Anne Cary Randolph Bankhead and John Bankhead. [1043]

1808 Dec. 28. THOMAS J. RANDOLPH, Museum, Philadelphia, to T. J., Washington. ALS. 1 p. Endorsed by T. J. Edgehill-Randolph Papers.
Insurrection in Amherst. Payments to Mr. McAlister and Mr. Purke. References to Mr. Pemberton, [Rubens?] Peale.   [1044]

1808 Dec. 29. CRAVEN PEYTON, Richmond, to T. J., Washington. ALS. 1 p. Endorsed by T. J. McGregor Library.
Request that T. J. inform [Andrew] Benade of money in Philadelphia bank. Hopes to have Henderson suit dismissed in Court of Appeals.   [1045]

1809 Jan. 1 [date received]. MARTHA RANDOLPH, Edgehill, to T. J., Washington. ALS. 1 p. Endorsed by T. J. Edgehill-Randolph Papers.
Requests for money received by Thomas Mann Randolph, Jr. Innoculation of Jefferson, Virginia, and Anne Randolph. Reference to Mr. Hackley.   [1046]

1809 Jan. 6. THOMAS MANN RANDOLPH, JR., Edgehill, to T. J., Washington. ALS. 2 pp. Endorsed by T. J. Edgehill-Randolph Papers.
Determination to sell Varina to pay his debts, possibly to a Mr. Patterson. Prefers to sell property rather than servants. Reference to Wilson C. Nicholas.   [1047]

1809 Jan. 9. T. J., Washington, to CRAVEN PEYTON. ALS. 1 p. File draft. Endorsed by T. J. McGregor Library.
Order on Gibson & Jefferson. Remittance to [Andrew] Benade. Wishes to sell part of Henderson's land between Colle and Milton, Va., to pay his debts.   [1048]

1809 Jan. 14. T. J., Washington, to WILLIAM EUSTIS, Boston. L. 1 p. Extract by N. P. Trist *ca.* 1830. Printed: Ford IX 235-236; L & B XII 222-229; TJR IV 120-121; B of R VI 144 (MS. in DLC).
Acknowledges receipt of Resolutions of the Republican Citizens of Boston. Will of the majority must prevail.   [1049]

1809 Jan. 18. CRAVEN PEYTON, Monteagle, Va., to T. J., Washington. ALS. 1 p. Endorsed by T. J. McGregor Library.
Sale of the Bennett Henderson estate lands owned by T. J. Better sale to people north of the Susquehanna.   [1050]

1809 Jan. 24. T. J., Washington, to CRAVEN PEYTON. ALS. 1 p. File draft. Endorsed by T. J. McGregor Library.
Instructions for selling portion of Henderson property. [Andrew] Benade acknowledged receipt of money.   [1051]

1809 Feb. 4. THOMAS J. RANDOLPH, Museum, Philadelphia, to T. J., Washington. ALS. 1 p. Endorsed by T. J. Edgehill-Randolph Papers.
Permission granted to study in the Philosophical Society. Trip to Washington. References to Caspar Wistar and [Rubens?] Peale.   [1052]

1809 Feb. 17. MARTHA RANDOLPH, Edgehill, to T. J., Washington. ALS. 2 pp. Endorsed by T. J. Edgehill-Randolph Papers.

Application for Mr. Moultree, son of Dr. James Moultree. Introducing Beverley Randolph, Martha's nephew. Innoculation of Benjamin and James. Geraniums, arbor vitae, and sweet-scented grass. Books for Mary Randolph. Hammocks sent by William Brown from Campeachy (*i.e.* Campeche) to Mrs. [Elizabeth] Trist. Mentions David R. Williams. [1053]

* 1809 Feb. 28. T. J., Washington, to JAMES WALLACE, Fauquier Court House. ALS. 1 p.

Request for wild geese, summer duck, balsam, cassia tree, sunbriar, and mammoth apple tree. [1054]

1809 Mar. 2. REPUBLICANS OF CONNECTICUT. RESOLUTIONS. D. 5 pp. Attested copy.

Approval of the Embargo and measures to avert war. Disapproval of conduct of Federalists and of action of members of Connecticut legislature in declaring acts of Congress unconstitutional; present convention represents individual opinion, not official action. Mentions George Washington. Signed by Jabez Fitch, Chairman. Attested copy by Jonathan Low, Secretary. [1055]

1809 Mar. 31. ELIZABETH TRIST, Farmington, to T. J., Monticello. ALS. 1 p. Endorsed by T. J. Edgehill-Randolph Papers.

Expressing her thanks to President Madison. [1056]

1809 Apr. 13. T. J., Monticello, to JONATHAN LOW, Hartford, Conn. L. 1 p. Extract by N. P. Trist *ca.* 1830. Printed: L & B XVI 364-365; B of R VI 280 (MS. in DLC).

Urges Connecticut Republicans to pledge themselves to the preservation of the union and the enforcement of its laws. [1057]

1809 May 25. T. J., Monticello, to WILSON CARY NICHOLAS. ALS. 1 p. Photostat. Original owned by Harold J. Coolidge. Printed: Ford IX 252; B of R X 137 (MS. in DLC).

Urges his support of Madison. Revoking of British Orders-in-Council and the Napoleonic Decrees. Possibility of war. Annexation of the Floridas and Cuba. [1058]

1809 May 29. THOMAS J. RANDOLPH, Philadelphia, to T. J., Monticello. ALS. 1 p. Endorsed by T. J. Edgehill-Randolph Papers.

Articles received from Etienne LeMaire. Complains that he has not heard from Martha, Thomas Mann Randolph, Jr., Ellen, Anne, or Mr. Bankhead. Mentions Dr. Barton. [1059]

1809 June 20. T. J., Monticello, to THOMAS J. RANDOLPH, Philadelphia. ALS. 1 p. Photostat. Original unknown.

Reasons why he has not written. Death of Dr. Woodhouse. Plans for T. J. R.'s return home. Payment of T. J. R.'s expenses. Book for Mary. References to [Rubens?] Peale, Etienne LeMaire. [1060]

1809 Aug. 6. CRAVEN PEYTON, Monteagle, Va., to T. J. ALS. 1 p. Endorsed by T. J. McGregor Library.

Hopes to sell some of Jefferson's land to John Akers. Is being pushed by creditors; would like to transfer titles to Henderson lands to Jefferson.   [1061]

1809 Aug. 22. T. J. to CRAVEN PEYTON. ADS. 1 p. File draft. Endorsed by T. J. McGregor Library.

Declaration that Peyton not held responsible if Frances, Lucy, or Nancy C. Henderson should fail to ratify the sale of their shares in the Bennett Henderson estate when they come of age.   [1062]

1809 Oct. 2. T. J., Monticello, to HENRY DEARBORN. ALS. 1 p. Photostat. Original owned by Harold J. Coolidge.

Introducing Thomas Mann Randolph, half-brother of T. J.'s son-in-law of the same name.   [1063]

1809 Dec. 7. RANDOLPH JEFFERSON to T. J., Monticello. ALS. 1 p. Endorsed by T. J. Carr-Cary Papers. Printed: Mayo 15.

Requesting gig harness needed to visit wife's brother, who is dying.   [1064]

1809 Dec. 8. T. J., Monticello, to JOHN WAYLES EPPES, Washington. ALS. 1 p. Printed: Randall III 319.

News of Francis Eppes II. Disappointment at offers of British Minister, Francis J. Jackson. Reference to Virginia Randolph.   [1065]

1809 Dec. 8. T. J., Monticello, to RANDOLPH JEFFERSON. ALS. 1 p. File draft. Endorsed by T. J. Carr-Cary Papers. Printed: Mayo 16.

Sends gig harness by Squire (servant). Invitation to Randolph and his sister (Anna Marks?) to visit Monticello.   [1066]

1809 Dec. 12. JOHN GARLAND JEFFERSON, Amelia, Va., to T. J., Monticello. ALS. 2 pp. Endorsed by T. J. McGregor Library.

Difference of opinion regarding an office for John Garland Jefferson. Sorry to have missed him in Amelia.   [1067]

1809 Dec. 27. BURGESS GRIFFIN, Poplar Forest, to T. J., Monticello. ALS. 2 pp. Endorsed by T. J. McGregor Library.

Report on the corn, wheat, and tobacco crops. Plastering work at Poplar Forest. Samuel Scott has begun building illegally on Stith's entry. References to [Samuel J.] Harrison, Mr. Richerson (Richardson?), and Thomas Mann Randolph, Jr.   [1068]

1809. JOHN BARNES, Georgetown, to T. J., Washington. AD and ADS. 4 items. 2 endorsed by T. J. McGregor Library.

Bills and accounts submitted by Barnes as financial and purchasing agent for T. J.   [1069]

1809-1816. TADEUSZ KOSCIUSZKO'S ACCOUNTS. 11 items. Edgehill-Randolph Papers.

Copies of accounts and their covering letters sent to T. J. by John Barnes, who handled Kosciuszko's financial affairs for Jefferson. Includes letters to and from Baring Brothers, Jonathan Smith, and George Williams. [1070]

[1810] Jan. 4 [incorrectly dated 1809]. ARCHIBALD THWEATT, Petersburg, to T. J., Monticello. ALS. 1 p. Endorsed by T. J. Edgehill-Randolph Papers.

Concerns the will of R. S. (Richard Stith?). Summons by Mr. Ladd to Richmond to state the accounts. [1071]

1810 Jan. 12. JOHN BARNES, Georgetown, to T. J., Monticello. ALS. 2 pp. Endorsed by T. J. Edgehill-Randolph Papers.

Remittance owed to General Kosciuszko. T. J.'s accounts. Remittance from Mrs. Beckley. [1072]

1810 Jan. 17. T. J., Monticello, to GIBSON & JEFFERSON, Richmond. ALS. 1 p. Photostat. Original owned by Mrs. Virginius Dabney. Another MS. in VHi.

Draft on Gibson & Jefferson by John Barnes. [1073]

1810 Jan. 21. JOHN WAYLES EPPES, Washington, to T. J., Monticello. ALS. 1 p. Edgehill-Randolph Papers.

Release to be executed for Colonel Bentley. Passage of Nathaniel Macon's bill. [1074]

1810 Jan. 25. JOHN BARNES, Georgetown, to T. J., Monticello. ALS. 5 pp. Endorsed by T. J. Edgehill-Randolph Papers.

Congratulations on good crops. Loss on General Kosciuszko's mislaid certificates. Payment from Mrs. Beckley delayed. Includes John Barnes' account with General Kosciuszko, 1809-1810. [1075]

1810 Jan. 25. T. J., Monticello, to JOHN GARLAND JEFFERSON. L. 2 pp. 19th century copy. Carr-Cary Papers. Printed: Ford IX 270-271; L & B XII 353-355; B of R VI 239 (MS. in DLC).

Did not offer John Garland Jefferson a job because of self-made rule not to give an office to a relative. Discussion of nepotism. [1076]

1810 Feb. 14. JOHN BARNES, Georgetown, to T. J., Monticello. ALS. 2 pp. Endorsed by T. J. Edgehill-Randolph Papers.

Payment of General Kosciuszko, mentioning Baring Brothers, Bowie & Kurtz, and Hoffingan & Co. [1077]

1810 Mar. 14. T. J., Monticello, to THOMAS J. RANDOLPH, Philadelphia. ALS. 2 pp. File draft. Endorsed by T. J. Edgehill-Randolph Papers.

Pros and cons of T. J. R.'s proposal to study half of each day in his own room. References to Mr. Girardin and to Mr. Wood. [1078]

1810 Mar. 16. GEORGE JEFFERSON, Richmond, to T. J., Monticello. ALS. 1 p. Endorsed by T. J. Photostat. Original owned by Mrs. Virginius Dabney.

Draft received from Charles Johnston. No news of Shoemaker's flour. [1079]

1810 Mar. 19. GEORGE JEFFERSON, Richmond, to T. J., Monticello. ALS. 1 p. Photostat. Endorsed by T. J. Original owned by Mrs. Virginius Dabney.
Payment to Jones & Howell. Receipt of plaster of Paris for T. J.   [1080]

1810 Apr. 2. JOHN WAYLES EPPES, Washington, to T. J., Monticello. ALS. 1 p. Endorsed by T. J. Edgehill-Randolph Papers.
Trouble with his knee. Arrangements with England for European trade. Plan to meet T. J. at Eppington. References to [Charles?] Pinckney, Wellesley, David Erskine, and Francis Eppes.   [1081]

1810 May 7. JOHN WAYLES EPPES to T. J., Monticello. ALS. 2 pp. Endorsed by T. J. Edgehill-Randolph Papers.
Request that T. J. send Francis Eppes to Eppington.   [1082]

1810 May 7. ARCHIBALD THWEATT, Petersburg, to T. J., Monticello. ALS. 1 p. Endorsed by T. J. Edgehill-Randolph Papers.
Business with Mr. Ladd delayed by rheumatism.   [1083]

1810 June 4. THOMAS J. RANDOLPH, Richmond, to T. J., Monticello. ALS. 1 p. Endorsed by T. J. Edgehill-Randolph Papers.
Purchase of oil. Plans for summer vacation. Confined to bed by cut of Achilles tendon.   [1084]

1810 June 4. ARCHIBALD THWEATT, Petersburg, to T. J., Monticello. ALS. 3 pp. Endorsed by T. J. Edgehill-Randolph Papers.
Payment due the executors of John Fleming's estate for purchase of "Ursala" should be applied to the debt Fleming owed the Wayles estate. References to Martha Wayles and her first husband, Bathurst Skelton.   [1085]

1810 June 8. RANDOLPH JEFFERSON, Stony Point, Virginia, to T. J., Monticello. ALS. 1 p. Endorsed by T. J. Carr-Cary Papers. Printed: Mayo 17.
Visit to Monticello delayed by broken axletree. Mentions Captain Patterson of Warren, Virginia.   [1086]

1810 June 11. T. J., Monticello, to RANDOLPH JEFFERSON. ALS. 1 p. File draft. Endorsed by T. J. Carr-Cary Papers. Printed: Mayo 18.
Invitation to visit Monticello before T. J. leaves for Poplar Forest.   [1087]

1810 June 27. T. J., Monticello, to JOSEPH C. CABELL, Warminster. ALS. 1 p. Endorsed. Printed: Cabell 1-2.
Recommends correspondence with Thomas Cooper, one of the ablest men in America. Mentions Joseph Priestley.   [1088]

1810 July 23. JOSEPH C. CABELL, Edgewood, to T. J., Monticello. ALS. 3 pp. Endorsed by T. J. Deposit by Philip B. Campbell. Printed: Cabell 2-5.
Unwillingness to enter into an agreement with Judge Cooper regarding collection of minerals. His knowledge only that of an amateur. His collection lent to William and Mary and to [Louis H.?] Girardin.   [1089]

1810 Aug. 19. ARCHIBALD THWEATT, Petersburg, to T. J., Monticello. ALS. 1 p. Endorsed by T. J. Edgehill-Randolph Papers.

Mr. Ladd's report regarding debt due the Wayles estate from the Fleming estate. Requests hiring of an associate in Richmond, George Hay or Mr. Williams. Mentions Edmund Randolph.   [1090]

*1810 Sept. 10. T. J., Monticello, to JOHN B. COLVIN. L. 4 pp. 19th century copy. Carr-Cary Papers. Printed: Ford IX 279-282; L & B XII 418-422; T. J. R. IV 149-152; B of R VI 92.

Observance of written law must at times give way to laws of necessity. Examples from Washington's actions at Yorktown and happenings in his own administration. References to Aaron Burr, purchase of Florida, John Randolph, *Chesapeake* Affair, and James Wilkinson.   [1091]

1810 Sept. 25-26. T. J., Monticello, to CAESAR A. RODNEY, Wilmington, Del. ALS. 3 pp. Endorsed. Printed: L & B XII 424-427; B of R VI 396 (MS. in DLC).

Information as to whether Edward Livingston could maintain an action in Richmond for a trespass committed in New Orleans (Batture controversy). Consultation with James Madison, Robert Smith, and Albert Gallatin on this matter. Recommends Levi Lincoln to replace the deceased William Cushing on the Supreme Court. References to George Hay, William Wirt, and L. W. Tazewell.   [1092]

1810 Sept. 28. GEORGE JEFFERSON, Richmond, to T. J., Monticello. ALS. 1 p. Endorsed by T. J. Photostat. Original owned by Mrs. Virginius Dabney.

Shipment of window glass by [John] Craven. Mentions Mr. Shoemaker.   [1093]

1810 Oct. 1. T. J., Monticello, to JOHN H. COCKE, Bremo. ALS. 1 p. Endorsed. Cocke Papers.

Receipt of two ewes for himself and six for Col. [William?] Fontaine.   [1094]

1810 Nov. 1. JOHN WAYLES EPPES, Mill Brook, to T. J., Monticello. ALS. 2 pp. Endorsed by T. J. Edgehill-Randolph Papers.

Reporting sale of Eppington plantation and removal to Mill Brook. Money due from the Wayles estate to the Hanbury estate. Mr. Robertson doubtful that T. J. will receive any of debt owed to him. Plans for Francis' visit to Monticello when J. W. E. is in Washington.   [1095]

1810 Nov. 23. T. J., Monticello, to CHARLES HOLT, New York. ALS. 1 p.

Refuses subscription to *The Columbian*, preferring local newspapers, Tacitus, and Horace. Presents tribute to the *Bee*, Holt's former paper.   [1096]

1810. THOMAS MANN RANDOLPH, JR., and MARTHA J. RANDOLPH. DEED to JOHN WATSON, Albemarle County. AD by T. J. 2 pp. File draft. Endorsed by T. J. McGregor Library.

Conveying the tract of land in Bedford County received from T. J. Land surveyed by Joseph Slaughter, bounded by the lands of John Watts, Mr. Ballard, Mr. Burton, Mr. Hobson, and Mr. Moseley.   [1097]

1811 Jan. 5. T. J., Monticello, to JOHN WAYLES EPPES. ALS. 2 pp. Printed: Ford IX 289-291; B of R VI 143 (MS. in DLC).

Encloses material on the boundaries of Louisiana. (For enclosure, see 15 January 1804). Advises seizure of East Florida immediately to forestall Great Britain. Francis Eppes' education.   [1098]

1811 Jan 7. JOHN BARNES, Georgetown, to T. J., Monticello. ALS. 2 pp. Edgehill-Randolph Papers.

T. J.'s order on Jonathan Smith, cashier of the Bank of Pennsylvania, for payment to Kosciuszko.   [1099]

1811 Jan. 21. JOHN WAYLES EPPES, Washington, to T. J., Monticello. ALS. 1 p. Endorsed by T. J. Edgehill-Randolph Papers.

Returning a pamphlet that was in the hands of [Henry] Clay. Predicts failure of the bill for renewal of charter of the Bank of the United States.   [1100]

1811 Jan. 26. T. J., Monticello, to DESTUTT DE TRACY. L. 3 pp. Extract by N. P. Trist *ca.* 1830. Another MS. in DLC.

Dissents with Tracy regarding preference of plural over a single executive. Importance of state governments as barriers of liberty. Dangers of and securities against secession.   [1101]

1811 Mar. 3. T. J., Monticello, to PETER MINOR. L. 1 p. Typescript copy. Original owned by Miss Belle Bidgood.

Offers aid to Rivanna Navigation Company, since his mill dam is an obstruction in the river.   [1102]

1811 Mar. 11. T. J., Monticello, to GEORGE JEFFERSON, Richmond. ALS. 2 pp. File draft. Endorsed by T. J. Photostat. Original owned by Mrs. Virginius Dabney.

Congratulations on his being named to the Lisbon consulship. Instructions regarding the proprieties of accepting his commission. Order for turpentine to fight scab in his sheep flock.   [1103]

1811 Mar. 11. T. J., Monticello, to GEORGE JEFFERSON. ALS. 1 p. Photostat. Original owned by Mrs. Virginius Dabney. Another MS. in VHi.

Reasons why Patrick Gibson (an Englishman by birth) cannot be appointed consul at Lisbon instead of George Jefferson.   [1104]

1811 Mar. 16. SAMUEL CARR, Dunlora, to T. J., Monticello. ALS. 1 p. Endorsed by T. J. Carr-Cary Papers.

Purchase of horse from Mr. Clarkson. Thanks for beans.   [1105]

1811 Mar. 16. T. J. ORCHARD RECORD. AD. 1 p. Edgehill-Randolph Papers.
Plan of orchard with note on how vacancies are to be filled.   [1106]

1811 Mar. 17. SAMUEL J. HARRISON, Lynchburg, to T. J., Monticello. ALS. 1 p. Endorsed by T. J. McGregor Library.

Will pay in Richmond installments due for the land. Burgess Griffin has not yet finished prizing the tobacco into casks.   [1107]

1811 Mar. 18. T. J., Monticello, to SAMUEL J. HARRISON, Lynchburg. ALS. 1 p. File draft. Endorsed by T. J. McGregor Library.
Will be glad to have payment for land through Gibson & Jefferson, Richmond. [1108]

1811 Mar. 20. JOHN WAYLES EPPES, Mill Brook, to T. J., Monticello. ALS. 3 pp. Endorsed by T. J. Edgehill-Randolph Papers.
Opposition to Madison in Congress. Request for melon seeds. Wheat and tobacco crop. Francis Eppes to return with Tom. [1109]

1811 Apr. 3. JOHN BARNES, Georgetown, to T. J., Monticello. ALS. 3 pp. Endorsed by T. J. Edgehill-Randolph Papers.
Payment to General Kosciuszko doubtful becaues of difficulties in remitting bills of exchange. Tobacco withheld from shipment because of the precarious foreign situation. [1110]

1811 Apr. 7. PETER CARR, Carr's Brook, to T. J., Monticello. ALS. 1 p. Endorsed by T. J. Carr-Cary Papers.
[George?] Divers and [Nimrod?] Bramham unwilling to help in subscription to relieve William Duane. Little help expected from William Wirt. [1111]

1811 Apr. 15. JOHN BARNES, Georgetown, to T. J., Monticello. ALS. 2 pp. Endorsed by T. J. Edgehill-Randolph Papers.
Bill of exchange drawn by Bowie & Kurtz on William Murdock, London, sent to Hoffingan & Co., Paris, General Kosciuszko's banker. Debt owned by Mrs. Beckley. Draft from Gibson & Jefferson. [1112]

1811 Apr. 30. BENNETT H. HENDERSON, Shelby County, Ky., to CRAVEN PEYTON, Milton, Va. ALS. 2 pp. McGregor Library.
Requests information regarding amount of land deeded for him by James L. Henderson. Wishes to dispose of his Milton holdings; fears James deeded more than he should have. Requests forwarding of two protested notes given by John Henderson to him, one on James and one on Isham Henderson. [1113]

1811 May 26. T. J., Monticello, to ANNE CARY BANKHEAD. ALS. 1 p. Photostat. Original owned by Harold J. Coolidge. Printed: SNR 349-350.
Comments on the book *Modern Griselda*. Brief life of the flowers compared to man's existence. Speaks of his own death. References to John Bankhead, Charles Bankhead, Cornelia Randolph, and Ellen Randolph. [1114]

1811 June 18. JOHN BARNES, Georgetown, to T. J., Monticello. ALS. 2 pp. Endorsed by T. J. Edgehill-Randolph Papers.
T. J.'s accounts, with references to General Kosciuszko, Mr. Barry, Gibson & Jefferson. [1115]

1811 June 18. T. J., Monticello, to HUGH CHIS[H]OLM. ALS. 1 p. File draft. Endorsed by T. J.
Requests his attendance to help Mr. Salmonds in the construction of a pierhead. Mentions James Madison. [1116]

*1811 June 20. CHARLES L. BANKHEAD, Port Royal, to T. J., Monticello. ALS. 2 pp. Endorsed by T. J. Edgehill-Randolph Papers.

John Bankhead declines purchase of William Short's lands. Bankhead attempting to fix sale price for his land in Bedford County to [William?] Radford. Colonel Randolph's success with the mill. Mentions Charles Clay.   [1117]

1811 July 6. JOHN BARNES, Georgetown, to T. J., Monticello. ALS. 6 pp. Endorsed by T. J. Edgehill-Randolph Papers.

Difficulties in making remittances to General Kosciuszko by a bill of exchange. Growth of Washington as a commercial city compared with Baltimore and Alexandria. Offers to supply T. J. with every article, wet or dry.   [1118]

1811 July 10. T. J., Monticello, to DAVID B. WADEN, Washington. ALS. 1 p. Endorsed.

Request that Mr. Warden take to France a copy of the *Review of Montesquieu*.
[1119]

1811 July 12. T. J., Monticello, to MRS. LEWIS. ALS. 1 p. Photostat. Original owned by H. J. Coolidge.

Gift of figs. Accepts offer of cucumbers.   [1120]

1811 July 26. WILSON J. CARY, Cary's Brook, Va., to T. J., Monticello. ALS. 1 p. Endorsed by T. J. (Attached to letter from Peter Carr dated 7 April 1811.) Carr-Cary Papers.

Requests delivery of merino ram to which he is entitled.   [1121]

1811 July 28. T. J., Monticello, to WILSON J. CARY. ALS 1 p. File draft. Endorsed by T. J. Carr-Cary Papers.

Remedy for curing diseased ewes. Visit to Bedford delayed by attack of rheumatism. Martha Randolph and Martha Carr ill. References to Col. [Miles] Cary and Mrs. Cary.   [1122]

1811 Aug. 4. CRAVEN and JANE PEYTON, Albemarle County. DEED to T. J. D. 5 pp. Endorsed by T. J. Witnessed by H. Peyton, Thomas Jefferson [son of Randolph Jefferson], and John B. Stout. Recorded by John Nicholas and attested by Alexander Garrett, Clerks of Albemarle County. McGregor Library.

Deed to all shares of property purchased from heirs of Bennett Henderson, deceased. Mentions: Bennett H., Charles, Eliza, Elizabeth, Frances, Isham, James L., John, Lucy, and Nancy Henderson, Sarah Henderson Kerr, Richard Anderson, Joseph Brand, James Bramham, John R. Kerr, James Lewis, and Richard Seabrook.   [1123]

1811 Aug. 21. T. J., Poplar Forest, to BROWN & ROBERTSON. ALS. 1 p. File draft. Endorsed by T. J. McGregor Library.

Payments for Burgess Griffin's purchases for Poplar Forest. Hopes for partial payment from sale of wheat now in Mr. Mitchell's hands.   [1124]

1811 Aug. 29. SEVENTY-SIX ASSOCIATION, Charleston, S. C., to T. J. LS. 1 p. Endorsed by T. J., with his mathematical calculations on *verso*. Deposited by C. S. Hutter, Jr.

Submitting, in accordance with Association rules, a copy of a Fourth of

July address by Benjamin A. Markley. Signed for the Association by Joseph
Johnson, J. B. White, William Lance, Joseph Kirkland, and Myer Moses. [1125]

1811 Aug. 31. PETER CARR, Carr's Brook, to T. J., Monticello. ALS. 1 p.
Endorsed by T. J. Carr-Cary Papers.
   Sends fine boar pig of Chinese or Parkinson breed, recommended by Judge
[David?] Holmes and General Smith of Winchester, Va. Martha Carr dying.
                                                                    [1126]

1811 Sept. 2. FRANCIS EPPES, Mill Brook, to T. J., Monticello. ALS. 1 p.
Endorsed by T. J. Edgehill-Randolph Papers.
   Eppes, aged ten, writes to his grandfather, mentioning Martha Randolph.
                                                                    [1127]

1811 Sept. 6. T. J., Monticello, to RANDOLPH JEFFERSON. ALS. 1 p. File
draft. Endorsed by T. J. Carr-Cary Papers. Printed: Mayo 19.
   Death of their sister, Martha Carr.   [1128]

1811 Sept. 12. T. J., Monticello, to JOHN SHORE. ALS. 1 p. Photostat. Original
owned by Mrs. Cameron Duncan.
   Sending him a phial of vaccine which he has just received from Benjamin
Waterhouse (who received it from Edward Jenner of London). Results of
vaccinating his servants and those belonging to John Wayles Eppes and Thomas
Mann Randolph, Jr.   [1129]

1811 Oct. 6. RANDOLPH JEFFERSON to T. J., Monticello. ALS. 1 p. Endorsed by T. J. Carr-Cary Papers. Printed: Mayo 20.
   Death of their sister Martha Carr. Busy getting wheat to Richmond market,
sowing new crop. Recent illness. Mentions Mr. Pryor.   [1130]

*1811 Dec. 5. T. J., Poplar Forest, to SAMUEL J. HARRISON. ALS. 1 p.
File draft. Endorsed by T. J. McGregor Library.
   Sends papers dealing with dispute with Samuel Scott regarding land in
Campbell County. List of papers: Richard Tullos' and T. J.'s patents, surveys
by William P. Martin, Richard Smith (Stith?), and Edward Tate. (See July
1812 for copies of some of these.) Mentions Burgess Griffin.   [1131]

1811 Dec. 5. T. J., Poplar Forest, to BENJAMIN RUSH. ALS. 3 pp. Photostat.
Original in New York, Private Collection. Printed: L & B XIII 114-117; TJR
IV 166-168; B of R VI 399 (MS. in DLC).
   Concerning the break between John Adams and himself. Expresses willingness
to resume correspondence should the occasion arise, but will not include Abigail
Adams in this "fusion of mutual affection". Reference to Mr. Coles. [1132]

1811 Dec. 7. T. J. DEED to WILLIAM RADFORD and JOEL YANCEY,
Campbell County. AD. 2 pp. File draft. McGregor Library.
   Conveying land in Bedford County in execution of certain covenants entered
into by Charles L. Bankhead and Anne Randolph Bankhead.   [1133]

1811 Dec. 31. T. J., Monticello, to JEREMIAH A. GOODMAN, Poplar Forest. ALS. 1 p.

People arrived from Poplar Forest. Sending articles needed by Dick (servant). Needs oxen from Poplar Forest. Recommends shipment of tobacco and wheat to market by ox-cart. Requests inventory of stock at both places. Mentions Mr. Darnell.   [1134]

[1811?]. T. J. NOTE ON DESTUTT DE TRACY'S *Review of Montesquieu.* ADS. 1 p. McGregor Library.

The note, identifying the manuscript by Destutt de Tracy, is with the manuscript owned by the McGregor Library.   [1135]

[1811 *et seq.*]. POPLAR FOREST PAPERS. 66 items. Many in Jefferson's hand or having his notes. McGregor Library.

Deeds, surveys, plats, field notes, memoranda. In 1811 a boundary dispute which arose with Samuel Scott, one of the abutting property owners (who was believed to have encroached on land Jefferson had sold to Samuel J. Harrison of Lynchburg) involved searching of all early patents and surveys in the neighborhood, some dating from 1762. In 1811 also, Jefferson was engaged in road building and other extensive improvement on his Poplar Forest tract. Some of the documents are mathematical calculations and field notes, others are elaborately certified surveys. The following names in the documents as landowners, surveyors, witnesses, etc.: Mr. Antrim, Mr. Atkins, Mr. Ballard, Charles L. Bankhead, Bedford County, Mr. Blankinship, Absalom Bradley, Mr. Brian, Mr. Brooks, Mr. Brown, Richard Callaway, Campbell County, G. Carr, Mr. Chetwood (Chitwood), Isham Chisholm, [Bowling] Clarke, [Charles] Clay, Samuel Cobb, Mr. Couch, Mr. Davies, Jarvis Dawson, Will Drew, I. Frost, J. Frost, Fry & Company, B. Griffin, Mr. Gill, Jeremiah Goodman, Mr. Hardwick, Gilbert Harold, Samuel J. Harrison, Ben Howard, James Hubbard, Benjamin Johnson, Christopher Johnson, Jarvis Johnson, Richard Johnson, Mr. Jones, Lunenberg County, Charles Lynch, William P. Martin, Mr. Mitchell, Mr. Moreman, Thomas Moseley, Mr. Murray, John Organ, M. Pate, Mr. Penn, Reuben Perry, William Radford, Thomas Jefferson Randolph, Thomas Mann Randolph, Jr., Mr. Robertson, Daniel Robinson, Samuel Scott, Mr. Shackle, Joseph Slaughter, Richard Smith, Mr. Sprice, [James] Steptoe, Richard Stith, Isham Talbot, Edmund Tate, Mr. Thompson, Mr. Thomson, J. Thomson, Archibald Thweatt, Richard Tullos, Mr. Turpin, Benjamin Waller, Mr. Watts, John Wayles, Thomas Whittington, John Wilkerson, and Joel Yancey.   [1136]

1811-1819. T. J. POPLAR FOREST GARDEN RECORD. AD. 2 pp. McGregor Library.

Memorandum of flowers, trees, fruits, and bushes planted and growing at Poplar Forest. List of mountains in the order in which they are seen from Poplar Forest.   [1137]

1812 Jan. 14. T. J., Monticello, to RANDOLPH JEFFERSON. ALS. 1 p. File draft. Endorsed by T. J. Carr-Cary Papers. Printed: Mayo 21.

Sends bougie and medical advice. Death of brother-in-law, Hastings Marks.

Sister, Anna Scott Marks, in poor health. Watch sent to Richmond. References to Dr. Casper Wistar and Dr. Walker. [1138]

1812 Jan. 15. JOHN BARNES, Georgetown, to T. J., Monticello. ALS. 2 pp. Endorsed by T. J. Edgehill-Randolph Papers.

No information received as to whether General Kosciuszko or his bankers, Hoffingan & Co., received remittances of 1810 and 1811. [1139]

1812 Feb. 8. RANDOLPH JEFFERSON, Woodlawn, Va., to T. J., Monticello. ALS. 1 p. Endorsed by T. J. Carr Cary Papers. Printed: Mayo 22.

His health improved; Anna Marks in poor health. Requests shepherd puppy. Watch lost in Fass Bender's fire. [1140]

1812 Feb. 13. JOHN BARNES, Georgetown, to T. J., Monticello. ALS. 5 pp. Endorsed by T. J. Edgehill-Randolph Papers.

Receipt of money by General Kosciuszko's banker for the year 1810. Expresses pleasure that T. J.'s debts have been reduced. Plans to retire to Philadelphia and be succeeded by William Morton. Asks T. J.'s recommendation of Morton to Madison for the post of Collector of Georgetown. Information from George Taylor regarding purchase of bills of exchange on Paris. [1141]

1812 Feb. 20. ARCHIBALD ROBERTSON, Lynchburg, to T. J., Monticello. ALS. 1 p. Endorsed by T. J. McGregor Library.

Sudden death of William Brown requires payment of T. J.'s debt. [1142]

1812 Feb. 26. JOHN BARNES, Georgetown, to T. J., Monticello. ALS. 1 p. Endorsed by T. J. Edgehill-Randolph Papers.

Purchase of bills of exchange for General Kosciuszko. [1143]

[1812] Mar. 1. T. J., Monticello, to JEREMIAH GOODMAN, Poplar Forest. ALS. 1 p. Deposited by C. S. Hutter, Jr. Another MS. in MHi.

Instructions to the overseer of Poplar Forest. Need for yoke of oxen at Monticello. Burnet seed to be procured from Mr. Duval. Lettuce seed to be planted. Mentions Major Flood, [Burgess] Griffin, and Moses (servant). [1144]

1812 Mar. 1. T. J., Monticello, to ARCHIBALD ROBERTSON, Lynchburg. ALS. 1 p. File draft. Endorsed by T. J. McGregor Library.

Partial payment of his debt to Brown & Robertson by draft on Samuel J. Harrison. Bedford tobacco pledged to pay bank debt incurred when president. [1145]

1812 Mar. 13. SAMUEL J. HARRISON, Lynchburg, to T. J., Monticello. ALS. 2 pp. Endorsed by T. J. Also a T. J. autograph copy. 1 p. McGregor Library.

Accepts draft in favor of Brown, Robertson & Co. Withholding last payment on Campbell County land until title cleared, due to Samuel Scott's suit regarding valuable portion of tract. [1146]

1812 Mar. 27. JOHN BARNES, Georgetown, to T. J., Monticello. ALS. 2 pp. Endorsed by T. J. Edgehill-Randolph Papers.

Payment on T. J.'s account of bills rendered by Mr. Foxall J. Barry, J.

Milligan, and R. Weightman partially defrayed by Gibson & Jefferson's order on the Bank of Columbia. Bills of exchange for General Kosciuszko.   [1147]

1812 Mar. 29. T. J., Monticello, to PATRICK GIBSON, Richmond. ALS. 1 p. McGregor Library.

Remittances to Benjamin Jones of Philadelphia, iron-monger, and to Ezra Sarjeant of New York, printer, to be defrayed by the sale of T. J.'s flour.
[1148]

1812 Apr. 2. T. J., Monticello, to SAMUEL J. HARRISON, Lynchburg. ALS. 3 pp. Endorsed by T. J. Two T. J. autograph copies. McGregor Library. Printed: Harrison 66-68.

Protests his refusal to pay for land. Will force him into failure. Declares Samuel Scott's claim ridiculous.   [1149]

1812 Apr. 13. RANDOLPH JEFFERSON to T. J., Monticello. ALS. 1 p. Endorsed by T. J. Carr-Cary Papers. Printed: Mayo 23.

His watch safe with Fass Bender. Asks for shepherd puppy. Health improved. References to R. Patteson and Dr. .Walker.   [1150]

1812 Apr. 20. JOHN BARNES, Georgetown, to T. J., Monticello. ALS. 4 pp. Endorsed by T. J. Edgehill-Randolph Papers.

Letter forwarded to John Morton. Purchase of bills of exchange for General Kosciuszko. Date of his retirement to Philadelphia uncertain. Growth of retail business in Washington and Georgetown.   [1151]

1812 Apr. 27. SAMUEL J. HARRISON, Lynchburg, to T. J. ALS. 2 pp. Endorsed by T. J. McGregor Library.

Retains his opinion on right to clear land title before payment. Will accept trust deed on part of Poplar Forest tract as security.   [1152]

1812 May 11. JOHN BARNES, Georgetown, to T. J., Monticello. ALS. 2 pp. Endorsed by T. J. Edgehill-Randolph Papers.

Purchase of bills of exchange from [John] Morton. Money received from Gibson & Jefferson transmitted to E. I. Dupont and to General Kosciuszko. References to Messrs. B. and G. Williams and to Mr. [Isaac?] Coles.   [1153]

1812 May 12. T. J. to JEREMIAH GOODMAN. AL. 1 p. Deposited by C. S. Hutter, Jr.

Instructions to the overseer of Poplar Forest regarding grass and lettuce seed, young trees, fruit bushes, and beer. Sheep to be sent to Mr. Caruthers of Rockbridge.   [1154]

1812 May 13. T. J., Poplar Forest, to SAMUEL J. HARRISON, Lynchburg. ALS. 1 p. File draft. Endorsed by T. J. McGregor Library.

On his way to Poplar Forest by upper road will pass through land T. J. intends to convey to him.   [1155]

1812 May 14. T. J., Poplar Forest, to BOWLING CLARKE. ALS. 1 p. File draft. Endorsed by T. J. McGregor Library.

Requests help in inquiry regarding title of land in Campbell County, purchased by John Wayles from Richard Stith. Land now claimed by Samuel Scott. Mentions Richard Tullos and Richard Smith.   [1156]

1812 May 14. T. J., Poplar Forest, to WILLIAM P. MARTIN. ALS. 1 p. File draft. Endorsed by T. J. McGregor Library.

Requests copies of entries and surveys of land in Campbell County claimed by Samuel Scott. Mentions Christopher Anthony, Richard Stith, Edmund Tate, Mr. Timberlake, Richard Tullos, and [John] Wilkerson.   [1157]

1812 May 16 [date received]. WILLIAM P. MARTIN to T. J. ALS. 2 pp. Endorsed by T. J. McGregor Library.

List of entries, surveys on land adjoining Poplar Forest tract in litigation between Samuel Scott and T. J. and Samuel Harrison. References to Christopher Anthony, William Callaway, Mr. Johnson, Jesse Locke, Thomas Moore, William Peters, Mr. Quarles, Richard Stith, Edmund Tate, Richard Tullos, John Wayles, John Wilkerson, John Wiley.   [1158]

1812 May 17. T. J., Poplar Forest, to [JOSEPH] SLAUGHTER. ALS. 1 p. File draft. Endorsed by T. J. McGregor Library.

Request for Colonel Watts' bond and for a statement of the account between [Charles L.] Bankhead and Slaughter.   [1159]

1812 May 18. JOHN BARNES, Georgetown, to T. J., Monticello. ALS. 3 pp. Endorsed by T. J. Edgehill-Randolph Papers.

Correspondence with Messrs. B. and G. Williams and with John Morton of Morton & Russell, Bordeaux, regarding purchase of bills of exchange to remit to General Kosciuszko's banker, Hoffingan & Co.   [1160]

1812 May 18. T. J. to CHARLES CLAY and WILLIAM NORVELL, Trustees for Samuel J. Harrison. ADS. 2 pp. File draft. Endorsed by T. J. Witnessed by Joseph Slaughter, Colin Buckner, and Mr. Rose. McGregor Library.

Deed for a tract of land in Bedford County to serve as security for land conveyed to Harrison (boundaries are disputed by Samuel Scott). Mentions John Gill, Benjamin Johnson, and Nicholas Johnson.   [1161]

1812 May 18. JAMES C. STEPTOE to [JAMES STEPTOE]. ALS. 1 p. Endorsed by T. J. McGregor Library.

No record of conveyance from Richard Stith to John Wayles. Found deed John Dayles (i.e., Wayles?) to Warren McCauley. Surveyor's records in hands of Matthew Pate, present surveyor. (Search made in consequence of litigation with Samuel Scott regarding Poplar Forest boundary).   [1162]

1812 May 19. T. J., Poplar Forest, to SAMUEL J. HARRISON. ALS. 1 p. File draft. Endorsed by T. J. McGregor Library.

Proposition respecting [Charles L.] Bankhead's tobacco. Procedure for defense against Samuel Scott's suit.   [1163]

1812 May 27. T. J., Monticello, to CHARLES BLAGROVE. ALS. 1 p. File draft. Endorsed by T. J. McGregor Library.

Requests search for record of transfer of land, Richard Stith to John Wayles, needed in suit brought by Samuel Scott. Fees to be paid by Gibson & Jefferson, Richmond. [1164]

1812 May 27. BOWLING CLARKE, Hills Creek, Campbell County, to T. J., Monticello. ALS. 2 pp. Endorsed by T. J. McGregor Library.

Information regarding Richard Stith's conveyance to John Wayles. References to Mr. Ferris, Burgess Griffin, Nicholas Lewis, Zachariah Morris, and Richard Tullos. [1165]

1812 May 27. T. J., Monticello, to ARCHIBALD THWEATT. ALS. 2 pp. File draft. Endorsed by T. J. McGregor Library.

Returns copy of Warden's exceptions. Requests search of John Wayles' books and papers for record of Richard Stith's entry in land in Campbell County, now in dispute between T. J. and Samuel Scott. [1166]

1812 June 3. T. J., Monticello, to JOHN WAYLES EPPES. ALS. 2 pp. Photostat. Original owned by Mrs. Irene Hallam. Printed: Randall III 369.

Requests first consideration in the sale of Pantops. Half of debt brought on by Washington residence is paid. Suggestion that Francis be placed in Peter Carr's school. [1167]

1812 June 4. CHARLES BLAGROVE, Land Office, to T. J., Monticello. ALS. 1 p. Endorsed by T. J. McGregor Library.

Returns plat and survey of Campbell County land. Can find no patent in name of John Dayles (i.e., Wayles) for this land. [1168]

1812 June 10. T. J. to [JAMES] LEITCH. ALS. 1 p.
Order for wax, a hair broom, and blue nankeen. [1169]

1812 June 15. T. J., Monticello, to CHARLES BLAGROVE, Land Office. ALS. 1 p. File draft. Endorsed by T. J. McGregor Library.

Acknowledges return of certificates. Error in search for patent made under Dayles instead of Wayles. [1170]

1812 June 15. T. J., Monticello, to ZACHARIAH MORRIS, Farmville, Va. ALS. 1 p. File draft. Endorsed by T. J. McGregor Library.

Asks for any recollections of purchase and payment for land bought by John Wayles from Richard Stith, and of Stith's original entry. Details of suit brought by Samuel Scott. Mentions Poplar Forest, Richard Tullos, and Mr. Blankenship. [1171]

1812 June 23. CHARLES BLAGROVE, Land Office, to T. J. ALS. 1 p. Endorsed by T. J. McGregor Library.

Searched record of patents, surveys in late Secretary's office, found no record in name of John Wayles. (Search made in connection with Samuel Scott suit.) [1172]

1812 June 23. ARCHIBALD THWEATT, Eppington, Va., to T. J., Monticello. ALS. 3 pp. Endorsed by T. J. Enclosure: Receipt (2 copies) 1 p. McGregor Library.

Sends copy of Richard Stith's receipt to John Wayles for payment for land in dispute with Samuel Scott. No evidence of Stith's entry found. Mentions John Wayles Eppes, James Donald. [1173]

1812 June 27. JOHN BARNES, Georgetown, to T. J., Monticello. ALS. 2 pp. Endorsed by T. J. Edgehill-Randolph Papers.

Money supplied to Davy (servant?). Dun horse's lameness may delay Davy's return. Health of T. J.'s family. [1174]

1812 July 3. T. J., Monticello, to ARCHIBALD THWEATT. ALS. 2 pp. File draft. Endorsed by T. J. McGregor Library.

In connection with Samuel Scott's suit, requests search for survey of Stith's entry and for John Wayles' land book, containing history of his land titles. References to John Wayles Eppes, Frank Harris, and [Henry] Skipwith. [1175]

1812 July 8. T. J., Monticello, to CHARLES BLAGROVE. ALS. 1 p. File draft. Endorsed by T. J. McGregor Library.

Asks for authenticated copy of his grant of 100 acres in Campbell County, dated 22 May 1797. [1176]

1812 July 11. T. J. ANSWER in the SUIT of SAMUEL SCOTT vs. T. J. and SAMUEL J. HARRISON. ADS. 4 pp. Rough draft. Endorsed by T. J. McGregor Library.

Detailed memorandum of defense against Samuel Scott's suit. History of disputed patent, proofs to be obtained, exhibits to be presented in court, law and equity in the case. References to: Christopher Anthony, Bedford County, Campbell County, Burgess Griffin, Benjamin Howard, Martha Wayles Jefferson, William P. Martin, Mr. Mead, Poplar Forest, Thomas Mann Randolph, Jr., Richard Smith (incorrect spelling for Stith), James Steptoe, Richard Stith, Isham Talbot, Edmund Tate (Tait), Richard Tullos, John Wayles, Thomas Whittington. [1177]

1812 July 13. T. J., Monticello, to GEORGE HAY. ALS. 1 p. File draft. Endorsed by T. J. McGregor Library.

Information regarding the Scott suit which T. J. wishes Hay to undertake together with William Wirt. Recommends purchase of William Short's land near Monticello. Mentions co-defendant, Samuel Harrison. [1178]

1812 July 13. T. J., Monticello, to WILLIAM WIRT. ALS. 1 p. File draft. Endorsed by T. J. McGregor Library.

Information regarding Samuel Scott's suit in which Wirt and George Hay are to serve as T. J.'s attorneys. Mentions co-defendant, Samuel Harrison. [1179]

1812 July 16. T. J., Monticello, to GEORGE HAY. ALS. 1 p. File draft. Endorsed by T. J. McGregor Library.

Samuel Scott suit. Law in [James?] Pleasants' collection of acts voids all entries unless surveyed before November 1798. Reference to case of Vincent *vs.* Conrad in Hall's *American Law Journal* series.   [1180]

1812 July 21. GEORGE HAY, Richmond, to T. J., Monticello. ALS. 1 p. Endorsed by T. J. McGregor Library.

Samuel J. Harrison's title good. Sends instructions regarding Samuel Scott's suit. Appreciates offer of William Short's lands but is located on Chickahominy. Mentions James Monroe.   [1181]

1812 July 21. WILLIAM WALLER HENING, Clerk, Superior Court of Chancery, Richmond. DS. 1 p. 2 copies. Endorsed. McGregor Library.

Summons to ──────────── in case of Samuel Scott *vs.* T. J. and Samuel J. Harrison.   [1182]

1812 July 30. JOHN WATSON and DAVID I. LEWIS, Justices of the Peace of Albemarle County, to DAVID MICHIE, Sheriff. D. 3 pp. (partly in T. J.'s hand). Endorsed by T. J. Photostat. Original at Monticello.

Warrant for restitution of land between Milton, Va., and the Rivanna River, formerly part of the Bennett Henderson estate, to T. J. Statement of delivery of warrant to T. J.'s attorney, David Higginbotham, signed [Thomas?] Garth and R. Garland. Mentions William Ballard, James Barksdale, James Clark, William Crenshaw, Frederick Gilliam, Reuben Grady, Abraham Johnson, Charles Huckstep, John Key, James Leitch, William Leitch, Nicholas Lewis, Peter Minor, Jesse Rey, Joel Shiflett, Benjamin Thurmond, John Watson. William Wood.   [1183]

1812 July. T. J. MEMORANDUM. AD. 1 p. McGregor Library.

Notes regarding deeds to the Bennett Henderson estate lands. References to Craven Peyton, Jane Peyton, and Bennett H. Henderson.   [1184]

1812 Aug. 1. SAMUEL J. HARRISON, Lynchburg, to T. J. ALS. 1 p. Endorsed by T. J. McGregor Library.

Encloses answer to Samuel Scott's suit for T. J.'s examination.   [1185]

1812 Aug. 2. ARCHIBALD THWEATT, Richmond, to T. J., Monticello. ALS. 2 pp. Endorsed by T. J. McGregor Library.

Sends Richard Stith's original receipt to John Wayles for land now disputed by Samuel Scott. Extracts from Wayles' memorandum book showing payment of Stith's fees. References to [Henry] Skipworth, Charles E. May (Hay?), and John Wayles Eppes.   [1186]

1812 Aug. GRIST MILL ESTIMATE. D. 1 p. Endorsed by T. J., Edgehill-Randolph Papers.

Memorandum by W. and R. Mitchell of terms for grinding T. J.'s wheat. [1187]

[1812 *ca.* Aug.]. T. J. COPIES OF EXHIBITS IN ANSWER TO SCOTT'S SUIT. ADS. 3 pp. McGregor Library.

a. 11 January 1771. Receipt to John Wayles by James Donald for currency for 99 acres of land near Ivy Creek. Signed Richard Stith, surveyor.

b. 19 December 1795. Thomas Jefferson. Receipt to Surveyor of Campbell

County for receiving land warrants, surveying, certificates. Receipted, Richard Stith, Surveyor.

c. 23. December 1795. Survey. 100 acres of land, Campbell County, Ivy Creek, bounded by Wilkinson, Johnson, [Richard] Tullos. Plat. Richard Stith, Surveyor. Wm. Peter Martin, C. C.

d. 5, 19 December 1795. Land Office Treasury warrant for 100 acres. Jefferson's entry for above lands. Surveyed, Richard Stith. Recorded, land office, 1796, by Charles Blagrove, Registrar. Grant issued 1797, attested 1812.

e. 15 November 1796. Letter from Samuel Scott, Campbell County, offering to buy land on Ivy Creek. Suggests 2 or 3 men as judges. Refers to B[owling] Clark[e], Jefferson's overseer.

f. 26 December 1803. Survey for Edmund Tate of 54¾ acres in Campbell County on Ivy Creek. Mentions Wilkerson, Johnson (now Couch), Tullos. Assigned to Samuel Scott. Wm. P. Martin, Surveyor.

g. 15 November 1809. Survey of T. J.'s land in Campbell County by William P. Martin, Surveyor. Mentions Wilkerson, Couch, Tullos, Samuel Scott.   [1188]

[1812 ca. Aug.]. T. J. PAPERS in CHANCERY SUIT, SCOTT vs. JEFFERSON and HARRISON. AD. 3 items, 14 pp. File drafts. Endorsed by T. J. McGregor Library.

a. Samuel Scott's petition to Creed Taylor, judge of the Superior Court of Chancery for the Richmond district, stating history of his title to 50 acres of land in Campbell County, Va.

b. Separate answer of Samuel J. Harrison to the above.
c. Separate answer of Thomas Jefferson to the above.

Names mentioned: Christopher Anthony, Bedford County, Campbell County, Benjamin Howard, Thomas Humphreys, William P. Martin, Poplar Forest, Thomas Mann Randolph, Jr., Richard Smith, Richard Stith, Edmund Tate (Tait), Isham Talbot, Mr. Timberlake, John Wayles, Mr. Wilkerson (Wilkinson).   [1189]

1812 Sept. 2. SAMUEL J. HARRISON, Lynchburg, to T. J., Poplar Forest. ALS. 1 p. Endorsed by T. J. McGregor Library.
Sends answer to Samuel Scott's bill. Price of wheat, Richmond.   [1190]

*1812 Sept. 2. Poplar Forest, to SAMUEL J. HARRISON, Lynchburg. ALS. 1 p. File draft. Endorsed by T. J. McGregor Library.
Requests signature on his answer to Samuel Scott, before sending it to George Hay and William Wirt.   [1191]

1812 Sept. 2. T. J., Poplar Forest, to JOSEPH SLAUGHTER. ALS. 1 p. File draft. Endorsed by T. J.. McGregor Library.
Requesting that he act as commissioner in taking depositions in suit brought against him by Samuel Scott.   [1192]

1812 Sept. 2. JOSEPH SLAUGHTER to T. J., Poplar Forest. ALS. 1 p. Endorsed by T. J. McGregor Library.

Agrees to take depositions in Scott suit. Magistrates are Capt. William Irvine, Joel Leftwich, David Sanders, and Jabez Leftwich. New London not in this county.   [1193]

1812 Sept. 4. T. J., Poplar Forest, to BURGESS GRIFFIN. ALS. 1 p. File draft. Endorsed by T. J. McGregor Library

Deposition in Samuel Scott's suit. Mentions Mr. Bradford (William Radford?), Mr. Claxton, Samuel J. Harrison, and [Joel] Yancey.   [1194]

1812 Sept. 4. T. J., Poplar Forest, to WILLIAM P. MARTIN. ALS. 1 p. File draft. Endorsed by T. J. McGregor Library.

Depositions for Samuel Scott's suit. Wishes to verify signatures of Richard Stith and Samuel Scott. Mentions Mr. Bradford (William Radford?), Mr. Claxton, James Donald, and Joel Yancey.   [1195]

1812 Sept. 4. T. J., Poplar Forest, to THOMAS WHITTINGTON. ALS. 1 p. File draft. Endorsed by T. J. McGregor Library.

Depositions in the Samuel Scott suit.   [1196]

1812 Sept. 5. BURGESS GRIFFIN, Old Glebe, Bedford County, to T. J., Poplar Forest. ALS. 1 p. Endorsed by T. J. McGregor Library.

Will attend meeting at Mr. Claxton's to give depositions in the Samuel Scott suit.   [1197]

1812 Sept. 10. T. J., Poplar Forest, to JAMES STEPTOE, Clerk of Bedford County. ALS. 2 pp. File draft. Endorsed by T. J. McGregor Library

Depositions for Samuel Scott's suit. Asks for testimony on condition of records in clerk's office in 1772 which would account for lack of Richard Stith's entry. Also wishes verification of handwriting of James Donald and Richard Stith.
                                                                                  [1198]

1812 Oct. 3. JOHN BARNES, Georgetown, to T. J., Monticello. ALS. 1 p. Endorsed by T. J. Edgehill-Randolph Papers.

Order on the cashier of the Bank of Pennsylvania to General Kosciuszko. [1199]

1812 Oct. 13. JOHN BARNES, Georgetown, to T. J., Monticello. ALS. 3 pp. Endorsed by T. J. Edgehill-Randolph Papers.

Expresses regret at T. J.'s fall; suggests applications of flannel as remedy. Remittance to General Kosciuszko. T. J.'s intended journey to Bedford County.   [1200]

1812 Oct. 18. T. J., Monticello, to PETER MINOR. ALS. 1 p. McGregor Library.

Purchase of Mr. Gilmore's horse. Reference to T. J. Randolph.   [1201]

1812 Oct. - Dec. T. J. MEMORANDUM ON WHEAT FROM POPLAR FOREST. AD. 2 pp. Endorsed by T. J. Edgehill-Randolph Papers.

"The whole crop of 1812 except the seed" equalled 1096 barrels.   [1202]

1812 Nov. 11. T. J., Poplar Forest, to ARCHIBALD ROBERTSON. ALS. 1 p. File draft. Endorsed by T. J. McGregor Library.

Payment of taxes in Bedford County through draft on Gibson & Jefferson, Richmond. Prospects of paying his account. [1203]

1812 Nov. 25. ABNER CALLAWAY to T. J., [Monticello]. ALS. 1 p. Endorsed by T. J. Edgehill-Randolph Papers.

Requesting a loan of 200 bricks, to be returned with those lent to Colonel Watts. [1204]

1812 Dec. 8. BURGESS GRIFFIN to T. J., Poplar Forest. ALS. 1 p. Endorsed by T. J. Edgehill-Randolph Papers.

Carter B. Page holds T. J.'s bond in Richmond. [1205]

1812 Dec. 9. JOHN BARNES, Georgetown, to T. J., Monticello. ALS. 3 pp. Endorsed by T. J. Edgehill-Randolph Papers.

Recommending that T. J. lease flour mill to John Eliason since Mr. Shoemaker has broken his lease. No news of John Morton or General Kosciuszko. [1206]

*1812 Dec. 13. T. J. DEED to BENJAMIN JOHNSON, Bedford County. AD. 2 pp. File draft. Endorsed by T. J. Witnessed by Lemuel Johnson, Jeremiah A. Goodman, Nirwood Daniel, Stephen Butler, and Lilbourn Johnson.

Exchange of lands in Bedford and Campbell Counties for mutual benefit. Mentioned: John Gill, David Johnson, John H. Moreman, Samuel Poindexter, Daniel Robertson, and John Wayles. [1207]

[1812]. LIST OF MILITIA SUBSCRIPTIONS. D. 2 pp. Maury Papers.

Subscribers beside T. J. for raising an Albemarle Company included: Charles Bankhead, R. M. Bell, J. Bishop, Chiles M. Brand, Peter Carr, G. Carr, John Craven, Charles Day, Dixon Dedham, James Dinsmore, George Divers, Charles Everette, James Garnett, Alexander Garrett, Elijah Garth, John M. Guy, John Kelly, William Kelly, Samuel Leitch, Reuben Mansfield, Wilson Medearis, Thomas J. Randolph, William Watson, John Wayman, John Winn. [1208]

1812-1813. W. & R. MITCHELL. GRISTMILL ACCOUNT. 2 items, 1 T.J.AD. Endorsed by T. J. Edgehill-Randolph Papers.

Account rendered to T. J. for wheat and flour. Terms for grinding wheat. [1209]

1812-1821. POPLAR FOREST ACCOUNTS. 4 items. 2 endorsed by T. J. Edgehill-Randolph Papers.

Account of tobacco sold to Samuel J. Harrison in 1812; Joel Yancey, overseer, statement of amount due Charles Clay, 27 April 1816; Robert Mitchell to Joel Yancey covering T. J.'s account, 26 September 1820; E. C. Mettlar to Joel Yancey concerning William Mitchell's account against Jefferson, 11 October 1821. [1210]

[1812-1824]. T. J. et al. to [JAMES] LEITCH, Charlottesville. ALS. 5 items.

Orders to Leitch for a cross-cut saw, olive oil, hand irons, rice, and 4 yds. of diaper; three from T. J., one from T. J. Randolph, and one from Martha Randolph.   [1211]

1813 Jan. 5. T. J., Monticello, to JOSEPH C. CABELL, Richmond. ALS. 1 p. Endorsed. Printed: Cabell 5-6.

Asks protection from a petition presented to the legislature by the Rivanna Company for an enlargement of their powers. Threatens T. J.'s mill.   [1212]

1813 Jan. 6. JOHN BARNES, Georgetown, to T. J., Monticello. ALS. 2 pp. Endorsed by T. J. Edgehill-Randolph Papers.

John Eliason requests interview regarding leasing of T. J.'s mills. References to General Kosciuszko, John Morton, and T. M. Randolph, Jr.   [1213]

1813 Jan. 12. JOSEPH C. CABELL, Richmond, T. J., Monticello. ALS. 1 p. Endorsed by T. J. Deposited by Philip B. Campbell. Printed: Cabell 6.

Defense of T. J.'s rights against the petition of the Rivanna Company. References to [Philip P.?] Barbour and [Chapman] Johnson.   [1214]

1813 Jan. 12. T. J., Monticello, to JAMES RONALDSON. L. 2 pp. Fragment. 19th century copy. Edgehill-Randolph Papers. Printed: L & B XIII 204-206; Ford IX 370-373; B of R VI 397 (MS. in DLC).

Difficulties in attempting to introduce new plants and trees: the cork tree, the olive tree of Aix, sainfoin, and upland rice. Development of cotton and cotton weaving. Household manufacture.   [1215]

1813 Feb. 17. JOSEPH C. CABELL, Richmond, to T. J., Monticello. ALS. 2 pp. Endorsed by T. J. Deposited by Philip B. Campbell. Printed: Cabell 7-8.

Services by Cabell, [P. P.?] Barbour, and [Chapman] Johnson in the Virginia legislature in defense of T. J.'s rights against the bill petitioned by the Rivanna Company. Action in the Senate and House of Delegates. Use of T. J.'s canal by the company and exemption of T. J.'s and his customer's produce from tools were involved.   [1216]

1813 Feb. 24. RANDOLPH JEFFERSON, Woodlawn, to T. J., Monticello. ALS. 1 p. Endorsed by T. J. Carr-Cary Papers. Printed: Mayo 24.

Sends Squire for garden seeds. Invitation to visit. Delayed at Woodlawn by Mrs. [David] Pryor's illness.   [1217]

1813 Feb. 27. T. J., Monticello, to DABNEY CARR. ALS. 1 p. File draft. Endorsed by T. J. Carr-Cary Papers.

Requests that he bring a letter to attention of Edmund Randolph. Offer for his tenement excellent.   [1218]

1813 Mar. 2. T. J., Monticello, to RANDOLPH JEFFERSON. ALS. 1 p. File draft. Endorsed by T. J. Carr-Cary Papers. Printed: Mayo 25.

Send seeds for vegetable and flower garden. Will call on Randolph on way to Bedford if road passable.   [1219]

1813 Mar. 12. T. J., Monticello, to JOHN H. COCKE, Bremo. ALS. 1 p. Endorsed. Sends seed of broom and sprout kale plants. [1220]

1813 Mar 14. DABNEY CARR, Winchester, to T. J., Monticello. ALS. 1 p. Endorsed by T. J. Carr-Cary Papers.
Letter for Edmund Randolph forwarded through Dr. Grayson. Randolph lives with son-in-law, Bennett Taylor. [1221]

1813 Apr. 11. FRANCIS EPPES, Lynchburg, to T. J., Monticello. ALS. 1 p. Endorsed by T. J. Edgehill-Randolph Papers.
Scolding his grandfather for failing to write. [1222]

1813 Apr. 21. T. J., Monticello, to JOSEPH HORNSBY, [Kentucky]. ALS. 2 pp. File draft. Endorsed by T. J. McGregor Library.
Requests his aid in getting his title to Henderson land confirmed by Mrs. Thomas Hornsby, last of minor heirs of Bennett Henderson. William D. Meriwether has influenced Hornsby in this. Mentions Craven Peyton, William Pope Duval, and Gov. Christopher Greenup. [1223]

1813 Apr. 24. T. J., Monticello, to RODOLPHUS DICKINSON, Greenfield, Mass. ALS. 1 p. Another MS. in DLC.
Thanking him for a copy of his book, *View of Massachusetts Proper.* [1224]

1813 Apr. 29. JOHN BARNES, Georgetown, to T. J., Monticello. ALS. 1 p. Endorsed by T. J. Edgehill-Randolph Papers.
Letter of introduction for John Eliason, who is interested in managing T. J.'s mill. [1225]

1813 Apr. 29. JOHN BARNES, Georgetown, to T. J., Monticello. ALS. 1 p. Endorsed by T. J. Edgehill-Randolph Papers.
Encloses letter from George Williams of Baltimore with news of General Kosciuszko. [1226]

1813 Apr. 30. T. J., Poplar Forest, to ARCHIBALD ROBERTSON, Lynchburg. ALS. 1 p. File draft. Endorsed by T. J. McGregor Library.
Unable to make payment because he was caught by the blockade before the sale of his flour. Sale ordered through Patrick Gibson of Richmond. Export from Norfolk possible. [1227]

1813 May 1. ARCHIBALD ROBERTSON, Lynchburg, to T. J., Poplar Forest. ALS. 1 p. Endorsed by T. J. McGregor Library.
T. J.'s arrangements for repayment of debt satisfactory. Attempts to run flour through Dismal Swamp may raise prices; large quantity in Richmond keeps price low. [1228]

1813 May 25. JOHN WAYLES EPPES, Washington, to T. J., Monticello. ALS. 4 pp. Endorsed by T. J. Edgehill-Randolph Papers.
Negotiations on the exchange of T. J.'s land in Bedford for J. W. Eppes' Pan-

tops near Monticello. If exchange be made, Eppes wishes land in Bedford in fee simple without reversionary claims. Resentment at T. J.'s favoring the Randolphs. Francis Eppes in school at Lynchburg, boarding with Seth Ward. President's majority in Congress. Failure of General Dearborn. Fever among the troops. Surrender of York (Toronto).   [1229]

1813 May 25. T. J., Monticello, to RANDOLPH JEFFERSON. ALS. 2 pp. File draft. Endorsed by T. J. Carr-Cary Papers. Printed: Mayo 26-27.

Request for carp to stock his fish pond. Gift of a spinning-jenny. Plans for a visit at Snowden on way to Bedford County. Course of reading for James Lilburne Jefferson, Randolph's son. Suggestions for farming operations and crop rotation.   [1230]

1813 May 26. RANDOLPH JEFFERSON to T. J. ALS. 2 pp. Endorsed by T. J. Carr-Cary Papers. Printed: Mayo 28.

Carp for T. J.'s fish pond. James Lilburne Jefferson to begin course of reading. Grateful for spinning jenny. Invitation to Anna Scott Marks to visit. T. J.'s farming methods too difficult.   [1231]

1813 June 3. JOHN BARNES, Georgetown, to T. J., Monticello. ALS. 2 pp. Endorsed by T. J. Edgehill-Randolph Papers.

T. J.'s account with Barnes. Remittances received from Gibson & Jefferson and sent to General Kosciuszko. Recommending John Eliason. References to George Williams, John Morton, and Thomas Mann Randolph, Jr.   [1232]

1813 June 4. JOHN BARNES, Georgetown, to T. J., Monticello. ALS. 3 pp. Endorsed by T. J. Edgehill-Randolph Papers.

Recommending T. J. charge General Kosciuszko one year's interest for services rendered in regard to public stock. Includes an account, 1809 to 1813.   [1233]

1813 June 20. JOHN BARNES, Georgetown, to T. J., Monticello. ALS. 3 pp. Endorsed by T. J. Edgehill-Randolph Papers.

Suggests a remittance might be made to General Kosciuszko through George Williams of Baltimore and Russell & Morton of Bordeaux without resorting to a bill of exchange. Present rate of exchange. Defeat of Bonaparte in Russia. Lawless division of Poland by Austria, Prussia, and Russia.   [1234]

1813 June 20. T. J., Monticello, to RANDOLPH JEFFERSON. ALS. 1 p. File draft. Endorsed by T. J. Carr-Cary Papers. Printed: Mayo 29.

Bedford visit delayed. Suggests he send servant to Monticello to learn to use spinning jenny. Sends gardening book published in Washington which he has indexed for Randolph's wife. Gherkin seeds.   [1235]

1813 June 21. RANDOLPH JEFFERSON, Snowden, to T. J., Monticello. ALS. 2 pp. Endorsed by T. J. Carr-Cary Papers. Printed: Mayo 30.

Wife grateful for gardening book; her illness. No woman available to learn to spin. Expects Anna Scott Marks for visit. James Lilburne Jefferson has joined the volunteers. No carp available. Will send for ram in cooler weather.   [1236]

1813 June 24. T. J., Monticello, to JOHN WAYLES EPPES. ALS. 7 pp. Printed: Ford IX 388-395; L & B XIII 269-279; TJR IV 196-201.

Importance of the rule that taxation and loans go hand-in-hand, so as not to alienate the land from the next generation. Money should be issued by the government, not by private banks. Reference to Francis Eppes.   [1237]

1813 June 26. FRANK CARR, Charlottesville, to T. J., Monticello. ALS. 1 p. Endorsed by T. J. Carr-Cary Papers.

Encloses sample of antimony found in neighborhood. (The antimony was sent to Correa de Serra).   [1238]

1813 July 6. JOHN BARNES, Georgetown, to T. J., Monticello. ALS. 2 pp. Endorsed by T. J. Edgehill-Randolph Papers.

Method of remittance to General Kosciuszko: K. to draw a bill of exchange on Barnes.   [1239]

1813 July 8. DABNEY CARR, Winchester, Va., to T. J., Monticello. ALS. 1 p. Endorsed by T. J. Carr-Cary Papers.

Encloses deed from Edmund Randolph, whose health is low. (He died 13 September 1813).   [1240]

1813 July 11. RANDOLPH JEFFERSON, Snowden, to T. J., Monticello. ALS. 1 p. Endorsed by T. J. Carr-Cary Papers. Printed: Mayo 31.

Sends girl to learn to use spinning jenny. Expects visit.   [1241]

1813 July 11. T. J., Monticello, to BENJAMIN ROMAYNE. ALS. 1 p. Another MS. in DLC.

Expressing his thanks for a Republican oration sent to him by Dr. Romayne.   [1242]

1813 July 12. T. J., Monticello, to RANDOLPH JEFFERSON, Snowden. ALS. 1 p. File draft. Endorsed by T. J. Carr-Cary Papers. Printed: Mayo 32.

Progress of girl learning to spin. Plans for trip to Bedford, Snowden. Will send jenny.   [1243]

1813 July 21. THOMAS HORNSBY, Shelbyville, Ky., to T. J., Charlottesville. ALS. 3 pp. Endorsed by T. J. McGregor Library.

Sale of property of minor Henderson children to Craven Peyton was done without their knowledge or permission. Justifies his action regarding his wife, Frances Henderson Hornsby's share. Mentions Elizabeth Henderson, Charles Henderson, James L. Henderson, Joseph Hornsby, Christopher Greenup, and William Meriwether.   [1244]

1813 Aug. 8 [Date received, Aug. 7]. RANDOLPH JEFFERSON, Snowden, to T. J., Monticello. ALS. 1 p. Endorsed by T. J. Carr-Cary Papers. Printed: Mayo 33.

Requests loan of $40. Inquires about servant Fanny's progress in learning to spin.   [1245]

1813 Aug. 8. T. J., Monticello, to RANDOLPH JEFFERSON, Snowden. ALS. 1 p. File draft. Endorsed by T. J. Carr-Cary Papers. Printed: Mayo 34.

Borrowed money for Randolph Jefferson. Poor year for corn, wheat, and livestock. Progress of Randolph's servant in spinning. Advises that he wait to sell his wheat until winter drives off blockading ships.   [1246]

1813 Aug. 16. PETER MINOR, Ridgeway, to T. J., Monticello. ALS. 1 p.
Thanking Jefferson for his aid in getting Minor the position of principal assessor.   [1247]

1813 Aug. 27. T. J., Poplar Forest, to ARCHIBALD ROBERTSON, Lynchburg. ALS. 1 p. File draft. Endorsed by T. J. McGregor Library.
Sends draft on Gibson & Jefferson. Last year's flour sold at low price due to blockade. Poor crops this year. Order for sugar, tea, molasses, and a clamp for a dry rubbing brush.   [1248]

1813 Aug. 28. BROWN & ROBERTSON, Lynchburg, Va., to T. J., Poplar Forest. ALS. 1 p. Endorsed by T. J. McGregor Library.
Receipt of draft on Gibson & Jefferson. Sending all articles except molasses.   [1249]

1813 Sept. 8. T. J., Poplar Forest, to RANDOLPH JEFFERSON, Snowden. ALS. 1 p. File draft. Carr-Cary Papers. Printed: Mayo 35.
Sends spinning jenny. Plans for visit with Randolph. Mentions Henry Flood, Noah Flood, and the Gibsons.   [1250]

1813 Sept. 11. T. J., Poplar Forest, to JOHN WAYLES EPPES. ALS. 8 pp. Printed: L & B XIII 353-368; Ford IX 395-403 n; B of R VI 143 (MS. in DLC).
Opinions on government finance, taxes, and debts. Must defray the expenses of the war in our own time. Bank paper must be suppressed and the circulating medium restored to the nation. Detailed consideration of the rate of interest on government loans. Reference to Francis Eppes.   [1251]

1813 Sept. 20. CHARLES L. BANKHEAD to T. J., Monticello. ALS. 1 p. Endorsed by T. J. Edgehill-Randolph Papers.
Requests hamper of charcoal to dry his malt.   [1252]

1813 Sept. 20. T. J., Monticello, to JAMES MARTIN. L. 2 pp. Extract by N. P. Trist ca. 1830. Printed: Ford IX 419-421; L & B XIII 381-384; B of R VI 316 (MS. in DLC).
Preference for shorter term for senators. Conduct of Federalists in Massachusetts in this crisis. Her secession would be followed by humiliating return to the union.   [1253]

1813 Oct. 10. JOHN BARNES, Georgetown, to T. J., Monticello. ALS. 2 pp. Endorsed by T. J. Edgehill-Randolph Papers.
Remittances to General Kosciuszko. Purchase of exchange from George Williams. Payment of order to J. Smith.   [1254]

1813 Oct. 19. JOHN BARNES, Georgetown, to T. J., Monticello. ALS. 2 pp. Endorsed by T. J. Edgehill-Randolph Papers.
Difficulties in purchasing a bill of exchange from George Williams on Russell & Morton.   [1255]

1813 Nov. 6. T. J., Monticello, to JOHN WAYLES EPPES. ALS. 20 pp. File draft [?]. Partly printed: L & B XIII 404-432; TJR IV 211-227; Ford IX 403-417 n; B of R VI 143 (MS. in DLC).

Opposition to re-establishment of the Bank of the U. S. Relative advantages of paper money and specie as media of exchange. General government should have sole right of establishing banks of discount *for paper*. Question of the public debt. References to Adam Smith and David Hume. (A cancelled paragraph dealing with the establishment of the Bank of the United States follows the first paragraph of this draft. It appears in none of the printed editions listed above.)   [1256]

1813 Nov. 7. T. J., Monticello, to JOSEPH C. CABELL, Williamsburg. ALS. 2 pp. Endorsed. Enclosure: AD. 1 p. Partly printed: Cabell 8-9; B of R VI 58 (MS. in DLC).

Bill to extend powers of the Rivanna Co. Requests return of Say's *Traité d'economie politique*. References to Col. [Nimrod] Bramham, [George] Divers, and Dabney Minor.   [1257]

1813 Nov. 10. JOHN BARNES, Georgetown, to T. J., Monticello. ALS. 2 pp. Endorsed by T. J. Edgehill-Randolph Papers.

Purchase of bill of exchange from George Williams; acknowledgement by General Kosciuszko of money received from Russell & Morton.   [1258]

1813 Nov. 11. T. J., Monticello, to THOMAS HORNSBY, Shellbyville, Ky. ALS. 3 pp. File draft. Endorsed by T. J. McGregor Library.

Requests that he meet with Gov. Christopher Greenup to adjust the differences regarding confirmation of Frances Henderson Hornsby's deed for her share of the Bennett Henderson estate, a deed made while she was a minor. References to James L. Henderson, Eliza Henderson, Elizabeth Henderson, John Henderson, and Craven Peyton.   [1259]

1813 Nov. 29. JOSEPH C. CABELL, Williamsburg, to T. J., Monticello. ALS. 2 pp. Endorsed by T. J. Deposited by Philip B. Campbell. Printed: Cabell 10-12.

Bill concerning T. J. and the Rivanna River Co. will pass the Virginia Assembly. Disagrees with T. J. on the length of the charter. Prefers Jean Baptiste Say's book on political economy to Adam Smith's.   [1260]

1813 Dec. 6. T. J., [Monticello], to BARON ALEXANDER VON HUMBOLDT. ALS. 4 pp. Photostat. Original, New York, private collection. Printed: Ford IX 430-433; L & B XIV 20-25; B of R VI 224 (MS. in DLC).

Acquaintance with José Correa da Serra. Receipt of Von Humboldt's books on astronomical observations and on New Spain. Revolutions in Latin America may lead to military despotisms. Important that American governments be separated from the "broils of Europe". Unprincipled policy of England has prevented a peaceful policy with the Indians. Brutalization and extermination of Indians compared to treatment of Ireland. British Arrowsmith and American Pike guilty of plagiarism. Delay in the publication of the journal of the Lewis and Clark expedition. Gift of tobacco seed to Von Humboldt.   [1261]

1813 Dec. 8. JOSEPH C. CABELL, Richmond, to T. J., Monticello. ALS. 1 p.
Endorsed by T. J. Deposited by Philip B. Campbell. Printed: Cabell 12-13.
  Books forwarded through General Moore. Reelection of Governor Barbour
expected despite discontent throughout the state. Consultation with Charles
Everett and Jesse W. Garth relative to the petition of the Rivanna River Co.
                                                                    [1262]

1813 Dec. 12. JOHN BARNES, Georgetown, to T. J., Monticello. ALS. 2 pp.
Endorsed by T. J. Edgehill-Randolph Papers.
  Remittance to General Kosciuszko via George Williams and Morton & Russell
is not possible. Congratulations on Thomas M. Randolph, Jr.'s safe return.
                                                                    [1263]

1813 Dec. 25. ELIZABETH HENDERSON. DEPOSITION. ADS. 1 p. Endorsed
by T. J. McGregor Library.
  Deposition denying knowledge of sale of her daughter's property to Craven
Peyton by James L. Henderson until several years after the transaction.   [1264]

1813 Dec. 28. T. J., Monticello, to CHARLES CLAY. ALS. 1 p. McGregor
Library. Printed: B of R VI 86 (MS. in DLC).
  Price of Mr. Forbes' wool-carding and cotton-carding machines.   [1265]

1813 Dec. 30. DABNEY MINOR, Albemarle County, to JOSEPH C. CABELL,
Richmond. ALS. 1 p. Endorsed. Printed: Cabell 10.
  Agreement between T. J. and the Rivanna Company directors that bill be
passed. References to [Charles] Everett and E. Garth.   [1266]

*1813. T. J., Poplar Forest, to CHARLES JOHNSTON. ALS. 1 p. File draft.
Endorsed by T. J. Edgehill-Randolph Papers.
  Apologizing for his inability to pay his bond. References to [Burgess] Griffin.
                                                                    [1267]

1813. [W. & R. MITCHELL]. ACCOUNTS AGAINST T. J. D. 2 items. One
endorsed by T. J. Edgehill-Randolph Papers.
  Accounts of the milling of the Poplar Forest wheat crop.   [1268]

1814 Jan. 9. THOMAS HORNSBY, Shelbyville, Ky., to T. J., Monticello. ALS.
3 pp. Endorsed by T. J. McGregor Library.
  Sends Elizabeth Henderson's deposition regarding the shares of the minor
children of Bennett Henderson. Asks about John Henderson's mill race. Value
of land mortgaged to Craven Peyton as security for property near Big Bone Lick,
Ky., he purchased from James L. Henderson in Virginia. References to William
Meriwether and Christopher Greenup.   [1269]

1814 Jan. 16. T. J., Monticello, to THOMAS COOPER. L. 3 pp. Copy by Ellen
Randolph. Printed: L & B XIV 54-63 (minor variations); B of R VI 95 (MS.
in DLC).
  Congratulates him on his edition of Justinian's *Institutes,* but wishes he had
put his time into Bracton's *De Legibus Angliae.* Would like to see Blackstone's
work supplemented by specification of particular cases of which his principles
are the essence. Cannot give name of author of *Commentary on Montesquieu*
[Destutt de Tracy]; manuscript now in T. J.'s hands.   [1270]

1814 Jan. 17. T. J., Monticello, to JOSEPH C. CABELL. ALS. 2 pp. Endorsed. Printed: Cabell 13-16; L & B XIV 67-70; B of R VI 58 (MS. in DLC).

Encloses letters written to John Wayles Eppes regarding public debt, banks, and money. Advises gradual reduction of paper money in Virginia. Favors division of state into hundreds or wards. [1271]

1814 Jan. 23. JOSEPH C. CABELL, Richmond, to T. J., Monticello. ALS. 3 pp. Endorsed by T. J. Deposited by Philip B. Campbell. Printed: Cabell 16-18.

Expresses limited approval of a state banking system. Voted for chartering Bank of Virginia. Restriction of the residence of a member of the House of Representatives to the district from which he was elected. Bill respecting the Rivanna River Company. Reasons for the division of state into wards. [1272]

1814 Jan. 31. T. J., Monticello, to JOSEPH C. CABELL, Richmond. ALS. 2 pp. Endorsed. Printed: Cabell 19-21; Ford IX 451-453; L & B XIV 82-85; TJR IV 238-239; B of R VI 58 (MS. in DLC).

Receipt of Say's *Traité d'economie politique*. Opinions as to whether states may prescribe any qualifications for members of Congress not contained in the Constitution. Line of demarcation between powers of the state and national governments. Maintains an interest in only two subjects: public education, and the division of counties into wards or hundreds. [1273]

1814 Feb. 3. T. J., Monticello, to JEREMIAH GOODMAN, Poplar Forest. ALS. 1 p. Deposited from Monticello.

Remittance through Patrick Gibson of Richmond. Instructions for sowing clover, shipment of beef and tobacco, rationing of salt. No flour sold. Orders to kill all dogs in excess of two, since they are taxable. [1274]

1814 Feb. 5. JOSEPH C. CABELL, Richmond, to T. J., Monticello. ALS. 3 pp. Endorsed by T. J. Deposited by Philip B. Campbell. Printed: Cabell 21-23.

Assembly's action on residence requirements for Congressmen. Passage of the Rivanna River Company bill in form agreed upon by T. J. and [Dabney] Minor. Bill to charter bank at Wheeling. [1275]

1814 Feb. 9. JOHN BARNES, Georgetown, to T. J., Monticello. ALS. 1 p. Endorsed by T. J. Edgehill-Randolph Papers.

Inability to make remittance to George Williams for General Kosciuszko. [1276]

1814 Feb. 11. JOHN BARNES, Georgetown, to T. J., Monticello. ALS. 4 pp. Endorsed by T. J. Edgehill-Randolph Papers.

Confidence in the credit of the Bank of Pennsylvania; opposes disposal of General Kosciuszko's bank stock. Beneficial results of banks overshadow their evils. [1277]

1814 Feb. 23. T. J., Monticello, to JOHN BARNES, Georgetown. ALS. 1 p. Endorsed. Photostat. Original owned by Wayne M. Hart.

Orders to convert Kosciuszko's stock in the Bank of Pennsylvania to government stock. Lack of confidence in banks. Failure of the Manhattan Bank. [1278]

1814 Feb. 27. JOHN BARNES, Georgetown, to T. J., Monticello. ALS. 2 pp. Endorsed by T. J. Edgehill-Randolph Papers.

Conversion of General Kosciuszko's shares in the Bank of Pennsylvania to government stock. Remittance to General K. Importance of stopping the increase of banks. Effect of the failure of the Bank of Manhattan on other banks.
[1279]

1814 Mar. 6. JOSEPH C. CABELL, Carysbrook, to T. J., Monticello. ALS. 1 p. Endorsed by T. J. Deposited by Philip B. Campbell. Printed: Cabell 24.

Return of T. J.'s letters on banking and finance which have been shown to William C. Rives, [John?] Tucker, Thomas Ritchie, and [John H.] Cocke.   [1280]

1814 Mar. 8. JOHN BARNES, Georgetown, to T. J., Monticello. ALS. 2 pp. Endorsed by T. J. Edgehill-Randolph Papers.

Considers transfer of T. J.'s and General Kosciuszko's Bank of Pennsylvania stock into loan office certificates unwise.   [1281]

1814 Mar. 25. THOMAS J. RANDOLPH, Carysbrook, to T. J. ALS. 1 p. Endorsed by T. J. Edgehill-Randolph Papers.

Mr. Cary [Wilson J. Cary? Wilson M. Cary?] not at home.   [1282]

1814 Apr. 5. JOHN BARNES, Georgetown, to T. J., Monticello. ALS. 3 pp. Endorsed by T. J. Edgehill-Randolph Papers.

Figures proving Bank of Pennsylvania stock is preferable to loan office certificates.   [1283]

1814 Apr. 7 [date received]. PETER CARR to T. J., Monticello. ALS. 1 p. Endorsed by T. J. Carr-Cary Papers.

Introducing the son of Dr. John D. Orr, a student of [Louis H.] Girardin.
[1284]

1814 Apr. 16. JOHN BARNES, Georgetown, to T. J., Monticello. ALS. 3 pp. Endorsed by T. J. Edgehill-Randolph Papers.

More facts to prove it is preferable to keep General Kosciuszko's Bank of Pennsylvania stock rather than converting to government stock.   [1285]

1814 Apr. 19. T. J., Monticello, to JOHN H. COCKE, Bremo. ALS. 1 p. Endorsed. Cocke Papers. Printed: B of R VI 89 (MS. in DLC).

Offers to purchase a dark bay horse. Payment to be made after repeal of embargo permits sale of flour by Gibson & Jefferson. (Payment noted by Cocke's endorsement).   [1286]

1814 Apr. 27. JOHN BARNES, Georgetown, to T. J., Monticello. ALS. 2 pp. Endorsed by T. J. Edgehill-Randolph Papers.

Payment to General Armstrong for articles he forwarded for T. J. Madison has left for Montpelier. Reference to Mr. Harper and the Cossack dinners.
[1287]

1814 May 2. JOHN BARNES, Georgetown, to T. J., Monticello. ALS. 3 pp. Endorsed by T. J. Edgehill-Randolph Papers.

Agrees to conversion of General Kosciuszko's shares of Bank of Pennsylvania stock into government stock. Requests letter of introduction to James Monroe or to William H. Crawford in order to get a bill of exchange for remittance to General Kosciuszko.   [1288]

1814 May 2. JOHN BARNES, Georgetown, to T. J., Monticello. ALS. 1 p. Endorsed by T. J. Edgehill-Randolph Papers.
  Purchase of government stock for General Kosciuszko. Reference to the Bank of Columbia.   [1289]

1814 May 13. JOHN BARNES, Georgetown, to T. J., Monticello. ALS. 1 p. Endorsed by T. J. Edgehill-Randolph Papers.
  Exchange of Kosciuszko's Bank of Pennsylvania stock for loan office certificates. Letter from Mr. Taylor regarding bank stock, government stock, and bills of exchange.   [1290]

1814 May 18. JOHN BARNES, Georgetown, to T. J., Monticello. ALS. 2 pp. Endorsed by T. J. Edgehill-Randolph Papers.
  Sale of Kosciuszko's bank stock; purchase of government stock.   [1291]

1814 May 24. JOHN BARNES, Georgetown, to T. J., Monticello. ALS. 3 pp. Endorsed by T. J. Edgehill-Randolph Papers.
  Sale of Kosciuszko's Bank of Pennsylvania stock. Remittance to Kosciuszko. Barnes in debt to purchase the General's government stock.   [1292]

1814 June 14. T. J. in account with W. & R. MITCHELL. D. 1 p. Edgehill-Randolph Papers.
  Bill for flour.   [1293]

1814 June 16. JOHN BARNES, Georgetown, to T. J., Monticello. ALS. 3 pp. Endorsed by T. J. Edgehill-Randolph Papers.
  Sale of Kosciuszko's bank stock finally completed. Remittance to the General through Baring Brothers of London. Difficult trip from Philadelphia.   [1294]

1814 June 21. T. J., Poplar Forest, to ARCHIBALD ROBERTSON, Lynchburg. ALS. 1 p. File draft. Endorsed by T. J. McGregor Library.
  Unable to meet payments since last year's flour unsold and bad drought this year. Peace or neutral commerce will help the growing crop. Plans tobacco crop. Mentions Patrick Gibson.   [1295]

1814 June 22. JOHN BARNES, Georgetown, to T. J., Monticello. ALS. 1 p. Endorsed by T. J. Edgehill-Randolph Papers.
  Purchase of bill of exchange to send remittance to General Kosciuszko. Encloses account with T. J. Mentions Mr. Nourse.   [1296]

1814 June 22. T. J., Poplar Forest, to ARCHIBALD ROBINSON [ROBERTSON], Lynchburg. ALS. 1 p. File draft. Endorsed by T. J. McGregor Library.
  Patrick Gibson is remitting money due to Jeremiah A. Goodman through Robertson. Order for sugar.   [1297]

1814 June 22. ARCHIBALD ROBERTSON, Lynchburg, to T. J., Poplar Forest. ALS. 1 p. Endorsed by T. J. McGregor Library.

Hopes for payment from T. J. Will make remittance to Jeremiah Goodman.
[1298]

1814 June 24. T. J., Monticello, to JOHN WAYLES EPPES. L. 4 pp. Extract by Joseph C. Cabell. Cabell Papers.

Importance of loans and taxes going hand-in-hand. Paper money should be issued by government and backed by taxes, not by banks.   [1299]

1814 June 27. JOHN BARNES, Georgetown, to T. J., Monticello. ALS. 2 pp Endorsed by T. J. Edgehill-Randolph Papers.

Bowie & Kurtz' bill of exchange on William Murdock given to James Monroe to be transmitted to Baring Brothers for General Kosciuszko. Desire for peace among Federalists.   [1300]

1814 July 7. JOHN BARNES, Georgetown, to T. J., Monticello. ALS. 4 pp. Endorsed by T. J. Edgehill-Randolph Papers.

Remittances to Kosciuszko. Difficulties encountered and expenses incurred in conversion of Kosciuszko's bank of Pennsylvania stock into government stock. Notes that Kosciuszko's capital is increased but interest reduced by this transaction.   [1301]

1814 July 13. JOHN BARNES, Georgetown, to T. J., Monticello. ALS. 4 pp. Endorsed by T. J. Edgehill-Randolph Papers.

Growth of Philadelphia. Criticism of a gentleman not named. Great Britain's jealousy of our liberty and wealth.   [1302]

1814 July 29. JOHN BARNES, Georgetown, to T. J., Monticello. ALS. 3 pp. Endorsed by T. J. Edgehill-Randolph Papers.

Remittance to General Kosciuszko. Payment for his government stock. Result of the commissioners at Ghent awaited. Inability of Britain to subjugate the United States. References to James Monroe, Mr. Pleisentson (of Mr. Monroe's office), and William H. Crawford.   [1303]

1814 July. JOHN BARNES, Georgetown, to T. J., Monticello. ALS. 3 pp. Edgehill-Randolph Papers.

Visit from Mr. Taylor. Mr. S.'s house has fallen under the hammer of the auctioneer. Outcome of the war. Reference to Etienne Le Maire.   [1304]

1814 Aug. 5. T. J., Monticello, to JOHN HARTWELL COCKE, Bremo. ALS. 1 p. Endorsed. Printed: B of R VI 89 (MS. in DLC).

Unable to pay for horse by order on Gibson & Jefferson because flour not sold. Hopes for peace.   [1305]

1814 Aug. 14. PETER CARR, Carr's Brook, to T. J., Monticello. ALS. 2 pp. Endorsed by T. J. Carr-Cary Papers.

Meeting of the committee consisting of John Winn, James Leitch, John Nicholas, [Frank] Carr, and Alexander Garrett, for viewing sites for Albemarle Academy.   [1306]

1814 Aug. 16. JOHN BARNES, Georgetown, to T. J., Monticello. ALS. 2 pp. Endorsed by T. J. Edgehill-Randolph Papers.

Requesting remittance from T. J. to cover installment due on General Kosciuszko's government bonds. Defense of Washington against the British. [1307]

1814 Aug. 22. T. J., Monticello, to THOMAS HORNSBY, Kentucky. ALS. 1 p. File draft. Endorsed by T. J. McGregor Library.

Requests papers regarding Elizabeth Henderson's dower rights in the Bennett Henderson estate, especially with regard to John Henderson's mill race. Needs to repel fraudulent claim of [David] Michie. Mentions James L. Henderson and Christopher Greenup. [1308]

1814 Aug. 24. T. J., Monticello, to DABNEY CARR. ALS. 1 p. File draft. Endorsed by T. J. Carr-Cary Papers.

Depositions in the question between T. J. and [David] Michie. Flood damage suffered by Peter Carr, Samuel Carr, and Peter Minor. Danger to Washington. Hopes for peace. [1309]

1814 Aug. 29. JOHN BARNES, Georgetown, to T. J., Monticello. ALS. 4 pp. Endorsed by T. J. Edgehill-Randolph Papers.

Failure of Patrick Gibson to remit to Barnes in time to make payment on General Kosciuszko's government stock. Retreat of our army from Bladensburg through Washington and Georgetown. President's encouragement of troops. Barnes deserted by Mrs. Ratcliffe and the servants. [1310]

1814 Aug. 29. DANIEL F. CARR, Charlottesville, to T. J., Monticello. ALS. 1 p. Endorsed by T. J. Carr-Cary Papers.

Request for money. (Endorsed by T. J.: "gave ord. on Gibson & Jefferson for 50 D.") [1311]

1814 Aug. 29. T. J., Monticello, to DANIEL F. CARR, Charlottesville. ALS. 1 p. File draft. Endorsed by T. J. Carr-Cary Papers.

Order on Gibson & Jefferson of Richmond. [1312]

1814 Aug. 29. T. J., Monticello, to SAMUEL CARR. ALS. 1 p. File draft. Endorsed by T. J. Carr-Cary Papers.

Requesting that Roland Goodman be excused from military duty because of consumption. [1313]

1814 Sept. 7. T. J., Monticello, to PETER CARR. ALS. 8 pp. File draft. Printed: L & B XIX 211-221; Cabell 384-390; Niles Register X 34-35; Joseph C. Cabell Sundry Documents on a System of Public Education 12-18; B of R VI 71 (MS. in DLC).

Plans for public education throughout the state providing elementary schools for all, with general college and professional schools for scholars. Elaborate discussion of the curriculum for Albemarle Academy. [1314]

1814 Sept. 17. JOSEPH C. CABELL, Warminster, to T. J., Monticello. ALS. 3 pp. Endorsed by T. J. Deposited by Philip B. Campbell. Printed: Cabell 24-27.

Preparations for defense of Richmond against the British. Lack of money in treasury at Washington and Richmond. Loans from Bank of Virginia and from the Farmers' Bank to the state. Stopping of specie payment in these banks. Suggests Colonel Nicholas as next governor.   [1315]

1814 Sept. 23. T. J., Monticello, to JOSEPH C. CABELL. ALS. 3 pp. Endorsed. Printed: Cabell 27-30.

Congress should have sole right of emission of paper money, based on taxation. But approves state auditors issuing certificates of indebtedness which will pass as currency until Congress shall undertake these measures.   [1316]

1814 Sept. 30. T. J., Monticello, to JOSEPH C. CABELL, Richmond. ALS. 1 p. Endorsed. Printed: Cabell 30-31; L & B XIV 199; B of R VI 58 (MS. in DLC).

Disapproves of depositing in the bank money from sale of glebe lands and from the Literary Fund.   [1317]

[1814 Sept.]. MR. S[TACK] to T. J., Monticello. ALS. 1 p. Endorsed.

Regulations proposed for Albemarle Academy regarding tardiness, recitations, deportment, morals, and property damage.   [1318]

1814 Oct. 11. JOHN BARNES, Georgetown, to T. J., Monticello. ALS. 3 pp. Endorsed by T. J. Edgehill-Randolph Papers.

Banking crisis due to failure of Northern and Southern banks to cooperate. Failure of the late public loan. Confidence in final victory. Good fortune in transferring General Kosciuszko's bank stock into government stock.   [1319]

1814 Oct. 15. T. J., Monticello, to JAMES MADISON. L. 3 pp. Copy sent to Joseph C. Cabell with letter of 16 October. Printed: Ford IX 489-492; L & B XIV 202-207; B of R VI 309 (MS. in DLC).

Opinions on what should be our object in the war with Great Britain. Paper money emissions.   [1320]

1814 Oct. 16. T. J., Monticello, to JOSEPH C. CABELL, Richmond. ALS. 1 p. Endorsed. Enclosure: L. 3 pp. Copy. Printed: Cabell 31; B of R VI 58 (MS. in DLC).

Encloses copy of letter to James Madison regarding public finance.   [1321]

1814 Oct. 19. JOSEPH C. CABELL, Richmond, to T. J., Monticello. ALS. 1 p. Endorsed by T. J. Deposited by Philip B. Campbell. Printed: Cabell 32.

Issuing of state certificates to bolster public credit.   [1322]

1814 Oct. 23. T. J., Monticello, to JOHN HARTWELL COCKE. ALS. 1 p. Endorsed. Printed: B of R VI 89 (MS. in DLC).

Payment for horse. Expects long war. Reliance on militia.   [1323]

1814 Oct. 27. PATRICK GIBSON, Richmond, to T. J., Bedford County. ALS. 1 p. Endorsed by T. J. Edgehill-Randolph Papers.

Renewal of a note. Letter forwarded to T. J. through Samuel J. Harrison.
                                                                          [1324]

1814 Nov. 11. W and R. MITCHELL, Lynchburg, to T. J. ALS. 1 p. Endorsed by T. J. Edgehill-Randolph Papers.

Enclosing an account with balance due the Mitchells.   [1325]

1814 Nov. 11. ARCHIBALD ROBERTSON, Lynchburg, to T. J., Poplar Forest. ALS. 1 p. Endorsed by T. J. McGregor Library.

Will pay draft on Patrick Gibson to Mr. Clayter. Requests payment of account if possible.   [1326]

1814 Nov. 23. FRANCIS EPPES, Mill Brook, to T. J., Monticello. ALS. 1 p. Endorsed by T. J. Edgehill-Randolph Papers.

Inability to go to school. Wishes to see T. J.   [1327]

1814 Nov. 23. T. J., Monticello, to FRANCIS WALKER GILMER. ALS. 1 p. Endorsed. Another MS. in MHi. Printed: Davis, *Francis Walker Gilmer* 78.

Letter for Dr. Caspar Wistar. Hopes Gilmer will live permanently in Virginia where he will be without rivals in public life.   [1328]

1814 Dec. 2. WILLIAM MITCHELL. ESTIMATE for T. J. D. 1 p. Endorsed by T. J. Edgehill-Randolph Papers.

Mitchell's terms, per John McAllister, for grinding Jefferson's wheat.   [1329]

1814 Dec. 6. JOHN BARNES, Georgetown, to T. J., Monticello. ALS. 2 pp. Endorsed by T. J. Edgehill-Randolph Papers.

Copy of letter from Baring Brothers & Co., London, acknowledging acceptance of a bill of exchange on William Murdock in favor of General Kosciuszko. Barnes hopes the national credit will be upheld.   [1330]

1814 Dec. 18. JOHN BARNES, Georgetown, to T. J., Monticello. ALS. 1 p. Endorsed by T. J. Edgehill-Randolph Papers.

Scrip certificates left with [Joseph] Nourse to purchase government stock. Requests power of attorney to receive dividends.   [1331]

1814 Dec. 27. JOSEPH C. CABELL, Richmond, to T. J., Monticello. ALS. 3 pp. Endorsed by T. J. Deposited by Philip B. Campbell. Printed: Cabell 32-35.

Tracy's work on political economy. Possible solutions of the problems of financing the state government: loan from the Farmer's Bank; issuance of treasury notes by the state; or a private loan by citizens. Thomas Mann Randolph's petition to open the falls near Milton and charge tolls on traffic conflicts with the Rivanna River Charter. References to Charles Yancey and William Wood.   [1332]

1814 Dec. 29. RANDOLPH JEFFERSON to T. J., Monticello. ALS. 1 p. Endorsed by T. J. Carr-Cary Papers. Printed: Mayo 36.

Asks that watch and dog be sent by Stephen. Mentions Thomas Mann Randolph, Jr.   [1333]

[1814]. MR. STACK to T. J. AD. 1 p. Endorsed by T. J.
Proposed course of classical education for Albemarle Academy.   [1334]

1815 Jan. 5. T. J., Monticello, to JOSEPH C. CABELL, Richmond. ALS. 3 pp. Endorsed. Printed: Cabell 35-38; Ford IX 499-501; B of R VI 58 (MS. in DLC).

Paper money. Destutt de Tracy's *Review of Montesquieu.* Jean Baptiste Say plans to come to the U. S. Sends papers regarding petition of Albemarle

Academy and on public education throughout the state. Defensive war with the Rivanna Co. Mentions Peter Carr, Thomas Cooper, William Duane, Francis W. Gilmer, [Joseph] Milligan, printer of Georgetown, Thomas Mann Randolph, Jr., and William Cabell Rives.   [1335]

1815 Jan. 6. T. J., Monticello, to JEREMIAH A. GOODMAN, Poplar Forest. ALS. 2 pp. Photostat. Original owned by Mrs. Laird U. Park.

Receipt of hogs and wheat very unsatisfactory. Sends plows, bottled beer, and wool by Dick. Urges better care of his sheep. Mr. Watkins to make a wheat machine for T. J. Intermarriage among T. J.'s servants. Phill not to be punished for running away. Urgent that tobacco be sent to Richmond. References to [William] Mitchell, [Archibald] Robertson, and to the following servants: Phill, Hanah, Dick, Nanny, Reuben, Daniel, and Stephen.   [1336]

1815 Jan. 10. JOHN BARNES, Georgetown, to T. J., Monticello. ALS. 1 p. Endorsed by T. J. Edgehill-Randolph Papers.

Public stock in T. J.'s name belonging to General Kosciuszko.   [1337]

1815 Jan. 31. T. J., Monticello, to WILLIAM PLUMER. L. 1 p. Extract by N. P. Trist *ca.* 1830. Printed: L & B XIV 235-238; B of R VI 376 (MS. in DLC).

Thanks for Plumer's pamphlet. Treasonable action of Massachusetts.   [1338]

1815 Feb. 2. PETER CARR, Carr's Brook, Va., to T. J., Monticello. ALS. 6 pp. (including 5 pp. enclosure). Endorsed by T. J. Carr-Cary Papers.

Severe attack of rheumatism. Requests supply of port or claret. Copy of his will, dated 16 January 1815. Property to his wife, Hetty Smith Carr, for life, then divided among his children at her discretion. Specific bequests to his sisters Cary Carr, Mary Carr, to his nieces, Martha, Lucy Ann, Virginia, and Mary Jane Terrell, brothers, Samuel Carr and Dabney Carr, step-son, George P. Stevenson, son, Dabney Carr, nephew, Dabney Terrell. Recommends the advice of Wilson C. Nicholas. Witnessed by Christopher Hudson, Dabney Minor, and Virginia Terrell. Memorandum attached concerning sum owed by Robert Carter Nicholas and provisions for adjustment of estate between Ellen B. Carr, Dabney S. Carr, Jane M. Carr, and George P. Stevenson.   [1339]

1815 Feb. 13. RANDOLPH JEFFERSON, Snowden, to T. J., Monticello. ALS. 2 pp. Endorsed by T. J. Carr-Cary Papers. Printed: Mayo 37.

Sending Squire for dog. Requests return of his watch. Asks for scions of fruit trees and for vegetable seeds. Expects to be summoned in [Thomas Mann?] Randolph and Craven Peyton's suit.   [1340]

1815 Feb. 16. T. J., Monticello, to RANDOLPH JEFFERSON, Snowden. ALS. 1 p. File draft. Endorsed by T. J. Carr-Cary Papers. Printed: Mayo 38.

Sending watch, dog, vegetable seeds. Directions for the vegetables. Peace confirmed. Effect on wheat, tobacco, and corn prices.   [1341]

1815 Mar. 5. JOSEPH C. CABELL, Warminster, to T. J., Monticello. ALS. 4 pp. Endorsed by T. J. Deposited by Philip B. Campbell. Printed: Cabell 38-41.

Petition regarding the setting up of an academy in Albemarle County;

possible effect on William and Mary College. Hopes it will induce such men as Jean Baptiste Say to reside in Virginia. Disposition of his slaves from Corotoman taken by the British. References to Dr. [Charles?] Carr, Peter Carr, Admiral Cockburn, John A. Smith, Destutt de Tracy, David Watson, and Charles Yancey. [1342]

1815 Mar. 14. T. B. GREER. RECEIPT to T. J. D. 1 p. Endorsed by T. J. McGregor Library.

Bedford County tax receipts, by William Salmon for Greer. [1343]

1815 Mar. 17. T. J., Monticello, to HENRY DEARBORN. ALS. 3 pp. Endorsed. Photostat. Original owned by H. J. Coolidge. Printed: L & B XIV 287-289; Randall III 399; TJR IV 257-258.

Pleasure over the victory of New Orleans and the Peace of Ghent. Mentions the treason of William Hull, Dearborn's victories at York and Fort George. Apostasy of Massachusetts in forsaking the counsel of the two Adams for that of Strong. Hopes for visit from Dearborn and Caesar Rodney. [1344]

1815 Mar. 31. T. J., Monticello, to T. J. RANDOLPH. ALS. 1 p. Endorsed by T. J. Edgehill-Randolph Papers. Printed: *Va. Mag. Hist.* XLVI 119.

Ellen's visit to Warren delayed by death of a horse. Mrs. Marks' visit to Randolph Jefferson. [1345]

1815 Apr. 1. DEED OF TRUST ON CARLTON. Charles Lewis Bankhead and Anne Cary Bankhead, to John Bankhead, Thomas Mann Randolph, Jr., and Reuben Lindsay, all of Albemarle County. DS (AD by T. J.). 4 pp. Endorsed by T. J. Witnessed by Edmund Bacon, W. Ballard, Robin Goodman, and T. J. Randolph. Recorded 1 May 1815 and again 5 August 1822 by Alexander Garrett, Clerk of Albemarle, and 12 August 1822 by John Pendleton, Clerk of Caroline. Carlton Papers.

Deed of trust to tract of land called Carlton and to 37 servants, and cattle, hogs, furniture, and dwelling; to be used to pay the creditors of Anne C. and Charles L. Bankhead, and thereafter for the maintenance of Anne and Charles. Mentions John Kelly, James Leitch, Molly Lewis, Robert Streshly, and John J. Taylor. [1346]

1815 Apr. 1. TRIPARTITE INDENTURE between T. J. on the first part, Anne Cary Bankhead on the second part, and John Bankhead of Caroline County, Thomas Mann Randolph, Jr., and Reuben Lindsay. ADS by T. J. 2 pp. Endorsed. Witnessed by Robin Goodman, Edmund Bacon, and W. Ballard. Recorded 1 May 1815 by Alexander Garrett, Clerk of Albemarle County Court. Carlton Papers.

Deed to land in Albemarle County, to be held in trust by Bankhead, Lindsay, and Randolph for the maintenance of Charles L. Bankhead, Anne C. Bankhead, and their children. [1347]

1815 Apr. 2. RANDOLPH JEFFERSON, Snowden, to T. J., Monticello. ALS. 1 p. Endorsed by T. J. Carr-Cary Papers. Printed: Mayo 39.

Arrival of Anna Scott Marks. Sale of land to Charles A. Scott to pay off debts. Will send fish when possible. Visit of Thomas J. Randolph and young Wilson Nicholas.   [1348]

1815 Apr. 22. JOHN BARNES, Georgetown, to T. J., Monticello. ALS. 1 p. Endorsed by T. J. Edgehill-Randolph Papers.
    Remittances to General Kosciusczko *via* Baring Brothers, London. Prefers English bills of exchange. Hopes the arranging and packing of T. J.'s library is completed.   [1349]

1815 Apr. 25. JOHN BARNES, Georgetown, to T. J., Monticello. ALS. 2 pp. Endorsed by T. J. Edgehill-Randolph Papers.
    Collection of T. J.'s order on the Treasury. Purchase of set of exchange on London to pay Kosciuszko. Rates of exchange.   [1350]

*1815 May 15. BENNETT H. HENDERSON, Glasgow, Barren County, Ky., to T. J., Monticello. ALS. 2 pp. Endorsed by T. J. McGregor Library.
    Requests private settlement of his share of Bennett Henderson estate, which his brother James L. Henderson deeded to Craven Peyton while Bennett H. Henderson was a minor. William D. Meriwether has full power of attorney.
                                                                         [1351]

1815 May 23. T. J., Poplar Forest, to ARCHIBALD ROBERTSON, Lynchburg. ALS. 1 p. File draft. Endorsed by T. J. McGregor Library.
    Refers to error in accounts, bond left by Mr. Garland. Will consult papers at home.   [1352]

1815 May 23. ARCHIBALD ROBERTSON, Lynchburg, to T. J., Poplar Forest. ALS. 1 p. Endorsed by T. J. McGregor Library.
    Money remitted to Jeremiah A. Goodman. Glad the error in Griffin's bond discovered.   [1353]

1815 May 25. JOHN BARNES, Georgetown, to T. J., Monticello. ALS. 3 pp. Endorsed by T. J. Edgehill-Randolph Papers.
    Remittance sent to General Kosciuszko, a bill of exchange of Bowie & Kurtz on William Murdock. Comments on Bonaparte's counter-revolution.   [1354]

1815 May 25. T. J., [Poplar Forest], to CHARLES CLAY. AL. 1 p. Endorsed. Deposited by C. S. Hutter, Jr.
    Overseer for Poplar Forest.   [1355]

1815 May 27. J. PENN, Lynchburg, to T. J., Poplar Forest. ALS. 1 p. Endorsed by T. J. McGregor Library.
    In Archibald Robertson's absence, he has exchanged T. J.'s Treasury bills for Virginia bills, a few of which not current. Mentions Jeremiah A. Goodman.   [1356]

1815 May 27. T. J., Poplar Forest, to ARCHIBALD ROBERTSON, Lynchburg. ALS. 1 p. File draft. Endorsed by T. J. McGregor Library.
    Requests exchange of Treasury bills for Virginia bills at par so he can pay

his neighbors who refuse to accept Treasury bills at par. Jeremiah A. Goodman mentioned. [1357]

1815 May 28. T. J., Poplar Forest, to J. PENN for ARCHIBALD ROBERTSON, Lynchburg. ALS. 1 p. File draft. McGregor Library.

Appreciates attention to his request. Reserves privilege of returning any bank notes unacceptable to cerditor; sends Treasury notes by Jeremiah A. Goodman. [1358]

1815 May 28. J. PENN, Lynchburg, to T. J., Poplar Forest. ALS. 1 p. Endorsed by T. J. McGregor Library.

Sends bills in return for treasury bills brought by Jeremiah A. Goodman: Virginia bills, Bank of Columbia, Bank of Alexandria, all pass currently, and a few others refused only by planters. [1359]

1815 June 1. T. J., Poplar Forest, to ARCHIBALD ROBERTSON, Lynchburg. ALS. 1 p. File draft. Endorsed by T. J. McGregor Library.

Financial arrangements with Mr. [Charles] Clay and Gibson & Jefferson. Joel Yancey to superintend T. J.'s overseers. [1360]

1815 June 1. ARCHIBALD ROBERTSON, Lynchburg, to T. J., Poplar Forest. ALS. 1 p. Endorsed by T. J. McGregor Library.

Acknowledges draft on Gibson & Jefferson. Congratulates T. J. on fact that Joel Yancey will superintend his affairs. [1361]

1815 June 23. T. J., Monticello, to RANDOLPH JEFFERSON. ALS. 1 p. File draft. Endorsed by T. J. Carr-Cary Papers. Printed: Mayo 40.

Requests return of gig harness. Mentions Anna Scott Marks. [1362]

1815 June 23. RANDOLPH JEFFERSON, Snowden, to T. J., Monticello. ALS. 1 p. Endorsed by T. J. Carr-Cary Papers. Printed: Mayo 41.

Harness worn out, sends another replacing it. Regrets Martha Carr's death. [1363]

1815 July 6. JOHN WAYLES EPPES, Mill Brook, to T. J., Monticello. ALS. 1 p. Endorsed by T. J. Edgehill-Randolph Papers.

Plans for education of Francis Eppes. Good corn and wheat crops. [1364]

1815 Aug. 6. M. A. C. MONROE, Salem, Ky., to T. J., Monticello. ALS. 2 pp. Endorsed by T. J. Edgehill-Randolph Papers.

To her dear uncle. Failure to hear from T. J. or Martha Randolph. Her recent marriage. Request that he send money by Mr. Woods. [1365]

1815 Aug. 9. DABNEY CARR, Winchester, to T. J., Monticello. ALS. 1 p. Endorsed by T. J. Carr-Cary Papers.

Will have depositions taken, leaving nothing to [David] Michie's honesty. Republicans pray for success of France. Reports of Wellington's victory. [1366]

1815 Aug. 25. T. J., Poplar Forest, to CHARLES CLAY. ALS. 1 p. Deposited by C. S. Hutter, Jr.

Request that Clay visit Poplar Forest amidst the noise of hammers, saws, and planes. [1367]

1815 Aug. 30. DAVID THOMPSON, [Bedford County], to T. J. ALS 1 p. Endorsed by T. J. Edgehill-Randolph Papers.

Timber sawed for T. J.   [1368]

1815 Sept. 15. T. J. DEPOSITION in suit between Mitchie B. Jefferson, widow of Randolph Jefferson, and Thomas Jefferson, Robert Lewis Jefferson, Field Jefferson, Isham Randolph Jefferson, and James Lilburne Jefferson, sons of said Randolph Jefferson. ADS. 3 pp. Carr-Cary Papers.

Declaration regarding his part in writing Randolph Jefferson's first will, and his belief that it was not Randolph's intention to change that will while in sound and healthy mind. Debts run up by Mrs. Jefferson, by writing forged orders. Mentions Mr. Moon and Mr. Johnson, storekeepers; Zachariah Pryor; Anna Scott Marks.   [1369]

1815 Sept. 23. JOHN JEFFERSON, Pittsylvania County, to T. J., Poplar Forest. ALS. 1 p. Endorsed by T. J. Carr-Cary Papers.

Introducing Arthur Hopkins, grandson of sister Judith. His suit against Colonel James settled out of court.   [1370]

1815 Sept. 28. T. J., Poplar Forest, to DR. SAMUEL K. JENNINGS. L. 1 p. Printed copy.

Recommendations, with reservations, of Dr. Jennings' steam bath. Printed in a pamphlet on the nature of the remedy effected by these steam baths, with letters and certificates of recommendation from many notables.   [1371]

1815 Oct. 3. JOEL YANCEY to CHARLES CLAY. DS. 1 p. Endorsed by T. J. Edgehill-Randolph Papers.

Note, as Jefferson's agent, for $97.75 (paid 29 April 1816).   [1372]

1815 Oct. 6. T. J., Monticello, to PATRICK GIBSON, Richmond. ALS. 1 p. Endorsed by T. J. Photostat. Original owned by Mrs. Virginius Dabney.

Renewal of his note. Sheriff's call for taxes soon to be met.   [1373]

1815 Oct. 13. T. J., Monticello, to DR. ROBERT PATTERSON, Philadelphia. ALS. 1 p. Photostat. Original, St. Anthony's Hall, University of Virginia.

Directions for packing and shipping time-piece to Gibson & Jefferson; expenses to be paid by [John] Vaughan. Requests one of Patterson's artificial horizons made of platinum.   [1374]

1815 Oct. 13. T. J., Monticello, to BENJAMIN WATERHOUSE. L. 1 p. Extract by N. P. Trist ca. 1830. Another MS. in DLC. Printed: Ford IX 532-533.

Mortification of Federalists at ridiculous issue of Hartford Convention. [1375]

1815 Oct. 20. T. J., Monticello, to PATRICK GIBSON, Richmond. ALS. 1 p. Photostat. Original owned by Mrs. Virginius Dabney.

Loan from the bank to pay taxes in Bedford County.   [1376]

1815 Oct. 22. SPENCER ROANE, Richmond, to T. J., Monticello. ALS. 2 pp.

File draft. Printed: *John P. Branch Papers* II No. 1, 131-132; B of R VIII 473 (MS. in DLC).

Receipt of T. J.'s letter regarding Roane's opinion in case of *Martin vs. Hunter*. Expresses respect for T. J.'s opinion as a real authority.   [1377]

1815 Oct. 28. T. J., Monticello, to JOHN BANKHEAD, Spring Grove. ALS. 2 pp. File draft. Endorsed by T. J. Edgehill-Randolph Papers.

Charles Bankhead a drunkard. Recommendations for possible treatment. References to Martha Randolph, Thomas Mann Randolph, Jr., and to Anne Randolph Bankhead.   [1378]

1815 Oct. 28. T. J., Monticello, to PATRICK GIBSON, Richmond. ALS. 1 p. Endorsed by T. J. Photostat. Original owned by Mrs. Virginius Dabney.

Renewal of his notes. Payment provided through flour from his mill and tobacco from Bedford. Payment of taxes to Clifton Harris, sheriff. Remittance to Joseph Milligan, bookseller. Order for cask of Lisbon, bale of cotton. [1379]

1815 Nov. 15. WILSON CARY NICHOLAS and THOMAS J. RANDOLPH, Albemarle. BOND to JOHN WAYLES EPPES, Rockingham County. DS. 1 p. Endorsed. Edgehill-Randolph Papers.

Bond for $5500. Payment of $2750 plus interest noted on verso, 15 November 1816.   [1380]

1815 Nov. 18. JOHN BARNES, Georgetown, to T. J., Monticello. ALS. 1 p. Endorsed by T. J. Edgehill-Randolph Papers.

Remittances to General Kosciuszko delayed by his moving to Switzerland. Reference to Baring Brothers & Co.   [1381]

1815 Nov. 18. T. J., Poplar Forest, to CHARLES CLAY. ALS. 1 p. Facsimile. Original owned by Samuel McVitty.

Observations made at the Peaks of Otter. Sends paper mullberries, charming near a porch for dense shade. Mentions [Bowling?] Clarke.   [1382]

1815 Dec. 11. JOHN WAYLES EPPES, Mill Brook, to T. J., Monticello. ALS. 1 p. Endorsed by T. J. Edgehill-Randolph Papers.

Continuation of Francis Eppes' education in French and Latin at Monticello.   [1383]

1815 Dec. 12. T. J., Poplar Forest, to ARCHIBALD ROBERTSON, Lynchburg. ALS. 1 p. File draft. Endorsed by T. J. McGregor Library.

Order on Gibson & Jefferson covers payment to Joel Yancey, Jeremiah A. Goodman, and Mr. Cooney.   [1384]

1815 Dec. 23. T. J., Monticello, to JOSEPH C. CABELL, Richmond. ALS. 2 pp. Endorsed by T. J. Printed: Cabell 41-42 (minor variations); B of R VI 58 (MS. in DLC).

Solicits Cabell's aid for claim of Capt. Joseph Miller, formerly of England, who prays confirmation of the will of his half-brother, Thomas Reed. Asks also the aid of Thomas W. Maury and Mr. Baker. Disapproves seizure of Miller's funds by the Literary Fund.   [1385]

[1815]. T. J. AN ACT FOR THE ESTABLISHING OF a College in the county of Albemarle . . . to be called CENTRAL COLLEGE . . . AD. 3 pp. File draft. Endorsed by T. J. Printed: Cabell 391-393 (variant).

College to be governed by a Board of Visitors who will appoint a treasurer and proctor, establish professorships, lay down rules of government and discipline, fix fees, and in general do what they deem necessary and proper. (Act was adopted February 1816).   [1386]

1816 Jan. 16. JOSEPH C. CABELL, Richmond, to T. J., Monticello. ALS. 3 pp. Endorsed by T. J. Deposited by Philip B. Campbell. Printed: Cabell 43-45.

Expects no opposition to Mr. Miller's petition. Some resistance to the bill for establishing Central College. Questioning of powers given the professors to imprison students. Possibility of a school for the deaf and dumb, taught by a Mr. Braidwood, to be attached to the college. Recommends enlisting the cooperation of Chapman Johnson, William G. Poindexter, Edward Watts and John W. Green of the Senate. References to [Peter] Carr, [Thomas W.] Maury, and [Charles] Yancey.   [1387]

1816 Jan. 19. JOHN BARNES, Georgetown, to T. J., Monticello. ALS. 1 p. Endorsed by T. J. Edgehill-Randolph Papers.

Remittance to General Kosciuszko, possibly through Baring Brothers.   [1388]

1816 Jan. 23. JOSEPH C. CABELL, Richmond, to T. J., Monticello. ALS. 3 pp. Endorsed by T. J. Deposited by Philip B. Campbell. Printed: Cabell 45-47.

Objections to the Central College bill. Papers in Captain Miller's case with respect to the Reed estate. Copy of the bill to prevent obstructions in the navigable watercourses of Virginia. Appropriations for Literary Fund and for endowment of a professorship for teaching the deaf and dumb. Dr. Smith asks recommendation of a textbook on the principles of government for use at William and Mary. References to Chapman Johnson, John Locke, Jean Jacques Rousseau, Jean Baptiste Say, and Charles Yancey.   [1389]

1816 Jan. 24. JOSEPH C. CABELL, Richmond, to T. J., Monticello. ALS. 2 pp. Endorsed by T. J. Deposited by Philip B. Campbell. Printed: Cabell 50-51; B of R VI 58 (MS. in DLC); Adams II 66-67.

Requests permission to publish T. J.'s letter to Peter Carr regarding the establishment of Central College. Possible locations: Charlottesville, Staunton, or Lexington. Move to shift seat of government to Staunton. References to [Charles F.] Mercer.   [1390]

1816 Jan. 24. T. J., Monticello, to JOSEPH C. CABELL, Richmond. ALS. 3 pp. Endorsed. Printed: Cabell 47-49; B of R. VI 58 (MS. in DLC).

Matters concerning Central College; duties of its Proctor; public school system; disapproves of connection of Mr. Braidwood's school for the deaf and dumb with the college; refuses to write about Central College to gentlemen named, because his correspondence too burdensome.   [1391]

1816 Jan. 27. T. J., Monticello, to PATRICK GIBSON, Richmond. ALS. 1 p. File draft. Endorsed by T. J. Photostat. Original owned by Mrs. Virginius Dabney.

Draft on Gibson in favor of T. J. Randolph, to be paid for by the sale of flour. [1392]

1816 Jan. 29. DABNEY CARR, Winchester, to T. J., Monticello. ALS. 1 p. Endorsed by T. J. Carr-Cary Papers.

If Louis Girardin's continuation of John Burk's history does not contain T. J.'s account of Dabney Carr, Sr., (writer's father), will turn it over for William Wirt's book. Proposed inscription for Carr's tombstone left in Philip Mazzei's book. [1393]

1816 Jan. 31. T. J., Monticello, to JOSEPH C. CABELL, Richmond. ALS. 1 p. Endorsed. Printed: Cabell 51.

Encloses conveyances for which Joseph Miller's bill is hung up. [1394]

1816 Feb. 2. T. J., Monticello, to JOSEPH C. CABELL, Richmond. ALS. 5 pp. Endorsed. (Also an extract by N. P. Trist, 4 pp.). Printed: Cabell 52-56; L & B XIV 417-423; B of R VI 58 (MS. in DLC).

Encloses list of acts and journals, copies of which are in his library purchased by Congress. Comments on the bill on the obstruction in navigable waters. Hopes he can retain his canal. Recomments Destutt de Tracy's *Review of Montesquieu,* to John A. Smith as best elementary book on government. Central College Bill. Public school system for Virginia. Division of powers between federal, state, and local governments. Stresses dividing counties into wards, where every man may take active part in his government. [1395]

1816 Feb. 12. JOHN BARNES, Georgetown, to T. J., Monticello. ALS. 2 pp. Endorsed by T. J. Edgehill-Randolph Papers.

Remittance to General Kosciuszko. Copy of letter from Kosciuszko to Barnes mentioning bills of exchange sent to Baring Brothers & Co. [1396]

1816 Feb. 14. JOSEPH C. CABELL, Richmond, to T. J. ALS. 1 p. Endorsed by T. J. Deposited by Philip B. Campbell. Printed: Cabell 56.

Passage of bill for Central College, Mr. Miller's bill, and the bill respecting navigable waters. Reference to [John W.] Green. [1397]

1816 Feb. 16. DABNEY C. TERRELL, Baltimore, to T. J., Monticello. ALS. 1 p. Endorsed by T. J. Carr-Cary Papers.

Sailing for France delayed by freezing of basin. [Thomas] Mann Randolph has promise of midshipman's warrant. Albert Gallatin's letters expected. Governor of Pennsylvania does not intend demanding him. Mentions Mr. Stevenson and Martha J. Randolph. [1398]

*1816 Feb. 18. JAMES LILBURNE JEFFERSON, Scott's Ferry, to T. J., Monticello. ALS. 2 pp. 2 enclosures. Endorsed by T. J.

Attempts to get money from father's estate so far unsuccessful. Has rented ferry; wishes to rent part of Snowden. Plans to travel west. Step-mother, Mitchie B. Jefferson, has removed to mother's house. Enclosures: two bills for cloth and stockings from James Leitch and Bramham & Jones, one endorsed by T. J.: "J Lilburne Jefferson."   [1399]

1816 Feb. 21. JOSEPH C. CABELL, Richmond, to T. J., Monticello. ALS. 4 pp. Endorsed by T. J. Deposited by Philip B. Campbell. Printed: Cabell 57-60.

Passage of Captain Miller's bill and of bill respecting navigable water; rejection of lottery bill to purchase Triplett Estis' property. Possible appropriation of U. S. surplus to Literary Fund. Modifications in Central College Bill respecting powers of college proctor, glebe lands, and the Literary Fund. Translation of Jean Baptiste Say's *Traité d'économie politique*. Mentions William Cabell, John W. Green, Chapman Johnson, Thomas W. Maury, and Wilson C. Nicholas.
                                                                        [1400]

1816 Feb. 23. JOHN BARNES, Georgetown, to T. J., Monticello. ALS. 1 p. Endorsed by T. J. Edgehill-Randolph Papers.

High rates of exchange prevent a remittance to Kosciuszko.   [1401]

1816 Feb. 26. JOSEPH C. CABELL, Richmond, to T. J., Monticello. ALS. 2 pp. Endorsed by T. J. Deposited by Philip B. Campbell. Printed: Cabell 60-61.

Publication of T. J.'s letter to Peter Carr. Appropriation of Virginia's U. S. Government stock to education. Presbyterians in Lexington and Scotch-Irish in Staunton will object to Albemarle as site for university since they hope to move seat of government to Staunton. Washington College at Lexington the bantling of the Federalists. Trouble with Colonel Monroe about caucus for an electoral ticket. References to Wilson C. Nicholas and [Charles F.] Mercer.
                                                                        [1402]

1816 Feb. 26. T. J. *vs.* SAMUEL SCOTT. D. 1 p. Endorsed by T. J. McGregor Library.

Statement to balance due T. J. (from Scott?) after payment of land tax in Campbell County.   [1403]

1816 Feb. 28. T. J., Monticello, to JOSEPH C. CABELL, Richmond. ALS. 1 p. Endorsed. Printed: Cabell 62.

Recommending that he translate Jean Baptiste Say's *Traite d'economie politique*. Mentions Destutt de Tracy's *Review of Montesquieu* and William Duane.
                                                                        [1404]

1816 Feb. 28. T. J., Monticello, to FRANCIS WALKER GILMER. ALS. 1 p. Endorsed. Printed: B of R X 7 (MS. in DLC).

Documents he worked out regarding Louisiana boundaries from the Perdido to the Rio Bravo is now in his library, recently purchased by Congress. A copy is in the State Department files; and the *Virginia Argus* printed a statement similar to this. A manuscript history of the settlement of the country by Bernard de la Harpe, proving the French claims to the Bravo as opposed to the Spanish, is in the State Department files. Manuscript found in possession of the family of the late Governor Messier. Mentions [Thomas?] Cooper, St. Denys Crosat.   [1405]

1816 Mar. 18 [date received]. FRANK CARR to T. J., Monticello. ALS. 1 p. Endorsed by T. J. Carr-Cary Papers.

Jefferson's man, Moses, at Farley's with broken leg. Cannot be moved. [1406]

1816 Mar. 21. JOHN BARNES, Georgetown, to T. J., Monticello. ALS. 3 pp. Endorsed by T. J. Edgehill-Randolph Papers.

Presentation of money to Ellen Randolph. Purchase of stock in the Farmer's and Mechanic's Bank from its cashier, C. Smith, for General Kosciuszko. Remittance to the General. Reference to Joseph Nourse.   [1407]

1816 Mar. GEORGE CABELL. ACCOUNT against T. J. D. 1 p. Endorsed by T. J. Edgehill-Randolph Papers.

Bill for bacon, corn, and carrying tobacco.   [1408]

1816 Apr. 2. T. J., Monticello, to WILSON C. NICHOLAS. L. 2 pp. Extract by N. P. Trist ca. 1830. Printed: L & B XIV 446-456; B of R VI 354 (MS. in DLC) ; Md. Hist. Mag. VII 419 (extract) .

Advantages of dividing counties into wards for administrative and educational purposes. Mentions letters to Joseph C. Cabell and John Adams.   [1409]

[1816] Apr. 19 [incorrectly dated 1815]. JAMES LILBURNE JEFFERSON, Warren, to T. J., Monticello. ALS. 1 p. Endorsed by T. J. Carr-Cary Papers.

Judge ill. Mr. Booker reported him unable to hold court to try Randolph Jefferson's will. All essential witnesses ready.   [1410]

1816 May 15. T. J., Monticello, to PATRICK GIBSON, Richmond. ALS. 1 p. Endorsed by T. J. Photostat. Original owned by Mrs. Virginius Dabney.

Sale of T. J.'s flour. Payment to Mr. Robertson and for taxes in Albemarle.   [1411]

1816 May 23. FRANK CARR, Charlottesville, to T. J., Monticello. AD. 1 p. Endorsed by T. J. Carr-Cary Papers.

Bill for medical services to servants 1813-1816, totaling $151.   [1412]

1816 May 31. JOHN BARNES, Georgetown, to T. J., Monticello. ALS. 2 pp. Endorsed by T. J. Edgehill-Randolph Papers.

Sale of Kosciuszko's treasury notes and purchase of bank stock. Remittance to Kosciuszko delayed by high exchange rates. Banking services offered to Ellen Randolph. President Madison's visit to Annapolis and naval review. Mentions Dolly P. Madison.   [1413]

1816 June 12. DABNEY C. TERRELL, Geneva, Switzerland, to T. J., Monticello. ALS. 2 pp. Endorsed by T. J. Carr-Cary Papers.

Describes trip through low countries and France. Education in Geneva with Marc Auguste Pictet. Report in Moniteur that Mexicans and South Americans losing. Desire to go to Spain. Regards to Martha Randolph.   [1414]

1816 July 4. JOSEPH C. CABELL, Warminster, to T. J., Monticello. ALS. 3 pp. Endorsed by T. J. Deposited by Philip B. Campbell. Printed: Cabell 62-65.

Maine's method of preparing hawthorne hedges is best. References to James

Henderson, Isaac Newton, Dobson's *Encyclopedia,* and Lord Karmes' translation of Say's *Traité d'économie politique.* Implementation of General Assembly act requiring an accurate map of each county.   [1415]

1816 July 13. T. J., Monticello, to JOSEPH C. CABELL, Warminster, Va. ALS. 2 pp. Endorsed. Printed: Cabell 65-66.

Thanks for Maine's recipe for preparing hawthorn. Discussion of relative merits of hedgethorn, hawthorn, holly, pyracanthus, cedar for hedges. Translation of Say's *Traité d'économie politique.* Recommends son of W. D. Meriwether for surveying (preparatory to Böye's Nine-Sheet Map).   [1416]

1816 July 14. T. J., Monticello, to JOSEPH C. CABELL, Warminster. ALS. 1 p. Endorsed. Printed: Cabell 67.

Encloses letter on his political ramblings.   [1417]

1816 July 18. JOHN BARNES, Georgetown, to T. J., Monticello. ALS. 2 pp. Endorsed by T. J. Edgehill-Randolph Papers.

Remittance to General Kosciuszko. Mentions James Monroe.   [1418]

1816 Aug. 4. JOSEPH C. CABELL, Edgewood, to T. J., Monticello. ALS. 4 pp. Endorsed by T. J. Deposited by Philip B. Campbell. Partly printed: Cabell 67-69.

Superiority of thorn hedges. Surveying for the map authorized by the Assembly (Herman Böye's Nine-Sheet Map). Advisability of a convention to amend the Virginia Constitution, favored by westerners desiring to place the pecuniary burdens of government on the easterners and by Federalist bank stockholders wishing to charter fifteen banks. Books by Montesquieu, Destutt de Tracy, and Say as textbooks at William and Mary. References to Philip Doddridge, Mr. Meriwether, Thomas Mann Randolph, Jr., and John Augustine Smith.   [1419]

*1816 Aug. 5. JOHN BARNES, Georgetown, to T. J., Monticello. ALS. 2 pp. Endorsed by T. J. Edgehill-Randolph Papers.

Account of General Kosciuszko's resources. Bill of exchange for the General sent to Baring Brothers & Co., London. Transferral of government stock into bank stock. Exchange bought from Smith & Biddle, Richmond, drawn by A. P. Heinrich, Baltimore, on John Rapp, London.   [1420]

1816 Aug. 10. JOHN BARNES, Georgetown, to T. J., Monticello. ALS. 1 p. Endorsed by T. J. Edgehill-Randolph Papers.

Transfer of General Kosciuszko's government stock into bank stock.   [1421]

1816 Sept. 3. T. J., Monticello, to JOSEPH C. CABELL. ALS. 1 p. Endorsed. Another MS. in MHi. Printed: Cabell 70.

Returns Cabell's papers. Requests his letter be kept out of public papers. [1422]

1816 Oct. 3. JOHN BARNES, Georgetown, to T. J., Monticello. ALS. 2 pp. Endorsed by T. J. Edgehill-Randolph Papers.

Difficulties in transferring Kosciuszko's stock into his own name. Request for powers of attorney from Kosciuszko and T. J. Collection of dividends from the Bank of Columbia. [1423]

1816 Oct. 14. T. J., Monticello, to JOHN BANKHEAD. ALS. 1 p. File draft. Endorsed by T. J. Edgehill-Randolph Papers.

Concerning Charles Bankhead's alcoholism and consequent insanity. His plantation going to ruin. Mentions Thomas Mann Randolph, Jr. [1424]

1816 Oct. 21. JOHN BARNES, Georgetown, to T. J., Monticello. ALS. 2 pp. Endorsed by T. J. Edgehill-Randolph Papers.

Receipt of T. J.'s and Kosciuszko's powers of attorney. Remittance to Kosciuszko. Note forwarded to [Joseph] Milligan. [1425]

*1816 Dec. 2. JOHN BARNES, Georgetown, to T. J., Monticello. ALS. 3 pp. Endorsed by T. J. Edgehill-Randolph Papers.

Difficulties in replacing a protested bill of exchange sent to Kosciuszko. Transfer to Kosciuszko's name of his Bank of Columbia stock and government stock. Reference to Baring Brothers of London, Smith & Biddle of Richmond, and Buckley & Abbott of New York. [1426]

*1816 Dec. 23. JOHN BARNES, Georgetown, to T. J., Monticello. ALS. 2 pp. Endorsed by T. J. Edgehill-Randolph Papers.

Form for transfer of government stock and Bank of Columbia stock from T. J.'s name to Kosciuszko's. Bill of exchange, received from Smith & Biddle to replace one protested, on its way to Baring Brothers. [1427]

1816 Dec. 23. JOHN WAYLES EPPES, Mill Brook, to T. J., Monticello. ALS. 1 p. Endorsed by T. J. Edgehill-Randolph Papers.

Martin (servant) to stay at Monticello until skilled in turning wood. Health improving. Greetings from Martha Eppes. [1428]

[ca. 1816?]. [WILSON CARY NICHOLAS] to T. J., [Monticello]. AL. 2 pp. Edgehill-Randolph Papers.

Concerning T. J.'s effort to renew cordiality between James Monroe and Nicholas broken when Nicholas supported Madison for the presidency. [1429]

1817 Jan. 1. T. J., Monticello, to JOSEPH C. CABELL, Richmond. ALS. 1 p. Endorsed. Partly printed: Cabell 70-71; B of R VI 59 (MS. in DLC).

Requests his attention to the petition of the Viscount Barziza, grandchild of Lucy Ludwell Paradise, for his share in her estate. Requests him to oppose Capt. [W. D.?] Meriwether's petition for turnpike from Rockfish Gap to Moore's Ford. [1430]

1817 Jan. 7. JOHN BARNES, Georgetown, to T. J., Monticello. ALS. 1 p. Endorsed by T. J. Enclosure: DS. 7 pp. Edgehill-Randolph Papers.

Enclosing Barnes' account with Kosciuszko for the years 1815 and 1816, with his notes to Kosciuszko relative to the account. [1431]

1817 Jan. 12. JOSEPH C. CABELL, Richmond, to T. J., Monticello. ALS. 2 pp. Endorsed by T. J. Deposited by Philip B. Campbell. Printed: Cabell 71-73.

Cabell to oppose the petition to which T. J. is opposed, and attend to Count Barziza's petition. Translation of Say's *Traité d'économie politique*. Copy of a banking bill enclosed. Failure to increase the Literary Fund as recommended by the governor. Col. [Samuel?] Taylor author of petition from Port Royal. Appointment of Cabell as a Visitor of Central College. Difficulty in obtaining money for colleges. Possible site for the University in Staunton. References to Thomas W. Maury.   [1432]

1817 Jan. 13. JOHN BARNES, Georgetown, to T. J., Monticello. ALS. 1 p. Endorsed by T. J. Edgehill-Randolph Papers.

Difficulty in changing government stock and Bank of Columbia stock to Kosciuszko's name. Encloses powers of attorney for this purpose.   [1433]

1817 Jan. 24. T. J., Monticello, to JOHN WAYLES EPPES, Mill Brook. ALS. 1 p. Deposited by Robert H. Kean.

Education of Francis Eppes. Martin (servant) learning to turn posts tolerably. Pleased that Eppes is returning to the U. S. Senate. References to Anne Bankhead, Martha Randolph, and Martha Eppes.   [1434]

1817 Jan. 25. VERDICT IN THE CASE OF T. J. *vs.* MINOR HEIRS OF BENNETT HENDERSON. DS. 2 pp. Endorsed by T. J. McGregor Library.

Award by Dabney and Peter Minor, arbiters in controversy between T. J. and Frances, Lucy, and Nancy C. Henderson, minor heirs of Bennett Henderson, regarding rent on lands belonging to said minor heirs and held illegally by T. J. T. J. to pay $766.80 for rent. Receipt for amount from W. D. Meriwether, attorney for heirs. Mentions Craven Peyton, James L. Henderson, and John Henderson.   [1435]

1817 Feb. 7. JOHN BARNES, Georgetown, to T. J., Monticello. ALS. 2 pp. Endorsed by T. J. Edgehill-Randolph Papers.

Kosciuszko's account. Transfer of government and Bank of Columbia stock to his name completed.   [1436]

1817 Feb. 9. JOSEPH C. CABELL, Richmond, to T. J., Monticello. ALS. 1 p. Endorsed by T. J. Deposited by Philip B. Campbell. Printed: Cabell 73-74.

Rejection of Count Barziza's petition. Is attending to Turnpike Bill. Hewing down of mammoth bank bill. References to Thomas W. Maury, [Joseph] Milligan (bookseller), William C. Rives, Tracy's *Political Economy*, and Archibald Thweatt.   [1437]

1817 Feb. 19. JOSEPH C. CABELL, Richmond, to T. J., Monticello. ALS. 1 p. Endorsed by T. J. Deposited by Philip B. Campbell. Partly printed: Cabell 74.

Report on Turnpike Bill, bill to call a convention, bill to equalize senatorial districts (modelled after bill reported by T. J., Pendleton, and Wythe in 1779), and the University Bill. Mentions Archibald Thweatt and Charles Yancey. [1438]

1817 Feb. 28. JOHN BARNES, Georgetown, to T. J., Monticello. ALS. 1 p.
Endorsed by T. J. Enclosure: AD. 1 p. Edgehill-Randolph Papers.
   Covering copy of a form required to receive interest on Kosciuszko's public
stock.   [1439]

1817 Mar. 5. T. J., Monticello, to T. M. RANDOLPH, JR., Varina. ALS. 1 p.
Endorsed by T. J. Edgehill-Randolph Papers.
   Request from Judge Peters for a model of T. M. R.'s hillside plow. Anne Bank-
head's health. References to John Bankhead, Joseph C. Cabell, Captain Clarke,
Thomas W. Maury, Dabney Minor, and Charles Yancey.   [1440]

1817 Mar. 26. JOHN BARNES, Georgetown, to T. J., Monticello. ALS. 1 p.
Endorsed by T. J. Edgehill-Randolph Papers.
   Inclosing a copy of the *National Messenger* which contains two letters from
President Adams to Judge [William] Cushing. Mentions T. Dalton.   [1441]

1817 Mar. 30. JOSEPH C. CABELL, Edgewood, to T. J., Monticello. ALS. 1 p.
Endorsed by T. J. Deposited by Philip B. Campbell. Printed: Cabell 75.
   Sends Maine's recipe for preparation of haws found in Brown's *Rural Affairs*.
                                                               [1442]

1817 Apr. 13. T. J., Monticello, to JAMES DINSMORE. ALS. 1 p. File draft.
Endorsed by T. J.
   Asking him to superintend the building of Central College. Board of Visitors:
James Madison, James Monroe, John H. Cooke, Joseph C. Cabell, David Watson,
and T. J. Mentions John Neilson.   [1443]

1817 Apr. 22. JAMES DINSMORE, Petersburg, to T. J. ALS. 1 p. Endorsed by
T. J.
   Accepts job superintending construction of Central College, with John Neil-
son. Plan for house for James Monroe. Gift of two books from Capt. Robert
Simington, Baker's *Chronicle* and the *History of the Holy Wars*, 1684.
                                                               [1444]

1817 Apr. 23. JOSEPH C. CABELL, Bremo, to T. J., Monticello. ALS. 2 pp.
Endorsed by T. J. Deposited by Philip B. Campbell. Printed: Cabell 75-76.
   Inability to attend meeting of the Board of Visitors of Central College.
References to Bedford and Goochland counties, Enniscorthy, John H. Cocke,
James Madison, and David Watson.   [1445]

1817 Apr. 25. T. J., Poplar Forest, to ARCHIBALD ROBERTSON, Lynchburg.
ALS. 1 p. File draft. Endorsed by T. J. McGregor Library.
   Plans for reducing his debts have failed in past due to Embargo, war, and
drought. Wheat and tobacco crops promising. Draft on Gibson & Jefferson will
pay for drafts on Robertson in favor of Nimrod Darnell, William Miller, and
Robert Miller.   [1446]

*1817 Apr. 28. JOHN WAYLES EPPES, Mill Brook, to T. J., [Poplar Forest].
ALS. 2 pp. Endorsed by T. J. Edgehill-Randolph Papers.
   Grape slips from North Carolina for T. J. Plans to locate Francis Eppes at

Richmond as superior to Lynchburg. Letter to Colonel Burton from Gen. Calvin Jones regarding the scuppernong grape. Shipment of wine by Colonel Burton through Mr. Gibson of Richmond. T. M. Randolph, Jr.'s chance in the election. News of Martha Randolph and Thomas J. Randolph. Eppes obliged to give up wine and spirits.   [1447]

1817 Apr. T. J. ACCOUNT AGAINST WILLIAM MITCHELL. AD. 1 p. Edge-hill-Randolph Papers.
    Account balancing wheat sent to Mitchell for flour and bacon received. [1448]

1817 May 1. T. J., Monticello, to JOHN H. COCKE, Bremo. ALS. 1 p. Endorsed. Cocke Papers. Printed: B of R VI 89 (MS. in DLC).
    Meeting of the Board of Visitors. Mentions Enniscorthy, Joseph Cabell, James Madison, James Monroe, and David Watson.   [1449]

1817 May 1. T. J., Monticello, to JOHN WAYLES EPPES. L. 1 p. Typescript copy. Original owned by Edward B. Eppes. Another MS. at CSmH.
    Payment to Mr. Burton for Scuppernong wine. Revolution in England unavoid-able. Meeting of the visitors of Central College: Joseph C. Cabell, John H. Cocke, T. J., James Madison, James Monroe, and David Watson. Hopes to start work in languages at Central College next spring.   [1450]

1817 May 9. FRANK CARR, Bentivar, to T. J., Monticello. ALS. 1 p. Endorsed by T. J. Carr-Cary Papers.
    Requesting his aid in forwarding letters to [Richard?] Terrell in Europe.
                                                                      [1451]

1817 May 9. T. J., Monticello, to WILLIAM THORNTON. ALS. 2 pp. Endorsed by T. J.
    Cast of Ceracchi's bust of T. J. Plans for Central College buildings. Contains rough sketch of T. J.'s early idea for the ground plans.   [1452]

*1817 May 12. JOHN BARNES, Georgetown, to T. J., Monticello. ALS. 2 pp. Endorsed by T. J. Edgehill-Randolph Papers.
    Encloses letters from Koskiuszko, Baring Brothers & Co., and Buckley & Cobbate. Plans for visit to Monticello delayed by arrival of his grandchildren, J. A. Duryee, a Yale graduate, and Maria Duryee. References to Timothy Dwight, Joseph Milligan, and his nephew, Samuel Milligan.   [1453]

1817 May 27. JOHN BARNES, Georgetown, to T. J., Monticello. ALS. 1 p. Endorsed by T. J. Edgehill-Randolph Papers.
    Visit to Monticello. Books from Joseph Milligan.   [1454]

1817 June 4. JOHN BARNES, Milton, to T. J., Monticello. ALS. 1 p. Endorsed by T. J. Edgehill-Randolph Papers.
    Awaits a horse or carriage to climb Monticello mountain.   [1455]

1817 June 13. T. J., Monticello, to BARON F. H. A. VON HUMBOLDT. L. 1 p. Extract by N. P. Trist, ca. 1830. Printed: Ford X 88-89; L & B XV 126-129; B of R VI 224 (MS. in DLC).
    Necessity of majority rule must be learned in Spanish America.   [1456]

1817 June 14. T. J., Monticello, to FRANCOIS DE BARBÉ MARBOIS, L. 1 p. Extract by N. P. Trist *ca.* 1830. Printed: L & B XV 129-131; B of R VI 314 (MS. in DLC).

Belief in the strength of republican structure of the U. S. as its size grows, contrary to Montesquieu. [1457]

1817 June 23. JOHN M. PERRY. CONTRACT with ALEXANDER GARRETT. DS. 3 pp. Endorsed. Witnessed by William Wertenbaker. Endorsed as approved by T. J.

Perry's agreement to do all carpenter and joiner's work on a pavilion at Central College for the same prices paid by James Madison to James Dinsmore for work at Montpelier. [1458]

1817 June 23. JOHN M. and FRANCES T. PERRY, Albemarle County. DEED to ALEXANDER GARRETT, Proctor of CENTRAL COLLEGE. D. S. (T. J. AD). 4 pp. Seals. Recorded by William Wertenbaker, Clerk.

Deed to 196¾ acres of land one mile above Charlottesville on the Staunton Road for the use of Central College. Acknowledgment of deed by Mrs. Frances T. Perry, 7 July 1817, witnessed by Micajah Woods and William Woods. [1459]

1817 June 26. CRAVEN PEYTON, Monteagle, Va., to T. J., Monticello. ALS. 1 p. Endorsed by T. J. McGregor Library.

Asks legal opinion on deed from Lewis to Lewis. Sends copy of Wickham's and William Wirt's opinions. Note by T. J.: Peyton is *bona fide* purchaser and C. L. Lewis guilty of fraud by his silence. [1460]

1817 July 1. T. J., Poplar Forest to PATRICK GIBSON, Richmond. ALS. 1 p. Endorsed by T. J. Photostat. Original owned by Mrs. Virginius Dabney.

Enclosing notes he has signed. [1461]

1817 July 8. JOHN BARNES, Georgetown, to T. J., Monticello. ALS. 3 pp. Endorsed by T. J. Edgehill-Randolph Papers.

Sale of watches for Louis Leschute, mentioning watchmakers and repairmen, Mr. Eckles and Morris Tobias of London. [1462]

1817 July 11. JOHN BARNES, Georgetown, to T. J., Monticello. ALS. 2 pp. Endorsed by T. J. Edgehill-Randolph Papers.

Adjustment of T. J.'s account. Mr. Wheat's report that he has seen Thurston. Thanks for his visit to Monticello. [1463]

1817 July 17. JOHN BARNES, Georgetown, to T. J., Monticello. ALS. 1 p. Endorsed by T. J. Edgehill-Randolph Papers.

Remittance enclosed for Louis Leschute. Books from Joseph Milligan forwarded to Mr. Gray, Fredericksburg. [1464]

1817 July 19. T. J., Monticello, to JOHN H. COCKE, Bremo. ALS. 1 p. Endorsed. Printed: B of R VI 89 (MS. in DLC).

Board of Visitors' meeting. Beginning of construction work at Central College. Mentions James Madison. [1465]

1817 July 21. T. J., Monticello, to JAMES OLDHAM, Richmond. ALS. 1 p. Deposited from Monticello. Another MS. in MHi.

Receipt of mahogany. Order for locks, handles, and bolts, to be paid for by Patrick Gibson.   [1466]

1817 July. JOHN BARNES, Georgetown. ACCOUNT with T. J., Monticello. ADS. 1 p. Edgehill-Randolph Papers.

Account for the years 1814-1817. Mentions [John] Armstrong, Gales & Seaton, Gibson & Jefferson, Tadeusz Kosciuszko ,and Dolly Madison.   [1467]

1817 Aug. 4 T. J., Monticello. CIRCULAR LETTER to James Pleasants, John W. Eppes, William B. Giles, Randolph Harrison, Thomas Newton, William A. Burwell, and Archibald Thweatt. ALS. 3 copies. 2 pp. Printed: *Va. Mag. Hist.* XXIX 445-447. The copy sent to Newton is in the McGregor Library; the copy sent to Giles and the master draft are in the general collection.

Soliciting funds for Central College. Advantages of location; general plans; personnel of Board of Visitors.   [1468]

1817 Aug. 12. T. J., Poplar Forest, to SAMUEL HARRISON, Lynchburg. L. 2 pp. Typescript copy. Original owned by Francis Burton Harrison.

Introducing M. and Mme. A. F. de Laage, lately removed to Lynchburg from Charlottesville.   [1469]

1817 Aug. 18. JOSEPH C. CABELL, Edgewood, to T. J., Monticello. ALS. 3 pp. Endorsed by T. J. Deposited by Philip B. Campbell. Printed: Cabell 76-78.

Catalog of English books sold by Barrois at Paris. Subscriptions to Central College from Albemarle, Amherst, Campbell, Lancaster, Northumberland, Richmond, and Westmoreland counties. Death of Cabell's mother. Comments of T. J.'s manuscript on meteorological subjects. References to William Brent, George Cabell, John Camm, Hill Carter, Sterling Claiborne, Ellyson Currie, Thomas Eubanks, David S. Garland, Spottswood Garland, William J. Lewis, James Madison, Roderick McCullock, William Pope, Robert Rives, Mr. Ritchie, Henry St. George Tucker, Robert Walker, and Edmund Winston.   [1470]

1817 Aug. 31. T. J., Poplar Forest, to HUGH CHISHOLM. ALS. 1 p. File draft. Endorsed by T. J.

Progress of construction at Central College. Superiority of stone- and brickworkers near Lynchburg.   [1471]

1817 Sept. 9. T. J., Poplar Forest, to JOSEPH C. CABELL, Edgewood. ALS. 1 p. Endorsed. Printed: Cabell 79-80; L & B XVII 417-418; B of R VI 59 (MS. in DLC). Enclosure: AD. 14 pp. Partly printed: Cabell App. 413-417. Two other drafts of enclosure in Cabell Papers.

Encloses bill for establishing a system of public education. Remarks on legal phraseology. Lawyers' double talk compared to simple English of the ancient statutes which T. J. tried to use in 1776. Bill provides for primary schools for all at common expense, colleges spaced at convenient distances throughout the state, and as a capstone a University in the central part of the state. List of white inhabitnats of the state divided into the nine collegiate districts.   [1472]

1817 Sept. 10. T. J., Poplar Forest, to JOSEPH C. CABELL, Edgewood. ALS.
1 p. Endorsed. Printed (minor variation): Cabell 80-81; B of R VI 59 (MS.
in DLC).

Returns Barrois' catalog. Requests he not be known as author of the bill for
elementary schools. Has written to Christopher Clarke and Charles Johnston
regarding subscriptions to Central College. Mentions [Thomas] Cooper. [1473]

1817 Sept. 16. THOMAS COOPER, Philadelphia, to T. J., Monticello. ALS.
4 pp. Endorsed by T. J.

Present position at the University of Pennsylvania precarious because students
in medicine forced to hear Dr. John R. Coxe's lectures in preference to his.
Has been offered post at William and Mary which he will accept if they meet
his conditions concerning his library and mineral collection. Would like to
see medical school set up in Virginia, perhaps in Richmond. Mentions Burwell
Bassett and John Augustine Smith. [1474]

1817 Sept. 17. THOMAS COOPER, Philadelphia, to T. J., Monticello. ALS. 1 p.
Endorsed by T. J.

Will write as soon as he can give decision about offer of professorship at
Central College. Discusses Destutt de Tracy' Eléments d'idéologie, which
Maclure imported for [Joseph C.?] Cabell. [1475]

1817 Sept. 19. THOMAS COOPER, Philadelphia, to T. J., Monticello. ALS. 3 pp.
Endorsed by T. J. Another MS. in DLC.

No reply from Varro in Frankfort, Ky. Discusses possibility of accepting professorship at Central College. Filling of other faculty posts at the college. Has
refused position at William and Mary. Possibility of medical college at Richmond.
Mentions Correa da Serra and Burwell Bassett. [1476]

1817 Sept. 23. T. J., Monticello, to THOMAS COOPER, Philadelphia. ALS. 1 p.
File draft. Endorsed by T. J.

Hopes he will accept offer at Central College. Correa da Serra and Robert
Walsh will be in Charlottesville. [1477]

1817 Sept. 24. ARCHIBALD THWEATT, Eppington, to T. J. ALS. 2 pp. Endorsed by T. J. Edgehill-Randolph Papers.

Subscriptions for Central College not encouraging in Petersburg. Recommends a
lottery. War taxes, prematurely ended, might have been applied to the Literary
Fund. [1478]

1817 Sept. 30. THOMAS COOPER, Philadelphia, to T. J., Monticello. ALS. 1 p.
Endorsed by T. J.

Unable to visit T. J. because of work on lectures and correcting press for
William Wirt's Life of Patrick Henry. Refusal of position at William and Mary.
Classical tutor for Central College. Mentions Mr. Sanders [Robert Saunders?]
of Williamsburg. [1479]

1817 Sept. 30. JOHN WAYLES EPPES, Mill Brook, to T. J., Poplar Forest. ALS.
2 pp. Endorsed by T. J. Edgehill-Randolph Papers.

Visits by relatives, Mr. Burton, Mr. Lane, and families, illness among servants, and pressure of the tobacco crop prevent his visiting T. J. Will subscribe to Central College. Plans for Francis to attend in the spring. His own illness. References to Ellen, Cornelia, and Martha Randolph.   [1480]

1817 Oct. 5. T. J., Monticello, to SAMUEL J. HARRISON. ALS. 1 p. File draft. Endorsed by T. J.
Cornerstone being laid at Central College. Urges that David Knight leave at once for his work.   [1481]

1817 Oct. 7. JOSEPH C. CABELL, Charlottesville, to T. J., Monticello. ALS. 1 p. Endorsed by T. J. Deposited by Philip B. Campbell. Printed: Cabell 81.
Delay in arriving at Board of Visitors meeting due to the meeting of the Association for an Agricultural Society. References to John H. Cocke, James Madison, James Monroe, Judge [Archibald?] Stewart, and David Watson. [1482]

1817 Oct. 7. T. J., Monticello, to JOSEPH C. CABELL, David Watson, and John H. Cocke, Charlottesville, Va. ALS. 1 p. Endorsed. Circular. Printed: Cabell 81.
Calls meeting of Board of Visitors to consider letter from Thomas Cooper. Mentions James Madison and James Monroe. Note from Cabell and Cocke to Watson on same sheet suggesting change in time of Agricultural Society Meeting.   [1483]

1817 Oct. 14. JOSEPH C. CABELL, Edgewood, to T. J., Monticello. ALS. 2 pp. Endorsed by T. J. Deposited by Philip B. Campbell. Printed: Cabell 82-83.
Plan for schools and colleges throughout the state of Virginia. Copy of membership list of Cincinnati left at Monticello. John Wayles Eppes endeavoring to secure subscribers at Buckingham Court House. Advises delay on the report to the Agricultural Society. Mentions John H. Cocke, Thomas Mann Randolph, Jr., and Arthur Young's *Annals*   [1484]

1817 Oct. 14. T. J., Monticello, to [FRANCIS WALKER] GILMER. ALS. 2 pp. Endorsed. Another MS. in DLC.
Dupont de Nemours' treatise worth publishing; suggests Robert Walsh publish it in his *American Register*. Discusses translation of French passage. Correa da Serra to live in Washington with Walsh. Thomas Cooper and George Ticknor possible professors at Central College. Hopes legislature will select Central College as site of University.   [1485]

1817 Oct. 24. T. J., Monticello, to JOSEPH C. CABELL. ALS. 2 pp. Endorsed. Printed: Cabell 83-85; L & B XIX 250-252; B of R VI 59 (MS. in DLC).
Plan for a system of education "within the compass of our funds." Refuses to sacrifice public good for local interest by including petty academies and colleges throughout the state in his plans. Progress of construction at Central College slow. Mentions [William Cabell] Rives.   [1486]

1817 Oct. 24. THOMAS COOPER, Philadelphia, to T. J., Monticello. ALS. 3 pp. Endorsed by T. J.
Withholds his decision regarding Central College position. If lectures can be arranged with Dr. John R. Coxe, may stay at University of Pennsylvania. Asks

about classical tutor, Stack, formerly of Carlisle College, known by William Duane. Recommends an Irishman formerly employed by Robert Patterson, as best mathematician in United States. James Semple, Rector of William and Mary College, has sent notice of election to professorship of chemistry, despite his declining. [1487]

* 1817 Oct. 24. T. J., Monticello, to PATRICK GIBSON, Richmond. ALS. 1 p. Endorsed by T. J. Photostat. Original owned by Mrs. Virginius Dabney.

T. J.'s draft in favor of Mr. Southall and drafts for taxes in Albemarle and in Bedford will be paid by flour sent to Richmond by Mr. Colclaser, one of T. J.'s mill tenants. [1488]

1817 Oct. 26. T. J., Monticello, to JOHN WAYLES EPPES, Mill Brook, Va. ALS. 1 p. Another MS. in DLC.

Has watch from Leschot for Martha Eppes. Recommends all repair be done by Leschot. Recommends Monroe's plan for militia. Wisdom of economy and clearing of debts in time of peace. [1489]

1817 Oct. 30. T. J., Monticello, to PATRICK GIBSON. ALS. 1 p. Endorsed by T. J. Photostat. Original owned by Mrs. Virginius Dabney.

Renewal of his note by the Bank of Virginia. Flour being shipped for T. J. by Mr. Colclaser in the hands of [Bernard] Peyton. [1490]

1817 Nov. 7. T. J., Monticello, to JOSHUA MEIGS, Washington. ALS. 1 p. McGregor Library.

Recommending Thomas Eston Randolph for the office of Postmaster, Richmond, replacing Dr. [William] Foushee. [1491]

1817 Nov. 10. THOMAS COOPER, Philadelphia, to T. J., Monticello. ALS. 1 p. Endorsed by T. J.

Will accept William and Mary offer renewed by Mr. Brown unless Central College can offer salary the following spring. [1492]

1817 Nov. 10. JOHN WOOD, Richmond, to T. J., Monticello. ALS. 3 pp. Endorsed by T. J.

Enquires about classics position offered him at Central College. Would prefer mathematics chair. Sends notice of Greek-English lexicon by Gilbert Wakefield. Mentions Thomas Mann Randolph, Jr. [1493]

1817 Nov. 11. T. J., Monticello, to NELSON BARKSDALE. ALS. 1 p. Endorsed.

Agreement with David Knight for work at Central College to be paid for by draft on Alexander Garrett. Mentions Samuel J. Harrison. [1494]

1817 Nov. 15. T. J., Monticello, to PATRICK GIBSON, Richmond. ALS. 1 p. Endorsed by T. J. Photostat. Original owned by Mrs. Virginius Dabney. Another MS. at VHi.

Johnson's delay in shipment of T. J.'s flour. [1495]

1817 Nov. 20. THOMAS COOPER, Philadelphia, to T. J., Monticello. ALS. 1 p. Endorsed by T. J.

Unless salary assured from Central College from April next, must accept William and Mary offer.　　　　　　　　　　　　　　　　　　　　　　　　[1496]

1817 Nov. 25. T. J., Poplar Forest, to THOMAS COOPER, Philadelphia. ALS. 2 pp. File draft. Endorsed by T. J.

Hopes Philadelphia students can have option to attend his lectures so he can remain at University of Pennsylvania until Central College ready. Might arrange for professorship of physical sciences to start sooner than planned to accommodate him. No one near Lynchburg remembers Stack. Plans to have distinguished professors from Edinburgh for Central College.　　　　　　　　　　　　[1497]

1817 Nov. 26. T. J., Poplar Forest, to JOHN WOOD, Richmond. ALS. 2 pp. File draft. Endorsed by T. J.

Letter to Wood was from self and not from Visitors of Central College. Understood his answer as refusal of classics professorship. Plans to procure professors from Europe. Thanks for information on Gilbert Wakefield's Greek-English Lexicon.　　　　　　　　　　　　　　　　　　　　　　　　[1498]

1817 Nov. 27-28. JOHN ORGAN. Poplar Forest Survey. ADS. 2 items. Endorsed by T. J. McGregor Library.

Notes on the land lines of Poplar Forest. Survey of roads from Campbell Court House to Poplar Forest.　　　　　　　　　　　　　　　　　　　　　[1499]

1817 Dec. 3. JOSEPH C. CABELL, Richmond, to T. J., Monticello. ALS. 3 pp. Endorsed by T. J. Deposited by Philip B. Campbell. Partly printed: Cabell 85-87.

Subscriptions to Central College from [Henry St. George?] Tucker and John Coalter. Plan for primary schools throughout the state. Opposition to Central College from Federalists, bigots, members of the Society of Cincinnati, and from friends of Washington College at Lexington. William and Mary people are liberal. References to Judge Brooke, John W. Green, Armistead Hoomes, Chapman Johnson, and Edward Watts.　　　　　　　　　　　　　　　　　[1500]

*1817 Dec. 6. THOMAS COOPER, Philadelphia, to T. J., Poplar Forest. ALS. 3 pp. Endorsed by T. J.

Accepts professorship of chemistry, mineralogy, philosophy, and law beginning following summer. Trustees of University of Pennsylvania rejected proposals to share John R. Coxe's students. William and Mary has elected Hare to post offered to Cooper. Adam Seybert, Mr. Cloud, or Zaccariah Collins will value his mineral collection before shipment. Relative merits of Edinburgh, Oxford, Cambridge, Eton, Westminster, Harrow, and Winchester as sources of faculty. Lauds advice of Sir William Jones on translating foreign languages. Mr. Stack now at Centerville, Md.　　　　　　　　　　　　　　　　　　　　　　　[1501]

1817 Dec. 7. THOMAS COOPER, Philadelphia, to T. J., Monticello. ALS. 1 p. Endorsed by T. J.

Accepts post at Central College. Confirms his letter of yesterday sent to Poplar Forest.　　　　　　　　　　　　　　　　　　　　　　　　　　　[1502]

1817 Dec. 10. MATTHEW BROWN, Lynchburg, to T. J., Poplar Forest. ALS.
1 p. Endorsed by T. J.
Estimate for making and laying bricks at Central College. Mentions Samuel
J. Harrison.   [1503]

1817 Dec. 13. JOSEPH C. CABELL, Richmond, to ROBERT G. SCOTT, Chairman of the Committee of Schools and Colleges. ALS. Draft. 5 pp. Endorsed.
[Copy sent to T. J.]. Deposited by Philip B. Campbell. Printed: Cabell 94-96.
Jefferson's ideas regarding the bill providing for the establishment of primary
schools, academies, colleges, and a university. Discussion of whether education
should be compulsory.   [1504]

1817 Dec. 13. T. J., Poplar Forest, to JAMES MONROE. ALS. 1 p. File draft.
Endorsed by T. J.
Forwards for his approval copy of report of Visitors of Central College to
Governor of Virginia. Plan for a general scheme of education, ward schools,
colleges, one university. Urges conciliation of Charles Fenton Mercer, author of
rival plan.   [1505]

1817 Dec. 17. JOSEPH ANTRIM. PLASTERER'S BID. AD. 1 p. Endorsed by
T. J.
Proposal for plastering at Central College.   [1506]

1817 Dec. 18. T. J., Poplar Forest, to JOSEPH C. CABELL. ALS. 1 p. Endorsed.
Printed: Cabell 87-88; B of R VI 59 (MS. in DLC).
Subscriptions and donations to Central College. Report of the Visitors to the
Governor. General education bill for Virginia. Thomas Cooper has accepted
position at Central College.   [1507]

1817 Dec. 19. T. J., Poplar Forest, to JOSEPH C. CABELL, Richmond.. ALS.
1 p. Endorsed. Printed: Cabell 88-89; B of R VI 59 (MS. in DLC).
High wages of bricklayers in Lynchburg. Asks Richmond prices. Reply must
be immediate so he can answer Matthew Brown of Lynchburg.   [1508]

1817 Dec. 20. MATTHEW BROWN, Lynchburg, to T. J., Poplar Forest. ALS.
1 p. Endorsed by T. J.
Brickwork at Central College. Mentions David Knight.   [1509]

[1817] Dec. 23 [date received]. FRANK CARR to T. J., Monticello. ALS. 1 p.
Endorsed by T. J. Carr-Cary Papers.
Returns letters of Messrs. [James C.?] Picket[t] and Albert Gallatin. Reference
to [Richard?] Terrell.   [1510]

1817 Dec. 29. JOSEPH C. CABELL. Richmond, to T. J., Monticello. ALS. 6 pp.
Endorsed by T. J. Deposited by Philip B. Campbell. Printed: Cabell 89-94.
Opposition by members of the Society of Cincinnati to Central College, preferring to give funds to Washington College. Presbyterians oppose because T. J.
is an infidel. Opposition in the Assembly to setting up a system of public
education in Virginia. Encloses copy of letter sent to Robert Scott, Chairman of

Committee for Schools and Colleges. Site for the University. Report on the Literary Fund. References to Francis T. Brooke, William Cabell, John Coalter, Thomas Cooper, Mr. Garrett, Chapman Johnson, Wilson C. Nicholas, [Alfred H.?] Powell, Spencer Roane, Henry Tucker, and Edward Watts.   [1511]

1817 Dec. 30. JOHN BARNES, Georgetown, to T. J., Monticello. ALS. 1 p. Endorsed by T. J. Edgehill-Randolph Papers.

Death of General Kosciuszko.   [1512]

1817 Dec. 30. T. J., Monticello, to [JAMES MADISON]. ALS. 2 pp. Printed: B of R VI 310 (MS. in DLC).

Report of the Visitors of Central College to the Governor. Subscriptions. Delays writing to Edinburgh until the legislature acts. Recommends Dr. Cooper's appointment to the chairs of physiology and law, but suspension of those functions at first and allowing him to teach languages.   [1513]

1817 Dec. 31. T. J., Monticello, to JOSEPH C. CABELL, Richmond. ALS. 1 p. Endorsed. Printed: Cabell 98-99; B of R VI 59 (MS. in DLC).

Requests information regarding lands of Mr. Poinsot des Essarts. Report [regarding Central College] sent to Mr. Madison.   [1514]

[1817 Dec.]. T. J. ADVERTISEMENT FOR BIDS ON CENTRAL COLLEGE. ADS. 1 p.

Contracts for brickwork. Mentions Matthew Brown, Clifton Harris.   [1515]

1817-1826. T. J. DRAWINGS AND PLANS OF THE UNIVERSITY OF VIRGINIA. 75 items, the majority T. J. AD. Partly printed: Lambeth, *Thomas Jefferson as an Architect.*

Fiske Kimball's *Thomas Jefferson, Architect,* pp. 200-204, lists and identifies 32 pieces numbered (1-32), 17 pieces numbered "Plate I" to "Plate 15" [and "No. 16" and "No. 17"], 23 other pieces of drawings, memoranda, and calculations, 16 lettered a-p and 7 unlabelled. The group includes several plans and drawings of Poplar Forest and Monticello. (See also [7] above). We note only the following additions to Mr. Kimball's inventory:

No. 20. Pavilion No. VIII East. On *verso,* dimensions and specifications noted by T. J.

No. 32. Arcade of base of Rotunda, rather than East Range as stated in Kimball, p. 202.

Three additional drawings:

A. An XVIIIth "Plate." Elevation of south front of Rotunda and wings, showing elevation of Pavilions IX and X. Tinted ink drawings with shadows rendered in gray. (No perspective; no other pavilions shown).

B. Proposed pavilion, two stories, with dormitories attached. Detached dormitory on similar plan. Ink drawings of elevations and floor plans.

C. Early ground plan for University with dimensioned floor plans of Range. Proposed elevation of oldest Pavilion (VII), Doric on Tuscan. Ink drawings.

[1516]

1817-1826. T. J. MINUTES of the BOARD OF VISITORS of CENTRAL COL-
LEGE and the UNIVERSITY OF VIRGINIA. ADS. MS. Vol. 105 pp. (including
11 pp. in other hands signed by T. J.). Printed: L & B XIX 361-499.

Official minutes of the University of Virginia Board of Visitors, kept by T. J.
as Rector from 1817-1826. The earlier notes are signed by T. J. and other members of the Board, Joseph C. Cabell, John H. Cocke, James Madison, James
Monroe, and David Watson. Members of the Board in later years who did not
sign: James Breckenridge, Chapman Johnson, George Loyall, and Robert L.
Taylor. The University of Virginia also owns preliminary notes made by T. J.
for later copying (35 pp.), as well as the copies of the minutes belonging to
Joseph C. Cabell, John H. Cocke, James Monroe, and James Breckenridge. Some
of the notes date from 1814, with the minutes of the Trustees of Albemarle
Academy. The minutes after the spring meeting of 1826 (pp. 107-185) in this
volume are in the hand of the Secretary of the Board, Nicholas P. Trist. (See
"Bibliography of Unprinted Official Records" in sixth *Annual Report of the
Archivist*, Univ. of Va., 1935-36).   [1517]

[1817-1826]. T. J. "OPERATIONS AT AND FOR THE COLLEGE." AD. 1 vol.
29 pp. Partly printed: Lambeth plates VI, VII, XIII.

Pocket memorandum book containing specifications, ink drawings, and other
data used and compiled by T. J. while directing the construction of the University of Virginia (Central college until 1819). There is a ground-plan, with all
proposed buildings indicated by letter; description of proposed buildings, style
of architecture, measurements, materials to be used, and the amount of brick
or stone required.   [1518]

[*ca.* 1818 Jan. 2]. T. J. to JAMES MADISON, DAVID WATSON, and JOHN H.
COCKE. ALS. 2 pp. Enclosure: AD. 2 pp. Cocke Papers.

Encloses copy of report of the Board of Visitors to the governor. Requests their
approval of Thomas Cooper's appointment to physiological professorship, with
an *ad interim* appointment to the classical school. Bricklayers' terms. Subscriptions. Enclosure: estimate of the objects of application of Central College funds.
                                                                      [1519]

1818 Jan. 5. JOSEPH C. CABELL, Richmond, to T. J., Monticello. ALS. 3 pp.
Endorsed by T. J. Enclosure: C. Tompkins, ALS. 2 pp. Deposited by Philip
B. Campbell. Partly printed: Cabell 99-101.

Encloses letter from Major Christopher Tompkins regarding the price of
bricklaying for Central College. Essay in the *Enquirer* by Mr. Giles. Prospects
not good for the general education bill. Receipt of the papers of Poinsot des
Essarts. Information regarding subscriptions to Central College from William
Brent, Mr. Currie, and Creed Taylor. References to Wilson C. Nicholas, James
P. Preston, Mr. Brown (bricklayer), and Mr. Night (bricklayer).   [1520]

1818 Jan. 6. T. J. to [JAMES P. PRESTON]. AD. 7 pp. Endorsed: "James Monroe."

Report to the governor of Virginia, concerning the progress and prospects of
Central College. Financial report. Copy sent to James Monroe for his approval.
                                                                      [1521]

1818 Jan. 7. T. J., Monticello, to THOMAS COOPER. ALS. 2 pp. File draft. Endorsed by T. J.

Pleased by Cooper's acceptance of physiological professorship. Cooper to open classical school in July. Plan to establish additional professorships when funds permit.   [1522]

1818 Jan. 9. T. J., Monticello, to ROBERT WALSH, Washington. ALS. 2 pp. Another MS. in DLC.

Enjoyed John Playfair's presentation of mathematical history; asks him to print unedited Destutt de Tracy manuscript, *Principes logiques,* in the *American Register.* Dr. Cooper's acceptance of Central College post. Invitation to visit Monticello with Correa da Serra.   [1523]

1818 Jan. 12. J. HORWITZ, Philadelphia, to T. J., Monticello. ALS. 2 pp. Endorsed by T. J. Enclosure: printed leaflet. 4 pp.

Application for professorship of oriental literature, German, and Hebrew. Enclosure: prospectus for the first American edition of Van der Hooght's Hebrew Bible.   [1524]

1818 Jan. 14. T. J., Monticello, to JOSEPH C. CABELL, Richmond. ALS. 5 pp. File draft. Endorsed by T. J. Partly printed: Ford IX 98-101; Cabell 102-106.

Financing a general education system for Virginia.   [1525]

1818 Jan. 15. T. J., Monticello, to JOSEPH C. CABELL, Richmond. ALS. 1 p. Endorsed. Printed: Cabell 107.

Financial aid for Central College from the legislature.   [1526]

1818 Jan. 15. FRANCIS WALKER GILMER, Winchester, to T. J., Monticello. ALS. 1 p. Endorsed by T. J.

Central College subscriptions.   [1527]

1818 Jan. 22. JOSEPH C. CABELL, Richmond, to T. J., Monticello. ALS. 3 pp. Endorsed by T. J. Enclosure: Creed Taylor ALS. 1 p. Endorsed by Cabell. Deposited by Philip B. Campbell. Partly printed: Cabell 108-110.

Search regarding land will be carried out for T. J. in the Register's Office. Copy of the Report of the Visitors circulated in the Assembly. Copy of T. J.'s letters regarding primary schools given to Robert Scott, Chairman of the Committee on Schools and Colleges. Motion to move the capital. Opposition to Central College by the Washington College people. Recommends that William Brent, John T. Brooke, John H. Cocke, and George Poindexter run for the Assembly. Bank loan being negotiated. Recommends annuity from the Literary Fund as best income for Central College. Encloses note from Chancellor Creed Taylor regarding T. J.'s proposed system of public education. References to Jesse W. Garth, James Madison, Robert Mallory, Dabney Minor, and James Monroe.   [1528]

1818 Jan. 23. JOSEPH C. CABELL, Richmond, to T. J., Monticello. ALS. 1 p. Endorsed by T. J. Deposited by Philip B. Campbell. Printed: Cabell 111.

Disappointment in the bill reported by the Committee of Schools and Colleges.

Visitors will be personally responsible for a bank loan to Central College. Movement of seat of government from Richmond to the West postponed. [1529]

1818 Jan. 23. THOMAS COOPER, Philadelphia, to T. J., Monticello. ALS. 1 p. Endorsed by T. J.

Death of Caspar Wistar may change situation at University of Pennsylvania, since Dr. John R. Coxe wishes to take *materia medica* chair. [1530]

1818 Jan. 30. JOSEPH C. CABELL, Richmond, to JOHN BROCKENBROUGH. ALS. 1 p. Copy sent by Cabell to T. J. Endorsed. Deposited by Philip B. Campbell. Printed: Cabell 114-115.

To the President of the Bank of Virginia, covering reports by the Visitors of Central College, given to enable the bank to judge the merits of a loan sought in anticipation of subscriptions. [1531]

1818 Jan. 31. JOHN BROCKENBROUGH, Richmond, to JOSEPH C. CABELL, Richmond. ALS. 1 p. Deposited by Philip B. Campbell. Printed: Cabell 115-116.

Agreeing to lend money to Central College for 60 days with renewal of notes possible. [1532]

1818 Feb. 1. JOSEPH C. CABELL, Richmond, to T. J., Monticello. ALS. 2 pp. Endorsed by T. J. Deposited by Philip B. Campbell. Printed: Cabell 112-113.

Fears failure of general education bill for Virginia. Requests T. J. to draw bill for annuity from Literary Fund for endowment of professorships. Inquires with regard to Des Essarts' land patents. References to Robert Scott, Samuel Taylor, and [George J.] Davison. [1533]

1818 Feb. 1. JOSEPH C. CABELL, Richmond, to T. J., Monticello. ALS. 2 pp. Endorsed by T. J. Deposited by Philip B. Campbell. Printed: Cabell 113-114.

Loan offered by John Brockenbrough, President of the Bank of Virginia, better than can be obtained from Benjamin Hatcher of the Farmer's Bank. Necessity for the Visitors to sign the notes as individuals. References to Wilson C. Nicholas and David Watson. [1534]

1818 Feb. 6. JOSEPH C. CABELL, Richmond, to T. J., Monticello. ALS. 3 pp. Endorsed by T. J. Deposited by Philip B. Campbell. Partly printed: Cabell 116-118.

Inquiies regarding Poinsot des Essarts' land patents. Back-country opposition to T. J.'s general education bill. Opposition to Central College from friends of Lexington and Staunton. Recommends selection of men such as General [John George] Jackson in the Northwest of Virginia and William Burwell from the Southwest. References to Mr. Johnson, General Kosciuszko, and Peter Carr. [1535]

1818 Feb. 6. T. J., Monticello, to THOMAS COOPER, Philadelphia. ALS. 1 p. File draft. Endorsed by T. J.

Laments death of Dr. Caspar Wistar. Engagement with Central College will not prevent Cooper's accepting better position at Pennsylvania caused by vacancy. [1536]

1818 Feb. 10. JOSEPH C. CABELL, Richmond, to T. J., Monticello. ALS. 3 pp.
Endorsed by T. J. Deposited by Philip B. Campbell. Printed: Cabell 119-121.
   T. J.'s letter published in the *Enquirer* to help the general education bill,
omitting T. J.'s estimate of the large amount of money necessary. Reference to
William Cabell, Wilson C. Nicholas, and Lewis Somers (*i.e.*, Summers). [1537]

1818 Feb. 11. ARCHIBALD THWEATT, Richmond, to T. J., Monticello. ÅLS.
1 p. Endorsed by T. J. Edgehill-Randolph Papers.
   Interest of the Wayles estate in Byrd's Lottery.   [1538]

1818 Feb. 12. JOSEPH C. CABELL, Richmond, to T. J., Monticello. ALS. 1 p.
Endorsed by T. J. Deposited by Philip B. Campbell. Printed: Cabell 121-122.
   Introducing Lewis Summers of Kanawha County.   [1539]

1818 Feb. 13. JOSEPH C. CABELL, Richmond, to T. J., Monticello. ALS. 3 pp.
Endorsed by T. J. Deposited by Philip B. Campbell. Partly printed: Cabell 122-
123.
   Enquiries regarding Poinsot des Essarts' land. Failure of T. J.'s general educa-
tion bill, with only a small appropriation for education of the poor, due to
interests from Lexington and Staunton and to the Presbyterians, aided by a
junto from the middle country delegation (Charles Yancey, Thomas Miller,
Robert Mallory, and Charles Everett). Possibility of an appropriation for
Central College. References to Francis T. Brooke, Dabney Carr, John W. Green,
Thomas Hill, and Chapman Johnson.   [1540]

1818 Feb. 16. T. J., Monticello, to JOSEPH C. CABELL, Richmond. ALS. 2 pp.
Endorsed. Printed: Cabell 124-125; B of R VI 59 (MS. in DLC).
   Regrets his "intermedling" in the education bill. Subscriptions for Central
College. Requests all of Board of Visitors to visit him whenever near Monticello
to help make decisions between formal meetings.   [1541]

1818 Feb. 17. RANDOLPH HARRISON, Clifton, Va., to T. J., Monticello. ALS.
1 p. Endorsed by T. J.
   Central College subscriptions. Mentions Mr. Baker, Thomas Jefferson Randolph, and George Skipwith.   [1542]

1818 Feb. 17. ARCHIBALD THWEATT, Richmond, to T. J., Monticello. ALS.
1 p. Endorsed by T. J. Edgehill-Randolph Papers.
   Inability to collect any subscriptions or to subscribe himself to the Central
College fund.   [1543]

1818 Feb. 20. JOSEPH C. CABELL, Richmond, to T. J., Monticello. ALS. 2 pp.
Endorsed by T. J. Deposited by Philip B. Campbell. Printed: Cabell 125-126.
   Bill providing for education of poor, an appropriation for the University, and
the setting up of the Rockfish Gap Commission passed the Senate.   [1544]

1818 Feb. 20. THOMAS COOPER, Philadelphia, to T. J., Monticello. ALS. 2 pp.
Endorsed by T. J.
   Expects an opening at University of Pennsylvania. Appreciative of Central

College's liberal conduct. Medical faculty has recommended Augustine Smith of Williamsburg for Wistar's post. Plans to come to Virginia with Correa da Serra. [1545]

1818 Feb. 22. JOSEPH C. CABELL, Richmond, to T. J., Monticello. ALS. 2 pp. Endorsed by T. J. Deposited by Philip B. Campbell. Partly printed: Cabell 127.
　　Passage of the Rockfish Gap Bill. Asks T. J. to serve as a commissioner. Appointments in the hands of the president and directors of the Literary Fund, three fifths of whom are from beyond the mountains. Urges immediate work on buildings of Central College because of opposition from Federalists, Presbyterian clergy, and the entire back country. Mentions James Madison. [1546]

1818 Feb. 24. JAMES PLEASANTS, JR., Washington, to T. J., Monticello. ALS. 1 p. Endorsed by T. J.
　　Subscriptions to Central College. [1547]

1818 Feb. 26. T. J., Monticello, to JOSEPH C. CABELL, Richmond. ALS. 1 p. Endorsed. Printed: Cabell 128-129; B of R VI 59 (MS in DLC).
　　James Madison will serve on Rockfish Gap Commission. Thinks it better for Cabell to serve rather than himself. [1548]

[1818 Feb.]. ROCKFISH GAP COMMISSION. A Bill appropriating part of the revenue of the Literary Fund, and for other purposes. Printed D. 4 pp. MS. notes by T. J.
　　Bill setting up the Rockfish Gap Commission for the establishment of the University of Virginia and the selection of a site. [1549]

1818 Mar. 11. JOSEPH C. CABELL, Fluvanna County, to T. J., Monticello. ALS. 2 pp. Endorsed by T. J. Deposited by Philip B. Campbell. Printed: Cabell 129.
　　Selection of members of the Rockfish Gap Commission. Visit to Monticello. [1550]

1818 Mar. 13. T. J., Monticello, to JOHN WAYLES EPPES. ALS. 1 p.
　　Recommends Francis Eppes II be sent to Mr. Dasheel (Dashiell?) in New London, Va., until Central College opens. Birth of a sixth grandson. Patsy doing well. Plans for meeting Francis. [1551]

1818 Mar. 15. JOSEPH C. CABELL, Warminster, to T. J., Monticello. ALS. 3 pp. Endorsed by T. J. Deposited by Philip B. Campbell. Printed: Cabell 130-132.
　　Rivalry between Washington College, Rockbridge College, and Central College as to the site for the University. Offer by a Mr. Robinson of Lexington to leave his estate to the University if located there. Requests T. J. to urge Wilson J. Cary, John H. Cocke, Randolph Harrison, and Washington Trueheart to serve in House of Delegates as friends of Central College. References to John Wayles Eppes. [1552]

1818 Mar. 20. T. J., Monticello, to JOHN ARMSTRONG. ALS. 1 p. File draft. Endorsed by T. J. Another MS. in Polish Roman Catholic University (Kosciuszko Papers).
　　Requests information for a biography of Tadeusz Kosciuszko to be written by Mr. Gullien. Administration of General Kosciuszko's estate. [1553]

1818 Mar. 25 [date received]. ANNE CARY BANKHEAD to T. J., Monticello. ALS. 1 p. Endorsed by T. J. Edgehill-Randolph Papers.
Covers Mr. Lightfoot's letter requesting a favor of T. J.   [1554]

1818 Mar. 28. FRANK CARR, Bentivar, to T. J., Monticello. AL. 1 p. Endorsed by T. J. Carr-Cary Papers.
Returning a letter to T. J. Mentions a letter to [Richard?] Terrell.   [1555]

1818 Mar. 31. JOSEPH C. CABELL, at Mrs. Tinsley's, to T. J., Monticello. ALS. 1 p. Endorsed by T. J. Deposited by Philip B. Campbell. Printed: Cabell 132.
Lending Jefferson a copy of the Oxford and Cambridge guide.   [1556]

1818 Apr. 10. T. J., Monticello, to FRANCIS WALKER GILMER. ALS. 1 p. Endorsed. Printed: Davis, *Francis Walker Gilmer* 125; B of R X 7 (MS. in DLC).
Urges him to try for the legislature rather than the cul-de-sac, William and Mary College. Visit of Correa da Serra and Thomas Cooper.   [1557]

1818 May 15. BENNETT H. HENDERSON, Glasgow, Barren County, Ky., to T. J., Monticello. ALS. 2 pp. Endorsed by T. J. McGregor Library.
Requests private settlement of his share of Bennett Henderson estate, which his brother James L. Henderson deeded to Craven Peyton while Bennett H. Henderson was a minor. William D. Meriwether has full power of attorney.
        [1557a]

1818 June 12. T. J., Monticello, to BERNARD PEYTON. ALS. 1 p. File draft. Endorsed by T. J.
Requests procuring of a workman, Mr. Jones, to examine slate quarries and to work at Central College.   [1558]

1818 June 15. FRANK CARR, Bentivar, to T. J., Monticello. AL. 1 p. Endorsed by T. J. Carr-Cary Papers.
Covering a letter for [Richard?] Terrell.   [1559]

1818 June 18. JOHN M. PERRY, Central College, to T. J., Monticello. ALS. 1 p. Endorsed by T. J.
Requesting instructions for bricklayers.   [1560]

1818 June 24. THOMAS COOPER, Philadelphia, to T. J., Monticello. ALS. 1 p. Endorsed by T. J.
Choice for chemistry chair to be made soon at University of Pennsylvania. Sends syllabus of lectures.   [1561]

1818 July 4. JOSHUA M. STOKES, Petersburg, to T. J., Monticello. ALS. 1 p. Endorsed by T. J.
Applies for work as painter, glazier at University.   [1562]

1818 July 10. D. HICKEY. BID for PLASTERING and STONEWORK. ADS. 1 p. Endorsed.
Rates to be charged on Mr. A. S. Brockenbrough's "new houses" (Central College buildings).   [1563]

1818 July 12. SAMUEL J. HARRISON to T. J. AL. 1 p. [On *verso*: letter to Dr. J. Wharton, Jr., 29 July 1819].

Excuses for not being able to dine with T. J. [1564]

1818 July 18 [date received]. FRANK CARR, [Bentivar], to T. J., Monticello. AL. 1 p. Endorsed by T. J. Carr-Cary Papers.

Enclosing a letter to [Richard?] Terrell. [1565]

1818 July 30. JOSEPH C. CABELL, Warminster, to T. J., Monticello. ALS. 1 p. Endorsed by T. J. Deposited by Philip B. Campbell. Printed: Cabell 132-133.

Sends by his brother William the signatures of Central College subscribers in Nelson County, agreeing to the conveyance of the property of Central College to the Commonwealth of Virginia, if the University of Virginia is located on the site of the college. [1566]

1818 Aug. 1-4. T. J. REPORT of the ROCKFISH GAP COMMISSION. AD. 42 pp. Printed with variations: Cabell 432-447; *Report of the Commissioners for the University of Virginia, assembled at Rock-Fish Gap . . . 1818.*

T. J.'s preliminary draft of the Rockfish Gap Report. Importance of education to the general welfare. Curriculum for the University. Calculation of center of population to prove that Central College is the proper site for the University. [1567]

[1818 Aug. 4?]. T. J. to [ROCKFISH GAP COMMISSION?]. AD. 1 p.

Undated formal expression of leave-taking, thanking them for acknowledging his feeble services and for the spirit of order and harmony of the board. [1568]

1818 Aug. 31-1819 Mar. 15. N. TURNER, C. TOMPKINS, B. TATE, Richmond, to T. J. DS. 1 p. Endorsed by T. J.

Recommendations for William Phillips, bricklayer. [1569]

1818 Sept. 11. J. HORWITZ, Philadelphia, to THOMAS COOPER, Philadelphia. ALS. 1 p. Endorsed by T. J.

Requests him to remind Mr. Jefferson that if college at Charlottesville is to have same standing as Harvard, Yale, Princeton, it will need professor of oriental literature. [1570]

1818 Oct. 3. THOMAS COOPER, Monticello, to T. J., Monticello. ALS. 3 pp. Endorsed by T. J.

Observations regarding Central College post. Assuming he is to hold chairs of experimental philosophy, chemistry, mineralogy, and law, asks questions regarding: apparatus, defraying expense of experiments, private tutoring, living quarters for family, vacation, salary, cost of moving. [1571]

1818 Oct. 4. T. J., Monticello, to THOMAS COOPER. ALS. 2 pp. File draft. Endorsed by T. J.

Answers Cooper's questions of 3 October, under the assumption that Central College is chosen as the University of Virginia. [1572]

1818 Oct. 6. THOMAS COOPER, Fredericksburg, to T. J. ALS. 3 pp. Endorsed by T. J.

Salary offered at Central College unsatisfactory. Injustice done T. J. by George Ord in his life of Alexander Wilson in Wilson's *Ornithology*. Mentions Correa da Serra. [1573]

1818 Oct. 17. JOHN WAYLES EPPES, Mill Brook, to T. J., Monticello. ALS. 3 pp. Endorsed by T. J. Edgehill-Randolph Papers.

Pleasure at T. J.'s return to health. Plans for Francis Eppes' education. Payment of his subscription to the Central College fund. References to Mr. Dashiell, a teacher, and to Mr. Baker. [1574]

1818 Oct. 24. JOSEPH C. CABELL, Edgewood, to T. J., Monticello. ALS. 1 p. Endorsed by T. J. Deposited by Philip B. Campbell. Printed: Cabell 133-134.

Invitation to Warminster; urges him not to tax his health. [1575]

1818 Oct. 27. T. J., Monticello, to HENRY DEARBORN, Boston. ALS. 2 pp. Endorsed. Photostat. Original owned by Harold J. Coolidge.

Libelous statements in Ord's preface to Wilson's *Ornithology*, regarding T. J.'s refusal to send Wilson on Pike's expedition. Requests inquiry by Dearborn as to why Stuart has detained T. J.'s portrait. Mentions explorations by Lewis and Clark, William Dunbar, and Thomas Freeman. Mentions James Wilkinson. [1576]

1818 Nov. 7. JOHN M. PERRY. DEED to NELSON BARKSDALE, PROCTOR of CENTRAL COLLEGE. DS. 1 p. Endorsed by T. J. Witnessed by Alexander Garrett.

Deed for land in Albemarle County, near Charlottesville, for Central College. Approved by T. J. [1577]

1818 Nov. 10. JAMES DINSMORE to T. J., Monticello. ALS. 2 pp. Endorsed by T. J.

Report on the qualities of tin roofing at Central College. [1578]

1818 Nov. 18. JOSEPH C. CABELL, Enniscorthy, to T. J., Monticello. ALS. 2 pp. Endorsed by T. J. Deposited by Philip B. Campbell. Printed: Cabell 134-135.

Illness prevents visit to Monticello. Rockfish Gap Report. Reason why he cannot make the trip to Europe for the college. Possibility he may run for the House of Representatives. Information regarding the bill for locating the University. Mentions [Samuel] Carr, Isaac Coles, William F. Gordon, Spencer Roane, Francis T. Brooke. [1579]

1818 Nov. 18. JAMES DINSMORE to T. J., Monticello. ALS. 1 p.

Cost of pine shingling calculated by Dinsmore and John M. Perry. [1580]

1818 Nov. 20. T. J., Monticello, to JOSEPH C. CABELL, Richmond. ALS. 1 p. Endorsed. Printed: Cabell 136; B of R VI 59 (MS. in DLC).

Letter to the Speaker of the Senate containing Rockfish Gap Report. Necessity for special agent to secure in Europe professors for Central College. [1581]

1818 Nov. 23. T. J., Monticello, to the MARQUIS DE LAFAYETTE. ALS. 2 pp. Photostat. Original owned by Mrs. Laird U. Park. Printed: L & B XIX 268-270; Ford-Bixby 243-244; B of R VI 255 (MS. in DLC).

T. J.'s ill health. Approval of the present French Constitution. Discounts reports of aggression in Florida. Prospects for Mr. Poirey's claims for compensation for services during the Revolution. Copy of translation of Destutt de Tracy's work on political economy.   [1582]

1818 Dec. 8. JOSEPH C. CABELL, Richmond, to T. J., Monticello. ALS. 2 pp. Endorsed by T. J. Deposited by Philip B. Campbell. Printed: Cabell 137-138.

Progress of the Rockfish Gap Report in the General Assembly. Attitudes of the William and Mary and Lexington interests. Cabell's health. References to Samuel Carr, William F. Gordon, Samuel Taylor, and Philip R. Thompson.   [1583]

1818 Dec. 14. JOSEPH C. CABELL, Richmond, to T. J., Monticello. ALS. 2 pp. Endorsed by T. J. Deposited by Philip B. Campbell. Partly printed: Cabell 138-139.

Progress of the bill to decide the site of the University. Prospects of Central College. Report of T. J.'s authorship of the bill gives appearance of dictation. References to Linn Banks, Samuel Taylor, and Robert T. Thompson.   [1584]

1818 Dec. 17. JOSEPH C. CABELL, Richmond, to T. J., Monticello. ALS. 1 p. Endorsed by T. J. Deposited by Philip B. Campbell. Printed: Cabell 139-140.

Central College fixed as the site of the University in the bill reported to the House of Delegates. Combination of western delegates opposed to Central College. Publication of T. J.'s calculation of the center of population based on census of 1810. References to Wilson C. Nicholas and William Cabell.   [1585]

1818 Dec. 17. JOSEPH C. CABELL, Richmond, to T. J., Monticello. ALS. 1 p. Endorsed by T. J. Deposited by Philip B. Campbell. Printed: Cabell 141.

Senator Davidson [Davison?] of Clarksburg in favor of Central College.   [1586]

1818 Dec. 18. DABNEY COSBY, Staunton, to T. J., Monticello. ALS. 2 pp. Endorsed by T. J.

Offers services as bricklayer, brickmaker to college.   [1587]

1818 Dec. 24. JOSEPH C. CABELL, Richmond, to T. J., Monticello. ALS. 3 pp. Endorsed by T. J. Deposited by Philip B. Campbell. Printed: Cabell 141-144.

Delay of the University bill. Opposition from friends of William and Mary, who demand $5000 per annum for William and Mary as price of their concurrence, from those who wish education left to individual enterprise, and from those who wish Literary Fund devoted to the poor. Various methods of calculating the center of population. References to the *Edinburgh Review*, William S. Archer, James Hunter, Chapman Johnson, Francis Preston, Adam Smith, Dugald Stewart, and Colonel Tatham.   [1588]

1818. BEDFORD COUNTY SHERIFF. Bill for POPLAR FOREST TAXES. ADS. 1 p. Endorsed by T. J.

Bill for taxes on 4000 acres of land, 53 slaves, and 16 horses. Paid by Joel

Yancey, T. J.'s overseer; receipted by Joseph D. Stratton, Deputy to Joel
Leftwich, Sheriff.   [1589]

[1818]. T. J. A BILL FOR THE ESTABLISHMENT OF AN UNIVERSITY.
AD. 4 pp. Printed (with additions): Cabell 447-450; *Enactments relating to . . .
the University of Virginia*, 1831.
   Bill to make Central College the University of Virginia. Board of Visitors to
erect, preserve, and repair buildings, appoint faculty and staff, prescribe the
course of education, and establish rules of government and discipline.   [1590]

1818-1819. T. J. UNIVERSITY OF VIRGINIA Balance Sheet. AD. 1 p.
   Income: subscriptions, glebe lands, and annual endowment. Costs: land purchases from John M. Perry and [W. D.?] Garth, wages, salaries, bricks.   [1591]

[1818-1823?]. W. H. WILMER to HUGH NELSON, Washington, D. C. ALS. 1 p.
Endorsed by T. J.
   Letter of introduction for Monsieur Calvo who wishes to apply for position
at Central College.   [1592]

1819 Jan. 1. T. J., Monticello, to JOSEPH C. CABELL, Richmond. ALS. 2 pp.
Endorsed. Printed: Cabell 145-146; B of R VI 59 (MS. in DLC).
   Center of white population in Virginia, calculated to determine best site for
the University.   [1593]

1819 Jan. 4. A. MACDONALD, Philadelphia, to T. J., Monticello. ALS. 1 p.
Endorsed by T. J.
   Applies for position as amanuensis or humble servant in any capacity.   [1594]

1819 Jan. 5. THOMAS COOPER, Philadelphia, to T. J., Monticello. ALS. 1 p.
Endorsed by T. J.
   Acknowledges receipt of [Rockfish Gap] Report. Workmen for the University.
T. J.'s health. Mentions William Short and Thomas Mann Randolph, Jr.   [1595]

1819 Jan. 6. ERASMUS STRIBLING, Staunton, to [T. J., Monticello]. ALS.
2 pp. Endorsed by T. J.
   Recommendation of Dabney Cosby, bricklayer.   [1596]

1819 Jan. 7. JOSEPH C. CABELL, Richmond, to T. J., Monticello. ALS. 3 pp.
Endorsed by T. J. Deposited by Philip B. Campbell. Printed: Cabell 146-149.
   Cabell's labors in the General Assembly on behalf of the University Bill.
T. J.'s health. References to John Brockenbrough, Chancellor John W. Green,
Thomas C. Hoomes, W. C. Nicholas, Mr. Pannel, Thomas Mann Randolph, Jr.,
Spencer Roane, Mr. Slaughter, John Taliaferro, Samuel Taylor, Chancellor
[Creed] Taylor, and Philip Thompson.   [1597]

1819 Jan. 7. JOHN WAUGH, Staunton, to ALEXANDER GARRETT, Charlottesville. ALS. 1 p. Endorsed by T. J.
   Recommendation of Dabney Cosby, bricklayer.   [1598]

1819 Jan. 8. JOHN WAYLES EPPES, Washington, to T. J., Monticello. ALS.
1 p. Endorsed by T. J. Edgehill-Randolph Papers.
Acknowledging receipt of Tracy's *Political Economy* and of the *Rockfish Gap
Report.* Inquiry about T. J.'s health. [1599]

1819 Jan. 18. JOSEPH C. CABELL, Richmond, to T. J., Monticello. ALS. 2 pp.
Endorsed by T. J. Deposited by Philip B. Campbell. Printed: Cabell 149-152.
University Bill passes the House of Delegates with Central College fixed as the
site. Various methods of determining the center of population favor Central
College. Cabell's recent illness. References to Briscoe G. Baldwin, Dabney Carr,
Armistead Hoomes, and James Hunter. [1600]

*1819 Jan. 20. T. J. Monticello, to RICHARD DUKE. ALS. 1 p. Photostat. En-
dorsed. Original owned by Mrs. George Gilmer.
Offering him the post of Proctor of the University. Mentions Nelson Barksdale
and Alexander Garrett. [1601]

1819 Jan. 21. JOSEPH C. CABELL, Richmond, to T. J., Monticello. ALS. 1 p.
Endorsed by T. J. Deposited by Philip B. Campbell. Printed: Cabell 152-153.
Progress of the University Bill in the Senate. Bill to connect the eastern and
western waters. Cabell's ill-health. References to Judge John Coalter, George Hay,
Armistead Hoomes, Chapman Johnson, Alfred Powell, John Taliaferro, and
Philip Thompson. [1602]

1819 Jan. 25. JOSEPH C. CABELL, Richmond, to T. J., Monticello. ALS. 1 p.
Endorsed by T. J. Deposited by Philip B. Campbell. Printed: Cabell 153.
Passage of the University Bill. Cabell's illness. References to John Coalter,
Chapman Johnson, and Edward Watts. [1603]

1819 Jan. 25. T. J., Monticello, to JOHN H. COCKE. ALS. 1 p. Cocke Papers.
Requesting him to come to Monticello because of business of extreme urgency.
[1604]

1819 Jan. 26. ALEXANDER GARRETT, [Charlottesville], to T. J., Monticello.
ALS. 1 p. Endorsed by T. J.
James Dinsmore agrees to work by Latrobe's price book. Passage of University
Bill in Senate. [1605]

1819 Jan. 28. DABNEY COSBY, Staunton, to JOHN BOWYER, Richmond. ALS.
1 p. Endorsed by T. J.
Asks for recommendation to assist his application for employment at Central
College. [1606]

1819 Jan. 28. T. J., Monticello, to JOSEPH C. CABELL, Richmond. ALS. 1 p.
Endorsed. Printed: Cabell 154; B of R VI 59 (MS. in DLC).
Passage of the University Bill. Need for extensive funds to execute the plan.
[1607]

1819 Feb. 1. SAMUEL CARR, Richmond, to T. J., Monticello. ALS. 2 pp. Endorsed by T. J. Carr-Cary Papers. Enclosure: AD. 1 p.
Recommends George Watson as anatomy professor; list of trustees of Uni-

versity of Pennsylvania who might recommend him. Success of the University Bill. Need for further funds. Recommends Dabney Cosby as mechanic. Appropriation of money for primary schools. Mentions Thomas Mann Randolph, Jr., and Francis Gilmer.   [1608]

1819 Feb. 2. THOMAS COOPER, Philadelphia, to T. J., Monticello. ALS. 1 p. Endorsed by T. J.

Salary offered by Visitors too small; will hold decision for final offer. Important law suit pending in United States Circuit Court prevents leaving in October.   [1609]

1819 Feb. 4. JOSEPH C. CABELL, Richmond, to T. J., Monticello. ALS. 4 pp. Endorsed by T. J. Deposited by Philip B. Campbell. Printed by Cabell 155-159, misdated as of 4 December.

Advises against moving now for the derelict portion of the School Fund. Copy of reports on the navigation of the James and on connection of eastern and western waters. Sketch of services rendered by the following friends of the University: William Brockenbrough, William H. Brodnax, Francis T. Brooke, Samuel Carr, John Coalter, [Francis W.?] Gilmer (author of essays signed "a Virginian"), John W. Green, George Hay, Armistead Hoomes, Garrett Minor, Wilson C. Nicholas, George Nicholson, Mr. Pannel, the Rev. Mr. Rice (author of essay signed "Crito"), Mr. Ritchie, Judge Spencer Roane, James Robertson, Jr., Mr. Scott, Captain Slaughter, Mr. Stannard, John Taliaferro, Chancellor [Creed] Taylor, Philip Thompson. Mentions also William S. Archer, Thomas Mann Randolph, Jr., and James Madison. (Thirteen lines made illegible, probably prior to publication of N. F. Cabell's book).   [1610]

1819 Feb. 8. JOHN BROWN, Spring Farm, Va., to T. J., Monticello. ALS. 2 pp. Endorsed by T. J.

Recommendation of Dabney Cosby for work at University of Virginia.   [1611]

1819 Feb. 8. JOSEPH C. CABELL, Richmond, to T. J., Monticello. ALS. 1 p. Endorsed by T. J. Deposited by Philip B. Campbell. Printed: Cabell 159-161.

Revenue of the Literary Fund not equal to appropriations.   [1612]

1819 Feb. 13. JAMES P. PRESTON. COMMISSION to T. J. DS. 1 p. Endorsed by T. J. Seal.

T. J.'s commission as Visitor of the University of Virginia.   [1613]

1819 Feb. 15. JOSEPH C. CABELL, Richmond, to T. J., Monticello. ALS. 3 pp. Endorsed by T. J. Printed: Cabell 161-163.

Appointment of James Breckenridge, Joseph Cabell, John H. Cocke, Chapman Johnson, James Madison, and Robert B. Taylor as Visitors of the University of Virginia. Cabell's health. Untrue report that Cabell is to go to Europe to seek professors. Advises delay in opening the University until sufficient buildings are ready. References to Samuel Taylor, Armistead Hoomes, [Samuel] Carr, and Henry St. George Tucker.   [1614]

1819 Feb. 17. THOMAS APPLETON, Leghorn, Italy. CONTRACT for UNIVERSITY with Michele and Giacomo Raggi. DS. 4 pp. Photostat. Endorsed by

T. J. Original privately owned. Notarized by Thomas F. B. Donati. Certified by Edward Swords, Chancellor, U. S. Consulate.

Contract for sculpture (marble columns) to be done at the University of Virginia. [1615]

1819 Feb. 19. T. J., Monticello, to JOSEPH C. CABELL, Richmond. ALS. 1 p. Endorsed. Printed: Cabell 164-165; B of R VI 59 (MS. in DLC).

Pleasure at choice of the Visitors: James Breckinridge, Robert B. Taylor, John H. Cocke, Cabell, Chapman Johnson, James Madison, and T. J. Construction to be undertaken at University. Mentions Thomas Cooper. [1616]

1819 Feb. 19. T. J., Monticello, to JOHN H. COCKE, Bremo. ALS. 1 p. Endorsed. Cocke Papers.

Inviting Cocke to travel with him to the Board of Visitors' meeting at James Madison's. Mentions Joseph Cabell, Colonel Lindsay, and David Watson. [1617]

1819 Feb. 22. JOSEPH C. CABELL, Richmond, to T. J., Monticello. ALS. 2 pp. Endorsed by T. J. Deposited by Philip B. Campbell. Printed: Cabell 165-167.

Meeting of the Board of Visitors of University; appointment of Dr. Cooper one of great delicacy and importance; recommends delay in opening until several eminent professors are secured. Difficulties in securing adequate funds from the Assembly. References to James Breckenbridge, John H. Cocke, Isaac Coles, James Madison, Robert B. Taylor, and David Watson. [1618]

1819 Feb. 25. THOMAS APPLETON, Leghorn, Italy. DRAFT on JOHN HOLLINS, Baltimore. ADS. 1 p. Endorsed. Printed: B of R VIII 23 (MS. in DLC).

Draft on Hollins in favor of Thomas Perkins, drawn for account of T. J. (Expenses incurred for the Raggi Brothers in purchase of marble for University). [1619]

1819 Mar. 1. T. J., Monticello, to JOSEPH C. CABELL. ALS. 3 pp. Endorsed. Partly printed: Cabell 167-169; B of R VI 59 (MS. in DLC).

Report to the Governor and Council of the Board of Visitors meeting. Progress of negotiations with Thomas Cooper. Denies rumors of Cooper's intemperance. University finances. Mentions Correa da Serra. [1620]

1819 Mar. 2. JOHN ADAMS to [T. J.]. L. 1 p. Copy in the hand of T. J. Printed: B of R VIII 13 (MS. in DLC).

Praising Destutt de Tracy's *Treatise on Political Economy*. [1621]

1819 Mar. 3. JAMES BULLOCK, Lynchburg, to [T. J., Monticello]. ALS. 2 pp. Endorsed by T. J.

Recommendation for David White, plasterer. [1622]

1819 Mar. 3. T. J., Monticello, to [SIMON] CHAUDRON. ALS. 1 p. Photostat. Original owned by Miss Estelle Chaudron. Printed: B of R VI 79 (MS. in DLC).

Best wishes on his removal to the Tombigbee River. [1623]

1819 Mar. 3. T. J., Monticello, to THOMAS COOPER, Philadelphia. ALS. 2 pp. File draft. Endorsed by T. J.

Tentative offer to Cooper. Final offer must await Board of Visitors meeting. Stoves for faculty residences.   [1624]

1819 Mar. 3. WILLIAM S. REID, JOHN M. GORDON, GEORGE CABELL, and JOHN BULLOCK, Lynchburg. DS. 1 p. Endorsed by T. J.

Recommendations of David White, plasterer.   [1625]

1819 Mar. 4. CHARLES JOHNSTON, Lynchburg, to T. J., Monticello. ALS. 1 p. Endorsed by T. J.

Recommends David White, plasterer.   [1626]

1819 Mar. 6. T. J., Monticello, to JOSEPH C. CABELL, Richmond. ALS. 1 p. Endorsed. Printed: Cabell 170.

Advertisement concerning the University to be put in the *Enquirer*.   [1627]

1819 Mar. 8. JOSEPH C. CABELL, Richmond, to T. J., Monticello. ALS. 3 pp. Endorsed by T. J. Deposited by Philip B. Campbell. Partly printed: Cabell 170-172.

State funds for the University. The Literary Fund. Professorship offered to Thomas Cooper. References to John H. Cocke, Isaac Coles, Alexander Garrett, James Madison, and James P. Preston.   [1628]

1819 Mar. 9. ARCHIBALD STUART, Staunton, to T. J., Monticello. ALS. 2 pp. Endorsed by T. J.

Congratulations on law establishing the University. Recommends Dabney Cosby as bricklayer. Conspiracy of Messrs. Jordan, Brown, Hawkins, and Darst, to get monopoly of brickwork at the University. Request from Messrs. Tucker and Kinney for papers in Jefferson's possession.   [1629]

1819 Mar. 10. CHRISTOPHER HUDSON, Mount Air, Va., to T. J., Monticello. ALS. 1 p. Endorsed by T. J.

Recommendation of David White, plasterer.   [1630]

1819 Mar. 10. DAVID WHITE. PLASTERER'S BID. ADS. 1 p. Endorsed by T. J.

Prices for plastering at the University.   [1631]

1819 Mar. 11. T. J., Monticello, to DABNEY CARR. ALS. 1 p. File draft. Endorsed by T. J. Carr-Cary Papers.

Advertisement (for workmen for the University?) for Winchester newspaper.
                                                                            [1632]

1819 Mar. 12. JOSEPH C. CABELL, Richmond, to T. J., Monticello. ALS. 2 pp. Endorsed by T. J. Deposited by Philip B. Campbell. Printed: Cabell 173-174.

Advertisement for workmen for the University inserted in the *Enquirer*. Alexander Garrett's draft on Literary Fund will be honored. Importance of securing Arthur S. Brockenbrough as proctor. Cabell's health improved. Mentions Mary Cabell, Mr. Montcarel, and Wilson C. Nicholas.   [1633]

1819 Mar. 13. THOMAS COOPER, Philadelphia, to T. J., Monticello. ALS. 4 pp. Endorsed by T. J.
Unlikely that Europeans will come to teach at the University of Virginia at income inferior to that common in this country. Terms under which he will go to the University. Mentions Nathaniel Bowditch, Parker Cleaveland, Zaccheus Collins, Dr. Holly, Dr. Meade, Mr. McNulty, Robert Patterson, Charles W. Peale, Mr. Shaw, and John Vaughan.   [1634]

1819 Mar. 13. WILSON CARY NICHOLAS, Richmond, to T. J., Monticello. ALS. 2 pp. Endorsed by T. J.
Stresses abilities of Arthur S. Brockenbrough. Urges he be secured as proctor to oversee construction. Mentions Alexander Garrett.   [1635]

1819 Mar. 14. DABNEY COSBY, Staunton, to T. J., Monticello. ALS. 1 p. Endorsed by T. J.
Mr. Bolinger's prices for boring logs.   [1636]

1819 Mar. 16. LEVI TAYLOR, Baltimore, to NELSON BARKSDALE, University of Virginia. ALS. 1 p. Endorsed by T. J.
Application for work as stonecutter.   [1637]

1819 Mar. 17. JAMES C. FISHER, Edward Burd, John Vaughan, John Read, Philadelphia, to NELSON BARKSDALE, University of Virginia. DS. 1 p. Endorsed by T. J.
Recommending Richard Ware as a carpenter for the University of Virginia.
                                                                         [1638]

[1819] Mar. 17. M. M. RANDOLPH, Tuckahoe, to THOMAS MANN RANDOLPH, JR., Richmond. ALS. 2 pp. Endorsed by T. J.
Recommendation for Daniel R. Calverly, painter, for work at Central College.
                                                                         [1639]

1819 Mar. 20. CHRISTOPHER BRANCH, Manchester, to [T. J., Monticello]. ALS. 2 pp. Endorsed by T. J.
Application for carpentry work at the University.   [1640]

1819 Mar. 20. ROBERT MILLS, Baltimore, to T. J., Monticello. ALS. 1 p. Endorsed by T. J.
Recommending Richard Ware, master carpenter, to Nelson Barksdale, Proctor of the University of Virginia. Progress on Washington Monument.   [1641]

1819 Mar. 20. JACOB H. WALKER, Smyrna, Del., to NELSON BARKSDALE, Charlottesville. ALS. 1 p. Endorsed by T. J.
Application for work as carpenter. Asks advance over wages in Matthew Carey's price book.   [1642]

1819 Mar. 22. JOHN BROCKENBROUGH, Richmond, to [T. J., Monticello]. ALS. 1 p. Endorsed by T. J.
Recommends Mr. Hickey, plasterer, for University.   [1643]

1819 Mar. 22. PATRICK GIBSON, Richmond, to T. J., Monticello. ALS. 1 p.
Endorsed by T. J.

Recommends Mr. Hickey as plasterer. Mentions Mr. Haxall, former employer,
and [John] Brockenbrough. [1644]

1819 Mar. 23. JOHN PARHAM, Philadelphia, to NELSON BARKSDALE, University of Virginia, or to THOMAS JEFFERSON, Monticello. LS. 3 pp. Endorsed by T. J.

Offers to do carpentry work at the University. Matthew Carey's price book
not known. Those now in use belong to the new and old Carpenters' Hall. Mentions W. Duane, Captain Dunlap, Captain Hardy, Thomas Pratt, Dr. Pilmore,
W. Strickland, Burton Wallace, and Dr. Wylie. [1645]

1819 Mar. 23. THOMAS MANN RANDOLPH, JR., Varina, to T. J., Monticello.
ALS. 1 p. Endorsed by T. J. Edgehill-Randolph Papers.

Introducing Mr. Calverly. Delayed in Richmond. Wheat crop, flowers, bushes,
and birds at Varina. [1646]

*1819 Mar. 23. [VICTOR ADOLPHUS] SASSERNO, Nice, France, to T. J., Mon-
ticello. ALS. 3 pp.

Concerning his problems as U. S. Consul. Unable to raise the $2000 bond
required of U. S. Consuls. No provision for office expenses in his instructions.
Few advantages for maritime commerce at Nice. Mentions Mr. Jackson of
New York. [1647]

1819, Mar. 24. CHILION ASHMEAD, Baltimore, to NELSON BARKSDALE,
Charlottesville. ALS. 1 p. Endorsed by T. J.

Application for painting and glazing work at University. Benjamin H. Latrobe
will recommend him. Cannot send proposals until he gets price book from
Alexandria, Va. [1648]

1819 Mar. 24. CURTIS CARTER and W. B. PHILLIPS, Richmond, to [T. J.,
Monticello]. LS. 1 p. Endorsed by T. J.

Terms for bricklaying at the University of Virginia. [1649]

1819 Mar. 24. WILLIAM HAWLEY, JR., Winchester, to NELSON BARKS-
DALE, Charlottesville. ALS. 1 p. Endorsed by T. J.

Terms for painting, glazing, and paper hanging at the University of Virginia.
[1650]

1819 Mar. 25. R. SCHAER, Washington, D. C., to T. J., Monticello. ALS. 3 pp.
Endorsed by T. J.

Offers to sell philosophical apparatus and collection of minerals, shells,
antiques, and books to the University of Virginia. [1651]

1819 Mar. 26. WILLIAM T. GRAY, Fredericksburg, to [T. J., Monticello]. ALS.
1 p. Endorsed by T. J. Another MS. in DLC.

Recommends Thomas Smith, painter. [1652]

1819 Mar. 26. E. W. HUDNALL, Buckingham County, to [T. J., Monticello]. ALS. 2 pp. Endorsed by T. J.
Submits terms for painting and glazing. Can be recommended by Littlebury Moon, Charles Irving, George Booker, Alexander Trent, and William Perkins.
[1653]

1819 Mar. 26. NORBORNE RATCLIFFE, Richmond, to [T. J., Monticello]. ALS. 2 pp. Endorsed by T. J.
Proposal for brickwork at the University of Virginia.   [1654]

1819 Mar. 26. RICHARD WARE, Charlottesville, to NELSON BARKSDALE. ALS. 1 p. Endorsed by T. J.
Proposal to undertake carpenters' work below prices in Matthew Carey's price book of 1812.   [1655]

1819 Mar. 27. JOHN ADAMS, Richmond, to JAMES BRECKENRIDGE. ALS. 1 p. Endorsed by T. J.
Recommends Russell Dudley, a carpenter, associate of Otis Manson, architect, for work at the University.   [1656]

1819 Mar. 27. JAMES DINSMORE, Charlottesville, to [T. J., Monticello]. ALS. 2 pp. Endorsed by T. J.
Construction of the University of Virginia. Wage scale set by Matthew Carey's price book unfair.   [1657]

1819 Mar. 27. JAMES DINSMORE and JOHN M. PERRY to the BOARD OF VISITORS, UNIVERSITY OF VIRGINIA. ADS. 1 p. Endorsed by T. J.
Report on the springs in the University grounds.   [1658]

1819 Mar. 27. JAMES OLDHAM, Charlottesville, to NELSON BARKSDALE, University of Virginia. ALS. 1 p. Endorsed by T. J.
Terms for doing carpentry work at the University.   [1659]

1819 Mar. 27. JOHN M. PERRY to BOARD OF VISITORS, UNIVERSITY OF VIRGINIA. ALS. 1 p. Endorsed by T. J.
Submits estimate on brickwork and carpentry at the University. Mentions M[atthew] Brown, and Matthew Carey's *Philadelphia Price Book*.   [1660]

1819 Mar. 29. DABNEY COSBY, Charlottesville, to NELSON BARKSDALE, University of Virginia. ALS. 1 p. Endorsed by T. J.
Terms for brickwork at the University.   [1661]

1819 Mar. 29. JOHN PERCIVAL, to [T. J., Monticello]. ALS. 1 p. Endorsed by T. J.
Terms for carpentry work. Objects to scale set in Matthew Carey's price book.   [1662]

1819 Mar. 29. THOMAS SMITH, Charlottesville, to NELSON BARKSDALE, University of Virginia. ALS. 2 pp. Endorsed by T. J.
Proposals for painting, glazing. Returning to Fredericksburg until news of proposal announced.   [1663]

1819 Mar. 30. ABRAHAM WOGLOME, Philadelphia, to NELSON BARKS-
DALE, University of Virginia. ALS. 1 p. Endorsed by T. J.
In response to advertisement in Philadelphia *Democratic Press*, submits pro-
posals for brickwork.   [1664]

[1819 Mar.]. DANIEL R. CALVERLY, [Richmond], to [T. J., Monticello]. ALS.
1 p. Endorsed by T. J.
Submits proposal for painting, glazing.   [1665]

1819 Apr. 1. JAMES DINSMORE and JOHN M. PERRY, University of Virginia, to NELSON BARKSDALE. ALS. 1 p. Endorsed by T. J.
Withdrawing earlier proposals. Will work for terms in Matthew Carey's
price book.   [1666]

1819 Apr. 2. T. J., Monticello, to THOMAS COOPER, Philadelphia. ALS. 2 pp.
File draft. Endorsed by T. J.
Decision of Visitors to open classical school under usher to be named by
Cooper, perhaps Mr. Stack. Will serve as nursery for the University. Need for
tinsmith and silversmith in Charlottesville. Plan for the University seal. [1667]

1819 Apr. 3. JOHN NEILSON, Upper Bremo, to BOARD OF VISITORS, University of Virginia. ALS. 1 p. Endorsed by T. J.
Regrets that he must decline further carpenter's work at present.   [1668]

1819 Apr. 3. JAMES OLDHAM, Charlottesville, to T. J., Monticello. ALS. 1 p.
Endorsed by T. J.
Changes terms submitted for work at the University. Possibility that workers
may erect cabins on the grounds. Mentions James Dinsmore and John M.
Perry.   [1669]

1819 Apr. 4. T. J., Monticello, to ROBERT S. GARRETT. ALS. 1 p.
Thanks for recommendations of Don Marcus Escopinachi, Dr. Speed, and of
Mr. Bonfils. Except for Dr. Cooper, the University will hire no professors
until construction is complete.   [1670]

1819 Apr. 6. RICHARD M. BURKE, Richmond, to NELSON BARKSDALE,
University of Virginia. ALS. 2 pp. Endorsed by T. J.
Seeking work as carpenter and joiner at the University of Virginia.   [1671]

1819 Apr. 8. DANIEL FLOURNOY, Chesterfield County, to [T. J., Monticello].
ALS. 1 p. Endorsed by T. J.
Submits proposals for brickwork at University.   [1672]

1819 Apr. 9. T. J., Monticello, to MR. BOLINGER. ALS. 1 p. File draft. Endorsed by T. J.
Accepts offer to pipe water to University.   [1673]

1819 Apr. 9. T. J., Monticello, to CURTIS CARTER and W. B. PHILIPS,
Richmond. ALS. 1 p. File draft. 2 copies. One endorsed by T. J.
Terms for brickwork at the University.   [1674]

1819 Apr. 9. T. J., Monticello, to THOMAS COOPER, Philadelphia. ALS. 1 p. File draft. Endorsed by T. J.
Stoves for the University. Important letter for Richard Ware, carpenter. Mentions Mr. Leschot of Charlottesville and Bernard Peyton. [1675]

1819 Apr. 9. T. J., Monticello, to RICHARD WARE, Philadelphia. ALS. 1 p. File draft. Endorsed by T. J.
Accepts his proposal for carpentry work. Information regarding wages, working conditions, and living quarters for the workers. Matthew Carey's price book. [1676]

1819 Apr. 11. THOMAS COOPER, Philadelphia, to T. J., Monticello. ALS. 3 pp. Endorsed by T. J.
Advertisement for stoves placed in *Democratic Press* and in *Poulson's American Daily Advertiser*. Recent illness. Stack will undertake grammar school in Charlottesville. Urges confining choice to Oxford if professors to be sought in Europe. Will try to accept terms of the University. Offers received to edit selection of English common law reporters and an agricultural dictionary. [1677]

1819 Apr. 11. T. J. to RANDOLPH HARRISON. ALS. 1 p. File draft. Endorsed by T. J.
Acknowledges his zeal in obtaining subscriptions for the University. More funds needed. Requests deposit of subscriptions in the University account in the Bank of Virginia. [1678]

1819 Apr. 14. DAVID COBBS to [T. J. Monticello]. ALS. 1 p. Endorsed by T. J.
Proposal for piping water. [1679]

1819 Apr. 15. THOMAS COOPER, Philadelphia, to T. J., Monticello. ALS. 1 p. Endorsed by T. J.
Receipt of money for stoves from Mr. Leschot. Mr. Stack leaving for Charlottesville. Information about Minerva for the University of Virginia seal. [1680]

1819 Apr. 17. JOSEPH C. CABELL, Richmond, to T. J., Monticello. ALS. 2 pp. Endorsed by T. J. Deposited by Philip B. Campbell. Printed: Cabell 174-176.
Recommends A. S. Brockenbrough as Proctor. Despite admiration for T. J.'s plans for the pavilions and lawn, recommends different style for hotels and ranges. Provision for lecture rooms in separate buildings from pavilions. Fire at Monticello. Reference to John H. Cocke. [1681]

1819 Apr. 18. THOMAS COOPER, Philadelphia, to T. J., Monticello. ALS. 2 pp. Endorsed by T. J.
Richard Ware will accept Jefferson's terms. Difficulty in procuring brickmakers. Brickmaker Cribbs recommends burning bricks in kilns to improve the quality. Mentions Mr. James, Quaker of Philadelphia. [1682]

1819 Apr. 20. RICHARD WARE, Philadelphia, to T. J., Monticello. ALS. 1 p. Endorsed by T. J.
Letter received through Thomas Cooper. Difficulties in finding brickmaker; brick prices. [1683]

1819 Apr. 22. THOMAS COOPER, Philadelphia, to T. J., Monticello. ALS. 1 p.
Endorsed by T. J.
  Still unwell. John Vaughan to buy stoves to ship to Bernard Peyton, Rich-
mond. Wing of Monticello destroyed by fire.   [1684]

1819 Apr. 24. CHARLES CLAY, Petty Grove, to T. J., Poplar Forest. ALS. 1 p.
Endorsed by T. J. Edgehill-Randolph Papers.
  Comments on T. J.'s ale. Gift of vegetables. Thanks for directions on "the
assignments" (of lands?).   [1685]

1819 Apr. 26. CHARLES CLAY, Petty Grove, to T. J., Poplar Forest. ALS. 1 p.
Endorsed by T. J. Edgehill-Randolph Papers.
  Recommends that the deeds be witnessed. (Possibly a reference to deed of
trust to Poplar Forest, 15 September 1819).   [1686]

1819 Apr. 27. GEORGE BLAETTERMANN, London, to T. J., Monticello.
ALS. French. 2 pp. Endorsed by T. J.
  Applies for professorship of modern languages at the University of Virginia.
Mentions Mr. Bevan, James Ogilvie, Mr. Preston, and George Ticknor. [1687]

1819 Apr. 28. CHARLES CLAY, [Petty Grove], to T. J., Poplar Forest. ALS. 1 p.
Endorsed by T. J. Edgehill-Randolph Papers.
  Asks how the revocation is to be executed and published.   [1688]

1819 May 3. T. J., Monticello, to JOHN H. COCKE, Bremo. ALS. 1 p. Endorsed.
Cocke Papers. Printed: B of R VI 89 (MS. in DLC).
  Requests aid a second time in stocking his fish pond. Suggests Cocke's son
attend Mr. Stack's classical school in Charlottesville with Mr. Laporte as boarding housekeeper. Arrival of Arthur S. Brockenbrough. Tadeusz Kosciuszko's will
to be proven.   [1689]

1819 May 3. JOHN H. COCKE, Bremo, to T. J., Monticello. ALS. 4 pp. Endorsed
by T. J.
  Detailed recommendations for changes in University construction plans
Suggests diverting money from Tadeusz Kosciuszko's will into American Coloni
zation Society. Mentions information collected by Miles and Burgess on the
coast of Africa.   [1690]

1819 May 4. T. J., Monticello, to WILSON J. CARY. ALS. 1 p. File draft.
Endorsed by T. J. Carr-Cary Papers.
  Mr. Stack, who is recommended by Thomas Cooper, to open classical school
at Charlottesville; advises that Wilson Miles Cary be placed there. [1691]

1819 May 7. WILSON J. CARY, Carybrook, to T. J., Monticello. ALS. 1 p
Endorsed by T. J. Carr-Cary Papers.
  Requests enrollment of Wilson Miles Cary in Mr. Stack's classical school.
Wishes him to board with [P.] Laporte to learn French. Mentions John H.
Cocke.   [1692]

1819 May 12. T. J. Action regarding Kosciuszko's will. (See under 1798 May 5.)
                                                                     [1693]

1819 May 14. T. J., Monticello, to WILSON CARY NICHOLAS. ALS. 1 p. Endorsed.

Avails self of Nicholas' offer of endorsement of note to the Farmer's Bank. Thomas Jefferson Randolph moving to Tufton.   [1694]

1819 May 15. JOHN WAYLES EPPES, Mill Brook, to T. J., Monticello. ALS. 2 pp. Endorsed by T. J. Edgehill-Randolph Papers.

Sending whin seed. Routes from Bedford to Monticello via Canton, Va., and Scot's Ferry. Pleasure at renewed intercourse with T. J.   [1695]

1819 May 17. T. J., Monticello, to ARTHUR S. BROCKENBROUGH. ALS. 1 p. Endorsed. Printed: B of R VI 51 (MS. in DLC).

Recommends substitution of Curtis Carter as a brick worker for Richard Ware, who has been jailed for debt in Philadelphia. Dr. Cooper to send house-joiners from Philadelphia. Pavilions and dormitories on East Lawn to be substituted for work on West Lawn.   [1696]

1819 May 22. WILSON J. CARY, Carybrook, to T. J., Monticello. ALS. 1 p. Endorsed by T. J. Carr-Cary Papers.

Sends Wilson Miles Cary to grammar school in Charlottesville. Payment of Board delayed until tobacco sold in Richmond.   [1697]

1819 May 28. T. J., Monticello, to ARTHUR S. BROCKENBROUGH. ALS. 1 p. Endorsed.

Arrival of Richard Ware. Superior bricklayers available at Philadelphia. [1698]

1819 June 5. T. J., Monticello, to ARTHUR S. BROCKENBROUGH. ALS. 1 p. Endorsed. Another MS. in DLC.

T. J.'s plans for pavilions. Contract for laborers. Trip to Bedford. Advantages of Philadelphia laborers.   [1699]

1819 June 15. T. J., Monticello, to CHARLES F. KUPFER, Boston. ALS. 1 p. File draft. Endorsed by T. J.

Window glass for the University. Mentions Smith and Riddle, agents in Richmond, and Bernard Peyton.   [1700]

1819 June 17. T. J., Monticello, to ARCHIBALD S. BULLOCH, Savannah, Ga. ALS. 1 p. McGregor Library. Printed: B of R VI 55 (MS. in DLC).

Pleased that Bulloch has named his son for him.   [1701]

1819 June 21. THOMAS COOPER, Philadelphia, to T. J., Monticello. ALS. 3 pp. Endorsed by T. J.

John Vaughan to ship stoves for University. Seal for University drawn by Thomas Sully, but Mr. Rasch's price for engraving too high. Bass Otis' portrait of T. J. excellent. Mineral collection and botanical garden for the University. Correa da Serra recommends Thomas Nuttal as botanist. Three editorial offers no longer available: edition of English reporters given to [Charles Jared] Ingersoll; agricultural dictionary and edition of Virginia law reporters given up.

Opinion on effect of paper swindling. Two papers in next *Analectic Magazine*, on the present movement among the manufacturers and on lithography. [1702]

1819 June 21. JAMES OLDHAM to T. J., Monticello. ALS. 1 p. Endorsed by T. J.
Sends draft of window frames. Asks instructions on cornice, ceiling of portico, and columns of pavilion. Asks to borrow Jefferson's Palladio.   [1703]

1819 June 24. DABNEY S. CARR, Baltimore, to T. J., Monticello. ALS. 1 p. Endorsed by T. J. Carr-Cary Papers.
Arrival of Italian sculptors, Michael and Giacomo Raggi; plan for their trip to the University. Mentions John Hollins, Thomas Appleton, Robert Patton, and Garrett Minor.   [1704]

1819 June 24. THOMAS ESTON RANDOLPH, Ashton, to T. J., Monticello. ALS. 1 p. Endorsed by T. J. Edgehill-Randolph Papers.
Delay in payment of rent due for the mill.   [1705]

1819 June 27. T. J., Monticello, to ARTHUR S. BROCKENBROUGH. ALS. 2 pp. Endorsed. Another MS. in DLC.
Disagreement with workmen, John M. Perry, Whateley, Curtis Carter, and William Phillips. Advises use of Philadelphia workmen who will work for less. Construction details.   [1706]

1819 June 28. T. J., Monticello, to FRANCIS W. GILMER. AL[S clipped]. 1 p. Endorsed. Another MS. in MHi.
Cannot give information on the 1776 revision of Virginia laws. Visit of Correa da Serra. Proposed trip to Bedford County. Mentions George Wythe.   [1707]

1819 June 29. T. J., Monticello, to ARTHUR S. BROCKENBROUGH. ALS. 1 p. Endorsed.
Dormitories and cellars for the workmen at the University promised by Perry.   [1708]

1819 July 1. JOHN HOLLINS. BILL to B. WILLIAMSON. D. 1 p.
Account for expenses incurred by the Raggi brothers.   [1709]

1819 July 1. JAMES DINSMORE to T. J., Monticello. ALS. 1 p. Endorsed by T. J.
Instructions regarding the columns for the University. Mentions Arthur S. Brockenbrough.   [1710]

1819 July 2. T. J., Monticello, to ARTHUR S. BROCKENBROUGH. ALS. 2 pp. Endorsed.
Reimbursement to John Hollins of Baltimore for money advanced to cover expenses of the Raggi brothers. Preparations needed for sculptors and brick makers. Mentions Thomas Appleton, Captain Concklin, Alexander Garrett, and Wilson Cary Nicholas.   [1711]

1819 July 5. J. WHARTON, JR., Stevensburgh, Culpeper County, to T. J., Monticello. ALS. 2 pp. Endorsed by T. J.

Applies for chair of medicine at the University of Virginia. Studied at Edinburgh; is well recommended.   [1712]

1819 July 6. JOHN M. PERRY, University of Virginia, to T. J., Monticello. ALS. 1 p. Endorsed by T. J.

Order for balance due for brickwork, including that on Mrs. Garner's house.
                                                                            [1713]

1819 July 7. T. J., Monticello, to JOHN H. COCKE, Bremo. ALS. 3 pp. Endorsed. Printed: B of R VI 89 (MS. in DLC).

Catalog of the best editions of the Greek and Latin classics. Expenses incurred for the Raggi brothers. Work planned for the Raggi brothers. Plans to visit Bedford County. Boys in the grammar school receive excellent instruction from Mr. Stack and Mr. Laporte. Mentions Robert Taylor and Mr. Cardelli. [1714]

1819 July 8, 11, and 16. T. J., Monticello, to JAMES BRECKENRIDGE. ALS. 4 pp.

Report on progress at the University of Virginia. Professors' gardens in rear of pavilions. Construction of the hotels and pavilions. Classical school run by Mr. Stack, with Mr. Laporte boarding the students. George Blaettermann, Nathaniel Bowditch, Thomas Cooper, Thomas Nuttal, and George Ticknor considered for faculty. Arrival of Raggi brothers to do sculpture. The marble in the quarry not the right quality for Ionic or Corinthian capitals. Work proceeds miserably. Paying the printed prices as the fair living prices.   [1715]

1819 July 11. T. J., Monticello, to THOMAS COOPER, Philadelphia. ALS. 1 p. File draft. Endorsed by T. J.

One of T. J.'s granddaughters (Cornelia Randolph?) has drawn sketch uniting two of Bass Otis' designs for the University seal to be engraved by cheaper workman. Interested in Thomas Nuttal for University faculty if a native. Philadelphia workmen expected. Opinion on paper money.   [1716]

1819 July 14. T. J., Monticello, to ARTHUR S. BROCKENBROUGH. ALS. 1 p. Endorsed. Another MS. in DLC.

Further payments for Michael Raggi to be remitted to Thomas Perkins at the request of Thomas Appleton. Progress of the carving.   [1717]

1819 July 21. ROWLAND REYNOLDS, Hampton, to T. J., Monticello. ALS. 3 pp. Endorsed by T. J.

Applies for classical professorship at the University of Virginia. Education at Trinity College, Dublin, Ireland and experience at the Rev. Gilbert Austin's academy in Dublin, at the Hampton Academy, and with private pupils. List of Greek and Latin classics he has read. Copy of his diploma, signed by Johs. Barrett, Thomas Elsington, Fra. Hodgkinson, Robert Phipps, and Thomas Prior. Mentions letter from [Thomas A.] Emmet to Bishop [Benjamin] Moore. [1718]

1819 July 28. T. J., Poplar Forest, to [ARTHUR S. BROCKENBROUGH]. ALS. 1 p. Endorsed. Another MS. in DLC.

Information from John Hollins of Baltimore, regarding arrival of marble from Leghorn, Italy, on board the Brig *Strong* belonging to Mchael and Giacomo Raggi. Duties to be paid.   [1719]

1819 July 28. THOMAS COOPER, Philadelphia, to T. J. ALS. 1 p. Endorsed by T. J.

Binns has sent copy of Declaration of Independence. Mr. Cloud and Mr. W. Humbell on mineral committee (to appraise Cooper's collection?); Mr. Collins unable to serve. Seal in engraver's hands. Correa da Serra will report on Thomas Nuttal, who is English by birth. Will advertise for tinsmith. [1720]

1819 July 29. T. J., Poplar Forest, to [ARTHUR S. BROCKENBROUGH]. ALS. 2 pp. Endorsed.

Forwards a letter from a Mr. Stokes. Information from John Gorman, stone-cutter, relative to prices and time required for stonecutting and sculpturing.
                                                              [1721]

1819 July 29. T. J., Poplar Forest, to J. WHARTON, JR. ALS. 1 p. File draft. Endorsed by T. J.

University of Virginia not yet ready to appoint professors.   [1722]

1819 Aug. 7. D. MARIANO, Lexington, Ky., to T. J., Monticello. ALS. 3 pp. Endorsed by T. J.

Application for professorship of modern languages and music at the University of Virginia. Teaches now at Transylvania University. Opinion on music teaching in the U. S. Offers to help T. J. in his translation of Carlo Botta's *History of the War of American Independence.*   [1723]

1819 Aug. 7. T. J., Poplar Forest, to ROWLAND REYNOLDS, Hampton. ALS. 1 p. File draft. Endorsed by T. J.

University of Virginia not yet ready to appoint faculty. Returns letter of [Thomas] Emmet to Bishop [Benjamin] Moore.   [1724]

1819 Aug. 9. T. J., [Poplar Forest], to CHARLES CLAY. L. 1 p. Typescript copy (apparently from a catalog notice) in Edward L. Stone MSS.

Approves the judgement in the case of the Negroes (case of illness or death caused by medicine). Attack of rheumatism.   [1725]

1819 Aug. 9. JEREMIAH SULLIVAN and THOMAS PETTIGRUE, Washington, to T. J. ALS by Sullivan. 1 p. Endorsed by T. J.

Applying for position as carver. Mentions Mr. Cardelli and Giovanni Andrei.
                                                              [1726]

1819 Aug. 10. GIOVANNI ANDREI, Washington, to T. J. ALS. 1 p. Endorsed by T. J. Italian.

Recommendation of Jeremiah Sullivan, stonecutter.   [1727]

1819 Aug. 17. T. J., Poplar Forest, to ARTHUR S. BROCKENBROUGH, Charlottesville. ALS. 1 p. Endorsed.

Forwarding two letters, one from [Giovanni] Andrei. Recommends the stone-work of John Gorman.   [1728]

1819 Aug. 24. T. J., Poplar Forest, to MARTHA RANDOLPH. ALS. 1 p. File draft. Endorsed by T. J. Edgehill-Randolph Papers. Another MS. in NNP.
Plans for his return to Monticello. Rheumatism better. Instructions for sending a siesta chair. Corn crop. References to Johnny Hemings, Henry (servant), James Leitch, Mrs. Trist, and Wormley (servant).   [1729]

1819 Aug. 25. SAMUEL J. HARRISON, Lynchburg, to T. J. ALS. 1 p. Endorsed by T. J.
Recommends James Wade for piping water to University of Virginia.   [1730]

1819 Aug. 29. T. J., Poplar Forest, to ARTHUR S. BROCKENBROUGH. ALS. 1 p. Endorsed. Another MS. in DLC.
Recommending James Wade of Lynchburg for conducting water to the University.   [1731]

1819 Aug. 29. T. J., Poplar Forest, to ROWLAND REYNOLDS, Hampton. ALS. 1 p. File draft. Endorsed by T. J.
Asks if he would be interested in teaching in classical school now in Charlottesville in the event present teacher, Stack, leaves.   [1732]

1819 Sept. 1. T. J., Poplar Forest, to ARTHUR S. BROCKENBROUGH. AL. 2 pp. Endorsed. Another MS. in DLC.
Engagements for brickwork and woodwork at the University with Curtis Carter, James Dinsmore, James Oldham, John M. Perry, William Phillips, and the Philadelphia workmen. Remission of money to the wives of the Raggi brothers. Corinthian capitals. Construction work at Poplar Forest. References to John Vaughan.   [1733]

1819 Sept. 10. T. J. to D. MARIANO. ALS. 1 p. File draft. Endorsed by T. J.
Nomination of professors being deferred until building completed.   [1734]

1819 Sept. 12. ROWLAND REYNOLDS, Hampton, to T. J. ALS. 1 p. Endorsed by T. J.
Declines offer to head classical school in Charlottesville.   [1735]

1819 Sept. 13. THOMAS COOPER, Philadelphia, to T. J. ALS. 1 p. Endorsed by T. J.
Stoves and University seal to be forwarded. Accepting *ad interim* offer to lecture at Lexington, Kentucky. Articles signed "Indagator" in *Analectic Magazine* opposes tariff. Correa da Serra well. Mentions John Vaughan.   [1736]

1819 Sept. 15. T. J. DEED of TRUST on POPLAR FOREST. ADS. 1 p. File draft. Endorsed by T. J. Edgehill-Randolph Papers. Original owned by C. S. Hutter, Jr.
Poplar Forest deeded to Bernard Peyton and Andrew Stevenson, Directors of Bank of the United States, Richmond, as security for a loan to Wilson Cary Nicholas, endorsed by T. J. and T. J. Randolph.   [1737]

1819 Sept. 16. CONSTANTINE S. RAFINESQUE, Lexington, Ky., to T. J., Monticello. ALS. 3 pp. Endorsed by T. J.
Application for professorship at the University of Virginia in French, Italian,

materia medica, natural philosophy, geometry, map drawing, natural history, drawing, political economy, etc. Lists qualifications; tells life history. Offers Dewitt Clinton, Zaccheus Collins, and Samuel L. Mitchell as references. Appends application to the Board of Visitors.   [1738]

1819 Sept. 17 [date received]. MICHELE and GIACOMO RAGGI to T. J., Monticello. ALS. Italian. 2 pp. Endorsed by T. J.
   Suggest savings possible by their making the marble columns for the University in Leghorn, Italy.   [1739]

1819 Oct. 4. CHAPMAN JOHNSON to [T. J.]. ALS. 1 p. Endorsed by T. J.
   Situation seems to require postponement or cancellation of Thomas Cooper's appointment, to save salary until institution opens. Suggests sending him copy of Visitors' resolution.   [1740]

1819 Oct. 8. T. J., Monticello, to JOHN H. COCKE, Bremo. ALS. 1 p. Endorsed. Cocke Papers.
   Covering letter to Thomas Cooper for his approval. Suffering from colic and rheumatism.   [1741]

1819 Oct. 11. THOMAS COOPER, Philadelphia, to T. J., Monticello. ALS. 3 pp. Endorsed by T. J.
   Stove casting and seal sent to T. J. Uncertain of going to Lexington, Kentucky. Medical school would succeed in Virginia with summer lectures at Charlottesville, winter lectures at Norfolk. Offers to defer coming to Charlottesville. Hopes to be Commissioner if Bankruptcy Law passes. Mentions John Vaughan.
                                                                [1742]

1819 Oct. 15. T. J. and JOHN H. COCKE to THOMAS COOPER. LS. 3 pp. File draft. Endorsed by T. J.
   Communication, by instructions of Board of Visitors, to explain delay in opening of the University of Virginia. Additional buldings, not hitherto planned, prevent hiring of professors. Richard Ware mentioned.   [1743]

1819 Oct. 16. T. J., Monticello, to JAMES LEITCH. ALS. 1 p. Photostat. Original owned by Mrs. J. Sharshall Grasty.
   Order to deliver cotton yarn fit for Negro cloth to bearer, Burwell (a servant).
                                                                [1744]

1819 Oct. 22. THOMAS COOPER, Philadelphia, to T. J., Monticello. ALS. 2 pp. Endorsed by T. J.
   Visitors' inability to fulfill contract leaves him without support, since position of bankruptcy commissioner failed to materialize. Dr. Robert Patterson giving his chemistry course. May have to accept permanent position elsewhere. Pleased at T. J.'s recovery from severe illness. Regards to John H. Cocke and the Board of Visitors.   [1745]

1819 Oct. 25. THOMAS COOPER, Philadelphia, to T. J., Monticello. ALS. 1 p. Endorsed by T. J.
   Position at Lexington, Ky., filled by Dr. Blythe. Therefore, proposes salary

advance and permission to live in University of Virginia buildings immediately.
[1746]

1819 Nov. 2. JOSEPH C. CABELL, Bremo, to T. J., Monticello. ALS. 1 p.
Endorsed by T. J. Deposited by Philip B. Campbell. Printed: Cabell 177.
Returns copy of plan of Poplar Forest. Financial requirements prevent his
moving to the neighborhood of the University at the present time. T. J.'s
illness.   [1747]

1819 Nov. 4. T. J. MEMORANDUM on the RAGGI BROTHERS. AD. 2 pp.
Terms of employment, expenses, sums advanced to their wives. Mentions
Thomas Appleton.   [1748]

1819 Nov. 7. T. J., Monticello, to CONSTANTINE S. RAFINESQUE, Lexington,
Ky. ALS. 1 p. File draft. Endorsed by T. J.
Long illness deferred reply. Visitors of University of Virginia plan to use all
funds for building, and are deferring appointment of faculty.   [1749]

1819 Nov. 19. T. J., Monticello, to THOMAS COOPER. ALS. 1 p. File draft.
Endorsed by T. J.
Letter formally engaging Dr. Cooper to teach at the University of Virginia.
Quarters provided for him.   [1750]

1819 Nov. 24. THOMAS COOPER, Philadelphia, to T. J., Monticello. ALS. 1 p.
Endorsed by T. J.
Plans for removing to the University of Virginia. Details regarding the
advance of his salary. Law suit won but lands unsalable. Regards Quaker petition to Congress on the Missouri question, drawn by Mr. Walsh, as mischievous
interference.   [1751]

1819 Dec. 4. T. J., Monticello, to FRANCIS WALKER GILMER. ALS. 1 p.
Endorsed. Another MS. in MHi.
Requests any payment due to John Wayles estate be paid to Archibald
Thweatt, son-in-law of Francis Eppes, who brought the original suit when T.
J. was in France. Inquiries about getting preference in payment of Wilson Cary
Nicholas' debt.   [1752]

1819 Dec. 8. T. J. vs. RIVANNA COMPANY. D. 18 pp. Endorsed by T. J.
Copy attested by William L. Eskridge, Clerk of Court of Chancery. Edgehill·
Randolph Papers.
Record in Virginia Supreme Court of Chancery at Staunton. Decision that
proof before court not sufficient, and therefore a commission set up to determine
whether any damage might be done to T. J.'s canal and mills by the use of
his canal by the Rivanna Company. George Divers, William D. Meriwether,
Nimrod Bramham, Dabney Minor, and John Welles, directors of the company.
[1753]

1819 Dec. 10. F. R. HASSLER, Newark, N. J., to T. J., Monticello. ALS. 3 pp.
Endorsed by T. J.
Application for chair of mathematics or natural philosophy at University of
Virginia. Lists experience at West Point, Union College (Schenectady, N. Y.),

work on boundary line at 45° parallel and on coast survey. Judge Yates of N. Y. will give him reference. Possesses library and apparatus. Mentions Robert Patterson and Mr. Troughton of London.   [1754]

1819 Dec. 18. THOMAS COOPER, Philadelphia, to T. J., Monticello. ALS. 1 p. Endorsed by T. J.

Has seal for University. Sets out for Columbia, S. C., to be professor of chemistry at Columbia College for one year.   [1755]

1819 Dec. 24. THOMAS COOPER, Philadelphia, to T. J., Monticello. ALS. 1 p. Endorsed by T. J.

Sends copy of *Democratic Press* on the Missouri Question. University of Virginia seal sent by Mr. Stack. Arrangements for advance on his salary at the University of Virginia. Mentions John Vaughan and J. Conolly.   [1756]

1819 Dec. 27. JAMES CUTBUSH, Washington, D. C., to T. J., Monticello. ALS. 3 pp. Endorsed by T. J.

Applies for professorship of chemistry or natural sciences. Lists publications. Character of a university set by its professors; cites University of Pennsylvania's flourishing under William Shippen, Caspar Wistar, and Benjamin Rush. Thomas Cooper treated unfairly.   [1757]

[*ca.* 1819. ARTHUR S. BROCKENBROUGH]. CONSTRUCTION ESTIMATE. AD. 1 p. Endorsed by T. J.

Estimate of cost of building one range of dormitories.   [1758]

[1819?]. [ARTHUR S. BROCKENBROUGH]. MEMORANDUM on plastering prices. AD. 1 p. Endorsed by T. J.

Prices quoted by Hugh Chisholm for work at the University.   [1759]

[*ca.* 1819]. T. J. THE LIFE AND MORALS OF JESUS OF NAZARETH. 1 vol. in several hands including Martha Randolph, Cornelia Randolph Trist, Mary Trist, and Martha Jefferson Trist Burke.

Copied from a volume (now in the National Museum), which Jefferson made by clipping from two copies of the Gospels verses dealing with Christ's life and moral precepts. (The University of Virginia Library owns the two Bibles from which the clippings were excerpted).   [1760]

[1819?]. T. J. PLAT OF UNIVERSITY OF VIRGINIA lands. AD. 1 p. 3 copies. 1 in Cabell Papers. Endorsed by T. J.

Land surveyed by William Woods.   [1761]

[*ca.* 1819]. T. J. Table of CONSTRUCTION COSTS. AD. 1 p.

Lists of prices for bricklayers, carpenters, plasterers, painters, glaziers, submitted by Joseph Antrim, Daniel Calverly, Curtis Carter, Dabney Cosby, Hugh Chisholm, James Dinsmore, Mr. Hudnall, John Neilson, James Oldham, John M. Perry, Mr. Percival, William Phillips, Mr. Smith, Richard Ware, and Mr. White. Also listed are Northern prices and Washington prices.   [1762]

1819-1820. T. J. and ARTHUR S. BROCKENBROUGH. Memoranda on tne RAGGI BROTHERS. 2 items, 1 a T. J. AD.

Notes on costs of Michele Raggi to the University of Virginia, and payments to him and to Giacomo Raggi. [1763]

[1820] Jan. 10 [incorrectly dated 1819]. JOHN W. WEBSTER, Boston, to T. J., Monticello. ALS. 3 pp. Endorsed by T. J.

Offering to sell his mineral collection, highly recommended by George Gibbs and Parker Cleaveland. [1764]

1820 Jan. 22. T. J., Monticello, to JOSEPH C. CABELL, Richmond. ALS. 1 p. Endorsed. Printed: Cabell 178; Ford X 154-155; W (1) VII 65; B of R VI 59 (MS. in DLC).

Bitter letter resenting niggardliness of Virginia as opposed to Kentucky, which has a flourishing university. Subscriptions of Cabell, John H. Cocke, [George?] Divers, John Harris, James Madison, and his own set aside to pay Thomas Cooper's salary. [1765]

1820 Jan. 24. T. J. to ALEXANDER GARRETT, Charlottesville. ALS. 2 pp. Endorsed.

Requests remittance to John Vaughan of Philadelphia, to be remitted to Thomas Appleton, Leghorn, Italy, on account of Michael and Giacomo Raggi. T. J.'s receipt for same, 13 February 1820, mentioning William Dandridge, Cashier of the Bank of Virginia. [1766]

1820 Feb. 3. JOSEPH C. CABELL, Richmond, to T. J., Monticello. ALS. 1 p. Endorsed by T. J. Deposited by Philip B. Campbell. Printed: Cabell 180-181.

Funds for the University from Literary Fund and elsewhere. Health of his wife, Mary. Reference to T. M. Randolph, Jr. [1767]

1820 Feb. 5. FRANCIS BLOODFOOD, Albany, to T. J., Monticello. ALS. 3 pp. Endorsed by T. J.

Offering to sell Dr. Benjamin DeWitt's mineral collection. Mentions Archibald Bruce and George Gibbs. [1768]

1820 Feb. 7. ALEXANDER GARRETT. ESTIMATE of UNIVERSITY COSTS. DS. 2 pp. Endorsed. Deposited by Philip B. Campbell.

Amount necessary to finish University construction estimated at $80,000 over and above expected subscriptions. [1769]

1820 Feb. 10. THOMAS COOPER, Columbia, S. C., to T. J., Monticello. ALS. 1 p. Endorsed by T. J.

Requests information as to when Mrs. Cooper and he are to come to Charlottesville. South Carolina and Virginia suffer from lack of good preparatory schools. [1770]

1820 Feb. 15. JOHN NEILSON, University of Virginia, to T. J., Monticello. ALS. 1 p. Endorsed by T. J.

Request that T. J. arbitrate a disagreement with John H. Cocke on Neilson's contract. Progress on Pavilion V. [1771]

1820 Feb. 17. JOSEPH C. CABELL, Richmond, to T. J., Monticello. ALS. 1 p.
Endorsed by T. J. Deposited by Philip B. Campbell. Printed: Cabell 181-182.
Attempts to obtain money for the University from the Assembly. References to
William and Mary, Burwell Bassett, James Breckenridge, James Dickinson,
George Hay, and Chapman Johnson.   [1772]

1820 Feb. 18. T. J., Monticello, to FRANCIS BLOODFOOD, Albany. ALS. 1 p.
File draft. Endorsed by T. J.
University of Virginia not sufficiently advanced to purchase mineral collection.
                                                             [1773]

1820 Feb. 24. JOSEPH C. CABELL, Richmond, to T. J., Monticello. ALS. 1 p.
Endorsed by T. J. Deposited by Philip B. Campbell. Printed: Cabell 182-183.
Encloses bill just passed regarding funds for the University. References to James
Breckenridge, William F. Gordon, and Chapman Johnson.   [1774]

1820 Feb. 24-Mar. 23. T. J. and William Munford. Documents relative to a
LOAN FOR THE UNIVERSITY OF VIRGINIA. T. J. AD (in part). 7 pp.
Stitched.
Act authorizing Visitors of the University of Virginia to borrow money to
finish building. Passed 24 February 1820.
Extract from minutes of meeting of the President and Directors of Literary
Fund, 28 February 1820, certified by William Munford, Clerk. Concerns letter
from James Breckenridge, Joseph C. Cabell, and Chapman Johnson, requesting
a loan.
ALS, T. J. to Thomas Mann Randolph, Jr., President of the Literary Board,
10 March 1820, with detailed discussion of terms of a loan of $60,000.
Extract of the minutes of the meeting of the Literary Fund Directors, 23
March 1820, certified by William Munford, Clerk granting a loan of $40,000.
Mentions James Breckenridge, Joseph C. Cabell, Chapman Johnson, and T. J.
                                                             [1775]

1820 Mar. 1. THOMAS COOPER, Columbia, S. C., to T. J., Monticello. ALS. 3
pp. Endorsed by T. J.
Request for pracise information on where he stands with respect to the University of Virginia. In view of criticism in the Rev. J. H. Rice's *Evangelical Magazine,* is willing to resign. Position would be insecure after T. J.'s and James
Madison's death.   [1776]

1820 Mar. 8. T. J., Monticello, to CRAVEN PEYTON, Monteagle. L. 1 p. Typescript copy. Original owned by C. Vernon Eddy.
Inability to pay debt because of failure of Bedford (Poplar Forest) crop and
flour rents. His debtors unable to pay him. Requests that he "forgive us our
trespasses as we forgive those who trespass against us."   [1777]

1820 Mar. 12. T. J., Monticello, to JOHN VAUGHAN, Philadelphia. ALS. 1 p.
Endorsed. Photostat. Original owned by Robert Hyatt. Another MS. in DLC.
Payment to Thomas Cooper. Thanks for copy of William Tilghman's agricul-
tural orations [before the Philadelphia Society for Promoting Agriculture]. [1778]

1820 Mar. 13. T. J., Monticello, to THOMAS COOPER, Columbia, S. C. ALS. 3 pp. File draft. Endorsed by T. J.

Error in sum sent to John Vaughan for Cooper has been corrected. Rev. J. H. Rice's diatribe against Cooper should be ignored. Only opposition to University is from Presbyterian clergy (not laity) and from William and Mary. Baptists, Anglicans, and Methodists entirely friendly to University.   [1779]

1820 Mar. 21. THOMAS COOPER, Columbia, S. C., to T. J., Monticello. ALS. 1 p. Endorsed by T. J.

Regrets institution cannot open until 1822. Advised John Vaughan of mistake in draft. Cannot decide on coming to University of Virginia until he sees Mrs. Cooper.   [1780]

1820 Mar. 24. T. J., Monticello, to THOMAS COOPER, Columbia, S. C. ALS. 1 p. File draft. Endorsed by T. J.

Covering a letter for [William J.] Coffee.   [1781]

1820 Mar. 24. T. J., Monticello, to JAMES LEITCH, Charlottesville. ALS. 1 p. Photostat. Original owned by Edward C. Boykin.

Order for dry goods and milk pans.   [1782]

1820 Mar. 25. PRESIDENT and DIRECTORS of the LITERARY FUND. Resolutions. D. 3 pp. Endorsed by T. J.

Resolutions on terms and form of security for loan of $40,000 to the University of Virginia. Binds T. J. as Rector and James Breckenridge, Joseph C. Cabell, John H. Cocke, Chapman Johnson, James Madison, and Robert Taylor as Visitors.   [1783]

1820 Mar. THOMAS COOPER, Philadelphia. DRAFT on the Bursar of the UNIVERSITY OF VIRGINIA. ADS. 2 pp. Endorsed and approved by T. J.

Draft in anticipation of his salary at the University of Virginia in favor of John Vaughan. Receipt 13 April from John H. Eustace to Alexander Garrett for letter containing a check. Vaughan's receipt.   [1784]

1820 Apr. 9. T. J., Monticello, to JOHN H. COCKE, Bremo. ALS. 1 p. Endorsed. Printed: B of R VI 89 (MS. in DLC).

Action of Board of Visitors makes it necessary to write to Thomas Cooper, reversing previous stand on the Rev. J. H. Rice's attack. Asks Cocke's approval of his letter.   [1785]

1820 Apr. 10. T. J., Monticello, to the PRESIDENT of the LITERARY FUND. ALS. 1 p. File draft. Endorsed by T. J. Enclosures: AD. 3 items. Endorsed.

Accepts loan on behalf of Board of Visitors of University of Virginia on terms proposed, but requests dates of repayment be deferred to permit completion of buildings by 1822. Enclosures: a scheme of application of the funds of the University; proposed applications of the funds of the University; Mr. Jefferson's estimate of the cost of buildings.   [1786]

1820 Apr. 15. ELIJA HUFFMAN and Aaron Fray. UNIVERSITY PLUMBING ESTIMATE. D. 1 p. Endorsed.
Agreement to bore pipes for University's water supply. [1787]

1820 Apr. 24. THOMAS COOPER, Columbia, S. C., to T. J., Monticello. ALS. 1 p. Endorsed by T. J.
Prejudice of clergy may be due to review of Joseph Priestley's writings. Trustees at Columbia willing to hire him on same terms as at Virginia, but clergy may be busy there too. [1788]

[ca. 1820 Apr.]. T. J., Monticello, to [ARTHUR S. BROCKENBROUGH]. ALS. 1 p. Endorsed.
Requests estimate for completing three additional pavilions, five hotels, and additional dormitories. (Report to Literary Fund, April 1820, contains these figures). [1789]

1820 May 1. ARTHUR S. BROCKENBROUGH, University, to T. J., Monticello. ALS. 1 p. Endorsed by T. J.
Difficulties regarding location of Hotel A at the University. Mentions James Oldham, John M. Perry, and George W. Spooner. [1790]

1820 May 1. T. J., Monticello, to PRESIDENT of LITERARY FUND. ALS. 1 p. File draft. Endorsed by T. J.
Asks immediate reply to proposal for additional loan for University of Virginia. [1791]

1820 May 3. THOMAS COOPER, Columbia, S. C., to T. J., Monticello. ALS. 2 pp. Endorsed by T. J.
Trustees of South Carolina College unanimously voted him professorship of geology, mineralogy, or law to add to present of chemistry, subject to approval of legislature. Recommended purchasing his collection of minerals Asks news of Correa da Serra. Regrets controversy raised on his account, and that he cannot go to Virginia. Robert Walsh calling for renewal of Missouri question. [1792]

[1820 May 31]. T. J. MEMORANDUM ON INDEBTEDNESS. D. 2 items. Edgehill-Randolph Papers.
Statement of interest and principal to fall due from 1820 to 1826 on T. J. and T. J. Randolph's bonds. [1793]

1820 June 7. ARTHUR S. BROCKENBROUGH, University, to T. J., Monticello. ALS. 2 pp. Endorsed by T. J.
Requests instructions on tin gutters for dormitories, ornaments on pavilions, house for the Raggi brothers, marble for the columns, brickwork, and laying of pipe for water supply. [1794]

1820 June 20. RUFUS WOODWARD, New Haven, Conn., to T. J., Monticello. ALS. 1 p. Endorsed by T. J.
Asks basis on which applications for professorships at University of Virginia will be received. Is tutor at Yale College. [1795]

1820 June 22. T. J., Monticello, to ROBERT MILLS. ALS. 1 p. Printed: B of R VI 326 (MS. in DLC).

Engineering operations of Commonwealth of Virginia in hands of Thomas Moore and Isaac Briggs. Design for the Washington Monument. Date of opening of the University uncertain. His ill health. [1796]

1820 June 27. T. J., Monticello, to JAMES MONROE. ALS. 1 p. Endorsed. Deposited by Frank Littleton.

Proposals for changes to Monroe's house (Oak Hill?). [1797]

1820 June 30. T. J., Monticello, to JOHN WAYLES EPPES, Mill Brook, Va. ALS. 6 pp. Another MS. in MHi.

Delay in opening of seminary because of its conversion into a public university. Terms of loan to University tie up all funds for next five years; hopes for remitting of loan. Francis Eppes' education with Mr. Stack and Mr. Ragland. Recommends he go to Columbia College to study under Cooper rather than to Eastern colleges. Plans for selling slaves to Eppes to pay his debts. Hopes for compromise in his commitment for Wilson Cary Nicholas' debt. Insists that women slaves be included in sale, which will produce addition capital in the future. Part of Poplar Forest to be given to Francis Eppes. Accepts his offer of the harpsichord for Poplar Forest. Invites Eppes to visit Monticello to see the University. Describes present and projected buildings. [1798]

1820 July 12. THOMAS COOPER, Philadelphia, to T. J., Monticello. ALS. 3 pp. Endorsed by T. J.

Indefinite yet as to whether he will accept permanent position at South Carolina. Discusses cost and curriculum at South Carolina College. Dislike for the New England character. Hope Stephen Elliot of Charleston will replace the deceased principal, Jonathan Maxcy. Gloomy about religious intolerance. Rev. [John Jacob?] Janeway's refusal to baptize grandchild of Peter S. Duponceau because of irregular church attendance. Reexamination of his works fails to show opposition to Christianity. Mentions Pierre Jean George Cabanis, Mr. Nulty, Joseph Priestley, and Benjamin Rush. [1799]

1820 July 29. T. J., Monticello, to JOHN WAYES EPPES, Mill Brook. ALS. 3 pp. Another copy: AL. 2 pp. File draft.

Thomas Cooper's information regarding expenses, curriculum, and staff at South Carolina College. Stephen Elliot a leading botanist and Nulty second to Nathaniel Bowditch in mathematics. Recommends Francis Eppes go there when Stack's school closes. Recommends John H. Cocke's Bremo Seminary for the younger children. Accepts proposal of loan to be repaid in Negroes in two years, men, women, and children. Proposed visit to Mill Brook. Francis Eppes' health. Mentions Correa da Serra, and Mr. Richardson of the Bremo Seminary. [1800]

1820 July 30 [date received]. PRESIDENT and TRUSTEES of the LITERARY FUND. Resolutions. D. 1 p. Endorsed by T. J.

Resolutions regarding payment of last installment of the loan to the University of Virginia. [1801]

1820 Aug. 13. T. J., Monticello, to WILLIAM MUNFORD, LITERARY FUND.
ALS. 1 p. File draft. Endorsed by T. J.

Requests copy of previous bond, so new one can be executed in same fashion.
Resolutions of Literary Fund Board received too late to comply with date of
application for loan.   [1802]

1820 Aug. 19. JOHN WAYLES EPPES, Mill Brook, to T. J., Monticello. ALS.
2 pp. Endorsed by T. J. Deposited by Robert H. Kean.

Agreement to lend T. J. $4000, with interest payable annually and the princi-
pal to be paid in Negroes. Francis Eppes' education at Columbia College and at
the University of Virginia. Admiration for Thomas Cooper. Best route Monticello by Buckingham Court House. Crops universally fine.   [1803]

1820 Sept. 1 [date received]. MICHELE and GIACOMO RAGGI to T. J. and
JOHN H. COCKE. ALS. 2 pp. Endorsed by T. J. Italian.

Propose three different schemes for completing marble work for the University: in Charlottesville, at Leghorn, Italy, or at Carrara, Italy.   [1804]

1820 Sept. 5. T. J., Monticello, to JOHN H. COCKE, Bremo. ALS. 1 p. Endorsed.
Printed: B of R VI 90 (MS. in DLC).

Recommending contract with Raggis for marble columns be relinquished, since
Thomas Appleton can procure them more cheaply in Italy. Mentions Arthur S.
Brockenbrough.   [1805]

1820 Sept. 6. CHARLES PINCKNEY, Charleston, to T. J., Monticello. L. 1 p.
Extract by N. P. Trist ca. 1830. Printed: B of R VIII 456 (MS. in DLC).

The increase and rise of our country. Opinions on the Missouri question. Importance of state governments.   [1806]

1820 Sept. 7. T. J. and JOHN H. COCKE to ARTHUR S. BROCKENBROUGH.
LS. 1 p. Endorsed. Another copy: T. J. AL. 1 p.

Recommending ending the contract with Raggi brothers, Raggis to pay
expenses of the return voyage.   [1807]

1820 Sept. 16. T. J., Poplar Forest, to JOHN H. COCKE, Bremo. ALS. 1 p.
Endorsed. Printed: B of R VI 89 (MS. in DLC).

Requesting him to audit the books of the Bursar and Proctor before the
Board of Visitors' meeting. Dinner at Monticello before the meeting.   [1808]

1820 Sept. 16. T. J., Poplar Forest, to THOMAS MANN RANDOLPH, JR. ALS.
1 p. File draft. Endorsed by T. J.

Loan from the Literary Fund to the University of Virginia.   [1809]

1820 Sept. 26. MICHELE RAGGI, Washington, to T. J., Charlottesville. ALS.
3 pp. Endorsed by T .J. Italian.

Complaints of his treatment, bad food, delay in getting marble blocks, lack of
understandng. Propose to finish term working at Washington or to do all
columns at Carrara.   [1810]

1820 Sept. 30. T. J., Monticello, to CHARLES PINCKNEY, Charleston. L. 2 pp. Extract by N. P. Trist *ca.* 1830. Printed: Ford X 161-163; L and B XV 279-281; B of R VI 372 (MS. in DLC).

The Missouri question a Federalist plot to divide the country on geographic lines on basis of slavery, "as if we were advocates for it". Right of posterity to throw away happiness given by those gone before. [1811]

1820 Oct. 3. JOSEPH C. CABELL, Charlottesville, to T. J., Monticello. ALS. 1 p. Endorsed by T. J. Deposited by Philip B. Campbell. Printed: Cabell 183.

Verification of Alexander Garrett's account. [1812]

1820 Oct. 10. THOMAS APPLETON, Leghorn, Italy, to T. J., Monticello. L. 1 p. Extract by T. J.

Cost of Corinthian capitals. Payment to be remitted through Samuel Williams of London. [1813]

1820 Oct. 12. THOMAS MANN RANDOLPH, JR., Richmond, to T. J. ALS. 1 p. Endorsed by T. J.

Sends form of bond to be executed by the Visitors. Explanation of date on the bond. Plan to visit Albemarle. Mentions William Munford. [1814]

1820 Oct. 19. ARTHUR S. BROCKENBROUGH, University, to T. J., Monticello. ALS. 2 pp. Endorsed by T. J.

Deals with construction problems of the Hotels. Wishes to correct his report to the Visitors. Mentions James Oldham. [1815]

1820 Oct. 20. T. J., Monticello, to RICHARD RUSH. L. 2 pp. Extract by N. P. Trist *ca.* 1830. Printed: L and B XV 281-284; B of R VI 400 (MS. in DLC).

Division in the country with regard to slavery pushed by the Federalists. Secession would not last long. Importance of U. S. standing as an example of unity to the world. [1816]

1820 Oct. 21. T. J. BOOK LIST. ADS. 1 p. McGregor Library.

List of books ordered (probably for the University of Virginia Library) principally Anglo-Saxon, ecclesiastical and religious. (Most of these appear in the 1828 catalogue of the University of Virginia Library). [1817]

[1820 Oct.]. T. J. ESTIMATE of cost of COLUMNS for UNIVERSITY. AD. 1 p.

Estimates cost of columns for several pavilions and the library (Rotunda). [1818]

1820 Nov. 9. T. J., Monticello, to THOMAS MANN RANDOLPH, JR. ALS. 1 p. File draft. Endorsed by T. J. Another copy: LS. 1 p.

Letter covering the accounts of the Bursar and Proctor. Explains certain corrections by the Proctor. [1819]

1820 Nov. 26. D. MARIANO, Washington, to T. J. ALS. 1 p. Endorsed by T. J.

His second application for a position at the University of Virginia. Gives as references [John Quincy?] Adams, Mr. Holley, and [James?] Monroe. [1820]

1820 Nov. 28. T. J., Poplar Forest, to JOSEPH C. CABELL. ALS. 4 pp. Endorsed.
Enclosure: AD. 2 pp. Endorsed. Printed: Cabell 184-189; Ford X 165-168; TJR IV
333-336; L & B XV 289-294; B of R VI 59 (MS. in DLC).

Encloses estimate of cost of University when completed. Gigantic efforts ot
New York in education shown by Clinton. Plan for elementary education for
Virginia. Letter to be communicated to James Breckenridge, William F. Gordon,
Chapman Johnson, and William Cabell Rives. Enclosure: statement of probable
cost of buildings.   [1821]

1820 Nov. 29. T. J., Poplar Forest, to FRANCIS WALKER GILMER. ALS. 1 p.
Endorsed. Printed: B of R X 7 (MS. in DLC).

Regrets at the departure of Correa da Serra. Wishes well for revolutionary
movements in Brazil, but hopes they will not affect Correa's good fortunes. [1822]

1820 Dec. 18. THOMAS GIMBREDE, U. S. Military Academy, West Point, to
T. J., Monticello. ALS. 1 p. Endorsed by T. J.

Application for position at University teaching drawing.   [1823]

1820 Dec. 20. JOSEPH C. CABELL, Richmond, to T. J., Monticello. ALS. 1 p.
Endorsed by T. J. Deposited by Philip B. Campbell. Partly printed: Cabell
189-190.

Attack on Governor Randolph's character. Money from the Assembly for University. Requests fuller accounts by Bursar, Mr. Garrett. References to James
Breckenridge, Mary Cabell, Chapman Johnson.   [1824]

1820 Dec. 22. JOSEPH C. CABELL, Williamsburg, to T. J., Monticello. ALS.
2 pp. Endorsed by T. J. Deposited by Philip B. Campbell. Partly printed:
Cabell 190-192.

Resolution giving grants to William and Mary, Hampton-Sidney, Washington
College, New London Academy, and the University will defeat the claims of
the University on the Literary Fund. Attitude of James Breckenridge, John
Bowyer, John Coalter, George W. Crump, Philip Doddridge, David S. Garland,
William F. Gordon, Mr. [Richard] Morris, Thomas Miller, Isaac Otey, Jr., Judge
Spencer Roane, Mr. [William?] Taylor, and David Watson. Alexander Garrett's
account for the University. Comments on Governor Randolph's message. [1825]

1820 Dec. 25. T. J., Monticello, to JOSEPH C. CABELL. ALS. 1 p. Endorsed.
Printed: Cabell 192-193; B of R VI 59 (MS. in DLC).

Sends copy of letter to Thomas Mann Randolph, Jr., explaining an apparent
difference in the Visitors' Report and the Proctor's estimate of the amount
necessary to complete buildings. (See 9 November 1820). Ascendancy of Massachusetts in the U. S. is due to education.   [1826]

1820 Dec. 25. T. J., Monticello, to THOMAS MANN RANDOLPH, JR. ALS.
1 p. File draft. Endorsed by T. J.

Explanation and apology for an error in the report of the Board of Visitors.
                                                                       [1827]

1820 Dec. 26. T. J., Monticello, to ALBERT GALLATIN, Paris. L. 2 pp. Extract by N. P. Trist *ca.* 1830. Printed: Ford X 175-178; B of R VI 170 (MS. in DLC).

Possibilities involved in the Missouri question. While Virginia and Pennsylvania hold together, the Atlantic states can never separate.   [1828]

1820 Dec. 28. T. J., Monticello, to D. MARIANO. ALS. 1 p. File draft. Endorsed by T. J.

Plans for professorships still undecided. When buildings completed, must rely on legislature for funds to open.   [1829]

1820 Dec. 29. T. J., Monticello, to THOMAS GIMBREDE, West Point, N. Y. ALS. 1 p. File draft. Endorsed by T. J.

Universiy of Virginia not yet ready to employ professors.   [1830]

[1820]. JAMES MADISON to T. J., Monticello. ALS. 1 p. Tracing, from original in private hands.

Congratulations on loan for the University. Suggests that work begin without formal meeting of the Board of Visitors.   [1831]

[1820?]. T. J. NOTES for the CONSIDERATION of the BOARD of VISITORS. AD. 1 p. Endorsed by T. J.

Estimates of proposed application of revenue. Proposals to the legislature regarding funds and appropriations. Supplementary sources of income. [1832]

1821 Jan. 4. JOSEPH C. CABELL, Richmond, to T. J., Monticello. ALS. 2 pp. Endorsed by T. J. Printed: Cabell 194-195.

Funds for the University. Doctrine that all colleges receiving funds should be under the control of the legislature. References to William and Mary, Mr. Bassett, Samuel Blackburn, Philip Doddridge, David S. Garland, Thomas Griffin, Chapman Johnson, Thomas Miller, [James?] Smith, Richard Venable, and Henry E. Watkins.   [1833]

1821 Jan. 11. ARCHIBALD THWEATT, Eppington, to T. J., Monticello. ALS. 1 p. Endorsed by T. J. Edgehill-Randolph Papers.

Letter from Judge Spencer Roane, asking a favor.   [1834]

1821 Jan. 18. JOSEPH C. CABELL, Richmond, to T. J., Monticello. ALS. 2 pp. Endorsed by T. J. Deposited by Philip B. Campbell. Printed: Cabell 196-197.

Little prospect of gaining additional funds for the University. References to Mr. Broadnax, [Richard?] Morris, and [Samuel] Taylor.   [1835]

1821 Jan. 25. JOSEPH C. CABELL, Richmond, to T. J., Monticello. ALS. 2 pp. Endorsed by T. J. Deposited by Philip B. Campbell. Printed: Cabell 197-199.

Funds for the University. Plans to leave public life at end of present session. References to James Breckenridge, [Nathaniel?] Claiborne, John H. Cocke, Chapman Johnson, and James P. Preston.   [1836]

1821 Jan. 30. T. J., Monticello, to JOSEPH C. CABELL, Richmond. ALS. 2 pp. Endorsed. Another MS. in DLC. Printed: Cabell 199-200.

Request that Visitors call a meeting to prevent lapsing of Chapman Johnson's commission as Visitor. Mentions James Breckenridge, John H. Cocke, James Madison, Thomas Mann Randolph, Jr., and Robert B. Taylor.   [1837]

1821 Jan. 30-Feb. 13. UNIVERSITY OF VIRGINIA Board of Visitors. DS. 1 p. Endorsed by T. J.

Call for a special meeting of the Board on 1 April 1821, signed by James Breckenridge, Joseph C. Cabell, T. J., Chapman Johnson, James Madison, and Robert B. Taylor.   [1838]

1821 Jan. 31. T. J., Monticello, to JOSEPH C. CABELL, Richmond. ALS. 2 pp. Endorsed. Another MS. in DLC. Printed: Cabell 201-203; TJR IV 340-341; L & B XV 310-313.

Details of a loan for the University. Urging James Breckenridge, Cabell, and Chapman Johnson to "die in the last ditch" for the University. Mentions John H. Cocke.   [1839]

1821 Feb. 8. JOSEPH C. CABELL, Richmond, to T. J., Monticello. ALS. 1 p. Endorsed by T. J. Deposited by Philip B. Campbell. Printed: Cabell 203-204.

Agrees to be a candidate for Assembly again. Funds for the University. References to Samuel Blackburn, James Breckenridge, Chapman Johnson, and William Selden.   [1840]

1821 Feb. 15. T. J., Monticello, to JOSEPH C. CABELL, Richmond, ALS. 1 p. Endorsed. Printed: Cabell 204; B of R VI 59 (MS. in DLC).

Letter sent to James Breckenridge should be shown within the circle of discretion.   [1841]

1821 Feb. 20. JOSEPH C. CABELL, Richmond, to T. J., Monticello. ALS. 2 pp. Endorsed by T. J. Deposited by Philip B. Campbell. Printed: Cabell 204-206.

Meeting of the Board of Visitors. Funds for the University. Passage of James River Bill by House of Delegates. References to William Archer, James Breckenridge, William Brodnax, Armistead Currie, David S. Garland, Chapman Johnson, Robert Mallory, T. M. Randolph, Jr., Samuel Taylor, and Robert B. Taylor.   [1842]

1821 Feb. 22. JOSEPH C. CABELL, Richmond, to T. J., Monticello. ALS. 1 p. Endorsed by T. J. Deposited by Philip B. Campbell. Printed: Cabell 206.

Funds for the University. References to Samuel Blackburn, [Nathaniel?] Claiborne, and David S. Garland.   [1843]

1821 Feb. 22. T. J., Monticello, to JOSEPH C. CABELL, Richmond. ALS. 1 p. Endorsed. Printed: Cabell 207; B of R VI 60 (MS. in DLC).

Pamphlet proving that William and Mary was intended to be a seminary of the Church of England. Statutes require all Visitors to be of the Church of England.   [1844]

1821 Feb. 25. JOSEPH C. CABELL, Richmond, to T. J., Monticello. ALS. 2 pp. Endorsed by T. J. Deposited by Philip B. Campbell. Printed: Cabell 208-209.

Passage of bill providing funds for the University. Mentions Samuel Blackburn, James Breckenridge, John Bowyer, William B. Chamberlayne, George W. Crump, Armistead Currie, William F. Gordon, James Hunter, Chapman Johnson, George Loyall, Richard Morris, Mr. Stephenson, and David Watson.
[1845]

1821 Mar. 9. T. J., Monticello. DEPOSITION concerning JOSHUA FRY. D. 3 pp. Copy. Endorsed. Witnessed by John Watson and Thomas J. Randolph.

T. J.'s recollections concerning the property of Joshua Fry, given in connection with an ejection suit in Greenup Circuit Court, Ky., John Doe for John Fry vs. Thomas and Samuel Bell.
[1846]

1821 Mar. 10. JOSEPH C. CABELL, Richmond, to T. J., Monticello. ALS. 2 pp. Endorsed by T. J. Deposited by Philip B. Campbell. Printed: Cabell 210-212.

Advises building no more buildings than those for which there is money in hand. Urges Jefferson to use his influence in the election of friends of the University. References to James Breckenridge, William H. Brodnax, Samuel Taylor, Littleton Tazewell, and Mr. Watts.
[1847]

1821 Mar. 12. T. J., Monticello, to JOHN H. COCKE, Bremo. ALS. 1 p. Endorsed. Cocke Papers. Printed: B of R VI 90.

Call for a special meeting of the Board of Visitors to prevent Chapman Johnson's commission from lapsing. Sends pumpkin and asparagus seeds from [Caesar] Rodney.
[1848]

1821 Mar. 23. PETER S. DUPONCEAU, Philadelphia, to T. J., Monticello ALS. 3 pp. Endorsed by T. J.

Introducing Lardner C. Vanuxem, candidate for professorship of chemistry and mineralogy at the University of Virginia, recommended by Thomas Cooper. [1849]

1821 Mar. 24. ARCHIBALD STUART, Staunton, to T. J., Monticello. ALS. 1 p. Endorsed by T. J.

Recommendation of Dabney Cosby's brickwork. Regrets failure to send firkin of butter.
[1850]

1821 Mar. 24. JOHN VAUGHAN, Philadelphia, to T. J., Monticello. ALS. 4 pp. Endorsed by T. J.

Recommends Lardner C. Vanuxem, recently returned from abroad, for a professorship. Highly recommended by Thomas Cooper. Mentions Correa da Serra, Peter S. DuPonceau, James Madison, and James Monroe.
[1851]

1821 Mar. 28. T. J., Monticello, to ARTHUR S. BROCKENBROUGH, Charlottesville. ALS. 1 p. Endorsed.

Introducing Thomas Sully, the portrait painter. Requests estimate on cost of the marble columns and of the library. On back is "An Estimate for the cost of Stone work."
[1852]

1821 Mar. 28 [date received.] CLAUDE CROZET, West Point, to T. J., Monticello. ALS. 3 pp. Endorsed by T. J. French.

Application for position teaching mathematics, philosophy, military science, and architecture at the University of Virginia.   [1853]

1821 Mar. 29. ARTHUR S. BROCKENBROUGH, University, to T. J., Monticello. ALS. 2 pp. Endorsed by T. J.

Sends estimate of cost of columns and of Rotunda.   [1854]

1821 Mar. 31. T. J., Monticello, to CLAUDE CROZET, West Point, N. Y. ALS. 1 p. File draft. Endorsed by T. J.

University not ready to employ professors.   [1855]

1821 Mar. 31. T. J., Monticello, to PETER S. DUPONCEAU, Philadelphia. ALS. 1 p. File draft. Endorsed by T. J.

Impressed with qualifications of Lardner C. Vanuxem; appreciates Du Ponceau's and Thomas Cooper's recommendations. Opening of University and appointment of professors indefinitely deferred.   [1856]

1821 Apr. 1. JOSEPH C. CABELL, Edgewood, to T. J., Monticello. ALS. 1 p. Endorsed by T. J. Deposited by Philip B. Campbell. Printed: Cabell 212.

Reasons for inability to attend meeting of the Board of Visitors. Note sent by [Valentine?] Southall.   [1857]

1821 Apr. 1. T. J., Monticello, to JOHN H. COCKE, Bremo. ALS. 1 p. Endorsed. Printed: B of R VI 90 (MS. in DLC).

Excusing Cocke from attending the meeting of the Board of Visitors because of illness. Acknowledges carp and kale seed. Mentions James Breckenridge, Joseph C. Cabell, Chapman Johnson, James Madison, and Robert B. Taylor.   [1858]

1821 Apr. 1. JAMES W. WIDDERFIELD, University, to T. J., Monticello. ALS. 1 p. Endorsed by T. J.

After working for four years as journeyman, applies for carpentry work on his own at University. Mentions James Dinsmore, John Neilson, and John M. Perry.   [1859]

1821 Apr. 2. GIACOMO RAGGI, University, to T. J., Monticello. ALS. 1 p. Endorsed by T. J. Italian.

Order for money to be paid to his wife.   [1860]

1821 Apr. 8. T. J., Monticello, to JOHN VAUGHAN, Philadelphia. ALS. 1 p. File draft. Endorsed by T. J.

Impressed with Lardner C. Vanuxem and with his recommendations from Peter S. DuPonceau, Thomas Cooper, and Vaughan. Appointment of faculty indefinitely delayed. Acknowledgment received from Thomas Appleton for remittance last year, but none from Mr. Dodge. Places less confidence in Dodge than in [Etienne?] Cathalan.   [1861]

1821 Apr. 9. T. J., Monticello, to JOHN H. COCKE, Bremo. ALS. 1 p. Endorsed. Enclosure: AD. 1 p. Cocke Papers. Printed: B of R VI 90 (MS. in DLC).

Sends copy of proceedings of meeting of Board of Visitors. Remittance to Thomas Appleton for capitals. Arthur S. Brockenbrough settling accounts to see if money available to begin Rotunda. References to James Breckenridge, Joseph Cabell, Chapman Johnson, and James Madison. Enclosure: extract of proceedings. [1862]

1821 Apr. 16. T. J., Monticello, to THOMAS APPLETON. ALS. 2 pp. File draft. Endorsed by T. J. Enclosure: AD. 1 p. Printed: B of R VI 15 (MS. in DLC).

Order for Ionic and Corinthian capitals; payment being made through bill from Bernard Peyton of Richmond to Samuel Williams of London. Specifications for these on enclosure. Payments to Giacomo Raggi's wife. No more money due to Michael Raggi, but he may work on columns at Carrara if Appleton wishes. Requests information on cost of capitals for the Rotunda as represented in Andrea Palladio. [1863]

1821 Apr. 16. WILLIAM H. CRAWFORD, Washington, to T. J., Monticello. ALS. 3 pp. Endorsed by T. J.

John Calhoun states that amount due to Virginia for advances during War of 1812 cannot be ascertained. Has written to Peter Hagner to speed up matter. [1864]

1821 Apr. 20. T. J., Monticello, to ARTHUR S. BROCKENBROUGH. ALS. 1 p. Endorsed. Another MS. in DLC.

Recommends purchase of cement from Andrew Smith. Glass for the University. [1865]

1821 Apr. 28. JOSEPH C. CABELL, Henrico County, to T. J., Monticello. ALS. 2 pp. Endorsed by T. J. Deposited by Philip B. Campbell. Printed: Cabell 212-214.

Cabell's illness. Requests information regarding last meeting of the Board of Visitors. Success of Samuel Blackburn, James Breckenridge, David S. Garland, Mr. Maury of Buckingham, and Joseph Shelton in the recent election. Funds for the University. [1866]

1821 Apr. 30. JAMES MONROE, Washington, to T. J., Monticello. ALS. 1 p. Endorsed by T. J.

Amount of claim of the Commonwealth of Virginia against the U. S. less than T. J. hoped. Claims presented by C. Selden, Virginia agent, will be paid soon. Hopes no unfavorable effect on the opening of the University. [1867]

1821 May 7. THOMAS M. HALL, Philadelphia, to T. J., Monticello. ALS. 2 pp. Endorsed by T. J.

Disappointed at present state of the University. Grateful for T. J.'s attention to documents placed in his care. [1868]

1821 May 31. T. J., Monticello, to ALEXANDER GARRETT. ALS. 1 p. Garrett Papers.

Encloses letter that may be of some help to Garrett, although T. J. has no

personal relation with Governor [Lewis] Cass and no acquaintances in Detroit.
[1869]

1821 June 11. JOHN HARNER, Harner's Mill, to T. J., Monticello. ALS. 1 p.
Endorsed by T. J. Edgehill-Randolph Papers.
Presenting a pair of buck's antlers.   [1870]

1821 June 16. T. J. BOND to JAMES LYLE. DS. 1 p. Endorsed. Edgehill-
Randolph Papers.
Bond for $2400. Receipts, dated 15 January and 15 July 1827, for $1803 from
Thomas Jefferson Randolph noted on *verso*.   [1871]

1821 June 23. THOMAS COOPER, Columbia, S. C., to T. J., Monticello. ALS.
1 p. Endorsed by T. J.
Evaluation of facilities, curriculum, and faculty of South Carolina College,
comparing the professor of mathematics to Nathaniel Bowditch, Audraine, and
Nulty. Virginia legislature must have liberality to compete with them. Progress
of Francis Eppes. Lectures in chemistry, mineralogy, criticism, Belles Lettres.
[1872]

1821 June 25. JOHN F. D'OLIVEIRA FERNANDEZ, Norfolk, to T. J., Monticello. ALS. 3 pp. Endorsed by T. J.
Appreciates good wishes for his own and country's welfare. Recommends Dr.
[Robert?] Andrews for professorship at the University. Regrets delay in opening
of University, unnecessary in view of the resources of Virginia. Recommends fee
system of University of Coimbra, Portugal, together with a law requiring that all
pastors, lawyers, and physicians practicing in the Commonwealth be graduated
from the University. Hopes Jefferson will live to see the opening of the University.   [1873]

1821 June 26. T. J., Monticello, to THEODORICK BLAND. ALS. 1 p. Printed:
B of R VI 38.
Opening date of University deferred until one year after the legislature re-
mits the debt. Information on faculty, curriculum, and costs for benefit of
Bland's son.   [1874]

1821 June 27. T. J., Monticello, to JUDGE SPENCER ROANE. L. 2 pp. Extract by N. P. Trist *ca.* 1830. Printed: L & B XV 326-329; B of R VI 393 (MS.
in DLC).
Approval of John Taylor's *Construction Construed*. States coordinate rather
than subordinate to federal government. Peculiar happiness of our system is on
appeal to the ballot rather than the cannon.   [1875]

1821 July 11. [BERNARD PEYTON?]. EXTENSION of LOAN. AD. 1 p.
Endorsed by T. J. Edgehill-Randolph Papers.
Extending the deed of trust [on Poplar Forest] to additional notes for $4000
and $2500 at the Farmer's Bank.   [1876]

1821 July 21. T. J., Monticello, to THOMAS MANN RANDOLPH, JR. ALS.
1 p. File draft. Endorsed by T. J. Another MS. in DLC.
Application for loan from the Literary Fund approved by act of the General
Assembly.   [1877]

1821 July 30. T. M. RANDOLPH, JR., Richmond, to T. J., Monticello. ALS.
1 p. Endorsed by T. J. Edgehill-Randolph Papers.
Meeting of the Board of the Literary Fund.   [1878]

1821 July. Rector and Visitors of the UNIVERSITY of VIRGINIA. BOND to
the DIRECTORS of the LITERARY FUND. T. J. AD. 1 p.
Rough draft of bond for loan of $30,000.   [1879]

1821 Aug. 3. Rector and Visitors of the UNIVERSITY of VIRGINIA. BOND to
President and Directors of the LITERARY FUND. ADS by T. J. 2 pp. Seal.
Witnessed by Nicholas P. Trist and William Bankhead.
Bond for a loan of $29,100. Notation: "1822. Jan. gave a bond for 30,900. D.
verbatim as this except at to the sum."   [1880]

1821 Aug. 5. JOSEPH C. CABELL, Edgewood, to T. J., Monticello. ALS. 2 pp.
Endorsed by T. J. Deposited by Philip B. Campbell. Printed: Cabell 215-216.
Cabell's illness. Request for complete statement of all University accounts for
the next General Assembly. Attacks on the University by the Presbyterians of
Hampton-Sydney and the Episcopalians of William and Mary. Washington Col-
lege to receive Robinson's estate.   [1881]

1821 Aug. 14. T. J., Monticello, to JOHN BROCKENBROUGH. ALS. 1 p.
File draft. Endorsed by T. J.
Warrant for $14,550 to be placed to the credit of the University of Virginia
at the Bank of Virginia. Mentions John H. Cocke. Mentions verbatim copy
addressed to Philip N. Nicholas, President of the Farmer's Bank of Virginia.
                                                              [1882]

1821 Aug. 15. T. J. and JOHN H. COCKE, Monticello, to Joseph C. Cabell,
Warminster. LS. 1 p. Endorsed. Circular. Printed: Cabell 216-217.
Proposing to defer regular autumnal meeting of the Board of Visitors until
Wednesday preceding the meeting of the Assembly, when a clear and satisfactory
report on construction can be given.   [1883]

1821 Aug. 15. T. J., Monticello, to JOHN H. COCKE, Bremo. ALS. 1 p.
Endorsed.
Sends letters regarding the Board of Visitors' meeting for his signature. Trip
to Bedford County. Congratulations on the change of his condition [his marri-
age].   [1884]

1821 Aug. 15. T. J., Monticello, to JAMES E. HEATH, Auditor of Virginia. ALS.
1 p. File draft. Endorsed by T. J.
Encloses order from the President and Directors of the Literary Fund for
$29,100 for the use of the University.   [1885]

1821 Aug. 15-30. T. J., JOHN H. COCKE, JAMES MADISON, CHAPMAN
JOHNSON, and JOSEPH C. CABELL. DS. 3 items.
Call for a special meeting of the Board of Visitors. Three identical copies, each
signed by T. J. and Cocke, with one additional signature on each.   [1886]

1821 Aug. 17. T. J., Monticello, to HENRY DEARBORN. L. 1 p. Extract by
N. P. Trist *ca.* 1830. Printed: Ford X 191-192; L & B XV 329-330; B of R VI
118 (MS. in DLC).

Missouri question has bought back the Hartford Convention men to power.
Union strengthened with westward expansion.   [1887]

1821 Aug. 19. T. J., Monticello, to NATHANIEL MACON. L. 1 p. Extract by
N. P. Trist *ca.* 1830. Printed: Ford X 192-193; B of R VI 285 (MS. in DLC).

Two necessary measures: checking invasion of states' rights by federal judiciary
and paying the national debt.   [1888]

1821 Aug. 20. JOHN BROCKENBROUGH, Bank of Virginia, Richmond, to
T. J. ALS. 1 p. Endorsed by T. J.

Sum of $14,550 deposited to the credit of the University of Virginia.   [1889]

1821 Aug. 25. CHAPMAN JOHNSON, Staunton, to T. J., Monticello. ALS. 2.
pp. Endorsed by T. J.

Approves special meeting of Visitors. Recommends appointment of temporary
accountant as aid to Proctor.   [1890]

1821 Aug. 31. JOSEPH C. CABELL, Edgewood, to T. J., Monticello. ALS. 1 p.
Endorsed by T. J. Deposited by Philip B. Campbell. Printed: Cabell 217-218.

Meeting of the Board of Visitors. Cabell's health. Reference to Mary Cabell.
                                                                      [1891]

1821 Sept. 4. JAMES BRECKENRIDGE, Fincastle County, to T. J., Monticello.
ALS. 1 p. Endorsed by T. J.

Approving special meeting of Visitors.   [1892]

1821 Sept. 11. T. J., Monticello, to [DANIEL BRENT, Washington, D. C.]. ALS.
1 p.

Order to send Brazilian ores by John Barnes. Prices of Cardelli's busts of
Madison and Monroe.   [1893]

1821 Sept. 16. T. J., Monticello, to JOHN WAYLES EPPES, Mill Brook. ALS.
2 pp.

Course of study for Francis Eppes at Columbia College, S. C.   [1894]

1821 Sept. 30. T. J., Monticello, to the BOARD of VISITORS. LS. 2 pp. Circular.
Enclosure: AD. 2 pp. The University of Virginia owns the copies sent to Cabell
and to Cocke, and a typescript of the letter sent to Breckenridge (original
owned by Samuel McVitty). Printed: Cabell 219-221.

Detailed report on the cost of various buildings from information presented
by Arthur S. Brockenbrough. Funds to be used for the library (Rotunda).
Enclosure: "A view of the whole expenses of the Funds of the University."
                                                                      [1895]

1821 Oct. 3. T. J., Monticello, to GIACOMO RAGGI. ALS. 1 p. File draft.
Endorsed by T. J.

News received from Thomas Appleton of the death of Raggi's wife in Carrara,

Italy. Requests orders on money being held for him. No news of Michael Raggi.
[1896]

1821 Oct. 6. GEORGE BLAETTERMANN, London, to RICHARD RUSH. L.
2 pp. Copy. Endorsed by T. J.
Honored by preference for professorship at the University of Virginia. Considers himself engaged. [1897]

1821 Oct. 8. GEORGE BLAETTERMANN, London, to RICHARD RUSH. L.
2 pp. Copy. Endorsed by T. J.
Conveys thanks to Jefferson. Eager to teach rising citizens of a country whose government is founded on the rights of man. [1898]

1821 Nov. 2. T. J., Monticello, to ARTHUR S. BROCKENBROUGH. ALS. 1 p.
Endorsed.
Choice of arbiters for the settlement of James Oldham's account. References to [George?] Divers and [Dabney?] Minor. [1899]

1821 Nov. 3. T. J., Monticello, to ARTHUR S. BROCKENBROUGH. ALS. 1 p.
Endorsed.
Arbitration of a dispute with workers at the University by [George?] Divers and [Dabney?] Minor. [1900]

1821 Nov. 6. ARCHIBALD THWEATT, Eppington, to T. J., Monticello. ALS.
1 p. Endorsed by T. J. Edgehill-Randolph Papers.
Requests permission to publish T. J.'s letter on the judiciary. [1901]

1821 Nov. 21. JOSEPH C. CABELL, Williamsburg, to T. J., Monticello. ALS.
1 p. Endorsed by T. J. Deposited by Philip B. Campbell. Printed: Cabell 222-223.
Absence from the meeting of the Board of Visitors due to illness. Advisability of finishing all University buildings. University finances. References to Chapman Johnson and Dr. [John A.] Smith of Williamsburg. [1902]

1821 Nov. 22. T. J. to ARTHUR S. BROCKENBROUGH. DS. 1 p. Endorsed.
Receipt for money paid for hoisting machine for University. [1903]

1821 Nov. 23. T. J., Monticello, to NATHANIEL MACON. L. 1 p. Extract by
N. P. Trist ca. 1830. Printed: L & B XV 340-342; B of R VI 285 (MS. in DLC).
Attack on states' rights by the federal judiciary. Virginia too much out of favor to protest at this time. [1904]

1821 Nov. 30. RECTOR AND VISITORS, UNIVERSITY of VIRGINIA. PETITION to the U. S. CONGRESS. ADS. 3 pp. File draft. Endorsed by T. J.
Printed: Central Gazette, 4 Jan. 1822.
Petition to abolish tariff on scientific books imported from abroad [1905]

1821 Dec. 1. JOHN T. KIRKLAND, Cambridge, Mass., to T. J., Monticello. DS.
3 pp. Endorsed by T. J.
Petition from "divers Colleges, Academies, and literary and scientific Societies"

to Congress to remove tariff on books. Letters from President Kirkland of Harvard College transmitting printed petition, asking signatures.   - [1906]

1821 Dec. 5. T. J., Monticello, to HUGH NELSON. ALS. 1 p. File draft. Endorsed by T. J.

Forwards copy of petition to Congress sent from Harvard College; has been asked to get signatures of institutions of South and West. Proposed it to Chapel Hill, N. C., Columbia, S. C., Athens, Ga., Transylvania, Ky. Printers do not need protective tariff.   [1907]

1821 Dec. 8. JOHN WAYLES EPPES to T. J., Monticello. ALS. 3 pp. Endorsed by T. J. Edgehill-Randolph Papers.

Eppes' ill health. Disrespect shown Dr. Cooper by Columbia students. Requests slips of purple grape. Proposal for exchange of his land for T. J.'s Bedford lands so that Francis Eppes can settle on the Bedford estate.   [1908]

1821 Dec. 9. T. J., Monticello, to JAMES BRECKENRIDGE. ALS. 1 p. Endorsed. Printed: B of R VI 46 (MS. in DLC).

Copy of Greenlee's plat will make his patent good against a junior claim. Meeting of Board of Visitors, with John H. Cocke, Chapman Johnson, and James Madison attending. State of the University published in papers. Decision on commencing the library deferred.   [1909]

1821 Dec. 16. JAMES HARRIS and ROBERT MCCULLOCK, Charlottesville, to T. J., Monticello. LS. 1 p. Endorsed by T. J.

Proposal for supplying lumber for central building of college.   [1910]

1821 Dec. 26. T. J., Monticello, to JOHN T. KIRKLAND, President, HARVARD COLLEGE. ALS. 1 p. File draft. Endorsed by T. J.

Petition to abolish tariff on books similar to that on Kirkland's circular sent to Congress. Hopes Georgia, Kentucky, North Carolina, and South Carolina will do likewise. Happy for the occasion of cooperating with other literary institutions.   [1911]

[ca. 1821]. T. J. to ARTHUR S. BROCKENBROUGH. AL. 1 p. Endorsed.

Regarding the Temple of Fortuna pavilion at the University of Virginia.
                                                                                                [1912]

[1821?] T. J. MEMORANDUM on D. MARIANO. AD. 1 p.

[Thomas] Sully's opinion of D. Mariano.   [1913]

[1821?]. MEMORANDUM ON TAXATION. D. 4 pp.

Taxes on land, slaves, horses, carriages, licenses, law processes, seals of courts, notary seals, tobacco, and military fines in all Virginia Counties. Comparison of representation and taxation of trans-Allegheny, Valley of Virginia, Piedmont, and Tidewater.   [1914]

1822 Jan. 3. T. J., Monticello, to JOSEPH C. CABELL and CHAPMAN JOHNSON, Richmond. ALS. 1 p. Endorsed. Partly printed: Cabell 228; B of R VI 60 (MS. in DLC).

Encloses copy of letter to [Thomas] Griffin answering his letter on the subject of the University.   [1915]

[1822] Jan. 3 [incorrectly dated 1821]. JOSEPH C. CABELL. Richmond, to T. J., Monticello. ALS. 5 pp. Endorsed by T. J. Deposited by Philip B. Campbell. Printed: Cabell 223-227.

Cabell in better health. Action in the Assembly regarding funds for the University. Move to shift seat of government to Staunton. Governor Randolph's differences with his Council. References to Hampden-Sydney College, Washington College, William Archer, Samuel Blackburn, Thomas Griffin, Chapman Johnson, Garrett Minor, [Richard?] Morris, Mr. Ritchie, Mr. Saunders, and Henry E. Watkins.   [1916]

1822 Jan. 3. T. J., Monticello, to JAMES OLDHAM. ALS. 1 p. Endorsed.

Suggests the difficulty with Arthur S. Brockenbrough be settled by arbitration.
                                                                          [1917]

1822 Jan. 5. T. J., Monticello, to JOSEPH C. CABELL or CHAPMAN JOHNSON, Richmond. ALS. 1 p. Endorsed. Enclosure: AD. 1 p. Endorsed. Printed: Cabell 228.

Enclosing a memorandum regarding funds for the University for 1822.   [1918]

1822 Jan. 6. T. J., Monticello, to THOMAS MANN RANDOLPH, JR. ALS. 1 p. File draft. Endorsed by T. J.

Has executed and mailed the bond. Recommends cancelling University debt and giving derelict funds for the library so that the University may open soon. Strong opposition reported by Cabell.   [1919]

1822 Jan. 7. JOSEPH C. CABELL, Richmond, to T. J., Monticello. ALS. 3 pp. Endorsed by T. J. Deposited by Philip B. Campbell. Partly printed: Cabell 229-231.

Funds for the University. Reasons for Thomas Griffin's resolution. Opposition from the clergy. References to William and Mary, Hampden-Sydney, Chapman Johnson, Bishop [Richard Channing] Moore, Richard Morris, Rev. Mr. Rice, and Henry E. Watkins.   [1920]

1822 Jan. 14. T. J., Monticello, to JOSEPH C. CABELL, Richmond. ALS. 1 p. Endorsed. Another copy: AL. 1 p. File draft. Deposited by Philip B. Campbell. Printed: Cabell 237.

Leaves to Cabell and his colleagues the decision as to methods of gaining relinquishment of the University debt.   [1921]

1822 Jan. 14. JOSEPH C. CABELL, Richmond, to T. J., Monticello. ALS. 4 pp. Endorsed by T. J. Deposited by Philip B. Campbell. Partly printed: Cabell 231-237.

Funds for the University. Advises conciliation of the clergy who are uneasy because of the predominance of the Socinians at Cambridge (Harvard), the appointment of Thomas Cooper in South Carolina, and the discovery that George Ticknor and Nathaniel Bowditch are Unitarians. References to Chapman Johnson and David Watson.   [1922]

1822 Jan. 17. T. J., Monticello, to JOHN WAYLES EPPES, Mill Brook. ALS. 2 pp.

Requesting Eppes to send House and Senate Journals, American State Papers,

and certain other newspapers and public documents, 1789-1809, to be used in a project he is planning [the writing of "some notes and explanations of particular and leading transactions which history should know"; T. J. to John Wayles Eppes, 23 October 1821, DLC]. Oppressiveness of his correspondence. Reasons for refusal to exchange lands: his age; part of Bedford County lands held in trust by Bank of the United States for his endorsement for Wilson C. Nicholas; situation not inconvenient for Francis Eppes. Sends silk tree and bowwood tree for Mrs. Eppes. Will delay paying interest on his debt to Eppes.
[1923]

1822 Jan. 19. T. J., Monticello, to JAMES LEITCH, Charlottesville. ALS. 1 p. Order for a sifter and some rice.   [1924]

1822 Jan. 21. JOSEPH C. CABELL, Richmond, to T. J., Monticello. ALS. 2 pp. Endorsed by T. J. Deposited by Philip B. Campbell. Printed: Cabell 238-239.

Funds for the University. Estimate of revenue from the Literary Fund. References to John Bowyer, Chapman Johnson, and Charles Fenton Mercer.
[1925]

1822 Jan. 25. T. J., Monticello, to JOSEPH C. CABELL, Richmond. ALS. 1 p. Endorsed. Printed: Cabell 239-240; B of R VI 60 (MS. in DLC).

Asserts that the University will have an enrollment of over 200 soon after it opens from every state south of the Ohio, Missouri, and Potomac. Urges suspension of payment of interest on the University debt.   [1926]

1822 Feb. 3. JOSEPH C. CABELL, Richmond, to T. J., Monticello. ALS. 2 pp. Endorsed by T. J. Deposited by Philip B. Campbell. Printed: Cabell 240-241.

Funds for the University. The Kentucky Mission. States' Rights. References to Samuel Blackburn, Thomas Griffin, Chapman Johnson, and Richard Morris.
[1927]

1822 Feb. 8. T. J., Monticello, to ARTHUR S. BROCKENBROUGH. ALS. 1 p. Endorsed.

Payment of University debt. Cornices for the rooms of the western hotels. Friezes by William J. Coffee.   [1928]

1822 Feb. 11. JOSEPH C. CABELL, Richmond, to T. J., Monticello. ALS. 3 pp. Endorsed by T. J. Deposited by Philip B. Campbell. Printed: Cabell 242-244.

Funds for the University. The Literary Fund. References to James Breckenridge, [Charles?] Cocke, Chapman Johnson, Thomas Miller, and Richard Morris. [1929]

1822 Feb. 13. T. J., Monticello, to JAMES LEITCH, Charlottesville. ALS. 1 p. Photostat. Original owned by Mrs. J. Sharshall Grasty.

Order for linen and clothing. Mentions Burwell (servant).   [1930]

1822 Feb. 25. JOSEPH C. CABELL, Richmond, to T. J., Monticello. ALS. 1 p. Endorsed by T. J. Deposited by Philip B. Campbell. Printed: Cabell 244-245.

Funds for the University. References to John Bowyer, Chapman Johnson, Richard Morris, Samuel Taylor, and David Watson.   [1931]

1822 Mar. 6. JOSEPH C. CABELL, Williamsburg, to T. J., Monticello. ALS. 7 pp. Endorsed by T. J. Deposited by Philip B. Campbell. Printed (in part): Cabell 245-251.

Failure to pass various bills to provide funds for the University. Reports of extravagance in construction of the buildings. Attack on the Literary Fund based on the waste of the Primary School Fund. References to Arthur S. Brockenbrough, Samuel Blackburn, John Bowyer, Mr. Clay, Thomas Griffin, Chapman Johnson, Richard Morris, and David Watson.   [1932]

1822 Mar. 10. JOSEPH C. CABELL, Williamsburg, to T. J., Monticello. ALS. 3 pp. Endorsed by T. J. Deposited by Philip B. Campbell. Printed: Cabell 251-254.

Meeting of the Board of Visitors. Funds for the University. Convinced that all buildings should be completed to give favorable impression. Incidental effects of the move to shift the capital from Richmond to Staunton. Attitude of the Federalist Party. References to Wilson J. Cary, George Crump, Thomas Griffin, Chapman Johnson, James Madison, and John Tyler.   [1933]

1822 Mar. 22. FRANCIS EPPES, Columbia, S. C., to T. J., Monticello. ALS. 2 pp. Endorsed by T. J. Edgehill-Randolph Papers

Lack of funds forces him to leave school early. Description of his studies. References to John Wayles Eppes' finances.   [1934]

1822 May 8. T. J., Monticello, to ALEXANDER GARRETT. ALS. 1 p. Endorsed.

Sends Thomas Appleton's account for marble capitals and sums to be paid Giacomo Raggi. Note by Garrett: check sent to Bernard Peyton on Farmer's Bank of Virginia. Receipt by Alexander Garrett to Arthur Brockenbrough for the money.   [1935]

1822 May 13. FRANCIS EPPES, Mill Brook, to T. J., Monticello. ALS. 2 pp. Endorsed by T. J.

John Wayles Eppes can spare money only for Francis Bacon's *Abridgement* and Coke on Littleton. Bad crops, father's ill health make economy essential. Course of study in law. Invites Martha Randolph and T. J. to visit Mill Brook.   [1936]

1822 May 13-Aug. 30. T. J. ESTIMATE OF BRICKS for 6 shafts of Doric columns. AD. 2 pp.

Calculations. Ordered from John M. Perry.   [1937]

1822 June 28. WILLIAM LAMBERT, Washington, to T. J., Monticello. ALS. 1 p. Endorsed by T. J. Enclosure: ADS. 7 pp.

Method of determining longitude by occultations, solar eclipses, tedious but accurate. Sends method of calculation for use of University. Enclosure: "To find the Moon's parallaxes in longitude and latitude, independent of the altitude and longitude of the nonagesimal."   [1938]

1822 July 5. JOHN QUINCY ADAMS, Washington, to T. J., Monticello. DS. 1 p. Endorsed by T. J.

Transmits copy of public journals and documents to each state university.

Noted by T. J.: *State Papers of 1818, Secret Journals of Congress, Journals of Federal Convention, Census for 1820.*   [1939]

1822 July 6. WILLIAM LAMBERT, Washington, to T. J., Monticello. ALS. 1 p. Endorsed by T. J.

Acknowledges his valued note. Does not wish to burden him with astronomical labors, merely wishes to aid university in native state by supplying them accurate method for calculations of longitude.   [1940]

1822 July 11. WILLIAM LAMBERT, Washington, to T. J., Monticello. ALS. 1 p. Endorsed by T. J. Enclosure: ADS. 7 pp.

Sends additional contribution to University of Virginia: "Calculations of the longitude of the Capital in the City of Washington from Greenwich Observatory, in England, from the beginning of the Solar Eclipse of August 27th 1821, Examined and revised."   [1941]

1822 July 20. T. J., Monticello, to JOHN WAYLES EPPES, Mill Brook. ALS. 2 pp.

Regrets Eppes' illness. Disapproves of Francis Eppes' plan for early marriage but recommends acquiescence. Promises the house at Poplar Forest and a plantation with it, but since it is security for his commitment, cannot give a deed. Recommends Francis live with friends for a year before incurring expense of housekeeping.   [1942]

1822 Aug. 25. JAMES OLDHAM, University, to T. J., Monticello. ALS. 1 p. Endorsed by T. J.

Flooring planks arrived. Sends drawing of method of grooving floors.   [1943]

1822 Aug. 28. T. J., Monticello, to HENRY CLAY. ALS. 2 pp. File draft. Endorsed by T. J. Edgehill-Randolph Papers.

Engaging Clay's professional services in the collection of Thomas Deye Owings' bond to the late Wilson Cary Nicholas. Involvement of T. J. and Thomas J. Randolph as endorsers of Nicholas' notes. References to John Brown of Lexington, Colonel Morrison, and Dabney Terrell.   [1944]

1822 Sept. 5. T. J., Monticello, to JOHN QUINCY ADAMS, Washington. ALS. 1 p. File draft. Endorsed by T. J.

As Rector of University of Virginia, acknowledges volumes presented to it.
                                                                        [1945]

1822 Oct. 3. JOSEPH C. CABELL, Edgewood, to T. J., Monticello. ALS. 1 p. Endorsed by T. J. Deposited by Philip B. Campbell. Printed: Cabell 254-255.

Illness prevents attendance at the Board of Visitors meeting. Auditing of the University's accounts by Martin Dawson. References to John H. Cocke.
                                                                        [1946]

1822 Oct. 4. WILLIAM LAMBERT, Washington, to T. J., Monticello. ALS. 1 p. Endorsed by T. J. Enclosure: ADS. 3 pp.

Presents table for use of University of Virginia, "A Table of Logarithms for reducing the Moon's equatorial horizontal parallax from a sphere to an oblate spheroid, admitting the ratio of the equatorial diameter to the polar axis of the Earth, to be as 320 to 319." [1947]

1822 Oct. 7. T. J. REPORT as RECTOR of the UNIVERSITY of Virginia to the PRESIDENT and Directors of the LITERARY FUND. D. 1 p. Clipping from the Charlottesville *Central Gazette* of 10 January 1823.

Progress of construction. Provision for religious instruction at the University. Audit of the University's books. (See entry of 23 December). [1948]

1822 Oct. 11. T. J., Monticello, to ARTHUR S. BROCKENBROUGH, University of Virginia. ALS. 2 pp. Endorsed.

Sends copy of resolution of Board of Visitors, authorizing building of the library, and of an advertisement for the Richmond *Enquirer* and Charlottesville *Central Gazette* regarding collection of University subscriptions in arrears. [1949]

1822 Oct. 11. THOMAS M. RANDOLPH (of Ashton), Norfolk, to T. J., Monticello. ALS. 1 p. Endorsed by T. J. Edgehill-Randolph Papers.

Requests that T. J. use his influence with the President and Secretary of the Navy to help Randolph's brother-in-law, Beverly Browne, become naval storekeeper at the Gosport Navy Yard. All wine sold by Captain Crane. (This is Thomas Mann Randolph, Jr., II, younger half-brother of Thomas Mann Randolph, Jr.). [1950]

1822 Oct. 25. DABNEY C. TERRELL, Louisville, Ky., to T. J. Monticello. ALS. 2 pp. Endorsed by T. J. Carr-Cary Papers.

Lien on ironworks in Montgomery will shield T. J. from loss as endorser of Wilson Cary Nicholas, if Owings' bond is awarded to Thomas Jefferson Randolph. Pestilence in Louisville. Mentions Henry Clay, Mr. Green, Mr. Leigh, and William Morrison. [1951]

1822 Oct. 31. FRANCIS EPPES, Mill Brook, to T. J., Monticello. ALS. 3 pp. Endorsed by T. J. Edgehill-Randolph Papers.

Plan for borrowing money to set up his plantation. Information from Colonel Burton about Carolina wine, made by Ebinezer Pettigrew of Edenton and George Spruel of Plymouth, sold by Thomas Cox & Co. Study of Coke. John Wayles Eppes' health. [1952]

1822 Nov. 21. T. J., Monticello, to ARTHUR S. BROCKENBROUGH. ALS. 1 p. Endorsed.

University accounts with Thomas Appleton and Giacomo Raggi. Reference to Alexander Garrett. [1953]

1822 Dec. 7. PETER MAVERICK, New York, to T. J., Monticello. ALS. 1 p. Endorsed by T. J.

Forward 250 prints of the plan of the University of Virginia to Bernard Peyton, retaining plate for future orders. Includes bill. [1954]

1822 Dec. 12. T. J., Monticello, to ARTHUR S. BROCKENBROUGH. ALS. 1 p. Endorsed.

Payment to Peter Maverick for his engraving of the University of Virginia ground plan. University accounts. References to Bernard Peyton. [1955]

1822 Dec. 19 [date received]. ARTHUR S. BROCKENBROUGH to T. J., Monticello. ALS. 1 p. Endorsed by T. J.

Statement of University accounts. Possible contracts for the library building with James Dinsmore, John Neilson, Thorn & Chamberlain, and John M. Perry. Has sent Alexander Garrett's account to Martin Dawson.   [1956]

1822 Dec. 19. JOSEPH C. CABELL, Richmond, to T. J., Monticello. ALS. 1 p. Endorsed by T. J. Deposited by Philip B. Campbell. Printed Cabell 255-257.

Funds for the University. Literary Fund finances very unfavorable. Cabell's health improved. Glad T. J.'s wound improving. References to Wilson J. Cary, David S. Garland, William F. Gordon, Chapman Johnson, Thomas Mann Randolph, Jr., [William Cabell] Rives, and Judge St. George Tucker.   [1957]

1822 Dec. 23. JOSEPH C. CABELL, Richmond, to T. J., Monticello. ALS. 3 pp. Endorsed by T. J. Deposited by Philip B. Campbell. Printed: Cabell 257-259.

Cost of building the library estimated by James Dinsmore. Funds for the University. Purchase of books and apparatus. Settlement of the Proctor's accounts. References to John Bowyer, Alexander Garrett, William F. Gordon, James Hunter, George Loyall, and [William Cabell] Rives.   [1958]

1822 Dec. 23. T. J., RECTOR of the UNIVERSITY of VIRGINIA, to the PRESIDENT and Directors of the LITERARY FUND. D. 1 p. Clipping from the Charlottesville *Central Gazette* of 10 January 1823.

Letter transmitting the report of 7 October (*q.v.*). Additional information on the financial status of the University.   [1959]

1822 Dec. 25. GIACOMO RAGGI, New York, to T. J., Monticello. ALS. 1 p. Endorsed by T. J.

Awaits arrival of ships from Livorno with the University's marble capitals. Mentions Thomas Appleton.   [1960]

1822 Dec. 28. T. J., Monticello, to JOSEPH C. CABELL. ALS. 3 pp. Endorsed. Printed: Cabell 260-262; B of R VI 60 (MS. in DLC).

Urges securing of money for the building of the library as of more importance than the remission of the University's debt. To secure a faculty of the highest order, must have distinguished structures. Estimates of the cost of the library by John M. Perry, John Gorman, James Oldham, James Dinsmore, and Arthur S. Brockenbrough. Extreme difficulty in writing. Mentions William Gordon, Chapman Johnson, George Loyall, and William C. Rives.   [1961]

1822 Dec. 30. JOSEPH C. CABELL, Richmond, to T. J., Monticello. ALS. 3 pp. Endorsed by T. J. Deposited by Philip B. Campbell. Partly printed: Cabell 263-265.

Funds for the University. Cost of the library. Error in the Proctor's accounts. References to Briscoe G. Baldwin, John Bowyer, Wilson J. Cary, John H. Cocke, Peter M. Daniel, David S. Garland, William F. Gordon, Chapman Johnson, Daniel Sheffey, Allen Taylor, and Henry E. Watkins.   [1962]

[*ca.* 1822]. T. J. ESSAY ON THE ANGLO-SAXON. AD. 64 pp. Printer's directions in another hand. Another copy: Rough draft. AD. 55 pp.

Essay for facilitating instruction in the Anglo-Saxon and modern English dialects, prepared for the use of the University of Virginia. Contains sections on Anglo-Saxon alphabet, orthography, grammar, numbers, pronunciation, and a specimen (the book of *Genesis*) of the form in which Anglo-Saxon writings might be published.   [1963]

1823 Jan. 3. WILLIAM J. COFFEE, New York, to T. J., Monticello. ALS. 3 pp. Endorsed by T. J. Edgehill-Randolph Papers.

Maverick's engraving of University ground plan. Instructions for installing ornaments for *Poplar Forest* and the University pavilions. T. J.'s recent fall. References to Arthur S. Brockenbrough, and John Hemmings.   [1964]

1823 Jan. 9. JOSEPH C. CABELL, Richmond, to T. J., Monticello. ALS. 1 p. Endorsed by T. J. Deposited by Philip B Campbell. Printed: Cabell 265-266.

Funds for the University. University's popularity shown in elections in Mecklenburg, Lunenburg, Brunswick, Greenville, Henrico, Norfolk, and Essex counties. References to Mr. Clopton, James Hunter, Arthur Lee, and Addison Powell.   [1965]

1823 Jan. 11. T. J., Monticello, to ARTHUR S. BROCKENBROUGH. ALS. 1 p. Endorsed.

Lodgings for John Gorman, a workman at the University.   [1966]

1823 Jan. 13. T. J., Monticello, to JOSEPH C. CABELL, Richmond. ALS. 2 pp. Endorsed by T. J. Printed: Cabell 266-268.

Requests that Cabell, Chapman Johnson, and George Loyall sign a special call for a Board of Visitors meeting as soon as the lower house passes the bill financing the library building. Martin Dawson's estimate of University debts higher than Arthur S. Brockenbrough's. Financing of a state system of education. Primary education most important, the University next, secondary schools the least. Mentions James Breckenridge, John H. Cocke, and James Madison.
                [1967]

1823 Jan. 22. T. J., T. J. RANDOLPH, and SAMUEL CARR. BOND to the PRESIDENT and MASTERS of the COLLEGE of WILLIAM and MARY. DS. 2 pp. Witnessed by Francis Eppes and D. O. Carr. Edgehill-Randolph Papers.

Loan to T. J. Randolph to discharge Wilson C. Nicholas' bond to the Bank of the United States.   [1968]

1823 Jan. 23. JOSEPH C. CABELL, Richmond, to T. J., Monticello. ALS. 3 pp. Endorsed by T. J. Deposited by Philip B. Campbell. Printed: Cabell 268-270.

Funds for the University and for colleges and primary schools throughout the state. Question of moving the capital from Richmond. References to Hampden-Sydney College, William F. Gordon, [William Cabell] Rives, and Samuel Taylor.
                [1969]

1823 Jan. 27. THOMAS J. O'FLAHERTY, Rappahannock Academy, Caroline County, to THOMAS COOPER, President, South Carolina College. L. 4 pp. Copy [sent to T. J.?]. Greek, Latin, French, and English.

Applying for a position at South Carolina College, with information on his education, experience, and devotion to the principles for which Robert Emmet

died. Impossibility of returning to Ireland under present conditions. Letter of
introduction from William Sampson.   [1970]

1823 Jan. 28. T. J., Monticello, to JOSEPH C. CABELL, Richmond. ALS. 2 pp.
Endorsed. Printed: Cabell 270-271.

Agrees to place University first, later to come forward as patron of the
primary schools. Disapproves special favors for Hampden-Sydney. Requests
written approval from Board of Visitors for engaging workmen for library.
Mentions Chapman Johnson, George Loyall, and William C. Rives.   [1971]

*1823 Jan. R. WALKER and JOEL YANCEY. APPRAISAL. D. 1 p. Endorsed.
Valuation of the slaves at Poplar Forest, made in connection with a settlement
between Jefferson and Francis Eppes.   [1972]

1823 Feb. 3. JOSEPH C. CABELL, Richmond, to T. J., Monticello. ALS. 3 pp.
Endorsed by T. J. Deposited by Philip B. Campbell. Printed: Cabell 272-273.

Meeting of the Board of Visitors. Loan bill for the University secure. Mr.
Brockenbrough's accounts. References to Philip Doddridge and Thomas Griffin.
                                                                     [1973]

1823 Feb. 4. T. J., Monticello, to JOSEPH C. CABELL. L. 2 pp. File draft [by
Ellen Wayles Randolph?]. Endorsed by T. J. McGregor Library.

Attacks on Brockenbrough's honesty by James Oldham, a worker at the University, sent to Thomas Griffin of the House of Delegates.   [1974]

1823 Feb. 5. JOSEPH C. CABELL, Richmond, to T. J., Monticello. ALS. 1 p.
Endorsed by T. J. Deposited by Philip B. Campbell. Printed: Cabell 274.

Passage of the University Bill. References to William F. Gordon, Chapman
Johnson, and George Loyall.   [1975]

1823 Feb. 11. JOSEPH C. CABELL, Richmond, to T. J., Monticello. ALS. 3 pp.
Endorsed by T. J. Deposited by Philip B. Campbell. Printed: Cabell 274-277.

No attention paid to James Oldham's charges against Arthur Brockenbrough.
Chapman Johnson's failure to attend meetings of Board of Visitors. University
finances. Application from Dr. Jones, formerly of the College of William and
Mary, for the chemistry chair at the University of Virginia. References to
Briscoe Baldwin, John Bowyer, Philip Doddridge, David S. Garland, William F.
Gordon, George Loyall, Daniel Sheffey, Allen Taylor, and Joseph Watkins.
                                                                     [1976]

1823 Feb. 15. WILLIAM J. COFFEE, New York, to T. J. D. 1 p. Edgehill-
Randolph Papers.

Bill for Poplar Forest ornaments.   [1977]

1823 Feb. 21. T. J., Monticello, to JOHN H. COCKE, Bremo. ALS. 1 p. Endorsed. Cocke Papers.

Requests his attendance to discuss the hiring of workmen for the Rotunda,
since legislature has permitted a $60,000 loan. Expects written authorization from
James Breckenridge, Joseph Cabell, George Loyall, and James Madison. Mentions
Arthur Brockenbrough, James Dinsmore, and John Neilson.   [1978]

1823 Feb. 25. MARTHA JEFFERSON, Spring Grove, Lunenberg County, to T. J., Monticello. ALS. 4 pp. Endorsed by T. J. Carr-Cary Papers.

Requesting her cousin's aid in settling the affairs of her deceased brother, George Jefferson. Believes that John Garland Jefferson and Patrick Gibson are being unfair to her. [1979]

1823 Feb. 26. JOSEPH C. CABELL, Williamsburg, to T. J., Monticello. ALS. 2 pp. Endorsed by T. J. Deposited by Philip B. Campbell. Printed: Cabell 277-278.

Law regarding seats on the Board of Visitors. Contracts for the library should be for a definite amount. References to Chapman Johnson and John Augustine Smith. [1980]

1823 Mar. 9. T. J., Monticello, to SIDNEY MORSE, New Haven. ALS. 1 p. Photostat. Endorsed. Original owned by B. D. Foster.

Expressing thanks for a copy of Morse's "Geography". Age prevents his offering detailed criticism of tables, but notes omission of William and Mary from list of colleges. [1981]

1823 Mar. 10. THOMAS J. O'FLAHERTY, Rappahannock Academy, Caroline County, to T. J., Monticello. ALS. 3 pp. Endorsed by T. J. Greek, Latin, French, English.

Application for chair of languages at University of Virginia. Transmits four letters, to be returned, from Robert S. Garnett, Thomas Cooper, and himself. [1982]

1823 Mar. 12. T. J., Monticello, to ARTHUR S. BROCKENBROUGH, University. ALS. 1 p. Endorsed. Enclosure: DS. 3 pp. Endorsed. Another copy. AL. 1 p.

Returns contracts (for work on the Rotunda) with James Dinsmore, John Neilson, and Thorn & Chamberlain. Requests statement of funds as work progresses. Enclosure: contracts with Dinsmore and Neilson. [1983]

1823 Mar. 12. T. J., Monticello, to BOARD OF VISITORS, UNIVERSITY of VIRGINIA. Circular. LS. 1 p. Endorsed. Copies sent to Cocke and to Cabell. Printed: Cabell 278-279.

Contracts made by Arthur S. Brockenbrough with Thorn & Chamberlain, John Neilson, and James Dinsmore for work on the Rotunda. [1984]

1823 Mar. 24. JOSEPH C. CABELL, Williamsburg, to T. J., Monticello. ALS. 3 pp. Endorsed by T. J. Deposited by Philip B. Campbell. Printed: Cabell 280-282.

Contracts for the library. Funds for the purchase of books and apparatus. References to John H. Cocke and Chapman Johnson. [1985]

1823 Mar. 26. T. J., Monticello, to THOMAS J. O'FLAHERTY, Rappahannock Academy. ALS. 2 pp. File draft. Endorsed by T. J.

Returns papers which have been communicated to James Madison. Cannot appoint professors until University's debt is discharged. On *verso*: calculations (for servants' clothing?). [1986]

1823 Mar. 27. T. J., Monticello, to CREED TAYLOR, Farmville. ALS. 1 p. Creed Taylor Papers. Another MS. in MHi.

Merits of the Journal of the Law School sent to T. J. by Taylor. (The law school referred to is one conducted by Taylor at his estate, Needham).   [1987]

*1823 Apr. 1. T. J. FINANCIAL STATEMENT. AD. 2 pp. Edgehill-Randolph Papers.

Expenses and income in Albemarle and Bedford. Plans for payment of his own debts by 1827, of Wilson C. Nicholas' by 1830, and "the lands will all be saved". List of his creditors: [Joseph] Antrim, Edmund Bacon, Bank of the United States, Bank of Virginia, Joseph Bishop, Brands' executors, Branham & Bibb, Youen Carden, Hugh Chisholm, Dabney Cosby, Martin Dawson, Dodge & Oxnard, Francis Eppes, John Wayles Eppes, Farmer's Bank, John Gorman, Mr. Gough, Elijah Ham, [Frederick W.?] Hatch, David Higginbotham, John Jones, James Leitch, Leroy & Bayard, James Lyle, Charles Massie, B. Miller, John Neilson, Mr. Pini, Hanah Proctor, Dr. Ragland, James Rawlings, Archibald Robertson, University of Virginia, Dr. Watkins, Mr. Welsh, John Winn, and Joel Yancey.   [1988]

1823 Apr. 5. T. J., Monticello, to ROBERT WALSH, Philadelphia. ALS. 1 p.

Regrets that physical disability prevents him from providing material for Walsh's projected biography. Biography ought not to be written while the subject is alive, because of difficulty in being properly critical and because he should have access to the letters of the person while writing. ". . . the letters of a person . . . form the only full and genuine journal of his life; and few can let them go out of their own hands while they live. a life written after these hoards become opened to investigation must supercede any previous one." Correa a member of the Cortes and in poor health, disapproves of our administration.   [1989]

1823 Apr. 6. T. J. MEMORANDUM on FINANCES of the UNIVERSITY. AD. 1 p. File draft. Endorsed by T. J.

Arthur S. Brockenbrough's and Martin Dawson's estimate of debts, subscriptions, annuity, prospects of help from legislature, and immediate loans needed for Rotunda.   [1990]

1823 Apr. 11. T. J., Monticello, to JOHN ADLUM. ALS. 1 p. Deposited from Monticello.

Acknowledging a gift of wine. Refuses comment on Adlum's book on wine culture.   [1991]

1823 Apr. 12. T. J., Monticello, to JAMES BRECKENRIDGE, Fincastle, Va. ALS. 1 p. Endorsed. Printed: B of R VI 47 (MS. in DLC).

Sends receipt for Chapman Johnson's subscription to the University. Hopes Breckenridge's election to the legislature will ensure remission of University's debt. Estimate of present debt.   [1992]

1823 Apr. 22. T. J., Monticello, to ARTHUR S. BROCKENBROUGH. ALS. 1 p. Endorsed.
Instructions for James Dinsmore and John Neilson on the entablature of the Rotunda.   [1993]

1823 Apr. 24. GEORGE BLAETTERMANN, London, to T. J., Monticello. ALS. 2 pp. Endorsed by T. J.
Requests information as to when he should begin his work at the University. Has toured Germany, France, and Holland collecting materials for lectures. Wishes to know if his books may enter duty free.   [1994]

1823 Apr. 30. T. J., Monticello, to WILLIAM J. COFFEE. ALS. 1 p. File draft. Endorsed by T. J. Edgehill-Randolph Papers.
Payment for ornaments for the University. Mix-up in shipment. Reference to Bernard Peyton.   [1995]

1823 May. 3. T. J., Monticello, to SAMUEL SMITH, Baltimore. LS. 2 pp. Endorsed. Printed: L & B XV 430-433; Ford X 251-252; *Virginia Advocate* 9 July 1830; B of R VI 436 (MS. in DLC).
Recommends tax on whiskey to discourage its consumption, but not on imported wines. Belief in support of infant industries only when they can in the future become strong. Refuses to express an opinion on the next election.   [1996]

1823 May 5. JOHN NEILSON, University, to T. J., Monticello. ALS. 1 p. Endorsed by T. J.
Problems concerning the north front of the Rotunda.   [1997]

1823 May 8. JOHN BROWN, JR., Auditor's Office, Richmond, to T. J., Monticello. ALS. 1 p. Endorsed by T. J.
Literary Fund Board has authorized loan of $40,000 to the University. Regrets his delay prevented T. J.'s trip to Poplar Forest. Mentions Alexander Garrett.
                                                                          [1998]

1823 May 10. T. J. CERTIFICATE. DS. 1 p. (multilated).
Alexander Garrett certified as Bursar of the University of Virginia.   [1999]

[1823 May 10?]. T. J. to the TREASURER OF VIRGINIA. AD. 2 pp.
Authorizing Alexander Garrett, Bursar of the University of Virginia, to receive funds from the Literary Fund and to transact business for the Board of Visitors.
                                                                          [2000]

1823 May 11. RECTOR AND VISITORS of the UNIVERSITY. BOND to the PRESIDENT and DIRECTORS of the LITERARY FUND. D. 2 pp. Signed by T. J. File draft. Endorsed by T. J. Witnesses: Thomas J. Randolph and W. W. Southall.
Bond for $40,000. Conditions of repayment. Note at bottom: "Nov. 21. 23. executed a bond for 5000. D. copied verbatim from this except as to sum." [2001]

1823 May 12. CLAUDIUS F. GOJON, Hyde Park, N. Y., to T. J., Monticello. ALS. 1 p. Endorsed by T. J.
Application for a position at the University of Virginia teaching French,

Spanish, and Italian. Lists experiences at the University of France and at Dr. Allen's Academy. Refers him to P. S. DuPonceau.   [2002]

1823 May 28. T. J., Monticello, to CLAUDIUS F. GOJON, Hyde Park. ALS. 1 p. File draft. Endorsed by T. J.
Opening of University uncertain, and appointment of professors delayed. [2003]

1823 May 30. T. J., Monticello, to THOMAS COOPER, Columbia, S. C. ALS. 2 pp. Endorsed.
Hopes Cooper will come to the University of Virginia despite revival of persecutions from the *genus irritabile vatum. Columbian Register* of May 10th contains no article by Ignatius Thompson but does have a message from the Governor of Connecticut.   [2004]

1823 June 7. T. J., Monticello, to MARTHA JEFFERSON, Spring Grove, Lunenburg County. ALS. 2 pp. File draft. Endorsed by T. J. Carr-Cary Papers.
Advice concerning the settlement of George Jefferson's estate. His high regard for her father, George Jefferson, and brothers, George Jefferson and John Garland Jefferson. Mentions Patrick Gibson.   [2005]

1823 June 16. T. J., Monticello, to ARTHUR S. BROCKENBROUGH. ALS. 1 p.
Sends drawings to correct ill effect of angles in passage of the Rotunda. [2006]

1823 June 20. T. J., Monticello, to ARTHUR S. BROCKENBROUGH. AL. 1 p.
Letter of introduction for Mr. Miralla of South America, who is bringing papers from T. J.   [2007]

1823 June 24. JOSEPH C. CABELL, Edgewood, to T. J., Monticello. ALS. 3 pp. Endorsed by T. J. Deposited by Philip B. Campbell. Another copy: 3 pp. File draft. Endorsed by Cabell. Cabell Papers.
Requesting T. J.'s advice on plan of jail for Nelson County.   [2008]

1823 June 25. T. J., Monticello, to Messrs. JOHN WINN, WILLIAM C. RIVES, DANIEL M. RAILEY, JOHN M. RAILEY, JOHN ORMOND, HORACE BRAM-HAM, AND GEORGE W. NICHOLAS. L. 1 p. Typescript copy. Original owned by Miss Jane Randolph Mcdonell. Printed: Ford-Bixby 276-277.
Age and debility prevent his attending Fourth of July celebration.   [2009]

1823 July 4. T. J. MEMORANDUM on CAPITALS for the UNIVERSITY. AD. 1 p. Endorsed by A. S. Brockenbrough.
Thomas Appleton's account for the capitals; account of Jonathan Thompson, Collector of New York, for duty and freight; Thomas Bell's account for freight.
                      [2010]

1823 July 5. T. J., Monticello, to SAMUEL J. HARRISON, Lynchburg. ALS. 1 p. Another MS. in MHi. Printed: Harrison 88.
Forwards extract of a letter from George Ticknor of Harvard, complimenting the scholarship, zeal, and character of Harrison's son, Jesse Burton Harrison.
                      [2011]

1823 July 18. JOSEPH C. CABELL, Edgewood, to T. J., Monticello. ALS. 2 pp. Endorsed by T. J. Deposited by Philip B. Campbell.

Thanking T. J. for his aid in planning the Nelson County jail. References to Mr. Crawford, Mr. Peck, and William Philips.   [2012]

1823 July-Aug. ARTHUR S. BROCKENBROUGH. MEMORANDUM on CAPITALS. AD. 1 p. Endorsed by T. J.

Cost of the capitals delivered at the University. Mentions Bernard Peyton, Thomas Appleton, Lyman Peck.   [2013]

1823 Aug. 3. THOMAS J. O'FLAHERTY, Rumford Academy, to JAMES MONROE. ALS. 3 pp. Endorsed by T. J. Greek, Latin, French, and English.

Application for position at the University of Virginia. Encloses letters from T. J., John Roane, and Thomas Cooper.   [2014]

1823 Aug. 6. JOSEPH C. CABELL, Edgewood, to T. J., Monticello. ALS. 5 pp. Endorsed by T. J. Enclosure: AD. 2 pp. Deposited by Philip B. Campbell.

Selection of the site of the Nelson County jail. Details of its plan. References to Arthur Brockenbrough, William Cosby, Mr. Crawford, Mr. Nelson, John Perry, William Phillips. Enclosure: memorandum of the contract made 29 July 1823 between Robert Rives, Joseph C. Cabell, and Thomas Massie, Jr., for the court of Nelson County, and William B. Phillips, who agrees to build the jail. Contract refers to Jefferson's plan.   [2015]

1823 Aug. 8. JOHN ROANE, King William County, to JAMES MONROE, Washington. ALS. 1 p.

Recommends Thomas J. O'Flaherty for professorship at the University. [2016]

1823 Aug. 10. T. J., Monticello, to ARTHUR S. BROCKENBROUGH. ALS. 1 p. Endorsed.

Change in his drawing of the library room of the Rotunda.   [2017]

1823 Aug. 11. T. J., Monticello, to ARTHUR S. BROCKENBROUGH. ALS. 1 p.
Door for the Rotunda.   [2018]

1823 Aug. 11. ARTHUR S. BROCKENBROUGH, University, to T. J., Monticello. ALS. 1 p. Endorsed by T. J.

Construction details regarding main door of Rotunda. Fire at the state penitentiary.   [2019]

1823 Aug. 27. T. J., Monticello, to E. S. DAVIS, Abbeville, S. C. AL. 1 p. File draft. Endorsed by T. J.

Forwards plan of University with printed explanations. Reports progress of construction. Hopes legislature will enable University to open by liberating funds. University to be *alma mater* of South and West.   [2020]

1823 Sept. 2. T. J., Monticello, to ARTHUR S. BROCKENBROUGH, University. ALS. 1 p.

Terms of agreement with Giacomo Raggi for bases of columns. Mentions Mr. Negrin, John Neilson, and James Dinsmore.   [2021]

1823 Sept. 4 [date received]. JOHN WAYLES EPPES, [Mill Brook], to T. J., [Monticello]. ALS. 1 p. Endorsed by T. J. Edgehill-Randolph Papers.

Requesting payment of balance due him.   [2022]

1823 Sept. 14. JOHN W. GREEN, Culpeper, to DR. WATKINS. ALS. 1 p. Endorsed by T. J.

Recommending Mr. and Mrs. John Gray as boarding-house keepers for the University.   [2023]

[1823 Sept. 17]. T. J., Monticello, to ARTHUR S. BROCKENBROUGH. ALS. 1 p. Endorsed.

Recommending that Giacomo Raggi be given an advance, secured by alabaster and marble which he has permission to sell. Receipt for $50 signed by Raggi.
                                                                          [2024]

*1823 Sept. 23. [ARTHUR S. BROCKENBROUGH] to T. J., Monticello. AL. 1 p. File draft. Endorsed by Brockenbrough.

Arrival of Corinthian and Ionic capitals from Italy.   [2025]

1823 Sept. 25. ARTHUR S. BROCKENBROUGH, University, to T. J., Monticello. ALS. 1 p. Endorsed by T. J.

Arrival of Corinthian and Ionic capitals from Italy. Itemizes variations from directions given. Inferior to those done by Michael Raggi.   [2026]

1823 Sept. 26, FRANK CARR, Red Hill, to T. J. ALS. 1 p. Endorsed by T. J. Carr-Cary Papers.

Sends three potato pumpkins and a cushaw squash with cultivation directions.
                                                                          [2027]

1823 Sept. ARTHUR S. BROCKENBROUGH. CONTRACT with GIACOMO RAGGI. AD by T. J. 2 pp. Endorsed.

For carving of Corinthian bases for University of Virginia columns, to be executed by Raggi under the direction of Thomas Appleton.   [2028]

1823 Oct. 8. T. J., Monticello, to THOMAS APPLETON, Leghorn, Italy. ALS. 2 pp. File draft. Endorsed by T. J.

Capitals received approved on the whole, but certain details unsatisfactory. Contract with Giacomo Raggi for Rotunda capitals. Requests price of bases for columns, wooden columns for interior, and marble squares for floor. Asks for engraving of Pantheon. Payment to be remitted by Bernard Peyton through Samuel Williams of London.   [2029]

1823 Oct. 27. JOSEPH C. CABELL, Edgewood, to T. J., Monticello. ALS. 1 p. Endorsed by T. J. Deposited by Philip B. Campbell. Partly printed: Cabell 282-283.

Coffey's and Roscoe's books on prisons. Unable to find the *Oxford and Cambridge Guide.* New purchase of land will make it necessary to withdraw from the Senate.   [2030]

1823 Nov. 2. T. J., Monticello, to ARTHUR S. BROCKENBROUGH. ALS. 1 p.

Transfer of title of the University lands from the Proctor to the Rector and Visitors.   [2031]

1823 Nov. 13. T. J., Monticello, to JOSEPH C. CABELL, Warminster. ALS. 1 p. Endorsed. Printed: Cabell 283.

Consultation with James Madison regarding a substitute for Cabell (in making the trip to Europe to engage faculty for the University) . [2032]

1823 Nov. 20. T. J., Monticello, to ARTHUR S. BROCKENBROUGH. ALS. 1 p. Endorsed.

Settlement of James Oldham's and John Neilson's account. Requests estimate of money available for professors. [2033]

1823 Nov. 22. T. J., Monticello, to ARTHUR S. BROCKENBROUGH. ALS. 1 p. Endorsed.

Order to remit funds for the Rotunda columns to Thomas Appleton, Leghorn, Italy, through Bernard Peyton, Richmond. [2034]

1823 Nov. 22. JOSEPH C. CABELL, Richmond, to T. J., Monticello. ALS. 1 p. Endorsed by T. J. Deposited by Philip B. Campbell. Printed: Cabell 284.

Personal affairs delay his attending Assembly meetings. Returns Roscoe's work on prisons. University bill to be pushed by James Breckenridge and T. M. Randolph, Jr. [2035]

1823 Nov. 28. ARTHUR S. BROCKENBROUGH, University, to T. J., Monticello. ALS. 1 p. Endorsed by T. J.

Estimate of expenses for the University of Virginia for 1824, unless brickmaking is resumed. Martin Dawson's charges will be slight in future. [2036]

1823 Dec. 3. JOSEPH C. CABELL, Richmond, to T. J., Monticello. ALS. 1 p. Endorsed by T. J. Deposited by Philip B. Campbell. Printed: Cabell 285.

Bill to remove the University debt. References to Colonel Boyd, William F. Gordon, James Pleasants, and Thomas Mann Randolph, Jr. [2037]

1823 Dec. 28. T. J., Monticello, to ARTHUR S. BROCKENBROUGH. ALS. 1 p. Endorsed.

Number of hands required for the next year's work at the University. [2038]

1823 Dec. 29. JOSEPH C. CABELL, Richmond, to T. J., Monticello. ALS. 1 p. Endorsed by T. J. Deposited by Philip B. Campbell. Printed: Cabell 286.

Funds for the University. References to Thomas Miller and Thomas Mann Randolph, Jr. [2039]

1823 Dec. 31. T. J. MEMORANDUM on FUNDS of the UNIVERSITY. AD. 3 pp.

State of funds for 1823, estimate for 1824, annual income, annual expenses, and probable expenses of a student. [2040]

[1823]. T. J. MEMORANDUM on APPLICATION of UNIVERSITY FUNDS. AD. 2 pp.

Detailed account of funds and debts 1820-1823. Interest payments projected to 1839. [2041]

[1823?]. T. J. Memorandum of SPECIFICATIONS for a building at the UNIVERSITY of VIRGINIA, [Rotunda?]. AD. 1 p. [2042]

[1823]. T. J. OPINION on the WILL of JOHN WAYLES EPPES. AD. 2 pp. Annotations in another hand. Ambler Papers.

Deals with right of Francis Eppes to that part of John Wayles Eppes' estate which J. W. E. possessed in right of his first wife, Maria Jefferson Eppes. Mentions Martha B. Eppes, John Wayles Eppes' second wife; Mr. Burton, an executor; Pantops, a part of John Wayles Eppes' land.   [2043]

[ca. 1823]. T. J. UNIVERSITY CONSTRUCTION ORDER. D. 1 p. Copy by Arthur S. Brockenbrough. Endorsed.

Instructions to bricklayers and carpenters at work on the Rotunda.   [2044]

1824 Jan. 2. T. J., Monticello, to ARTHUR S. BROCKENBROUGH. ALS. 1 p. Endorsed.

Introducing Mr. Ralston of Philadelphia and Captain Chapman, who wish to see the University of Virginia.   [2045]

1824 Jan. 26. JOSEPH C. CABELL, Richmond, to T. J., Monticello. ALS. 2 pp. Endorsed by T. J. Deposited by Philip B. Campbell. Printed: Cabell 287-288.

Funds for the University. Purchase of books. Reference to Thomas Mann Randolph, Jr.   [2046]

1824 Jan. 29. JOSEPH C. CABELL, Richmond, to T. J., Monticello. ALS. 2 pp. Endorsed by T. J. Deposited by Philip B. Campbell. Partly printed: Cabell 288-290.

Passage of the University bill. Funds for purchase of library and apparatus. Recommending Claude Crozet as professor of mathematics and Dabney Carr as professor of law. Mentions Alexander Garrett.   [2047]

1824 Feb. 3. T. J., Monticello, to JOSEPH C. CABELL, [Richmond]. ALS. 3 pp. Endorsed. Printed: Cabell 290-292; L & B XVI 4-8; TJR IV 386-388; B of R VI 60 (MS. in DLC).

Funds for the University of Virginia. Reappointment of the Board of Visitors. Funds for library and apparatus. Importance of choosing faculty on merit alone rather than from favoritism, which practice has lowered standards at the College of Philadelphia and at Edinburgh University. Has never appointed relation to office, because always found someone else better qualified.   [2048]

1824 Feb. 15. C. S. RAFINESQUE, Lexington, Ky., to T. J., Monticello. ALS. 2 pp. Endorsed by T. J. Enclosures: AD. 4 pp. and 1 clipping from *Cincinnati Literary Gazette*.

Renews application for professorship of botany, zoology, mineralogy, geology, physics, geometry, mental philosophy, ancient history of America, archaeology, phonology, and philology. Enclosures: catalog of his principal works; newspaper articles by Rafinesque, dealing with American anthropology and with a new tree of Kentucky, *cladrastis fragrans*.   [2049]

1824 Feb. 19. JOSEPH C. CABELL, Richmond, to T. J., Monticello. ALS. 2 pp. Endorsed by T. J. Deposited by Philip B. Campbell. Printed: Cabell 293-294.

Logrolling attempt: University bill and the bill to recharter the Farmer's

Bank. References to James Breckenridge, Alexander Garrett, William F. Gordon, and Thomas Mann Randolph, Jr.   [2050]

1824 Feb. 25. T. J., Monticello, to ARTHUR S. BROCKENBROUGH. ALS. 1 p. Endorsed.

Request for 1200 bricks to be placed to the account of John M. Perry. [2051]

1824 Mar. 4. ARTHUR S. BROCKENBROUGH, University, to T. J., Monticello. ALS. 1 p. Note by T. J. on text.

List necessary expenditures for the University. Sends balance sheet up to 31 December [1823].   [2052]

1824 Mar. 4. T. J., Monticello, to ARTHUR S. BROCKENBROUGH, University. AL. 1 p. Endorsed.

Estimate of income and expenses for the year 1823. Mentions Martin Dawson.
                                                    [2053]

1824 Mar. 7. JOSEPH C. CABELL, Richmond, to T. J., Monticello. ALS. 3 pp. Endorsed by T. J. Deposited by Philip B. Campbell. Partly printed: Cabell 294-296.

Funds for the University from the debt due Virginia from the Federal government. Francis Walker Gilmer's scheme of professorships. References to James Barbour, William F. Gordon, [George?] Hay, Chapman Johnson, James Madison, and Thomas Mann Randolph, Jr.   [2054]

[1824 Mar. 10?]. T. J. MEMORANDUM ON DEBTS. AD. 1 p. Edgehill-Randolph Papers.

Memorandum concerning the renewal of his notes held by the Bank of the U. S., the Farmer's Bank, and the Bank of Virginia.   [2055]

1824 Mar. 16. T. J., Monticello, to ALEXANDER GARRETT, Charlottesville. ALS. 1 p. Fragment. Endorsed. Garrett Papers.

Note concerning University of Virginia debts.   [2056]

1824 Mar. 17. JOSEPH C. CABELL, Williamsburg, to T. J., Monticello. ALS. 3 pp. Endorsed by T. J. Deposited by Philip B. Campbell. Printed: Cabell 296-299.

Complete victory of the friends of the University in the Assembly. Downfall of William and Mary seems certain. Suggests hiring of certain of the William and Mary faculty: John A. Smith, Mr. Campbell, James B. Rogers, and James Semple. References to John Bowyer, James Breckenridge, Alexander Garrett, William F. Gordon, Chapman Johnson, George Loyall, James Madison, and Thomas Mann Randolph, Jr.   [2057]

1824 Mar. 24. JOHN GRISCOM, New York, to T. J., Monticello. ALS. 3 pp. Endorsed by T. J.

Selection of chemical and philosophical apparatus adapted to the needs of the University of Virginia. Sources of apparatus: New York, London, Paris. [2058]

1824 Mar. 24. GRANVILLE SHARP PATTISON, Baltimore, to T. J., Monticello. ALS. 7 pp. Endorsed by T. J.

Discussion of relative merits of dissection and wax models in teaching anatomy; practices of Caspar Wistar and Philip S. Physick. Urges good medical library. Will send list of books needed and a collection of bones.   [2059]

1824 Mar. 27. FRANKLIN BACHE, Philadelphia, to T. J., Monticello. ALS. 2 pp. Endorsed by T. J.

Applies for chemistry vacancy mentioned by Thomas Cooper. Mentions T. J.'s friendship for his father. Benjamin Franklin Bache. Reference to [Lardner] Vanuxem.   [2060]

1824 Mar. 28. ARTHUR S. BROCKENBROUGH, University, to T. J., Monticello. ALS. 2 pp. Endorsed by T. J.

Suggests changes in the galleries of the Rotunda, on which James Dinsmore and John Neilson are working without his permission. Noted by Jefferson: "disapproved".   [2061]

1824 Mar. 29. T. J., Monticello, to ARTHUR S. BROCKENBROUGH. ALS. 1 p. Endorsed.

Plans for the library. References to John Neilson and James Dinsmore. [2062]

1824 Mar. 29. GEORGE WASHINGTON SMYTH, Washington, to T. J., Monticello. ALS. 3 pp. Endorsed by T. J.

Applies for tutorial position at the University. Describes education at Glasgow, at Trinity College, Dublin, and at Oxford. Sends copies of recommendations from B. Lloyd, professor of mathematics, and the Reverend Thomas Gannon. Mentions the Reverends C. Boyton, J. Gutch, Henry Harte, and James Kennelly.
                                                              [2063]

1824 Mar. 31. ROBERT HARE, Philadelphia, to T. J., Monticello. ALS. 2 pp. Endorsed by T. J. Enclosure: AD. 2 pp.

Sends list of chemical apparatus adequate for the University of Virginia. Enclosure: "Catalogue of Apparatus."   [2064]

1824 Apr. 1. JOSEPH C. CABELL, Washington, to T. J., Monticello. ALS. 2 pp. Endorsed by T. J. Deposited by Philip B. Campbell. Printed: Cabell 299-301.

Attempt to get recognition of the University's claim to money owed Virginia by the United States. Monroe's recommendation of [James G?] Percival and [John] Torrey for the University faculty. References to James Barbour, William H. Crawford, Chapman Johnson, and William Wirt.   [2065]

1824 Apr. 5. ARTHUR S. BROCKENBROUGH, University, to T. J., Monticello. ADS. 1 p. Endorsed by T. J.

Estimate of cost of Rotunda to date. Payments to Thorn & Chamberlain, contract with Giacomo Raggi, itemized list of building materials.   [2066]

1824 Apr. 8. JOSEPH C. CABELL. Edgewood, to T. J., Monticello. ALS. 1 p. Endorsed by T. J. Deposited by Philip B. Campbell. Printed: Cabell 301-302.

Returning a horse loaned by T. J. Reference to Col. John Coles and to Mr. Maclure.   [2067]

1824 Apr. 9. MARY GARNER. DEED TO ARTHUR S. BROCKENBROUGH. DS. 1 p. Endorsed. Witnessed by John M. Perry. Approved by T. J.
Conveying land in Albemarle County to the University of Virginia. [2068]

1824 Apr. 9. DANIEL A. PIPER and MARY A. F. PIPER. DEED to ARTHUR S. BROCKENBROUGH. DS. 1 p. Endorsed. Witnessed by John M. Perry. Approved by T. J.
Conveying land in Albemarle County to the University of Virginia. [2069]

1824 Apr. 9. T. J., Monticello, to BOARD OF VISITORS, UNIVERSITY OF VIRGINIA. LS. 1 p. Endorsed. Circular. Copies sent to Cabell and Cocke. Printed: Cabell 302-303.
Number of professors that can be hired. Estimated expenses for 1824. [2070]

1824 Apr. 10. T. J., Monticello, to FRANKLIN BACHE, Philadelphia. ALS. 1 p. File draft. Endorsed by T. J.
Board of Visitors will consider his application in October. Glad the son of his late friend, Benjamin Franklin Bache, is qualified. [2071]

1824 Apr. 16. JOSEPH C. CABELL, Bremo, to T. J., Monticello. ALS. 1 p. Endorsed by T. J. Deposited by Philip B. Campbell. Printed: Cabell 303-304.
Agreeing to the engagement of the anatomical professor from Europe. Pleased to see the number of foreign professors is to be limited. Note by John H. Cocke: "I concur with Mr. Cabell in the above." [2072]

1824 Apr. 18. ALEXANDER GARRETT, Charlottesville, to T. J., Monticello. ALS. 1 p. Endorsed. Garrett Papers. Another MS. in CSmH.
Sends letters from accountant of Literary Fund and from cashier of Farmer's Bank of Virginia. Asks instructions regarding a loan from the Bank of Virginia. Mentions Chapman Johnson. [2073]

*1824 Apr. 23. FRANCIS EPPES, Poplar Forest, to T. J., Monticello. ALS. 2 pp. Endorsed by T. J.
Concerning John Wayles Eppes' estate. Fruit and tobacco crops. Request for pyracanthus root. [2074]

1824 Apr. 26. T. J. LETTER INTRODUCING FRANCIS WALKER GILMER. ADS. 1 p. File draft. Endorsed by T. J.
Introducing Gilmer, and granting him full authority to engage professors for the University of Virginia. [2075]

1824 Apr. 27. T. J., Monticello, to ARTHUR S. BROCKENBROUGH. ALS. 1 p. Endorsed.
Request for "ground plats" (Maverick's engraving?) of the University to be sent to Europe. Requests tin for his house. [2076]

1824 Apr. 30. FRANCIS WALKER GILMER, Richmond. RECEIPT to ALEXANDER GARRETT. ADS. 1 p. Endorsed. Approved by T. J.
Receipt for bills of exchange drawn by Joseph Mann on Gowan & Marx of

London for Gilmer's use as agent of the University to recruit faculty members, and for purposes of the University designated by instructions.   [2077]

1824 May 4. T. J., Monticello, to ARTHUR S. BROCKENBROUGH. ALS. 1 p. Endorsed.

Ill health prevents his leaving Monticello. If consultation necessary, requests Brockenbrough and Bergmin to come to Monticello.   [2078]

1824 May 5. JOSEPH C. CABELL, Williamsburg, to T. J., Monticello. ALS. 4 pp. Endorsed by T. J. Deposited by Philip B. Campbell. Printed: Cabell 305-308.

Attitude of the University toward the possible removal of William and Mary from Williamsburg to Richmond. Views on the subject held by William Armistead, Colonel Bassett, Chancellor Brown, [John B.?] Clopton, Dr. Charles Everett, N. Faulcon, Dr. Galt of Williamsburg, [James M.?] Garrett, Thomas Griffin, Mr. Johnson of Williamsburg, George Loyall, Thomas Macon, Bishop Moore, Hugh Nelson, Mr. Nicholas, Brazure W. Pryor, Archibald Ritchie, Judge James Semple, Mr. Scott, John W. Sourell, L. W. Tazewell, and John Tyler.   [2079]

1824 May 16. T. J., Monticello, to JOSEPH C. CABELL, Richmond. LS. 5 pp. Endorsed. Printed: Cabell 308-313 (with omissions); L & B XVI 35-42; B of R VI 60 (MS. in DLC).

Discussion of the removal of William and Mary from its present site to Richmond or a possible consolidation with the University. Would welcome the library and funds of William and Mary but not their faculty in case of consolidation. Suitability of Richmond and Norfolk as site of medical school. Mentions James Madison.   [2080]

1824 May 17. T. J., Monticello, to Thomas Appleton, Leghorn, Italy. ALS. 1 p. File draft. Endorsed by T. J.

Orders polished marble squares for Rotunda floor. Requests supervision of Giacomo Raggi's contract for bases of columns. Raggi left New York on ship *Cyane* for Gibraltar.   [2081]

1824 May 20. JAMES MADISON, Montpellier, to T. J. L. 1 p. Copy by J. C. Cabell. Deposited by Philip B. Campbell. Printed: Cabell 313; B of R IV 53 (MS. in DLC).

Urging that the friends of the University of Virginia be passive in regard to the removal of William and Mary from Williamsburg to Richmond, Petersburg, or the western part of the state.   [2082]

1824 May 25. T. J., Monticello, to [CLEMENT P.] McKENNIE, Charlottesville. AL. 3 pp.

Material about the University of Virginia for use in McKennie's newspaper, the *Central Gazette*: date of opening, dormitory facilities, courses offered, and fees.   [2083]

1824 May 31. SAMUEL WHITCOMB. NOTES on an INTERVIEW with T. J. AD. 6 pp. Photostat. Original owned by Frederick W. Wead.

Interview included right of Georgia to the Cherokee lands, character of Indians and Negroes, tariff, disposition of Great Britain toward Spain and the United States, religion, and theology. Brief account of interviews with Colonel James, P. P. Barbour, and James Madison. [2084]

1824 June 4. A. S. BROCKENBROUGH, University, to T. J., Montiecllo. ALS. 3 pp. File draft and recipient's copy. Endorsed by Brockenbrough and T. J. respectively.

Recommends a reservoir be placed on the Rotunda for fire-protection. Plans for the University's water supply. References to Mr. Chamberlain, John Perry, and A. B. Thorn. [2085]

1824 June 5. T. J., Monticello, to FRANCIS WALKER GILMER, [Cambridge, England]. ALS. 1 p. Endorsed. Another MS. in DLC.

Sends report on the plan of the University for Dr. [Dugald] Stewart and others. Failure of legislature to appropriate money for books and apparatus. Possibility that William and Mary may consolidate with the University. Sends acknowledgment to Major [John] Cartwright for a volume on the English Constitution that he sent. Suggests presenting copy of report on the University to Cartwright. [2086]

1824 June 13. JOSEPH C. CABELL, Warminster, to T. J., Monticello. ALS. 2 pp. Endorsed by T. J. Deposited by Philip B. Campbell. Printed: Cabell 314-315.

Illness of Mrs. [St. George] Tucker prevents his visiting T. J. at Monticello and the Madisons at Montpellier. Removal of William and Mary to Richmond. [2087]

1824 June 21. GEORGE BLAETTERMANN. CONTRACT with FRANCIS WALKER GILMER, attorney for the UNIVERSITY of VIRGINIA. DS. 3 pp. Endorsed.

Contract to teach French, Italian, German, English, Anglo-Saxon, modern history, and geography. Salary, prequisites, and conditions of the professorships. [2088]

1824 June 24. T. J., Monticello, to STEPHEN T. MITCHELL, Lynchburg. ALS. 1 p. Endorsed. Deposited by C. S. Hutter, Jr.

Agreeing to subscribe to Mitchell's newspaper. [2089]

1824 July 14. ARTHUR S. BROCKENBROUGH, University, to T. J., Monticello. ALS. 1 p. Endorsed by T. J.

Requests instructions for John Gorman, who is working on the Rotunda. James Dinsmore and John Neilson need funds. [2090]

1824 July 18. T. J., Monticello, to LYDIA H. SIGOURNEY, Hartford. LS 2. pp. Endorsed. Photostat. Original owned by St. Paul's School. Another MS. in NNP. Printed: *Mag. Amer. Hist.* XXI 431.

Belief in human progress and perfectibility. Advocates Indian rights. [2091]

1824 Aug. 10. T. J., Monticello, to ARTHUR S. BROCKENBROUGH. ALS. 1 p. Endorsed.

Request for copies of the Rockfish Gap Report and [Maverick's] plan of the University. [2092]

1824 Sept. 20. P. F. B. CONSTANT, Mount Airy College, Germantown, Pa., to ARTHUR S. BROCKENBROUGH, University of Virginia. ALS. 3 pp. Endorsed. Enclosure: Broadside.

Application for professorship of modern languages, geography, and history. Lists qualifications and education. Gives Robert Walsh, Jr., as reference. Enclosure: prospects of Mount Airy College, P. F. B. Constant, Principal. Label in T. J.'s hand "Candidates for Professorships." [2093]

1824 Sept. 28. ROBLEY DUNGLISON. CONTRACT with FRANCIS WALKER GILMER, attorney for the UNIVERSITY of VIRGINIA. DS. 1 p. Endorsed. Scals. Witnessed by George Long and Thomas H. Key.

Contract to teach anatomy, surgery, history and theory of medicine, physiology, *materia medica,* and pharmacy. Salary, perquisites, and conditions. [2094]

1824 Sept. 28. THOMAS HEWETT KEY. CONTRACT with FRANCIS WALKER GILMER, attorney for the UNIVERSITY of VIRGINIA. DS. 1 p. Endorsed. Seals. Witnessed by George Long and Robley Dunglison.

Contract to teach mathematics, navigation, architecture, astronomy. Salary, perquisites, and conditions. [2095]

1824 Sept. 28. GEORGE LONG. CONTRACT with FRANCIS WALKER GILMER, attorney for the UNIVERSITY of VIRGINIA. DS. 1 p. Seals. Endorsed. Witnessed by Thomas H. Key and Robley Dunglison.

Contract to teach Latin, Greek, Hebrew, rhetoric, *belles lettres,* ancient history, ancient geography. Salary, perquisites, and conditions. [2096]

1824 Oct. 1. CHARLES BONNYCASTLE. CONTRACT with FRANCIS WALKER GILMER, attorney for UNIVERSITY of VIRGINIA. DS. 2 pp. Seals. Endorsed. Witnesses: William Barksdale and B. M. Carter.

Contract to teach natural philosophy, mechanics, statics, hydrostatics, hydraulics, pneumatics, acoustics, optics, and astronomy. Salary, perquisites, and conditions. [2097]

1824 Oct. 4. HORACE WELLFORD, Charlottesville, to [Board of Visitors, UNIVERSITY of VIRGINIA]. ALS. 1 p. Endorsed by T. J.

Application for professorship of anatomy and physics. [2098]

1824 Oct. 5. T. J. RESOLUTIONS of the BOARD of VISITORS of the University. DS. 1 p. Endorsed.

Resolutions concerning the leasing of hotels and the rent to be paid. Copy sent to Brockenbrough. [2099]

* 1824 Oct. 12. T. J., Monticello, to FRANCIS WALKER GILMER, [London]. ALS. 4 pp. File draft. Endorsed by T. J. Endorsed with note of presentation from W. C. N. Randolph to Micajah Woods, 17 May 1899.

Advice on selection of professors. Prefers English, Irish, or Scotch to German professors. George Blaettermann's books to be passed duty-free. Funds from legislature for books. Lafayette's visit to Charlottesville and the University.

Hopes Gilmer will accept position at University. Requests copy of William Russell's book on Scottish universities. Presidential election between William H. Crawford and John Q. Adams. Mentions James Ivory and Sir John Leslie. [2100]

1824 Oct. 24. T. J., Monticello, to JOSEPH COOLIDGE, JR., Boston. ALS. 2 pp. Photostat. Original owned by Harold J. Coolidge. Another MS. in MHi. Printed: Ford X 323-324.

Abscessed jaw improved. Approval of Coolidge's marriage to Ellen Randolph. Inability to provide a dowry. Plan to use Milizia's book on architecture as a text at the University. General Lafayette's approaching visit. Reference to James Madison. [2101]

1824 Oct. 28. ARTHUR S. BROCKENBROUGH, University, to T. J., Monticello ALS. 1 p. Endorsed by T. J.

Returns papers and a copy of the Proctor's account for T. J.'s files. Recommends higher boarding rates to attract good hotel keepers. [2102]

1824 Nov. 1. T. J., Monticello, to JAMES MADISON. ALS. 1 p. Photostat. Original owned by John Skelton Williams. Printed: B of R VI 312 (MS. in DLC).

Inviting Mr. and Mrs. Madison to meet Lafayette at Charlottesville. Lafayette to go to Montpellier and Fredericksburg. No news from Francis Walker Gilmer. [2103]

1824 Nov. 5. T. J. REPLY TO A TOAST. Clipping from the 24 November issue of the *Portsmouth* [N. H.?] *Journal.*

Given at a dinner in Charlottesville in honor of General Lafayette. [2104]

1824 Nov. 21. T. J., Monticello, to FRANCIS WALKER GILMER. ALS. 1 p. Endorsed. Another MS. in DLC.

Distressed by news of Gilmer's ill health. Exemption of George Blaettermann's books from duties. Details on board and lodging prepared for the professors. Mentions Bernard Peyton, agent for the University in Richmond. [2105]

1824 Nov. 22. T. J., Monticello, to FRANCIS WALKER GILMER, New York. ALS. 1 p. Endorsed. Another MS. in DLC. Printed: Davis, *Francis Walker Gilmer* 240.

Urges him to accept faculty post at University of Virginia. [2106]

1824 Nov. 24. T. J., Monticello, to JOHN H. COCKE, Bremo. ALS. 1 p. Endorsed. Printed: B of R VI 90 (MS. in DLC).

Returns donation for purchase of Polyglot Bible through Alexander Garrett since Cummings & Hillard have sold it. Francis Walker Gilmer has engaged five professors. Visitors must meet to appoint others. [2107]

1824 Nov. 24. T. J., Monticello, to JAMES PLEASANTS, Richmond. ALS. 1 p. File draft. Endorsed by T. J.

University will open on 1 February 1825 since Gilmer has hired George Blaettermann, Charles Bonnycastle, Robley Dunglison, Thomas Key, and George Long, expected from Europe in a few days. [2108]

1824 Nov. 30. T. J., Monticello, to FRANCIS WALKER GILMER. ALS. 1 p. Endorsed. Another MS. in DLC.

Wishes to know port professors will enter, so as to secure remission of duty on books. Requests information on John Torrey's attitude toward chair of natural history. Urges Gilmer to accept chair of law.   [2109]

1824 Dec. 2. ARTHUR S. BROCKENBROUGH, University, to T. J., Monticello. ALS. 1 p. Endorsed by T. J.

Measurements of Rotunda dome. Sends Hotel contracts for his inspection.
                    [2110]

1824 Dec. 2. ARCHIBALD THWEATT, Eppington, to T. J., Monticello. ALS. 1 p. Endorsed by T. J. Edgehill-Randolph Papers.

Introducing Richard Kidder Meade, whose father wishes to manage boarding houses for the University of Virginia.   [2111]

1824 Dec. 4. T. J., Monticello, to FRANCIS WALKER GILMER. ALS. 1 p. Endorsed.

Wrote [Joseph] Anderson, state comptroller, to instruct collector to exempt professors' books from duty. Problems of immediate accommodations for professors.   [2112]

1824 Dec. 5. T. J., Monticello, to ARTHUR S. BROCKENBROUGH, University. ALS. 3 pp. Endorsed. Another MS. in DLC.

Sends suggested form for articles of agreement for leases of Hotels, covering all details of operation. Copy form is a lease with John Gray, Jr.   [2113]

1824 Dec. 6. A. MacDONALD, Philadelphia, to T. J., Monticello. ALS. 1 p. Endorsed by T. J.

Applies for post of librarian at University of Virginia. William Tilghman a reference.   [2114]

1824 Dec. 13–1825 Apr. 8. T. J. LETTER of APPOINTMENT for UNIVERSITY of VIRGINIA FACULTY. AD. 1 p. File draft. Endorsed by T. J. Another MS. in DLC.

Endorsed with the names of Professors George Blaettermann, Charles Bonnycastle, Robley Dunglison, John Patton Emmet, Thomas H. Key, and George Long.   [2115]

1824 Dec. 17. JOSEPH C. CABELL, Richmond, to T. J., Monticello. ALS. 3 pp. Endorsed by T. J. Deposited by Philip B. Campbell. Printed: Cabell 316-318.

Cabell's business at Corotoman. Assembly politics with respect to the bill to move the College of William and Mary to Richmond and funds for the University. References to [George] Bla[e]tterman[n], Francis T. Brooke, John Bowyer, William Brockenbrough, John Coalter, James M. Garnett, George Hay, Chapman Johnson, Mr. Leigh, Judge Marshall, James Madison, Thomas Mann Randolph, Jr., and Robert B. Taylor.   [2116]

1824 Dec. 21. JOSEPH C. CABELL, Richmond, to T. J., Monticello. ALS. 2 pp. Endorsed by T. J. Deposited by Philip B. Campbell. Printed: Cabell 318-320.

Decision to vote against the bill to remove William and Mary to Richmond. Medical education at the University. References to Chapman Johnson and Thomas Mann Randolph, Jr.   [2117]

1824 Dec. 22. T. J., Monticello, to JOSEPH C. CABELL, Richmond. ALS. 5 pp. Endorsed. Printed: Cabell 320-323; L & B XVI 84-89; B of R VI 60 (MS. in DLC).

Recommendations regarding the removal of William and Mary and division of her funds among ten collegiate districts. University should get $50,000 from Congress. Meeting of Visitors to appoint remaining faculty members. George Long's arrival.   [2118]

1824 Dec. 22. T. J., Monticello, to JOSEPH C. CABELL, Richmond. ALS. 1 p. Endorsed. Printed: Cabell 324.

Jefferson and Madison prefer George Tucker for chair of ethics. Bill for district colleges. Mentions Thomas Mann Randolph, Jr., and William F. Gordon.
                                    [2119]

1824 Dec. 24. BENJAMIN WATERHOUSE, Cambridge, Mass., to T. J., Monticello. ALS. 2 pp. Endorsed by T. J. Enclosure: Broadside. 1 p.

Recommends the Rev. Joseph P. Bertrum, who wishes to teach at the University of Virginia. Failure of John Adams "animal economy" but not his intellectual powers. Foresees trouble about inscription on Bunker Hill Monument. Republic ungrateful in not providing one for Samuel Adams. Enclosure: "Heads of a Course of Lectures on Natural History given annually (since 1788) in the University of Cambridge, by B. Waterhouse, M. D.."   [2120]

1824 Dec. 25. SAMUEL MARTIN, Campbell Station, Tenn., to T. J., Monticello. ALS. 1 p. Endorsed by T. J. Printed: Ford-Bixby 290-291.

Urges Jefferson to throw influence to Andrew Jackson. Clay should content himself with Mexican ministry.   [2121]

1824 Dec. 31. JOSEPH C. CABELL, Richmond, to T. J., Monticello. ALS. 3 pp. Endorsed by T. J. Deposited by Philip B. Campbell. Partly printed: Cabell 324-327.

Differences of opinion between Jefferson and Madison regarding the removal of the College of William and Mary to Richmond. Funds for the University. References to John Bowyer, Judge Dabney Carr, Francis W. Gilmer, William F. Gordon, George Loyall, Mr. Nicholas, James Pleasants, Thomas Mann Randolph, Jr., James Semple, John A. Smith, George Tucker, and John Tyler. [2122]

[1824]. LIST of APPLICANTS for chemistry PROFESSORSHIP at WEST POINT. D. 1 p. Endorsed by T. J.: "Torrey John to be professor of chemistry".

Applicants for situation vacated by death of James Cutbush include Franklin Bache, James F. Dana, J. Everett, Jacob Green, John Manners, James G. Percival, Arthur L. Porter, John Torrey, and G. Troost.   [2123]

1825 Jan. 3. WILLIAM C. SOMERVILLE, Stratford, Va., to T. J., Monticello. ALS. 3 pp. Endorsed by T. J. Seal. Enclosure: ADS. 16 pp.

Offers to sell his library of 3000 to 4000 volumes to the University of Virginia. Collection includes portrait of Washington by Gilbert Stuart and other portraits of Lafaytte and Peyton Randolph. Enclosure: catalog of books.   [2124]

1825 Jan. 5. T. J., Monticello, to H. P. VAN BIBBER, Northend, Va. ALS. 1 p. Endorsed. Photostat. Original privately owned. Another MS. in DLC.

Details on opening of the University, faculty, textbooks, entrance requirements.   [2125]

1825 Jan. 5. JOHN L. THOMAS, Charlottesville, to T. J., Monticello. ALS. 2 pp. Endorsed by T. J.

Applies for position as librarian. Alexander Garrett given as a reference. [2126]

1825 Jan. 6. JOSEPH C. CABELL, Richmond, to T. J., Monticello. ALS. 2 pp. Endorsed by T. J. Deposited by Philip B. Campbell. Printed: Cabell 328-329.

Letter from George Tucker regarding a teaching position at the University. Application from Mr. Kidd for the position of professor of ethics. Bill for removal of William and Mary to Richmond to be rejected. Funds for the University. References to James Barbour, William F. Gordon, Thomas Mann Randolph, Jr., James Madison, and Judge James Semple.   [2127]

1825 Jan. 8. WILLIAM LEE, Washington, to T. J., Monticello. ALS. 2 pp. Endorsed by T. J.

Offers University cabinet of conchology, mineralogy purchased by friend, Edward Wyer, in Spain. Dr. Wallace of Virginia offers to examine and report on it.   [2128]

1825 Jan. 9. T. J., Monticello, to ARTHUR S. BROCKENBROUGH. ALS. 1 p. Endorsed.

Enclose papers from [William] Coffee and text of an advertisement to be inserted in the Richmond *Enquirer,* the *Constitutional Whig,* and the principal paper of Fredericksburg concerning the opening of the University.   [2129]

1825 Jan. 9. T. J., Monticello, to JOHN L. THOMAS, Charlottesville. ALS. 1 p. File draft. Endorsed by T. J.

One of professors to act as librarian.   [2130]

1825 Jan. 11. T. J., Monticello, to JOSEPH C. CABELL, Richmond. ALS. 2 pp. Endorsed. Printed: Cabell 330-332; L & B XVI 97-100; TJR IV 411-412; B of R VI 60 (MS. in DLC).

Non-arrival of professors may delay opening of University. James Barbour hopeful of obtaining $50,000 from Congress for the University. Additional funds needed to complete Rotunda and anatomical theatre. Jefferson's actions to further the University have roused much personal antagonism.   [2131]

1825 Jan. 15. T. J., Monticello, to JOSEPH COOLIDGE, JR., Boston. ALS. 2 pp. Photostat. Original owned by Harold J. Coolidge. Another MS. in MHi. Printed: L & B XVIII 334-337; MHS *Coll* I 340-342.

Thanks for gift of books by Michael Russell and Joseph Bosworth. Agrees that William Hilliard be made the University's agent to purchase books in Europe. Recommends plates for a new edition of Wilson's *Ornithology*. Reported discovery in Athens of 2000 rolls of papyri of Greek authors. Expected arrival of new professors at the University. [2132]

*1825 Jan. 15. SAMUEL MARTIN, Campbell's Station, Tenn., T. J., Monticello. ALS. 1 p. Endorsed by T. J. Printed: Ford-Bixby 291.

Recommends setting up port near Norfolk to be named after Jefferson to rival New York. Begs Jefferson to use his influence for Jackson in presidential election. [2133]

1825 Jan. 16. JOSEPH C CABELL, Richmond, to T. J., Monticello. ALS. 2 pp. Endorsed by T. J. Deposited by Philip B. Campbell. Partly printed: Cabell 332-333.

Request that T. J. prepare a bill to prevent removal of William and Mary College to Richmond. Clergy, Richmond, and the Federalists all united in favor of removal. [2134]

1825 Jan. 16. T. J., Monticello, to JOHN GRISCOM, New York. ALS. 1 p. Printed: B of R VI 194 (MS. in DLC).

Returning a copy of Michael Russell's *View of Education in Scotland*. Expected arrival of professors from England. [2135]

1825 Jan. 17. A. DE LETAMENDI, St. Augustine, [Fla.], to T. J., Monticello. ALS. 2 pp. Endorsed by T. J.

Applies for professorship of foreign languages at University of Virginia. [2136]

1825 Jan. 17. T. J., Monticello, to WILLIAM C. SOMERVILLE, Stratford, Va. AL. 1 p. File draft. Endorsed by T. J.

Somerville's book catalog given to University's purchasing agent (Cummings and Hilliard). Funds dependent on Virginia's claim against Congress. [2137]

1825 Jan. 17 T. J., Monticello, to WILLIAM LEE, Washington. ALS. 1 p. File draft. Endorsed by T. J.

Will hold offer of Edward Wyer's mineral collection under consideration; funds dependent on claim of state of Virginia on Congress. [2138]

1825 Jan. 19. T. J., Monticello, to JOSEPH C. CABELL, Richmond. ALS. 1 p. Endorsed. Another MS. in DLC. Printed: Cabell 334.

Calls meeting of Board of Visitors of University to approve loan required for work on Rotunda, loan to be backed by subscriptions due. Mentions Arthur Brockenbrough, John H. Cocke, Alexander Garrett, and James Madison. [2139]

1825 Jan. 22. T. J., Monticello, to JOSEPH C. CABELL, Richmond. ALS. 1 p.
Endorsed. Another MS. in DLC. Printed (with omissions) : Cabell 335. Enclosure:
AD. 6 pp. Printed: Cabell Appendix 499-501.

Sends draft of bill for the discontinuance of the College of William and Mary
and the establishment of colleges at Williamsburg, Hampden-Sydney, Lynchburg, Richmond, Fredericksburg, Winchester, Staunton, Fincastle, Louisburg,
and Clarksburg. Distribution of William and Mary's funds. Enclosure: draft of
bill.   [2140]

1825 Jan. 22. WILLIAM LEE, Washington, to T. J., Monticello. ALS. 2 pp.
Endorsed by T. J.

Concerning possible sale of Edward Wyer's mineral collection to University
of Virginia. Mentions Dr. Wallace.   [2141]

1825 Jan. 25. FRANCIS WALKER GILMER, Richmond, to the RECTOR and
VISITORS of the UNIVERSITY of VIRGINIA. ADS. 3 pp. Endorsed by T. J.

Financial report on his mission to Europe. Funds paid by bankers Gowan and
Marx to George Blaettermann, Charles Bonnycastle, Mr. Bohn (bookseller),
Mr. Cary (optician), Robley Dunglison, Thomas H. Key, and John Tuther.
Incloses letters and catalogs of books and instruments from Dr. Parr, Mr. Harris,
and the Rev. John Tynes.   [2142]

1825 Jan. 28. JOSEPH C. CABELL, Richmond, to T. J., Monticello. ALS. 1 p.
Endorsed by T. J. Deposited by Philip B. Campbell. Printed: Cabell 336.

Removal of William and Mary to Richmond. Articles in the *Whig* on the
funds of William and Mary and the decision of the Court of Appeals in the
case of Bracken and the College. References to Alexander Garrett and John A.
Smith.   [2143]

1825 Jan. 30. JOSEPH C. CABELL, Richmond, to T. J., Monticello. ALS. 1 p.
Endorsed by T. J. Deposited by Philip B. Campbell. Printed: Cabell 336-337.

News of Ship *Competitor*. Requests authorities to support the division of
William and Mary's money. Mentions Dartmouth College case.   [2144]

1825 Feb. 3. T. J., Monticello, to JOSEPH C. CABELL, Richmond. ALS. 2 pp.
Endorsed. Printed: Cabell 339-341. Enclosure: AD. 2 pp. Cabell Papers (enclosure only).

Faculty should prescribe textbooks for most courses, but that of government
should be set by Board of Visitors to prevent dissemination of Federalist principles. Necessity for investigating the sum of education rendered in each county in
primary schools. Financing the medical theatre. Enclosure: resolution requiring
annual statement of schooling rendered in each county, together with a sample
form for the report.   [2145]

1825 Feb. 3. JOSEPH C. CABELL, Richmond, to T. J., Monticello. ALS. 2 pp.
Endorsed by T. J. Deposited by Philip B. Campbell. Printed: Cabell 337-338.

Publication of a letter from T. J. to help prevent removal of the College of
William and Mary to Richmond. Consideration of Francis W. Gilmer and

Chancellor [St. George] Tucker for the law chair at the University. Suggests the professor of law be also given a small chancery district. References to Scervant Jones and Richard Morris. [2146]

1825 Feb. 4. WILLIAM H. CRAWFORD, Washington, to T. J., Monticello. ALS. 4 pp. Endorsed by T. J.

Recommends Dr. Henry Jackson, youngest brother of Gen. James Jackson, for professorship of natural history and philosophy. Sends seed from Italy and sample of Cremona flax received from Thomas Appleton. [2147]

1825 Feb. 7. JOSEPH C. CABELL, Richmond, to T. J., Monticello. ALS. 2 pp. Endorsed by T. J. Deposited by Philip B. Campbell. Partly printed: Cabell 341-342.

Defeat of plan to remove William and Mary to Richmond. Plan for a general education system. [2148]

1825 Feb. 11. JOSEPH C. CABELL, Richmond, to T. J., Monticello. ALS. 3 pp. Endorsed by T. J. Deposited by Philip B. Campbell. Partly printed: Cabell 343-345.

Defeat of the bill to remove William and Mary to Richmond. Delay in arrival of the University faculty. T. J.'s resolutions relative to primary schools. Expresses disapproval of a constitutional convention for Virginia. Opposition to Cabell in his senatorial district. References to John Bowyer, Judge Francis T. Brooke, Col. Benjamin Cabell, John H. Cocke, David S. Garland, William F. Gordon, George Loyall, and Thomas Mann Randolph, Jr. [2149]

1825 Feb. 11. JOSEPH C. CABELL, Richmond, to T. J., Monticello. ALS. 1 p. Endorsed by T. J. Deposited by Philip B. Campbell. Printed: Cabell 346.

Funds for the University from interest claim of the Commonwealth of Virginia. References to George Loyall and Littleton W. Tazewell. [2150]

1825 Feb. 16. T. J. ADVERTISEMENT of the OPENING of the UNIVERSITY OF VIRGINIA. AD. 2 pp. Printed: Richmond *Enquirer* 22 Feb. 1825.

Information regarding fees, courses, and provisions for housing and board. (The advertisement appeared in the *Enquirer* over the name of the Proctor, Arthur S. Brockenbrough). [2151]

1825 Feb. 18. JOSEPH C. CABELL, Richmond, to T. J., Monticello. ALS. 1 p. Endorsed by T. J. Deposited by Philip B. Campbell. Printed: Cabell 346-347.

Arrival of the University faculty. Meeting of the Board of Visitors. References to Chapman Johnson, Francis Gilmer, George Loyall, and John H. Cocke. [2152]

1825 Feb. 19. ANDREW KEAN, Charlottesville, to T. J., Monticello. ALS. 1 p. Endorsed by T. J.

Applies for position of librarian for son, John V. Kean, lists his qualifications. Lancelot Minor, Horatio G. Winston, and George W. Trueheart of Louisa recommend him. [2153]

1825 Feb. 21. JOSEPH C. CABELL, Richmond, to T. J., Monticello. ALS. 1 p.
Endorsed by T. J. Deposited by Philip B. Campbell. Printed: Cabell 347.

Faculty positions offered to [Henry St. George?] Tucker and to George Tucker.
References to Judge John Coalter and [St. George] Tucker.   [2154]

1825 Mar. 4. ARTHUR S. BROCKENBROUGH. ACCOUNT for 1824. ADS.
1 p. Endorsed by T. J.

Proctor's statement of the funds of the University as of 31 December 1824.
                                                                         [2155]

[1825 Mar. 7]. T. J., Monticello, to ARTHUR S. BROCKENBROUGH, University. AD. 1 p. Endorsed.

Notice to students of opening of University to be published in *Central
Gazette, Enquirer, National Intelligencer.*   [2156]

1825 Mar. 8. T. J., Monticello, to ALEXANDER GARRETT. ALS. 1 p. Garrett
Papers.

Enclose Visitors' ratification of loan of $5000 from Farmer's Bank. Directs
remittance to Thomas Appleton through Bernard Peyton of Richmond and
Samuel Williams of London for columns.   [2157]

1825 Mar. 9. T. J., Monticello, to ARTHUR S. BROCKENBROUGH. ALS. 1 p.
Endorsed. Another MS. in DLC.

Letter to Alexander Garrett contains instructions for payment to Thomas
Appleton (for Giacomo Raggi's work on columns) through Bernard Peyton.
Second letter of this date.   [2158]

1825 Mar. 9. T. J., Monticello, to ARTHUR S. BROCKENBROUGH, University. ALS. 2 pp. Endorsed.

Resolutions of the Visitors concerning the $50,000 to be received from Con-
gress. Accounting procedures. Part of fund to be used for preparation of a room
to receive books. Number of bricks necessary for medical theatre.   [2159]

1825 Mar. 9. T. J., Monticello, to GEORGE TUCKER, Lynchburg. ALS. 1 p.
Endorsed. Deposited by Mrs. Edward Gamble.

Appointment of Tucker as Professor of the School of Moral Philosophy.
Arrival of five professors from England. Opening of the University.   [2160]

1825 Mar. 12. FRANCIS WALKER GILMER, Richmond, to T. J., Monticello.
ALS. 3 pp. File draft. 2 copies. Endorsed by Gilmer. Printed: B of R VIII 268
(MS. in DLC).

University's obligation concerning the bond forfeited by Charles Bonnycastle
in accepting University position. Salary arrangements with Robley Dunglison
and Thomas H. Key. Details regarding shipment of books and instruments to
University. Mentions George Barlow, Dollond Co., Alexander Garrett, London,
Gowan & Marx, and Munich.   [2161]

1825 Mar. 15. T. J. FINANCIAL STATEMENT on the UNIVERSITY. AD.
2 pp.

Funds as of 1 January 1825, and estimate for 1826.   [2162]

1825 Mar. 16. T. J., Monticello, to ARTHUR S. BROCKENBROUGH. ALS. 1 p. Endorsed. Another MS. in DLC.

Recommends macadam roads for the University.   [2163]

1825 Mar. 30. T. J. to JOHN V. KEAN. ALS 1 p. File draft. Endorsed by T. J.

Appointment as librarian at salary of $150 per year. Statement of his duties.   [2164]

1825 Mar. 31. ARTHUR S. BROCKENBROUGH, Charlottesville, to T. J., Monticello. LS. 2 pp. Endorsed by T. J.

Note for $5000, negotiable at Farmer's Bank of Virginia. Receipted by Alexander Garrett, Bursar, and William Nekervis, Cashier of Farmer's Bank. [2165]

1825 Apr. 2. T. J., Monticello, to ARTHUR S. BROCKENBROUGH. ALS. 1 p. Endorsed.

Request for printed copies of the rules enacted by the Board of Visitors. [2166]

1825 Apr. 5. T. J., Monticello, to HORACE HOLLY, Lexington, Ky. ALS. 1 p. Endorsed. McGregor Library. Another MS. in DLC.

Rules for discipline at the University of Virginia. Opening of the University. Express hope for the success of the University of Transylvania.   [2167]

1825 Apr. 12. T. J., Monticello, to JOSEPH COOLIDGE, JR. ALS. 2 pp. Photostate. Original owned by Harold J. Coolidge. Printed: L & B XVIII 337-339; M H S *Coll* I 343-345; Univ. of Va. *Alumni Bulletin* V 3 (partial).

Opening of the University. The faculty. Bell for the University. William Hilliard engaged to buy a library for the University to the value of $15,000. Receipt of books sent by Coolidge for the University. Coolidge's visit to Monticello.   [2168]

1825 Apr. 13. T. J., Monticello, to JOHN SPEAR SMITH, Baltimore. AL[S clipped]. 1 p. Endorsed.

Jefferson's gift to Smith's son. Numbers enrolled at the University of Virginia. Disciplinary problems. Accepts the Bayle [dictionary?] and Edinburgh Atlas for the University Library.   [2169]

[1825 Apr. 14]. T. J. LIST of BOOKS donated to the UNIVERSITY of VIRGINIA by JOSEPH COOLIDGE, JR., of Boston. AD. 1 p. Endorsed.   [2170]

1825 Apr. 15. T. J., Monticello, to BOARD of VISITORS, UNIVERSITY of VIRGINIA. LS. 3 pp. Circular. Endorsed. Enclosure: AD. 2 pp. The library owns the copies sent to Cabell and to Cocke. Printed: Cabell 348-350.

Necessity of purchasing from John Perry the strip of land that divides the two parcels of University property in order to secure the water supply. All faculty except George Tucker and law professor have arrived. Necessity for disciplining students. Enclosure: estimate of University income and expenditures, 1824-1827.   [2171]

1825 Apr. 19. JOHN ADAMS, Quincy, to T. J., Monticello, ALS. 1 p. Copy perhaps by one of the Sigourneys. Photostat. Original owned by St. Paul's School. Printed: *Mag. Amer. Hist.* XXI 432.

Letter of introduction for Mr. and Mrs. Charles Sigourney (Lydia Sigourney). [2172]

1825 Apr. 21. T. J., Monticello, to ARTHUR S. BROCKENBROUGH. ALS. 2 pp. Endorsed. Another MS. in DLC.

Opposing the holding of religious services in University buildings. [2173]

1825 Apr. 28. T. J., Monticello, to ARTHUR S. BROCKENBROUGH, University. ALS. 2 pp. Endorsed.

Draft of advertisement requesting book donations for the University library to be inserted in the *Central Gazette* and Richmond *Enquirer.* Advertisement mentions donations from [John?] Hansford of King George County, Bernard Moore Carter of London, and Joseph Coolidge, Jr., of Boston. [2174]

1825 May 4. THOMAS APPLETON, Leghorn. ACCOUNT rendered to T. J. ADS. 2 pp. Endorsed. Stamped and signed by Jonathan Thompson, Collector of New York.

Account for work on marble columns. [2175]

1825 May 6. JOSEPH C. CABELL, Norfolk, to T. J., Monticello. ALS. 1 p. Endorsed by T. J. Deposited by Philip B. Campbell. Printed: Cabell 351.

Approves purchase of John M. Perry's land for the University. [2176]

1825 May 8. T. J., Monticello, to ARTHUR S. BROCKENBROUGH, University. ALS. 1 p. Enclosure: AD. 1 p. Another MS. in DLC.

Encloses draft of handbill to answer routine questions on the courses and expenses of the University. [Clement P.?] McKennie to print handbill. [2177]

1825 May 13. T. J., Monticello, to BOARD of VISITORS, UNIVERSITY of VIRGINIA. LS. 2 pp. Endorsed. Circular. The University owns copies sent to Cabell and to Chapman Johnson. Printed (with omissions): Cabell 351-353.

Qualifications of Judge W. A. G. Dade for the law professorship discussed with Judge [Archibald] Stuart, Howe Peyton, and John H. Cocke, after Francis W. Gilmer had refused it. [2178]

1825 May 14. T. J. to ARTHUR S. BROCKENBROUGH. ADS. 1 p.

Authorization to execute bond to John M. Perry in consideration of 132 acres of land sold to the University. Receipt by Perry for $2411 attached. [2179]

1825 May 19. JAMES MADISON, Montpellier, to T. J., Monticello. ALS. 1 p. Endorsed by T. J.

Law chair to be offered to William A. G. Dade. [2180]

1825 May 22. T. J., Monticello, to ARTHUR S. BROCKENBROUGH, University. ALS. 1 p. Endorsed.

Instructions to deposit $18,000 in the United States Bank of Philadelphia to the account of William Hilliard of Boston, agent of the University of Virginia for the purchase of books. [2181]

1825 May 22. JOHN LESLIE, London, to RICHARD RUSH, Philadelphia. ALS. 3 pp. Endorsed by T. J.

Inquires whether he is to criticise the plan of the educational system at Virginia and to collect philosophical instruments as Francis Walker Gilmer had intimated. Requests official population documents for United States for a projected book. [2182]

1825 May 23. T. J., Monticello, to CHARLES SIGOURNEY, Charlottesville. ALS. 1 p. Photostat. Original owned by St. Paul's School.

Invitation to dine at Monticello. [2183]

1825 May 24. FRANCIS WALKER GILMER, Richmond, to T. J., Monticello. ALS. 2 pp. File draft? Another MS. in MoHi.

University's responsibilities regarding Charles Bonnycastle's forfeited bond. Censure from professors because of his state of health. [2184]

1825 May 25. JOSEPH C. CABELL, Norfolk, to T. J., Monticello. ALS. 2 pp. Endorsed by T. J. Deposited by Philip B. Campbell. Printed: Cabell 353-354.

Approves choice of William A. G. Dade for the law chair. Splendid prospects for the University. Greetings from Mr. Maclure in Paris. [2185]

1825 May 31. T. J., Monticello, to ARTHUR S. BROCKENBROUGH. ALS. 1 p. Endorsed. Another MS. in DLC.

Introducing Dr. Waterhouse of Cambridge. Use of macadam method on University roads. Address of Judge Dade. [2186]

1825 May 31. T. J., Monticello, to WILLIAM A. G. DADE, Dumfries, Va. ALS. 2 pp. File draft and recipient's copy.

Offering him the law chair at the University; citing advantages of the post. [2187]

1825 June 2. T. J., Monticello, to ALEXANDER GARRETT, University. ALS. 1 p. Endorsed. Garrett Papers.

Asks if deposit to William Hilliard's credit has been made. Is sending catalog of books to Hilliard. [2188]

1825 June 3. T. J., Monticello, to WILLIAM HILLIARD, Boston. ALS. 1 p. Endorsed. McGregor Library. Another MS. in DLC.

Purchase of books for the library of the University. Lists books desired as well as the "Harvard duplicates". [2189]

1825 June 3. T. J. CATALOG of BOOKS for the UNIVERSITY of VIRGINIA LIBRARY. 1 vol. 86 pp. in the hand of Virginia Randolph, annotated by T. J.

List of books, with date and place of publication, size, and price estimated in some cases. At the end is the following in Jefferson's hand: "The preceding catalogue is that of the books with the purchase of which Mr. Wm. Hilliard is

charged on behalf of the University of Virginia./Th: Jefferson Rector/June 3.
1825."   [2190]

1825 June 5. T. J., Monticello, to THOMAS MANN RANDOLPH, JR. ALS.
1 p. File draft. Endorsed by T. J. Edgehill-Randolph Papers.
Advising Randolph about his financial status; begging him to return to his
family and to take up public life when called.   [2191]

1825 June 6. ARTHUR S. BROCKENBROUGH, University, to T. J., Monticello. ALS. 2 pp. Endorsed by T. J.
Requests instruction on finishing library in the Rotunda. John P. Emmet
dissatisfied with his laboratory facilities. [John] Brockenbrough has made remittance to William Hilliard.   [2192]

1825 June 6. T. J., Monticello, to FRANCIS WALKER GILMER, Richmond.
ALS. 1 p. Endorsed.
If William A. G. Dade refuses law chair, Gilmer, the first choice, may have it.
Charles Bonnycastle's bond settled. William Hilliard to purchase books for
University.   [2193]

1825 June 7. T. J., Monticello, to ARTHUR S. BROCKENBROUGH. ALS. 1 p.
Endorsed.
Rooms for John P. Emmet's chemistry experiments. Encloses draft of a
balluster (not found with the letter).   [2194]

1825 June 9. ARTHUR S. BROCKENBROUGH, University, to T. J., Monticello. ALS. 1 p. Endorsed by T. J.
Construction necessary to prevent free access to library by all people.   [2195]

1825 June 13. T. J., Monticello, to ARTHUR S. BROCKENBROUGH. ALS.
1 p. Endorsed.
Request that Bernard Peyton procure a bill of exchange payable to Rufus
King, Ambassador of the U. S. in London, for the purchase of books and
apparatus for the University.   [2196]

[1825 June 15?]. ARTHUR S. BROCKENBROUGH, University, to T. J. AL.
1 p. (On same sheet as T. J.'s letter of June 13). Another MS. in CSmH.
Requests permission to publish T. J.'s letter of 21 April 1825 regarding the use
of University buildings for religious services.   [2197]

1825 June 18. CUMMINGS, HILLIARD & CO., Boston, to BOARD of VISI-
TORS, UNIVERSITY of VIRGINIA. D. 1 p. Endorsed by T. J.
Invoice of books shipped aboard the *Enterprise,* Captain Cason, to Bernard
Peyton in Richmond.   [2198]

1825 June 19. T. J., Monticello, to HENRY DEARBORN, Boston. ALS. 2 pp.
Endorsed. Printed: B of R VI 118 (MS. in DLC).
Regrets Dearborn's accident. His own health poor. Opening of University of
Virginia with splendid faculty, but without president or theological schools.

Invites Mr. and Mrs. Dearborn for visit. Soldiers sent by Governor George M. Troup of Georgia into Creek country. Ellen Randolph Coolidge goes to Boston soon. [2199]

1825 June 20. T. J., Monticello, to ARTHUR S. BROCKENBROUGH. AL. 1 p. Endorsed. Another MS. in DLC.

Opposing publication of his letter of 24 April. Purchasing bills of exchange to be used for purchase of apparatus in England. Reference to Bernard Peyton. [2200]

1825 June 21. T. J., Monticello, to [GENERAL JOSEPH G. SMITH?]. ALS. 1 p.

Refers him to Cummings & Hilliard, who may purchase some of his books for the University library. Grateful for loan of Philibert de Lorme's *Architecture*. [2201]

1825 June 23. T. J., Monticello, to GEORGE THOMPSON, Harrodsburg, Ky. ALS. 2 pp. Photostat. Original: N. Y. Private Collection.

News of himself, his health, his family, and the University of Virginia. Power of federal government should be limited. Refuses to enter into the question that agonizes Kentucky. Mentions Thomas J. Randolph. [2202]

1825 June 27. T. J., Monticello, to ARTHUR S. BROCKENBROUGH. ALS. 1 p. Endorsed.

Introducing Emanuel Miller who wishes to enter the schools of Professors Long, Blaettermann, and Key and who brings a bill of credit from Chandler, Price, & Morgan of Philadelphia. [2203]

1825 June 27. T. J., Monticello, to ARTHUR S. BROCKENBROUGH. ALS. 1 p. Endorsed.

Stables at the University. Deed for John M. Perry's land. [2204]

1825 June 27. ARTHUR S. BROCKENBROUGH, University, to T. J., Monticello. ALS. 1 p. Endorsed by T. J.

Location of stables and East Range. Requests copy of contract with John M. Perry, since he wishes to use barn for rye. [2205]

[1825] June 28. T. J., Monticello, to [THEODORUS] BAILEY, ALS. 1 p.

Requests him to forward letter to London by packet. [2206]

1825 June 29. T. J., Monticello, to ROBLEY DUNGLISON. ALS. 1 p. Deposited by Mrs. John Staige Davis. Another MS. in DLC.

Policy regarding vacations for the University. [2207]

1825 June 30. T. J., Monticello, to PETER BARLOW, Royal Military Academy, Woolwich, England. ALS. 3 pp. Printed: Univ. of Va. *Alumni Bulletin* Ser. 2 VII 56-58; B of R VI 27 (MS. in DLC).

Requests his aid in securing apparatus for the University. Money placed in London subject to orders of Rufus King. If Charles Bonnycastle's bond forfeited, that amount must be subtracted from the total. List of apparatus and in-structions for shipment. Mentions Francis Walker Gilmer.   [2208]

1825 July 2. T. J., Monticello, to ARTHUR S. BROCKENBROUGH, University. ALS. 1 p. Endorsed.
Requests bill of exchange be sent to Rufus King for purchase of anatomical apparatus.   [2209]

1825 July 8. THOMAS MANN RANDOLPH, JR., to T. J., Monticello. ALS. 4 pp. Edgehill-Randolph Papers.
His estrangement from Martha. Use of T. J.'s name in a meeting at the court house in Charlottesville regarding the convention at Staunton and general suffrage. Use of T. J.'s letter with regard to the title papers to the public land dating from T. J.'s governorship. Financial relations between himself and Thomas Eston Randolph. Causes of T. M. Randolph's financial straits. References to Hamilton and the Federalist plot of 1798.   [2210]

1825 July 9. T. J., Monticello, to THOMAS MANN RANDOLPH, JR. ALS. 1 p. File draft. Endorsed by T. J. Edgehill-Randolph Papers. Another MS. in DLC. Printed: Richmond *Enquirer* 14 Sept. 1827.
Assuring Randolph of his affection. His deafness gives the appearance of reserve. No objection to Randolph's use of his opinions on suffrage or of his letter regarding public lands. Urges him to return to his family.   [2211]

1825 July 12. THOMAS APPLETON, Leghorn, Italy. ACCOUNT rendered to T. J. ADS. 1 p. Endorsed.
Account for marble columns.   [2212]

1825 July 14. KERR & CASKIE, Manchester, Va., to JAMES DUNLAP, London. DS. 2 pp. Endorsed. Notes by T. J. on back.
Bill of exchange in favor of Thomas Tredway. Endorsed by Tredway to Rufus King; purchased by University to pay for anatomical apparatus.   [2213]

1825 July 23. T. J., Monticello, to ARTHUR S. BROCKENBROUGH. ALS. 1 p. Endorsed.
Date of remittance to Thomas Appleton. Marble capitals expected daily.   [2214]

1825 July 23. ARTHUR S. BROCKENBROUGH, University, to T. J., Monticello. ALS. 1 p. Endorsed by T. J.
William Coffee's prices for cornice too high, but Joseph Antrim says no one else in New York does such work. Dr. [Thomas M.] Boswell of Gloucester, Va., has presented mineral collection now in John P. Emmet's charge. Asks procedure in recording such gifts.   [2215]

1825 July 24. T. J., Monticello, to ARTHUR S. BROCKENBROUGH. ALS. 1 p. Endorsed. Another MS. in DLC.
William Coffee's prices for the Corinthian ornaments. Minerals for John P. Emmet. Arrival of marble bases expected on the Ship *Caroline*, Captain Farmer.   [2216]

1825 July 28. T. J., Monticello, to RUFUS KING, London. ALS. 1 p. Endorsed. 2 enclosures. Another MS. in DLC.

Bills of exchange deposited with King for the use of Thomas Callaway, who is purchasing anatomical equipment for Robley Dunglison. Enclosures: Two bills of exchange, one dated 27 June 1825 for £1350, the other 14 July 1825 for £675, drawn by Kerr & Caskie on James Dunlap of London in favor of Thomas Tredway.   [2217]

1825 Aug. 4. T. J., Monticello, to BOARD of VISITORS, UNIVERSITY of VIRGINIA. LS. 1 p. Endorsed. Circular. The library owns copies sent to Cocke, Cabell, and Chapman Johnson. Printed: Cabell 355.

Henry St. George Tucker, P. P. Barbour, Dabney Carr, and William A. G. Dade having declined the law chair, Francis W. Gilmer, the first choice, now agrees to accept. Accounts for spending of $50,000 for library and apparatus. References to Cummings & Hilliard, John P. Emmet, and Rufus King. [2218]

1825 Aug. 5. T. J., Monticello, to FRANCIS WALKER GILMER. ALS. 1 p. Endorsed. Another MS. in DLC.

W. A. G. Dade having declined law chair, has asked Visitors to authorize Gilmer's appointment.   [2219]

1825 Aug. 5. GEORGE HANCOCK, Fotheringay, Montgomery County, to T. J., Monticello. ALS. 1 p. Endorsed by T. J.

Offers sell mineral collection and library to University.   [2220]

1825 Aug. 7. T. J., Monticello, to WILLIAM HILLIARD, Boston. ALS. 1 p. Endorsed.

Instructions and list of books for the University of Virginia library. Recommends use of Clarke's catalogue of law books (1819).   [2221]

1825 Aug. 10. T. J., Monticello, to THOMAS APPLETON, Leghorn, Italy. ALS. 1 p. File draft. Endorsed by T. J.

Payment for marble columns made for University by Giacomo Raggi and others. Requests an exact statement of balance due after bills of exchange remitted through Samuel Williams and Mr. Bailey.   [2222]

1825 Aug. 13. T. J., Monticello, to GEORGE HANCOCK, Fotheringay, Va. ALS. 1 p. File draft. Endorsed by T. J.

Refusing his offer to sell mineral collection.   [2223]

1825 Aug. 17. T. J., Monticello, to RUFUS KING, London. ALS. 1 p. Endorsed. Another MS. in DLC.

Forwarding a duplicate bill of exchange for purchase of University of Virginia anatomical apparatus.   [2224]

1825 Aug. 19. JOSEPH C. CABELL, Edgewood, to T. J., Monticello. L. 1 p. Copy attested by N. F. Cabell. Deposited by Philip B. Campbell. Printed: Cabell 356.

Approves appointment of Francis W. Gilmer as professor of law.   [2225]

1825 Aug. 26. T. J., Monticello, to ARTHUR S. BROCKENBROUGH. ALS.
1 p. Endorsed. Another MS. in DLC.

Accounts of Dr. Boswell, Gowan & Marx, and Bohn with the University of
Virginia. Preparations for Francis Walker Gilmer as a member of the faculty.
[2226]

1825 Aug. 27. T. J., Monticello, to ELLEN WAYLES RANDOLPH COOLIDGE,
[Boston]. ALS. 2 pp. Photostat. Original owned by Harold J. Coolidge. Printed:
L & B XVIII 340-342; M H S *Coll* I 352-354.

Void she has left at Monticello. Coolidges' trip through New York and New
England parallels that made by T. J. and Madison in 1791. Good behavior of
students at the University. Clock for the Rotunda. T. J.'s poor health.   [2227]

1825 Aug. 29. RUFUS KING, London, to T. J., Monticello. LS. 2 pp. Endorsed
by T. J. Another copy: contemporary copy. 2 pp. Another MS. in DLC.

Has banked University's funds with Baring Brothers & Co. Bonnycastle's
forfeited bond taken up with George Canning. References to Mr. Knowles,
executor of the late Professor Bonnycastle, and to John Adams Smith, U. S.
chargé in London.   [2228]

1825 Aug. 30 T. J., Monticello, to ARTHUR S. BROCKENBROUGH. ALS. 1 p.
Endorsed.

Arrival in New York of marble bases and paving squares for the University and
of chimney pieces for Monticello. Reference to Bernard Peyton.   [2229]

1825 Aug. 31. T. J., Monticello, to WILLIAM HILLIARD, Boston, ALS. 2 pp.
Endorsed. McGregor Library. Another MS. in DLC.

Complaints regarding the Encyclopedia and other books sent by Hilliard.
Necessity for purchasing the best editions. Lack of texts for students.   [2230]

1825 Sept. 5. RUFUS KING, London, to T. J., Monticello. L. 2 pp. Copy.
Endorsed by T. J. Another MS. in DLC.

Bill of exchange by Kerr & Caskie on James Dunlop in favor of Thomas
Tredway received and deposited with Baring Brothers & Co. Letters sent to
Mr. Callaway and Peter Barlow. No word from George Canning on Charles
Bonnycastle's bond.   [2231]

1825 Sept. 6. HENRY A. S. DEARBORN, Custom House, Boston, to T. J.,
Monticello. ALS. 3 pp. Endorsed by T. J.

Will see to transferring marble capitals arrived on Brig *Farnsworth* from
Thomas Appleton of Leghorn, Italy, to vessel for Richmond. Mentions Bernard
Peyton. Notes on back by T. J. concerning tariff due.   [2232]

1825 Sept. 9. JONATHAN THOMPSON, New York, to T. J., Monticello. ALS.
2 pp. Endorsed by T. J.

Freight and duty on marble from Leghorn for the University of Virginia,
shipped aboard the Sloop *Eliza Allen*, Captain Allen, to Bernard Peyton. [2233]

1825 Sept. 10. T. J., Monticello, to the BOARD OF VISITORS, UNIVERSITY of VIRGINIA. LS. 1 p. Endorsed. Circular. Copies sent to Cocke and Cabell. Another MS. in DLC. Printed: Cabell 356-357.
Requesting that Visitors meet with him at Monticello prior to formal meeting, which his health will prevent his attending. [2234]

1825 Sept. 13. T. J., Monticello, to ARTHUR S. BROCKENBROUGH. ALS. 1 p. Endorsed.
Arrival of marble capitals in Boston. Duties payable at Boston and New York. [2235]

1825 Sept. 13. T. J., Monticello, to HENRY A. S. DEARBORN, Boston. ALS. 1 p. Endorsed. Photostat. Original owned by Mrs. Laird U. Park. Printed: B of R VI 119 (MS. in DLC).
Duty on marble capitals for the University that have arrived at Boston. [2236]

1825 Sept. 20. T. J., Monticello, to ARTHUR S. BROCKENBROUGH, University. ALS. 2 pp. Endorsed. Another MS. in DLC.
Sends accurate statement of articles properly chargeable to library funds. Money put in Francis Walker Gilmer's hands not included. Requests statement of debts and funds on hand to pay them. Mentions Thomas Appleton, Henry A. S. Dearborn, John P. Emmet, and Cummings & Hilliard. [2237]

1825 Sept. 21. T. J., Monticello, to THOMAS VOIGHT, [Philadelphia?]. ALS. 1 p. File draft. Endorsed by T. J.
Requests estimate on cost of clock and bell for University. [2238]

1825 Sept. 22. HENRY A. S. DEARBORN, Custom House, Boston, to T. J., Monticello. LS. 3 pp. Endorsed by T. J.
Suggests giving bond for duties on marble capitals, while petitioning Congress to remit duties. Lists insurance placed on columns and charges paid. [2239]

1825 Oct. 1. ARTHUR S. BROCKENBROUGH, University, to T. J. ALS. 1 p.
Covers letter from William J. Coffee, agreeing to reduce prices on cornices. Letter from Coffee to Brockenbrough, 25 September, on verso. [2240]

1825 Oct. 1. T. J., Monticello, to ARTHUR S. BROCKENBROUGH. ALS. 1 p. Endorsed.
Request for numbers of students enrolled in each school for T. J.'s report to the Visitors. Figures noted at bottom by Brockenbrough for Professors Blaettermann, Bonnycastle, Dunglison, Emmet, Key, Long, and Tucker. [2241]

1825 Oct. 3. JONATHAN THOMPSON, New York, to T. J., Monticello. ALS. 1 p. Endorsed by T. J.
Duties on the marble received on the Ship Caroline for the University of Virginia. Reference to Bernard Peyton. [2242]

[1825 Oct. 4]. THOMAS H. KEY and GEORGE LONG to RECTOR and VISITORS, UNIVERSITY of VIRGINIA. LS (ALS by Key). 2 pp. Endorsed by T. J.
Offering resignations, having lost confidence after student riot. (See Bruce, History of the University of Virginia II 298 ff.). [2243]

1825 Oct. 7. WILLIAM HILLIARD, Boston, to T. J., Monticello. ALS. 1 p.
Endorsed by T. J. Enclosure: D. 2 pp.

Sends case of books for University, the invoice for which is enclosed. Problems
involved in securing various editions of certain works. Hilliard unable to go
abroad personally because commission lowered. Books enclosed for [M. W. D.]
Jones and [Valentine] Southall.   [2244]

1825 Oct. 7. T. J. RESOLUTION of the BOARD OF VISITORS, UNIVERSITY
of VIRGINIA. DS. 1 p. Endorsed by A. S. Brockenbrough.

Duties of the Proctor. Attorney-in-fact for the University responsible for
property, breaches of the peace, trespasses by students or others on University
grounds. Copy sent to Brockenbrough.   [2245]

1825 Oct. 9. T. J., Monticello, to ARTHUR S. BROCKENBROUGH. ALS. 1 p.
Endorsed.

Reimbursement of Henry A. S. Dearborn for the money advanced for the
University of Virginia marble.   [2246]

1825 Oct. 11. T. J., Monticello, to FRANCIS WALKER GILMER. AL[S clipped].
1 p. Endorsed.

Offers him the chair of law.   [2247]

1825 Oct. 12. T. J., Monticello, to ARTHUR S. BROCKENBROUGH. ADS.
1 p. Endorsed.

Remittances to Henry A. S. Dearborn, Boston, and Jonathan Thompson, New
York, for duties and freight on the University marble. Request for copies of
the printed enactments of the Board of Visitors, and for all the land deeds of
the University. Instructions regarding construction.   [2248]

1825 Oct. 12. T. J., JOHN H. COCKE, JAMES MADISON, CHAPMAN JOHN-
SON, JAMES BRECKENRIDGE, GEORGE LOYALL, and JOSEPH C. CABELL.
BOND to UNITED STATES OF AMERICA. DS. 1 p. Endorsed. Witnessed by
Arthur S. Brockenbrough.

Guaranteeing payment to Collector of Boston for capitals imported on Brig
Farnsworth, J. Harmor Master.   [2249]

[1825] Oct. 13. T. J., Monticello, to JOSEPH COOLIDGE, JR., Boston. ALS.
3 pp. Photostat. Original owned by H. J. Coolidge. Another MS. in MHi.
Printed: L & B XVIII 342-346: M H S *Coll* I 356-359.

Price for the University clock and bell. Student riot at the University. T. J.'s
health. Greetings to Ellen.   [2250]

1825 Oct. 15. ANDREW YATES, Schenectady, to T. J., Monticello. Printed
prospectus. 2 pp.

Proposal for a polytechny at Chitenengo, N. Y., for education in application
to useful arts.   [2251]

1825 Oct. 21. T. J., Monticello, to ARTHUR S. BROCKENBROUGH. ALS.
1 p. Endorsed. Another MS. in DLC.

Money advanced by Thomas Appleton to one of the Raggi brothers. [2252]

1825 Oct. 21. HENRY A. S. DEARBORN, Boston, to T. J., Monticello. ALS. 2 pp. Endorsed by T. J. 2 enclosures.

Payment received for the marble capitals. Enclosures: bills from Henry Hovey & Co. and the Franklin Insurance Co. [2253]

1825 Oct. 25. T. J., Monticello, to GEORGE W. LEWIS. ALS. 4 pp. Endorsed. Deposited by Mrs. Lucien D. Winston. Printed: L & B XVI 124-129; B of R VI 268 (MS. in DLC).

Recommendation for a course of study in ancient and modern history. David Hume's bias in his *History of England*. Recommends Coke's *Littleton* as the best elementary work in law. Mentions Francis Walker Gilmer. [2254]

1825 Nov. 4. T. J., Monticello, to WILLIAM HILLIARD, Boston. ALS. 2 pp. Endorsed. McGregor Library.

Instructions regarding editions of various books for the library. Complaints by students and by George Blaettermann at lack of texts. [2255]

1825 Nov. 10. MARTIN DAWSON, Milton, to T. J., Monticello. ALS. 1 p. Endorsed.

Explains state of University funds. Mentions Joseph C. Cabell and John H. Cocke. [2256]

1825 Nov. 11. PETER BARLOW, Woolwich, England, to T. J., Monticello. ALS. 3 pp. Endorsed by T. J.

Apparatus for University of Virginia. Prices exceed some of Charles Bonnycastle's estimates. Mentions Rufus King. [2257]

1825 Nov. 12. T. J., Monticello. MEMORANDUM to ARTHUR S. BROCKEN-BROUGH. ALS. 1 p. Endorsed.

Instructions relative to smoke houses and wood yards for the faculty, firewood for class rooms, student regulations, student accounts, and money remitted by Samuel Williams to Thomas Appleton. [2258]

1825 Nov. 14-26. T. J., Monticello, to ELLEN WAYLES COOLIDGE. ALS. 4 pp. Photostat. Original owned by H. J. Coolidge. Printed: L & B XVIII 346-352; M H S *Coll* I 359-363.

Discipline restored at the University after student riot. News of the loss of Ellen's baggage received from John Hemmings. Offers to give to Joseph Coolidge, Jr., the writing desk on which the Declaration of Independence was written. Clock for the University to be made by Mr. Willard when funds permit. Request that the Coolidge buy codfish, tongue, and cognac for him. References to Benjamin Waterhouse and George Ticknor. [2259]

1825 Nov. 15. T. J., Monticello, to ARTHUR S. BROCKENBROUGH. ALS. 1 p. Endorsed. Another MS. in DLC.

Accounts with [Martin] Dawson and Jonathan Thompson. Instructions regarding the building of smoke houses. [2260]

1825. Nov. 17. JONATHAN THOMPSON, New York, to T. J., Monticello. ALS. 1 p. Endorsed by T. J.

Receipt of money for expenses incurred for the University of Virginia. (Attached is ALS 12 November from W. Dandridge, Bank of Virginia, to Arthur S. Brockenbrough regarding University of Virginia funds).   [2261]

1825 Nov. 18. T. J., Monticello, to JOSEPH COOLIDGE, JR., Boston. ADS and DS. 1 p. 2 copies. Photostat. Originals owned by H. J. Coolidge. Another MS. in DLC.

Card sent with writing desk, made by Ben Randall of Philadelphia, on which T. J. wrote the Declaration of Independence.   [2262]

1825 Nov. 20. RUFUS KING, London, to T. J. L. 2 pp. Contemporary copy. Endorsed.

Virginia will not be called upon for the forfeiture of Charles Bonnycastle's bond. Instruments ordered from Mr. Barlow. Reference to George Canning.

[2263]

1825 Dec. 7. JOSEPH C. CABELL, Richmond, to T. J., Monticello. ALS. 2 pp. Endorsed by T. J. Deposited by Philip B. Campbell. Printed: Cabell 357-358.

Death of his brother-in-law, Dr. Carter, prevents his attendance at Board of Visitors' meeting. New regulations at the University. References to John H. Cocke, Thomas Cooper, Chapman Johnson, George Loyall, and [George] Tucker.

[2264]

1825 Dec. 8. WILLIAM G. WALL, New York, to T. J., Monticello. ALS. 2 pp. Endorsed by T. J.

Requests information on terms of art professorship at University of Virginia, offered to him by Mr. Brown. Offers [Robert?] Greenhow, [David] Hossack, [James] Renwick, and [John] Trumbull as references.   [2265]

1825 Dec. 13. T. J., Monticello, to ARTHUR S. BROCKENBROUGH. ALS. 1 p. Endorsed. Another MS. in DLC.

Instructions regarding professors' salaries, proctor's quarters and salary, store rooms, and a post office at the University.   [2266]

1825 Dec. 25. RUFUS KING, London, to T. J., Monticello. LS. 1 p. Endorsed by T. J. Another contemporary copy.

Sends dispatch from George Canning concerning the Bonnycastle bond, notice of which has been given to Peter Barlow. Mr. Warwick of Virginia to ship the apparatus for the University.   [2267]

1825 Dec. 27. T. J., Monticello, to ARTHUR S. BROCKENBROUGH. ALS. 1 p. Endorsed.

Request for copies of the last University of Virginia advertisement.   [2268]

1825 Dec. 31. WILLIAM H. ELLIOTT, Charlotte Court House, Va., to T. J., Monticello. ALS. 1 p. Endorsed by T. J.

Applies for position of librarian. Mentions Henry St. George Tucker.   [2269]

1825. ARTHUR S. BROCKENBROUGH, PROCTOR, UNIVERSITY OF VIRGINIA. DEED TO T. J., JAMES MADISON, JAMES BRECKENRIDGE, CHAPMAN JOHNSON, JOSEPH C. CABELL, JOHN HARTWELL COCKE, and GEORGE LOYALL, VISITORS. AD by T. J. 3 pp. Draft.

Conveying title of University lands from the Proctor to Rector and Visitors. Four parcels of land formerly owned by John M. and Francis T. Perry, and by Daniel A. and Mary A. F. Piper.   [2270]

[1825]. T. J. STATEMENT OF CASH ADVANCED TO PROFESSORS OF UNIVERSITY OF VIRGINIA. AD. 1 p. Endorsed.

Advances to George Blaettermann, Charles Bonnycastle, Robley Dunglison, Thomas Hewett Key, and George Long from October through December 1824.   [2271]

1826 Jan. 2. T. J., Monticello, to WILLIAM G. WALL, New York. ALS. 1 p. File draft. Endorsed by T. J.

John P. Emmet will answer his enquiries concerning art position at University.   [2272]

1826 Jan. 3. T. J., Monticello, to ARTHUR S. BROCKENBROUGH. ALS. 1 p. Endorsed. Another MS. in DLC.

Placement of the temporary bell. Book shelves needed. University advertisements.   [2273]

1826 Jan. 8. JEFFERSON NEILSON, Transylvania University, Ky., to T. J., Monticello. ALS. 1 p. Endorsed by T. J.

Asks requirements for entering senior class.   [2274]

1826 Jan. 12. T. J., Monticello, to WILLIAM F. GORDON. L. 2 pp. Extract by N. P. Trist, ca. 1830. Printed: Ford X 358-359; B of R VI 186 (MS. in DLC).

Is weakened in body and mind by infirmities. States' rights usurped by the Federal Government. References to the South Carolina Resolutions, Van Buren's motion, and Baylies' proposition.   [2275]

1826 Jan. 15. JOHN A. TALIAFERRO, Charlottesville, to T. J. ALS. 1 p. Endorsed by T. J.

Sends references from Charles Hill and John Wood as candidate for office of librarian.   [2276]

1826 Jan. 16. MANN A. PAGE, Fredericksburg, to T. J., Monticello. ALS. 1 p. Endorsed by T. J.

Applies for position of librarian to defray his expenses as student.   [2277]

1826 Jan. 17. FRANCIS TOMQUIST, New York, to T. J., Monticello. ALS. 3 pp. Endorsed by T. J. Enclosure: AD. 2 pp.

Sends catalog of instruments for sale, including telescope made by William Herschel. New York Athenaeum also interested. Enclosure: catalog.   [2278]

1826 Jan. 20. T. J., Monticello, to JOSEPH C. CABELL. ALS. 1 p. Photostat. Original owned by Harold J. Coolidge.

Encloses circular concerning candidates for the law professorship. Requests Cabell's aid in getting lottery bill through the legislature. Proposes extension to

the University of the Riot Act of 1786 for purposes of maintaining discipline.
[2279]

1826 Jan. 20. T. J., Monticello, to the BOARD OF VISITORS, UNIVERSITY of
VIRGINIA. LS. 3 pp. Endorsed. Circular. Copy sent to Cocke. Cocke Papers.
MS. in DLC.

Qualifications of P. P. Barbour, William A. C. Dade, William Preston, William
C. Rives, [John?] Robertson, and Dabney Terrell for the law professorship.
[2280]

1826 Jan. 23. T. J., Monticello, to FRANCIS WALKER GILMER. ALS. 1 p.
Endorsed. Printed: Davis 250.

Dr. Robley Dunglison forbids his visiting Gilmer. Urges him to take care of
himself.   [2281]

1826 Jan. 30. JOSEPH C. CABELL, Richmond, to T. J., Monticello. ALS. 3 pp.
Endorsed by T. J. Deposited by Philip B. Campbell. Partly printed: Cabell 360-
361.

Conference between George Loyall, Chapman Johnson, and Cabell regarding
delay in the appointment of a law professor. Action regarding the William and
Mary Bill. Conference regarding T. J.'s debts. References to Judge Francis T.
Brooke, Judge Dabney Carr, Judge John Coalter, Judge John W. Green, and
John T. Lemare.   [2282]

1826 Jan. 30. T. J., Monticello, to WILLIAM WERTENBAKER, Charlottesville.
ALS. 1 p. Another copy: AL. 1 p. File draft.

Offering temporary appointment as librarian, replacing John V. Kean. Outlines duties.   [2283]

1826 Feb. 3. JOSEPH C. CABELL, Richmond, to T. J., Monticello. ALS. 1 p.
Endorsed by T. J. Deposited by Philip B. Campbell. Printed: Cabell 362.

Meeting of T. J.'s friends in support of the lottery. David S. Garland's bill
for educational funds.   [2284]

[1826] Feb. 3. T. J. RANDOLPH, Richmond, to T. J. ALS. 2 pp. Endorsed by
T. J. Edgehill-Randolph Papers.

Progress of the bill to permit the Jefferson lottery. Kindness of Judges
Brooke, Cabell, Green, and Carr. [In the University Carr-Cary Papers there is a
letter dated 24 March 1826, C. J. Carr to Messrs. Dobbin, Murphy, and Bose,
requesting publication of an article signed John Hancock, requesting aid for
Mr. Jefferson, benefactor of the people of the United States].   [2285]

1826 Feb. 4. T. J., Monticello, to JOSEPH C. CABELL, Richmond. ALS. 2 pp.
Endorsed. Printed: Cabell 363-364.

With no hope of further funds from General Assembly, has instructed
Brockenbrough to reserve all funds for library in Rotunda and for anatomical
theatre. Likelihood that Congress will not remit duties on marble columns.
Establishment of secondary schools throughout the state. Necessity of an annual
report on the primary schools from each county.   [2286]

1826 Feb. 7. T. J., Monticello, to JOSEPH C. CABELL, Richmond. ALS. 2 pp. Endorsed. Printed: Cabell 365-367; Ford X 372-374; B of R VI 60 (MS. in DLC).

Action of the General Assembly concerning his bankruptcy. Possibility of moving to Bedford County, selling Monticello. Disclaims letter appearing in in Richmond *Enquirer* signed "An American Citizen", which declares he feels the legislature has been niggardly toward the University. Mentions James Madison. [2287]

1826 Feb. 8. JOSEPH C. CABELL, Richmond, to T. J., Monticello. ALS. 4 pp. Endorsed by T. J. Deposited by Philip B. Campbell. Partly printed: Cabell 367-369.

T. J.'s plan for location of colleges throughout the state better than that of David S. Garland. Motion made by George Loyall regarding T. J.'s lottery. [2288]

1826 Feb. 8. T. J., Monticello, to THOMAS J. RANDOLPH. L. 1 p. Copy. Carr-Cary Papers. Printed: Ford X 374-375; SNR 414-416; B of R VI 383 (MS. in DLC).

Expressing his affection for T. J. R.'s part in giving him a happy life. Gloom about future prospects with his debts not covered by assets. His misfortunes due to fluctuations in value of money and to long farming depression. Regrets that his family, especially Martha, should be turned out penniless. (On same sheet: T. J. Randolph, Tufton, Va., to Dabney Carr, Baltimore, 18 July 1826, concerning the publication of this letter from Jefferson to make clear to the public the reason for the Jefferson lottery, with a suggested introduction by N. P. Trist. Letter contains discussion of his own financial difficulties.) [2289]

1826 Feb. 10. JOSEPH C. CABELL, Richmond, to T. J., Monticello. ALS. 4 pp. Endorsed by T. J. Deposited by Philip B. Campbell. Printed: Cabell 370-372.

Action in the Assembly with regard to T. J.'s lottery. Bill to establish colleges throughout the state. References to James Madison, Chapman Johnson, and Hampden-Sydney College. [2290]

1826 Feb. 13. RUFUS KING, London, to T. J., Monticello. ALS. 1 p. Endorsed by T. J.

Encloses Warwick's account for instruments. [2291]

1826 Feb. 14. T. J., Monticello, to JOSEPH C. CABELL, Richmond. ALS. 1 p. Endorsed. Printed: Cabell 373-374.

Secondary education bill. Grateful for the efforts of his friends on the lottery bill, especially for the report of the Committee of Finance. [2292]

1826 Feb. 15. JOSEPH C. CABELL, Richmond, to T. J. ALS. 1 p. Endorsed by T. J. Deposited by Philip B. Campbell. Printed: Cabell 374-375.

T. J.'s lottery bill. Bill to establish colleges throughout the state. [2293]

1826 Feb. 20. JOSEPH C. CABELL, Richmond, to T. J., Monticello. ALS. 2 pp. Endorsed by T. J. Deposited by Philip B. Campbell. Printed: Cabell 375-376.

Passage of T. J.'s lottery bill, with list of the votes of the senators. Bill for establishment of colleges throughout the state. Reference to Samuel Taylor. [2294]

1826 Mar. 3. T. J., Monticello, to THOMAS WALKER MAURY. L. Contemporary copy. 1 p. Endorsed.

Assurances that he retains his schoolboy affections for James Maury. T. J.'s health broken and faculties impaired. [2295]

1826 Mar. 4. FRANCIS BROOKE, [Fredericksburg], to T. J., Monticello. ALS. 2 pp. Endorsed by T. J.

Recommends John T. Lomax of Fredericksburg for law professorship vacated by death of Francis Walker Gilmer. Lists qualifications, including graduation from William and Mary. [2296]

1826 Mar. 4. FRANCIS BROOKE, Fredericksburg, to JAMES MADISON, Montpelier. ALS. 2 pp. Endorsed by T. J.

Same subject as letter this date to Jefferson. [2297]

1826 Mar. 13. WILLIAM CABELL RIVES, Washington, to T. J., Monticello. ALS. 2 pp. Endorsed by T. J.

Bill to remit duties on marble columns approved by Ways and Means Committee of the House of Representatives. Expects eventual passage of bill. [2298]

1826 Mar. 16. JOHN W. GREEN, Culpeper, to T. J., Monticello. ALS. 1 p. Endorsed by T. J.

Recommends John T. Lomax of Fredericksburg for law professorship. [2299]

1826 Mar. 16-17. T. J. WILL. ADS. 4 pp. Photostat. Original in the Albemarle County Court House. Printed in facsimile: L & B XIX x. Recorded 7 August 1826 by Alexander Garrett, Clerk.

To his grandson, Francis Eppes, a portion of the Poplar Forest tract. All other property is subject to payment of debts, with the residue after payment going to Thomas J. Randolph, Nicholas P. Trist, and Alexander Garrett for the support of Martha J. Randolph and her heirs. Nothing to Thomas Mann Randolph, Jr., to ensure that the assets will not go for payment of his debts. Thomas J. Randolph is appointed sole executor, Trist and Garrett to act in the event of T. J. R.'s death. Codicil dated 17 March gives a gold watch to each grandchild, freedom to his servants, Burwell, John Hemings, and Joe Fosset. Madison Hemings and Eston Hemings apprenticed to John Hemings until the age of 21 when they are to receive their freedom. To T. J. Randolph a silver watch, and all his business and literary papers; to the University of Virginia his library, with a portion of it going to Nicholas P. Trist and Joseph Coolidge, Jr.; to James Madison a walking stick. Recommends to his daughter the care of her aunt, Anna Scott Marks. [2300]

1826 Mar. 19. T. J., Monticello, to ELLEN RANDOLPH COOLIDGE, Boston. ALS. 1 p. Photostat. Original owned by Harold J. Coolidge. Printed: L & B XVIII 352-354; M H S Coll I 373-374.

Sends cuttings from the Taliaferro apple. Thanks for the piano, brandy, fish, tongues, and sounds. [2301]

1826 Mar. 24. T. J., Monticello, to [NATHANIEL MACON]. L. 1 p. Copy. Photostat. Original owned by H. J. Coolidge. Also MS. copy. 1 p. Carr-Cary Papers. Printed: B of R VI 285 (MS. in DLC).
Introducing his grandson, Thomas J. Randolph.   [2302]

1826 Mar. 25. ARCHIBALD STUART, Staunton, to T. J., Monticello. ALS. 3 pp. Endorsed by T. J.
Recommends Gen. [Briscoe G.?] Baldwin for law professorship. Distinguished figure at the bar, highly successful in the army, political views acceptable (*i.e.*, Republican).   [2303]

1826 Mar. 26. T. J., Monticello, to [JOHN ADAMS]. L. 1 p. Copy. Photostat. Original owned by Harold J. Coolidge. Also MS. copy. 1 p. Carr-Cary Papers. Printed: L & B XVI 159-160; B of R VI 9 (MS. in DLC).
Introducing his grandson, Thomas J. Randolph.   [2304]

1826 Mar. 31. [ARTHUR S. BROCKENBROUGH]. UNIVERSITY FINANCIAL STATEMENT. AD. 4 pp. Endorsed.
Copy of statement of receipts and expenditures of the University made for T. J.   [2305]

1826 Mar. 31. T. J., Monticello, to [ROBLEY DUNGLISON]. ALS. 1 p. Endorsed. Deposited by Mrs. John Staige Davis.
Request for more detailed information regarding books to be ordered for the University library.   [2306]

[1826 Apr. 3-4]. T. J. MEMORANDUM to the BOARD of VISITORS, UNIVERSITY of VIRGINIA. AD. 2 pp. File draft.
Reasons for his objections to the creation of a president of the University.   [2307]

1826 Apr. 7. JON. BOUCHER CARR to T. J., Monticello. ALS. 1 p. Carr-Cary Papers.
Agrees to consult with T. J. regarding irregular practices of the University students. Reference to Alexander Garrett.   [2308]

1826 Apr. 7. T. J., Monticello, to the FACULTY of Professors of the UNIVERSITY OF VIRGINIA (addressed to Dr. Robley Dunglison). ALS. 1 p. Deposited by Mrs. John Staige Davis. Another MS. in DLC.
Action of the Board of Visitors regarding diplomas and the University code of regulations.   [2309]

1826 Apr. 16. JOHN H. COCKE, Charlottesville, to T. J., Monticello. ALS. 3 pp. Endorsed by T. J.
Recommendations concerning buildings and grounds: drainage, offal depots, replacement of timber used during construction, macadamizing roads. Mentions Arthur S. Brockenbrough, Robley Dunglison, and George W. Spotswood.   [2310]

1826 Apr. 21. T. J., Monticello, to CHARLES BONNYCASTLE. ALS. 1 p. File draft. Endorsed by T. J.
Recommends use of lap boards instead of tables to give room for more students.   [2311]

1826 Apr. 21. T. J., Monticello, to JOSEPH C. CABELL. L. 1 p. Circular. Copy. Endorsed. Printed: Cabell 377.

William Wirt declined office proposed to him. John T. Lomax has accepted law professorship.   [2312]

[1826 Apr. 27]. T. J. to [JOHN P. EMMET]. ALS. 2 pp. File draft. Printed: L & B XVI 163-167; B of R VI 141 (MS. in DLC).

Instructions regarding setting up of a school of botany with plans for a botonical garden. Correa de Serra recommended course combining Linnaeus and Jussieu.   [2313]

1826 Apr. JEFFERSON LOTTERY TICKET (number 1936) issued at Richmond. D. 1 p. Deposited by Thomas P. Grasty.

Signed by Yates & McIntyre for the managers, John Brockenborough (sic), Philip N. Nicholas, and Richard Anderson.   [2314]

[ca. 1826 Apr.]. "AMICUS". NOTICES CONCERNING JEFFERSON SUBSCRIPTION. D. 2 items. Carr-Cary Papers.

Stating that T. J. will accept money raised by subscription for his relief. In the same hand, notice of a meeting in Exchange Hall, [Richmond?] for the purpose of relief for T. J.   [2315]

1826 May 2. T. J., Monticello, to ARTHUR S. BROCKENBROUGH. ALS. 1 p. Endorsed.

Necessity of making payment to Henry A. S. Dearborn, Collector of Boston.
                                                                            [2316]

1826 May 5. T. J., Monticello, to A. S. BROCKENBROUGH. ALS. 1 p. Endorsed.

Instructions regarding the setting up of the capitals, repairing leaky roofs, plastering, and making of library tables. References to Mr. Broke (i. e. A. H. Brooks), a tin worker, and to John H. Cocke.   [2317]

1826 May 5. T. J., Monticello, to [FERDINAND R. HASSLER]. ALS. 1 p. McGregor Library. Another MS. in DLC.

Refers him to Professors Thomas H. Key and Charles Bonnycastle in regard to possible use of his mathematics book as a text at the University. Orders a copy for himself.   [2318]

1826 May 5. T. J. RECOMMENDATION for JESSE B. HARRISON. L. 1 p. Copy by N. P. Trist sent to John H. Cocke. Cocke Papers.

Recommending Harrison for professorship of French and Spanish at the University of North Carolina. This copy made in 1827 when Harrison was considered for post at University of Virginia.   [2319]

1826 May 13. WILLIAM CABELL RIVES, Washington, to T. J., Monticello. ALS. 2 pp. Endorsed by T. J.

Passage of bill remitting duties paid on marble columns. Separate post office for University approved. Mentions Arthur S. Brockenbrough.   [2320]

1826 May 20. T. J., Monticello, to JOHN H. COCKE, Bremo. ALS. 2 pp. Endorsed.

Dissatisfied with conditions of University. Lists matters needing attention: Rotunda leaks; water supply inadequate because of pipe problems; gas lights needed; remission of duties on columns; botanical garden; clock. Mentions John P. Emmet and Mr. Ziegler. [2321]

1826 May 28. T. J., Monticello, to JOHN H. COCKE, Charlottesville. ALS. 1 p. Endorsed.

Requests consultation with Cocke and Alexander Garrett regarding University papers. [2322]

1826 May 28. T. J. UNIVERSITY FINANCIAL STATEMENT. AD. 1 p.

Estimate of resources and expenses of the University 1826-1828, with references to 1829-1831. [2323]

[ca. 1826 May]. T. J. INSTRUCTIONS TO ARTHUR S. BROCKENBROUGH. AD. 1 p. Endorsed by T. J.

Instructions regarding work on the University's Rotunda, clock and bell, macadamizing roads, water supply, botanical garden, purchasing of chemicals and gas lights for Dr. Emmet's use, and copy of enactments for each student. Pencilled annotations by Brockenbrough of cost of various items. [2324]

1826 June 4. T. J., Monticello, to JOSEPH COOLIDGE, JR., Boston. ALS. 2 pp. Photostat. Original owned by H. J. Coolidge. Printed: L & B XVIII 354-357; U. Va. *Alumni Bulletin* V 112; M H S *Coll* I 374-377.

Instructions for the making of the University clock by Mr. Willard. University's need for a workman who can bore for water to immense depths. Student discipline. [2325]

1826 June 5. T. J., Monticello, to ELLEN WAYLES COOLIDGE, Boston. ALS. 1 p. Photostat. Original owned by H. J. Coolidge. Printed: Ford X 387-390.

News of the neighborhood. Greetings to Cornelia Randolph. [2326]

1826 June 22. T. J., Monticello, to ARTHUR S. BROCKENBROUGH, University. ALS. 1 p. File draft and recipient's copy. Endorsed by T. J. and Brockenbrough respectively.

[Simon] Willard to construct clock and purchase bell for the University. Remittance to be made through Joseph Coolidge, Jr. of Boston. [2327]

1826 June 22. T. J., Monticello, to JOSEPH COOLIDGE, JR., Boston. AL. 1 p. Photostat. Original owned by Harold J. Coolidge. Another MS. in DLC.

Remittance for Mr. Willard, clockmaker. Greetings to Ellen Coolidge. [2328]

1826 [ante July]. T. J. UNIVERSITY OF VIRGINIA BALANCE SHEET. AD. 2 pp. [2329]

1826 July 4. ALEXANDER GARRETT, Monticello, to MRS. ALEXANDER GARRETT, Charlottesville. ALS. 1 p. Garrett Papers.

Announcing death of Jefferson. Burial plans. Reactions of Martha Randolph and the rest of the family. [2330]

[*ca.* 1826 July]. THOMAS JEFFERSON RANDOLPH. ACCOUNT OF THOMAS JEFFERSON'S LAST ILLNESS AND DEATH. AD. 2 pp. Edgehill-Randolph Papers.   [2331]

[ca. 1826]. [THOMAS J. RANDOLPH?]. APPRAISAL OF T. J.'s PROPERTIES. D. 2 pp.

Valuation of slaves, livestock, farm tools, and carriages, made after Jefferson's death, mentioning omission of five slaves freed by T. J.'s will. In at least two hands.   [2332]

MISCELLANEOUS UNDATED ITEMS

T. J. APOTHECARY'S SCALE. AD. 1 p.

Scale of equivalent weights. On *verso*: version of song, "Bumpers Squire Jones", in hand of Martha Randolph. (See *Gentlemen's Magazine*, XIV 612).

[2333]

T. J. COPY OF A BALLAD. AD. 2 pp. Printed: Percy III no. 12.

Although Jefferson has been credited frequently with the authorship of a ballad, *The King of France,* this copy is a fragment of an old English ballad, *Valentine and Ursine* or *Valentine and Orson,* which is printed in Bishop Thomas Percy's *Reliques of Ancient English Poetry* as number 12 in his 3rd series, book 3. In his catalogue of 1783, Jefferson lists Percy's work as one of the volumes he intended to purchase. [2334]

T. J. AUTOGRAPH to MR. BOTTA. ALS. 1 p. Photostat. Original owned by St. Paul's School. [2335]

T. J. DRAWINGS. 10 pp. 8 T. J. AD. Section D printed: Fiske Kimball, "Jefferson and the Public Buildings of Virginia", *Huntington Library Quarterly* XII 3 (May 1949) figures 6-7, pp. 308-309, incorrectly attributed to the Coolidge Collection.

Rough drafts, finished plans, and specifications for various buildings.

A. Two-story building. Elevation, first and second floor plans. Pen drawings, ink wash. Marked "Plan C".

B. Three-story building. Elevation, three floor plans. Pen drawings, ink wash.

C. Five floor plans; pencil sketches with ink specifications, showing varying arrangements of centrally located circular and elliptical rooms. Perhaps drawings for unidentified residences; or tentative sketches proposed for the Capitol and Governor's House in Richmond (actually constructed from other plans); or more probably sketches for the President's House in Washington, made in preparation for anonymous submission of an entry in the competition announced by the Commissioners of Federal Buildings, 1792.

D. First and second floor plans for a square residence with north and south porticoes, wings connected to the main building by arcades; ink drawings. Students of Jeffersonian architecture have identified these drawings as (1) tentative studies for the President's House and (2) tentative studies for the Governor's House at Richmond. (See Fiske Kimball's article cited above). It may be noted that the one parlor shown occupies less than one ninth of the first floor, which is largely occupied by bedrooms, a nursery, etc.—a much simpler plan than that of the Governor's House at Williamsburg—suggesting that this plan may be for an unidentified country residence.

E. Floor plan and cross section of elevation of a residence. Elevation labelled "Thos. Jefferson Archt. Longitudinal Section. Robt. Mills delr." Ink drawings showing details of interior.

F. See [7] and [1516] above for drawings of Monticello and Poplar Forest. [2336]

T. J. DRAWING and SPECIFICATIONS for a GAME BAG. D. 1 p. Edgehill-Randolph Papers.   [2337]

T. J. DRAWING and SPECIFICATIONS for SERPENTINE WALL of the UNIVERSITY OF VIRGINIA. AD. 1 p. Photostat. Original owned by Samuel H. McVitty. Printed: *Corks and Curls* (Univ. of Va. annual) 1934 320-321. [2338]

[T. J.]. NOTES ON CONSTRUCTING AN ELLIPSE. D. 1 p. 19th century copy. Edgehill-Randolph Papers.   [2339]

T. J. NOTES ON HERBS. AD. 1 p. Edgehill-Randolph Papers.   [2340]

T. J. NOTES on a SURVEY in FAUQUIER COUNTY, VA. AD. 1 p. Photostat. Original unknown.   [2341]

PART II

A Supplementary Calendar of
Manuscripts Acquired 1950–1970

Editor's note: Asterisks refer the reader to Errata, page 497.

Introduction to Part II

THE supplementary calendar describes the Jefferson manuscripts acquired by the University of Virginia since 1950, when the library published the original edition of *The Jefferson Papers of the University of Virginia*. Publication of the supplement, with the accompanying reissue of the original calendar, makes available to scholars a complete set of indexed abstracts of the university's present holdings.

We have followed the style of entry set by Mrs. Thurlow and Mr. Berkeley in the original calendar, with certain exceptions. First, we have added in the first paragraph of each entry more detailed information concerning ownership. Second, we have added in the first paragraph the accession number used by the library for purposes of identification. This number is preceded by the symbol #. Third, we have had to be content with listing only the most readily accessible printed text of items that have been printed.

About two dozen entry numbers do not appear in the supplement. These items were deleted for various reasons after final copy had been prepared for the press.

We have included a small group of manuscripts of which the library holds photographic copies, even though the originals are in other libraries. These manuscripts include, most notably, the correspondence with Thaddeus Kosciuszko, in the National Museum of Cracow, Poland, and Jefferson's official vouchers as Governor of Virginia, in the Virginia State Library. Both of these groups of manuscripts have unique value for users of the library's manuscript collections, and neither is commonly accessible outside the institution that holds the originals.

Many items in the supplement belong to the Edgehill-Randolph Collection (#5533), which is an additional deposit of family papers owned by three of Jefferson's descendants: Miss Olivia Alexander Taylor, Miss Margaret Randolph Taylor, and Mrs. Edwin Page Kirk. Manuscripts in this important collection are listed as "Edgehill-Randolph Papers," not as deposits of the owners. With other family papers in the library, the Edgehill-Randolph Collection makes available a large archive for research on Jefferson's domestic life, on his business affairs, and on his career after his term as president of the United States.

We are indebted to Messrs. James A. Bear, Jr., Francis L. Berkeley, Jr., Julian P. Boyd, Dumas Malone, Frederick D. Nichols, and, especially, the late John Cook Wyllie for various forms of valued assistance with this project. Miss Donna Lynn Purvis prepared the final typescript of the supplement.

C. Clinton Sisson and Mrs. Jeanne K. Sisson have prepared the combined index to both parts of the complete calendar.

Our greatest debt is to Miss Ann L. Stauffenberg who with patience and perseverance helped with the final editing, indexing, and proofreading. Gratitude is also due in large measure to the other members of the Manuscripts Department staff who re-read the original manuscripts against the Calendar's text and made many necessary corrections and revisions; particularly, Edmund Berkeley, Jr., Miss Vesta L. Gordon, Gregory A. Johnson, Michael F. Plunkett, Miss Mary Faith Pusey, William G. Ray, and Douglas W. Tanner.

The Thomas Jefferson Memorial Foundation, through a generous grant, made possible the initial work of compilation, for which we gratefully acknowledge its support.

Finally, for the university, we are pleased to express gratitude to the many donors and depositors whose thoughtful gifts and loans to the library have built the Jefferson Collections and whose continuing interest has guaranteed the accessibility of manuscript materials for the study of Jefferson's life, opinions, and contributions to the university and the nation.

J. C. and A. F.

1767–1852. ACCOUNT BOOK KEPT BY T. J. AND OTHERS. AMS. *Ca.* 145 pp. Owned by Robert Hill Kean. #186-a.

I. 23 pages, 1767 Aug. 19–1770 June 30, T. J.'s personal accounts in his hand. II. 26 pages, 1786–1792 June 21: "The Est. of Thomas Jefferson Esqr. in Account with Nicholas Lewis" in unidentified hand. III. 68 pages, 1783–1791, accounts of various persons with T. J.'s estate in unidentified hand, with 1 page of Martha Carr's account in T. J.'s hand. IV. fragment (p. 659) in T. J.'s hand. V. 3 pages, "Alphabet to all accounts from J. Key's superintendance to Mr. Lewis's inclusive," in T. J.'s hand. VI. 1 page, "Alphabet to the Merchant's accounts" in T. J.'s hand. VII. 10 pages, 1794–1797, accounts for the "Nailery" in unidentified hand. VIII. Other later accounts and sketches by members of the Randolph family.   [2341-a]

1769 Feb. 5. T. J., Shadwell, to THOMAS TURPIN. ALS. 2 pp. #7769. Printed: Boyd I, 23–24.

Legal studies of Phillip Turpin. Building of Monticello. Will visit Turpin on way to Williamsburg.   [2342]

[1769–1770]. T. J. EARLY SKETCH FOR MONTICELLO. AD. 2 pp. Photostat. 4½″ x 5½″. Original owned by T. J. Memorial Foundation. #5385. See Nichols, Item 46.

Front elevation showing double porches; first floor plan.   [2343]

[1769–1772]. T. J. TABLE OF MILEAGES, STAUNTON TO WARM SPRINGS. AD. 2 pp. McGregor Library. #3620.

Lists Garner's, McDowell's, Stribling's Spring, Crawford, Laporte, Mrs. Berry's, Hodge's, Bell's, Kincaid's, Lange's, Harnest's at Panther Gap, Cloverdale, Bratton's, Williams's Spring, Scotchtown, Fawcet's, Shaw's, McLung's, and Dry Branch Gap.   [2344]

[1769–1772]. T. J. TABLE OF MILEAGES, WARM SPRINGS TO CHAR-LOTTESVILLE. AD. 1 p. Microfilm. Original owned by James Monroe Museum and Memorial Library, Fredericksburg. #3159.

Lists McLung, Shaw's, Fawcet's, Scotchtown, Cloverdale, Lange, [Kincaid's?], Hodges, McDowell, Staunton, Waynesboro, Morrison's, Yancey, Hardings, Wood's.   [2345]

[1770–1774]. T. J. CONSTRUCTION MEMORANDUM. AD. 2 pp. Edgehill-Randolph Papers. #5533.

Lists furnishings for Monticello, some to be gotten from Phillip Mazzei. Cost of Shadwell locks. Prices at mill. Bricks needed to complete Monticello.   [2346]

[1771–1772]. T. J. EARLY DRAWING OF MONTICELLO. AD. 1 p. Photostat. 13¾″ x 18¾″. Original owned by Mrs. Edwin Page Kirk. #5291. See Nichols, Item 47.

Study for final elevation of the first version.   [2347]

1773 May 22. T. J. MEMORANDUM REGARDING TOMB OF DABNEY CARR. AD. 2 pp. Owned by Dabney J. Carr, III. #6425. Printed: SNR, 27–28 (partially).

Inscriptions for tomb, foot of grave, and upper part of stone. Quotes David Mallet's *Excursion* and Ossian's Temora. Mentions Charlottesville, Va., John and Jane Carr of Louisa County, Martha Jefferson, Peter and Jane Jefferson, and T. J. [2348]

1774 Oct. 3. ANDERSON BRYAN SURVEY MAP OF LANDS OF E[DWARD] CARTER. ADS. 3 pp. Endorsed by T. J. Map: 15″ x 15¾″. Text: 10¼″ x 7½″. Edgehill-Randolph Papers. #5533.

Albemarle County land to be purchased by T. J. (This land, 483 acres on Montalto adjacent to Monticello, bought by T. J. in 1777 for £190.)   [2350]

1775 Nov. 7. T. J., Philadelphia, to FRANCIS EPPES, the Forest, Charles City County, Va. AL. 1 p. Owned by T. J. Memorial Foundation. #6596. Printed: Boyd I, 252.

Surrender of Chambly. Arms taken at Chambly to be used at St. John's, Montreal, and upper ports of St. Lawrence River. Arnold's success not known. Commotion in South Carolina. No news from Virginia. Mentions Mrs. William Byrd and Mrs. Elizabeth Wayles Eppes.   [2351]

[1775]. T. J. NOTES ON MARBLE FOR FIREPLACES AT [MONTICELLO]. AD. Fragment. 1 p. McGregor Library. #3620.   [2352]

1777 May 2. GEORGE CARRINGTON MAP OF THE COUNTY OF CUMBERLAND. In hand of T. J. DS. 1 p. 16″ x 12¾″. Edgehill-Randolph Papers. #5533.
                                                                        [2353]

1778 June 26. T. J., Albemarle County, to JERMAN BAKER, Petersburg. ALS. 1 p. #5856.

Encloses record of tickets received by John Wayles. Col. William Byrd signed page, but account is inaccurate.   [2354]

1778 Oct. 29. THOMAS WALKER PETITION IN BEHALF OF PETER JEFFERSON AND THOMAS MERIWETHER TO VIRGINIA GENERAL ASSEMBLY. AD. 1 p. Photocopy. Original owned by Virginia State Library. #7790.

To survey and sell land on New River, bought in 1748 by Thomas Meriwether, David Meriwether, Peter Jefferson, and Thomas Walker from William Gray and Ashford Hughes.   [2355]

1778 Nov. 13. EDMUND RANDOLPH, Williamsburg, to [T. J.?] ALS. 1 p. Owned by T. J. Memorial Foundation. #7443-e.

Re T. J.'s notifying his relation, [Randolph?] Jefferson, of court order requiring latter to give security for costs in his suit against Reade's administrators, which order was obtained by Mr. Carrington. Notes on verso re Joyce Shifflet.   [2355-a]

[1778]. T. J. to [?]. AL. Fragment. 1 p. Letterpress copy. Intermediate page only; beginning and end missing. Edgehill-Randolph Papers. #5533.

Surveying matters involving Anderson Bryan, Col. Randolph, and Staples. Claims on Col. Randolph and James Marks. Mentions Williamsburg and Albemarle County.   [2356]

1779 June 22. T. J., Williamsburg, to ST. GEORGE TUCKER. ALS and accompanying documents. 2 pp. Photostats. Originals owned by O. O. Fisher. #3449. Printed: Boyd III, 12–13.

As Tucker has interest in the American states and Bermuda, T. J. sends copies of resolution of Virginia Council regarding exchange of aid. T. J. covertly suggests if Bermuda will supply "Brobdinagian" bushels of salt, America will respond with Indian corn.

Accompanying the letter are: 1779 June 21, ACT OF ASSEMBLY authorizing the trade of grain for salt. ADS signed by Archibald Blair, Clerk of Council (18th-century copy). Also, 1780 Sept. 26, CERTIFICATE by BENJAMIN POWELL, Williamsburg justice of the peace, declaring that Tucker received T. J.'s letter.
                                                                          [2358]

1779 Aug. 15. T. J. to Parish of St. Anne, Albemarle. ADS. 1 p. Photostat. Deposit of T. J. Memorial Foundation. #5385-a.

Recommendation for Rev. Charles Clay.   [2359]

1779 Oct. 25. T. J., In Council, to FRANCIS TAYLOR, Barracks, Albemarle County. ALS. 1 p. Photostat. Original owned by O. O. Fisher. #3449. Printed: Boyd III, 121.

Commissions. Captains: Burnley, Purvis, Porter, Burton, White, Herndon. Lieutenants: Slaughter, Taylor, Paulett, Pettus. Ensigns: Winston, Slaughter, Paulet. Has no provisions, but Board of War may help.   [2360]

1779 Nov. 6. T. J., Williamsburg, to [WALTER?] CROCKETT, COUNTY LIEUTENANT OF PRINCE WILLIAM. LS. 1 p. Photostat. In clerk's hand. Signed by T. J. Original owned by Mrs. Joseph P. Crockett. #6242-a. Cf. Boyd III, 162.

Officer for Western Battalion to be commissioned. To proceed with first half of battalion to Albemarle; Crockett to follow with remainder. Mentions Sampson Mathews in Augusta and auditors in Virginia.   [2361]

[177–]. T. J. NOTES FROM MINUTES OF COUNCIL AND GENERAL COURT FOR 1625. AD. Fragments. 3 pp. #4705.   [2362]

[177–]. T. J. NOTES ON VIRGINIA LAWS, 1623–1773. AD. 2 pp. Owned by Gordon Trist Burke. #5385-u.

Items secured from office of House of Burgesses, Peyton Randolph through R. Hickman, Richard Bland, Charles City Office, John Page of Rosewell, and Pervis.   [2363]

1780 Jan. 12. T. J. LAND GRANT TO ROBERT CARTER NICHOLAS. DS. 1 p. Edgehill-Randolph Papers. #5533.

Nine and one half acres, an island in Fluvanna River, Albemarle County.   [2364]

1780 June 30. T. J., Richmond, to JAMES BUCHANAN. ANS. 1 p. Owned by Dumfries Burgh Museum, Scotland. #4916. Printed: Boyd XV, 592.

Orders wine.   [2365]

1780 Sept. 1. T. J. LAND GRANT TO JOHN CAROLILE. DS. 1 p. Photostat. Original owned by Mr. and Mrs. Jerry G. Helms. #5270.

  50 acres in Augusta County.   [2366]

1780 Nov. 22. T. J. RECEIPT TO MARY LEWIS. ADS. 1 p. Owned by Miss Mary V. Perley. #3668.

  Funds in Old Continental and State currency received of Mr. Lewis from Mary Lewis' collection in Albemarle for donation to soldiers.   [2368]

1780 Nov. 24. T. J., Richmond, to ROBERT LAWSON, Petersburg. ALS. 1 p. Photostat. Original owned by O. O. Fisher. #3449. Printed: Boyd IV, 151.

  Letter, 22 Nov., from Thomas Nelson at Richneck, enclosing note from New-port's news point, indicates that enemy ships are standing for Capes. Must rein-force Southern army to overcome Cornwallis' expected move on Camden.   [2369]

1780 Dec. 18. T. J. To VIRGINIA MEMBERS OF CONGRESS [JAMES MADI-SON & THEODORICK BLAND, JR.]. L. 3 pp. French translation in unidentified hand. Owned by T. J. Memorial Foundation. #5385-b. Printed: with English trans-lation, Hutchinson and Rachal, *Papers of James Madison*, II, 245–48. In French, Boyd XV, 598–99.

  French forces in Chesapeake Bay at Hampton Roads near Hampton and York-town. Burwell's ferry and West Point to Jamestown should be defended. Mentions Cumberland, Pamunkey River, King and Queen Court House, Hoods, Portopotank and Mattaponi.   [2370]

1780. GOVERNOR'S OFFICIAL VOUCHERS TO VIRGINIA AUDITORS. DS. Signed by T. J. 3 items. Each item 1 p. Microfilm. Originals owned by Virginia State Library. #6655.

  Name Mr. Scott and John Brown.   [2372]

1781 Jan. 2. T. J., Richmond, to THOMAS READ, COUNTY LIEUTENANT OF CHARLOTTE. LS. 2 pp. In clerk's hand. Signed by T. J. Photostat. Original owned by O. O. Fisher. #3449. Printed: Boyd IV, 298.

  Militia to rendezvous at Petersburg to repel British troops. Invasion Law.   [2373]

1781 Jan. 12. T. J., Richmond, to [JAMES WOOD]. ALS. 1 p. Photostat. Original owned by Julian W. Glass, Jr. #4562. Printed: Boyd IV, 347.

  British troops have retired down James River. German prisoners to return to barracks in Albemarle.   [2373-a]

1781 Feb. 13. T. J., Richmond, to [JAMES WOOD]. ALS. 1 p. Photostat. Original owned by Julian W. Glass, Jr. #4562. Printed: Boyd IV, 607.

  Enlistments to guard German prisoners in Albemarle must be extended. Mr. Brown has money for maintenance of Germans.   [2373-b]

1781 Feb. 18. T. J., Richmond, to [JAMES WOOD]. LS. In secretary's hand; signed by T. J. Original owned by Julian W. Glass, Jr. #4562. Printed: Boyd IV, 652.

  Cornwallis, having been at Boyd's Ferry on the 14th, approaches. Convention troops must be removed. Prisoners from Cow-pens to be at Staunton. Troops to remain below the Blue Ridge.   [2373-c]

1781 Mar. 1. T. J. LAND GRANT TO ELIZABETH THEEDS. DS. 1 p. Owned by Office of Clerk of Albemarle County Court. #5145.

161 acres on Rivanna River. Mentions John Shiflet, Stephen Phillips, Baptist Road, Ivy Creek, Samuel Ray, Alexander Markie, and Joseph Burnett. [2374]

1781 Apr. 5. JAMES BARBOUR, Culpeper, to [T. J.]. ALS. 1 p. Coles Collection. #6350. Printed: Boyd V, 587–88.

Asks that militiamen be relieved for corn planting. [2375]

1781 Apr. 5. T. J., In Council, to [THOMAS] WALKER, JOHN WALKER, and NICHOLAS LEWIS, Albemarle. ALS. 1 p. Owned by T. J. Memorial Foundation. #7443-e.

Asks recipients to act on Congress' plan for settlement of Col. Wood's account. Encloses resolution (not present) of Va. Council of State requesting that action. [2375-a]

1781 Apr. 9. RICHARD HENRY LEE, Chantilly, to [T. J.]. ALS. 2 pp. Coles Collection. #4421. Printed: Boyd XV, 606.

Mr. Whitlock found him with Militia by Potomac River. Skirmished with British who now go to Alexandria. British advance on tobacco stores on Yeocomico River. [2376]

1781. GOVERNOR'S OFFICIAL VOUCHERS TO VIRGINIA AUDITORS. DS. Signed by T. J. 66 items. Each item 1 p. Microfilm. Originals owned by Virginia State Library. #6655.

Recipients and cosigners: James Anderson, William Armistead, Evan Baker, Col. Bannister, Charles Bradford, John Bellfield, Bonner, Robert Boush, William Brackenridge, John Brown, John Browne, Thomas Bryant, Arthur Campbell, Obediah Clarke, John Coots, Anthony Crowe, William Davies, Charles Dick, Daniel Dodson, Lewis Duval, Milton Ford, Thomas Hambleton, George Harmer, Benjamin Harrison, William Harrison, Capt. Kincaid, John Lathim, Lewis & Thornton, Mrs. MacIntosh, Joseph Martin, George Matthews, James F. Moore, George Muter, Simon Nathan, Matthew Pope, Edmund Read, George Rice, Duncan Rose, David Ross, Edmund Roud, Col. Russell, Col. Senf, Capt. Singleton, John Sloane, Granville Smith, David Standeford, Baron Steuben, John Stewart, John Syme, Col. Temple, Vanbebbers, Peter Waggoner, John Walker, Levin Walker, John Webb, Gen. Weedon, Robert Yancey, Capt. Young. Certain items mention hospitals, gunpowder, gun factory, U.S. Navy. References to prisoners in New York, forks of James River, Powell Valley, Richmond, Botetourt. [2377]

1782 Apr. 10. THOMAS MANN RANDOLPH, SR. to T. J. ALS. 1 p. #5385-s.

No beer by Jupiter since brewer is visiting wife. Col. Cary appreciates pecan trees; Mr. Carter raising rabbits at Shirley. Regrets fire. Mentions Mrs. Jefferson and Mr. Tucker. [2378]

1782 Aug. 16. T. J. LEGAL OPINION IN WAYLAND CASE. D. 1 p. Contemporary transcript. Photocopy. Original owned by Madison County Court House, #7653. Copy attested by Clerk. (Original ADS of T. J. subsequently purchased. #9524) Printed: John Cook Wyllie, "The Second Mrs. Wayland, An Unpublished Jefferson Opinion on a Case in Equity," *American Journal of Legal History*, IX (1965), 64–68.

Will does not protect Mrs. Wayland, who must claim legal rights. Cites Garbland vs. Mayot 2 Vernon 105, Cook vs. Cook ibid. 545, Bateman vs. Roach 9 Modern Cases in Law and Equity 104, and Coleman vs. Seymour 1 Vesey 209.   [2379]

[1782]. MARTHA WAYLES JEFFERSON PROSE COMMENT ON THE FLIGHT OF TIME. With addition in hand of T. J. and note by Martha J. Trist Burke. AD. 1 p. Photocopy. Original owned by James Monroe Museum and Memorial Library, Fredericksburg. #3159. Printed: Boyd VI, 196.
Sentiment on death and eternal separation.   [2380]

[1782]. T. J. INSCRIPTION FOR TOMB OF MARTHA WAYLES SKELTON JEFFERSON. AD. 2 pp. Owned by T. J. Memorial Foundation. #5118. See SNR, 41.
Mentions John Wayles. With construction directions. Quotes *Iliad*.   [2381]

[1782]. T. J. SKETCH WITH LATIN NOTE ON HUMAN SUFFERING. 2 pp. Original owned by T. J. Memorial Foundation. #5118.
Translation of note in unidentified hand. Sketch for monument.   [2382]

[1782]. T. J. POEM TO MARTHA WAYLES SKELTON JEFFERSON. AD. 1 p. Microfilm. Original owned by James Monroe Museum and Memorial Library, Fredericksburg. #3159.
"A Death-Bed Adieu."   [2383]

1783 Jan. 6. T. J., Philadelphia, to COL. JAMES WOOD, Winchester. ALS. 1 p. Photostat. Original owned by Julian W. Glass, Jr. #4562. Printed: Boyd XV, 608.
Will leave Col. Wood's sword with James Madison when he goes to Europe.   [2383-a]

1783 June. T. J. to MR. FRAZER. AD. 2 pp. Fragments. #6225.
Bill of scantling to the sawyer at Monticello.   [2384]

1783 July 29. T. J., Monticello, to PHILIP TURPIN. L. 11 pp. 18th-century copy. #6443. Printed: Boyd VI, 324–30.
Turpin's medical studies in Great Britain and Paris, service in Royal Navy, efforts to join American forces. Mentions Cowpens, Charleston, Fort Washington, London, Long Island, New York, Staten Island; Benedict Arnold, Sir Guy Carleton, Lord Cornwallis, Mr. Griffin, Governor Nelson, the Utaws, George Washington; Acts of Virginia Assembly, Foster's Crown Law, Governor's Proclamation, Manuscript Records of Congress.   [2385]

1783 Dec. 31. T. J., Annapolis, Md., to WILSON CARY NICHOLAS. L. 2 pp. 19th-century copy. #5025.
Grammar school in Albemarle. Dr. Witherspoon at Princeton and Irish persons at Philadelphia know of no available teachers. Seeking one in Scotland. Expects war in Europe. Mentions Turkey, France, Prussia, Great Britain, Ireland, Holland. Congress not yet assembled.   [2386]

1784 Apr. 15. MARTHA J. CARR, Spring Forest, to T. J. ALS. 1 p. Photostat. Original owned by Mrs. John Shelton White. #4757-d. Printed: Boyd XV, 612–13.
Visited Bear Castle with Peter Carr and saw Mr. Overton. Mr. Stuart told Mr.

Bolling that Mr. Short had found school for Peter. Mr. Short wrote from Monticello that Mr. Key should send him to Liberty Hall, Rockbridge County. Mr. Wilton at Eppington. Health of Nancy at Fairfields, Lucy, Martha, and Mr. Bolling. Jenny Cary has daughter.   [2387]

1785 May 6. MARTHA J. CARR to T. J. ALS. 2 pp. Endorsed by T. J. Photostat. Original owned by Mrs. John Shelton White. #4757-d. Printed: Boyd XV, 618–19.

Martha's health. Nancy's package. Mr. Bolling did not see Col. LeMaire; Mrs. Eppes did. Health of Maria and Dabney Carr. Peter with James Maury, as James Madison wished. Mr. and Mrs. Bolling to go to Chesterfield. Tom Bolling and Mary Bolling Lewis of Fairfields dead.   [2388]

1785 June–1789 June. T. J. WEATHER RECORD. AD. 2 pp. McGregor Library. #3620.

Years in France.   [2389]

1785 July 5. T. J., Paris, to JAMES MONROE. AL. 1 p. Microfilm. Original owned by James Monroe Museum and Memorial Library, Fredericksburg. #3159. Printed: Boyd VIII, 261–62.

Mr. Adams carried earlier letter. Emperor in Italy. Dutch agents in Vienna. Constantinople troops refuse to use European arms. No news of Mr. Lamb. No progress in Barbary proceedings. Diplomatic cipher code message.   [2390]

1785 Aug. 20. T. J., Paris, to MARTHA J. CARR. ALS. 2 pp. Letterpress copy. Owned by Mrs. Carroll Stribling. #4810. Printed: Boyd XV, 620–21.

Mazzei brought letter. Condolence to Thomas and Mary J. Bolling. Maria to come. Letter from Peter Carr at Williamsburg. Books from London. Mr. Maury praises him. Dabney Carr's position. Samuel Carr's health. Martha well, speaking French. David Humphries, Mr. Short, T. J. do not speak French so well. Will send silk for Anna Scott Jefferson. James Madison to forward letters. No news of Eppington.   [2391]

1785 Aug. 30. T. J., Paris, to FRANCIS EPPES. ALS. 3 pp. Letterpress copy. Edgehill-Randolph Papers. #5533. Printed: Boyd XV, 621–23.

Letters to Francis and Elizabeth Wayles Eppes not answered. Jacques LeMaire, who wrote from Richmond about Maria, carried letters. Daniel and Theodorick Fitzhugh bring seeds. Daniel Fitzhugh to see Eppes in Richmond. Wants Maria sent. Nurses, ships, and voyages. Isabel would be a good nurse, or a young lady going to France or England. Nurse need come only to Havre, l'Orient, or Nantes. Martha's French better than that of David Humphries, William Short, or T. J. Emperor and Dutch settled quarrel. Possible trouble with Turks. Mentions Hors-du-monde, James Hemings.   [2392]

1785 Sept. 22. T. J., Paris, to [ELIZABETH WAYLES] EPPES. ALS. 2 pp. Letterpress copy. Edgehill-Randolph Papers. #5533. Printed: Boyd XV, 624–25.

Daniel and Theodorick Fitzhugh stayed longer than expected. Dr. Currie reports Maria and all are well. Maria's trip to France. Mr. Fitzhugh brings seeds. Mentions Mr. and Mrs. Skipwith and Maria.   [2393]

1785 Oct. 14. T. J., Paris, to SAMUEL HENLEY. ALS. 2 pp. Photocopy. Original owned by Paul Mellon. #7289-b. Printed: Boyd VIII, 634–35.

Books from Henley. Mentions Mr. Bradford and Mr. Gwatkin. Williamsburg fire. William and Mary College's altered curriculum. Mentions George Wythe and professors James McClung and Charles Bellini.   [2393-a]

1785 Nov. 5. T. J. PASSPORT FOR JOHN LAMB. DS. 1 p. Photostat. Original owned by O. O. Fisher. #3449.
Travel in France.   [2394]

1785 Nov. 14. T. J. AND THOMAS WALKER PETITION TO VIRGINIA GENERAL ASSEMBLY. D. 2 pp. Photocopy. #7790. Original owned by Virginia State Library.
T. J., heir to Peter Jefferson, and Thomas Walker, agent of Loyal Company, ask to survey and sell land bought 1748 by Peter Jefferson for Thomas Meriwether, David Meriwether, and Thomas Walker from Ashford Hughes and others.   [2395]

[1785]. T. J. FURNITURE LIST. AD. 4 pp. McGregor Library. #2958.
In France, perhaps for U.S. ministry.   [2397]

1786 Mar. 25. T. ROBINSON, London, to T. J., London. ALS. 1 p. Owned by the Misses Margaret and Olivia Taylor. #8937.
Specifications for a tool chest.   [2397-a]

1786 April 26. GRACE ROBERTS RECEIPT to T. J. DS. 1 p. Edgehill-Randolph Papers. #5533.
Lodging at Mrs. Connor's.   [2398]

1786 May 5. MARTHA J. CARR to T. J. ALS. 2 pp. Endorsed by T. J. Photostat. Original owned by Mrs. John Shelton White. #4757-d. Printed: Boyd XV, 626–27.
Health of T. J., Mrs. Skipwith, Peter Carr with Mr. Maury, Dabney Carr, Jenny Carr. Samuel Carr not seen. Bolling family at Fairfields. Has Bernard Moore settled bond for Dabney Carr's law books? Mentions Elizabeth Wayles Eppes, Eppington, Monticello, Williamsburg.   [2399]

[1786]. LACEY, JEWELLER OF LONDON, BUSINESS CARD. D. 1 p. Endorsed by T. J. Owned by Mrs. Edwin Page Kirk. #5291.
Purchased tea tray.   [2402]

[1786]. JAMES SHRAPNELL, GOLDSMITH OF CHARING CROSS, BUSINESS CARD. D. 1 p. Endorsed by T. J. Owned by Mrs. Edwin Page Kirk. #5291.
Purchased butter boats, pudding dish.   [2403]

[1786]. THOMAS ROE, LINEN DRAPER OF THE STRAND, BUSINESS CARD. D. 1 p. Endorsed by T. J. Owned by Mrs. Edwin Page Kirk. #5291.
Purchased calico.   [2404]

[1786]. J. THOMAS, JEWELLER OF LONDON, BUSINESS CARD. D. 1 p. Endorsed by T. J. Owned by Mrs. Edwin Page Kirk. #5291.
Purchased sword chains.   [2405]

[1786]. JOHN GRANT, JEWELLER OF LONDON, BUSINESS CARD. D. 1 p. Endorsed by T. J. Owned by Mrs. Edwin Page Kirk. #5291.
Purchased coffee urn.   [2406]

[1786]. WILLIAM SUTTON, JEWELLER OF LONDON, BUSINESS CARD. D. 1 p. Endorsed by T. J. Owned by Mrs. Edwin Page Kirk. #5291.
Purchased coffee jar.   [2407]

[1786]. WILLIAM LEIGH, JEWELLER OF LONDON, BUSINESS CARD. D. 1 p. Owned by Mrs. Edwin Page Kirk. #5291
Purchased stewing dish and top.   [2408]

[1786]. SAMUEL WILDMAN, JEWELLER OF LONDON, BUSINESS CARD. D. 1 p. Endorsed by T. J. Owned by Mrs. Edwin Page Kirk. #5291.
Purchased silver cross.   [2409]

[1786]. E. PUGH, JEWELLER OF LONDON AND TO PRINCESS AMELIA, BUSINESS CARD. D. 1 p. Endorsed by T. J. Owned by Mrs. Edwin Page Kirk. #5291.
Purchased small silver cross.   [2410]

[1786]. ALEXANDER MACKINTOSH, SADLER OF LONDON, BUSINESS CARD. D. 1 p. Endorsed by T. J. Owned by Mrs. Edwin Page Kirk. #5291.
Purchased bit.   [2411]

[1786]. MR. PRICE, JEWELLER OF LONDON, BUSINESS CARD. D. 1 p. Endorsed by T. J. Owned by Mrs. Edwin Page Kirk. #5291.
Purchased silver candlestick.   [2412]

[1786?]. SAMUEL SMITH to T. J. L. 4 pp. Wilson Cary Nicholas copy. Edgehill-Randolph Papers. #5533.
T. J. should abandon commercial involvement in European affairs if he wants to represent U.S. government. Cites Mr. Livingston. Mr. R. leaving England soon for Virginia.   [2413]

[1786?]. T. J. to [?]. ALS. Fragment. 1 p. Letterpress copy. Last page only. Edgehill-Randolph Papers. #5533.
Letter from Gibraltar. Trouble in Morocco. Writes to Mrs. Barclay at Richmond. Goes to Philadelphia, hoping to find a letter from Mr. Barclay.   [2414]

[1786?]. T. J. SPECIFICATIONS FOR M. DE C[ORNY]'S TRAVELLING COPY PRESS. AD. 4 pp. Edgehill-Randolph Papers. #5533. Cf. Boyd X, 400n.   [2414-a]

[post-1786]. T. J. NOTES DESCRIBING CHIP CUT FROM SHAKESPEARE'S CHAIR. AD. 1 p. Photostat. Original owned by Mrs. Robert E. Graham. #5832.
T. M. Randolph, Jr. cut chip while visiting Stratford-on-Avon, England.   [2415]
1787 Jan. 2. MARTHA J. CARR to T. J. ALS. 3 pp. Endorsed by T. J. Photostat. Original owned by Mrs. John Shelton White. #4757-d. Printed: Boyd XV, 632–34.
Mr. Madison, now member of Congress, has not forwarded all letters. Maria well, does not want to go to France. Isabel may not go. Health of Peter Carr, Nancy, and Bolling and Charles Lewis families. Jenny Cary says French Consul at Williamsburg may go next summer. Mr. Smith commends Dabney. Samuel Carr not seen. Mrs. Eppes could not bring Maria to Monticello. Inquires after Martha. Mentions Eppington and Wilson Nicholas.   [2416]

1787 Feb. 26. MARTHA J. CARR, Spring Forest, to T. J. ALS. 1 p. Endorsed by
T. J. Photostat. Original owned by Mrs. John Shelton White. #4757-d. Printed:
Boyd XV, 634–35.

Mr. Madison to bring letters, including one for Peter Carr. Maria at Eppington.
Health of Mr. Randolph of Dungeness, his eldest son in Scotland, and Jenny Cary.
Mrs. Marshall, née Ambler, insane. Mrs. Page of Rosewell and Mrs. Nicholas dead.
[2417]

1787 Apr. 27. MARTHA J. CARR to T. J. ALS. 2 pp. Photostat. Original owned
by Mrs. John Shelton White. #4757-d. Printed: Boyd XV, 636–37.

Maria going to France. Sad to leave Eppington and Mrs. Eppes. Saw Sam Carr.
Servant murdered baby of Mr. Stannard who married daughter of Ned Carter.
Nancy well. Lucy Randolph married Frenchman.   [2418]

[1787] June 28. T. J. to MARTHA JEFFERSON, l'Abbaye royale de Panthemont.
ALS. 1 p. Owned by Gordon Trist Burke. #5385-n. Printed: Boyd XI, 503.

Madame de Traubenheim says Martha unwell. Maria in England.   [2419]

1787 July 6. T. J. to MARTHA JEFFERSON, l'Abbaye royale de Panthemont.
ALS. 1 p. Photostat. Original owned by John R. Burke. #5422. Printed: Boyd
XV, 638.

Will ride with Martha and Miss Annesley.   [2421]

1787 Dec. 3. MARTHA J. CARR, Spring Forest, to T. J. ALS. 3 pp. Endorsed by
T. J. Photostat. Original owned by Mrs. John Shelton White. #4757-d. Printed:
Boyd XV, 639–41.

Peter Carr to carry letter to Mr. Madison. Maria's trip. Judgment against Bernard Moore. Trip to Buck Island. Criticizes Hastings Marks. Jack Carr says Marks
and Hudson Martin to go to Kentucky. Sold cook, Lewis. Archibald Cary died.
Health of Cary's son Arche, and of Peter and Dabney Carr. Mrs. Bolling's son died.
Polly Cary married Mr. Peachy. Letter for Martha.   [2423]

[1787]. T. J. to [?]. ALS. 1 p. Fragment. Letterpress copy, last page only. Edgehill-
Randolph Papers. #5533.

Will write Mr. Randolph. War reported among France, England, and Holland.
John Wayles Eppes to study at William and Mary College. Letter from Mr. Carr.
[2424]

[1787]. T. J., Paris, to [MARTHA J. CARR]. AL. 1 p. Fragment. Letterpress copy.
Photostat. Original owned by Mrs. John Shelton White. #5670.

Wants report on Monticello fruit trees. Maria's trip to Paris.   [2425]

[1787]. T. J. MARGINAL NOTATIONS IN BARON D'HOLBACH'S *LE CHRIS-
TIANISME DÉVOILÉ*. AD. 2 pp. Photostat. Original owned by T. J. Memorial
Foundation. #5156.   [2426]

1788 June 16. T. J. to MARTHA JEFFERSON, l'Abbaye royale de Panthemont.
L. 1 p. 20th-century copy. Photostat. Original owned by Mrs. A. Slater Lamond.
#7803. Printed: Betts and Bear, 44–45.

Madame de Corney to take her to opera. Maria with T. J.   [2427]

1788 July 11. T. J., Paris, to N. LEWIS. ALS. 8 pp. Photostat. Original owned by O. O. Fisher. #3449. Printed: Boyd XIII, 339–44.

Wrote to Francis Eppes. Renting estates. European tobacco prices. Rent from Garth and Mousley in Bedford, and Hickman and Smith in Albemarle. Mr. Eppes to help sell Cumberland and Elkhill land to pay Jones and McCaul. Protection for slaves. Debts to Mr. Braxton, Dr. Walker, Mr. Smith, Donald Scott, Dr. Reid, Col. Bannister, Phripp and Bowden of Norfolk, Hierom Gaines, Frank Gaines, William Chisholm, Johnson, Watson and Orr, Robinson, Bennet, and Callaway. Mr. Donald will take note. Mentions Monticello and Virginia. Mrs. Lewis sent corn that surpasses Italian and French corns. Great George, Ursula, Betty Hemings, Martin, and Bob not to be hired out. [2428]

1788 Aug. 8. JOHN PARADISE POWER OF ATTORNEY TO NATHANIEL BURWELL. D. 2 pp. In hand of and signed by T. J. Photostat. Original owned by James C. Shipley. #5757-c.

Paradise, of James City County, now of Paris, appoints Burwell of Carter's Grove to manage affairs and to pay debt to Edward Bancroft and William Anderson of London. Witnessed by T. J., William Short, and Phillip Mazzei. [2429]

[1788]. T. J. NOTES ON VIRGINIA LAWS, 1661–1788. AD. 13 pp. Owned by Gordon Trist Burke. #5385-u. [2430]

1789 July 7. T. J., Paris, to MARQUIS DE LAFAYETTE. ALS. 1 p. Photocopy. Original owned by Paul Mellon. #7289-b. Printed: Boyd XV, 252.

Denies proposing to Mr. Necker to sell American corn and flour to France, as understood by Monsieur de Mirabeau. Told John Jay that Necker favored such sale. Extract of letter published in American gazette. Wishes Lafayette to convey facts to French assembly. [2430-a]

1789 Sept. 25. T. J., Paris, to WILLIAM BINGHAM. ALS. 2 pp. #5763. Printed: Boyd XV, 476–77.

Trip to America. Note from Mr. Milne of the cording and spinning operation of la Muette. No news of Mrs. Bingham. [2431]

[1789]. T. J. PLANS AND SPECIFICATIONS FOR HIS SPECTACLES. AD. 1 p. Owned by T. J. Memorial Foundation. #5158. Includes sketch. [2432]

1790 Jan. 6. T. J. to JOHN PARADISE. ALS. 2 pp. Fragment. Letterpress copy. 2nd and 3rd pp. only. Edgehill-Randolph Papers. #5533. Printed: Boyd XVI, 84–86.

Finances of Mr. and Mrs. John Paradise. Nathaniel Burwell's aid to them. Mentions Dr. Bancroft, Mr. Wilkinson. [2433]

1790 Jan. 25. T. J., Monticello, to THOMAS WALKER. AL. 3 pp. Fragment. Letterpress copy. Edgehill-Randolph Papers. #5533. Printed: Boyd XVI, 127–29.

T. J. and Randolph Jefferson settled estate of Peter Jefferson with John Nicholas. Provisions for sisters, Anna Scott Jefferson, and lands. Cost of T. J.'s education, some owed to Thomas Walker. Accounts with Dabney Carr, Kippen and Company, John Walker, and Francis Walker. [2434]

1790 Feb. 23. MARRIAGE CONTRACT OF THOMAS MANN RANDOLPH, JR. AND MARTHA JEFFERSON. DS. 1 p. Signed by T. J. Owned by Office of Clerk of Albemarle County Court. #5145. Cf. Boyd XVI, 191, note.   [2435]

1790 Feb. T. J. RECORD OF PLANTING. AD. 2 pp. McGregor Library. #3620.
Largely fruit trees.   [2436]

1790 Mar. 7. T. J., Richmond, to [ELIZABETH WAYLES] EPPES. L. 1 p. 19th-century copy. Edgehill-Randolph Papers. #5533. Printed: Boyd XVI, 208–9.
Wanted to visit Eppington, but must go to New York. Maria will stay with Mrs. Eppes. Maria's Spanish studies and *Don Quixote*.   [2437]

1790 Mar. 26. CONGRESSIONAL APPROPRIATION BILL. Signed by T. J., Secretary of State. DS. 2 pp. Photostat. Original owned by O. O. Fisher. #3449.
                [2438]

1790 Apr. 6. T. J. to GOVERNOR OF GEORGIA [EDWARD TELFAIR]. LS. 1 p. Photostat. Original owned by Jay W. Johns. #5315.
Acts of Congress on Western land claims of North Carolina and exportation of uninspected goods.   [2439]

1790 Apr. 11. T. J., New York to MARIA JEFFERSON. ALS. 1 p. Letterpress copy. Edgehill-Randolph Papers. #5533. Printed: Boyd XVI, 331–32.
Asks about *Don Quixote*. Mentions Mr. Randolph, Francis, and Elizabeth Wayles Eppes.   [2440]

1790 May 2. T. J., New York, to MARIA JEFFERSON. ALS. 1 p. Letterpress copy. Edgehill-Randolph Papers. #5533. Printed: Boyd XVI, 405.
No news from Maria, Martha, or Thomas Mann Randolph, Jr.   [2441]

1790 May 4. T. J., New York, to COL. NICHOLAS LEWIS. AL. 1 p. Owned by T. J. Memorial Foundation. #7443-e. Printed: Boyd XVI, 411.
Introduction for Judge James Wilson of federal Supreme Court who will be in Charlottesville on his circuit. Regards to Mrs. Lewis.   [2441-a]

1790 June 13. T. J., New York, to [ELIZABETH WAYLES] EPPES. L. 2 pp. 19th-century copy. Edgehill-Randolph Papers. #5533. Printed: Boyd XVI, 489.
Headache. Appreciates Mrs. Eppes's care of Maria. House of Representatives to remove to Baltimore, but Senate may not concur, wishing to go instead to Philadelphia. New York climate. Mentions Francis Eppes.   [2442]

1790 June 13. T. J., New York, to MARIA JEFFERSON. ALS. 1 p. Letterpress copy. Edgehill-Randolph Papers. #5533. Printed: Boyd XVI, 491–92.
Wants Maria's pudding when in Virginia. Foods, birds, maxims, and books. Headache.   [2443]

[1790 June 23]. T. J., New York, to ANGELICA CHURCH. ALS. 1 p. Fragment. Letterpress copy. 2nd page only. Edgehill-Randolph Papers. #5533. Printed: Boyd XVI, 549–50.
May move Maria to New York or Philadelphia when Congress moves. John

Trumbull and paintings in Philadelphia. Letter from Mme. de Corny. Mentions Mrs. Hamilton, Mr. Church, and Kitty Church. [2444]

1790 July 4. T. J., New York, to MARIA JEFFERSON. ALS. 1 p. Letterpress copy. Edgehill-Randolph Papers. #5533. Printed: Boyd XVI, 599.
Spanish lessons, chickens, books, crops, weather, and family. [2445]

1790 July 20. MARIA JEFFERSON, Eppington, to T. J., Philadelphia. ALS. 1 p. Edgehill-Randolph Papers. #5533. Printed: Boyd XVII, 239.
Aunt Skipwith recovering. Books: Barthélemy's *Anacharsis* and Gibbon's *Roman Empire*. Repairs to Monticello pianoforte. [2446]

1790 July 21. T. J., New York, to [WILLIAM] FITZHUGH, Chatham, Va. ALS. 1 p. Fragment. Letterpress copy. 1st page only. Edgehill-Randolph Papers. #5533. Printed: Boyd XVII, 241–42.
Bob Hemings to take account of Tarquin to Fitzhugh on way to Fredericksburg. Tarquin lame. Unfavorable rate of exchange prevents drawing on Amsterdam bankers for Tarquin's price. Mentions packets. [2447]

1790 July 25. T. J., New York, to MARIA JEFFERSON. ALS. 1 p. Letterpress copy. Edgehill-Randolph Papers. #5533. Printed: Boyd XVII, 271–72.
Maria owes him letters. Will see her and Francis and Elizabeth Wayles Eppes at Monticello. Mentions puddings and Spanish studies. [2448]

1790 July 25. T. J., New York, to [ELIZABETH WAYLES] EPPES. L. 1 p. 19th-century copy. Edgehill-Randolph Papers. #5533. Printed: Boyd XVII, 265–66.
Letters from Francis and her. Eppington to Richmond mail slow. Mentions Martha's maid. May establish Martha in Albemarle. Will consult with her about Maria at Monticello. [2449]

1790 Aug. 22. T. J., New York, to THOMAS MANN RANDOLPH, JR. L. 1 p. 19th-century copy. Edgehill-Randolph Papers. #5533.
Horse buying. Mentions Monticello. [2450]

1790 Oct. 8. T. J., Monticello, to FRANCIS EPPES, Eppington. L. 3 pp. 19th-century copy. Edgehill-Randolph Papers. #5533. Printed: Boyd XVII, 581–82.
Visited Richmond to buy Edgehill from Thomas Mann Randolph, Sr. for Thomas Mann Randolph, Jr., and to sell Cumberland lands to William Ronald. Will sell Elkhill. John Hanson's mortgage on Cumberland and Beaverdam lands. Received at Annapolis Hanbury's account against John Wayles. Cannot visit Eppington. Suggests that John Wayles Eppes go to Princeton College or to Philadelphia College, may use T. J.'s law books at Eppington or at Mr. Lewis's where James Monroe can assist him. Mentions Mr. and Mrs. Skipwith. [2451]

1790 Oct. 10. T. J., Monticello, to FRANCIS EPPES. L. 1 p. 19th-century copy. Edgehill-Randolph Papers. #5533. Printed: Boyd XVII, 584.
Debt settlement with Mr. Ross. Sale of Elkhill. [2452]

1790 Oct. 22. CUSTOMS DECLARATION. DS. Signed by T. J. 1 p. #5891.
Wine and papers in ship *Henrietta*, Benjamin Wicks, master, from Havre de Grace. Witnessed by Sharp Delany and Frederick Phily. [2454]

1790 Oct. 29. T. J., Monticello, to [REUBEN] LINDSAY. ALS. 1 p. Letterpress copy. Endorsed by T. J. Edgehill-Randolph Papers. #5533. Printed: Boyd XVII, 654.
Arbitration of affairs of Mr. Mercer.   [2455]

1790 Oct. 31. T. J., Monticello, to [ELIZABETH WAYLES] EPPES. ALS. 1 p. Letterpress copy. Edgehill-Randolph Papers. #5533. Printed: Boyd XVII, 658.
Departing for Philadelphia. Purchase of Edgehill from Thomas Mann Randolph, Sr. for Thomas Mann Randolph, Jr. Negotiations with Mr. Carter. Martha at Monticello, perhaps with Maria. Will see John Wayles Eppes in Philadelphia.
[2456]

1790 Oct. 31. T. J., Monticello, to ELIZABETH WAYLES EPPES. L. 1 p. 19th-century copy. Edgehill-Randolph Papers. #5533.
Duplicates item 2456.   [2457]

1790 Nov. 3. T. J., Monticello, to FRANCIS WALKER. AL. 1 p. Fragment. 1st page only; 2nd page missing. Edgehill-Randolph Papers. #5533. Printed: Boyd XVII, 676–77.
See Item 209.   [2458]

1790 Nov. 3. T. J., Monticello, to [JAMES] LYLE. L. 1 p. Fragment. 19th-century copy. Edgehill-Randolph Papers. Printed: Boyd XVII, 674–76.
Discusses Dr. Thomas Walker's and John Harvie's settlement of Alexander McCaul's claim against Peter Jefferson's estate.   [2458-a]

1790 Nov. 6. T. J. DEED FOR SLAVES GIVEN TO THOMAS MANN RANDOLPH, JR. AND MARTHA JEFFERSON RANDOLPH. DS. 1 p. Edgehill-Randolph Papers. #5533. Printed: Boyd XVIII, 12.
Conveys Suck and child Philip Evans, Scilla and children Suck, John, Dick, and George, and Molly, daughter of Mary. Witnessed by Nicholas Lewis and John Garland Jefferson.   [2459]

1790 Dec. 7. T. J., Philadelphia, to MARIA JEFFERSON, Monticello. ALS. 1 p. Letterpress copy. Edgehill-Randolph Papers. #5533. Printed: Boyd XVIII, 141–42.
Col. Bell at Charlottesville will forward reply. Letters to Thomas Mann Randolph, Jr., Martha, and Maria. Letter from Thomas Mann Randolph, Jr. at Richmond. House in Philadelphia.   [2460]

1790 Dec. 7. T. J., Philadelphia, to MARIA JEFFERSON. ALS. 1 p. Photostat. Original owned by Mrs. Francis E. Shine. #3509.
Duplicates item 2460.   [2461]

[1790]. T. J. to [DAVID MEADE RANDOLPH]. AL. Fragment. 1 p. Letterpress copy. Intermediate page only; beginning and end missing. Edgehill-Randolph Papers. #5533.
Payments to Kippen, Richard Randolph, Capt. William Meriwether, and Mr. Walker. Mr. Harvie and Mr. McCaul paid by Thomas Walker. Mentions Presque Isle.   [2462]

[1790]. T. J. NOTES ON CLIMATES OF PHILADELPHIA AND MONTICELLO. AD. 2 pp. McGregor Library. #3620.   [2463]

[1790]. T. J. NOTES ON EXPENSES. AD. 2 pp. Fragment. Edgehill-Randolph Papers. #5533.

Prices in Philadelphia. Note on verso mentions expenses of personnel in the Foreign Affairs and War and Marine offices.   [2464]

[1790]. T. J. DESIGN WITH SKETCH FOR DESK. AD. 1 p. #6225.   [2465]

[1790]. T. J. to FRANCIS EPPES. ALS. 1 p. Fragment. Letterpress copy. Last page only. Edgehill-Randolph Papers. #5533.

Will ask Martha to contact aunt. Mr. Short well. Greetings to Mr. and Mrs. Skipwith and Mrs. Eppes.   [2466]

[1790–1809]. T. J. TABLE OF MILEAGES, GEORGETOWN TO MONTICELLO. AD. 4 pp. Owned by T. J. Memorial Foundation. #5118.

Lists Bentivoglio, Gordon's, Orange Court House, Downey's Ford, Stevensburg, Norman's Ford, Elk run Church, Slate run Church, Gaines's, Bullrun, Songster's, Fairfax Court House, Falls Church, Rapidan, Robinson, Culpeper Court House, Hedeman, Jefferson, Fauquier Court House, Lacy's Leesburg, Knowland's Cross Roads, Frederick, Md., German's Gap, Kennerly's, Narrow Passage, Woodstock, Stover's, Zane's, Winchester, Threetons, McCormac's, Harper's Ferry, Strode's, Somerville's mill, Wren's, Ravensworth, Richard Fitzhugh, Greenwich, Madison's Cave, Gilbert's, Colchester, Dumfries, Thomas's, Jones's, Thomson's, Newgate, Georgetown ferry, and Alexandria.   [2467]

1791 Jan. 5. T. J., Philadelphia, to MARIA JEFFERSON, [Monticello]. ALS. 1 p. Letterpress copy. Edgehill-Randolph Papers. #5533. Printed: SNR, 158.

Scolds Maria for not having written. Mentions Charlottesville.   [2468]

1791 Jan. 5. T. J., Philadelphia, to MARIA JEFFERSON, [Monticello]. L. 1 p. 19th-century copy. Edgehill-Randolph Papers. #5533.

Duplicates item 2468.   [2469]

1791 Jan. 20. T. J., Philadelphia, to [FRANCIS] EPPES. ALS. 1 p. Letterpress copy. Edgehill-Randolph Papers. #5533.

Had hoped to see John Wayles Eppes, but house not done. Peace between Great Britain and Spain has affected American produce unfavorably. Mentions John Hanson, crops, Elizabeth Wayles Eppes. Increasing demand for wheat in France.   [2470]

1791 Jan. 20. T. J., Philadelphia, to [FRANCES] EPPES. L. 1 p. 19th-century copy. Edgehill-Randolph Papers. #5533.

Duplicates item 2470.   [2471]

1791 Feb. 16. T. J., Philadelphia, to MARIA JEFFERSON. ALS. 1 p. Letterpress copy. Edgehill-Randolph Papers. #5533. Printed: SNR, 159.

Martha's baby, Anne Cary Randolph. Sends John Gregory's *Comparative View* for Martha. Mentions Thomas Mann Randolph, Jr. and Jennie. Spanish and harpsichord lessons.   [2472]

1791 [mis-dated 1796] Feb. 27. MARIA JEFFERSON, Varina, to T. J. 19th-century copy of extract. 1 p. Owned by the Misses Margaret and Olivia Taylor. #8937.
  Compliments Martha Jefferson Randolph. Mentions Sallie Cropper.   [2472-a]

1791 Feb. 28. T. J. CUSTOMS DECLARATION. D. 1 p. Owned by T. J. Memorial Foundation. #5385-ac.
  Acknowledges account for samples of wine of Portugal imported from Lisbon on the ship *Phoebe Williams*. Duties owed to Collector, District of Pennsylvania.
    [2472-b]

1791 Mar. 9. T. J., Philadelphia, to MARIA JEFFERSON, Monticello. ALS. 1 p. Photostat. Original owned by Mrs. Francis E. Shine. #3509. Printed: SNR, 159–60; Betts, *Garden Book*, 160–61, extract.
  Birds and frogs. Asks for zoological and botanical information to compare climates of Pennsylvania and Virginia. Mentions Mrs. Randolph and Jenny. [2473]

1791 Mar. 14. THOMAS MANN RANDOLPH, JR., Monticello, to T. J., Philadelphia. ALS. 3 pp. Endorsed by T. J. Edgehill-Randolph Papers. #5533.
  Charlottesville-Richmond mail service. Crossing a dog and a wolf. His diary. Wants to read Buffon's *Histoire Naturelle* and the *Encyclopédie*. Health of Maria, Martha, and Anne Cary Randolph. Martha, Dr. John Gregory, and Mrs. Fleming disagree on baby food. Mentions Georgetown.   [2474]

1791 Apr. 24. T. J. to TOBIAS LEAR. ANS. 1 p. #6047.
  Mail for George Washington to Camden, Taylor's Ferry, and Mount Vernon.
    [2475]

1791 Apr. 24. T. J., Philadelphia, to MARIA JEFFERSON. ALS. 1 p. Letterpress copy. Edgehill-Randolph Papers. #5533. Printed: SNR, 163; Betts, *Garden Book*, 162, extract.
  Climates and ladies' veils. John Wayles Eppes with T. J. Botanical data. Mentions Thomas Mann Randolph, Jr., Martha, and Anne Cary Randolph.   [2476]

1791 Apr. 24. T. J., Philadelphia, to MARIA JEFFERSON. ALS. 1 p. Photostat. Original owned by Mrs. Harold W. Wilson. #5385-v.
  Duplicates item 2476.   [2477]

1791 May 6. T. J., Philadelphia, to MR. FULWAR SKIPWITH. L. 5 pp. 19th-century copy. Edgehill-Randolph Papers. #5533.
  John Wayles' responsibility in case of *Guineaman*. Effect of death of Col. Randolph. Obligation of Farrell and Jones in slave trade with Africa. Cites Freeman 344, Tutthill vs. Roberts. Mentions Mrs. Skipwith's trip to Sweet Springs.   [2478]

1791 May 8. T. J., Philadelphia, to MARIA JEFFERSON. ALS. 1 p. Letterpress copy. Edgehill-Randolph Papers. #5533. Printed: SNR, 164–65.
  Sends nankeen care of Mr. Brown, Richmond. Will answer Thomas Mann Randolph, Jr.'s letters to Monticello before joining James Madison in New York. Travel route: New York to Albany and Lake George, to Bennington, through Vermont to Connecticut River, thence to Hartford and New Haven and to New York and Philadelphia. Maria's riding lessons. Mentions Anne Cary Randolph.
    [2479]

1791 May 15. T. J., Philadelphia, to FRANCIS EPPES. L. 1 p. 19th-century copy. Edgehill-Randolph Papers. #5533. Printed: SNR, 165–66.

John Wayles Eppes and Capt. Stratton arrived. Letter to Mr. Fulwar Skipwith concerning *Guineaman*. Coming to Virginia, perhaps not Richmond. John Wayles Eppes's studies. Trip to Lake George, Lake Champlain. [2480]

1791 May 15. T. J., Philadelphia, to ELIZABETH WAYLES EPPES. L. 1 p. 19th-century copy. Edgehill-Randolph Papers. #5533. Printed SNR, 166.

Favor from John Wayles Eppes. Letter, this date, to Francis Eppes. Mentions Anne Cary Randolph. Would have left Maria with Mrs. Eppes, but Martha needed her at Monticello. [2481]

1791 June 26. T. J., Philadelphia, to MARIA JEFFERSON. ALS. 1 p. Letterpress copy. Edgehill-Randolph Papers. #5533. Printed: SNR, 169.

Geography of Lake George area. Received tobacco reports from Mr. Lewis and Mr. Hylton. Mentions Martha, Anne Cary Randolph, and Thomas Mann Randolph, Jr. [2482]

1791 July 14. T. J., Monticello, to [NATHANIEL] CHIPMAN. ALS. 1 p. Photocopy. Original owned by Victor B. Levit. #8265-b.

Commission as judge of District of Vermont sent at same time as those for attorney and marshal. Encloses a new commission signed by Washington. [2482-a]

1791 July 31. T. J., Philadelphia, to MARIA JEFFERSON. L. 1 p. 19th-century copy. Edgehill-Randolph Papers. #5533. Printed: SNR, 169–70.

Wants stores sent to Mr. Brown, Richmond, moved to Monticello. Sent commodes and chessmen. Petit says chessmen were sent. Asks about Maria's and Martha's music. [2483]

1791 Aug. 7. T. J., Philadelphia, to FRANCIS EPPES. ALS. 1 p. Fragment. Letterpress copy. 1st page only; 2nd page missing. Edgehill-Randolph Papers. #5533.
See item 2485. [2484]

1791 Aug. 7. T. J., Philadelphia, to FRANCIS EPPES. L. 2 pp. 19th-century copy. Edgehill-Randolph Papers. #5533.

Asks about Capt. Hylton's debts to Mazzei. John Wayles Eppes's law studies. Unsettled time of George Washington's trip to Virginia makes T. J.'s trip uncertain. Hopes to see Mr. and Mrs. Eppes at Monticello because cannot get to Eppington. Tobacco unprofitable. Will sell property to settle debt to John Hanson. Mentions friends at Hors-du-monde. [2485]

1791 Aug. 21. T. J., Philadelphia, to MARIA JEFFERSON. ALS. 1 p. Letterpress copy. Edgehill-Randolph Papers. #5533. Printed: SNR, 170.

Coming to Monticello. Thomas Mann Randolph, Jr. will get him a new horse. James Madison lends horse for trip to Virginia. Mentions Thomas Mann Randolph, Jr., Martha, and Anne Cary Randolph. [2486]

1791 Aug. 21. T. J., Philadelphia, to MARIA JEFFERSON. L. 1 p. 19th-century copy. Edgehill-Randolph Papers. #5533.
Duplicates item 2486. [2487]

1791 Aug. 31. T. J., Philadelphia, to THOMAS LIEPER. ALS. 1 p. Letterpress copy. Endorsed by T. J. Edgehill-Randolph Papers. #5533.

Money for trip. Shipment of tobacco expected on Capt. Stratton's ship.   [2488]

1791 Oct. 5. T. J., Philadelphia, to FRANCIS EPPES. L. 2 pp. 19th-century copy. Edgehill-Randolph Papers. #5533.

To Philadelphia with Maria. To Virginia in Spring to settle with John Hanson. Cannot find Mazzei's account against Hylton. Perhaps with Blair. Samuel Woodson and Robert Lewis defaulted on bond; have not paid Eppes money spent on Maria. To pay John Wayles Eppes. Books from Europe for John Wayles Eppes. Mr. Skipwith says Wigan, Bevin's administrator, sues T. J. and Eppes. Health of Mrs. Eppes.   [2489]

1791 Oct. 6. T. J., Monticello, to FRANCIS WALKER. ALS. 1 p. Fragment. Letterpress copy. 1st page only. Edgehill-Randolph Papers. #5533.

Mr. Lyle to supply copy of Kippen and Company account with estate of Peter Jefferson prior to first accounts with Mr. Nicholas. Letter from Lyle, Manchester, calls for delay until T. J. returns from Philadelphia. Accounts with Mr. Harvie and Dr. Walker.   [2490]

1791 Oct. 7. T. J. to JAMES STRANGE. ALS. 1 p. Fragment. Letterpress copy. With ANS, Letterpress copy, 1791 Oct. 7, T. J. to N. POPE. Edgehill-Randolph Papers. #5533.

Pope to pay note from proceeds of suits in Henrico District Court against Robert Lewis and Samuel Woodson of Goochland. Returns to Philadelphia. Pope to pay Strange or Donald Scott.   [2491]

1791 Oct. 25. T. J., Philadelphia, to MATTHEW MAURY. ALS. 1 p. Letterpress copy. Endorsed by T. J. Edgehill-Randolph Papers. #5533.

Encloses payment promised in letter from Monticello, in care of Maury's brother, Fredericksburg. Redeemable in U.S. Collector's Office.   [2492]

1791 Nov. 6. T. J., Philadelphia, to FRANCIS EPPES. L. 1 p. 19th-century copy. Edgehill-Randolph Papers. #5533.

Mail difficulties. Bevin's suit. John Wayles Eppes well, reading Coke on Littleton. George Washington's speech indicates Congress' work load. Mentions Maria, Mrs. Eppes.   [2493]

1791 Nov. 7. GEORGE WASHINGTON COMMISSION TO THOMAS JOHNSON OF MARYLAND AS ASSOCIATE JUSTICE OF U.S. SUPREME COURT. DS. Signed by T. J. 1 p. Photostat. Original owned by Bradley T. Johnson. #5594-a.   [2494]

1791 Nov. 13. T. J., Philadelphia, to FRANCIS EPPES. L. 1 p. Fragment. 19th-century copy. Edgehill-Randolph Papers. #5533.

Will pay John Wayles Eppes for horse gotten by Francis Eppes. To breed a Jack with Mazzei's Jenny. [Break in text.] Will pay his British debts; objects to paying those of others. Irregularity in Bevin suit may release T. J. and Francis Eppes. Maria well, writes to Elizabeth Wayles Eppes. John Wayles Eppes's studies. [2495]

1791 Dec. 4. T. J., Philadelphia, to JOHN DOBSON. ALS. 2 pp. Fragment. Letter-press copy. Pages 1 and 2 only. Edgehill-Randolph Papers. #5533.
   See Item 316. [2496]

1791. T. J. NOTES ON TREES, FLOWERS, AND SHRUBS OF PRINCE WILLIAM COUNTY, VA. AD. 2 pp. McGregor Library. #3620. [2497]

[1791–1794]. T. J. NOTES ON WINES. AD. 4 pp. Photostat. Original owned by Herbert R. Strauss. #6643-a.
   Bordeaux, Lisbon, Burgundy. Recommends Mr. Fenwick, U.S. Consul at Bordeaux and purchasing agent at Amsterdam. [2498]

1792 Mar. 11. T. J., Philadelphia, to FRANCIS EPPES. L. 1 p. 19th-century copy. Edgehill-Randolph Papers. #5533.
   Demand on Mr. Bannister. Account of sale: slaves brought little, but, with profit from sale of Cumberland land, will cover installment to John Hanson. Sale of Elkhill and debts, including those due Jones and Hanbury. Mentions Mr. Lewis. Health of Maria and John Wayles Eppes. Mentions Elizabeth Wayles Eppes. [2499]

1792 Apr. 9. THOMAS MANN RANDOLPH, JR., Monticello, to T. J. ALS. 1 p. Endorsed by T. J. Edgehill-Randolph Papers. #5533.
   Letter for British partners. Hares damaged orchard. Gilmer ill. [2500]

1792 Apr. 11. T. J. to SENATORS AND REPRESENTATIVES FROM VIRGINIA. AN. 1 p. Microfilm. Original owned by James Monroe Museum and Memorial Library, Fredericksburg. #3159.
   Collection of British debts in Virginia courts. [2501]

1792 May 11. T. J., Philadelphia, to MARTHA JEFFERSON RANDOLPH. L. 1 p. 19th-century copy. Edgehill-Randolph Papers. #5533.
   Correspondence with Thomas Mann Randolph, Jr. Congress adjourned. James Monroe will bring watch, Paine's *Rights of Man*, and T. J.'s copy of Johann Caspar Lavater's *Aphorisms*. Mrs. Pine to England; Maria to Mrs. Brodeau. George Washington to Mount Vernon. T. J. to Monticello. Mentions Anne Cary Randolph. [2502]

1792 June 14. T. J., Philadelphia, to THOMAS PINCKNEY. ALS. 2 pp. Fragment. Last 2 pages only. Photostat. Location of original not known. #3449. Printed: L and B VIII, 375–77.
   Personnel for mint. Wants Drost and Boulton. Mr. Morris can hire in France. [2503]

1792 June 15. T. J., Philadelphia, to NATHANIEL BURWELL, the Grove, near Williamsburg. ALS. 1 p. #5727.
   Mrs. Paradise asks inventory of estate in Virginia. Paradise trustees in England can collect proceeds from sale of public lands. [2504]

1792 July–1793 Oct. 16. T. J. ACCOUNT BOOK. AD. 1 p. Partly in unidentified hand. #6004.
   Farm business. Account for work done by William. [2505]

1792 Sept. 10. T. J., Monticello, to DANIEL HYLTON. ALS. 3 pp. Fragment. Letterpress copy. Break in text between pages numbered 2 and 4. Edgehill-Randolph Papers. #5533.

Will sell Elkhill if Greenbrier profits not adequate. Mr. Banks can sell regardless of mortgages. For purposes of litigation, Greenbrier County might be in the East Indies. Elkhill safer with T. J. Dr. Taylor's bond. T. J. to Philadelphia. Martin may have purchaser. Mr. Banks wrote from Alexandria. [2506]

1792 Sept. 23. T. J. MEMORANDUM FOR MR. CLARKSON. AD. 3 pp. Edgehill-Randolph Papers. #5533.

Household affairs involving butcher, Ben Calvard or Calvert, Thomas Mann Randolph, Jr., John Quarles, Robert Smith, Thomas Norris, John Henderson's executors, Thomas Massey, Nicholas Lewis, Joseph Mansfield, wheat, Sheriff of Albemarle, Peter Marks, Richmond, Va., Daniel Wood, Mr. Clarkson, fencing, hemp and cotton growing, slaves, stone cutting, limestone, tools, wheel making, woodcutting, sand moving, log houses, Mr. Henderson, Randolph family supplies, Christmas livestock lists, grain sales, and orchard grubbing. [2507]

1792 Sept. 25. T. J. to NICHOLAS LEWIS. ADS. Owned by T. J. Memorial Foundation. #7443-e.

Receipt for books and papers relative to superintendence of T. J.'s affairs from 1783. [2507-a]

1792 Nov. 2. T. J., Philadelphia, to THOMAS MANN RANDOLPH, Jr. ALS. 2 pp. Owned by T. J. Memorial Foundation. #4726-a.

Health of Anne Cary Randolph and Thomas Jefferson Randolph. Mr. and Mrs. James Monroe, James Madison, and members of Congress arrived. Republican victory in Pennsylvania. Monocrats displeased. Mentions Martha and Maria. [2508]

1792 Nov. 2. T. J., Philadelphia, to THOMAS MANN RANDOLPH, JR. L. 2 pp. 19th-century copy. Edgehill-Randolph Papers. #5533.

Duplicates item 2508. [2509]

1792 Nov. 2. T. J., Philadelphia, to COL. GAMBLE. L. 1 p. 19th-century copy. Edgehill-Randolph Papers. #5533.

Order from Mr. Vaughan on John Hopkins payable to Gamble for account of Mr. Derieux. [2510]

1792 Nov. 14. T. J., Philadelphia, to M. DUMAS. ALS. 1 p. Photostat. Original owned by O. O. Fisher. #3449.

Plans to retire. Directs mail to successor. [2511]

1792 Dec. 19. T. J., Philadelphia, to [FRANCIS] EPPES. L. 1 p. 19th-century copy. Edgehill-Randolph Papers. #5533.

Proceeds from John Wayles's estate to be placed with James Brown, Richmond. Horse breeding. Retreat of Duke of Brunswick. John Wayles Eppes well. Mentions Mrs. Eppes. [2512]

1792 Dec. 25. T. J., Philadelphia, to [ROBERT] RUTHERFORD. ALS. 5 pp. Owned by George Green Shackelford. #3525-h.

Motions concerning weights and measures, now pending in Senate committee, and formerly considered by House of Representatives committee. [2513]

[1792] T. J. to MARIA JEFFERSON. AN. 1 p. Owned by Miss Florence P. Kennedy. #5385-o.

Wants Mrs. Pine's price for portrait of James Madison. [2514]

1793 Jan. 24. THOMAS MANN RANDOLPH, JR., Monticello, to T. J., Philadelphia. ALS. 3 pp. Endorsed by T. J. Edgehill-Randolph Papers. #5533.

T. J. Wrote to Randolph Jefferson. James Kinsolving bought Dinah and children from Clarkson. Col. Lewis and Col. Bell set value. Bedford sale. Kinsolving joined by John Burnley. Limestone and wood cutting, orchard grubbing. Stable to be built. Martha's report of Charlottesville fire premature. Dyvers and Lindsey lost heavily. Will tell Mr. Hylton at Richmond about stalactite. Clothes for Negroes at neither Monticello nor Mr. Brown's. Anne Cary Randolph ill; Gilmer treating. Martha writes to Maria. French victory. [2515]

1793 Feb. 18. T. J., Philadelphia, to THOMAS MANN RANDOLPH, JR. L. 2 pp. 19th-century copy. Contains N, 19th-century copy, n.d., T. J. to THOMAS MANN RANDOLPH, JR. Edgehill-Randolph Papers. #5533. Printed: Betts, *Farm Book*, 98, extract, and 165, extract.

Randolph's letter to Maria. Monticello work. Bedford sale. Will secure Maryland tenant for land on Shadwell side of river; will hire Negroes to tenant. To Head of Elk when Congress adjourns. Horse, Brimmer. Joseph accidentally killed Matchless. Now has old pair and Tarquin, to be sold. Capt. Swaille of schooner *Mary* bound Norfolk to Richmond brings servants' clothes care Mr. Brown. Note adds that model threshing machine comes by Capt. Weymouth, ship *Ellice*, New York to Norfolk, care Col. Gamble. Machine to be moved from Richmond. [2516]

1793 Feb. 27. T. J., Philadelphia, to FRANCIS EPPES. L. 1 p. 19th-century copy. Edgehill-Randolph Papers. #5533.

More time for John Wayles Eppes because Commissioners to Indian Treaty delayed. Mr. Cary's executor to send money for moving. Mentions Elizabeth Wayles Eppes. [2517]

1793 Mar. 10. T. J., Philadelphia, to DR. CURRIE. L. 1 p. 19th-century copy. Edgehill-Randolph Papers. #5533.

Mr. Barton replaced by Mr. Sergeant who will answer suit against Griffin. Military land rights west of Ohio and Act of Congress affecting them. W. Ronald's affairs. T. J. protected by land mortgage and Beaverdam land transaction. [2518]

1793 Mar. 17. T. J., Philadelphia, to FRANCIS EPPES. L. 2 pp. 19th-century copy. Edgehill-Randolph Papers. #5533.

John Wayles Eppes's trip to the Indian Treaty. Has given up Philadelphia house; moving furniture to Virginia. John Wayles Eppes should study at Williamsburg. Books from Ireland addressed to T. J. care James Brown, Richmond. Packages from England. Carr money. Mentions Mrs. Eppes and Eppington. [2519]

1793 Mar. 17. T. J., Philadelphia, to FRANCIS EPPES. ALS. 1 p. Fragment. Letterpress copy. 1st p. only. Edgehill-Randolph Papers. #5533.

Duplicates item 2519. [2520]

1793 Mar. 21. T. J., Philadelphia, to SAMUEL COOPER JOHONNET. LS. 2 pp. Owned by George Green Shackelford. #3525-y.

Orders precautions to be taken by Consular Service in event of war in Europe. Consuls' surety bonds. Forwarding of mail to Secretary of State at Philadelphia.
[2520-a]

1793 Apr. 14. T. J., Philadelphia, to PETER CARR. L. 1 p. 19th-century copy. Edgehill-Randolph Papers. #5533.

Letter for Dabney Carr advising him to secure Coke's *Institutes*, a law dictionary, and White Kennett's *Compleat History of England*. Peter Carr controls Negroes. Mentions Virginia, Thomas Mann Randolph, Jr., Martha, "Timon."   [2521]

1793 Apr. 14. T. J., Philadelphia, to JOHN WAYLES EPPES. L. 1 p. 19th-century copy. Edgehill-Randolph Papers. #5533.

Account of Peter Gordon, shoemaker. Beverly Randolph at Baltimore. George Washington expected at Philadelphia. Mentions Maria, Francis, and Elizabeth Wayles Eppes.   [2522]

1793 Apr. 20. T. J., Philadelphia, to THOMAS PINCKNEY. ALS. 1 p. 1st page only. Photostat. Location of original not known. #3449. Printed: L and B IX, 66–67; TJR III, 228–29.

William Penn mail. No progress with Mr. Hammond. Wants Mr. Droz for mint.
[2523]

1793 Apr. 28. T. J., Philadelphia, to MARTHA JEFFERSON RANDOLPH. L. 2 pp. Trist copy. Microfilm. Original owned by James Monroe Museum and Memorial Library, Fredericksburg. #3159.

No news from Monticello. Maria ill. Bizarre scandal rumored in Richmond *Gazette*. Mentions Thomas Mann Randolph, Jr.   [2524]

1793 May 16. MARTHA JEFFERSON RANDOLPH, Monticello, to T. J. ALS. 2 pp. Endorsed by T. J. Edgehill-Randolph Papers. #5533.

Connection of herself and Thomas Mann Randolph, Jr. with Bizarre scandal. Mentions Richard Randolph, Anne Cary Randolph of Bizarre, and David Randolph. Livestock and gardening. Mentions Maria.   [2525]

1793 June 24. T. J., Philadelphia, to THOMAS MANN RANDOLPH, JR. L. 2 pp. 19th-century copy. Edgehill-Randolph Papers. #5533. Printed: Ford VI, 316–18.

George Washington at Mount Vernon. Maria has mumps. Manager from Elkton. Maryland tenants. May ask Clarkson to take east side of river. Effects in France of Dumouriez's desertion. Brittany insurrection, possible war between England and France. Threshing machine. Mentions Maria.   [2526]

1793 July 14. T. J. to [JAMES MADISON]. L. 1 p. 19th-century copy. Edgehill-Randolph Papers. #5533.

Congress to convene. Must meet Madison in Philadelphia or at Monticello. Trouble with French Minister and with England. Letter to James Monroe. [2527]

1793 Aug. 11. T. J. to HENRY KNOX. L. 1 p. 19th-century copy. Edgehill-Randolph Papers. #5533.

Asking Knox to direct enclosure to Judge Symes of Jersey. Proposition for publishing rules of Aug. 3 (Genet affair?) in newspapers with suggested preface. [2527-a]

1793 Aug. 11. T. J. to THOMAS MANN RANDOLPH. L. 1 p. 19th-century copy. Edgehill-Randolph Papers. #5533.
Requesting Randolph to deliver confidential letter to James Madison. [2527-b]

1793 Aug. 12. T. J., Monticello, to MR. RITTENHOUSE. ANS. 1 p. #6411.
To see him again. Mentions Mrs. Rittenhouse. [2528]

1793 Sept. 15. T. J., Schuylkill, to DR. CURRIE. L. 1 p. 19th-century copy. Edgehill-Randolph Papers. #5533.
Letter to Mr. Sergeant. Mentions fever and Mrs. Currie. Hopes to leave Philadelphia. [2529]

[1793?] Sept. 15. T. J., Schuylkill, to MARTHA JEFFERSON RANDOLPH. L. 1 p. 19th-century copy. Edgehill-Randolph Papers. #5533.
Fever killed Dupont, French Consul, and Wright, the painter. Lieper said dead. J. Barclay ill. Hamilton and wife well. Banks open. Mentions George Washington and Congress. [2530]

1793 Dec. 15. T. J., Philadelphia, to MARIA JEFFERSON. ALS. 1 p. Photostat. Original owned by Mrs. Harold W. Wilson. #5385-v. Printed: SNR, 188–89.
Letter to Thomas Mann Randolph, Jr. Letters from Martha and Maria. Mr. Watson makes writing desk. Saw Sally Cropper who was at Trenton at Mrs. Fullerton's house. Maid died of fever. Wants horse at Fredericksburg. Eli Alexander of Elkton to operate plantation under Byrd Rogers. [2531]

[1793]. T. J. to MARTHA JEFFERSON RANDOLPH. ALS. 1 p. Fragment. Letterpress copy. Last page only. Edgehill-Randolph Papers. #5533.
Fragmentary reference to Thomas Mann Randolph, Jr. Maria writes to Mr. Randolph. [2532]

[1793]. T. J. NOTES ON MR. CLAY'S THRESHING MACHINE. AD. 2 pp. Edgehill-Randolph Papers. #5533.
Poetry on verso. [2533]

[1793]. T. J. NOTES ON ARTHUR YOUNG'S LETTER TO THE PRESIDENT OF JAN. '92. D. 4 pp. 19th-century copy of extract. #4024.
Cost of slave labor, referring to Buffon's tables, compared to cost of free labor in England, using Suffolk as example. [2533-a]

1794 Apr. 16. T. J. SURVEY MAP OF ROAD FROM SECRETARY'S FORD. AD. 1 p. 8" x 12⅜". Edgehill-Randolph Papers. #5533. Cf. Betts, *Garden Book*, Plate XIV.
Road to the Thoroughfare. [2534]

1794 Apr. 26. T. J. to JOHN GARLAND JEFFERSON. ALS. Press copy. Final 2 pp. only. [First page at MHi.] Edgehill-Randolph Papers. #5533.
Settlement of unidentified estate. Advising suit against Gen. Harrington as

executor. Ignorance of North Carolina laws, judges, and courts. Infants' legal rights. Recourse open to federal district and supreme court of U.S.   [2534-a]

1794 June 8. T. J., Eppington, to [?]. ALS. 1 p. #7447.
   Account with Donald and Burton from Charlottesville. Mentions Clow and Company.   [2535]

1794 July 29. T. J. SURVEY MAP OF FIELDS AT LEGO. AD. 1 p. 8" x 12⅜". Edgehill-Randolph Papers. #5533. Cf. Betts, *Garden Book*, Plate XV.
   Shows boundary with river.   [2536]

1794 Aug. 28. T. J., Monticello, to FRANCIS EPPES, Eppington. ALS. 2 pp. Owned by T. J. Memorial Foundation. #5385-r.
   Mr. Jones's Monroe papers omit deeds on R. and D. Randolph. John Marshall sent note on *Guineaman*. May go to Bedford. Receipt in John Randolph case. Mentions Elizabeth Wayles Eppes, Thomas Mann Randolph, Jr., Martha, Mr. Wickham, Mr. Innes, Mr. and Mrs. Skipwith.   [2537]

1794 Dec. 24. T. J. DEED OF MANUMISSION TO ROBERT HEMINGS. ADS. 1 p. #5589.
   Frees Hemings, son of Betty Hemings. Witnessed by Dabney Carr and John Nicholas.   [2537-a]

[1794]. T. J. to [?]. ALS. Fragment. 1 p. Letterpress copy. Last page only. Edgehill-Randolph Papers. #5533.
   Tobacco sold to Messrs. Adams, Perkins, Buchannan, and Brown. Richmond merchant has books.   [2538]

1795 May 8. T. J., Monticello, to COL. CALLIS, Louisa. ALS. 1 p. Photostat. Original owned by John P. McGuire, Jr. #3367.
   May buy slave Nance from Mr. and Mrs. Hastings Marks. Wants Callis to arrange purchase.   [2539]

1795 June 16. THREE T. J. SURVEY MAPS, UNIDENTIFIED. AD. Each item 1 p. 7¾" x 9¼"; 7¾" x 9¼"; 12⅜" x 8". Edgehill-Randolph Papers. #5533. [2540]

1795 Aug. 12. T. J., Monticello, to JOSIAH DONATH, Philadelphia. ALS. 1 p. #3456.
   Bohemian glass.   [2541]

1795 Sept. 16. T. J., Monticello, to JOHN BARNES. ALS. 1 p. Letterpress copy. Edgehill-Randolph Papers. #5533.
   Letter of introduction for Mr. Peyton, merchant of Milton, to trade in Philadelphia. Barnes to send tea, glasses, tin plates, solder, and pure tin by Peyton. J. Bringhurst knows supply of pure tin.   [2542]

1795 Oct. 1. T. J., Monticello, to BUSHROD WASHINGTON, Richmond. ALS. 2 pp. #6755.
   Banks's suit against T. J. as former governor of Virginia.   [2543]

1795–1796. T. J. FARM BOOK. AD. 2 pp. #3946. Cf. Betts, *Farm Book*, 47, 48.
   Bread lists for Monticello, Mr. Petit, and Mr. Page. Labor lists for Monticello,

Tufton, Shadwell, and Lego. General clothing list. Lists white workers Mr. Buck, Mr. Watson, Mr. Bailey. [2544]

1796 Feb. 5. T. J. DEED OF MANUMISSION TO JAMES HEMINGS. ADS. 1 p. #5589. Printed: Betts, *Farm Book*, 15, 16.

Frees Hemings, son of Betty Hemings. Witnessed by John Carr and Francis Anderson. [2545]

1796 Feb. 21. T. J. POWER OF ATTORNEY. ADS. 2 pp. Photocopy. Original owned by Victor B. Levit. #8265-b.

John Barnes to act for William Short in collecting interest on stock from the Treasury or Bank of the U.S. Witnessed by Thomas Bell, justice of the peace for Albemarle County; certified by John Nicholas. [2545-a]

1796 Dec. 27. T. J., Monticello, to EDWARD RUTLEDGE. ALS. 3 pp. Photocopy. Original owned by Paul Mellon. #7289-b. Partially printed: L and B IX, 352–55.

Wishes to obtain cowpeas from Charleston, S. C., to be shipped to Charles Johnston & Co., Richmond. Draft paid by John Barnes of Philadelphia. Lieth machine for threshing wheat. Rice. Reluctance to run in Election of 1796; suffers from slanders. Mentions newspapers, John Adams, Rutledge's son, and Thomas Pinckney. [2545-b]

1797 Mar. 11. T. J., Philadelphia, to MARIA JEFFERSON. AL. 1 p. Letterpress copy. Edgehill-Randolph Papers. #5533.

See Item 588. [2546]

1797 June 14. T. J. to MARIA JEFFERSON. AL. 1 p. File draft. Edgehill-Randolph Papers. #5533.

Her marriage to John Wayles Eppes. Offers Pantops. Can make road to Edgehill to make it close as Monticello. Congressional debates. [2547]

1797 July 18. T. J., Monticello, to JOHN BARNES. ALS. 1 p. Letterpress copy. Edgehill-Randolph Papers. #5533.

Box containing mammoth's tooth and another bone which Mr. Johnston has in Philadelphia. Tooth to be addressed to Prince of Parma, delivered to Yrujo, Spanish minister. Notes, one paid to Charles Johnston and Company. Mentions Mr. Short. [2548]

1797 Aug. 28. T. J., Monticello, to ST. GEORGE TUCKER, Williamsburg. ALS. 2 pp. Photostat. Original owned by O. O. Fisher. #3449. Printed: L and B IX, 417–19.

Santo Domingo revolt. Concern about slave revolts in U.S. Financing government in U.S. and Europe. [2549]

1797 Oct. 8. T. J., Monticello, to JOHN BARNES. ALS. Photocopy of press copy. Original owned by Thomas Jefferson Coolidge and Miss Ellen Coolidge Burke. #5156-a.

Encloses power of attorney for Barnes to draw on William Short's dividends for payment to James Monroe in Philadelphia. [2549-a]

1797 Oct. 12. MARRIAGE INDENTURE OF JOHN WAYLES EPPES AND MARIA JEFFERSON. In hand of T. J. AD. 2 pp. Letterpress copy. Edgehill-Randolph Papers. #5533.

Binds Francis, Elizabeth Wayles, and John Wayles Eppes of Chesterfield and Thomas and Maria Jefferson. Francis Eppes conveys land at Bermuda Hundred on James River and at Martin's Swamp next to David Meade Randolph's land. T. J. conveys Pantops, formerly Smith land on Rivanna River in Albemarle, slaves, etc. Witnessed by Richard Richardson, Hugh Chisolm, and Matthew Toler.   [2550]

1797 Oct. 12. MARRIAGE INDENTURE OF JOHN WAYLES EPPES AND MARIA JEFFERSON. In hand of T. J. AD. 1 p. Fragment. 1st page only. Letterpress copy. Edgehill-Randolph Papers. #5533.

Binds Thomas and Maria Jefferson of Albemarle and Francis, Elizabeth Wayles, and John Wayles Eppes of Chesterfield. T. J. conveys Angola on Appomattox River, Cumberland. Francis Eppes conveys Bermuda Hundred, Chesterfield. T. J. conveys Pantops, formerly Smith land, on Rivanna River, bounded by Lego, formerly Edwin Hickman land, and slaves.   [2551]

1797 Dec. 31. T. J. TO MR. TAZEWELL. ALS. 1 p. #6918.

Letter for Mr. Henry. Mr. Blount and Mr. Beckley may read it.   [2552]

1797. T. J. to FRANCIS EPPES. ALS. 2 pp. File draft. Edgehill-Randolph Papers. #5533.

Marriage of Maria Jefferson and John Wayles Eppes. Will make settlement like that with Thomas Mann Randolph, Jr. and Martha Jefferson Randolph. Rather than Poplar Forest, giving Pantops opposite Monticello. Angola exchange; interests in Bedford. Monticello roofing.   [2553]

[Post-1797]. T. J. to MARIA JEFFERSON EPPES. Lettercover. 1 p. #6004. [2554]

1798 Jan. 7. T. J., Philadelphia, to MARIA JEFFERSON EPPES, Eppington. L. 3 pp. 19th-century copy. Photostat. Original owned by M. Howard Bradley. #5085. Printed: SNR, 207–8.

Letters from John Wayles Eppes and Kitty Church. Discusses harmony in marriage. Mr. Bolling's drunkenness at Chestnut Grove. Virginia estates.   [2555]

1798 Feb. 5. T. J., Philadelphia, to DAVID LONGWORTH, New York. ALS. 1 p. Photostat. Original owned by Albert Adam Bieber. #6279.

Received in Virginia letter about Fénelon's *Télémachus*. Edition equal to those from Europe.   [2556]

1798 Feb. 15. T. J., Philadelphia, to JOHN BARNES. ALS. 1 p. Edgehill-Randolph Papers. #5533.

Bill of exchange to Samuel H. Smith.   [2557]

1798 Feb. 26. MARTHA JEFFERSON RANDOLPH, Belmont, to T. J. 19th-century copy of extract. 2 pp. Owned by the Misses Margaret and Olivia Taylor. #8937.

Martha established at Belmont after move from Varina. Thomas Mann Randolph, Jr. has wheelwright, carpenter, smith, and other workmen. Mr. and Mrs. P. Carr visiting. Ellen's health.   [2557-a]

1798 Mar. 8. T. J., Philadelphia, to THOMAS MANN RANDOLPH, JR. AL. 1 p. Fragment. First page only. Letterpress copy. Edgehill-Randolph Papers. #5533. Printed: Betts, *Garden Book*, 260–61, extract.

George Jefferson to handle letter. Mr. Page and George know how to handle seed when arrived at Charlottesville or Milton. Box for Mr. Strickland. French Directory acted against Philadelphia's English merchants. [2558]

1798 Apr. 1. T. J., Philadelphia, to MARIA JEFFERSON EPPES. AL. 1 p. File draft. Owned by Mrs. Harold W. Wilson. #5385-v.

Would make her private secretary at Monticello. Letter from John Wayles Eppes. Richmond mail. Orders for Quarrier to deliver chariot. May visit Eppington. Work at Monticello. Congress to adjourn late. Mr. Trist rents George Nicholas' house in Charlottesville. [2559]

1798 [Apr. 30]. THADDEUS KOSCIUSZKO to T. J. D. Draft in T. J.'s hand. 1 p. Photocopy. Original owned by National Museum, Cracow, Poland. #9013-a.

Power of attorney. [2559-a]

1798 May 5. T. J. to JOHN BARNES. ALS. 1 p. Edgehill-Randolph Papers. #5533.

Bill of exchange to James Cary. [2560]

1798 May 17. T. J., Philadelphia, to MARTHA JEFFERSON RANDOLPH. ALS. 1 p. Letterpress copy. Edgehill-Randolph Papers. #5533. Printed: SNR, 210–11, extract.

Letter to Thomas Mann Randolph, Jr. Maria and John Wayles Eppes should go to Richmond from Monticello. Politics. Randolph children likely to forget T. J. [2561]

1798 May 18. T. J., Philadelphia, to MARIA JEFFERSON EPPES. ALS. 1 p. Letterpress copy. Edgehill-Randolph Papers. #5533.

Letter from Mr. Eppes. Congress to adjourn. Wants Maria and John Wayles Eppes to go to Monticello. Harpsichord at Monticello. Mentions Eppington, Eppes family. [2562]

1798 June 14. T. J., Philadelphia, to JOHN STEELE, COMPTROLLER OF U.S. ALS. 1 p. #5845.

Sum due William Short from U.S. Treasury to be paid John Barnes. Mentions Bank of U.S. [2563]

[1798–1800]. THOMAS MANN RANDOLPH, JR. MEMORANDUM. AMS. On verso of lettercover in T. J.'s hand to Thomas Mann Randolph, Jr. #6089-a.

English reasons for war with France. [2564]

1799 Jan. 3. T. J., Philadelphia, to ALEXANDER GARRETT. ALS. 1 p. #3695.

Assistant Postmaster General needs date of mail irregularity reported by Garrett and Mr. Watson. [2565]

1799 Jan. 9. T. J., Philadelphia, to JOHN BARNES. ADS. 1 p. Edgehill-Randolph Papers. #5533.

Bill of exchange to John Francis. [2566]

1799 Jan. 22. T. J. to JOHN BARNES. ADS. 1 p. Edgehill-Randolph Papers. #5533.
Bill of exchange to Mrs. Gardner, washer woman. Receipted by Jacob Lawrence for Mrs. Gardner.   [2567]

1799 Jan. 25. T. J., Philadelphia, to HENRY REMSEN. ALS. 1 p. McGregor Library. #3258.
Letter by British packet. Logan's trip to France. John Barnes will pay funds due. Mentions Virginia, Hamburg, Paris, newspapers.   [2568]

1799 Jan. 28. T. J. to JOHN BARNES. ADS. 1 p. Edgehill-Randolph Papers. #5533.
Bill of exchange to Stevens Thomson Mason. Receipted by Richard Williams for Stevens Thomson Mason.   [2569]

1799 Feb. 7. T. J., Philadelphia, to MARIA JEFFERSON EPPES. AL. 1 p. Signature cut. Owned by Miss Florence P. Kennedy. #5385-o. Printed: SNR, 216–17.
Quotes Ossian. Trip to Monticello. Eppington, via Fredericksburg and Richmond, too far. T. J. thinks she is at Montblanco. Letter to John Wayles Eppes.
                                                                                  [2570]

1799 Feb. 7. T. J., Philadelphia, to MARIA JEFFERSON EPPES. L. 1 p. Letterpress copy. Edgehill-Randolph Papers. #5533.
Duplicates item 2570.   [2571]

1799 Feb. 24. EDMUND PENDLETON, Virginia, to T. J. ALS. 2 pp. Endorsed by T. J. #5775.
Too ill to go to Philadelphia. Pendleton's republican ideas to be published in Richmond. Virginia politics.   [2572]

1799 May 13. T. J. to JAMES MONROE. ALS. 1 p. Microfilm. Original owned by James Monroe Museum and Memorial Library, Fredericksburg. #3159.
Grievances of people of Charlottesville and Milton to go to Mr. Divers.   [2573]

1799 June 8. T. J. LETTERCOVER, Signed, to HENRY REMSEN, New York. Photocopy. Original owned by Bruce E. Engstler. #7786.   [2574]

1799 June 14. T. J., Monticello, to JOHN BARNES. ADS. 1 p. Edgehill-Randolph Papers. #5533.
Bill of exchange to Dr. David Jackson.   [2575]

1799 Sept. 5. T. J., Monticello, to WILSON CARY NICHOLAS. ALS. 2 pp. Edgehill-Randolph Papers. #5533. Printed: L and B X, 130–32.
Discussed Kentucky-Virginia resolutions with Madison. Persuaded by Madison to omit references to secession. Loss of John Nicholas and visit of John Marshall to Kentucky create problems.   [2576]

1799 Oct. 1. T. J. LEASE OF SHADWELL TO CRAVEN PEYTON. ADS. 2 pp. Owned by Office of Clerk of Albemarle County Court. #5145. Printed: Betts, *Farm Book*, 166–68.
Witnessed by James Dinsmore, Robert Bolling, and Richard Richardson. Mentions Monticello.   [2577]

1799 Nov. 28. T. J., Albemarle County, to [?]. ANS. 1 p. McGregor Library. #4898.
   John Haden to guide Chickasaw Indians to see Governor in Richmond.   [2578]

1799 Dec. 29. JAMES MADISON to T. J. L. 1 p. Extract. 19th-century copy.
Edgehill-Randolph Papers. #5533.
   See item 2706.   [2579]

1799 Dec. 30. T. J., Philadelphia, to JOHN STEELE, COMPTROLLER OF THE
U.S. ALS. 1 p. Photostat. Original owned by Frank Ix, Jr. #6820.
   William Short's U.S. Treasury account payable to John Barnes.   [2580]

[1799]. T. J. to [?]. ALS. Fragment. 1 p. Letterpress copy. Last page only. Edgehill-
Randolph Papers. #5533.
   Wheat crop. Mentions Mr. Donald and Philadelphia.   [2581]

1800 Jan. 1. T. J. to JOHN BARNES. ADS. 1 p. Edgehill-Randolph Papers. #5533.
   Bill of exchange to Tench Coxe. Receipted by Ezekiel Foreman for Tench Coxe.
                                                                        [2582]

1800 Jan. 13. T. J., Senate Chamber, to MR. PARKER, Franklin Court. ALS. 1 p.
#8002.
   Houdon's equestrian statue of Washington in the Capitol at Richmond. Prices
in Paris, Rome, and Florence. Mentions sculptor Ceracchi.   [2582-a]

1800 Feb. 10. T. J., Philadelphia, to JOHN BARNES. ADS. 1 p. Edgehill-Randolph
Papers. #5533.
   Bill of exchange to Maurice Rogers.   [2583]

1800 Feb. 12. T. J., Philadelphia, to JOHN BARNES. ADS. 1 p. Edgehill-Randolph
Papers. #5533.
   Bill of exchange to John Hawkins.   [2584]

1800 Feb. 26. T. J. to JOHN BARNES. ADS. 1 p. Edgehill-Randolph Papers. #5533.
   Bill of exchange to T. J.   [2585]

1800 Feb. 28. T. J., Philadelphia, to GEORGE WYTHE. ALS. 2 pp. Photostat.
Original owned by Henry N. Flynt. #4669.
   Parliamentary irregularities of Continental Congress and U.S. House of Representatives. Senate better. Encloses text of T. J. *Manual of Parliamentary Practice*
for Wythe's corrections.   [2586]

1800 Mar. 4. T. J., Philadelphia, to HENRY REMSEN. ALS. 1 p. Letterpress copy.
Owned by Mrs. Edwin Page Kirk. #5291.
   Envoys at Lisbon. Sell tobacco to Mr. Lieper, not to French. Bordeaux and
London prices. West Indies stock. John Barnes to pay draft. New York market.
Congress to adjourn.   [2587]

1800 Mar. 24. JOHN KELLY RECEIPT to T. J. AD. 1 p. Edgehill-Randolph Papers. #5533.
   Nails and brads delivered by R. Richardson.   [2588]

1800 Aug. 11. T. J., Monticello, to PHILIP NORBORNE NICHOLAS. ALS.
Labelled "duplicate." 1 p. #8404.
Architectural plan for Nicholas' house. Peter Carr's plan.   [2588-a]

1800 Aug. 30. T. J., Monticello, to JOHN BEELE BOARDLY. ALS. 1 p. Owned
by George Green Shackelford. #3525-d.
Mrs. Randolph, whom Boardly knew in England, holds marriage contract annuity payable by Peter Randolph, Peyton Randolph, and Philip Grymes. Peter
Randolph's estate insolvent. Edmund Randolph is Peyton Randolph's heir. Suit
filed against Philip Grymes, who can claim against Edmund Peyton, who cannot
pay.   [2589]

1800 Dec. 17. REMBRANDT PEALE to T. J., Washington. ALS. 3 pp. Endorsed
by T. J. Owned by T. J. Memorial Foundation. #5385-k.
Wants to study in Europe as did John Trumbull. Prefers diplomatic post in
France to one in Italy.   [2590]

1800 Dec. 23. T. J., Washington, to JOHN WAYLES EPPES. ALS. 1 p. McGregor
Library. #4979.
Congress assembled. Housing costs more than at Philadelphia. Senate opposition
to French treaty. Judiciary. Territorial governments. Votes of Vermont, Kentucky,
Tennessee uncertain. Republican candidates have more votes than Federalists, Mr.
Adams and Mr. Pinckney. Mr. Powell builds nailery. Mentions Col. Burr, Maria,
and Edgehill.   [2591]

[1800]. T. J. NOTES ON MILEAGES. AD. 2 pp. #6225.
Lists Monticello, Thornton Gap, Ruffner's, Cunningham's Mill, Rockfish Gap,
Kennerley's, Madison's Cove, Jones's, Gilbert's, Narrow Passage, Rappidan, Robin-
son River, Brown's Culpeper Court House, Hedgeman River, Fauquier Court
House, Germantown, [Pa.?], Widow Nevill's, West's Ordinary, Leesburg, Know-
land's Ferry, Zane's, Winchester, Threetons, McCormack's, Harper's Ferry, Fred-
erictown, [Md.?], Bentley's. Taverns listed, Leesburg: McEntire's, Indian King;
Frederictown: Crush's, Sycamore Tree; Tawney Town: Mrs. Charlton's, Caleb's,
Bacchus and Threetons; Petersburg: Kurtz's, The Swan; McAllister's Town: Rhen-
egher's; Yorktown: White's, Sign of the Lemon; Lancaster: Rickhart's, The Bear.
Other towns: Alexandria, Colchester, Dumfries, Lansdowne, Elkrun Church,
Piscotaway, Port Tobacco, Howe's Ferry, Port Royal, Bowling Green, Hanover
Court House, Goodall's, Richmond.   [2592]

[1800]. T. J. SKETCH FOR HOUSE AND DEPENDENCY. AD. 1 p. Fragment.
Addressed on verso to T. J., Albemarle. #6225. See Nichols, Item 465.   [2593]

1801 Feb. 7. THOMAS MANN RANDOLPH, JR. to T. J. ALS. 1 p. Endorsed by
T. J. Edgehill-Randolph Papers. #5533.
Coming election. Dinsmore's account. Mentions Lillie [Gabriel Lilly?] and Dr.
Bache.   [2594]

1801 Feb. 22. T. J., Washington, to JOHN WAYLES EPPES. ALS. 2 pp. Owned by
Miss Florence P. Kennedy. #5385-o.
Mr. Tyler took letter to Maria. Eppes family at Monticello. Bedford stock.

Gibson and Jefferson to pay for horses. Horses from Dr. Walker, Mr. Bell, and Mr. Haxhall. Cost of Presidency. Col. Hoomes's horses. Federalists weak. Senate may reject nominations. No European news.   [2595]

1801 Mar. 14. T. J., Washington, to THADDEUS KOSCIUSZKO. ALS. 1 p. Photo-copy. Original owned by National Museum, Cracow, Poland. #9013.
John Barnes wrote about Kosciuszko's financial affairs. Bank stock converted to U.S. government loan. Republican majority. Land for Kosciuszko near Monticello. Mentions Mr. Dawson and Mr. Pichon.   [2595-a]

1801 Mar. 27. T. J., Washington, to MESSRS. EDDY, RUSSELL, THURBER, WHEATON, AND SMITH, Providence. ALS. 1 p. Photostat. Original owned by C. H. Merriman, Jr. #7644. Printed: L and B X, 248–49.
Acknowledges congratulations on election. Will uphold Constitution for good of people.   [2596]

1801 Mar. 31. THOMAS CARPENTER ACCOUNT WITH T. J. 1 p. Endorsed by T. J. Bears ANS, 1801 Mar. 31, T. J. to JOHN BARNES. Edgehill-Randolph Papers. #5533.
Paid by bill of exchange.   [2598]

1801 Apr. 11. T. J., Monticello, to MARIA JEFFERSON EPPES. ALS. 1 p. Photo-stat. Original owned by Mrs. Harold W. Wilson. #5385-v. Printed: SNR, 236–37.
Letter to Mr. Eppes about horses at Bermuda Hundred. Davy Bowles comes for them. John works for Lilly; Goliah is gardener. Invites her to Washington. Bacon to arrive from Bedford before she reaches Monticello.   [2599]

1801 May 1–July 1. THOMAS CARPENTER ACCOUNT WITH T. J. 1 p. DS. Endorsed by T. J. Edgehill-Randolph Papers. #5533.
Paid by John Barnes.   [2600]

1801 May 11. T. J. to JOHN BARNES. ADS. 1 p. Edgehill-Randolph Papers. #5533.
Bill of exchange to Joseph Rapin.   [2601]

1801 May 12. T. J. to JOHN BARNES. ADS. 1 p. Edgehill-Randolph Papers. #5533.
Bill of exchange to Colin C. Wills.   [2602]

1801 June 17. T. J. to JOHN BARNES. ADS. 1 p. Edgehill-Randolph Papers. #5533.
Requests money in U.S. bills.   [2602-a]

1801 June 19. MARTHA J. RANDOLPH, Edgehill, to T. J., Washington. ALS. 3 pp. Endorsed by T. J. Edgehill-Randolph Papers. #5533.
Family meeting at Monticello. Storm destroyed skylights at Monticello. Char-lottesville and Milton damaged. Mrs. Randolph and Mrs. Lilburn Lewis had trouble with Martha Jefferson Carr about T. J.'s stockings.   [2603]

1801 June 24. T. J., Washington, to MARIA JEFFERSON EPPES. ALS. 1 p. Photo-stat. Original owned by Mrs. Harold W. Wilson. #5385-v. Printed: SNR, 237.

Letter to John Wayles Eppes. Maria's trip to Monticello. Martha well. Hail storm broke windows at Edgehill. Broken skylights at Monticello. Wants Maria and Martha to come to Washington in fall. Mentions Mrs. Eppes and Eppington.

[2604]

1801 Sep. 5. T. J. to JOHN BARNES. ADS. 1 p. Edgehill-Randolph Papers. #5533.
Bill of exchange to E. Lemaire.   [2605]

1801 Oct. 9. T. J. to JOHN BARNES. ADS. 1 p. Edgehill-Randolph Papers. #5533.
Bill of exchange for hat and value of jacket to Edward Lemaire.   [2606]

1801 Oct. 11. T. J., Washington, to JOHN BARNES. ADS. 1 p. Edgehill-Randolph Papers. #5533.
Bill of exchange to Joseph Dougherty.   [2607]

1801 Nov. 1. T. J., Washington, to EDWARD LIVINGSTON. ALS. 1 p. Photocopy. Original owned by Victor B. Levit. #8265-b.
Will not reply to letter from Denniston & Chatham regarding Duane case. States his position on the unconstitutionality of Alien and Sedition laws.   [2607-a]

1801 Nov. 7. T. J., Washington, to JOHN BARNES. ADS. 1 p. Edgehill-Randolph Papers. #5533.
Bill of exchange to E. Lemaire.   [2608]

1801 Nov. 9. T. J., Washington, to JOHN BARNES. ADS. 1 p. Edgehill-Randolph Papers. #5533.
Bill of exchange to E. Lemaire.   [2609]

1801 Nov. 16. T. J., Washington, to JOHN BARNES. ADS. 1 p. Edgehill-Randolph Papers. #5533.
Bill of exchange to E. Lemaire.   [2610]

1801 Dec. 12. JAMES DINSMORE, Monticello, to T. J. L. 1 p. 19th-century copy. Owned by Mrs. Augustina David Carr Mills. #4869.
Mr. Wanscher at Monticello. Mr. Perry brings timber. Peace between Great Britain and France.   [2611]

1801 Dec. 14. T. J., Washington, to JOHN BARNES. ADS. 1 p. Edgehill-Randolph Papers. #5533.
Bill of exchange to E. Lemaire.   [2612]

1801 Dec. 18. T. J. to JOHN BARNES. ADS. 1 p. Edgehill-Randolph Papers. #5533.
Bill of exchange to Joseph Dougherty.   [2613]

1801 Dec. 18. T. J., Washington, to JAMES TAYLOR, Norfolk. ALS. 1 p. Owned by T. J. Memorial Foundation. #5090.
Madeira wine.   [2613-a]

[1801]. T. J. to JAMES MADISON. ANS. 1 p. #5951.
Asks that he correct enclosed writings.   [2615]

[1801–1809]. T. J. SHIP'S PAPERS. DS. 1 p. Photostat. Original owned by O. O. Fisher. #3449.
Also signed by James Madison. [2616]

1802 Jan. 1. JAMES DINSMORE, Monticello, to T. J. L. 1 p. 19th-century copy. Owned by Mrs. Augustina David Carr Mills. #4869.
Work at Monticello. Mr. Wanscher finishing cellar. [2616-a]

1802 Jan. 15. THOMAS CARPENTER ACCOUNT WITH T. J. DS. 1 p. Endorsed by T. J. Bears ANS., 1802 Jan. 15, T. J. to JOHN BARNES. Edgehill-Randolph Papers. #5533.
Bill of exchange to Thomas Carpenter. [2617]

1802 Jan. 23. JAMES DINSMORE, Monticello, to T. J. L. 1 p. 19th-century copy. Owned by Mrs. Augustina David Carr Mills. #4869.
Juneo dead; family well. Work at Monticello. John Perry in Fluvanna. Mentions Mr. Oldham and Critta. [2620]

1802 Jan. 26. T. J., Washington, to JOHN BARNES. ANS. 1 p. Photocopy. Original owned by Victor B. Levit. #8265-b.
Order to pay William Duane. [2620-a]

1802 Jan. 29–Apr. 26. THOMAS CARPENTER ACCOUNT WITH T. J. DS. 1 p. Endorsed by T. J. Edgehill-Randolph Papers. #5533. [2621]

1802 Feb. 2. T. J., Washington, to JOHN BARNES. ADS. 1 p. Edgehill-Randolph Papers. #5533.
Bill of exchange to Thomas Newton. [2622]

1802 Feb. 8. T. J., Washington, to JOHN BARNES. ADS. 1 p. Edgehill-Randolph Papers. #5533.
Bill of exchange to E. Lemaire. [2623]

1802 Feb. 8. T. J., to JOHN BARNES. ADS. 1 p. Edgehill-Randolph Papers. #5533.
Bill of exchange to Joseph Dougherty. [2624]

1802 Feb. 12. JAMES DINSMORE, Monticello, to T. J. L. 1 p. 19th-century copy. Owned by Mrs. Augustina David Carr Mills. #4869.
Work at Monticello. Prince Ruspoli visited Mrs. Randolph. Mr. Wanscher needs money. [2625]

1802 Feb. 15. T. J., Washington, to JOHN BARNES. ALS. 1 p. Edgehill-Randolph Papers. #5533.
Bill of exchange to E. Lemaire. [2626]

1802 Mar. 3. [Date received]. THOMAS JEFFERSON RANDOLPH to T. J. ALS. 2 pp. Endorsed by T. J. #6225.
Latin improves. Goes in spring to Latin school with Beverly Randolph. [2627]

1802 Mar. 18. JAMES MONROE, Richmond, to T. J. ALS. 1 p. #4776-a.
Report of Committee of House of Delegates concerning General Assembly action on Alien and Sedition Laws. Mentions U.S. Senate. [2628]

1802 Apr. 6. T. J. LAND GRANT TO JAMES GRAY. DS. 1 p. Photostat. Original owned by O. O. Fisher. #3449.
Land in Northwest Territory. Countersigned by James Madison.   [2629]

1802 Apr. 7. T. J., Washington, to JOHN BARNES, Georgetown. ADS. 1 p. Edgehill-Randolph Papers. #5533.
Bill of exchange to William Parkinson. Receipted by Charles Peale Polk. [2630]

1802 May 22. T. J. to JOHN BARNES. ADS. 1 p. Edgehill-Randolph Papers. #5533.
Bill of exchange to T. J. Receipted by J. Dougherty.   [2631]

1802 June 11. CHARLES TRAVERS, Richmond, INVOICE TO T. J., Washington. DS. 1 p. Edgehill-Randolph Papers. #5533.
Books shipped by Gibson and Jefferson on ship *Good Welcome* from James River, Richmond, to Washington, D.C.   [2632]

1802 June 14–July 20. THOMAS CARPENTER ACCOUNT WITH T. J. AD. 1 p. Endorsed by T. J. Edgehill-Randolph Papers. #5533.
For clothing.   [2632-a]

1802 June 21. T. J., Washington, to JOHN BARNES. ADS. 1 p. Edgehill-Randolph Papers. #5533.
Bill of exchange to Thomas Carpenter.   [2633]

1802 June 22. T. J., Washington, to JAMES DINSMORE, Monticello. ALS. 1 p. #2650-a.
Work for Mr. Fitch. Doors at Monticello. Sketches of servants' quarters. Coming to Monticello.   [2634]

1802 June 26. T. J. to JOHN BARNES. ADS. 1 p. Edgehill-Randolph Papers. #5533.
Bill of exchange to T. J.   [2635]

1802 June 26. T. J., Washington, to JAMES MONROE. ALS. 1 p. Photostat. Original owned by I. Witkins. #3627.
Moses Myers, Richard Evers, Arthur Lee, Littleton W. Tazewell of Williamsburg considered for Commissioners of Bankruptcy in Norfolk. Henry Hiort, Thomas Willock, John Dunn present Commissioners. May all be Republicans. T. J. to Monticello.   [2636]

1802 July 7. T. J., Washington, to JOHN F. MERCER. ALS. 1 p. Photocopy. Original owned by Victor B. Levit. #8265-a.
Reviews Act of Congress, 1802 May 1, for borrowing money by Commissioners of Washington, to be paid by sale of lots in Washington, guaranteed by Treasury of U.S. Debt due state of Maryland.   [2636-a]

1802 July 20. T. J. to JOHN BARNES. ADS. 1 p. Edgehill-Randolph Papers. #5533.
Bill of exchange to T. J. Receipted by Joseph Dougherty.   [2637]

1802. Aug. 27. T. J., Monticello, to STEPHEN R. BRADLEY, Vermont. ALS. 1 p. #5845.

Republicans to be Commissioners of Bankruptcy. Nominations from Bradley and Judge Smith. Persons should live near meeting place of U.S. Court. Secretary of State to handle distant cases.   [2639]

1802 Sept. 4. MR. FITCH'S SURVEYING NOTES. AD. 2 pp. Endorsed by T. J. Edgehill-Randolph Papers. #5533.   [2640]

1802 Sept. 6. T. J. to THOMAS WELLS, JR. ADS. 1 p. Edgehill-Randolph Papers. #5533.
Note payable in Virginia currency. Assigned to Frederick Harris, John J. Hawkins, and P. Hoffman.   [2640-a]

1802 Sept. 13. STEPHEN R. BRADLEY, Westminister, Vermont, to T. J. ALS. 2 pp. File draft. #5845.
Republicans Mark Richards and Reuben Atwater of Westminister, James Elliot of Brattleborough, and Oliver Gallop of Hartland for Commissioners of Bankruptcy. Judge Smith should name four for other side of mountains; should alternate meetings between U.S. Court and state capitol. Federalist machinations in legislative elections.   [2641]

1802 Oct. 14. T. J., Washington, to JOHN BARNES, Georgetown. ADS. 1 p. Edgehill-Randolph Papers. #5533.
Bill of exchange to Thomas Monroe. Receipted by Thomas Monroe and Thomas Turner.   [2642]

1802 Oct. 18. T. J., Washington, to NATHANIEL MACON, SPEAKER OF U.S. HOUSE OF REPRESENTATIVES, Warrenton, North Carolina. ALS. 1 p. Photostat. Original owned by O. O. Fisher. #3449.
Republicans to be Commissioners of Bankruptcy. Newburn, Wilmington, and Edenton to be considered.   [2643]

1802 Oct. 19. T. J. to JOHN BARNES. ADS. 1p. Edgehill-Randolph Papers. #5533.
Bill of exchange to T. J.   [2644]

1802 Oct. 24. T. J. to JOHN BARNES. ADS. 1 p. Edgehill-Randolph Papers. #5533.
Bill of exchange to T. J., payable to E. Lemaire. Receipted by J. Dougherty.   [2645]

1802 Nov. 2. T. J., Washington, to JOHN BARNES. ADS. 1 p. Edgehill-Randolph Papers. #5533.
Bill of exchange to Thomas Carpenter.   [2646]

1802 Nov. 12. T. J., Washington, to JOHN BARNES. ALS. 1 p. Edgehill-Randolph Papers. #5533.
Money due Martin Wanscher in Alexandria. Pay in bills of Alexandria or Washington bank. Wonders if Bank of Columbia will pass them.   [2647]

1802 Dec. 1. T. J., Washington, to [JAMES] DINSMORE. ALS. 1 p. #6540.
Work at Monticello. Nailboys to leave Mr. Stewart and go to Mr. Lilly. Lilly to be supplied with nail making equipment. Roofing tin. Work in progress, including that of Messrs. Oldham, Fitch, and Perry. Mentions Mr. Higginbotham.   [2649]

1802 Dec. 16. T. J., Washington, to JOHN BARNES, Georgetown. ADS. 1 p. Edgehill-Randolph Papers. #5533.
   Bill of exchange to Mr. McLaughlin. Receipted by Edgar Patterson.   [2650]

1802 Dec. 16. T. J., Washington, to JOHN BARNES. ADS. 1 p. Edgehill-Randolph
Papers. #5533.
   Bill of exchange to Thomas Carpenter.   [2651]

1802 Dec. 23. JOHN WAYLES EPPES, Richmond, to T. J. ALS. 3 pp. Endorsed by
T. J. Edgehill-Randolph Papers. #5533.
   Virginia General Assembly. Stevens T. Mason is U.S. Senator. George Hay and
Calendar fought. Mentions *Recorder*. Federalist and Republican feud. Taxes. Trea-
sury surplus. Mr. Page in Richmond.   [2652]

1803 Jan. 6. T. J. to JOHN BARNES. ADS. 1 p. Edgehill-Randolph Papers. #5533.
   Bill of exchange to T. J.   [2653]

1803 Feb. 21. T. J., Washington, to JOHN WAYLES EPPES, Bermuda Hundred.
ALS. 1 p. Photostat. Original owned by Mrs. Francis E. Shine. #3509.
   To meet Eppes and Maria at Monticello. Lilly works on canal. Dislikes borrow-
ing from Federalist banks.   [2654]

1803 Feb. 23. T. J., Washington, to CRAVEN PEYTON, by Mr. Hunter, Albemarle. ALS. 1 p. Photostat. Original owned by Mrs. G. T. Errickson. #3449-a. Published: Greene County, New York, *Examiner-Record*, 9 Jan. 1958, p. 2-A.
   Banker in Georgetown enables him to enclose draft on Gibson and Jefferson to
cover debt.   [2655]

1803 Feb. 24. THOMAS JEFFERSON RANDOLPH to T. J. ALS. 1 p. Endorsed
by T. J. #6225.
   No measles. Virginia speaks well. Ellen learns French. Cornelia sends love.
Wants geography book.   [2655-a]

1803 Feb. 25. T. J., Washington, to JOHN BARNES, Georgetown. ADS. 1 p.
Edgehill-Randolph Papers. #5533.
   Bill of exchange to James Hamilton and/or J. Campbell for College of Carlisle.
                                                                          [2656]

1803 Apr. 21. T. J., Washington, to BENJAMIN RUSH. ALS. 3 pp. McGregor
Library. #2958-b.
   See item 834.   [2658]

1803 Apr. 25. T. J., Washington, to MARIA JEFFERSON EPPES. ALS. 1 p. Letterpress copy. Edgehill-Randolph Papers. #5533.
   To present religious views in defense against libels. Wrote to Philadelphia for
Dr. Priestley's *General History of the Christian Church*. John Wayles Eppes wrote
from Bermuda Hundred that Francis Eppes over measles. Wants Martha and
Maria at Monticello. Mr. and Mrs. P. Carr visited on way to Baltimore. Nelly Carr
sick, returning to Dunlora. Mentions Eppington.   [2659]

1803 [ca. Apr. 26]. T. J. to JOHN BARNES. ADS. 1 p. Edgehill-Randolph Papers. #5533.
Bill of exchange to Thomas Carpenter.   [2659-a]

1803 May 4. T. J., Washington, to VICTOR DUPONT, New York. ALS. 1 p. #5796.
Bills on U.S. Bank to pay for wines from France.   [2660]

1803 May 12. T. J., Washington, to JOHN WAYLES EPPES. ALS. 1 p. Letterpress copy. Edgehill-Randolph Papers. #5533.
No news of Mr. Hancocke. Sent money for Eppes to George Jefferson. Problems, some involving Thomas Mann Randolph, Jr., of exchanging Eppes's Bedford lands for Lego. Will lease Lego to Eppes in exchange for Bedford rents. Mentions Petty, Shadwell. Wants Maria at Monticello.   [2661]

1803 June 2. T. J., Washington, to JOHN BARNES, Georgetown. ADS. 1 p. Edgehill-Randolph Papers. #5533.
Bill of exchange to William Stewart.   [2662]

1803 June 9. T. J. to JOHN BARNES, Georgetown. ADS. 1 p. Edgehill-Randolph Papers. #5533.
Bill of exchange to Alexander Terrasse.   [2663]

1803 June 19. JOHN BARNES MEMORANDUM TO T. J. AD. 1 p. Endorsed by T. J. Edgehill-Randolph Papers. #5533.
T. J.'s bank negotiations.   [2664]

1803 June 19. T. J., Washington, to JOHN BARNES. ADS. 1 p. Edgehill-Randolph Papers. #5533.
Bill of exchange to Martin Wanscher. Receipted by John W. Pratt, Georgetown.
                                                                         [2665]

1803 July 8. T. J. to JOHN BARNES. ADS. 1 p. On bill from J. B. Anderson, Washington, 1803 June 27. Edgehill-Randolph Papers. #5533.
Bill of exchange to J. B. Anderson for frames for medallions and print of Washington.   [2666]

1803 July 15. T. J., Washington, to JOHN BARNES. ADS. 1 p. Edgehill-Randolph Papers. #5533.
Bill of exchange to Wilson Bryan.   [2667]

1803 Sept. 8. T. J., Monticello, to JOHN BARNES, Georgetown. ADS. 1 p. Edgehill-Randolph Papers. #5533.
Bill of exchange to Robert Leslie.   [2668]

1803 Oct. 9. T. J., Washington, to JOHN BARNES. ADS. 1 p. Edgehill-Randolph Papers. #5533.
Bill of exchange to Joseph Dougherty.   [2669]

1803 Oct. 18. T. J. to JOHN BARNES. ADS. 1 p. Edgehill-Randolph Papers. #5533.
Bill of exchange to T. J. Mentions Monticello.   [2670]

1803 Oct. 30. THOMAS JEFFERSON RANDOLPH, Edgehill, to T. J. ALS. 1 p.
Endorsed by T. J. Owned by Mrs. Edwin Page Kirk. #5291.

Mr. Dinsmore left Monticello to go to Philadelphia. Work on canal and well
house. Goldsmith's Grecian and Roman histories, Thucydides. Mentions Thomas
Mann Randolph, Jr. and John Wayles Eppes.   [2671]

1803 Nov. 27. T. J. to JOHN BARNES. ADS. 1 p. Edgehill-Randolph Papers.
#5533.

Bill of exchange to William Stewart.   [2672]

1803 Dec. 9. T. J. to JOHN BARNES. ADS. 1 p. Edgehill-Randolph Papers. #5533.

Bill of exchange to Wilson Bryan. Assigned to Mr. Layman.   [2673]

1803 Dec. 18. T. J., Washington, to JOHN BARNES, Georgetown. ADS. 1 p.
Edgehill-Randolph Papers. #5533.

Bill of exchange to Charles Coffin, Jr., for College of Tennessee.   [2674]

1803 Dec. 19. T. J. to JOHN BARNES. ADS. 1 p. Edgehill-Randolph Papers. #5533.

Bill of exchange to E. Lemaire.   [2675]

1804 Jan. 7. T. J. to JOHN BARNES. ADS. 1 p. Edgehill-Randolph Papers. #5533.

Bill of exchange to Mr. Doolittle. Receipted by Mr. Jackson.   [2675-a]

1804 Jan. 9. T. J. to JOHN BARNES. ADS. 1 p. Edgehill-Randolph Papers. #5533.

Bill of exchange to E. Lemaire.   [2676]

1804 Jan. 23. T. J. to MARTHA JEFFERSON RANDOLPH. ALS. 1 p. Letterpress
copy. Edgehill-Randolph Papers. #5533.

Snow storm stopped Milton mail. Congress not meeting. John Wayles Eppes may
go to Maria. Congress having dinner to honor Louisiana acquisition. No foreign
guests. Offensive to Merry and Yrujo. Libels by Federalist newspapers.   [2677]

1804 Jan. 29. T. J., Washington, to MARIA JEFFERSON EPPES, Edgehill near
Milton. ALS. 1 p. Photostat. Original owned by Mrs. Harold W. Wilson. #7437.
Printed: SNR, 253–54; Betts, *Garden Book*, 294, extract.

Milton mail no longer to be mixed with New Orleans mail. Congress adjourns
in March; Mr. Eppes may leave sooner. Bantams from Algiers for Anne Cary
Randolph. East India fowl. Mentions Pantops.   [2678]

1804 Feb. 20. T. J., Washington, to JOHN BARNES. ADS. 1 p. Edgehill-Randolph
Papers. #5533.

Bill of exchange to E. Lemaire.   [2681]

1804 Feb. 26. T. J., Washington, to MARIA JEFFERSON EPPES, Edgehill. AL.
1 p. File draft. Owned by Mrs. Harold W. Wilson. #5385-v. Printed: SNR, 254;
Betts, *Garden Book*, 295, extract.

Maria's baby. Meeting of Congress prevented his coming. John Wayles Eppes
and Thomas Mann Randolph, Jr., come at adjournment. Wants her to go to
Monticello. Mentions Mr. Lilly, Goliah, and gardening.   [2682]

1804 Feb. 26. T. J., Washington, to MARIA JEFFERSON EPPES, Edgehill. ALS. 1 p. File draft. Edgehill-Randolph Papers. #5533.
Duplicates item 2682.   [2683]

1804 Mar. 3. T. J., Washington, to MARIA JEFFERSON EPPES. ALS. 1 p. File draft. Edgehill-Randolph Papers. #5533. Printed: SNR, 255.
Inaction of Congress prevents being with her in her illness. John Wayles Eppes comes.   [2684]

1804 Mar. 6. T. J. to JOHN BARNES. ADS. 1 p. Edgehill-Randolph Papers. #5533.
Bill of exchange to T. J. for use of John Rogers in Richmond. Receipted by Joseph Dougherty.   [2685]

1804 Mar. 15. T. J. to JOHN BARNES. ADS. 1 p. Edgehill-Randolph Papers. #5533.
Bill of exchange to John (Negro). Trip to Monticello.   [2686]

1804 Mar. 15. T. J., Washington, to JOHN WAYLES EPPES, Edgehill. ALS. 1 p. #6860.
Light food and cordial wines as cures for Maria's fever. Wants her at Monticello until Pantops is ready. T. J. will forward oats to Benson, postmaster at Fredericksburg. Mentions Martha Jefferson Randolph.   [2686-a]

1804 Mar. 17. T. J., Washington, to JOHN BARNES. ALS. 1 p. Edgehill-Randolph Papers. #5533.
Bill of exchange to Joseph Dougherty for Martin Wanscher. Invites Barnes to dinner.   [2687]

1804 Mar. 26. EDWARD FRETHY TO T. J. ANS. 1 p. Endorsed by T. J. Bears ANS, 1804 Mar. 26, T. J. to JOHN BARNES. Edgehill-Randolph Papers. #5533.
Frethy's bill and T. J.'s payment.   [2688]

1804 Mar. 26. T. J. to JOHN BARNES. ADS. 1 p. Edgehill-Randolph Papers. #5533.
Bill of exchange to Joseph Dougherty.   [2689]

1804 May 14. T. J., Washington, to MARTHA J. RANDOLPH. ALS. 1 p. File draft. Edgehill-Randolph Papers. #5533.
Trip to Washington. Mentions Orange Court House, horse Castor, Fauquier Court House, Col. Wren, and John. Garden seed. Mentions Thomas Mann Randolph, Jr.   [2690]

1804 May 19. DABNEY CARR, Charlottesville, to T. J. ALS. 1 p. Edgehill-Randolph Papers. #5533.
Payments to Johnson.   [2691]

1804 June 24. T. J., Washington, to JOSIAH DONATH, Philadelphia. ALS. 1 p. #4529.
Glass sent care of Gibson and Jefferson, Richmond.   [2692]

1804 July 1. JOHN TAYLOR, Caroline, to T. J. ALS. 1 p. Endorsed by T. J. #5734.
Sends turnips.   [2693]

1804 July 16. T. J. to JAMES MADISON. ADS. 1 p. Edgehill-Randolph Papers. #5533.
  Draft on Office of Discount and Deposit, Washington.   [2694]

1804 July 29. JOHN WAYLES EPPES, Eppington, to T. J. ALS. 1 p. Endorsed by T. J. #4715.
  Francis Eppes and Maria well. Betsy's child sick. Cannot come to Monticello Mentions Martha.   [2695]

1804 Aug. 15. T. J., Monticello, to G. C. DELACOSTÉ, New York. ALS. 1 p. Photostat. Original owned by Bernard W. Southgate, III. #6504.
  Cannot aid New York Museum of Sculpture, Painting, etc.   [2696]

1804 Nov. 6. T. J., PAPERS FOR SHIP *NEW YORK*. DS. 1 p. Photostat. Original owned by O. O. Fisher. #3449.
  Matthew Dunnell, Master. Countersigned by James Madison and David Gelston.   [2697]

1804 Nov. 6. T. J., Washington, to MARTHA JEFFERSON RANDOLPH. ALS. 1 p. Photostat. Original owned by Mrs. Robert Graham. #5832-a.
  Sends magazine. Mr. Randolph's arrival in Washington. One house of Congress complete, but no Senate. Election of 1804. Desires to quit politics for family life. Mentions Mr. Eppes, Francis Eppes, and Maria Jefferson Eppes at Eppington. Messages to Anne Randolph and to Ellen Randolph for whom he has bantams.   [2697-a]

1804 Nov. 12. T. J., Washington, to DABNEY CARR. ALS. 1 p. File draft. #6563.
  Money for Craven Peyton.   [2698]

1804 Nov. 26. ELIZABETH TRIST, New Orleans, to T. J., Washington. ALS. 3 pp. #5385-n.
  Henry Brown and Mrs. Trist had fever. Mrs. Claibourne, Mrs. Gunley, and Mr. Gelston died. Mr. Dubourg handling Gelston's affairs. Needs money from England to settle Iberville plantation, which Spain holds. Squatters at Natchez plantation. James Monroe did not visit. Has Mr. Brigg's likeness of T. J. Mentions Mary Trist, William Brown, Thomas Mann Randolph, Jr., Martha, John Wayles Eppes. [2699]

1804 Dec. 24. T. J., Washington, to JAMES OLDHAM, Richmond. ALS. 1 p. #7708.
  Seeking edition of Palladio in Philadelphia and Baltimore. Ryland Randolph of Turkey Island had one which David Randolph might locate. Note in unidentified hand: "For the Rev. Dr. Packard with the respects of T. R. Slack." Addressed on verso, Mechums River, Va., to Rev. William Packard, Theological Seminary, Virginia.   [2700]

1804–1813. T. J. LEGAL BRIEF IN CASE OF JEFFERSON vs. MICHIE. D. 248 pp. 19th-century copy. Owned by Mrs. Augustina David Carr Mills. #4869.
  Suit against David Michie of Buck Island concerning claims of Elizabeth Henderson and her minor children to lands and mill formerly owned by Bennett Henderson at Milton. Brief contains letters or depositions of James Henderson, Richard Price, James Lewis, Elizabeth Henderson, John Henderson, Craven Peyton, Charles Henderson, David Michie, Kemp Catlett, William Wood, James Barbour, Elijah

Hogg, and Martin Dawson. Appeal heard by George Wythe in Richmond. Contains documents certified in courts of Shelby County, Kentucky. Contains letters, David Michie to T. J., dated 1812 June 18, 1812 June 21, 1812 June 27, 1812 July 20, 1813 April 23, and 1813 May 30. Contains letters, T. J. to David Michie, dated 1812 June 20, 1812 June 22, 1812 June 27, 1812 July 20, 1813 April 20, and 1813 May 30.

[2700-a]

[1804] T. J. *SUBSCRIPTION TO THOMAS SCOTT'S FAMILY BIBLE* (Philadelphia: William W. Woodward [1804]). ADS. 1 p. Owned by T. J. Memorial Foundation. #5196-a   [2700-b]

1805 Jan. 26. THOMAS MANN RANDOLPH, JR., Edgehill, to T. J., Washington. ALS. 1 p. Endorsed by T. J. #5589.
     Martha's and children's health.   [2701]

1805 Feb. 3. T. J. to MATTHEW CARY, Philadelphia. ANS. 1 p. #5799.
     Mr. Reibelt of Baltimore sent French New Testament. Needs Greek and English New Testaments from Philadelphia. Would like the Benjamin Johnson–Robert Carr Bible.   [2702]

1805 Feb. 23. JACOB CROWNINSHIELD to T. J. ANS. 1 p. Owned by George Green Shackelford. #3525-i.
     Time for visit.   [2703]

1805 Mar. 7. T. J., Washington, to MATTHEW CARY. ALS. 1 p. #4601.
     Draft on Philadelphia bank for books. Wants new edition of Bible that Cary has available.   [2704]

1805 Mar. 14. T. J., PAPERS FOR SHIP *CHATHAM*. DS. 1 p. Photostat. Original owned by O. O. Fisher. #3449.
     James B. Wasson, master. New York to Liverpool. Countersigned by James Madison, David Gelston. Text in French, Spanish, English, and Dutch.   [2705]

1805 Mar. 26. T. J. to WILSON CARY NICHOLAS. L. Extract. 2 pp. Unidentified hand copy. On sheet with L., Extract, unidentified hand copy, 1799 Dec. 29, JAMES MADISON to T. J. Edgehill-Randolph Papers. #5533. [Calendared as Item 2579].
     Prostration of Federalism. Republicans are dividing, but political divisions natural.
     Madison sends questionable report that North Carolina Legislature discussed Virginia Resolution.   [2706]

1805 Apr. 3. T. J., Monticello, to [?]. ANS. 1 p. #6047.
     Probably to John Barnes. Orders payment to Mr. Lenthal.   [2707]

1805 Apr. 5. T. J., Monticello, to JOHN BARNES. ALS. 1 p. Owned by Mrs. Edwin Page Kirk. #5291.
     Mr. Taggert's bill. Paint from Philadelphia at Richmond.   [2708]

1805 July 23. WILLIAM WIRT, Williamsburg, to T. J. ALS. 3 pp. McGregor Library. #5622.

Wants T. J.'s remembrances for biography of Patrick Henry. Offers as references Peter and Dabney Carr. Would also like short sketches of Henry's colleagues. [2709]

[1805] Aug. 4. [Subsequently dated 1812 Apr. 12.] T. J., Monticello, to WILLIAM WIRT. ALS. 1 p. McGregor Library. #5622.

Praises Henry for giving "first impulse to the ball of revolution" and for oratory, but criticizes ignorance of law and avarice. [2710]

*1805 Aug. 4. [Subsequently dated 1812 Apr. 12.] T. J. RECOLLECTION OF PATRICK HENRY. AMS. 6 pp. McGregor Library. #5622. Printed: Ford IX, 339–45.

Met Henry at Nathaniel West Dandridge's home in Hanover while traveling to William and Mary College. Henry's legal training inadequate. Peyton Randolph, John Randolph, and Robert C. Nicholas reluctantly signed license; George Wythe would not sign. Henry, Burgess for Hanover, stopped John Robinson's loan office scheme. Henry's support for George Johnston's resolution against English Parliament's stamp tax crushed power of Peyton Randolph, Richard Bland, Edmund Pendleton, Robert C. Nicholas, George Wythe, Peter Randolph, etc. T. J. Burgess for Albemarle when Lord Botetourt Governor of Virginia. Henry and T. J. agreed on principles while serving in House of Delegates. Henry and Richard Henry Lee poor performers at first Continental Congress. Edmund Pendleton and Benjamin Harrison reported that William Livingston, Governor of New Jersey, John Jay, and John Dickinson surpassed Henry and Lee. Address to King and people of Great Britain. When Lord Dunmore called Peyton Randolph to Virginia Assembly concerning Lord North's proposals, T. J. replaced Randolph in Continental Congress. Mentions George Washington and Declaration of Independence. Henry appointed Colonel of Virginia Convention's 1st regiment. Lived at Roundabout in Louisa. Hunted deer in Fluvanna. Bought land of Mr. Lomax on Smith River. Yazoo speculations brought condemnation from Virginia Legislature. Case of Jones and Walker. British debts. Henry opposed U.S. Constitution and hated George Washington. Hamilton's funding system. Henry declined mission to Spain, hoped to be Secretary of State. Deserted Republicanism for Federalism. [2711]

[1805]. T. J. SPECIFICATIONS FOR ROOF AT POPLAR FOREST. AD. 1 p. #3893.

Includes sketches of ridge beams. [2712]

[1805–1806]. T. J. PLANS AND 5 SKETCHES. AD. 3 pp. McGregor Library. #3352.
For phaeton. [2713]

[1805–1810]. T. J. to CORNELIA RANDOLPH, Dr. Bankhead's, Port Royal, Va. AN. 1 p. #5385-u.
Canons of conduct. [2714]

1806 Mar. 5. T. J. to SENATE OF U.S. ALS. 1 p. Photostat. Original owned by O. O. Fisher. #3449.

Letters of Secretary of State, James Madison; Minister Plenipotentiary at Paris, John Armstrong; and Henry Waddell, in case of ship New Jersey. [2715]

1806 Apr. 21. T. J. PAPERS FOR SHIP *ONTARIO*. DS. 2 pp. Photostat. Original owned by Johnson Crawford, Jr. #4309.

George Hitch, Master. Ship of New Bedford, Mass. Note on verso, signed by William Lyman, U.S. Consul at London, transfers command from David Nye, Jr., to George Hitch, Jr.   [2716]

1806 June 20. T. J., Washington, to CHRISTIAN MAYER. ALS. 1 p. #4532. Printed: Betts, *Garden Book*, 320.

Corn. Mr. Reibelt was to order books from France, but Mayer did it instead.   [2717]

1806 July 1. T. J., Washington, to WILLIAM ROSCOE. ALS. 1 p. Photostat. Original owned by City of Liverpool Public Library. #5128.

Roscoe's *History of the Pontificate of Leo X* compared to *Life of Lorenzo de Medici*. Americans do not have time for scientific pursuits.   [2718]

1806 July 13. T. J., Washington, to JOHN H. FREEMAN. ALS. 1 p. #7708.

Leaving for Edgehill and Monticello. Packages from Richmond. Work at mill, garden, and by Milton road. Mr. Burwell's horses and servant.   [2719]

1806 Aug. 3. T. J., SURVEY OF MONTICELLO. AD. 1 p. 8¼" x 10". Edgehill-Randolph Papers. #5533.   [2720]

1806 Sept. 29. T. J., Monticello, to DAVID HIGGINBOTHAM, Milton. ALS. 1 p. #3537.

William Stewart account. Mr. Lilly unavailable. Profit from nailery to apply to debt.   [2721]

1806 Nov. 31. CAESAR A. RODNEY, Philadelphia, to T. J. ALS. File draft. 3 pp. Owned by George Green Shackelford. #5661-a.

Encloses letter from his father Thomas Rodney on situation in the West. Mentions letters from Allan McLane on problems of collecting revenue at port of Wilmington, and judicial decisions affecting revenue laws. Rodney fears Judiciary is undermining the Administration. Cevallos ordered all communication between Madison and Spanish legation turned over to Yrujo. Willingness to replace Judge William Paterson.   [2722]

1806 Dec. 6. T. J., Washington, to MAYER AND BRANTZ. ALS. 1 p. #6047.

Books and bill of lading. Encloses draft on U.S. bank at Baltimore.   [2723]

1806 Dec. 20. THOMAS SEYMOUR, JONATHAN BULL, SYLVESTER WELLS, NATHANIEL PATTEN, DANIEL ALCOTT, THOMAS TISDALL, and HENRY SEYMOUR, Hartford, Conn., to T. J. ALS. 5 pp. Endorsed by T. J. Owned by T. J. Memorial Foundation. #6895.

Federalist libels against Republicans. Interference of churchmen in politics and corruption of Federalist newspapers.   [2724]

1806. WILLIAM ROSCOE to T. J. ALS. 2 pp. File draft. Photostat. Original owned by City of Liverpool Public Library. #5128-a.

Sends *Life and Pontificate of Leo X*, by way of Ra[lph?] Eddens of Philadelphia.   [2725]

1807 Jan. 1. EDMUND BACON, Monticello, to T. J. ALS. 1 p. Endorsed by T. J. Edgehill-Randolph Papers. #5533.

Nail rod. Books from Richmond by Mr. Johnson. Gardening and brickmaking as Mr. Chisolm directed. Hogs and sheep.   [2727]

1807 Feb. 5. T. J. to CAESAR A. RODNEY. AL. 1 p. Photostat. Location of original not known. #3449.

Yrujo suit against William Duane, editor of the *Aurora*.   [2728]

1807 Feb. 18. WILLIAM A. BURWELL to T. J. ALS. 1 p. Owned by the Misses Margaret and Olivia Taylor. #8937.

Dispute between Thomas Mann Randolph, Jr. and T. J.   [2728-a]

1807 Feb. 20. WILLIAM A. BURWELL to T. J. ALS. 1 p. Owned by the Misses Margaret and Olivia Taylor. #8937.

Dispute between Thomas Mann Randolph, Jr. and T. J.   [2728-b]

1807 Feb. 28. WILLIAM A. BURWELL to T. J. ALS. 1 p. Owned by the Misses Margaret and Olivia Taylor. #8937.

Health and state of mind of Thomas Mann Randolph, Jr. Joseph brings carriage.
                                                                            [2728-c]

[1807] Mar. 3. W. A. BURWELL to T. J. ALS. 1 p. Original owned by the Misses Margaret and Olivia Taylor. #8937.

Thomas Mann Randolph, Jr's. regrets for having left T. J. and Randolph's state of mind.   [2728-d]

1807 Mar. 20. T. J. to MARTHA J. RANDOLPH. ALS. 1 p. Draft copy. Edgehill-Randolph Papers. #5533.

T. J.'s headache. Health of Mr. Randolph, Lemaire, and Mr. Freeman.   [2729]

1807 Mar. 30. T. J., Washington, to CAESAR A. RODNEY. ALS. 1 p. Photostat. Location of original not known. #3449.

Lost paper found. To Monticello.   [2730]

1807 May 22. EDMUND BACON, Monticello, to T. J. ALS. 1 p. Endorsed by T. J. Edgehill-Randolph Papers. #5533.

Work at mill. Mr. Perry works on scow and Mr. Maddox on toll mill. Thorn hedges.   [2731]

1807 May 29. DABNEY CARR, Charlottesville, to T. J. ALS. 2 pp. Endorsed by T. J. Edgehill-Randolph Papers. #5533.

Perry's bond. Baltimore creditors of John Speer, assignee, demand Maddox's draft to E. Alexander which was presented at Monticello. Judgment against Stewart and Walker. Mentions Melinda and Samuel Carr.   [2732]

1807 June 2. T. J. PAPERS FOR SHIP *GOOD INTENT*. DS. 1 p. #6693-a.

Christopher Meader, master. Baltimore to Havana. Countersigned by James Madison and Samuel Sterrett.   [2733]

1807 June 6. EDMUND BACON to T. J. ALS. 2 pp. Endorsed by T. J. Edgehill-Randolph Papers. #5533.

Flood damage to toll mill. Mr. Perry doing scow roof. Hedges. Purchase of sheep. Mr. Carr's and Mr. Craven's mules. Mentions Mr. Walker.   [2734]

1807 June 6. T. J., Washington, to JOHN BARNES. ALS. 1 p. Owned by T. J. Memorial Foundation. #7443-e.
Encloses check on the Bank of the U.S. Debt to Barnes. Barnes to collect Beckley's debt and credit T. J.   [2734-a]

1807 June 12. EDMUND BACON TO T. J. ALS. 2 pp. Endorsed by T. J. Edgehill-Randolph Papers. #5533.
Mill and canal flooding. Mentions Davy.   [2735]

1807 June 27. JAMES TUCKER, Norfolk, to T. J. L. 1 p. Typescript copy from *Norfolk Gazette and Public Ledger*. Location of original not known. #3439.
Resolution of officers sailing to and from ports of Norfolk and Portsmouth. [2736]

1807 July 3. EDMUND BACON, Monticello, to T. J. ALS. 1 p. Endorsed by T. J. Edgehill-Randolph Papers. #5533.
Monticello barn. Horse mended. Mentions Mr. Perry and James Clark.   [2737]

1807 July 8. T. J., Washington, to MASTERS AND OFFICERS SAILING TO AND FROM PORTS OF NORFOLK AND PORTSMOUTH. L. 1 p. Typescript copy from *Norfolk Gazette and Public Ledger*. Location of original not known. #3439. Printed: L and B XI, 261.
Defense of Fort Norfolk, Craney Island, Elizabeth and James Rivers.   [2738]

1807 July 26. T. J. to CAESAR A. RODNEY. AN. 1 p. Photostat. Location of original not known. #3449.
Robert Bowie and Mr. Wilkinson invited to dine.   [2739]

1807 Aug. 1. JOHN BORROWS to T. J. ADS. 1 p. Edgehill-Randolph Papers. #5533.
Bill for milk and cream.   [2740]

1807 Aug. 3. T. J. to JOHN BOYER. DS. 1 p. Oak Hill Papers. #3248.
Ensign's commission. Countersigned by James Madison.   [2741]

1807 Aug. 7. T. J. to ANNE LOUIS DE TOUSARD. ANS. 1 p. #4195.
Subscribes to *American Artillerist's Companion*.   [2742]

1807 Aug. 11. T. J., Monticello, to WILLIAM H. CABELL. ALS. 5 pp. Photocopy. Original owned by Paul Mellon. #7289-b. Printed: L and B XI, 318–23.
Philosophy and construction of the law relating to volunteers for armed forces.
                                                                           [2742-a]

1807 Sept. 18. T. J., Monticello, to CAESAR A. RODNEY, Wilmington, Del. AN. 1 p. Photocopy. Original owned by Victor B. Levit. #8265-b.
Unidentified legal matter.   [2742-b]

1807 Sept. 23. T. J. to JOHN BARNES. ADS. 1 p. Edgehill-Randolph Papers. #5533.
Promissory note on bank of Columbia.   [2742-c]

1807 Sept. EDMUND BACON ACCOUNT. AD. 1 p. Endorsed by T. J. Edgehill-Randolph Papers. #5533.

Payments to James Carr, Thomas Burress, Jacob Kooper, John Peyton, Richard Anderson, John Rogers, James Butler. [2743]

1807 Oct. 21. T. J., Washington, to JOHN BARNES. DS. 1 p. Edgehill-Randolph Papers. #5533.

Note payable at Bank of Columbia. [2744]

1807 Oct. 24. EDMUND BACON, Monticello, to T. J. AL. Fragment. 2 pp. Endorsed by T. J. Edgehill-Randolph Papers. #5533.

Accounts of Mr. Peyton and cooper. Mr. Craven's tobacco. Timothy planting. Corn. Work on dam. [Break in text]. Property sale. Mentions Mr. Shoemaker, Mr. Perry. [2745]

1807 Nov. 7. T. J., Washington, to JOHN MINOR. ALS. 1 p. Photocopy. Original owned by Mrs. James H. Johnson. #8917.

Mrs. Dangerfield's Negroes. Disagreement with England. Amendment of the Constitution for removal of judges, and Senate proposal for appointment of judges. Mentions L. W. Dangerfield and Sarah Dangerfield. [2745-a]

1807 Nov. 8. EDMUND BACON, Monticello, to T. J. ALS. 2 pp. Endorsed by T. J. Edgehill-Randolph Papers. #5533.

Davy to Washington. Corn from Mr. Craven, Robert Teril, Robert Burress, Mr. Peyton. Stewart drunk and working poorly. Garden work. No work at cooper's shop, Belt's home, or head gate. Mr. Maddox broke arm. [2746]

1807 Nov. 15. EDMUND BACON, Monticello, to T. J. AL. Fragment. 1 p. Endorsed by T. J. Edgehill-Randolph Papers. #5533.

Money to be sent by Mr. Craven. [2747]

1807 Nov. 25. T. J., Washington, to JAMES DINSMORE, Monticello. ALS. 1 p. Photostat. Original owned by W. Bedford Moore. #9487.

Davy bringing box of articles furnished by Dr. Ott. Lead has left Philadelphia. Has sent Mr. Bacon books and other packages for Monticello to be stored in greenhouse. [2747-a]

1807 Dec. 11. EDMUND BACON, Monticello, to T. J. AL. Fragment. 1 p. Endorsed by T. J. Edgehill-Randolph Papers. #5533.

Mrs. Dangerfield's runaway slaves. Mr. Belt wants new bolting cloth. Davy, not Mr. Perry, can make addition to the nursery. Mr. Grady's money. [2748]

1807 Dec. 16. T. J., Washington, to JOHN BARNES. DS. 1 p. Edgehill-Randolph Papers. #5533.

Note payable at Bank of Columbia. [2749]

1807 Dec. 18. EDMUND BACON, Monticello, to T. J. AL. Fragment. 1 p. Endorsed by T. J. Edgehill-Randolph Papers. #5533.

Runaway slaves not at Mrs. Dangerfield's. Wants T. J. to prevent his being made a soldier. [2750]

1807 Dec. 25. EDMUND BACON, Monticello, to T. J. ALS. 1 p. Endorsed by T. J. Edgehill-Randolph Papers. #5533.

Mrs. Lewis' account for turkeys, bacon, oats, and vegetables gotten by Edmund Bacon, Mr. Freeman, and Mr. Lilly. Hogs. Thomas Mann Randolph, Jr. took two wagon horses. [2751]

1808 Jan. 8. EDMUND BACON, Monticello, to T. J. AL. Fragment. 1 p. Edgehill-Randolph Papers. #5533.

Owes John Carr. Peter Minor buys nails from penitentiary. [Break in text]. Runaway slaves. [2752]

1808 Jan. 15. EDMUND BACON, Monticello, to T. J. AL. Fragment. 1 p. Endorsed by T. J. Edgehill-Randolph Papers. #5533.

Mr. Belt keeping his horse at the mill. Bigtail sheep flock increasing. [2753]

1808 Jan. 30. T. J. to SENATE OF U.S. ALS. 1 p. Photostat. Original owned by O. O. Fisher. #3449.

Treaties with Ottowas, Chippewas, Wyandots, and Potawatomis, made at Detroit, and with Choctaws at Pooshapukanuck. [2754]

1808 Feb. 19. T. J., Washington, to MR. DEBLOIS, Alexandria. ANS. 1 p. #4574.

Goods to Gibson and Jefferson, Richmond, by Capt. Johnson. [2755]

1808 Feb. 26. EDMUND BACON, Monticello, to T. J. ALS. 1 p. Endorsed by T. J. Edgehill-Randolph Papers. #5533.

Stewart's account. Dinsmore levels land. Corn from Mr. Mullins. Needs nail rod, as George Jefferson has none at Richmond. Mentions Mr. Walker, Thomas Mann Randolph, Jr. [2756]

1808 Mar. 4. EDMUND BACON to T. J. ALS. 2 pp. Endorsed by T. J. Edgehill-Randolph Papers. #5533.

Thorn hedges. Sowing oats in field bought from Mr. Craven. Corn planting. Small ewe that had been at Alexander's died. Joe wants tin for coopers. [2757]

1808 Mar. 7. T. J. to [WILSON CARY NICHOLAS]. AN. 1 p. Owned by the Misses Margaret and Olivia Taylor. #8937.

Check on the Bank of the U.S. for Burgess Griffin. [2757-a]

1808 Apr. 15. EDMUND BACON, Monticello, to T. J. ALS. 1 p. Endorsed by T. J. Edgehill-Randolph Papers. #5533.

Davy brings horse. Gardening. Mentions Mr. Chisolm and Mr. Dinsmore. Needs nail rod. [2758]

1808 May 4. T. J., Washington, to EDMUND BACON. ALS. 1 p. #6089-a.

Davy brings horse. T. J. comes later. Peter Hemings should cook for T. J., and Wormly should tend horses. Mentions Mr. Price. [2759]

1808 May 10. RANDOLPH HARRISON, Clifton, to [T. J.]. ALS. 2 pp. Endorsed by T. J. Edgehill-Randolph Papers. #5533.

Surveying land touching Elkhill between Byrd Creek and James River, bought from D. Ross. Meredith Price survey not correct. Cannot locate marker tree on Joshua's branch.   [2760]

1808 June 30. EDMUND BACON, Monticello, to T. J. ALS. 1 p. Endorsed by T. J. Edgehill-Randolph Papers. #5533.
   Mr. Peyton's account. Jerry gone to Bedford. Canal and boat. Mr. Maddox works at stables. Mentions horses, Mr. Chisolm.   [2761]

1808 July 8. EDMUND BACON, Monticello, to T. J. ALS. 1 p. Endorsed by T. J. Edgehill-Randolph Papers. #5533.
   Brown needs money from Bishop. Slaves working for Thomas Mann Randolph, Jr., and cutting oats. River and canal. Parney corn.   [2762]

1808 Sept. 4. T. J. LIST OF BOOKS GIVEN TO THOMAS JEFFERSON RANDOLPH. AD. 1 p. Edgehill-Randolph Papers. #5533.
   Homer, Vergil, Lucan, Claudian, Silius Italicus, Ovid, Juvenal, Perseus, Horace, Seneca the tragedian, Plautus, Terence, Ausonius, Caesar, Suetonius, Tacitus, Justin, Sallust, Boethius, Cicero, Hippocrates. Also, Greek and Latin New Testaments and *Orthodoxa Symbola*. Printers: Elzevir, Morelli, and Jansson.   [2763]

1808 Sept. 17. ANNE CARY RANDOLPH AND CHARLES BANKHEAD, MARRIAGE CONTRACT. AD. Draft copy in hand of T. J. 1 p. Edgehill-Randolph Papers. #5533.
   Binds Thomas Mann Randolph, Jr., Martha Jefferson Randolph, and affianced couple. Transfers Poplar Forest, Bedford County, lands to Bankhead. Verso: mathematical calculation and T. J.'s presidential mailing address.   [2764]

1808 Oct. 13. EDMUND BACON, Monticello, to T. J. ALS. 1 p. Endorsed by T. J. Edgehill-Randolph Papers. #5533.
   Mill dam. Garden work. Corn prices. Money for Johnson. Horse Fitch Partner lame.   [2765]

1808 Nov. 3. T. J., Washington, to T. J. RANDOLPH. ALS. 1 p. #6242.
   Letter from Martha J. Randolph. Bundle sent to Philadelphia, as well as box of books from Milton. Forgot to pack some Buffon volumes. T. J. wants his mamaluke bit plated in Philadelphia. Dr. Rush praises T. J. Randolph.   [2766]

1808 Nov. 5. T. J. RANDOLPH, Museum [Philadelphia], to T. J. ALS. 1 p. Endorsed by T. J. Edgehill-Randolph Papers. #5533.
   Watch repair. Will send to New York for crystal seal. Cannot get Bell's *Anatomy*; using Fyfe. Mentions Voight, Dr. Porter, Dr. Mitchell.   [2767]

1808 Nov. 17. EDMUND BACON, Monticello, to T. J. AL. Fragment. 1 p. Endorsed by T. J. Edgehill-Randolph Papers. #5533.
   Note to Mrs. Carter for John Pace's and Nicholas Gianniny's corn. Mr. Lammons, stone mason, not yet working. Davy wants to see his wife Christmas. [Break in text]. Mentions miller and Robert Teril.   [2768]

1808 Dec. 6. T. J., Washington, to OLIVER EVANS, Philadelphia. ALS. 1 p. Owned by George Green Shackelford. #5661.

Machinery used in T. J.'s mill was patented by Evans. T. J. to pay Evans' agent, John Moody, by draft on U.S. Bank at Philadelphia. [2769]

1808 Dec. 8. EDMUND BACON to T. J. ALS. 2 pp. Endorsed by T. J. Edgehill-Randolph Papers. #5533.

Mr. Walker's directions for bolting cloth. Garden work. Capt. Davis' money for livestock from Hancocke Allen's sale. Nail rod. [2770]

1808 Dec. 9. OLIVER EVANS, Philadelphia, to T. J., Washington. ALS. 2 pp. On verso of ALS, 1808 Dec. 6, T. J. to OLIVER EVANS. Owned by George Green Shackelford. #5661.

Thanks T. J. for payment sent to his agent, John Moody, for use in T. J.'s mill of machinery patented by Evans. Mentions Congressional act concerning his patents. His belief that the Mississippi River can be navigated with boats propelled by steam. [2771]

1808 Dec. 15. EDMUND BACON to T. J. ALS. 1 p. Endorsed by T. J. Edgehill-Randolph Papers. #5533.

Corn purchases, involving Higginbotham and Pace. Garden work. Returning from Washington, found steer left by Mr. Freeman with Mr. Willis near Orange Court House. Nail rod. [2772]

1808 Dec. 19. T. J., Washington, to RICHARD FITZHUGH, Ravensworth. ALS. 1 p. McGregor Library. #3763.

Introduces Alexander Wilson, to discuss birds with Mr. Coffer. [2773]

1808 Dec. 19. T. J., Washington, to THOMAS JEFFERSON RANDOLPH. ALS. Draft copy. 1 p. Edgehill-Randolph Papers. #5533.

Smallpox vaccine from Dr. Wistar for Edgehill. Funds with Mr. Peale. Homespun from Philadelphia. Mentions Mr. Ronaldson, clothes merchant. [2774]

1808 Dec. 21. EDMUND BACON, Monticello, to T. J. ALS. 1 p. Endorsed by T. J. Edgehill-Randolph Papers. #5533.

Davy leaves today. Nathaniel Hooe's runaway slave, Gabril, working for Bacon. Hooe agrees to Bacon's hiring Gabril for the coming year. Garden work. [2775]

1808 Dec. 29. EDMUND BACON, Monticello, to T. J. ALS. Fragment. 2 pp. Endorsed by T. J. Edgehill-Randolph Papers. #5533.

Davy left before aspens ready. Killed Negroes' dogs. Debates planting flax and cotton. Mr. Watkins comes. Phill Hubbard and Bedford Davy to do sawing. Mentions Mr. Chisolm, garden work, and Sheppard. [2776]

1809 Jan. 7. T. J., Washington, to ANDREW BENADE, Bethlehem, Pennsylvania. ALS. 1 p. Photostat. Original owned by Moravian College for Women Library, Bethlehem. #3111.

Draft to Craven Peyton. [2776-a]

1809 Jan. 12. EDMUND BACON, Monticello, to T. J. ALS. 2 pp. Endorsed by T. J. Edgehill-Randolph Papers. #5533.

Money from George Jefferson in Richmond. Money due Johnson Rowe, Richard Johnson, Anderson Rowe, Charles Houchens, and John Pace. Washington lamb flock. Purchases from Mr. Higginbotham at Milton. Garden work. Mr. Watkins arrived. Stone masons working. Davy brought no raspberries. Mrs. Dangerfield's Negroes. Runaway slave. T. J. note mentions Nicholas Giannini.   [2777]

1809 Jan. 19. EDMUND BACON, Monticello, to T. J. ALS. 1 p. Endorsed by T. J. Edgehill-Randolph Papers. #5533.

Garden work. Nail making. Mr. Watkins took Sheppard, Davy, and Bartlet. Moses, Joe, Jim Hubbard, Lewis, John, Wormly, and Wagner Davy working. [2778]

1809 Feb. 6. T. J., Washington, to EDMUND BACON. ALS. 1 p. Edgehill-Randolph Papers. #5533.

No Milton mail. Wants wool sample from Merino sheep.   [2779]

1809 Feb. 6. T. J. to CHARLES WORTHINGTON. DS. 1 p. Photocopy. Original owned by Victor B. Levit. #8265-b.

Draft on Office of Discount and Deposit, Washington.   [2779-a]

1809 Feb. 6. T. J. to JOHN COX. ADS. 1 p. Edgehill-Randolph Papers. #5533.

Draft on Office of Discount and Deposit, Washington.   [2779-b]

1809 Feb. 6. T. J. to SAMUEL HARRISON SMITH. ADS. 1 p. Edgehill-Randolph Papers. #5533.

Draft on Office of Discount and Deposit, Washington.   [2779-c]

1809 Feb. 6–Mar. 1. T. J. ACCOUNT WITH PETER MILLER. D. 1 p. In un-identified hand. #6004.

T. J.'s bread buying.   [2780]

1809 Feb. 9. EDMUND BACON, Monticello, to T. J. ALS. 1 p. Endorsed by T. J. Edgehill-Randolph Papers. #5533.

Wool sample enclosed. Corn buying.   [2781]

1809 Feb. 20. T. J., Washington, to EDMUND BACON. ALS. 1 p. #6918-a.

Bacon's trip to Washington delayed until arrival of Milton post. Wagon to carry corn and oats for horses, and bacon. Fodder, only, to be purchased on road. 8 horses and mules expected. 8 horses and 8 people returning to Monticello. [2781-a]

1809 Feb. 24. EDMUND BACON, [Monti]cello, to T. J. ALS. Fragment. 1 p. En-dorsed by T. J. Edgehill-Randolph Papers. #5533.

[Break in text]. Ditch digging and fence building.   [2782]

1809 Feb. 25. T. J., Washington, to THADDEUS KOSCIUSZKO. ALS. 2 pp. Photo-copy. Original owned by National Museum, Cracow, Poland. #9013.

Secretary, Mr. Coles, carries public dispatches. Losses of exports caused by em-bargo. U.S. may enter war if enemies' edicts not repealed before Congress meets. Kosciuszko's financial affairs. John Barnes disabled. Retirement from Presidency imminent.   [2782-a]

1809 Feb. 27. T. J. to SAMUEL LATHAM MITCHELL. ANS. 1 p. #6900.

Letter from T. M. Randolph, Jr., care of Mr. Barker.   [2783]

1809 Apr. 26. WILLIAM ROSCOE to T. J. ALS. File draft. 3 pp. Photostat. Origi-nal owned by City of Liverpool Public Library. #5128-a.

Introduces John Bradbury, to study natural history of Louisiana. *The Life and Pontificate of Leo X.*   [2784]

1809 Apr. 27. T. J., Washington, to ROBERT PATTERSON. ALS. 1 p. Photostat. Location of original not known. #3449.

Elias Boudinot to leave mint. Offers job to Patterson, allowing him also to continue work at the College (University of Pennsylvania).   [2785]

1809 May 24. T. J., Washington, to JAMES MADISON AND JOHN BARNES. DS. 1 p. Edgehill-Randolph Papers. #5533.

Note payable at Office of Discount and Deposit.   [2786]

1809 Sept. 18. T. J., Monticello, to JAMES MADISON, Montpelier. ALS. 1 p. #4793.

Edward Coles reports Madison goes to Washington. Benjamin Franklin Randolph ill, T. J. may go without Martha Randolph.   [2787]

1809 Nov. 28. T. J. MEMORANDUM. AD. 2 pp. McGregor Library. #3620.

Provisions for winter from Mrs. Lewis.   [2788]

1809 Dec. 22. WILSON CARY NICHOLAS, Warren, to T. J. ALS. File draft. 4 pp. #1729.

Acknowledges T. J. letter of Dec. 16 admonishing him for resigning from Congress. Ill health reason for leaving. Opposed to embargo. Prefers war rather than appeasement.   [2788-a]

1809 Dec. 29. T. J. PLAT OF LEGO. AD. 1 p. 11½″ x 9″. Photostat. Original owned by Miss Olivia Taylor. #5214.   [2789]

[1809]. T. J. LIST OF FARM ACREAGES AND SLAVES BORN 1743–1809. A.D. 2 pp. Microfilm. Original owned by James Monroe Museum and Memorial Library, Fredericksburg. #3159.

Land in Albemarle County from N. Lewis, Overton, Carter, Wells, and Brown. Lands identified by names Tufton, Portobello, Monticello, Hendersons, Ingrahams, Milton, Shadwell, Lego, Shadwell Mountain, Pouncey's, Limestone (Sharp's), Hardware. Lands in Bedford and Campbell Counties: Dan Robinson, Poplar Forest, Tomahawk, Callaway Patent, John Robinson's, Buffalo, Johnson. Lists slaves by date of birth.   [2789-a]

1809–1811. BURGESS GRIFFIN'S LIST OF BLANKETS AND BEDS AT POPLAR FOREST. AMS 2 pp. Endorsed by T. J. Edgehill-Randolph Papers. #5533.

Lists slaves.   [2791]

1810 Jan. 15. T. J., Monticello, to SAMUEL KERCHEVAL. ALS. 2 pp. Photostat. Original owned by Mr. and Mrs. R. W. Stoneburner. #4453. Printed: L and B XII, 341–43.

Academy in Frederick County.   [2793]

1810 Feb. 26. T. J., Monticello, to THADDEUS KOSCIUSZKO. ALS. 4 pp. Photocopy. Original owned by National Museum, Cracow, Poland. #9013. Printed: L and B XII, 365–70, extract.

Explains reticence in writing candidly while in Presidency. War in Europe.

Chesapeake affair. U.S. preparations for defense: military stores, sulphur, arms, artillery, founderies, military school, soldiers, seaport defenses at New York and New Orleans, gunboats. Recommendations to Congress for settlement of territory of Orleans by land grants not carried out, nor classing of militia by age. Privateers and pirates. Admiration of Madison. Retirement to Monticello, family, books. Schedule of day spent in correspondence, shops, garden, on horseback at farms, society of friends, and reading. Health. Discusses ploughs, harrows, seeding, harvesting, and politics with his neighbors. Education of young men living at Charlottesville. Personal finances and debt. John Barnes, Kosciuszko's stock, and T. J.'s financial indebtedness to Kosciuszko.   [2793-a]

1810 July 12. JOHN STEELE, Philadelphia, to T. J. ALS. 1 p. Endorsed by T. J. Edgehill-Randolph Papers. #5533.
Seeds care of Collector of Richmond.   [2794]

1810 Sept. 17. T. J., Monticello, VOUCHER TO CASHIER OF BANK OF PENN-SYLVANIA. ADS. 1 p. Owned by George Green Shackelford. #3525-p.
Funds due Thaddeus Kosciuszko paid to John Barnes.   [2795]

1810 Sept. 17. MARTHA C. LEWIS, LUCY B. LEWIS, ANN M. LEWIS, and CHARLES L. LEWIS, Livingston County, Kentucky, to T. J. ALS. 2 pp. Owned by the Misses Margaret and Olivia Taylor. #8937.
Death of Mrs. Charles L. Lewis. Move to Kentucky and conditions there. Loss of servants. Poor financial condition. Indebtedness to Mr. Peyton. Asks T. J.'s intervention also, Uncle Randolph, Mr. Randolph, P. Carr, and D. Carr. Mentions Aunt Carr, Mrs. Randolph, and Polly Carr. Description of Ohio River, shovel fish, buffalo fish, carp, and other fish.   [2795-a]

1810 Sept. 30. T. J., Monticello, to PETER MINOR. ALS. 9 pp. #4899. Printed: Betts, *Farm Book*, 376–78, extract.
Denies that must build canal lock at order of Directors of Rivanna Company. Crown grant makes river T. J.'s land, and inquests agreed that T. J.'s dam does not interfere with rights of others. Rappahannock River and Appomattox Mills disputes. Mentions Henry Williams, Milton, and Secretary's Ford.   [2796]

1810. T. J. INDENTURE WITH GEORGE DIVERS AND DIRECTORS OF RIVANNA COMPANY. AD. File draft. 2 pp. Edgehill-Randolph Papers. #5533.
Right of way over T. J.'s canal and river holdings from Secretary's Ford to Sandy Falls at Shadwell. Mentions Thomas Mann Randolph, Jr.   [2798]

1811 Feb. 7. T. J. TRIGONOMETRY PROBLEMS. AD. 2 pp. Edgehill-Randolph Papers. #5533.
Demonstration of instrument error at noon.   [2799]

1811 Feb. T. J. MEMORANDUM. AD. 1 p. Photostat. Original owned by Miss Ellen Coolidge Burke. #5096-b.
List of charges to ship flour from Lynchburg to Richmond: toll and drayage, storage and cooperage, and market price at Richmond, written on verso of flour shipping bill. Mentions corn, wheat, and Morris and Dunnington.   [2799-a]

1811 March 7. T. J., Monticello, to ROBERT PATTERSON. ALS. 1 p. #8923-a.
Nautical Almanac. Mentions John Garnett's edition and English edition. [2799-b]

1811 Apr. 1. T. J., Monticello, to GEORGE JEFFERSON. ALS. 1 p. Photostat.
Original owned by Jack N. Herod. #6365.
   William Johnson of Milton moving T. J.'s crop. Letter for James Oldham.
Samuel J. Harrison, in charge of T. J.'s Bedford tobacco, is to place money on one
of T. J.'s accounts. Bedford flour.   [2800]

1811 Apr. 16. T. J., Monticello, to THADDEUS KOSCIUSZKO. ALS. 2 pp. Photocopy. Original owned by National Museum, Cracow, Poland. #9013.
   Previous letter under State Department dispatches via John Armstrong or David
Ballie Warden. War between England and France; U.S. adherence to peace. U.S.
economy. Extinction of national debt. Imported items only to be taxed. Self-
sufficiency of household manufacturing means poor only have to pay salt tax.
Revenues applied to canals, roads, schools. Quaker system. Happiness and prosperity of citizens are first duties of government. Anti-war sentiments. Revolutions
in Spanish America. John Barnes and Kosciuszko's financial affairs.   [2800-a]

1811 Apr. 17. T. J. SURVEY MAP OF LINE BETWEEN LEGO AND PANTOPS.
AD. 1 p. 20¼" x 16½". Edgehill-Randolph Papers. #5533.   [2801]

1811 May 12. T. J., Monticello, to THADDEUS KOSCIUSZKO. ALS. 1 p. Photocopy. Original owned by National Museum, Cracow, Poland. #9013.
   Bills of exchange, one under Secretary of State's dispatches. Mentions Joel Barlow and John Barnes.   [2801-a]

1811 June 3. T. J., Monticello, to CORNELIA RANDOLPH. ALS. File draft. 1 p.
Edgehill-Randolph Papers. #5533.
   Mrs. Edgeworth's *Moral Tales.* Virginia and Mary taking care of Cornelia's silk-
worm. Mrs. Higginbotham gave dolls.   [2802]

1811 July 8. T. J., Monticello, to THADDEUS KOSCIUSZKO. ALS. 2 pp. Photocopy. Original owned by National Museum, Cracow, Poland. #9013.
   Reticent tone of letters during Presidency based on fear correspondence might
fall into hands of English or French. Kosciuszko's financial affairs. Mentions Joel
Barlow, David Ballie Warden, John Barnes, and London.   [2802-a]

1811 Aug. 16. T. J., Poplar Forest, to CHARLES CLAY. ALS. 1 p. Photostat.
Original owned by C. A. Mallory. #5465.
   Will meet Clay at Double Branches in road. Dinner with Mr. Steptoe. [2803]

1811 Sept. 8. T. J., Monticello, to CHARLES WINGFIELD. ALS. 1 p. Photostat.
Original owned by Mrs. Cornelius Timothy Smith, Jr. #3826.
   Wingfield to conduct funeral of Martha Jefferson Carr.   [2804]

1811 Sept. 12. T. J., Monticello, to DAVID HIGGINBOTHAM, Milton. ALS. 1 p.
Owned by Mr. and Mrs. Henry M. Taylor. #3330.
   George Jefferson to sell lot in Richmond which T. J. bought from Col. Byrd.

Boundaries formerly owned by Patrick Cutts and Robert C. Nicholas, later by Mr. Ambler. Other lots at Beverly town, Westham, including ferry landing.   [2805]

18[11] Nov. T. J. BILL OF SALE TO DAVID HIGGINBOTHAM. D. Fragment. 1 p. 19th-century copy. Owned by Mr. and Mrs. Henry M. Taylor. #3330.
    Land on James River at Richmond. Mentions Robert Carter Nicholas. Witnessed by Coleman Estes, Charles Vest, David Huckstep, and John Burks.   [2806]

1811 Dec. 24. T. J. to JAMES LEITCH. ANS. 1 p. Photostat. Original owned by T. J. Memorial Foundation. #5196.
    Orders thread.   [2807]

1812 Jan. 30. GIBSON AND JEFFERSON, Richmond, to T. J. ALS. 1 p. Endorsed by T. J. Edgehill-Randolph Papers. #5533.
    Mr. Ligon's tobacco and flour prices not correct. Mentions George Jefferson, Mr. Rutherfoord, and Mr. Mutter.   [2808]

1812 Feb. 3. T. J. to JAMES LEITCH. ANS. 1 p. Photostat. Original owned by T. J. Memorial Foundation. #5196.
    Orders teacups, coffee cups, saucers, and paper.   [2809]

1812 Feb. 15. T. J. to JAMES LEITCH. ANS. 1 p. Photostat. Original owned by T. J. Memorial Foundation. #5196.
    Clothing for Burwell (slave).   [2810]

1812 Feb. 27. PATRICK GIBSON, Richmond, to T. J. ALS. 2 pp. Endorsed by T. J. Edgehill-Randolph Papers. #5533.
    Albemarle tobacco prices. Mentions Mr. Bruce. Flour market. Goods from Alexandria by Johnson. Adam's plow. Nail rod.   [2811]

1812 Mar. 2. JAMES LIGON of GIBSON AND JEFFERSON, Richmond, to T. J., Monticello. ALS. 1 p. Endorsed by T. J. Edgehill-Randolph Papers. #5533.
    Mr. Johnson brings supplies.   [2812]

1812 Mar. 11. PATRICK GIBSON, Richmond, to T. J. ALS. 1 p. Endorsed by T. J. Edgehill-Randolph Papers. #5533.
    Tobacco prices. C. Peyton's Billy ordered seeds sent care of Mr. Higginbotham. Johnson brings nail rod. Flour sales. Washington reports suggest embargo.   [2813]

1812 Apr. 13. GIBSON AND JEFFERSON, Richmond, to T. J. ALS. 1 p. Endorsed by T. J. Edgehill-Randolph Papers. #5533.
    Sales to O. Philpotts, J. G. Gamble, Mr. Leiper, and W. Hancocke.   [2814]

1812 Apr. 16. GIBSON AND JEFFERSON, Richmond, to T. J. ALS. 1 p. Endorsed by T. J. Edgehill-Randolph Papers. #5533.
    Payments to Hay, Wirt, and Tazewell.   [2815]

1812 Apr. 20. T. J., Monticello, to PATRICK GIBSON. ALS. 1 p. #6918-a.
    Flour sales and prices.   [2815-a]

1812 Apr. 21 T. J. to JAMES LEITCH. ANS. 1 p. Photostat. Original owned by T. J. Memorial Foundation. #5196.
    Orders box of wafers.   [2816]

1812 May 24. T. J. to DAVID HIGGINBOTHAM, Milton. ALS. 1 p. Owned by Mr. and Mrs. Henry M. Taylor. #3330.

Byrd's trustees wrong about Richmond land, as Charles Carter's deed, in Henrico or General Court, shows.   [2817]

1812 June 9. GIBSON AND JEFFERSON, Richmond, to T. J. ALS. 1 p. Endorsed by T. J. Edgehill-Randolph Papers. #5533.

T. J.'s account, particularly draft against Harrison.   [2818]

1812 June 18. GIBSON AND JEFFERSON, Richmond, to T. J. ALS. 1 p. Endorsed by T. J. Edgehill-Randolph Papers. #5533.

O. Philpotts has not paid.   [2819]

1812 June 18 and 21. DAVID MICHIE to T. J. 2 L. In 2700-a.

1812 June 20 and 22. T. J. to DAVID MICHIE. 2 L. In 2700-a.

1812 June 23. JAMES LIGON for GIBSON AND JEFFERSON, Richmond, to T. J. ALS. 1 p. Endorsed by T. J. Edgehill-Randolph Papers. #5533.

Remittance made. Deposit made to order of James Hamilton of Williamsboro, North Carolina.   [2820]

1812 June 27 and July 20. T. J. to DAVID MICHIE. 2 L. In 2700-a.

1812 June 27 and July 20. DAVID MICHIE to T. J. 2 L. In 2700-a.

1812 June 28. T. J., Monticello, to THADDEUS KOSCIUSZKO. ALS. 3 pp. Photocopy. Original owned by National Museum, Cracow, Poland. #9013. Printed: L and B XIII, 168–72.

War of 1812. Relations with France. Possible burning of New York and London. Congreve rockets. England's economy. U.S. invasion of Canada. U.S. privateers. Trade relations with France. Artillery. Advanced state of manufacturing in U.S. Household machinery. Carding and spinning machines and looms for wool, cotton, and linen. Merino sheep. Kosciuszko's finances. Mentions John Barnes, Mr. Morton of Bordeaux, Indians, British intrigues with Col. Henry.   [2820-a]

1812 Aug. 5. T. J., Monticello, to THADDEUS KOSCIUSZKO. ALS. 1 p. Photocopy. Original owned by National Museum, Cracow, Poland. #9013. Printed: L and B XIII, 182–83.

Bill of exchange. U.S. invasion of Canada. U.S. to possess all of St. Lawrence except Quebec. U.S. privateers will do more damage to English commerce than combined European navies could.   [2820-b]

1812 Aug. 12. JAMES LIGON for GIBSON AND JEFFERSON, Richmond, to T. J. ALS. 1 p. Endorsed by T. J. Edgehill-Randolph Papers. #5533.

Encloses bank note. Spinning machine from New York.   [2821]

1812 Sept. 23. MRS. MOLLY LEWIS to T. J., Monticello. ALS. 1 p. Endorsed by T. J. Owned by Mrs. Edwin Page Kirk. #5291.

Joe to help her. Wishes barrels sent to be filled with surplus apples. Mentions Mr. Chisolm. T. J. note on verso: surveying calculations for Shadwell fields. [2822]

1812 Oct. 9. GIBSON AND JEFFERSON, Richmond, to T. J. ALS. 1 p. Endorsed by T. J. Edgehill-Randolph Papers. #5533.

Unless Congress intervenes, wheat and flour prices will rise.   [2823]

1812 Oct. 26. GIBSON AND JEFFERSON, Richmond, to T. J. ALS. 1 p. Endorsed by T. J. Edgehill-Randolph Papers. #5533.
Wheat and flour prices.   [2824]

1812 Nov. 2. GIBSON AND JEFFERSON, Richmond, to T. J. ALS. 1 p. Endorsed by T. J. Edgehill-Randolph Papers. #5533.
Note falling due. Wheat and flour prices.   [2825]

1812 Nov. 5. T. J., Monticello, to DAVID HIGGINBOTHAM, Milton, forwarded to Richmond. ALS. 1 p. Owned by Mr. and Mrs. Henry M. Taylor. #3330.
William Short's reply. Going to Bedford. To settle with Higginbotham on return about land matter.   [2826]

1812 Dec. 7. GIBSON AND JEFFERSON, Richmond, to T. J. ALS. 1 p. Edgehill-Randolph Papers. #5533.
T. J.'s bond to T. Gwathmey due for payment. Wheat and flour prices.   [2827]

1812. T. J. PRINTED VOLUME, *THE PROCEEDINGS OF THE GOVERN-MENT OF THE UNITED STATES IN MAINTAINING THE PUBLIC RIGHT TO THE BEACH OF THE MISSISSIPPI, ADJACENT TO NEW ORLEANS AGAINST THE INTRUSION OF EDWARD LIVINGSTON* (New York: Ezra Sargeant, 1812), 80 pp. Endorsed by T. J. to John G. Jackson, with T. J. marginal notations. McGregor Library, Jeffress Collection. Printed: L and B XVIII, 1–132.
                                                                               [2828]

[*Post*-1812.] T. J., Charlottesville, LETTERCOVER to NICHOLAS PHILIP TRIST, Donaldsonville, Louisiana. AD. 1 p. Owned by T. J. Memorial Foundation. #5385-n.   [2829]

1813 Jan. 8. T. J., Monticello, to JEREMIAH GOODMAN, Poplar Forest. ALS. 1 p. Photostat. Location of original not known. Deposit by T. J. Memorial Foundation. #5555.
Dick arrived via Lynchburg. Mr. Gibson and wheat. Tobacco at Lynchburg to Mr. Harrison. Mr. Perry too slow. Goodman's debts. Mentions Mr. Darnell, Richmond.   [2830]

1813 Jan. 12. T. J., Monticello, to JAMES RONALDSON, Philadelphia. ALS. 2 pp. Photostat. Original owned by Miss Sarah Mortimer. #5506-a. Printed: L and B XIII, 204–6; Betts, *Garden Book*, 505, extract.
Cork tree from Paris. Olives from Aix, sainfoin from Malta, and acorns from Marseilles. African rice in Georgia and Kentucky. Household manufactures. Marine hospitals, seamen, Mr. Gallatin. Grain trade with enemies. War in Iberian Peninsula and the Baltic.   [2831]

1813 Jan. 27. JAMES LIGON for GIBSON AND JEFFERSON, Richmond, to T. J. ALS. 1 p. Endorsed by T. J. Edgehill-Randolph Papers. #5533.
Funds to credit of James Hamilton of Williamsboro, North Carolina, in Bank of Virginia. Mentions Mr. Gibson.   [2832]

1813 Jan. 31. DAVID HIGGINBOTHAM BOND TO WILLIAM SHORT. In hand of T. J. AD. 2 pp. Owned by Mr. and Mrs. Henry M. Taylor. #3330.

Higginbotham, of Albemarle County, to pay Short, of Philadelphia, in U.S. dollars, through Bank of Richmond. Short assigns to Joseph and George [Marx?]. Witnessed by Carter H. Harrison. [2833]

1813 Jan. 31. DAVID HIGGINBOTHAM BOND TO WILLIAM SHORT. In hand of T. J. AD. 1 p. Owned by Mr. and Mrs. Henry M. Taylor. #3330.
Text as 2833; not assigned. Marked paid. [2834]

1813 Jan. 31. DAVID HIGGINBOTHAM BOND TO WILLIAM SHORT. In hand of T. J. AD. 1 p. Owned by Mr. and Mrs. Henry M. Taylor. #3330
Text as 2833; not assigned. Signature of David Higginbotham crossed out by Short, who notes on verso, 1816 May 4, that the obligation was satisfied with land found outside the Indian Camp estate limits. [2835]

1813 Feb. 10. PATRICK GIBSON, Richmond, to T. J. ALS. 1 p. Endorsed by T. J. Edgehill-Randolph Papers. #5533.
Mr. T. Taylor, presumably for Mr. Gallego, offers to buy land from T. J. Edmund Randolph at Winchester. Mr. Randolph's boat to bring powder. [2836]

1813 Feb. 27. DAVID HIGGINBOTHAM BOND TO WILLIAM SHORT. In hand of T. J. AD. 1 p. Owned by Mr. and Mrs. Henry M. Taylor. #3330.
Rent on the Indian Camp lands. [2837]

1813 Mar. 26. WILL OF ANNE SCOTT JEFFERSON MARKS. In hand of T. J. AD. 1 p. Edgehill-Randolph Papers. #5533.
Debts of Hastings Marks. Bequests to children of Martha Jefferson Randolph. Thomas Jefferson Randolph, executor. Witnessed by William McLung, Hugh Chisholm, and E. Bacon. [2838]

1813 Apr. 20 and May 30. T. J. to DAVID MICHIE. 2 L. In 2700-a.

1813 Apr. 23 and May 30. DAVID MICHIE to T. J. 2 L. In 2700-a.

1813 Apr. 28. PATRICK GIBSON, Richmond, to T. J. ALS. 1 p. Endorsed by T. J. Edgehill-Randolph Papers. #5533.
William Marshall, hired by Mr. Taylor to handle Mazzei's affairs. T. J. and Mr. Randolph must sign bill. Flour prices. [2839]

1813 May 4. PATRICK GIBSON, Richmond, to T. J. ALS. 1 p. Endorsed by T. J. Edgehill-Randolph Papers. #5533.
Bill of sale, drawn by William Marshall for Mr. Taylor, transferring Mazzei's lands, invalid, unless Mazzei U.S. citizen. Flour sale. [2840]

1813 May 6. T. J. to CHARLES CLAY. L. 1 p. Photostat of printed extract from unidentified newspaper. Deposit of T. J. Memorial Foundation. #5385-a.
Spinning machine. [2841]

1813 May 29. PATRICK GIBSON, Richmond, to T. J. ALS. 1 p. Endorsed by T. J. Edgehill-Randolph Papers. #5533.
Mazzei's power of attorney acceptable to Mr. Taylor. Flour prices. Burr has powder; other powder from T. White. [2842]

1813 May 30. T. J., Monticello, to JOHN ELIASON, Georgetown. ALS. 1 p. Owned by James D. Cox. #6449. Printed: Betts, *Farm Book*, 393, extract.

· [Thomas Eston] Randolph to keep mill. Terms of tenancy.   [2843]

1813 July 24. PATRICK GIBSON, Richmond, to T. J. ALS. 1 p. Endorsed by T. J.
Edgehill-Randolph Papers. #5533.

Paid Mr. Hooe and Judge Holmes. Chocolate by mail. David Higginbotham paid.
Forwards statement of sale to Mr. Taylor. Mr. Derieux, at Eagle Tavern, claims
Mazzei's property.   [2844]

1813 Aug. 4. PATRICK GIBSON, Richmond, to T. J. ALS. 1 p. Endorsed by T. J.
Edgehill-Randolph Papers. #5533.

Judah's note discounted. No money from O. Philpotts for tobacco, although
William Hay, Jr., sues.   [2845]

1813 Aug. 5. CHARLES L. LEWIS, Salem, Livingston County, Kentucky, to T. J.
ALS. 1 p. Endorsed by T. J. Owned by the Misses Margaret and Olivia Taylor.
#8937.

Asks financial help to be sent by Mr. Woods.   [2845-a]

1813 Aug. 8. T. J. to DAVID HIGGINBOTHAM. ANS. 1 p. Owned by Mr. and
Mrs. Henry M. Taylor. #3330.

Mr. Gamble wants to know about common on land in Richmond. Papers of
James Buchanan and Col. Byrd, and Carter's deed.   [2846]

1813 Aug. 14. PATRICK GIBSON, Richmond, to T. J. ALS. 1 p. Endorsed by T. J.
Edgehill-Randolph Papers. #5533.

Deed to Mr. Taylor when he returns from Springs.   [2847]

1813 Aug. 15. T. J., Monticello, to SAMUEL H. SMITH. ALS. 1 p. Owned by
George Green Shackelford. #5661-a.

Recommends Joseph Dougherty for position with Smith. *National Intelligencer*
subscription mentioning Mr. Gale. Regrets that Mrs. Smith had to leave country
for city life.   [2848]

1813 Aug. 29. WILLIAM CANBY to T. J. L. 1 p. Photocopy of 19th-century copy
owned by Isaac Jeanes. #4598-b.

Religious questions.   [2848-a]

1813 Sept. 18. T. J. to WILLIAM CANBY. L. 2 pp. Photocopy of 19th-century
copy owned by Isaac Jeanes. #4598-b. Printed: L and B XIII, 376–78.

Religious questions. Mentions Jesus, Richard Mott, Papists, Quakers, Presbyterians, Methodists, Baptists, Aristides, Cato, William Penn, John Tillotson, Euclid,
geometry, and St. Athanasius.   [2848-b]

1813 Sept. JOSEPH SLAUGHTER MAP OF TOMAHAWK CREEK LANDS. D.
1 p. 22″ x 12½″. Endorsed by T. J. Edgehill-Randolph Papers. #5533.   [2849]

1813 Oct. 6. T. J., Monticello, to PATRICK GIBSON. ALS. File draft. 2 pp. Mc-
Gregor Library. #4019.

Drafts from Bedford to Brown and Robertson, sheriff of Bedford, Nimrod
Darnell, and Jeremiah A. Goodman. Payments to Craven Peyton, David Higgin-

botham, William Garth (deputy sheriff of Albemarle) and Gales and Seaton (editors of *National Intelligencer*), Washington. Flour prices. Drought. Wheat, corn, tobacco. British blockade of Chesapeake Bay impossible to maintain in winter.
[2850]

1813 Oct. 13. PATRICK GIBSON, Richmond, to T. J. ALS. 1 p. Endorsed by T. J. Edgehill-Randolph Papers. #5533.
Attends to drafts. Encloses notes care of Mr. Higginbotham as mails undependable. Flour prices. Mr. H. paid for repairing T. J.'s watch.   [2851]

1813 [*ante*-Oct.] T. J. BLANK CONTRACT. ADS. 1 p. #4195. Cf. Betts, *Farm Book*, 86.
Lease for people of Milton to cut firewood between Milton and Colle.   [2852]

1813 Nov. 13. PATRICK GIBSON, Richmond, to T. J. ALS. 1 p. Endorsed by T. J. Edgehill-Randolph Papers. #5533.
Sends money. Flour prices.   [2853]

1813 Dec. 21. PATRICK GIBSON, Richmond, to T. J. ALS. 1 p. Endorsed by T. J. Edgehill-Randolph Papers. #5533.
T. J.'s note. Flour prices. Embargo has stopped West Indies trade.   [2854]

1813 Dec. 29. PATRICK GIBSON, Richmond, to T. J. ALS. 1 p. Endorsed by T. J. Edgehill-Randolph Papers. #5533.
Flour sales and wheat prices.   [2855]

1813–1814. T. J. ACCOUNT WITH DR. WILLIAM STEPTOE. ADS. 1 p. In hand of William Steptoe; endorsed by T. J. Edgehill-Randolph Papers. #5533.
Services rendered and medications prescribed. Patients include slaves Aggy, Maria, Ambrose, and Sally. Mentions Mr. Clay.   [2857]

1814 Jan. 19. PATRICK GIBSON, Richmond, to T. J. ALS. 1 p. Endorsed by T. J. Edgehill-Randolph Papers. #5533.
Sends money. Flour prices and sales, some to Alexandria, Va.   [2858]

1814 Feb. 1. T. J., Monticello, to MRS. ELIZABETH TRIST, at Mr. Gilmer's, near Henry Court House. ALS. 1 p. Photostat. Original owned by John R. Burke. #5422.
Ellen Wayles Randolph's translation of letter. Martha's new daughter Septimia Ann. Children have whooping cough. Thomas Mann Randolph, Jr. probably leaves in spring to campaign. T. J. Randolph's girl friend at Warren. Mr. Gilmer's brothers well. Dr. Gilmer left Milton for place bought from Key near Mr. Minor.
[2859]

1814 Feb. 8. PATRICK GIBSON, Richmond, to T. J. ALS. 1 p. Endorsed by T. J. Edgehill-Randolph Papers. #5533.
Nail rod, corks, and powder by Mr. Johnson. Flour prices. T. J. accounts with Samuel P. Adams, James Brown, Jr., and Ignatius J. Dick.   [2860]

1814 Feb. 26. PATRICK GIBSON, Richmond, to T. J. ALS. 1 p. Endorsed by T. J. Edgehill-Randolph Papers. #5533.

T. J.'s note falls due. New one enclosed for signature. Prospect of peace and trade with Holland influence tobacco market, but not flour prices.   [2861]

1814 Mar. 2. PATRICK GIBSON, Richmond, to T. J. ALS. 1 p. Endorsed by T. J. Edgehill-Randolph Papers. #5533.
Note may not be received. Will pay anyway, renew new one when received. Flour prices. Encloses money.   [2862]

1814 Mar. 4. MARTIN DAWSON & CO., Milton, to T. J., Monticello. ALS. 1 p. Endorsed by T. J. Edgehill-Randolph Papers. #5533.
T. J.'s note to Craven Peyton for corn purchases. Will accept draft on Richmond or cash at Charlottesville.   [2863]

1814 Mar. 13. PATRICK GIBSON, Richmond, to T. J. ALS. 1 p. Endorsed by T. J. Edgehill-Randolph Papers. #5533.
New procedure for handling T. J.'s notes. Encloses notes. Flour sales.   [2864]

1814 Mar. 26. PATRICK GIBSON, Richmond, to T. J. ALS. 1 p. Endorsed by T. J. Edgehill-Randolph Papers. #5533.
Notes received. Encloses bank notes.   [2865]

1814 Apr. 20. PATRICK GIBSON, Richmond, to T. J. ALS. 1 p. Endorsed by T. J. Edgehill-Randolph Papers. #5533.
Repeal of restrictions brought flour buyers. Awaiting armistice. Mr. Albert bought tobacco. Powder.   [2866]

1814 May 4. PATRICK GIBSON, Richmond, to T.J. ALS. 1 p. Endorsed by T. J. Edgehill-Randolph Papers. #5533.
Sends bank notes. Flour sales await armistice.   [2867]

1814 May 7. T. J., Monticello, to CRAVEN PEYTON, Monteagle. ALS. 1 p. Owned by John Peyton. #5843-c.
Encloses John Henderson's quitclaim for Peyton's use in defending against Elizabeth Henderson's claim that Peyton purchased for T. J. lands of minor Henderson children without her knowledge or permission. Mentions James Henderson, Thomas Hornsby.   [2867-a]

1814 June 13. PATRICK GIBSON, Richmond, to T. J. ALS. 1 p. Endorsed by T. J. Edgehill-Randolph Papers. #5533.
Flour prices declining.   [2868]

1814 June 13. T. J., Poplar Forest, to THOMAS LAW. ALS. 4 pp. #9561. Printed: L and B XIV, 138–44.
Received and read Law's *Second Thoughts on Instinctive Impulses*. Agrees with his philosophy of morality in man. Wollaston's theory whimsical. Truth, love of God not foundations of morality as atheists, Deists virtuous men. Diderot, d'Alembert, d'Holbach, Condorcet examples. Taste, egoism also false. Helvetius quoted, refuted. Man's innate moral instinct true basis of morality. Education a corrective for its absence. Virtue conditioned by utility. Lord Kames, in *Principles of Natural Religion*, says the same.   [2868-a]

1814 June 28. T. J., Monticello, to THADDEUS KOSCIUSZKO. ALS. 2 pp. Photocopy. Original owned by National Museum, Cracow, Poland. #9013.

Embargo and blockade prevent John Barnes from sending remittances to Kosciuszko. Insecurity of U.S. banks. Investment in Pennsylvania bank stock transferred to U.S. government loan. Peace between England and France. Great events at Paris. Mentions Mr. Morton, Boice & Kurtz, William Murdock of London, Messrs. Barings Brothers & Co. of London.   [2868-b]

1814 July 13. PATRICK GIBSON, Richmond, to T. J. ALS. 1 p. Endorsed by T. J. Edgehill-Randolph Papers. #5533.

Nail rod. T. J.'s account.   [2869]

1814 Aug. 13. T. J., Monticello, to CRAVEN PEYTON, Monteagle. ALS. 1 p. #9706.

Charles L. Lewis' deed.   [2870-a]

1814 Aug. 14. T. J., Monticello, to WILLIAM WIRT. ALS. 8 pp. McGregor Library. #5622. Printed: L and B XIV, 162–73.

Recollections of Patrick Henry. Topics: Loan Office scandal, Journals of House of Burgesses, Address to King, Memorials to Houses of Lords and Commons, Stamp Act, Royle's *Virginia Gazette*, Parson's Cause, Two-penny Act, Resolutions of 1765, T. J.'s revision of Virginia laws, Philips case, proposals for dictator. Names: John Robinson, James Maury, John Camm, Richard Bland, Nathaniel West Dandridge, John Littlepage, John Marshall, John Daly Burke, Peyton Randolph, Peter Randolph, George Wythe, Edmund Pendleton, Robert Carter Nicholas, Henry Lee, Richard Henry Lee, John Page, George Mason, George III of England, Edmund Randolph, Josiah Philips, Thomas L. Lee, John Taylor of Caroline, Andrew Moore, Edward Stevens. Places: Hanover, Williamsburg, Dismal Swamp, Staunton, Fredericksburg.   [2871]

1814 Aug. 24. PATRICK GIBSON, Richmond, to T.J. ALS. 1 p. Endorsed by T. J. Edgehill-Randolph Papers. #5533.

Impossible to send funds North. Transactions with Mr. Dufief and Mr. Barnes. Mr. Johnson brings cotton and castings. Nail rod. Mr. Randolph to send earthenware.   [2872]

1814 Sept. 27. T. J., Monticello, to PATRICK GIBSON. ALS. File copy. 1 p. #9562.

Wishes loan extension to cover taxes in Bedford. Credit of bank paper doubtful. Merchant support might help. Jugs from Mr. R. Randolph and glass from Capt. Oldham. Oil and corks from Gibson. Mentions flour, wheat, and tobacco. Trip to Bedford.   [2872-a]

1814 Sept. 30. PATRICK GIBSON, Richmond, to T. J., ALS. 2 pp. Endorsed by T. J. Edgehill-Randolph Papers. #5533.

Note received and enlarged. System of curtailing notes ended, but doubtless soon resumed. Bank measures necessary, merchants doing everything possible. Encloses money. Will send supplies by Johnson, pay Mr. Oldham for glass.   [2873]

1814 Oct. 27. PATRICK GIBSON, Richmond, to T. J., Monticello. ALS. 1 p.
Endorsed by T. J. Edgehill-Randolph Papers. #5533.

Encloses note for renewal. Forwards copy to Bedford by Samuel J. Harrison.
Drafts will be paid on presentation.   [2874]

1814 Nov. 12. T. J., Poplar Forest, to CHARLES CLAY. ANS. 1 p. Photostat. Deposit of T. J. Memorial Association. #5385-a.

Spectacles from Mr. McAlister in Philadelphia.   [2875]

1814 Dec. 7. PATRICK GIBSON, Richmond, to T. J. ALS. 1 p. Endorsed by T. J.
Edgehill-Randolph Papers. #5533.

Dr. Brockenbrough and John Harvie's note. No money from O. Philpotts. Tobacco and flour prices.   [2876]

1814 Dec. 14. PATRICK GIBSON, Richmond, to T. J. ALS. 1 p. Endorsed by T. J.
Edgehill-Randolph Papers. #5533.

Jacquelin Harvie paid John Harvie's note.   [2877]

1814 Dec. 23. T. J., Monticello, to PATRICK GIBSON. ALS. Draft copy [?]. 1 p.
On verso of lettercover to T. J., Monticello, via Milton. #5914.

John Harvie's payment. Tobacco and wheat. Ghent negotiations indicate Great
Britain to accept peace. Judgments against O. Philpotts. Directs payment to Jeremiah Goodman at Poplar Forest near Lynchburg.   [2878]

1814 Dec. 30. JEREMIAH A. GOODMAN, Poplar Forest, to T. J., Monticello. ALS.
3 pp. Endorsed by T. J. Edgehill-Randolph Papers. #5533.

Dick leaves for Monticello with supplies, wheat for mill. Wheat prices for Mr.
Mitchell. Phill Hubbard at Poplar Forest, perhaps to marry Hanna. Farm business.
Mentions Mr. Darnell, Lewis Brown, Mr. Clarkson, and Mr. Cole.   [2879]

1814. T. J. LIST OF SLAVES BORN 1743–1814. AD. 2 pp. Microfilm. Original
owned by James Monroe Museum and Memorial Library, Fredericksburg. #3159.
                                                                        [2880]

1815 Jan. 7. T. J., Monticello, to PATRICK GIBSON. ALS. Draft copy [?]. 1 p.
On verso of lettercover to T. J., Monticello. #5759.

Payment to T. J. Randolph. Flour and tobacco sales. Hopes British will not
delay treaty to get part of Maine.   [2881]

1815 Feb. 21. T. J., Monticello, to CHARLES CLAY. ALS. 1 p. #6410.

Sends T. J.'s lenses with Clay's spectacles. Victory at New Orleans.   [2883]

[Post-1815 Mar. 3.] J. Jervey, William Yeadon, Benjamin Elliott, and R. Y. Hayne,
Charleston, S.C., to T. J. ALS. 1 p. On verso of title page, John B. White, *An Oration . . . in Commemoration of the Federal Constitution* (Charleston, '76 Association, 1815). McGregor Library. #3576. McG. *A1807 .R39.

Dedication to T. J. of White's Republican address to Charleston '76 Association.
                                                                      [2883-a]

[1815 Mar. 14] THADDEUS KOSCIUSZKO to T. J. ALS. 2 pp. In French. Endorsed by T. J. #6237.

Believes T. J. has become Secretary of State again. Requests interest due him, and principal after formal peace with England. Advises establishment of a military college to insure republican spirit necessary for a free state. [2883-b]

1815 Mar. 29. PATRICK GIBSON, Richmond, to T. J. ALS. 1 p. Endorsed by T. J. Edgehill-Randolph Papers. #5533.

Sends money. Flour sales. Northern and European markets. Ship from France ruined Havana market. Shadwell flour. None from Bedford. Tobacco prices. [2884]

1815 Apr. 7. JEREMIAH A. GOODMAN, Poplar Forest, to T. J. ALS. 1 p. Endorsed by T. J. Edgehill-Randolph Papers. #5533.

Papers on Scott served to Bedford sheriff. Tobacco to Richmond, except that for Lynchburg sale. Wheat sales to pay Mr. Mitchell. [2885]

1815 May 10. PATRICK GIBSON, Richmond, to T. J. ALS. 1 p. Endorsed by T. J. Edgehill-Randolph Papers. #5533.

Encloses money. Flour sold to Tarleton Saunders. Tobacco sales. [2886]

1815 May 12. T. J., Monticello, to WILLIAM WIRT, Richmond. ALS. 1 p. McGregor Library. #5622.

Opinion reconsidered in case of Josiah Philips. Outlawry, attainder, immunity. [2887]

1815 Aug. 13. MARTHA JEFFERSON RANDOLPH, Monticello, to T. J. ALS. 1 p. Owned by T. J. Memorial Foundation. #7443-e.

Buckingham court business requiring T. J.'s attention. Illness in family. [2887-a]

1815 June 1. T. J., Poplar Forest, to Mrs. ELIZABETH TRIST, Mr. Gilmer's, near Henry Court House. ALS. 2 pp. #6995.

Victory at New Orleans proves popular support for Union there and in Kentucky, and Tennessee. Andrew Jackson's threatened removal: rule of law versus national survival. Bonaparte an usurper, Bourbons expelled, but people must rule. U.S. maxim not to meddle in European affairs. U.S. system distinct in interests, but connected in commerce. England governed by merchants, not by common sense. Will not permit U.S. to remain at peace, but will renew Orders in Council, resume impressment, force war on U.S. as they forced France to become nation of soldiers. Mr. and Mrs. Divers well. Peas in. Monticello family well. T. J. Randolph's marriage. Peter Carr's death. Mentions Mr. and Mrs. Peachy Gilmer. [2888]

1815 June 16. JEREMIAH A. GOODMAN, Lynchburg, to T. J., Monticello. ALS. 1 p. Endorsed by T. J. Edgehill-Randolph Papers. #5533.

His dismissal. Refers to Mr. Yancey. Wheat, oats, tobacco on own farm. [2889]

1815 July 5. PATRICK GIBSON, Richmond, to T. J., Monticello. ALS. 1 p. Endorsed by T. J. Edgehill-Randolph Papers. #5533.

Notes involving T. J., Benjamin Jones, John Vaughan, and John Harvie. Flour sales. Shipments from Shadwell and Bedford. Johnson brings cotton. [2890]

1815 July 17. PATRICK GIBSON and JAMES LIGON to T. J. ANS. 1 p. Endorsed by T. J. Edgehill-Randolph Papers. #5533.

Harry will bring cotton instead of Mr. Johnson. [2890-a]

1815 Aug. 5. T. J., Monticello, to WILLIAM WIRT, Richmond. ALS. 6 pp. McGregor Library. #5622. Printed: L and B XIV, 335–42.

Rhode Island Resolutions, mentioning Richard Henry Lee, Francis Lightfoot Lee, John Adams, Thomas Johnson, Edmund Randolph, William Fleming, John Fleming, John Robinson, Peyton Randolph, Edmund Pendleton, George Wythe, and Richard Bland. Virginia aristocracy isolated from European society. Wild Irish in Valley of Virginia between Blue Ridge and northern mountains. Social strata: aristocrats, half-breeds, pretenders, yeomanry, overseers. Bland's pamphlet, Dickinson's *Letters from a Pennsylvania Farmer*. Allows quotes in loan office, Josiah Philips cases, but not on Henry and Lee addresses. Benjamin Harrison, Robert C. Nicholas gave some information. T. J. role in Burgesses session welcoming Lord Botetourt. T. J. prepared answer in 1775 to Lord North's propositions at session called by Lord Dunmore. Mr. Nicholas represented James City County at Williamsburg. T. J. first met Patrick Henry in 1759–60 at Nathaniel West Dandridge's, whose sister Mrs. Spotswood married John Campbell.   [2891]

1815 Aug. 6. WILSON CARY NICHOLAS, Warren, to T. J. ALS. 1 p. Endorsed by T. J. Edgehill-Randolph Papers. #5533.

Randolph Jefferson dying, perhaps willing estate to wife, Mitchie B. Pryor Jefferson.   [2892]

1815 Aug. 28. PATRICK GIBSON, Richmond, to T. J., Poplar Forest. ALS. 1 p. Endorsed by T. J. Edgehill-Randolph Papers. #5533.

Will attend to draft. Sends note for renewal. Flour and wheat prices. Tobacco prices high despite news from England.   [2893]

1815 Sept. 21. PATRICK GIBSON, Richmond, to T. J. ALS. 1 p. Endorsed by T. J. Edgehill-Randolph Papers. #5533.

Requests reply to item 2893, which is copied on verso.   [2894]

1815 Nov. 8. EDMUND BACON, Monticello, to T. J. ALS. 2 pp. Endorsed by T. J. Edgehill-Randolph Papers. #5533.

Cider. Corn prices at Richmond. Sharp and Mr. Craven sold corn. Mr. Randolph urges buying. Wheat. Mr. Ham.   [2895]

1815 Dec. 8. T. J., Poplar Forest, to DR. WILLIAM STEPTOE. ALS. Draft copy. 1 p. Edgehill-Randolph Papers. #5533.

Unidentified sick boy.   [2896]

1815 Dec. 29. MARTIN DAWSON, Milton, to T. J., Monticello. ALS. 1 p. Endorsed by T. J. Edgehill-Randolph Papers. #5533.

Account with Dawson, mentions Edmund Bacon and John Bacon. Payment by draft on Richmond or cash. Partnership with John Watson.   [2897]

1815–1819. T. J. ACCOUNT. AD. 1 p. Microfilm. Original owned by James Monroe Museum and Memorial Library, Fredericksburg. #3159.

Household costs.   [2898]

1816 Jan. 13. T. J., Monticello, to JOHN ADLUM, near Georgetown. ALS. 1 p. #6033. Printed: Betts, *Garden Book*, 554–55, extract.

Wine sent while in Washington. Mr. Penn's fox grape cuttings to be sent care of William F. Gray, Fredericksburg, to Milton.   [2899]

1816 Jan. 31. T. J., Monticello, to HENRY JACKSON, CHARGÉ DES AFFAIRS OF U.S., PARIS. ALS. 1 p. #6995.

Thanks Jackson for kind words in letter to George Ticknor. T. J. sending Jackson letters to Ticknor, and Mr. Appleton, Consul at Leghorn. Dabney Terrell of Kentucky will deliver T. J.'s letters to Jackson on his way to Geneva.   [2900]

1816 Feb. 22. JOHN G. ROBERT for PATRICK GIBSON, Richmond, to T.J. ALS. 1 p. Endorsed by T. J. Edgehill-Randolph Papers. #5533.

Teneriffe wine from Dr. Fernandes, through Fox and Richardson, by Mr. Gilmer's boat.   [2901]

1816 Mar. 13. PATRICK GIBSON, Richmond, to T. J. ALS. 1 p. Endorsed by T. J. Edgehill-Randolph Papers. #5533.

Flour prices. Tobacco sales.   [2902]

1816 Mar. 18. PATRICK GIBSON, Richmond, to T. J. ALS. 1 p. Endorsed by T. J. Edgehill-Randolph Papers. #5533.

Tobacco prices. Flour prices. Sales to P. F. Smith, John M. Warwick and William Gilliat.   [2903]

1816 Apr. 27. JAMES LIGON for PATRICK GIBSON, Richmond, to T. J. ALS. 1 p. Endorsed by T. J. Edgehill-Randolph Papers. #5533.

Flour sales to William H. Hubbard and to Smith and Riddle. Mr. Warwick brought flour at Col. Randolph's instructions.   [2904]

[1816 Apr.] THADDEUS KOSCIUSZKO to T. J. AL. Draft in French. 4 pp. Photocopy. Original owned by National Museum, Cracow, Poland. #9013-a.

American victory over English. T. J.'s and Addison's [sic] reputation high in Europe. Discusses state of Poland and Alexander I's failure to recreate old boundaries. At Soleure, Switzerland. Personal finances in U.S. England respects U.S., not Europe, whose ministers corrupt. English and French commerce.   [2904-a]

1816 May 14. JOHN STEELE, Collector's Office, Philadelphia, to T. J. ALS. 1 p. Endorsed by T. J. Edgehill-Randolph Papers. #5533.

Wine and macaroni from Stephen Cathalan at Marseilles.   [2905]

1816 May 22. T. J., Monticello, to PETER MINOR. ANS. 1 p. Photocopy. Original owned by Mrs. Frank J. McHugh, Jr. #8134.

Invitation for peas and punch.   [2905-a]

1816 June 1. JOHN STEELE, Collector's Office, Philadelphia, to T. J. ALS. 1 p. Edgehill-Randolph Papers. #5533.

Goods from Stephen Cathalan on ship *Five Sisters*. Encloses bill of lading. [2906]

1816 Aug. 25. T. J., Monticello, to PETER MINOR. ALS. File draft. 1 p. With enclosed AD, n.d., T. J. STATEMENT to PETER MINOR. #5984.

Directors of Rivanna Company to discuss Shadwell Mills and lock. Mr. Meriwether's basin. To Bedford. Rivanna Company was authorized by Acts of Legislature, 1794, 1805, and 1806, to open Rivanna River to Milton, later to Moore's Ford opposite Charlottesville. T. J.'s dam blocks navigation; lock needed.   [2907]

1816 Sept. 4. T. J., Monticello, to WILLIAM WIRT. ALS. 2 pp. McGregor Library. #5622.

Wirt's *Sketches of . . . Patrick Henry*. Henry did not read Livy annually. May have read some Greek and Roman history. Perhaps read Stith's *History of the First Discovery and Settlement of Virginia*. Professor at William and Mary College Richard Graham, not Greeme. Henry counselor for Nathaniel West Dandridge, not James Littlepage. John Blair more important than Bolling Starke. To Bedford.
[2908]

1816 Sept. 29. T. J., Poplar Forest, to WILLIAM WIRT. ALS. 1 p. McGregor Library. #5622.

Revisions for Wirt's *Sketches of . . . Patrick Henry*. To Albemarle.   [2909]

1816 Sept. 29. T. J. REVISIONS TO WILLIAM WIRT'S [*SKETCHES OF . . . PATRICK HENRY*]. AD. 4 pp. McGregor Library. #5622.

Questions concerning William Livingstone, U.S. House of Representatives, John Jay, Richard Henry Lee. Edward Foy was Lord Dunmore's secretary. Thomas Nelson President of Assembly at William Nelson's death in Hanover. William Henry and John Syme cowards. John Page, member of committee, thought Patrick Henry a coward. Committee of Safety refused commands to William Byrd and Henry. Distrust between Patrick Henry and Edmund Pendleton. Compares Demosthenes and Henry. Henry glad to leave Congress at Philadelphia. George Washington's military law.   [2910]

1816 Oct. 2. WILLIAM WIRT, Richmond, to T. J. ALS. 1 p. McGregor Library. #5622.

Have *Sketches of . . . Patrick Henry* miscarried?   [2911]

1816 Oct. 8. T. J., Monticello, to WILLIAM WIRT. ALS. 2 pp. McGregor Library. #5622.

Manuscript received at Poplar Forest relates to time of T. J.'s service in Europe. Josiah Philips, Edmund Randolph, and Patrick Henry. St. George Tucker's *Blackstone's Commentaries*.   [2912]

1816 Oct. 21. JAMES LIGON for PATRICK GIBSON, Richmond, to T. J., Poplar Forest. ALS. 1 p. Endorsed by T. J. Edgehill-Randolph Papers. #5533.

Account.   [2913]

1816 Nov. 12. T. J., Poplar Forest, to WILLIAM WIRT, Richmond. ALS. 2 pp. McGregor Library. #5622.

Old Virginia aristocracy preserved by entail. Wirt's *Sketches of . . . Patrick Henry* should not be retrenched. Quarterly reviews will attack it, but those in Edinburgh may defend. Critics will compare it with Plutarch and Nepos. Proper canons of criticism.   [2914]

1816 Dec. 30. CRAVEN PEYTON, Monteagle, to T.J., Monticello. ALS. 1 p. Endorsed by T. J. Edgehill-Randolph Papers. #5533.

Will send deed.   [2915]

[1816–1826]. T. J. to JAMES LEITCH. AN. In unidentified hand. 1 p. Photostat. Original owned by T. J. Memorial Foundation. #5196.

Orders needles. [2916]

1817 Mar. 10. T. J., Monticello, to JAMES MADISON. ALS. 1 p. #3360.

Letter and seeds by Bessy. University of Virginia Board of Visitors. Madison to join John Hartwell Cocke, David Watson, Joseph Carrington Cabell, and James Monroe, at Monticello. [2917]

1817 Mar. 23. CRAVEN PEYTON, Monteagle, to T. J., Monticello. ALS. 1 p. Endorsed by T. J. Edgehill-Randolph Papers. #5533.

Has sold corn promised to T. J. [2918]

1817 Mar. 27. T. J., Monticello, to JOHN H. COCKE, Bremo. ALS. 1 p. Photocopy. #9513-a.

Scuppernong wine. Marseilles fig, paper mulberry, and cuttings of Lombardy poplar from France. Prickly locust (Robinia hispida) and snowberry bush brought from Pacific by Capt. Lewis. Mentions gooseberry bush. [2918-a]

1817 Apr. 8. ALBEMARLE COUNTY COURT ORDER ESTABLISHING COMMITTEE TO EVALUATE T. J. AND T. J. RANDOLPH PROPOSAL TO BUILD ROADS. D. 2 pp. Copy certified by Alexander Garrett, Clerk. Endorsed by T. J. AN. 2 pp. COMMENTS ON PROPOSED ROADS, MILEAGES OF SAME. Edgehill-Randolph Papers. #5533.

Road from Orange Fork near Lewis' Ferry on lands of Richard Sampson, T. J. Randolph, and T. J. to mouth of Chapel Branch. Road on Charles L. Bankhead's lands from near Charlottesville to Secretary's Ford, thence to mouth of Chapel Branch. Road from Moore's Creek to area of Colle. Committee: Joseph Coleman, Benjamin Childress, Andrew Hart, Robert McCullock, Jr., John Slaughter, Brightberry Brown, and Horsley Goodman. [2919]

1817 Apr. 10. JAMES MADISON, Montpelier, to T. J. ALS. 1 p. Endorsed by T. J. #3942.

Business in Washington prevents attending Central College. Board of Visitors. Mentions Bizet. To Monticello when Board meets next. [2920]

1817 May 5. RESOLUTION OF UNIVERSITY OF VIRGINIA BOARD OF VISITORS. DS. 1 p. Photocopy. In hand of James Madison; signed by T. J. #3430.

T. J. and John Hartwell Cocke jointly to be interim Central College Proctor. Also signed by John Hartwell Cocke, James Monroe, and James Madison. [2922]

1817 June 6. T. J., Monticello, to JOHN WAYLES EPPES. ALS. 1 p. Photostat. Original owned by Mrs. Francis E. Shine. #3509.

Mr. Wood's school. Francis to study arithmetic using Bezout, Latin, and Greek. Greetings from Mrs. Randolph to Mrs. Eppes. [2923]

1817 June 25. T. J., Monticello, to JAMES DINSMORE, Petersburg. ALS. 1 p. #3353.

Agreed upon Perry's site for Central College. Perry to do wood work. Chisolm to meet T. J. in Lynchburg to secure bricklayer. Hopes for subscriptions. Mentions Mr. Nelson. [2924]

1817 July 15. CHRISTOPHER L. BLACK, WILLIAM SINGLETON, HOUGH-TON SMITH, SAMUEL BURGESS, AND THOMAS D. CANDY, Charleston, South Carolina, to T. J., Monticello. ALS. 1 p. On verso of title page, **Benjamin Elliott**, *An Oration . . . in Commemoration of American Independence* (Charleston, '76 Association, 1817). McG. *A1807 .R39.

Benjamin Elliot's Republican address to Charleston '76 Association.   [2925]

1817 Aug. 11. JAMES LIGON for PATRICK GIBSON, Richmond, to T. J. ALS. 1 p. Endorsed by T. J. Edgehill-Randolph Papers. #5533.

Mr. Fisher not paid by Mr. Dufief. Flour sales. Mentions V. W. Southall.   [2926]

1817 Sept. 1. T. J., Poplar Forest near Lynchburg, to THOMAS COOPER. ALS. Draft copy. 4 pp. #7254-a.

Plans advancing for college of general science, supported by public subscription and perhaps by Virginia legislature, which granted constitution and made Governor its patron. Visitors James Monroe, James Madison, Joseph C. Cabell, John Hartwell Cocke, David Watson, and T. J. Construction underway near Charlottesville on pavilion for professor of languages. To teach Greek and Latin, history and rhetoric, perhaps French, Spanish, Italian, and German. Asks Cooper to recommend person. Not common school of Yankee Latin. Classical scholars among Irish immigrants and at Dublin College. Will plan other pavilions in the future. Mathematical and physiological sciences. Offers Cooper zoology, botany, mineralogy, chemistry, anatomy, and law. Mathematician from Europe. 200–300 students expected initially. William and Mary to deteriorate to grammar school because of poor climate. Charlottesville climate ideal. Free moral and political climate compensates for brawling Presbyterian and Baptist ministers. Invites visit. Fredericksburg and Charlottesville stage to bring Cooper to Monticello, to meet Mr. Correa.   [2927]

[1817 Sept. 15]. THADDEUS KOSCIUSZKO to T. J. AL. Draft. 2 pp. Photocopy. Original owned by National Museum, Cracow, Poland. #9013-a.

Asks T. J. to appoint someone to replace John Barnes upon his death to manage financial affairs in U.S. Mentions James Madison. Comments on oppression of Poland, and government of U.S. Urges military college.   [2927-a]

1817 Sept. 18. T. J., Poplar Forest, to SAMUEL J. HARRISON. ALS. 2 pp. #1771.

Recommending European wines. Offers letters to Cathalan, Consul at Marseilles, and Appleton, Consul at Leghorn. Mentions Capt. Bernard Peyton as importer. Describes Roussillon, Hermitage, Florence, and Claret of Marseilles wines.   [2927-b]

1817 Oct. 4. CRAVEN PEYTON, Monteagle, to T. J. ALS. 1 p. Endorsed by T. J. Edgehill-Randolph Papers. #5533.

Corn sales.   [2928]

1817 Oct. 27. PATRICK GIBSON, Richmond, to T. J. ALS. 1 p. Endorsed by T. J. Edgehill-Randolph Papers. #5533.

Flour. No cotton.   [2929]

1817 Nov. 10. PATRICK GIBSON, Richmond, to T. J. ALS. 1 p. Endorsed by T. J. Edgehill-Randolph Papers. #5533.

Flour sales to E. Williams and Joseph A. Weed. Reports from England of rise in flour prices stir local market. Note renewed in U.S. Bank. [2931]

1817 Nov. 22. JOHN ORGAN to JOEL YANCEY, Bedford. ALS. 1 p. Endorsed by T. J. Edgehill-Randolph Papers. #5533.

Will make survey. [2932]

1817 Dec. 10. EDMUND BACON, Monticello, to T. J. ALS. 2 pp. Endorsed by T. J. Edgehill-Randolph Papers. #5533.

John leaves in morning. Purchases, including corn, from Mr. Higginbotham, Mr. Bankhead, and John Fagg. Turkeys, coopers, carpenter. Payment received from Gibson and Jefferson. Apologizes for questioning T. J.'s judgment on interest due. Canal work. [2933]

1817 Dec. 11. PATRICK GIBSON, Richmond, to T. J. ALS. 1 p. Endorsed by T. J. Edgehill-Randolph Papers. #5533.

Flour sold to Robert K. Jones. [2935]

1817 Dec. 16. JAMES LIGON for PATRICK GIBSON, Richmond, to T. J., Monticello. ALS. 1 p. Endorsed by T. J. Edgehill-Randolph Papers. #5533.

Goods from Norfolk by Mr. Gilmore. [2936]

1817 Dec. 24. EDMUND BACON to T. J., Monticello. ALS. 1 p. Endorsed by T. J. Edgehill-Randolph Papers. #5533.

Brothers urge move to Missouri. Asks salary increase. Compares own to overseers of James Monroe, Tufton, Mr. Higginbotham, Mr. Burnley. [2937]

1817 Dec. 31. T. J., Monticello, to DAVID HIGGINBOTHAM. ALS. 1 p. #3537.

Mr. Short's reconveyance of Indian Camp lands to Higginbotham. [2938]

[*Post*-1817.] T. J. SURVEY OF UNIVERSITY SITE SHOWING ROTUNDA, "EAST STREET," AND "WEST STREET." AD. 1 p. 8" x 6¼"." See Nichols, Item 327.

In folder with other fragments, one 3½" x 5¾", giving dimensions for "Perry's Houses." [2938-a]

1818 Apr. 7. T. J. BILL TO JOHN BROWN, JUDGE OF CHANCERY AT STAUNTON, AGAINST RIVANNA COMPANY. D. 65 pp. In clerk's hand. #4899.

Previous inquests established that T. J.'s dam above Shadwell mill not harmful, or infringement of public rights. An aid to navigation, already did most of Rivanna Company's work by getting through South West mountains. Company built locks above mill, interfering with its water supply, and placed toll house near mill. Directors profiting at T. J.'s expense. Mentions Albemarle Co., Milton, Moore's ford, Secretary's ford, Sandy Falls, Potomac River, James River, Rappahannock River, Peter Jefferson, Thomas Mann Randolph, Peter Minor, John Brown, and directors George Divers, William D. Meriwether, Nimrod Bramham, Dabney Minor, and John Kelly. Appended letter, copy 1817 July 23, George Divers, Farmington, to T. J. claiming overriding rights of canal company. Appended document, copy, 1817 Aug. 7, T. J. approves insertion of above letter. Appended document, copy, 1818 April 7, Rivanna Company claims precedence. T. J. cannot include Rivanna River as his property. Mentions Ray's ford, Stuart & Coalter, Richard Sampson, Richard Farrar and Mr. Henderson. Copies certified by N. H. Lewis and William S. Eskridge.   [2939]

1818 May 3. T. J., Poplar Forest, to JOHN WAYLES EPPES. ALS. 2 pp. Photostat. Original owned by Mrs. Francis E. Shine. #3509.

Letter at Flood's. To Monticello. Mr. Dashiell will board Francis. Greek of Xenophon's *Cyropaedia* preferable to Lucian. Mr. Yancey can get books at Cotton's in Lynchburg. Bezout and Euclid. Francis to sleep alone to avoid itch common at Dr. Carr's school. Subscription papers for Central College. Literary Fund and University.   [2940]

1818 July 14. EDMUND BACON to T.J. ALS. 2 pp. Endorsed by T. J. Edgehill-Randolph Papers. #5533.

Land in West. Mentions Mr. Randolph.   [2941]

1818 July 27. NELSON BARKSDALE, PROCTOR OF CENTRAL COLLEGE, DEED TO PRESIDENT AND DIRECTORS OF LITERARY FUND. AD. 1 p. In hand of T. J. Signed by Barksdale. Owned by Charles E. Moran, Jr. #6269.

Transfers Central College lands and properties in Albemarle County to Literary Fund for benefit of University of Virginia as permitted by act of Legislature. Witnessed by Frank Carr, James Leitch, James Brown, and Alexander Garrett, Clerk of Albemarle County Court.   [2942]

1818 July 29. EDMUND BACON to T. J. ALS. 1 p. Endorsed by T. J. Edgehill-Randolph Papers. #5533.

Plows. No payment from Mr. Randolph. Payment from Mr. Dawson.   [2943]

1818 Aug. 13. JOHN STEELE, Customs House, Philadelphia, to T. J. ALS. 1 p. Endorsed by T. J. Edgehill-Randolph Papers. #5533.

Wine sent to Richmond. Sends bill of lading.   [2944]

1818 Oct. 19. MARTIN DAWSON, Milton, to T. J., Monticello. ALS. 1 p. Endorsed by T. J. Edgehill-Randolph Papers. #5533.

T. J. note to Edmund Bacon.   [2945]

[1818]. T. J. NOTES ON MADISON'S MAP. AD. Fragment. 1 p. McGregor Library. #3620.

Mentions Monticello, Potomac River, Willis's Mountain, and Blue Ridge Mountains.   [2946]

1819 Jan. 24. T. J., Monticello, to RICHARD DUKE, near Lindsay's Store. ALS. 1 p. Owned by Mrs. R. T. W. Duke. #6286.

Duties of Proctor of Central College. Nelson Barksdale suited for part of duties, but Alexander Garrett recommends Duke for other duties. To begin when Legislature approves University.

See item 1601, misdated 1819 Jan. 20.   [2947]

1819 Jan. 25. EDMUND BACON to T. J. ALS. 1 p. Endorsed by T. J. Edgehill-Randolph Papers. #5533.
Trip to the West. Market wagon.   [2948]

1819 Feb. 27. JAMES P. PRESTON, Council Chamber, Richmond, to T. J. ALS. 2 pp. Endorsed by T. J. #7254-a.
Appointment as Visitor of University.   [2949]

1819 Feb. 28. WILLIAM ROSCOE, Liverpool, to T. J., Monticello. ALS. File draft. 2 pp. Photostat. Original owned by City of Liverpool Public Library. #5128-a.
Submits for comment his pamphlets on the opening of the Liverpool Botanic Gardens, and on penal jurisprudence and the reformation of criminals. Mentions his life of Leo the Tenth, and Beccaria's *Essay on Crimes and Punishments.* [2950]

1819 Apr. 9. EDMUND BACON to T. J. ALS. 1 p. Endorsed by T. J. Edgehill-Randolph Papers. #5533.
Corn buying, some from Mr. Higginbotham. Draft on Richmond for debt. Powder from Mr. Osmond of Milton. T. J. mathematical notes on verso.   [2951]

1819 May 26. T. J., Monticello, to VICTOR ADOLPHUS SASSERNO, U.S. CONSUL, Nice, France. ALS. 2 pp. #6157.
Bellet wine. Nice wines. Mentions M. Spreafico. English terms for wines: Frontignan and Lunel of France, Pacharetti doux of Spain, Calcavalla of Portugal, Vin du Cap, Vin de Grave, Vin du Rhin, Vin de Hockheim, Madere sec, Pacharetti sec, vin d'Oporto, silky Madeira, and malmsey. Recent Marseilles wine acid. Desires former kinds shipped immediately care of Mr. Cathalan before Dec. winds drive ship off course to West Indies.   [2952]

1819 May 26. T. J., Monticello, to VICTOR ADOLPHUS SASSERNO, U.S. CONSUL, Nice, France. L. 3 pp. 19th-century French translation in unidentified hand. #6157.
See Item 2952.   [2953]

1819 June 1. MARTIN DAWSON, Milton, to T. J. ALS. 1 p. Endorsed by T. J. Edgehill-Randolph Papers. #5533.
T. J.'s suit against Rivanna Company. Mentions Daniel Colclaser, Ambrose Flannagan, William Bacon, Thomas D. Boyd, Joseph Gilmore, William F. Cardin, William D. Fitch, Thomas E. Randolph, William Johnson, and Edmund Bacon.
                                                                  [2954]

1819 June 2. EDMUND BACON to T. J., Monticello. ALS. 1 p. Endorsed by T. J. Edgehill-Randolph Papers. #5533.
Trip to the West.   [2955]

1819 June 14. EDMUND BACON to T. J. ALS. 1 p. Endorsed by T. J. Edgehill-Randolph Papers. #5533.
Financial transactions with Mr. Pollock, Mr. Craven, Mr. Maupin, and Bishop.
                                                                  [2956]

1819 June 22. JOHN ADAMS, Quincey, to T. J. L. 1 p. 19th-century copy. #2723-m. Printed: Adams, Charles Francis, *Works of John Adams* X, 380–81.

Mecklenburg Declaration of Independence cited from Essex *Register* and Raleigh *Register*. If had known about this at the time, would have spread in Whig newspapers and halls of Congress until T. J.'s Declaration of Independence. Better than Thomas Paine's *Common Sense*. Richard Caswell, William Hooper, and Joseph Hewes, Congressmen from North Carolina. [2957]

1819 June 30. EDMUND BACON to T. J., Monticello. ALS. 1 p. Endorsed by T. J. Edgehill-Randolph Papers. #5533.
Account with T. J. [2958]

1819 July 4. T. J., Monticello, to WILLIAM DAVENPORT, Philadelphia. ALS. 1 p. #4924.
Richmond bank note, not U.S. bank note, to pay bill sent through Mr. Patterson. Telescope. [2959]

1819 July 7. EDMUND BACON to T. J., Monticello. ALS. 1 p. Endorsed by T. J. Edgehill-Randolph Papers. #5533.
Trip to the West. [2960]

1819 July 9. T. J., Monticello, to JOHN ADAMS. L. 2 pp. Extract. 19th-century copy. #2723-m. Printed: L and B XV, 204–7.
Questions authenticity of Mecklenburg Declaration. Not reported by Thomas Ritchie or *National Intelligencer*. William Alexander, Richard Caswell, William Hooper, and Joseph Hewes all dead. Peter Horry's history of Francis Marion, Williamson, Ramsay, Marshall, Jones, Girardin, and Wirt do not mention it. Patrick Henry's similar resolutions greatly publicized. Dickinson a doubter, Hooper a Tory, and Hewes indecisive; Caswell strong Whig, but left early. Penn fixed Hewes. Doubts McKnitt a genuine name. [2961]

1819 July 26. EDMUND BACON, Monticello, to T. J. ALS. 2 pp. Endorsed by T. J. Edgehill-Randolph Papers. #5533.
Canal cleaned. No help from Mr. Randolph or Mr. Colclaser. Mill business. Barrels and corn. Money from Mr. Randolph and Mr. Pollock. Mentions Richmond, Mr. Meeks, Lego. Ailing horse. Jimmy and Shepherd sick. Flour shipment. [2962]

1819 Oct. 22. THOMAS COOPER, Philadelphia, to T. J. ALS. Draft. 2 pp. #8722.
See Item 1745. [2962-a]

1819 Oct. 28. T. J., Monticello, to [MATTHEW] CAREY. ANS. 1 p. #6389.
Epictetus of Elizabeth Carter and *Sophocles* of Robert Potter. Charles Thompson's translation of Old and New Testaments. [2962-b]

1819 Nov. 30. T. J., Monticello, to JAMES MADISON. ALS. 1 p. #6047.
Letters from Thomas Cooper. Mentions Mrs. Madison. [2963]

1819 Dec. 13. CRAVEN PEYTON, Monteagle, to T. J. ALS. 1 p. Endorsed by T. J. Edgehill-Randolph Papers. #5533.
Slave sale. [2964]

1819 Dec. 18. T. J., Monticello, to ARCHIBALD STUART, Staunton. ALS. 2 pp. Photostat. Original owned by Mrs. Peyton Cochran. #3762.
Mr. Fuller, met in Charlottesville, had poor proof of supposed discovery of the longitude. T. J. unwilling to make effort to check mathematical project at his age. Mentions Mrs. Stuart. [2965]

[1819]. T. J. SKETCH FOR SERPENTINE WALL. AD. 1 p. 2¾" x 8". #1871-a. Original of #2338. See Nichols, Item 315. [2966]

[1819]. T. J. PLAN FOR PAVILION X AT UNIVERSITY OF VIRGINIA. 12" x 13". #6944. See Nichols, Item 326-a.
Thomas S. Ridgeway statement on verso identifies as T. J.'s work. [2967]

[1819]. EDMUND BACON to T. J. ALS. 1 p. Endorsed by T. J. Edgehill-Randolph Papers. #5533.
Payment due John H. Craven, Maupin (the President's agent), Campbell, and Meeks. William D. Fitz of Milton holds notes. Land as financial security. T. J. endorsement mentions Jerry. [2968]

1820 Feb. 5. T. J., Monticello, to HENRY DEARBORN. ALS. 1 p. McGregor Library. #4397.
Gilbert Stuart portrait. Mentions Mrs. Randolph and Mrs. Dearborn. [2969]

1820 Feb. 16. MARTIN DAWSON, Milton, to T. J., Monticello. ALS. 1 p. Endorsed by T. J. Edgehill-Randolph Papers. #5533.
Note due Mr. Laporte at Richmond. [2970]

1820 Feb. 22. JOHN STEELE, Custom House, Philadelphia, to T. J. ALS. 1 p. Endorsed by T. J. Edgehill-Randolph Papers. #5533.
Wine by schooner *Industry* under Corson, care of Mr. Gibson, Richmond. Mr. Dodge's letter about ship *Emma Matilda*. [2971]

1820 Mar. 24. T. J. to JAMES LEITCH. ANS. 1 p. #9011.
Cotton, ticklenburg, osnaburg, and milk pans. [2971-a]

1820 Mar. 27. T. J., Monticello, to JOHN LAVAL, [Philadelphia]. ALS. 1 p. #6047.
Latin-Greek and La Porte du Theil editions of Aeschylus. Potter's translation of Euripides. Milton mail service. [2972]

1820 Mar. 31. JOHN STEELE. Custom House, Philadelphia, to T. J. ALS. 1 p. Endorsed by T. J. Edgehill-Randolph Papers. #5533.
Account with T. J. [2973]

1820 Apr. 11. T. J., Monticello, to MATTHEW CAREY. ALS. 1 p. Owned by George Green Shackelford. #3525-n.
New Olive Branch. Wants to exchange copy of Haines. Mentions Bernard Peyton of Richmond. [2974]

1820 Apr. 22. T. J., Monticello, to JOHN HOLMES. ALS. 2 pp. Photocopy. Original owned by Paul Mellon. #7289-b. Printed: L and B XV, 248–50.
Missouri question. Slavery, emancipation, expatriation, and evils of a geographical line. [2974-a]

1820 June 12. JOHN WAYLES EPPES, Buckingham, to T. J., Monticello. ALS. 3 pp. Endorsed by T. J. Photostat. Original owned by Mrs. Francis E. Shine. #3509.

University will not open in time for Francis Eppes. Prefers Virginia school and Virginian character. Yale University. T. J.'s problems with Wilson Cary Nicholas. Debts. Proposes to exchange U.S. Bank stock for T. J.'s. Negroes at Buckingham to be sent to Bedford for Francis. Francis left Laporte. Note on Richmond for Francis.   [2975]

1820 June 30. T. J. to JOHN WAYLES EPPES. ALS. Fragment. Draft copy. Last 2 pages only. Edgehill-Randolph Papers. #5533.

[Break in text]. Mentions Francis Eppes. Disposition of Bedford lands, including those of Thomas Mann Randolph, Jr. House like Pantops for Francis Eppes. To meet John Wayles Eppes at Poplar Forest after Visitors' meetings. Harpsichord from Millbrook to Poplar Forest for Martha and children. New Canton Road better than Buckingham Court House Road. University.   [2976]

1820 July 16. EDMUND BACON to T. J. ALS. 1 p. Endorsed by T. J. Edgehill-Randolph Papers. #5533.

Mr. Randolph's valuation of market wagon. Trip to the West. Beverly absent from carpenters.   [2977]

1820 Aug. 1. T. J. LEAF FROM HIS FARM BOOK. AMS. 2 pp. #7953.

Information for the 1820 Census at Monticello on recto. Verso lists slaves and clothing issued to them, 1820–21.   [2977-a]

1820 Oct. 26. MARTIN DAWSON, Milton, to T. J., Monticello. ANS. 1 p. Endorsed by T. J. Edgehill-Randolph Papers. #5533.

Bill of Mr. Edmund Meeks.   [2978]

1820 Nov. 7. T. J., Monticello, to ROBERT PATTERSON, by Mr. H. B. Trist, Philadelphia. ALS. 1 p. #6531.

Scholarship of H. B. Trist, son of H. B. Trist, grandson of Mrs. House.   [2979]

1820 Nov. 21. EDMUND BACON, Monticello, to T. J., Poplar Forest. ALS. 1 p. Endorsed by T. J. Edgehill-Randolph Papers. #5533.

Mr. Meeks leaving. Mentions Mr. Colclaser. Mr. Randolph in Richmond. [2980]

1820 Dec. 27. T. J., Monticello, to WILLIAM ROSCOE. ALS. 2 pp. Photostat. Original owned by City of Liverpool Public Library. #5128. Printed: L and B XV, 302–4.

Thanks him for his pamphlet on penal jurisprudence. Beccaria's principles are being attempted in U.S. University of Virginia. Tolerance of intellectual error. Upheavals in England puzzling. Queen must be a rallying point for discontented. James Maury is sending bust to T. J.   [2981]

1820 Dec. 30. T. J. to MR. BACON. ANS. 1 p. #6026.

Pork delivered to Mr. Minor.   [2982]

[1820]. T. J. NOTES ON CONSTRUCTION OF DINING HALL AND PARLOR. AD. 2 pp. Microfilm. Original owned by James Monroe Museum and Memorial

Library, Fredericksburg. #3159.

Building to be constructed at the University of Virginia.   [2983]

1821 Jan. 26. EDMUND BACON to T. J. ALS. 1 p. Endorsed by T. J. Edgehill-Randolph Papers. #5533.

Accounts. Mentions T. J. Randolph.   [2984]

1821 Jan. 27. T. J., Monticello, to MR. CARDELL. ALS. 1 p. Photostat. Original owned by O. O. Fisher. #3449.

Membership in American Academy of Language and Belles Lettres.   [2985]

1821 Jan. 28. EDMUND BACON to T. J., Monticello. ALS. 1 p. Endorsed by T. J. Edgehill-Randolph Papers. #5533.

Accounts.   [2986]

1821 Feb. 1. MARTIN DAWSON, Milton, to T. J., Monticello. ALS. 1 p. Endorsed by T. J. Edgehill-Randolph Papers. #5533.

Accounts with Joseph Gilmore, John Rogers, and Edmund Meeks.   [2987]

1821 Feb. 26. T. J., Monticello, to DABNEY CARR TERRELL. LS. 4 pp. In hand of Ellen Randolph. Signed by T. J. Photostat. Original owned by Mrs. John Shelton White. #4757-b.

Ellen's copy of a letter, 1814 Jan. 16, to Thomas Cooper of Carlisle, Pa., in which he outlined course of study for law, will be enclosed. Four epochs of English Law: Bracton (Common Law), Coke, Matthew Bacon, and Blackstone. Course begins with law at time of King James, goes to Bacon, then to Blackstone and Wooddeson. Baron Geoffrey Gilbert, Cooper's edition of Justinian's *Institutes* (for Roman law), Reeves' *History*, Vaughan's Reports of Gardener and Sheldon. Mentions Browne's *Compendium of the Civil and Admiralty Law, Jure Ecclesiastica*, and *Les Institutions du Droit et la Nature et des Gens de Rayneval*, Fonblanque's edition of Francis' *Treatise of Equity*.   [2988]

1821 Feb. 26 [misdated 1824 by Trist] T. J., Monticello, to DABNEY TERRELL. L. 2 pp. Extract by N. P. Trist. #5385-u. Printed: L & B XV, 318–22.

Copy of Item 2988 with added note praising J. H. Thomas' *A Systematic Arrangement of Lord Coke's First Institute of the Laws of England* . . . .   [2988-a]

1821 Feb. T. J. SLAVE BREAD LIST. AD. 1 p. Owned by T. J. Memorial Foundation. #4726-a.   [2989]

[1821] Mar. 31. T. J., Monticello, to CLAUDIUS CROZET, West Point, New York. ALS. 1 p. Photostat. Original owned by Mrs. Jay W. Johns. #6924.

University of Virginia professors.   [2990]

1821 June 16. T. J. PROMISSORY NOTE TO JAMES LYLE. DS. 1 p. Edgehill-Randolph Papers. #5533.

Witnessed by James M. Randolph and Tarleton Saunders.   [2991]

1821 June 27. T. J., Monticello, to THOMAS MANN RANDOLPH, JR., GOVERNOR OF VIRGINIA, Richmond. ALS. 1 p. #4610.

Martha brought Col. Taylor's letter to Judge Roane. Hail storm damage to crops between Monticello and Mechunk, including those of T. M. Randolph, Rogers, Gilmer. Trip to Bedford; work on mill. James Randolph studies Greek with T. J. and French with girls; soon to New London, Va. Funds for University and Proctor's account. Plans for Library. Literary Board. Martha not well. William and Anne Cary Randolph Bankhead at Monticello with children, except John.   [2992]

1821 July 27. THOMAS MANN RANDOLPH, JR., Richmond, to T. J. ALS. 3 pp. Endorsed by T. J. Edgehill-Randolph Papers. #5533.

Absences from Richmond of Mr. Pendleton, Sr., and Mr. Daniel delay Literary Board. Loan directed by Legislature. Negro revolt. Wheat, flour and tobacco prices. Mentions Winchester bushel. Careers in agriculture and law. Henrico lands. Edgehill for James Randolph. Ridicule by New England is the strongest ally of education and reason in area.   [2994]

1821 Aug. 12. T. J., Monticello, to [CRAVEN PEYTON]. ALS. 1 p. #9706.

Lame horse. Mr. Bacon's fodder accounts. Payment from Isham Randolph. Anne Bankhead and Charles Bankhead. To Bedford. Dr. Watkins to charge treatments to his sister to T. J.'s own account.   [2994-a]

1821 Aug. 15. T. J. NOTICE OF MEETING OF UNIVERSITY BOARD OF VISITORS. ADS. 1 p. #7254-a.

To arrange affairs before General Assembly meets. Also signed by John Hartwell Cocke and James Breckenridge.   [2995]

1821 Sept. 25. T. J., Monticello, to SAMUEL TAYLOR, Battletown, Jefferson County. ALS. 1 p. #3354.

Opening of University awaits action of Legislature on Literary Fund Loan. [2996]

1821 Sept. 27. T. J., Monticello, to JAMES MONROE, Highlands. ALS. 1 p. #3942.

Lewis' letter indicates James Barron is unprincipled.   [2997]

1821 Nov. 23. T. J., Monticello, to NATHANIEL MACON. ALS. 2 pp. Photostat. Original owned by O. O. Fisher. #3449.

Unauthorized publishing of his letters. Future corruption of U.S. government. Consolidating effect of judiciary. Missouri crisis.   [2998]

1821 Nov. 23. T. J., Monticello, to CLAUDIUS CROZET, West Point, New York. ALS. 1 p. Photostat. Original owned by Jay W. Johns. #6924.

Treatise on Descriptive Geometry.   [2999]

1821 Nov. 30. T. J., UNIVERSITY RECTOR, FOR UNIVERSITY VISITORS, to SENATORS AND REPRESENTATIVES FROM VIRGINIA. ALS. 1 p. Polygraph copy. #3734.

Wants Congress to repeal import duty on books.   [3000]

1821 Dec. 28. SAMUEL SMITH, Washington, to T. J. Randolph. ALS. 2 pp. Endorsed by T. J. Edgehill-Randolph Papers. #5533.

Unable to obtain copy of deed of conveyance from William Brust, clerk of court. Mentions Col. Morrison, Col. Nicholas and Mr. Clay.   [3001]

1822 Jan. 17. T. J., Monticello, to JOHN WAYLES EPPES. ALS. 2 pp. Draft copy. Edgehill-Randolph Papers. #5533.

Wants loan of certain books from list sent him by Eppes. Has *Journals* of Congress, etc., for 1789–1809. Correspondence burdens him: 1,267 letters in one year. Too old to exchange lands. Mentions Francis Wayles Eppes, Bedford, and Millbrook. Debt to Col. Nicholas. Sends trees. Lists books desired. Mentions Senate and House *Journals* for eighth through tenth Congresses, *American State Papers* on foreign relations, and *American Senatorial Debates*. [3002]

1822 Jan. 26. EDMUND BACON to T. J. ALS. 1 p. Endorsed by T. J. Edgehill-Randolph Papers. #5533.
Flour from Mr. Randolph and Mr. Craven. Corn at Shadwell mill. [3003]

1822 Jan. 25. T. J., Monticello, to MRS. KATHERINE DUANE MORGAN. ALS. 1 p. Facsimile. #6557.
Remembers her from Washington. Mentions Col. Morgan. [3004]

1822 Feb. 20. T. J., Monticello, to CONSTANTINE SAMUEL RAFINESQUE. ALS. 1 p. #4610.
University opening delayed. To present Rafinesque's offer to teach Natural History to Board of Visitors. [3005]

1822 Apr. 3. EDMUND BACON to T. J. ALS. 2 pp. Endorsed by T. J. Edgehill-Randolph Papers. #5533.
Paper from Mrs. Proctor and account from Mr. Vest. Mr. Stout reduced delivery. Corn and oats prices. James Monroe, through Mr. Watson, paid Negroes' hire. Grain from Mr. Carr. Jerry to Milton for cement from John Crad[d]ock. Fence rail. Mentions Gill. [3006]

1822 Apr. 18. EDMUND BACON to T. J. ALS. 1 p. Endorsed by T. J. Edgehill-Randolph Papers. #5533.
James Monroe's plan to pay debt through corn sales. Mr. Rogers to sell corn. Bishop to buy timber. Isaac hauling wood. Mentions Mr. Watson and coopers. [3007]

1822 June 13. T. J., Monticello, to JOHN ADLUM, Georgetown. ALS. 1 p. #6033.
Mr. Skinner may quote T. J. letters about Adlum's wines. Caumartin grape. North Carolina's Scuppernong Creek wine and European wines. Norfolk market brandies wine too often. [3009]

1822 June. T. J. NOTES ON COSTS OF UNIVERSITY BUILDINGS. AD. 1 p. #7254. [3010]

1822 June. EDMUND BACON to T. J., Monticello. ALS. 1 p. Endorsed by T. J. Edgehill-Randolph Papers. #5533.
Corn prices and purchases, partly from Mr. Rogers. Horse drover from Missouri at Charlottesville to sell Chickasaw horses and a mule. T. J. note due Edmund Bacon, heir to John Bacon, with Martin Dawson. [3010-a]

1822 Aug. 2. EDMUND BACON to T. J. ALS. 1 p. Endorsed by T. J. Edgehill-Randolph Papers. #5533.
Carriage price. Charlottesville carriage maker not good pricing agent; Mr.

Randolph better. Richmond price. T. J. Randolph says Edmund Randolph does not need Bacon at mill. Mentions Colclaser and plan to leave Virginia.   [3011]

1822 Aug. 6–1822 Aug. 29. T. J. NOTES ON SLAVES' WORK. AD. 1 p. On verso of lettercover to [?], Monticello. McGregor Library. #3620.
Ox and mule carts of stone hauled by Wormly, Jerry, Isaac, and Ned.   [3012]

1822 Sept. 12. EDMUND BACON to T. J. ALS. 1 p. Edgehill-Randolph Papers. #5533.
Money for iron and to pay William Bacon. Bedford cart.   [3013]

1822 Oct. 9. T. J., Monticello, to JAMES FREEMAN DANA. ANS. 1 p. #3919.
Pamphlets on the disease of cattle in a certain district, and on the new invention of a water burner. Giving one to agricultural society of which James Madison is president.   [3014]

1822 Dec. 1. T. J., Monticello, to JAMES MONROE, Washington. ALS. 1 p. McGregor Library. #4886.
Mr. Taylor's letter. Mentions Iturbide. Hopes Brazil and Mexico will "homologize with us." Arm improved. Aid to Gibson.   [3015]

1822 Dec. 23. PETER MAVERICK, New York, to T. J. ALS. 1 p. Endorsed by T. J. #2737.
Received payment from Col. Bernard Peyton for engraving and printing the plan of the University.   [3015-a]

[1822]. EDMUND BACON to T. J. ALS. 1 p. Edgehill-Randolph Papers. #5533.
Davy can help Joe. Estate of John Bacon.   [3016]

[1822–1828 October]. ACCOUNT BOOK KEPT AT MONTICELLO, WITH ENTRIES IN T. J.'S HAND. AD. 46 pp. Photostats. Original owned by Mrs. Robert E. Graham. #5832.
T. J. entries concern slaves. Other entries in hands of T. J. Randolph and Martha J. Randolph.   [3017]

1823 Feb. 16. T. J., Monticello, to JAMES MADISON. LS. 1 p. #3707.
Legislature empowered Literary Board to supply more funds to University. Mr. Cabell and Mr. Loyall approved acceptance of loans; if Madison approves, T. J. and John Hartwell Cocke can proceed to employ workmen without meeting of Board of Visitors.   [3019]

1823 Feb. 19. JAMES MADISON to T. J. ALS. 1 p. #6455.
Loan to University. Cannot work begin without formality of a Board of Visitors meeting?   [3020]

1823 Mar. 17. T. J. to MR. HUNTINGTON. ANS. 1 p. Photostat. Original owned by H. I. Hutton. #4303.
Invitation to dine at Monticello with Mr. Dodge of Marseilles.   [3021]

1823 Mar. 21. JAMES MADISON, Montpelier, to T. J. ALS. 2 pp. Endorsed by T. J. #4610.

Progress on Rotunda. Letter from Thomas J. O'Flaherty. Professor Edward Everett of Boston must seem heretic to New England.   [3022]

1823 May 10. T. J., Monticello, to BERNARD PEYTON. ALS. 1 p. #6885.
To Bedford. T. J. Randolph believes tobacco must have reached Richmond. Payments to Jacobs and Raphael. Nail rod.   [3023]

1823 June 9. T. J., Monticello, to WILLIAM B. GILES, Wig-wam, near Genito-bridge. ALS. 1 p. Photostat. Original owned by Herbert R. Strauss. #3508.
Papers to T. J. Randolph at Richmond. Financial problems caused by recent death of friend. Hopes to open University in time for Giles's son to attend. Legislature to determine opening date. T. J.'s fractured arm.   [3023-a]

1823 June 10. T. J., Monticello, to [?]. L. 1 p. 19th-century copy. Edgehill-Randolph Papers. #5533.
Recommends Dabney Overton Carr, son of Samuel Carr, for military studies.   [3024]

1823 July 4. T. J., Monticello, to JOSEPH C. CABELL, Edgewood near Warminister. ALS. 1 p. McGregor Library. #5452.
Plans for Cumberland jail. Literary Board to wait. Rotunda construction. Marble in transit New York to Richmond.   [3025]

[1823] Sept. 1. T. J., Monticello, to [JAMES WESTHALL] FORD, at Mr. Dyer's, Charlottesville. ANS. 1 p. Endorsed, 1858 March 3, by T. J. Randolph. #6073.
Ford to paint Mrs. Randolph's portrait at Monticello.   [3025-a]

[1823] Sept. 8. T. J. to [JAMES WESTHALL] FORD. ANS. 1 p. Endorsed, 1858 March 3, by T. J. Randolph. #6073.
Ford to paint the President's (James Monroe's) portrait. Assistance in moving Ford's instruments.   [3025-b]

1823 Sept. 30. T. J., Monticello, to WHOM IT MAY CONCERN. ALS. 1 p. Endorsed, 1858 March 3, by T. J. Randolph. #6073.
Recommends James W. Ford as portrait painter. Mentions portrait of James Monroe.   [3025-c]

1823 Nov. 12. T. J., Monticello, to JAMES PLEASANTS, GOVERNOR OF VIRGINIA, Richmond. ALS. 1 p. #3351.
Literary Board funds inadequate. Bursar needs supplement for Proctor.   [3026]

1823 Nov. 18. T. J. to MRS. LEWIS. ALS. 1 p. Owned by T. J. Memorial Foundation. #6895.
Muscat and Madeira wines. Mr. and Mrs. Martin to dine. Mrs. Randolph to visit.   [3027]

1823. T. J. to FREDERICK BEASLEY, PROVOST OF UNIVERSITY OF PENNSYLVANIA, Philadelphia. ALS. 1 p. Photostat. Original owned by Miss Sarah Mortimer. #5506.
Search of Truth in the Science of the Human Mind.   [3028]

1824 Jan. 9. JOHN STEELE, Collector's Office, Philadelphia, to T. J. ALS. 2 pp. Endorsed by T. J. Edgehill-Randolph Papers. #5533.

Wine from Dodge and Oxnard by brig *Caledonia* from Marseilles. Schooner *Hiram*, Thomas Dunike, Master, care of Collector of Port of Richmond. Account mentions Wilson Hunt.   [3029]

1824 Jan. 19. T. J., Monticello, to JOSEPH C. CABELL, Virginia Senate, Richmond. ALS. 1 p. #3296.

Interest charges on University funds. Whether to have 7 or 8 professors.   [3030]

1824 Jan. 22. T. J., Monticello, to JOSEPH C. CABELL, Virginia Senate, Richmond. ALS. 1 p. #3296.

Code of Regulations on distribution of courses among University professors. Encloses a copy AD. 2 pp. of T. J. ENACTMENTS TO BE PROPOSED TO VISITORS OF UNIVERSITY. Eight professors: ancient languages, modern languages, mathematics, natural philosophy, natural history, anatomy, moral philosophy, and law.   [3031]

1824 Jan. 23. T. J., Monticello, to JOSEPH C. CABELL, Virginia Senate, Richmond. ALS. 2 pp. #3296.

Funds for University, as reported in *Enquirer*. If Legislature can repeal endowment, University cannot compete with European schools. Not to be "common local academy" like Hampden-Sydney, Lexington, and Rumford.   [3033]

1824 Jan. 31. JOHN STEELE, Collector's Office, Philadelphia, to T. J. ALS. 1 p. Endorsed by T. J. Edgehill-Randolph Papers. #5533.

Draft on Bank of Pennsylvania care of Bernard Peyton.   [3034]

1824 Feb. 15. T. J., Monticello, to CHARLES WILLSON PEALE. ALS. 2 pp. McGregor Library. #5509.

Rembrandt Peale's work on painting of George Washington. University more beautiful than anything in U.S. or Europe. Museum.   [3035]

1824 Apr. 7. T. J. EXTRACTS FROM JOURNALS OF VISITORS OF UNIVERSITY. ADS. 2 pp. Owned by Mason Robertson. #7601.

Subjects to be taught by University professors; their duties and salaries.   [3037]

1824 Apr. 13. T. J., Monticello, to NICHOLAS TRIST. ALS. 2 pp. Owned by Gordon Trist Burke. #5385-n.

Legislature approved funds for University. Visitors want to open February, 1825. Professors from Europe. Work on Rotunda. Trist's work on catalogues. Mrs. Lewis, Mrs. Southall, and Dr. Ragland dead. Charlottesville's growth. Mentions Hore Browse Trist, Jr.   [3038]

1824 Apr. 26. T. J. POWER OF ATTORNEY TO FRANCIS WALKER GILMER ON BEHALF OF UNIVERSITY. ADS. 1 p. Owned by Mason Robertson. #7601.

Rector and Visitors appoint Gilmer to go to Great Britain and Europe to hire professors.   [3039]

1824 May 1. T. J., Monticello, to WILLIAM RUSSEL, New Haven, Connecticut. ALS. 1 p. Photocopy. Original owned by Paul Mellon. #7289-b.

Scheme of education for Virginia. Preparatory schools to teach classical languages, geometry, and geography not yet established. Department of grammar, rhetoric, and oratory at University of Virginia. Mentions professors at University, and pamphlet and grammar of composition. [3039-a]

1824 May 4. JOHN MICHAEL O'CONNOR, New York City, to T. J., Monticello. ALS. Draft [?]. 2 pp. Owned by T. J. Memorial Foundation. #5385-ac.
Translation of Gay de Vernon's *Treatise on the Science of War and Fortification*. Politics in U.S., liberty in Europe, election of 1800. Praises William Harris Crawford. [3039-b]

1824 May 13. T. J., Monticello, to BERNARD PEYTON, Richmond. ALS. 1 p. #6923.
Fountain pen like Mr. Cowan's. Richmond watchmaker, for Mr. Dyer. [3040]

1824 June 22. T. J., Monticello, to F. R. HASSLER, Jamaica, New York. ALS. 1 p. Barrett Collection. #3635.
Visitors to open University 1 February 1825. European scholars because American not suitably prominent. [3041]

1824 July 10. T. J., Monticello, to [?]. ALS. 1 p. #9371-b.
Recommends Col. Bernard Peyton for office in Richmond. Mentions Bedford. [3041-a]

1824 July 11. T. J., Monticello, to HENRY A. S. DEARBORN, Boston. ALS. 1 p. #9371-b.
Introduces Col. Bernard Peyton of Richmond, a commission merchant who travels to expand his business in North. [3041-b]

1824 Aug. 9. T. J., Monticello, to THOMAS J. O'FLAHERTY, Richmond. ALS. 1 p. #5600.
Busy at University. O'Flaherty's competence in Greek, Latin, French, and English. [3042]

1824 Aug. 16. T. J. to JAMES LEITCH. ANS. 1 p. Photostat. Original owned by T. J. Memorial Foundation. #5196.
Orders material for saddlecloth. [3043]

1824 Sept. 10. T. J., Monticello, to PETER MINOR. ALS. 1 p. #5280.
Grain samples from Mr. Gelston, New York, for Albemarle Agricultural Society. [3044]

1824 Sept. 25. T. J., Monticello, to JOSEPH ANTRIM, University of Virginia. ALS. 1 p. #8769.
Recommendation for Joseph Antrim as plasterer on basis of work at University of Virginia. [3044-a]

1824 Oct. 12. T. J., Monticello, to FRANCIS WALKER GILMER. ALS. 4 pp. Owned by E. R. W. McCabe. #4647.
Board of Visitors has no money. Scottish, English, Irish, German professors. Second-rate Europeans better than second-rate Americans. Ivory and Leslie acceptable. No duty on George Blaetterman's books. U.S. debt to Virginia. LaFayette

to visit Monticello, Montpelier, and University. Russel's *Views of the System of Education in the Universities of Scotland*, with appendix on England, published at Edinburgh. Endorsed by T. J. as never received by Gilmer, and returned to T. J.

[3045]

1824 Oct. 19. MARTHA JEFFERSON RANDOLPH, Monticello, for T. J., to JAMES LEITCH. ANS. 1 p. Photostat. Original owned by T. J. Memorial Foundation. #5196.

Orders sewing supplies.   [3046]

1824 Oct. 19. JAMES MADISON, Montpelier, to T. J. ANS. McGregor Library. #2716.

Returns Francis Walker Gilmer's letter which he has copied. Gilmer must not fail to bring professor of natural philosophy for the University.   [3046-a]

1824 Oct. 23. CORNELIA RANDOLPH, Monticello, for T. J., to JAMES LEITCH. ANS. 1 p. Photostat. Original owned by T. J. Memorial Foundation. #5196.

Orders screws and copperas.   [3047]

1824–1825. BANK DEBTS. D. 1 p. In unidentified hand. Endorsed by T. J. Owned by Mrs. Edwin Page Kirk. #5291.

Sums owed to Farmers Bank, United States Bank, and Virginia Bank.   [3049]

1825 Jan. 5. T. J., Monticello, to H. P. VAN BIBBER, Northend, Virginia. ALS. 1 p. Photocopy. Original owned by Paul Mellon. #7289-b.

University of Virginia. Professors of mathematics and natural philosophy expected shortly. Advertisement of University's opening in newspapers. Textbook sales. Qualifications to enter schools of Latin, Greek, mathematics, and natural philosophy.   [3050]

1825 Jan. 15. T. J. to JAMES LEITCH. ANS. 1 p. Photostat. Original owned by T. J. Memorial Foundation. #5196.

Orders brandy.   [3050-a]

1825 Jan. 27. T. J., Monticello, to ANDREW KEAN, Charlottesville. ALS. 1 p. #6402.

Urges Kean to remain at Charlottesville.   [3051]

1825 Feb. 17. T. J., Monticello, to FRANCIS WAYLES EPPES. ALS. 1 p. Draft copy. Edgehill-Randolph Papers. #5533.

News of fire damage at Poplar Forest from Ashton. J. Hemings to repair. Wood from Captain Martin. English professors at Hampton. University opens in March.

[3053]

1825 Feb. 18. T. J., Monticello, to MR. HILLIARD of CUMMINGS AND HILLIARD, Boston. ALS. 2 pp. #6185.

No book agent in Charlottesville. Suggests Meredith Jones. Foulis and Leipsic classics. Paris stereotype editions the best. Dufief's French and English dictionary. Boiste's French dictionary equal to that of Academy. Many French students, some Spanish students, few German and Italian. Cubi's Spanish Dictionary, Baltimore edition adequate. Professors from England in Hampton Roads. University opens

7 March. Langard's *History of England*. George Brodie's *History of the English Empire from the Accession of Charles I*. Turner's *History of the Anglo-Saxons*. Hume's *History of England*. Thomas' edition of Edward Coke's *First Institute* on Littleton.   [3054]

1825 Feb. 27. T. J., Monticello, to CAPTAIN WORMELEY. ALS. 1 p. #5528.
Letter from England.   [3055]

1825 Mar. 11. T. J., Monticello, to ARTHUR BROCKENBROUGH. ALS. 1 p. Photostat. Original owned by Albert H. Small. #8410.
Financial situation of University of Virginia. Difficulty in riding.   [3055-a]

1825 Mar. 12. T. J. to JAMES LEITCH. ANS. 1 p. Photostat. Original owned by T. J. Memorial Foundation. #5196.
Orders "wool cards" and mustard.   [3056]

1825 Mar. 31. T. J. to JAMES LEITCH. ANS. 1 p. Photostat. Original owned by T. J. Memorial Foundation. #5196.
Shirting for Burwell (slave).   [3057]

1825 Apr. 3. T. J., Monticello, to JOHN PATTERSON. ALS. 1 p. #5354.
Central Gazette and *Rules for Governing the University*. Philadelphia papers favor Philadelphia medical school and suppress University advertisements. Boston and New York papers better. Commends Patterson. T. J. Randolph's wife improves; Robley Dunglison treating her.   [3058]

1825 Apr. 4. T. J., Monticello, to THOMAS COOPER, Columbia, South Carolina. ALS. 2 pp. #8722.
Health. University of Virginia. Professors found by Francis Walker Gilmer. Professors Bonnycastle, Dunglison, Emmet, and Tucker. Courses in mathematics, natural philosophy, medicine, classics, French, Spanish, Italian, German, Swedish, Danish, Anglo-Saxon, chemistry, botany, zoology, ethics, and law. Library. Mentions Cambridge and Edinburgh Universities. University of South Carolina.
                                                                            [3058-a]

1825 Apr. 8. T. J. to JAMES LEITCH. ANS. 1 p. Photostat. Original owned by T. J. Memorial Foundation. #5196.
Orders bedticking.   [3059]

1825 Apr. 12. T. J., Monticello, to JOSEPH COOLIDGE, JR. ALS. File draft. 2 pp. Includes ALS. File draft, 1 p., [1825 Apr. 12], T. J. NOTES ON A CLOCK FOR THE UNIVERSITY OF VIRGINIA. #5262. Printed: L and B XVIII, 337–40.
Professors arrived; University opened March 7. English professors. Professors of chemistry and moral philosophy are Americans; professor of law not selected. Boston bell makers. Mr. Hilliard, University agent for library purchases. Board of Visitors appreciates gift of books. Coolidge's parents to visit. Mentions Mr. Ticknor. Enclosure describes clock for Rotunda and asks cost.   [3060]

1825 Apr. 23. T. J., Monticello, to TREASURER OF VIRGINIA. ALS. 1 p. #5712.
James Barbour advises that U.S. President deposited money for University to credit of Treasurer of Virginia in Branch Bank of U.S., Richmond. As University

Rector, T. J. to pay agent for books from Europe. Wrote to Governor of Virginia.
[3061]

1825 Apr. 25. T. J. to JAMES LEITCH. ANS. 1 p. Photostat. Original owned by T. J. Memorial Foundation. #5196.
Orders coffee. [3062]

1825 Apr. 30 or Feb. 17. JAMES MADISON to T. J. ALS. File draft. 1 p. Fragment. #6539.
Recommends Henry St. George Tucker for professor of law at University. Rockfish Gap conference. Mentions Joseph C. Cabell. [3063]

[*Post*-1825 May 9.] T. J. PLAT OF UNIVERSITY LANDS. AD. 1 p. 9″ x 13¾″. Bursar's Records. #5262. See Nichols, Item 327-a.
Purchases from John Perry, Daniel and Mary A. F. Piper, and Jesse W. Garth. Lands held by Alexander Garrett, Arthur S. Brockenbrough, and Nathan Barksdale as University Proctors. [3064]

1825 May 30. T. J. to JAMES LEITCH. ANS. 1 p. Photostat. Original owned by T. J. Memorial Foundation. #5196.
Orders salt. [3065]

1825 June 18. T. J. to JAMES LEITCH. ANS. 1 p. Photostat. Original owned by T. J. Memorial Foundation. #5196.
Orders cloth and thread. [3066]

1825 July 2. T. J., Monticello, to JOHN H. SHERBURNE. ALS. 1 p. #4532.
J. P. Jones memorabilia. Houdon's bust of Jones at Monticello. Artist from Washington might copy it. [3067]

1825 July 2. T. J., Monticello, to ROBLEY DUNGLISON. ALS. File draft. 1 p. McGregor Library. #4000. Printed: Dorsey, 34–35.
Health better. Payment to Dunglison. [3068]

1825 July 2. ROBLEY DUNGLISON, University, to T. J. ALS. 1 p. Endorsed by T. J. McGregor Library. #4000. Printed: Dorsey, 35.
T. J.'s health. Will accept no money. [3069]

1825 July 4. T. J., Monticello, to ROBLEY DUNGLISON. ALS. File draft. 1 p. McGregor Library. #4000. Printed: Dorsey, 36.
Wants to pay for future treatments. [3070]

1825 July 8. T. J., Monticello, to ROBLEY DUNGLISON. ALS. File draft. 1 p. McGregor Library. #4000. Printed: Dorsey, 36–37.
Health worse. [3071]

1825 July 18. ROBLEY DUNGLISON, University, to T. J. ALS. 2 pp. Endorsed by T. J. McGregor Library. #4000. Printed: Dorsey, 37.
To visit Monticello. Prescribes laudanum. [3072]

1825 July. T. J. FARM BOOK. D. 2 pp. Extract by N. P. Trist. Owned by Gordon Trist Burke. #5385-u.

Weather prognostics, notes on thermometers, table of weights.   [3073]

1825 Aug. 3. WILL OF ANNE SCOTT MARKS. In hand of T. J. ADS. 1 p.
Edgehill-Randolph Papers. #5533.
    Bequests to T. J. Randolph, Samuel Carr, and Martha J. Randolph. T. J. Randolph, executor. Witnessed by T. J. and Mary J. Randolph. Another will [not present] executed eight days later.   [3074]

1825 Aug. 4. T. J., Monticello, to ARCHIBALD ROBERTSON, Lynchburg. ALS.
1 p. #5190.
    Letter brought by Mr. Turner to T. J. Randolph. Payment of debt.   [3075]

1825 Aug. 5. JOSEPH AND ELLEN WAYLES COOLIDGE, Boston, to T. J. ALS.
2 pp. Endorsed by T. J. #5262.
    Simon Willard to make University clock. To come to Charlottesville to install. Clock for University at Cambridge, Representatives' Chamber at Washington, and New York.   [3076]

1825 Sept. 23. ROBLEY DUNGLISON, University, to T. J. ALS. 1 p. Endorsed by
T. J. McGregor Library. #4000. Printed: Dorsey, 39.
    Not to call at Monticello.   [3077]

1825 Sept. 30. T. J. to CHARLES BONNYCASTLE, University. ALS. 1 p. #4106.
"Ideas on the subject of a meridian for the University." Mentions Observatory, Rotunda, and American Philosophical Society *Transactions* sent to Univ. of Va. librarian John V. Kean.   [3078]

1825 Oct. 23. T. J., Monticello, to [FRANCIS WALKER GILMER]. ALS. 1 p.
#8743.
    Dissensions at University of Virginia. Fears schism among professors. Poor health. Regards to Mr. and Mrs. Divers.   [3078-b]

1825 Nov. 15. MARQUIS DE LAFAYETTE to T. J. ALS. 1 p. Endorsed by T. J.
#8885.
    Books to T. J. from Destutt de Tracy care of Mr. Connel. Brochure of French gentleman.   [3078-c]

1825 Nov. 17. T. J., Monticello, to ROBLEY DUNGLISON. AL. File draft. 1 p.
McGregor Library. #4000. Printed: Dorsey, 41–43.
    Condition of his health. Payment to Dunglison. The plan of a new medical school he encloses [not present] will show "a specimen of our proficiency in the art of puffery." Mentions Hippocratus.   [3079]

[1825] Nov. 18. Misdated 1824. ROBLEY DUNGLISON, University, to T. J. ALS.
1 p. Endorsed by T. J. McGregor Library. #4000. Printed: Dorsey, 43.
    Will accept no money. T. J.'s health.   [3079-a]

1825 Nov. 20. RUFUS KING, London, to T. J. ALS. 2 pp. Endorsed by T. J. #4106.
    Negotiations with Foreign Office re Charles Bonnycastle's bond successful. [3080]

1825 Nov. 26. T. J., Monticello, to ROBLEY DUNGLISON. ALS. 1 p. McGregor

Library. #4000. Printed: Dorsey, 44–45.

Draft on Mr. Raphael.   [3081]

1825 Nov. 29. T. J., Monticello, to REMBRANDT PEALE. ALS. 1 p. #8894.

Asks Peale's opinion of Cornelius DeBreet of Baltimore as a possible teacher of landscape painting for University of Virginia.   [3081-a]

1825 Dec. 21. ROBLEY DUNGLISON PRESCRIPTION FOR T. J. ANS. 1 p. Endorsed by T. J. McGregor Library. #4000. Printed: Dorsey, 48–49.

Rhubarb and magnesia. For severe pain, laudanum.   [3082]

1825 Dec. 26. T. J., Monticello, to WILLIAM B. GILES. L. 4 pp. 19th-century copy. #8722. Printed: L and B XVI, 146–51.

Usurpation of States rights by federal government. Federal court. Power over commerce, agriculture, and manufacture. Construction of roads and canals. Mentions John Quincy Adams, Federal party, and Hartford Convention. Progress of the University of Virginia, teaching of Latin, and University professors.   [3082-a]

[1825]. T. J. CLASS SCHEDULE FOR UNIVERSITY. AD. 1 p. Photostat. #3430.

Visitors of the University may visit any school.   [3083]

[1825]. T. J. NOTES ON PROFESSORS' HOUSING AT UNIVERSITY. AD. 2 pp. Microfilm. Original owned by Laurence G. Hoes. #3159.

Professors Long, Key, Emmet, Tucker, Blaetterman, Bonnycastle, and Dunglison. Tenants Edwin Conway, E. B. Chapman, Warner Minor, George W. Spotswood, John Gray, and John D. Richeson. Builders James Dinsmore, James Oldham, Mr. Nelson, Richard Ware, John M. Perry, and John Neilson.   [3084]

[1825]. T. J. NOTES ON UNIVERSITY CURRICULUM. AD. 2 pp. Microfilm. Original owned by James Monroe Museum and Memorial Library, Fredericksburg. #3159.

Subjects to be taught.   [3085]

1826 Jan. 9. T. J., Monticello, to C[LAIBORNE] W[ATTS] GOOCH, Richmond. ALS. 2 pp. #3921-b. Printed: L and B XVI, 151–53.

Federal powers better contained by South Carolina resolutions, Van Buren's motions, and Francis Baylies' propositions than by action of state of Virginia.
                                                                         [3085-a]

1826 Jan. 20. T. J., Monticello, to JOSEPH C. CABELL. ALS. 1 p. #9513-a.

Circular on law professor at University of Virginia. Thomas Jefferson Randolph is at legislature regarding T. J.'s debts and disposal of property. Asks Cabell's help.
                                                                         [3085-b]

1826 Feb. 1. T. J. PURCHASING LIST. AD. 1 p. Microfilm. Original in James Monroe Museum and Memorial Library, Fredericksburg. #3159.

Wines: Bergasses, Ledanon, Lienoux, Scuppernong, claret from Richmond, virgin oil of Aix, Muscat de Rivesalte, macaroni, and anchovies.   [3086]

1826 Feb. 7. T. J. RANDOLPH, Richmond, to T. J. ALS. 1 p. Endorsed by T. J. Edgehill-Randolph Papers. #5533.

Legislation on Jefferson Lottery.   [3087]

1826 Feb. 8. T. J., Monticello, to CHARLES BONNYCASTLE, University. ALS. 1 p. #4106.

Letters from Peter Barlow and Rufus King. Encloses copy [present] of LS, George Canning to Rufus King on subject of Bonnycastle's bond. Mentions George Canning and British government. [3088]

1826 Mar. 16–1826 Mar. 17. T. J. WILL. ADS. 4 pp. Owned by Albemarle County Court. #5145.

See Item 2300. [3089]

1826 Mar. 18. ROBLEY DUNGLISON to T. J. ALS. 1 p. Endorsed by T. J. Mc-Gregor Library. #4000. Printed: Dorsey, 51.

Taking catalogue to faculty meeting. Dispensary. [3090]

1826 Apr. 25. T. J. RANDOLPH, New York, to T. J. ALS. 1 p. Endorsed by T. J. Edgehill-Randolph Papers. #5533.

Support in New York and Boston weak. Lottery should succeed. Will write from Philadelphia. [3091]

1826 Apr. JEFFERSON LOTTERY TICKETS, issued at Richmond. D. 34 pp. Owned by the Misses Margaret and Olivia Taylor. #8937.

Signed by Yates and McIntyre for the managers, John Brockenbrough, Philip N. Nicholas, and Richard Anderson. [3091-a]

1826 June 4. T. J., Monticello, to JOSEPH COOLIDGE, JR. AL. 2 pp. File draft. #5262. Printed: L and B XVIII, 354–57.

Congress suspended tax on marble; Mr. Willard's work on University clock. Dial plate in Boston. Well driller. Student conduct. Probably included Item 3093. [3092]

1826 June 4. T. J. NOTES ON CONSTRUCTION OF UNIVERSITY CLOCK. AND BELL. ADS. 2 pp. #5262.

Probably a draft for an enclosure in Item 3092. [3093]

1826 June 15. JOSEPH COOLIDGE, JR., Boston, to T. J. ALS. 1 p. Endorsed by T. J. #5262.

Mr. Willard's work on clock. Bell. Received desk on which Declaration of Independence was written. [3094]

[1826] July 1–3. 3 UNIDENTIFIED LETTER WRAPPERS TO T. J., Monticello. Each 1 p. Owned by Gordon Trist Burke. #5385-a.

Sickroom notes on verso, dated July 1, 2, 3, purported to detail T. J.'s last illness. Endorsed by N. P. Trist. [3094-a]

1826 July 4. SUMMARY OF DEBT OF T. J. and T. J. RANDOLPH. D. 2 pp. In unidentified hand. Edgehill-Randolph Papers. #5533.

T. J. debts to James Lyle, Opie Norris through Higginbotham, Andrei Pinni as heir to Mazzei, Hiram Saunder, A. Robertson of Lynchburg, James Leitch, Richmond banks, Ludlow of New York, and T. J. Randolph. Total: $107,273.63. T. J. Randolph debts to William and Mary College, Richmond and Lynchburg banks, Kirby's executor, Norton's executor, Literary Fund, John Neilson, Robert Davis. Total $61,064.25. Mentions Marshall, Pantops, and Welks. [3095]

1826 July. T. J. NOTES CRITICIZING *LE SYSTÈME SOCIAL* OF BARON D'HOLBACH. D. 1 p. In hand of N. P. Trist. Owned by Gordon Trist Burke. #5385-u.   [3096]

1826 Aug. 1–1827 Jan. STATEMENT OF ACCOUNT OF T. J. ESTATE WITH JOHN WINN AND DAVIS. D. 3 pp. In unidentified hand. Edgehill-Randolph Papers. #5533.   [3097]

1827 Sept. 27. T. J. PLAN FOR ROTUNDA BELL AND CLOCK. In hand of N. P. Trist. D. 1 p. Edgehill-Randolph Papers. #5533. See Nichols, Item 371.
Explanatory note dated Monticello.   [3100]

1828 Mar. 9. T. J. ACCOUNT WITH T. J. RANDOLPH. D. 1 p. In hand of N. P. Trist. #5385-u.
Account for 1823 Jan. 1–1827 Jan. 1.   [3100-a]

[182–]. T. J. LIST OF BOOKS LENT TO FRIENDS. AD. 2 pp. Edgehill-Randolph Papers. #5533.
Mr. Short, Col. Lewis, Peter Carr, Mr. Wingfield, Mr. Stewart, Mr. Brown, Mr. Carr, Mr. McLung, Mr. McDowell, Mr. Mathews, F. Eppes, and Mr. Crawford. Addition in childish hand of T. J. Randolph.   [3101]

[182–]. T. J. LIST OF PAINTINGS, ETC., AT MONTICELLO. AD. 11 pp. McGregor Library. #2958.
Names 126 paintings, sculptures, medals, and other art works, often with artists and sources. Subjects are chiefly religious, classical, mythological, and historical.   [3102]

[182–]. T. J. LIST OF HIS ART OBJECTS. AD. 14 pp. Photostat. Original owned by Mrs. Edwin Page Kirk. #5291.
Names 48 paintings and art works, often with artists and sources. Subjects are chiefly religious, classical, mythological, and historical.   [3103]

n.d. T. J. NOTES ON DISTANCES IN POLES. AD. 1 p. Edgehill-Randolph Papers. #5533.
Survey of a road, partly on lands of N. M. L[ewis].   [3104]

n.d. T. J. NOTES ON FLOWER GARDENING. AD. 1 p. McGregor Library. #3620.   [3106]

n.d. T. J. NOTES ON BUILDING A PORTABLE FRAME FOR RIDGES. AD. Fragment. 1 p. McGregor Library. #3620.
With two sketches of this device for protecting young plants.   [3107]

n.d. T. J. NOTES ON DIGGING A HA! HA! MOAT. AD. 1 p. Microfilm. Original owned by James Monroe Museum and Memorial Library, Fredericksburg. #3159.
Lists slaves who are diggers of this trench.   [3108]

n.d. T. J. NOTES ON HORSE WHEELS AT LEGO AND TUFTON. AD. 1 p. On verso of similar notes in unidentified hand. McGregor Library. #3620.   [3109]

n.d. T. J. NOTES ON HOUSEHOLD SUPPLIES FOR ONE QUARTER. AD. 1 p. Microfilm. Original owned by James Monroe Museum and Memorial Library, Fredericksburg. #3159.

Spirits, whiskey, salt, brown sugar, white sugar, tea, coffee, cotton, and candles.
[3110]

n.d. T. J. NOTES ON HOW FAR THINGS ARE VISIBLE FROM MONTI-CELLO. AD. Fragment. 1 p. McGregor Library. #3620.
English and French measurements.
[3111]

n.d. NOTES ON MAKING A JOINT, WITH SAMPLE. AD. 3 pp. Edgehill-Randolph Papers. #5533. See Nichols, Item 379.
In unidentified hand on lettercover addressed to T. J.
[3112]

n.d. T. J. NOTE DESCRIBING LAND EXTENDING FROM RIVANNA RIVER TO MONTICELLO MOUNTAIN. AD. 1 p. Edgehill-Randolph Papers. #5533.
[3113]

n.d. T. J. NOTES ON LIVESTOCK. AD. 1 p. On verso of lettercover, [?] to T. J., Milton. McGregor Library. #3620.
[3114]

n.d. T. J. NOTES ON LIVESTOCK AT MONTICELLO, TUFTON, AND LEGO. AD. 1 p. On verso of lettercover, [?] to [?], ATTORNIES AT LAW, Charlottesville. McGregor Library. #3620.
[3115]

n.d. T. J. NOTES ON NAIL SIZES. AD. 1 p. Microfilm. Original owned by James Monroe Museum and Memorial Library, Fredericksburg. #3159.
[3116]

n.d. T. J. NOTES ON SUN. AD. 2 pp. Photostat. Owned by T. J. Memorial Foundation. #5118.
Mentions London, Paris, and Fry-Jefferson map. On verso are notes on winds, comparing Williamsburg and Monticello.
[3117]

n.d. T. J. NOTES ON TIN AND PLANKING NEEDED AT MONTICELLO. AD. 2 pp. Microfilm. Original owned by James Monroe Museum and Memorial Library, Fredericksburg. #3159.
[3118]

n.d. T. J. NOTES, UNIDENTIFIED. AD. 1 p. Microfilm. Original owned by James Monroe Museum and Memorial Library, Fredericksburg. #3159.
Perhaps index to mathematics book.
[3120]

n.d. T. J. to [?]. ALS. Letterpress copy. Fragment. 1 p. Last page only. Edgehill-Randolph Papers. #5533.
Hubbard (slave) better shoemaker for Bedford plantation than Peter. Tobacco to London via Richmond. Mentions Mr. Brown, Mr. Clay, cotton, clover, hemp, wheat, and slave sale.
[3122]

n.d. T. J. to [?]. ALS. Letterpress copy. Fragment. 1 p. Last page only. Edgehill-Randolph Papers. #5533.
Mentions Congressional campaign.
[3123]

n.d. T. J. to [?]. ALS. Letterpress copy. Fragment. 1 p. Last page only. Edgehill-Randolph Papers. #5533.
Land and Negro sales.   [3124]

n.d. T. J. to [?]. ALS. Fragment. 2 pp. #6085.
Scientific discussion.   [3125]

n.d. T. J. to [?]. ALS. Letterpress copy. Fragment. 1 p. Last page only. Edgehill-Randolph Papers. #5533.
Mr. Wythe too dear a friend to be impartial judge in a matter involving T. J. Returns to Virginia in fall.   [3126]

n.d. T. J. to [?]. ALS. Letterpress copy. Fragment. 1 p. Last page only. Edgehill-Randolph Papers. #5533.
Discourse on integrity.   [3127]

n.d. T. J. to [?]. ALS. Letterpress copy. Fragment. 1 p. Last page only. Edgehill-Randolph Papers. #5533.
Thanks for help on business at Le Havre and Paris.   [3128]

n.d. T. J. to [?]. ALS. Letterpress copy. Fragment. 1 p. Last page only. Edgehill-Randolph Papers. #5533.
Wants copper bell.   [3129]

n.d. T. J. MAP OF CANAL AND SAW MILL. AD. 1 p. 7¾″ x 9¾″. Edgehill-Randolph Papers. #5533. See Nichols, Item 487.   [3130]

n.d. T. J. MAP OF CHARLOTTESVILLE AND MILTON. AD. 1 p. 16½″ x 10″. Edgehill-Randolph Papers. #5533. See Nichols, Item 526.   [3131]

n.d. T. J. PLAT OF HARRISON FAMILY LAND. AD. 1 p. 15″ x 11″. Owned by Mrs. Edwin Page Kirk. #5291.
Mr. Harrison's mill and Woodson's Ferry.   [3132]

n.d. T. J. MAP OF JAMES RIVER AND FLUVANNA RIVER FROM RICHMOND TO MONTICELLO. AD. 1 p. 7¼″ x 14⅝″. Edgehill-Randolph Papers. #5533.   [3133]

n.d. T. J. PLAT OF NICHOLAS M. LEWIS' LAND. AD. 1 p. 3″ x 5¼″. Owned by Mrs. Edwin Page Kirk. #5291.   [3134]

nd. T. J. PLAT OF MONTICELLO. AD. 1 p. 11½″ x 15⅜″. Owned by T. J. Memorial Foundation. #5348.   [3135]

n.d. T. J. SURVEY MAP OF MONTICELLO. AD. 1 p. 15½″ x 20″. Edgehill-Randolph Papers. #5533.   [3136]

n.d. T. J. MAP OF EDGEHILL, SHADWELL, LEGO AND PANTOPS. AD. 1 p. 16⅜″ x 20⅜″. Edgehill-Randolph Papers. #5533.   [3137]

n.d. T. J. MAP AND SURVEY OF SHADWELL, PANTOPS, LEGO AND EDGEHILL. Fragment. AD. 2 pp. 9½″ x 16″. Edgehill-Randolph Papers. #5533.

Incomplete explanation on verso tracing chain of title to his land in Albemarle County.   [3138]

n.d. T. J. HAND COPY OF STAPLES'S PLAT OF SHADWELL, AND EDGE-HILL. ADS. 2 pp. 9⅞" x 7¾". Edgehill-Randolph Papers. #5533.   [3139]

n.d. T. J. PLAN FOR OCTAGONAL BUILDING. AD. 1 p. 4¾" x 8¼". Edgehill-Randolph Papers. #5533. See Nichols, Item 496.
Unidentified.   [3140]

n.d. T. J. SURVEY MAP. AD. 1 p. 12⅜" x 8". Edgehill-Randolph Papers. #5533.
Unidentified.   [3142]

n.d. T. J. SURVEY MAP. AD. 2 pp. 21" x 16½". Edgehill-Randolph Papers. #5533.
Unidentified.   [3143]

n.d. T. J. SURVEY NOTES. AD. 4 pp. Edgehill-Randolph Papers. #5533.
Unidentified.   [3144]

n.d. GRAPH PAPER. 1 p. Edgehill-Randolph Papers. #5533.
Said to have belonged to T. J.   [3146]

n.d. T. J. TABLE OF MILEAGES, MONTICELLO TO POPLAR FOREST, BED-FORD COUNTY. AD. 1 p. #6696.
Monticello, Carter's Bridge, Warren Ferry, Gibson's gate, Raleigh, Mrs. Flood's, H. Flood's, Hunter's, Candler's, Limestone Bridge, Poplar Forest, Campbell Court House, Flat Creek, Waterlick, Turnpike, my road, western gate, and Poplar Forest house.   [3147]

n.d. T. J. BLANK DINNER INVITATION WITH STAGE OR MAIL SCHED-ULE ON VERSO. AD. 2 pp. Edgehill-Randolph Papers. #5533.
Fredericksburg, Richmond, and Lynchburg.   [3148]

n.d. T. J. NOTES ON ELEVATIONS IN FRENCH AND ENGLISH TERMS. AD. 1 p. McGregor Library. #3620.
Mentions river, Monticello, and Montalto with [barometric readings?] at each site.   [3149]

n.d. T. J. MUSIC. AD. 3 pp. Owned by T. J. Memorial Foundation. #5118.
"The Adieu," "Love and Opportunity," "The Pleasures of the Town," "Minuet de la cour," "Air de l'Epreuve villageoise," and "Money Musk."   [3150]

n.d. T. J. MUSIC. AD. 2 pp. Monticello Music Collection; owned by T. J. Me-morial Foundation. #3177-a.
Not titled.   [3151]

n.d. T. J. POEMS. AD. 2 pp. #6004.
"Tweed Side" and "To Maggy My Love I Did Tell."   [3152]

n.d. T. J. COPY OF LORD BYRON'S *ENIGMA*. AD. 2 pp. #6696.   [3153]

n.d. T. J. EXTRACT FROM EDWARD YOUNG'S *THE BROTHERS*. AD. 1 p. #6643.

Poem.   [3154]

n.d. T. J. MARGINAL NOTES IN COPY OF *THE FIRST COLLECTION OF VOLUME THE SECOND OF THE MOSTE FAVOURITE MINUETS WITH THEIR BASSES* (London, n.d.). AD. 2 pp. Monticello Music Collection; owned by T. J. Memorial Foundation. #3177-a.

Method for tuning harpsichord.   [3155]

n.d. T. J. to THOMAS MANN RANDOLPH, JR., Monticello. LETTERCOVER. 1 p. Owned by George Green Shackelford. #5333.

Draft of letter in unidentified hand.   [3156]

n.d. [?] to T. J., Monticello. LETTERCOVERS. 5 items, each 1 p. #5385-t.

Includes one franked by William Wirt as Attorney General of U.S.   [3157]

n.d. [?] to T. J., Monticello. LETTERCOVERS. 2 items, each 1 p. Owned by T. J. Memorial Foundation. #5385-n.   [3158]

n.d. [N. P. TRIST'S] DESCRIPTION OF T. J.'S PRESSES AND THEIR CONTENTS. 2 pp. #5385-u.

On verso of lettercover postmarked n.y. Feb. 14.   [3159]

n.d. [?], to T. J. LETTERCOVER. 1 p. Owned by Gordon Trist Burke. #5385-u.
                                                                         [3160]

n.d. [?], to T. J. LETTERCOVER. 1 p. Owned by T. J. Memorial Foundation. #5385-f.

Care of Mr. Brown.   [3161]

n.d. T. J. UNIDENTIFIED MARKINGS. AD. 2 pp. Edgehill-Randolph Papers. #5533.

Perhaps wrappers. "1st day: plat" and "to be decyphered."   [3162]

n.d. T. J. ENDORSED WRAPPER: "SURVEYS OF SHADWELL." AD. 1 p. Edgehill-Randolph Papers. #5533.   [3163]

n.d. T. J. ENDORSED WRAPPER: "SURVEYS OF LEGO." AD. 1 p. Edgehill-Randolph Papers. #5533.   [3164]

n.d. T. J. LOGARITHM TABLES. AD. 2 pp. Microfilm. Original owned by James Monroe Museum and Memorial Library, Fredericksburg. #3159.

Sine, cosine, tangent, and cotangent tables on recto. More tables with triangular forms on verso.   [3165]

n.d. T. J. MATHEMATICAL NOTES. AD. 2 pp. Edgehill-Randolph Papers. #5533.

Method of cosecants.   [3167]

n.d. GEOMETRY PROBLEM. AD. 2 pp. Edgehill-Randolph Papers. #5533.

Has notes by T. J. at foot on method of drawing an octagon, and demonstration on verso.   [3168]

n.d. T. J. NOTES FOR USE OF BORDA'S CIRCLE. AD. 1 p. Edgehill-Randolph Papers. #5533.
Includes formula for correction of instrumental error.   [3169]

n.d. T. J. CHESS PROBLEM, STATED AND SOLVED. AD. 2 pp. Microfilm. Original owned by James Monroe Museum and Memorial Library, Fredericksburg. #3159.   [3170]

n.d. T. J. ACCOUNT WITH [?]. D. 1 p. In unidentified hand. Edgehill-Randolph Papers. #5533.
Mentions Norton and Col. Nicholas.   [3171]

n.d. 3 SCRAPBOOKS, EACH CONTAINING LETTERCOVERS ADDRESSED TO T. J. D. 3 vols. #5948.
Bookplate of William H. Clark, with legend, "Bought at the sale of the library of John Randolph of Roanoke by Wm. H. Clark of Halifax Co., Va. and presented by Mr. Clark to Miss Sarah Randolph of Edgehill."   [3172]

n.d. T. J., [Milton] to JAMES OLDHAM, at Mr. Gallego's, Richmond. Lettercover. 1 p. Photocopy. Original owned by Victor B. Levit. #8265-b.   [3173]

Index

Index

[Numbers refer to items, not to pages.]

Appointments, T. J.'s. See under Presidency, T. J.'s
Appomattox Mills, 2796
Appomattox River, Va., 2551
Arbitration, 2455
  Henderson case, 1435
  labor dispute, 1900, 1917
Arbor vitae, 1053
Archer, Polly, 609
  William S., 1588, 1610, 1842, 1916
Architectural plans
  T. J.'s
    general, 7, 583, 779, 1516, 2336, 2966, 3107, 3112, 3140
    Monticello, 1516, 2343, 2347
    Nelson County Jail, 2008, 2012, 2015
    Univ. of Va., 1452, 1516, 1518, 1681, 1699, 2006, 2017, 2018, 2338, 2938-a
    for Nicholas's house, 2588-a
    see also Sketches and drawings
Architecture textbook, 2101
Ardouin, Captain, 477
Aristides, 2848-b
Arithmetic, 269
Armistead, Robert, 901
  William, 2079, 2377
Armistice, 2866, 2877
Arms and armaments, 159, 2377, 2793-a, 2820-a
  captured at Chambly, 2351
  European, 2390
  supplied by Va., 40
Armstrong, General John, 1287, 1467, 1553, 2715, 2800-a
Army. See Great Britain, army; Militia; Standing armies; United States, Army; United States, Continental Line
Arnold, Benedict, 27, 2351, 2385
Arrowsmith, Aaron, 1261
Art objects, 2444, 2582-a
  list of, 3102, 3103
Art teacher, 3081-a
Articles of Confederation, 59, 68, 86, 188
Artillery, 2793-a, 2820-a
Artists, 3102, 3103
Ash trees, 1018
Ashlin, John, 393
Ashmead, Chilion, 1648

Ashton, Va., 1705, 3053
Asparagus, 562, 1848
Assessor, Minor appointed, 1247
Assignats, 344
Associates of late Dr. Bray, xvi
Assumption, debt, 282
Astronomy, 1261, 1938, 1940, 1941, 1947
Athanasius, St., 2848-b
Atheism, T. J. accused of, 661
Atheists, 2868-a
Athens, Ga., college, 1907
Athens, Greece, 2132
Atkins, Mr., 1136
Attorneys. See Lawyers; names of individuals
Atwater, Reuben, 805, 2641
Auditors, military, 2361
Audraine, Mr., 1872
Augusta, Ga., 41, 243, 829
Augusta County, Va., 2361
Aurora, 2728
Ausonius, Decimus Magnus, 2763
Austin, Mr., 303
  Rev. Gilbert, 1718
  William, 535
Austria, 67, 1234
Axletree, of carriage, 1086
Ayowais Indians. See Iowa

Baby food, 2474
Bacchus and Threetons Tavern, Taneytown, Md., 2592
Bache, Benjamin Franklin, 255, 313, 629, 631, 2060, 2071
  Franklin, 255, 2060, 2071, 2123
  William, 649, 663, 2594
  Mrs. William, 663
Back country. See Valley of Virginia; Western Virginia
Bacon, Edmund
  complaint concerning military conscription, 2750
  fodder accounts, 2994-a
  heir to John Bacon, 3008
  T. J.'s account with, 1988, 2945, 2958, 2984, 2986
  land sale considered, 2745
  letters from, 2727, 2731, 2734, 2735, 2737, 2745–48, 2750–53, 2756–58, 2761, 2762, 2765, 2768, 2770,

Bacon, Edmund (*cont.*)
    2772, 2775–78, 2781, 2782, 2895,
    2933, 2937, 2941, 2943, 2948,
    2951, 2955, 2956, 2958, 2960,
    2962, 2977, 2980, 2984, 2986,
    3003, 3006, 3007, 3010-a, 3011,
    3013
  letters to, 2759, 2779, 2982
  mentioned, 998, 1036, 2747-a, 2897, 2954
  overseer at Monticello, 1009, 1010
  travels, 2599, 2781-a, 2948, 2955, 2960, 2977
  witness to document, 1346, 1347, 2838
  Francis, 1936, 3102
  John, 2897, 3010-a
  Matthew, 2988
  William, 2954, 3013
Bacon, pork, 344, 1408, 1448, 2599, 2751, 2781-a
Baehr, Christian, 284, 291, 382
Bagby, Ellen, 35
Bailey, Mr., 2222
  Robert, 2544
  Theodorus, 2206
Baker, Dr., 857
  Mr., 348, 903, 1385, 1542, 1574
  Evan, 2377
  Jerman, 2354
  Richard, 1444
Baldwin, Mr., 667
  Briscoe G., 1600, 1962, 1976, 2303
Ballads, 2334
Ballanger, Mr., 466
Ballard, Mr., 1097, 1136
  William, 1183, 1346, 1347
Balloon ascents, 392, 397
Ballot, popular, 1875
Ballow, Mr., 307
  Thomas, 7
Balsam, 1054
Baltic Sea, 2831
Baltimore, Md., 3081-a
  as capital site, 175, 176
  as commercial center, 1118
  Bibles from, 2702
  carpenters' wages, 1642
  Carr family visits, 2659
  charitable committee of, 468
  commissioner of bankruptcy, 829
  creditors of John Speer in, 2732

  edition of Cubi's Spanish dictionary from, 3054
  Heinrich's home, 1420
  House of Representatives to remove to, 2442
  Maria Jefferson visits, 308
  letters from, 52, 1398, 1637, 1641, 1648, 1704, 2059
  letters to, 479, 692, 693, 717, 785, 973, 975, 1996, 2169, 2289
  marble from, 1719
  mentioned, 453, 884, 1226, 1619, 1711
  Palladio sketches sought in, 2700
  passengers for France, 477
  Beverley Randolph visits, 2522
  shipments of wine to, 489
  study of French in, 352
  U. S. bank, 2723
  George Williams in, 1234
Balusters, for Univ. of Va., 2194
Bancroft, Edward, 2429, 2433
Bank bills, 1432, 1437, 2799-b
Bank credit, 811
Bank discounts, 773
Bank negotiations, 2664
Bank notes, 750, 788, 837, 1359, 2872-a, 2959
Bank of Alexandria, 1359, 2647
Bank of Columbia, 2647, 2744, 2749
  crisis in, 748
  T. J.'s account with, 728, 735, 772, 773
  lack of paper, 772, 773
  mentioned, 696, 891, 1147, 1289
  notes of, 750, 1359, 2742-c
  stock issued, 1423, 1426, 1427, 1433, 1436
Bank of Manhattan, 1278, 1279
Bank of Pennsylvania, 666, 1004, 1199, 2795, 2868-b, 3034
  payment to Kosciuszko, 1099
  soundness of, 1277
  stock issued, 1278, 1279, 1281, 1283, 1285, 1290, 1292, 1301
Bank of Philadelphia, 2530, 2704
Bank of Richmond, 2372, 2833, 2863, 2897, 2951, 2959, 2975, 3095
Bank of the United States, 2563, 2660, 2734-a, 2757-a, 2931, 2959, 2975, 3049

visit to Monticello, 1454, 1455
wine consigned to, 826
Barometric readings, 3149
Barracks, Albemarle County, Va., 2360, 2373-a, 2377
Barrels, 2799-a, 2822, 2962
Barrett, Johs., 1718
Barrois, of Paris, bookseller, 282, 1470, 1473
Barron, James, 2997
Barruel, Augustin de, 648
Barry, J., 1115, 1147
Barter, of tobacco, 633
Barthélemy, Jean Jacques, 2446
Bartlet (slave), 2778
Barton, Benjamin, 105, 338, 340, 1059, 2518
Bartram, Mr., 629
Barziza, Viscount, 1430, 1432, 1437
Bassett, Burwell, 1474, 1476, 1772, 1833, 2079
Bateman vs. Roach, 2379
Battletown, Jefferson County, Va., 2996
Batture controversy, 1092
Bayard, Mr., 525
  see also Leroy & Bayard
Bayle, Pierre, 2169
Bayley, Captain, 241
Baylie, Francis, 2275, 3085-a
Bayou St. Jean, land on, 918
Beall, Mr., 79
Beans, 268, 1105
Bear Castle, Louisa County, Va., 2387
Beasley, Frederick, 3028
Beaverdam lands, 2451, 2518
Beccaria, Cesare Bonesano, 2950, 2981
Beckley, Mr., 2734-a
  Mrs., 1072, 1075, 1112
  John James, 2552
Bedding, 978, 2791, 3059
  see also Blankets; Sheets
Bedford County, Va.
  bacon shipped from, 2599
  Charles Bankhead's land in, 1117
  cart at plantation, 3013
  deeds. See under Deeds
  John Wayles Eppes's estate in, 2553, 2661
  flour production, 2800, 2884
  James I. Harrison of, 2874
  T. J.'s estate in, 2789-a, 2850, 3002

T. J.'s expenses and income from, 1988
T. J.'s trips to, 1004, 1200, 1243, 1699, 1707, 1714, 1884, 2537, 2826, 2872-a, 2907, 2908, 2992, 2994-a, 3023
land exchanged for Pantops, 1229
land in, 7, 18, 147, 573, 578, 584, 745, 840, 899, 1097, 1136, 1161, 1162, 1164, 1165, 1177, 1189, 1207, 1499, 1908, 2976
letter to, 1324, 2932
mentioned, 1219, 1230, 1235, 1445, 2287, 2776, 3041-a
Thomas Mann Randolph, Jr.'s estate in, 2976
rents from, 2428
route to Monticello, 1695
sale in, 404, 1117
sheriff, 2850, 2885
shipments from, 2890
shoemaker, 3122
slaves, 324, 325, 366, 2515, 2516, 2776, 2975
stock from, 2595
taxes, 1203, 1343, 1376, 1379, 1488, 1589, 2872-a
tobacco, 264, 1145, 1379
see also Albemarle County; Poplar Forest
Bedford Washington, Rachel's (slave), 2880
Bedinger, Mr., 892
Beds, 2791
Bee, The, 1096
Beef, 751, 1274
  see also Cattle; Livestock
Beer, 1336, 2378
Bell, Charles, 1040
  John, 2767
  R. M., 1208
  Samuel, 1846
  Thomas
    account with Univ. of Va., 2010
    ejection suit, 1846
    forwards mail, 2460
    funds for Garland Jefferson, 435, 437, 440
    horses purchased from, 712, 2595
    illness of, 566
    T. J.'s account with, 362, 400, 924
    justice of the peace, 2545-a

see also Bennett Henderson; Samuel
    Scott; names of areas, e.g., Flori-
    da
Bourbon family, 2888
Bournonville, Mr., 495
Boush, Robert, 2377
Bowden, Phripp &, 2428
Bowditch, Nathaniel, 1634, 1715, 1800,
    1872, 1922
Bowdoin, Mr., 282
Bowels, ailments of, 896
Bowie, Robert, 2739
Bowie & Kurtz, 1077, 1112, 1300, 1354
    see also Boice and Kurtz
Bowles, Davy, 656, 804, 864, 865, 2599
Bowling Green, Va., 2592
Bowwood tree, 1923
Bowyer, John, 1606, 1825, 1845, 1925,
    1931, 1932, 1958, 1962, 1976, 2057,
    2116, 2122, 2149
Boyd, Colonel, 2037
    James D., 2954
    Walter, 508
Boyd's Ferry, 2373-c
Böye, Herman, 1415, 1416, 1419
Boyer, John, 2741
Boykin, Edward C., 1782
Boyton, C., 2063
Bracken vs. William and Mary, 2143
Brackenridge, William, 2377
Bracton, Henry de, 1270, 2988
Bradbourn, William C., 1012
Bradbury, John, 2784
Bradford, Captain, 430
    Mr., 1194, 2393-a
    Charles, 2377
Bradley, Absalom, 1136
    John W., 1136
    Mrs. M. Howard, 2555
    Mary, 1136
    Stephen R., 2639, 2641
Brads, 2588
Braidwood, Mr., 1387, 1391
Bramham, Mr., 909
    Horace, 2009
    James W., 907, 935, 1123
    Nimrod, 907, 908, 1111, 1257, 1753,
        2939
Bramham & Bibb, 1988
Bramham & Jones, 1399
Branch, Christopher, 1640

Brand, Mr., 635, 1988
    Chiles M., 1208
    James, 967, 968
    Joseph, 1123
Brandy, 949, 2259, 2301, 3050-a
Brandywine, Va., 417
Brantz, Mayer &, 2723
Brattleborough, Vt., 2641
Bratton's, Va., 2344
Bray, Dr., Associates of, xvi
Braxton, Carter, 2428
Brazil, 1822, 1893, 3015
Bread, 2780
Bread lists, 2544, 2989
Breckenridge, James
    Board of Visitors, Univ. of Va.,
        1517, 1614, 1616, 1783, 1837,
        1838, 1858, 1862, 1967, 1978,
        2001, 2995
    bond from, 2249
    deed to, 2270
    letters from, 641, 1775, 1892
    letters to, 1656, 1715, 1841, 1895,
        1909, 1992
    mentioned, 1618, 1772, 1774, 1821,
        1824, 1825, 1836, 1840, 1842,
        1845, 1847, 1929, 2035, 2050,
        2057
    in Va. legislature, 1839, 1866
    John, 647
Breeches, 284, 291, 382
Breeding, of dog and wolf, 2474
Brehan, Marquise de, 120
Bremo, Fluvanna County, Va.
    letters from, 1445, 1690, 1747, 2072
    letters to, 1094, 1286, 1305, 1449,
        1465, 1617, 1689, 1714, 1741,
        1785, 1805, 1808, 1848, 1858,
        1862, 1884, 1978, 2321, 2918-a
Bremo Seminary, 1800
Brent, D. C., 831
    Daniel, 1893
    Robert, 933, 939
    William, 1470, 1520, 1528
Brewer, 2378
Brian, Mr., 1136
Bricks, 1204, 1251, 2346, 2727
    method of making, 1682
Brickwork, Univ. of Va., 1503, 1508,
    1509, 1515, 1519, 1560, 1587, 1596,
    1598, 1649, 1660, 1661, 1664, 1672,

Brown & Relf, 796
Brown & Robertson, 1124, 1145, 1146,
 1248, 1249, 2850
 see also William Brown; Archibald
 Robertson
Brown, Rives & Co., 733, 970
Browne, Arthur, 2988
 Beverly, 1950
 John, 2377
Brown's, Va., 2592
Brown's *Rural Affairs*, 1442
Bruce, Mr., 199, 2811
 Archibald, 1768
 Walter Coles, 20
Bruni, Miss, 588
Brunswick, Duke of, 386, 394, 534,
 2512
Brunswick County, Va., 437, 1965
Brussels, Belgium, 386
Brust, William, 3001
Brutus (newspaper), 787
Bryan, Anderson, 136, 141, 2350
 Wilson, 2667, 2673
Bryant, Thomas, 2377
Btocki, Count, 91
Buchanan, Mr., 240
 Mrs., 158
 James, 2846
 William, 688, 713, 975
Buck, John H., 2544
Buck Island, Albemarle County, Va.,
 139, 2423, 2700-a
Buckingham County, Va., 659, 1484,
 1653, 1803, 2887-a
 see also Randolph Jefferson
Buckingham Court House Road, Va.,
 2976
Buckley & Abbott, 1426, 1453
Buckner, Colin, 1161
Buck's horns, T. J.'s, 1870
Buffalo fish, 2795-a
Buffalo tract, Va., 2789-a
Buffon, Georges L. L. de, 229, 2474,
 2533-a, 2766
Bull, Jonathan, 2724
Bull Run, 2467
Bulloch, Archibald S., 1701
Bullock, David, 636
 Eliza. See Eliza Henderson
 James, 1013
 John, 909, 914, 915, 938, 1622,
 1625
 William Bellinger, 818

"Bumpers Squire Jones" (song), 2333
Bunce, Samuel, 709
Bunker Hill Monument, 2120
Bur Creek, Bedford County, Va., 2791
Burch, Samuel, 663
Burd, Edward, 1638
Burford, W. A., 758
Burgess, Samuel, 2925
 see also Miles & Burgess
Burgoyne, John, 36, 394
Burgundy (wine), 2498
Burials, 2348, 2349
Burk, John, 1393
 John Daly, 2871
 Richard M., 1671
Burke, Edmund, 263, 266
 Ellen Coolidge, 2549-a, 2799-a
 Gordon Trist, 2363, 2419, 2430,
 3094-a, 3159, 3160
 John R., 2421, 2859
 Martha Jefferson Trist, 2380
Burks, John, 1012, 2806
Burnet seed, 1144
Burnett, Joseph, 2374
Burnley, Mr., 2937
 Garland, 2360
 John, 2515
Burr, Mr., 2842
 Aaron, 673, 982, 994, 999, 1091,
 2591
Burrell. See Burwell
Burress, Robert, 2746
 Thomas, 2743
Burtin, Robert, 830
Burton, Mr., 1097, 1480, 2043
 Hutchins G., 1447, 1450, 1952
 James, 2360
 see also Donald & Burton
Burwell [Burrell] (slave), 1744, 1930,
 2300, 2810, 3057
Burwell, Mr., 942, 988, 2719
 Carter, 30
 Nathaniel, 30, 281, 2429, 2433, 2504
 Rebecca, 16
 William, 1535
 William A., 1468, 2728-a, 2728-b,
 2728-c, 2728-d
Burwell's Ferry, Va., 2370
Business affairs. See names of individu-
 als, e.g., John Barnes; James
 Brown; Gibson & Jefferson; Dan-
 iel Hylton; Thomas Jefferson
Business cards, 2402–12

1382, 1725, 2803, 2841, 2875,
2883
  mentioned, 929, 1117, 1136, 1360,
2359, 2857
  money due, 1210
  threshing machine, 2533
  trustee for Harrison, 1161
Mrs. Charles, 2841
Henry
  election of 1824, 2121
  T. J.'s lawyer, 1944
  law practice, 1951
  letter to, 1944
  mentioned, 1100
Clayter, Mr., 1326
Clearance papers. See Ships' papers
Cleaveland, Parker, 1634, 1764
Clergy, 1788, 1920, 2134, 2349, 2359,
2724
  see also Christianity; Religion
Clifton, Cumberland County, Va.,
1542, 2760
Climate, 238, 270, 2442, 2463, 2473,
2476
  see also Weather
Clinton, DeWitt, 1738
  George, 180, 183, 862, 1022
Clock and bell, for Univ. of Va., 2227,
2238, 2250, 2259, 2273, 2321,
2324, 2325, 2327, 2328, 3060,
3076, 3092–94, 3100
Clocks, 542, 569, 1374, 3076
Clopton, John B., 1965, 2079
Cloth. See Drygoods
Clothing
  account for, 2632-a
  Lilburne Jefferson's, 1399
  mentioned, 65, 69, 291, 1930, 2544,
2774, 2800-a
  slaves', 315, 317, 318, 397, 560, 2515,
2516, 2810, 2977-a
  see also names of items
Cloud, Mr., 1501, 1720
Clover, 250, 441, 528, 546, 564, 566,
579, 590, 675, 955, 1274, 3122
  seed, 528, 536, 627, 997, 1002
Cloverdale, Va., 2344, 2345
Clow & Co., 390, 2535
Coachman, T. J.'s, 650
Coalter, John, 1500, 1511, 1602, 1610,

1825, 1866, 2116, 2154, 2282
  see also Stuart and Coalter
Coast survey, 1754
Coats, orders for, 284
Cobb, Mr., 578
Cobbett, William, 376
Cobbs, David, 1679
  Samuel, 1136
  Samuel, Jr., 7
  Tom, 307
Cochran, J. Lynn, 858
  Mrs. Peyton, 2965
Cockburn, Sir George, 1342
Cocke, Charles, 1929
  John Hartwell
    Agricultural Society, 1484
    Board of Visitors, Univ. of Va.,
1443, 1450, 1468, 1517, 1614,
1616, 1783, 1837, 1886, 1909,
1967, 2001, 2139, 2319, 2917,
2927, 2995, 3019
    bond from, 2249
    Bremo Seminary, 1800
    deed to, 2270
    disagreement with Neilson, 1771
    letters from, 1690, 1743, 1807,
1883, 2310
    letters to, 1094, 1220, 1286, 1305,
1323, 1449, 1465, 1483, 1519,
1604, 1617, 1689, 1714, 1741,
1785, 1804, 1805, 1808, 1848,
1858, 1862, 1884, 1895, 1978,
1984, 2107, 2171, 2218, 2234,
2280, 2321, 2322, 2918-a
    marriage of, 1884
    mentioned, 1280, 1445, 1482, 1528,
1618, 1628, 1681, 1692, 1745,
1836, 1839, 1882, 1946, 1962,
1985, 2149, 2152, 2256, 2264,
2317
    opinion of Judge Dade, 2178
    Proctor, Univ. of Va., 2922
    procurement of faculty, Univ. of
Va., 2072
    to run for election, 1552
    subscription to Univ. of Va., 1765
Cockran, Charles B., 805
Codes, 56, 2390
Codfish, 2259
Coffee, 823, 923, 3062, 3110
Coffee, W. A., 2030

Coffee (*cont.*)
   William J.
      letters from, 1964, 1977, 2240
      letters to, 1781, 1995
      mentioned, 1928
      papers from, 2129
      price for cornices, 2215, 2216
Coffee cups, 2809
Coffee jar, 2407
Coffee urn, 2406
Coffer, Mr., 2773
Coffin, Charles, Jr., 2674
   Francis, 150, 151, 467
Cognac. See Brandy
Coimbra, University of, 1873
Coins, 187
Coke, Sir Edward, 16, 148, 154, 165,
     1936, 1952, 2254, 2493, 2521, 2988,
     2988-a, 3054
Col de Tende, Italy, 82, 115
Colclaser [Coleclasher], Mr., 1488, 1490
   Daniel, 2954, 2962, 2980, 3011
Cole, Mr., 2879
Colechester, Md., 2467, 2592
Coleclasher. See Colclaser
Coleman, Mr., 135
   Joseph, 2919
Coleman vs. Seymour, 2379
Coles, Mr., 302, 1006, 1132, 1153
   Edward, 2787
   Isaac, 20, 1579, 1618, 1628, 2782-a
   John, 2067
Coles Collection, 2376
Colfax, Colonel, 931
Colle, Albemarle County, Va., 221,
     282, 677, 1009, 1010, 1048, 2582,
     2919
Colleges. See names and locations of
     colleges
Colley, Nathaniel, 191, 279
Collier, Thomas, 829
Collins, Mr., 1720
   Zaccheus, 1501, 1634, 1738
Columbia, Bank of. See Bank of Co-
     lumbia
Columbia, S. C.
   letters from, 1770, 1776, 1780, 1788,
     1792, 1872, 1934
   letters to, 691, 1779, 1781, 2004,
     3058-a
   see also Columbia College; South
     Carolina College

Columbia, Va., 274, 283, 322, 323, 327,
     937
Columbia College, S. C., 1755, 1788,
     1803, 1894, 1907
   see also South Carolina College
Columbian, The, 1096
Columbian Register, 2004
Columns, for Univ. of Va., 1704, 1710,
     1711, 1714, 1715, 1717, 1726, 1733,
     1739, 1748, 1794, 1804, 1805, 1807,
     1810, 1813, 1818, 1862, 1863, 1935,
     1937, 1960, 2010, 2013, 2021, 2025,
     2026, 2028, 2029, 2034, 2066, 2081,
     2157, 2158, 2175, 2212, 2214, 2216,
     2222, 2229, 2232, 2233, 2235, 2236,
     2239, 2249, 2253, 2266, 2298, 2320,
     2321
Colvin, John B., 1091
Combs, 998
*Commentaries on the Laws of Eng-
     land*, 2988
Commerce
   European, 1081, 2470, 2831, 2904-a
   federal regulation of, 68, 294, 3082-a
   foreign, 294
   French-English threat to, 600
   treaties with France, 133
   Washington's speech on, 311
   West Indies, 493
   see also under names of countries
Commission merchants, 594, 3041-b
   see also John Barnes
Commissioners. See under subjects,
     e.g., Public buildings, commis-
     sioners of
Commissions, 2360, 2361, 2482-a, 2741
Committee to revise Va. laws, 29, 2871
Commodes, 2483
Common law, 640, 2576
Common law reports, 1677
Common Sense, 2957
*Comparative View of the State and
     Faculties of Man with the Animal
     World*, 2472
*Compendious View of the Civil Law,
     and of the Law of the Admiralty*,
     2988
*Compendium of the Anatomy of the
     Human Body*, 2767
Competitor (ship), 2144
Compleat History of England, 2521
Composition, 3039-a

County lieutenants, 2361, 2373, 2377

Cours, P., 659

Courses of study, recommended by T. J., 172, 992, 1230, 1231, 1894, 2254
see also letters to Dabney and Peter Carr; John Garland Jefferson

Courts, 2494, 2501, 2534-a, 2724, 2887-a, 2939
see also Judiciary; names of states, counties, cities

Cousin, Mr., 190

Coutts, Patrick, 2805

Cowan, Mr., 3040

Cowes, England, 131

Cowley, Hannah, 118, 121

Cowpeas, 2545-b

Cowpens, S. C., 2373-c, 2385

Cowper, Captain, 700

Cowpox, 728

Cox, Henry, 31
James D., 2843
John, 2779-b
Moses, 422, 424

Cox (Thomas) & Co., 1952

Coxe, Dr. John R., 1474, 1487, 1501, 1530
Tench
bill of exchange, 2582
letter of introduction, 259, 285, 287
letter from, 632
letters to, 472, 493, 496

Crackers, for Monticello, 821, 823

Craddock, John, 3006

Craig, James
clerk of Shelby County, Ky., 689, 798, 799, 897, 907, 914, 915
letter from, 954
mentioned, 953
Robert, 1025

Crane, Captain, 1950

Craney Island, Norfolk County, Va., 2738

Craven, John
T. J.'s overseer, 672, 711, 764, 837, 936, 955, 1093
purchases from, 955
subscription to militia, 1208
John H., 2734, 2745–47, 2757, 2895, 2956, 3003

Crawford, Mr., 225, 909, 2012, 2015, 3101

Johnson, Jr., 2716
William H.
election of 1824, 2100
letters from, 1864, 2147
mentioned, 1303, 2065, 3039-b
Secretary of Treasury, 1288

Crawford, Va., 2344

Cream, 2740

Creek Indians, 2199

Cremona flax, 2147

Crenshaw, William, 1183

Cribbs, Mr., 1682

Criticism, literary, 2914

"Crito" (pseudonym), 1610

Critta (slave), 778, 781, 2620

Crockett, Mrs. James P., 2361
Walter, 2361

Croft, Herbert, 613

Cropper, Sally, 545, 2472-a, 2531

Crops, 294, 2445, 2470, 2831
damages to, 845, 936, 2992
medicinal, 1416
prospects, 268, 634, 675, 1075, 1246, 1248, 1777, 1803
rotation of, 369, 671, 1230
transportation expense, 2799-a
see also Agriculture; names of crops

Crosat, Mr., 1405

Crosly, Mr., 490

Cross (silver), 2409, 2410

Cross, David, 2377

Crouch, Mr., 1002

Crowe, Anthony, 2377

Crown grant, 2796
see also Land grants

Crown Law, Foster's, 2385

Crowninshield, Jacob, 2703

Crozet, Claude [Claudius], 1853, 1855, 2047, 2999

Crump, George W., 1825, 1845, 1933

Crush's Tavern, Fredericktown, Md., 2592

Crystal seal, 2767

Cuba, 1058

Cubi y Soler, Mariano, 3054

Cucumbers, 714, 1120, 3107

Culpeper, Va., 893, 896, 2023, 2299, 2375, 2467, 2592, 2822, 2871

Culpeper Court House, 2592

Cumberland, Va., 2370

Cumberland County, Va., 31, 251, 500, 2353, 2428, 2451, 2499, 3025

Cumberland River, 1014
Cummings, Hilliard & Co., 2107, 2137,
    2198, 2201, 2218, 2237, 3054
  see also William Hilliard
Cunningham's Creek, 17
Cunningham's Mill, Va., 2592
Cups, 2809
Currency, 2368, 2640-a
  see also Money; Paper money; Rate
    of exchange
Currie, Armistead, 1842, 1845
    Ellyson, 1470, 1520
    James, 202, 246, 250, 293, 307, 333,
      2393, 2518, 2529
    Mrs. James, 2529
Curuger, Mr., 444
Cushaw squash, 2027
Cushing, William, 1092, 1441
Custis, Nelly, 311
Customs. See Tariffs
Customs declaration, 2454, 2472-b
Cutbush, James, 1757, 2123
Cutting, J. B., 105
    Nathaniel, 127, 129, 427
Cyane (ship), 2081
Cyclopedia, 2940
Cypress vines, 1018
Cyropaedia, 2940

Dabney, Mrs. Virginius, 1073, 1079,
    1093, 1103, 1104, 1373, 1376, 1379,
    1392, 1411, 1461, 1488, 1490, 1495
Dade, William A. G.
  considered for law professorship,
      2178, 2180, 2185, 2193, 2218,
      2219, 2280
  letter to, 2187
  mentioned, 2186
Dale, Mr., 794
Dalton, T., 1441
Dam, T. J.'s at Shadwell, 2745, 2765,
    2796, 2907, 2939
Dan River, 20
Dana, James Freeman, 2123, 3014
Dance, H., 907
Dandridge, Mr., 495
    Nathaniel West, 2711, 2871, 2891,
      2908
    W., 2261
Dangerfield, Mrs., 2745-a, 2748, 2750,
    2777

    L. W., 2745-a
    Sarah, 2745-a
Daniel (slave), 1336, 2791
Daniel, Mr., 2994
    Nirwood, 1207
    Peter M., 1962
Danish (language), 3058-a
Dannery, Mr., 492, 494
Danville, Duchess of, 314
Darden, Mr., 2802-a
Darlington (horse), 606
Darnell, Mr., 1134, 2830, 2879
    Nimrod, 1446, 2850
Darst, Mr., 1629
Dartmouth College case, 2144
Dashiell, Mr., 1551, 1574, 2940
Daugherty. See Dougherty
Davenport, William, 606, 750, 754,
    2959
Davidson, James, 1003
    John, 57
Davies, Mr., 1136
    Augustine, 134, 283, 315
    Mrs. Augustine, 313
    Nicholas, 7
    William, 2377
Davila, discourses on, 263, 360
Davis, Mr., 887, 2770
    E. S., 2020
    James, 914
    Mrs. John Staige, 2207, 2306, 2309
    Robert, 3095
  see also Weiss & Davis
Davison, Mr., 737
    George J., 1533, 1586
Davy (slave), 701, 1174, 2735, 2746,
    2747-a, 2748, 2758, 2759, 2768,
    2775–78
Dawson, Mr., 2595-a
    John, 7, 695, 2597
    Martin
      account with T. J., 1988, 2897,
        2943, 3010-a
      audits Univ. of Va. accounts, 1946
      estimates Univ. of Va. debts, 1967,
        1990
      Henderson suits, 907, 2700-a
      lands sold to, 909
      letters from, 2256, 2897, 2945,
        2954, 2970, 2978, 2987
      mentioned, 955, 1956, 2053
      Univ. of Va. accounts, 2036, 2260

2300, 2976
in Richmond, 1447
sent to Eppington, 1082
witnesses bond, 1968
John Wayles
asked to visit T. J., 2537
attends Indian council, 399, 2519
bonds of, 1380
books, 262, 2489
bridle for, 804
candidate for Congress, 780
candidate for Va. Assembly, 824
children of, 2684, 2695
education, 200, 296, 324, 431,
2424, 2451, 2456, 2470, 2480,
2485, 2493, 2495, 2517
estate of, 2043, 2074, 2553
finances, 309, 421, 745, 747, 1908,
1934, 1936, 1972, 1988, 2489,
2495
harvesting, 714, 778
health, 1480, 1908, 1936, 1942,
1952, 2499, 2512
horses, 2599
lands, 620, 621, 631, 747, 751,
1908, 2043, 2661
letters from, 439, 598, 620, 621,
645, 651, 653, 658, 665, 745,
767, 780, 783, 819, 820, 824,
833, 845, 877–81, 899, 903,
1031, 1035, 1074, 1081, 1082,
1095, 1100, 1109, 1175, 1229,
1364, 1383, 1428, 1434, 1480,
1574, 1599, 1695, 1803, 1908,
2022, 2652, 2695, 2975
letters to, 604, 608, 624, 634, 642,
695, 698, 701, 712, 762, 766,
770, 840, 847, 929, 990, 994,
1006, 1034, 1065, 1098, 1167,
1237, 1251, 1256, 1271, 1299,
1450, 1468, 1489, 1551, 1798,
1800, 1894, 1923, 1942, 2522,
2591, 2595, 2654, 2661, 2686-a,
2923, 2940, 2976, 3002
marriage to Maria Jefferson, 2547,
2550, 2551, 2553
mentioned, 55, 312, 394, 611, 616,
626, 652, 657, 663, 707, 768,
771, 814, 835, 860, 865, 1173,
1175, 1186, 1447, 1552, 2481,
2555, 2559, 2562, 2570, 2604,
2659, 2671, 2699

in Philadelphia, 2476
profession for, 254, 256
relationship with T. J., 1695
shoemaker for, 2522
slaves of, 642, 994, 1129, 2550, 2551
subscriptions for Central College,
1484
in U. S. Senate, 1434, 2678, 2683
vaccination of slaves, 1129
visits Monticello, 2561, 2562
Lucy, 61, 2387
Maria Jefferson
birth of child, 645, 2677, 2683
books, 335, 2443, 2445
death of, 886, 887
death of child, 652
education, 347, 2437, 2440, 2445,
2446, 2448, 2489
at Eppington, 296, 2417, 2437,
2442
health, 61, 431, 598, 609, 620, 626,
651, 653, 658, 745, 767, 780,
783, 824, 833, 865, 877–81,
884, 2388, 2493, 2499, 2508,
2524, 2526, 2684, 2686-a, 2695
lettercover to, 2554
letters from, 163, 168, 194, 232,
237, 244, 248, 269, 328, 778,
814, 2446, 2472-a
letters to, 160, 228, 233, 238, 272,
280, 288, 308, 446, 545, 588,
611, 616, 618, 631, 652, 657,
663, 673, 684, 707, 747, 766,
768, 771, 781, 804, 835, 2440,
2441, 2443, 2445, 2448, 2460,
2461, 2468, 2469, 2472, 2473,
2476, 2477, 2479, 2482, 2483,
2486, 2487, 2514, 2531, 2546,
2547, 2555, 2559, 2562, 2570,
2571, 2599, 2604, 2659, 2678,
2682–84
maid for, 2531
marriage to John Wayles Eppes,
2547, 2550, 2551, 2553
mentioned, 55, 76, 84, 90, 93, 148,
158, 164, 165, 167, 171, 189,
192, 219, 223, 227, 229, 236,
254, 271, 274, 282, 286, 312,
317, 324, 329, 332, 334, 337,
366, 384, 387, 394, 397, 399,
423, 445, 463, 512, 521, 530,
533, 534, 541, 549, 558, 564,

Fentress, John, 850, 851, 907, 914
Fenwick, Joseph
    draft, 527
    letters to, 247, 395, 448, 457, 509
    mentioned, 401
    U. S. Consul at Bordeaux, 415, 2498
Fernandes, Dr., 2901
Fernandez, John F. d'Oliveira, 1873
Ferries, 1399, 2805
    see also specific names, e.g., Boyd's
        Ferry; Scott's Ferry
Ferris, Mr., 344, 1165
Fertilizer, 338, 447
Fevers, 2529–31, 2699
Fiction, 22
Figs, 721, 1120, 2918-a
Finance
    Hamilton on, 1280
    T. J. on, 1280
    public. See United States, public
        debt
Finances, T. J.'s. See Accounts, T. J.'s;
    John Barnes; Thomas Jefferson,
    business affairs
Fincastle County, Va., 1892, 1992, 2140
Fireplaces, 2352
Fires, 2378, 2393-a
    Charlottesville, 2515
    Monticello, 1681, 1684
    Poplar Forest, 3053
    Williamsburg, 2393-a
Firewood, 750, 934, 1009, 1012, 2852
*First Collection of Volume the Second
    of the Moste Favourite Minuets
    with Their Basses*, 3177-a
Fiscal agents, T. J.'s. See John Barnes;
    James Brown; Gibson & Jefferson
Fiscal policy, Hamilton's, 231
Fish, 1348, 2795-a
    for pond, 1230, 1231, 1689
    gift from the Coolidges, 2301
    purchased by T. J., 702, 955
    see also names of fish
Fisher, Mr., 2926
    James C., 1638
    O. O., 2358, 2360, 2369, 2373, 2394,
        2428, 2438, 2511, 2549, 2616,
        2629, 2643, 2697, 2705, 2715,
        2754, 2985, 2998
Fishinger, R., 35
Fitch, Mr., 541, 779, 909, 2634, 2640,
    2649

Jabez, 1055
    William D., 1012, 2954
Fitch Partnir (horse), 2765
Fitzhugh, Daniel, 2392, 2393
    Peregrine, 601
    Richard, 2467, 2773
    Theodorick, 2392, 2393
    William, 152, 189, 193, 205, 2447
Five Sisters (ship), 2906
Flannagan, Ambrose, 2954
Flat Creek, Va., 3147
Flax, 2147, 2776
Fleischer, Mr., 14
Fleming, Mrs., 237, 2474
    John, 1085, 1090, 2891
    William, 2891
Fletcher, Thomas C., 907
Flood, Major, 1144
    Mr., 2940
    Mrs., 3147
    H., 3147
    Henry, 1250
    Noah, 1250
Floods, 2734, 2735
    Virginia's, of 1814, 1309
Flooring, 1943
Florence (wine), 2927-b
Florence, Italy, 2582-a
Florida
    acquisition of, 1006, 1016, 1058,
        1091, 1098
    boundary disputes, 36, 1405
    U. S. aggression, of 1818, 1582
Flour, 2872-a
    Bedford County, Va., 2800, 2884
    Embargo affects, 1027, 1028
    for Mayor of Marseilles, 372
    prices of, 2800, 2811, 2823–25, 2827,
        2839, 2842, 2850, 2851, 2853,
        2854, 2858, 2860, 2861, 2862,
        2868, 2876, 2893, 2902, 2903,
        2994
    purchase of, 3003
    sales of, 1079, 1148, 1227, 1228, 1274,
        1286, 1295, 1305, 1379, 1392,
        1411, 1488, 1490, 1495, 2430-a,
        2799-a, 2813, 2814, 2815-a, 2840,
        2855, 2864, 2866, 2867, 2881,
        2884, 2886, 2890, 2904, 2926,
        2935
    shipments of, 2884, 2929, 2962
    see also Wheat

Flour mills. See Mills, grist
Flournoy, Daniel, 1672
   Matthew, 689, 798, 799, 907, 914, 915
Flower gardening. See Gardens and
   gardening
Flowers, 77, 1114
   at Edgehill, 976, 1018, 1020
   at Poplar Forest, 1137
   in Prince William Co., Va., 2497
   seeds, 1219
   at Varina, 1646
   see also Gardens and gardening;
    names of flowers
Fluvanna County, Va., 1, 1550, 2620,
   2711
Fluvanna River, Va., 7, 2364, 3133
   see also James River
Fly, Hessian, 845, 847, 936
Flyte, Henry N., 2586
Fodder, 2781-a, 2994-a
Fontaine, Carter B., 30
   William, 1094
Fontblanque, J. de G., 2988
Food, 721, 758, 955, 1069, 2443
   see also names of foods
Forbes, Mr., 1265
   John M., 713
Ford, James Westhall, 3025-a, 3025-b,
   3025-c
Ford, at Milton, Va., 2377
Foreman, Ezekiel, 2582
Forest, the, Charles City County, Va.,
   2351
Forrest, Colonel, 285
Forster, Mr., 325
Fort George, 1344
Fort Norfolk, Va., 2738
Fort Washington, N. Y., 2385
Fort Wayne, 318
Fortuna Virilis, temple of, 1912
Fosset, Joe, freed by T. J., 2300
Fossil tooth, 593
Foster, B. D., 1981
   Sir Michael, 2385
   Richard, 47
Fotheringay, Va., 2220, 2223
Foulis (printers), 3054
Foundries, 2793-a
Fountain pen, 3040
Fourth of July, 470, 962, 1125, 2009
Foushee, William, 442, 1491
Fox & Richardson, 2901

Fox grape, 2899
Fox Indians, 956
Foxall, Mr., 1147
Foy, Edward, 2910
Frames, 2666
France
   affairs in, 336, 344, 392, 531, 534, 541,
    649, 2526
   George Blaettermann's tour
    through, 1994
   books from, 2717
   British prejudice, 121
   commerce, 2904-a
    with U. S., 133, 231, 390, 497, 515,
     600, 2428, 2430-a, 2470
   constitution approved, in 1818, 1582
   Consuls of, in U. S., 481, 491, 492,
    494, 2416, 2530
   Directory (governmental), 647, 2558
   Emperor of, 2390, 2392
   forces of, in Chesapeake Bay, 2370
   funds for, 2660
   imports from, 515
   Maria Jefferson's trip to. See under
    Maria Jefferson Eppes
   T. J.'s ministry to. See under Thom-
    as Jefferson, Political life
   Legislative assembly, 311, 2430-a
   M. Lenblhon bound for, 461
   letters from, for R. H. Lee, 36
   Louisiana claims, 1405
   measurements system, 3111, 3149
   mentioned, 1119, 2386
   Minister to, 375, 695, 2527
   Napoleon's threat to, 647, 2888
   National Convention, 390
   paper money, 219
   passengers for, 477, 479
   Rembrandt Peale and, 2590
   personnel for U. S. mint from, 2503
   relations with Great Britain, 447,
    900, 2611, 2868-b, 2888
   relations with U. S., 59, 360, 438,
    604, 605, 608, 611, 639, 640, 661,
    1029, 1034, 1058, 2802-a, 2820-a
   Revolution, 121, 122, 124, 131, 159,
    186, 229, 231, 311, 318, 511, 647
   ship from, 2884
   Dabney Terrell's trip to, 1398, 1414
   tobacco market, 390, 2587
   travel in, 2394
   treaties with, 133, 2591

France (*cont.*)
  trees and plants from, 2918-a
  University of, 2002
  wars, 395, 430, 431, 447, 610, 900,
     1366, 2424, 2515, 2526, 2564,
     2611, 2800-a, 2868-b
    see also Europe, War of 1790–1815
  weather, 2389
  West Indies colonies, 186, 313
  wines, 2498, 2952
Francis, John, 2566
  Richard, 2988
Frank, Mr., 493
Frankfort, Ky., 641, 647, 1476
Franklin, Benjamin, 49, 67, 129, 467
  William Temple, 185
Franklin Court, 2582-a
Franklin Insurance Co., 2253
Fray, Aaron, 1787
Frazer, Mr., 2384
Frederick (slave), 728
Frederick County, Va., 603, 2793
Fredericksburg, Va.
  college at, 2140
  William F. Gray at, 2899
  horses at, 2531
  T. J.'s trip to, 617
  laws revised, 2871
  letters from, 1573, 1652, 2277, 2297
  mentioned, 193, 310, 385, 541, 551,
     589, 650, 902, 1464, 1663, 2103,
     2299, 2447, 2571, 2686-a
  newspapers in, 2129
  travel through, 3148
  United States Collector, 2492
Fredericksburg and Charlottesville
    stage line, 2927
Fredericktown, Md., 2592
Frederictown, 2592
Freedom of press, 2724
Freedom of speech, 561
Freeman, Mr., 2719, 2751
  Mr. (legal codifier), 2478
  John, 2729
  John Holmes, 955, 2719
  Thomas, 1576
Freemon, Dr., 971
Freight, charges for, 2799-a
French (language), 352, 558, 1485,
    2391, 2392, 2655-a, 2705, 2927,
    2992, 3042, 3058-a
French dictionaries, 3054

French-English dictionary, 3054
  for cipher, 56
French New Testament, 2702
French Revolution. See Europe, War
  of 1790–1815; France, Revolution
French West Indies, 186, 313
Frenchman, 2418
Freneau, Philip, 313, 315, 327, 347,
  360, 366, 491, 534, 541
Frethy, Edward, 2688
Friends, Society of. See Quakers
Friezes, 928, 1928, 1977
Frogs, 2473
Fronsac, Duke de, 271
Frontignan (wine), 2952
Frost, J., 1136
  D., 1136
Froville, M., 364
Fruit, 2392
  at Monticello, 269, 659
  at Poplar Forest, 1137, 2074
  shipped to Monticello, 726
  trees, 410, 659, 714, 1137, 1154, 1340,
    2425, 2436
  see also Orchards; names of trees
Fry, Henry, 893, 896
  John, 1846
  Joseph, 371
  Joshua, 6, 7, 1846, 3117
Fry & Co., 1136
Fuller, Mr., 2965
Fullerton, Valerie, 366, 488, 545, 2531
Funding system, 2711
Funerals, 2804
Furniture, 219, 220, 223, 237, 245, 262,
  280, 430, 431, 460, 521, 537, 547,
  549, 551, 2346, 2397
Fyfe, Andrew, 2767

Gabriel (slave), 2775
Gage, Thomas, 26
Gaines, Bred., 643
  Frank, 2428
  Hierom, 362, 2428
Gaines's, Va., 2467
Gale, Joseph, 2848, 2850
Gales & Seaton, 1467
Gallatin, Albert
  letters from, 1398, 1510
  letters to, 1029, 1032, 1828

699, 727, 773, 788, 796, 801, 827,
830, 854, 855, 873, 884, 886, 889,
1024, 1035, 1048, 1108, 1112,
1115, 1147, 1153, 1164, 1203,
1232, 1248, 1249, 1286, 1305,
1311, 1312, 1360, 1361, 1384,
1446, 1467, 1979, 2595, 2632,
2655, 2692, 2755, 2818, 2820,
2933
T. J.'s agent in Richmond, 1374
letters from, 2808, 2812, 2814, 2815,
2818, 2819, 2821, 2823–25, 2827,
2832
letter to, 1073
William Short's account, 787
see also Patrick Gibson; George Jefferson
Gibson's gate, Va., 3147
Gig harness, 1064, 1066, 1362, 1363
Gilbert, Sir Geoffrey, 2988
Gilbert's, Va., 2467, 2592
Giles, Mr., 308
William B., 420, 561, 1016, 1468,
1520, 3023-a, 3082-a
Gilet, 291
Gill (slave), 2856, 3006
Gill, John, 1136, 1161, 1207
Gilliam, Frederick, 1183
Gilliat, William, 2903
Gilmer, Mr., 1201, 2901, 2992
Francis Walker
anonymous essays by, 1610
death of, 2296
funds given to, 2237
health, 2105, 2184, 2281, 2500
Leslie's survey of Univ. of Va.,
2182
letters from, 1527, 2161, 2184, 2247
letters to, 1328, 1405, 1485, 1557,
1707, 1752, 1822, 2086, 2100,
2105, 2106, 2109, 2112, 2193,
2219, 2281, 3045
mentioned, 1335, 1608, 2103, 2122,
2152, 2208, 2254, 2859
mission to Europe to engage Univ.
of Va. faculty, 2075, 2077,
2088, 2094–97, 2100, 2107,
2108, 2142, 3046-a, 3058-a
power of attorney, 3039
on Univ. of Va. faculty, 2054,
2100, 2109, 2146, 2178, 2193,
2218, 2225, 2226, 3078-b

George, 212, 433, 512, 564, 2515
Mrs. George, 1601
John, 2859
Lucy, 322
Mary House, 2888
Peachy Ridgway, 2888
see also McHenry, Gilmer, & Sterrett
Gilmore, Mr., 2936
Joseph, 2954, 2987
Gilpin, Mr., 731
George, 818
Gilsner, Mrs., 332
Gimbrede, Thomas, 1823, 1830
Ginani, Giuseppi, 317
Girardin, Mr., 1078
Louis H., 1089, 1284, 1393, 2961
Givin, Thomas, 689, 798, 799, 907
Glasgow, Ky., 1557-a
Glasgow, University of, 2063
Glass, 570, 585, 587, 599, 729, 1093,
1700, 1865, 2541, 2604, 2692,
2872-a, 2873
see also Glazing
Glass (tumblers), 726, 2542
Glass, Julian W., Jr., 2373-a, 2373-b,
2373-c, 2383-a
Glasses, eye. See Spectacles
Glazing, 1562, 1648, 1650, 1653, 1663,
1665
Glebe lands, 214, 1317, 1400, 1591
Gloster, Bedford Rachel's (slave), 2856
Gloucester, Va., 1005, 2215
Godwin, William, 648
Gojon, Claudius F., 2002, 2003
Goldsmith, Oliver, 2671
Goldsmiths, 2403
Goliah [Goliath] (slave), 2507, 2599,
2683
Gooch, Claiborne Watts, 3085-a
Mrs. William S., 160, 707, 781
Goochland, Va., 2491
Goochland County, Va.
Court of, 9
Court House, 2, 3, 4
deeds to land in, 1, 3, 31, 51, 53, 636
election of 1817, 1445
letters from, 215, 350, 358, 359, 383,
428, 437, 443, 535
letter to, 440
map, 5
mentioned, 370

Harper's Ferry, Va., 2467, 2592
Harpsichord, 606, 609, 611, 1006, 1798, 2472, 2562, 2976, 3155
Harrington, General, 2371, 2534-a
Harris, Mr., 735, 2142
    Clifton, 1379, 1515
    Frank, 1175
    Frederick, 2640-a
    James, 1910
    John, 1765
    see also Shelton & Harris
Harrison, Mr., 19, 2377
    Benjamin, 20, 33, 302, 2377, 2711, 2891
    Carter H., 2833
    Francis Burton, 1469
    Jesse Burton, 2011, 2319
    Randolph, 1468, 1542, 1552, 1678, 2760
    Samuel J., 1145, 1210, 1324, 1494, 1503, 2800, 2818, 2830, 2874
        letters from, 1107, 1146, 1152, 1185, 1564, 1730
        letters to, 1108, 1131, 1149, 1155, 1163, 1191, 1469, 1481, 2011, 2927-b
        Samuel Scott suit, 1068, 1136, 1158, 1161, 1177–79, 1181, 1189, 1190, 1194
    William, 2377
Harrison family, 3132
Harrison's mill, Albemarle County, Va., 3132
Harrodsburg, Ky., 2202
Harrow (school), 1501
Harrows, 2793-a
Harry (slave), 2890-a
Hart, Andrew, 2919
    Patrick, 519
    Wayne M., 1278
Harte, Henry, 2063
Hartford, Conn., 1057, 2091, 2479, 2724
Hartford Convention, 1375, 1887, 3082-a
Harvard College, 1570, 1906, 1907, 1911, 2011, 2189
Harvest, 714, 778
    see also names of crops
Harvey, Lewis, 820
Harvie, Gabriella, 184

Jacquilin, 2877
John, 136, 533, 563, 2458, 2458-a, 2490, 2876–78, 2890
    executor of Peter Jefferson, 10, 13, 141, 149, 209, 319
    land in Albemarle County, 136, 184, 225
    letters to, 141, 206
    R., 149
    Richard, 1024
Hassler, Ferdinand R., 1754, 2318, 3041
Hastings, Warren, 96
Hat factory, 946
Hatch, Frederick W., 1988
Hatcher, Benjamin, 1534
Havana, Cuba, 2733, 2884
Havre, France, 127, 129, 151, 364, 467, 3128
Havre de Grace, France, 2454
Hawkins, Mr., 425, 1629
    John J., 2584, 2640-a
Hawley, William, Jr., 1650
Hawthorn hedges, 1416, 1442
Haxall [Haxhall], Mr., 695, 712, 1644, 2595
Hay, Mr., 2815
    George, 1602, 1610, 1772, 2054, 2116, 2652
        T. J.'s attorney, 908, 945, 950, 985, 1092, 1178, 1179, 1191
        letter from, 1181
        letters to, 1178, 1180
    William, Jr., 2845
Hay, Wirt, & Tazewell, 2815
Hayne, Robert Young, 2883-a
Hazard, Captain William, 1003
Headaches, T. J.'s, 171, 175, 176, 207, 271, 990, 2442, 2443, 2729
Head gate, 2746
Head of Elk, Wilmington, Del., 2516
Heath, Colonel, 987
    Mr., 737
    James E., 1885
Hebrew Bible, 1524
Hebrides, 214
Hedeman, Va., 2467
Hedgeman River, Va., 2592
Hedges, 1415, 1416, 1419, 1442, 2731, 2734, 2757
Hedgethorn, 1416

Heidelberg, Germany, 100
Heinrich, A. P., 1420
Helms, Jerry G., 2366
Helvetius, Claude Adrien, 2868-a
Hemings, Betty, 2537-a
  Eston, 2300
  J., 3053
  James, 577, 2545
  John, 1729, 1964, 2559, 2300
  Madison, 2300
  Peter, 782
  Robert, 2537-a
Hemp, 3122
Henderson, Mr., 278, 2507, 2939
  Anne B., 785, 838
  Bennett, estate of, 581, 643, 677, 685,
    689, 716, 734, 736, 738, 741, 750,
    752–54, 774–76, 784, 785, 797–
    99, 809, 812, 815–17, 822, 825,
    830, 836, 838, 839, 843, 846, 850–
    52, 854, 855, 867, 870, 885, 888–
    90, 897, 898, 907–10, 913–15,
    926, 934, 935, 937–39, 945, 950,
    953, 954, 965, 970, 971, 1008–10,
    1013, 1039, 1045, 1048, 1050,
    1051, 1061, 1062, 1113, 1123,
    1183, 1184, 1223, 1244, 1259,
    1264, 1269, 1435, 1557-a, 2700-a
  Charles, 734, 738, 797, 799, 870, 871,
    907–9, 935, 1123, 1244, 2700-a
  Eliza, 736, 798, 799, 812, 907–9, 915,
    926, 935, 1123, 1259
  Elizabeth, 848, 914, 1269, 2867-a
    deeds from, 752, 798, 850, 851, 871
    Bennett Henderson estate, 581,
      797, 809, 843, 907–9, 935, 970,
      1123, 1244, 1259, 1264, 1308,
      2700-a
  Frances, 736, 799, 812, 907, 909, 914,
    935, 1013, 1062, 1123, 1244,
    1435
  Helman, 907
  Isham, 689, 734, 736, 738, 784, 792,
    798, 870, 907–9, 935, 1113, 1123
  James, 1415, 2700-a, 2867-a
  James L., 797, 798
    deeds, 689, 752, 799, 870, 914, 926
    Bennett Henderson estate, 643,
      718, 734, 736, 738, 741, 774,
      907–9, 935, 953, 1008, 1113,
      1123, 1244, 1259, 1264, 1269,
      1308, 1435, 1557-a

  protested note, 1113
  sale of land, 809
  John, 11, 362, 643, 797, 2507, 2867-a
    deeds, 784, 785, 838, 871, 970, 1013
    Bennett Henderson estate, 736,
      741, 754, 815, 854, 873, 909,
      935, 953, 1039, 1123, 1259,
      1269, 1435, 2700-a
    notes from, 1113
    Peyton vs. Henderson, 836, 839,
      842, 844, 846, 848, 859, 876,
      885, 907, 908, 934, 945, 1308
    property of, 977
  Lucy, 736, 799, 812, 907–9, 914, 935,
    1013, 1062, 1123, 1435
  Martha, 970
  Matthew, 907, 908, 977, 1010, 1039
  Nancy Crawford. See Nancy Craw-
    ford Henderson Nelson
  Richard, 907
  Sarah. See Sarah Henderson Kerr
  William, 843, 907, 908, 1123
Henderson & Connard, 907, 908
Henderson, McCaul, & Co., 586, 662,
  1024
see also James Lyle; Alexander Mc-
  Caul
Hendersons, Albemarle County, Va.,
  2789-a
Hening, William Waller, 1182
Henley, Samuel, 2393-a
Henri (servant), 379
*Henrici de Bracton de Legibus & Con-
  suetudinibus Angliae Libri Quing
  . . . ,* 2988
Henrico County, Va., 1, 147, 506, 819,
  1965, 2817, 2994
Henrietta (ship), 2454
Henry (slave), 1729, 2962
Henry, Colonel, 2820-a
  John, 2552
  Patrick, 89
    William Wirt's biography, 2709–
      11, 2871, 2891, 2908–12, 2914,
      2961
  William, 2910
  see also Montgomery & Henry
Henry Court House, Va., 2859, 2888
Herbs, 2340
Hermitage (wine), 2729-b
Herndon, Edward, 2360
Herod, Jack N., 2800

Horace (Quintus Horatius Flaccus), 1096, 2763
Horizons, artificial, 1374
Hornsby, Frances Henderson. See Frances Henderson
Joseph, 1223, 1244
Thomas, 1244, 1259, 1269, 1308, 2867-a
Horry, Mr. (of South Carolina), 161, 162
Peter, 2961
Hors du Monde, Va., 302, 2392, 2485
Horse carts, 3012
Horse drovers, 3010-a
Horse wheels, 3109
Horses
bit for, 2411, 2766
breeding, 2495, 2512
bridle for, 804
Brimmer, 2516
care of, 415, 990, 994, 2411, 2737, 2761, 2962, 2994-a
Castor, 767, 2690
Darlington, 606
Fitch Partnir, 2765
harness, 192, 729, 731, 1064, 1066, 1362, 1363
Matchless, 2516
mentioned, 408, 565, 1036, 1589, 1914, 2067, 2486, 2516, 2531, 2599, 2719, 2751, 2753, 2781-a
purchase of, 152, 193, 196, 198, 205, 288, 603, 606, 695, 698, 701, 712, 766, 767, 899, 929, 1006, 1031, 1034, 1035, 1105, 1201, 1286, 1305, 1323, 2377, 2447, 2450, 2486, 2595
riding lessons, 2479
Tarquin, 454, 460, 521, 530, 551, 2447, 2516
travel on, 290, 356, 451, 545, 549, 551, 656, 1174, 2531, 2759, 2793-a
Horwitz, J., 1524, 1570
Hose, 560
Hospitals, 1017, 2080, 2377, 2385, 2831
Hossack, David, 2265
Houchens, Mr., 2777
Houdon, Jean Antoine, 768, 2582-a, 3067
"Hours" (engraving), 109, 114
Household manufacturing, 1215, 2831

House, Mr., 2979
Houses, 422–424
Housing, 158, 532, 2460, 2519, 2529, 3084
costs, 2591
Hovey (Henry) & Co., 2253
Howard, Benjamin, 1136, 1177, 1189
Howe, Sir William, 36
Howe's Ferry, Va., 2592
Howell, Jones &, 968, 1000, 1080
Howlett, Samuel, 2666
Hubard (slave), 3122
Hubbard, James, 1136
Jim (slave), 2778
Phill (slave), 2776, 2879
William H., 2904
see also Van Staphorst & Hubbard
Huckstep, Charles, 1183
David, 2806
Hudnall, Mr., 1762
E. W., 1653
Hudson, Captain, 837
Christopher, 711, 1339, 1630
Huffman, Elija, 1787
Hughes, Mr., 565
Ashford, 2355, 2395
Hull, William, 1344
Humbell, W., 1720
Humboldt, Alexander von, 1261, 1456
Hume, David, 1256, 2254, 3054
Humphreys, David, 67
Thomas, 1189
Humphries, David, 2391, 2392
Hundreds (districts), 1271
Hunt, Wilson, 3029
Hunter, Mr., 385, 2655, 3147
James, 1588, 1600, 1845, 1958, 1965
see also Martin vs. Hunter
Huntington, Mr., 3021
Samuel, 39
Hutter, C. S., Jr., 28, 159, 710, 1125, 1355, 1367, 1737, 2089
Hutton, H. I., 3021
Hyde Park, N. Y., 2002, 2003
Hylton, Captain, 296
Mr., 2482
Daniel, 324, 325, 500, 533, 665, 2485, 2489, 2515
letter from, 442
letters to, 235, 252, 391, 403, 501, 2506
sale of Elkhill, 402–4, 441

Kosciuszko, Thaddeus (*cont.*)
    goods shipped to, 628, 630
    letters from, 1453, 2559-a, 2883-b, 2904-a, 2927-a
        see also finances
    letters to, 722, 2595-a, 2782-a, 2793-a, 2800-a, 2801-a, 2802-a, 2820-a, 2820-b, 2868-b
        see also finances
    mentioned, 1206, 1213, 1226, 1535
    opinion on rise of Poland, 600
    stock owned by, 660, 666, 1277–79, 1281, 1285, 1288–91, 1294, 1307, 1310, 1319, 1337, 1407, 1413, 1421, 1423, 1426, 1427, 1436, 1439
    will of, 607, 1689, 1690
Kupfer, Charles F., 1700
Kurtz, Boice &, 2868-b
Kurtz, Bowie &, 1077, 1112, 1300, 1354
Kurtz's Tavern, Petersburg, Va., 2592

Labor, 419, 672
    cost of, 2533-a
    disputes, 1900, 1917
    lists, 2544
Laboratory equipment. See Apparatus; Virginia, University of, laboratory equipment
Lacey, Mr. (jeweller), 2402
Lacy's, Va., 2467
Ladd, Mr., 1071, 1083, 1090
Lafayette, Marie Joseph, Marquis de
    deserters from, 48
    dinner in honor of, 2104
    inscribed book for, 62
    land grants to, 918
    letter from, 3078-c
    letters to, 156, 161, 919, 1582, 2430-a
    message to, 314
    portrait of, 2124
    visit to Virginia, 2100, 2101, 2103, 3045
Lake Champlain, N. Y., 270, 2480
Lake George, N. Y., 270, 272, 2479, 2480, 2482
Lamb, John, 241, 2390, 2394
Lambert, William, 1938, 1940, 1941, 1947
La Meutte, France, 2431
La Motte, M., 151, 153, 364, 449, 458, 509

Lammons, Mr., 2768
Lamond, Mrs. Slater, 2427
Lancaster, Dabney, 978
Lancaster, Penn., 522, 971, 1022, 2592
Lancaster County, Va., 1470
Lance, William, 1125
Land
    Charles L. Bankhead's, 1117, 1346, 1347
    books, 1175
    claims, 19, 2439
    glebe, 214, 1317, 1400, 1591
    grants, 12, 17, 41, 166, 225, 556, 578, 592, 635, 743, 744, 918, 919, 996, 1533, 2364, 2366, 2374, 2629, 2793-a, 2796
    John Wayles Eppes's, 620, 621, 631, 747, 751, 1908, 2043, 2661
    T. J.'s, 1, 8, 17, 18, 53, 141, 197, 225, 402, 412, 418, 571–73, 578, 580, 584, 636, 638, 677, 678, 734, 738, 741, 752, 753, 784, 785, 798, 799, 809, 812, 815, 817, 838, 840, 845, 870, 873, 876, 882, 888, 897, 899, 907–9, 914, 915, 926, 943, 950, 970, 1013, 1039, 1048, 1050, 1051, 1061, 1062, 1107, 1108, 1123, 1131, 1133, 1136, 1149, 1152, 1155–57, 1161, 1162, 1165–68, 1171, 1173, 1175, 1176, 1178–80, 1183–85, 1188, 1189, 1192–98, 1207, 1347, 1499, 1528, 1557-a, 1589, 1909, 1923, 2350, 2355, 2395, 2428, 2451–53, 2456, 2499, 2506, 2518, 2550, 2551, 2553, 2661, 2760, 2764, 2789-a, 2805, 2806, 2817, 2836, 2846, 2976, 3002, 3113, 3124, 3138
        see also Albemarle County; Bedford County; Campbell County; Bennett Henderson, estate of; Monticello; Poplar Forest; Samuel Scott
    laws, 311, 582
    offices, 571, 1170, 1172, 1188
    Ordinance of 1785, 67
    public, 166, 1092, 2210, 2211, 2504
    Thomas Mann Randolph, Sr.'s, 1, 25, 141, 506
    Thomas Mann Randolph, Jr.'s, 1, 147, 288, 768
    speculation, 52

ships' papers, 2616, 2697, 2705, 2733
subscription to Univ. of Va., 1765
sugar maples for, 371
sword left with, 2383-a
travel with T. J., 2479
Virginia and Kentucky Resolutions, 637, 2576
visit to Annapolis, 1413
Madison County, Va., 2379
Madison's Cave, Va., 2467, 2592
Madison's map, 2946
Magazine, 2697-a
Magnesia, 3082
Mahogany, 1466
Mahrattas, 334
Mail. See Postal service
Maine, 2881
Maine, Mr., 1415, 1416, 1442
Majority rule, 649, 1023, 1049, 1456
Mallet, David, 2348
Mallory, C. A., 2803
  Mrs. O. T., 2875
  Robert, 1528, 1540, 1842
Malmsey (wine), 2952
Malt, 1252
Malta, 2831
Mamaluke bridle bit, 2766
Mammoth, 2548
Managers, 2526
Manchester, England, 586, 662, 2490
Manchester, Va., 1640, 2213
Manfield, Joseph, 2507
Manhattan Bank, 1278, 1279
Mann, Joseph, 2077
Manners, John, 2123
Mansfield, Joseph, 362
  Reuben, 1208
Manson, Otis, 1656
Manual of Parliamentary Practice, 2586
Manuel, Will's (slave), 2880
Manufacturers, 1702
Manufacturing, 946, 1215, 2820-a, 3082-a
  see also Nailery
Manumission, 577, 607, 2300, 2537-a, 2545
Manure, 338, 447
Maple sugar, 314
Maple trees, 221, 275, 345, 371

Maps
  Albemarle County, Va., 141, 753, 2350, 2789, 2801, 3137-39, 3164
  Bedford County, Va., 7, 147, 573, 1136
  canal and mill, 3130
  Charlottesville, Va., 3131
  Cumberland County, Va., 2353
  Edgehill, Va., 3137-39
  Goochland County, Va., 5
  mentioned, 2946, 3117
  Milton, Va., 753, 3131
  rivers, 3133
  survey, 2350, 2534, 2536, 2540, 2801, 3136, 3138, 3143
    see also Land, surveys of
  Tomahawk Creek, 2849
  unidentified, 3145
  Univ. of Va., 1761, 3064
  Virginia, 1, 6, 92, 1415, 1416, 1419
  Virginia-North Carolina boundary, 6
Marble, 1719, 1805, 1935, 2013, 2024, 2025, 2028, 2110, 2175, 2212, 2232, 2233, 2235, 2236, 2242, 2246, 2248, 2352, 3025, 3092
  see also Columns; Raggi brothers
Marbois, François de Barbé, 1457
Marchesi, Luigi, 101
Maria (schooner), 710
Maria (sloop), 826
Marianne (ship), 477
Mariano, D., 1723, 1734, 1820, 1829, 1913
Marigolds, 1018
Marine Department, 2464
Marine hospitals, 1017, 2831
Mariniere, Mme. de la, 379
Marion, Francis, 2961
Markey, W., 758
Markie, Alexander, 2374
Markley, Benjamin A., 1125
Marks, Anne Scott Jefferson
  health, 1138, 1140, 2416, 2994-a
  invitation to Monticello, 1066
  Peter Jefferson's estate, 140, 2434
  T. J.'s devotion to, 2300
  letter of credit for, 502-4
  letter to, 504
  mentioned, 53, 93, 1002, 1231, 1345, 1362, 1369
  package for, 2388

Monroe, James (*cont.*)
    and Memorial Library, Fredericksburg, Va.
  Mrs. James, 663, 2508
  Joseph, 345
  M. A. C., 1365
  Thomas, 2642
Monsley, Walter, 225
Mont Blanco, Chesterfield County, Va., 621, 626, 657, 658, 663, 2570
Montalto, Albemarle County, Va., 2350, 3149
Montcarrel, M., 1633
Monteagle, Albemarle County, Va., 1014, 1050, 1061, 1460, 2867-a, 2870-a, 2915, 2918, 2928, 2964
Montesquieu, Charles, 1419, 1457
Montgomery, Ala., 1951
Montgomery & Henry, 465
Monticello, Albemarle County, Va.
  account books, 2341-a, 3017
  acreages, 2789-a
  architectural plans and drawings, 1516, 2343, 2347
  art objects at, 3102, 3103
  Board of Visitors, Univ. of Va., meets at, 2917
  books for, 262, 627, 2747-a, 3078-c
  Cabell visits, 1550
  Mrs. Dabney Carr visits, 2425
  Samuel Carr visits, 2399
  cellar, 2616-a
  census of 1820, 2977-a
  chimney pieces, 2229
  climate, 238, 2463, 3119
  clock repairs, 569
  construction, 292, 404, 578, 606, 626, 656, 699, 724, 726, 779, 894, 920, 923, 1466, 1713, 1943, 2342, 2346, 2352, 2516, 2553, 2559, 2611, 2616-a, 2620, 2625, 2634, 2649, 2671, 2737, 3118
  Thomas Cooper visits, 1557, 2927
  crops, 79, 349, 441, 606, 1010, 2545-b
  Eppes refuses residence at, 780
  Eppes's trips to, 712, 778, 783, 824, 903, 2448, 2537, 2561, 2562, 2595, 2686-a
  expenses and income from, 1988
  family meetings at, 673, 707, 719, 2448, 2449, 2603
  family occupants, 2888, 2992
  farming at, 268, 275, 579, 672, 2544
  fire at, 1681, 1684
  fish pond, 1689
  furniture for, 220, 537, 2346
  garden, 238, 315, 338, 423, 425, 1054
  greenhouse, 2747-a
  harpsichord at, 611
  icehouse at, 894
  Maria Jefferson's residence, and trips to, 2416, 2456, 2481, 2559, 2561, 2599, 2605, 2654, 2659, 2661, 2683
  Martha Jefferson's residence, 2481
  T. J.'s plans to return to, 189, 456, 618
  T. J.'s trips to, 192, 193, 271, 289, 486, 608, 652, 657, 684, 695, 771, 864, 1729, 2486, 2502, 2527, 2571, 2597, 2634, 2636, 2654, 2719, 2730, 2940
  Lafayette to visit, 3045
  letters from, 22–24, 134–43, 145, 146, 196–206, 208–13, 226, 257, 268, 269, 274, 297, 299–307, 331, 332, 345, 346, 349, 360, 370, 398, 426, 441, 443, 463, 489–97, 499–502, 504, 506, 512, 521, 556, 558–66, 568–70, 575–79, 583, 585, 587, 589–91, 613, 614, 616, 631, 634, 637, 639, 640, 642, 663, 666, 698, 700, 701, 745, 794, 800, 837, 850, 852, 855, 878, 885, 889, 901, 924, 925, 945, 959, 965, 972, 992, 1001, 1002, 1005–7, 1027–30, 1032–34, 1036, 1037, 1057–60, 1063, 1065, 1066, 1073, 1076, 1078, 1087, 1088, 1091, 1092, 1094, 1096, 1098, 1101–4, 1108, 1114, 1116, 1119, 1120, 1122, 1128, 1129, 1134, 1138, 1144, 1145, 1148, 1149, 1164, 1166, 1167, 1170, 1171, 1175, 1176, 1178–80, 1201, 1212, 1215, 1218–20, 1223, 1224, 1229, 1230, 1235, 1237, 1242, 1243, 1246, 1253, 1256, 1257, 1259, 1261, 1265, 1270–74, 1278, 1286, 1299, 1305, 1308, 1309, 1312–14, 1316, 1317, 1320, 1321, 1323, 1328, 1335, 1336, 1338, 1341, 1344, 1345, 1362, 1373–76, 1378, 1379, 1385, 1391, 1392, 1394, 1395, 1404–6,

627, 628, 721, 764, 821, 823, 923,
955, 998, 1118, 1211, 2483, 2561,
2562, 2872-a, 2971-a, 3078-c
theft at, 599
trees. See under Trees
Nicholas Trist writes from, 3100
visibility from, 3111
winds at, 3117
Monticello Mountain, Albemarle
County, Va., 3113
Monticello Music Collection, 3151,
3155
Montmarin Saint-Hérem, Armand
Marc, Compte de, 111, 159
Montpelier, Orange County, Va., 1007,
1287, 1458, 2087, 2103, 2297, 2787,
2920, 3022, 3045, 3046-a
Montreal, Canada, 2351
Moody, John, 2769, 2771
Moon, Mr., 1369
Littlebury, 1653
Moore, General, 1262
Andrew, 2871
Benjamin, 1718, 1724
Bernard, 84, 2399, 2423
E., 908
Edward, 907, 908
Joseph, 47
James F., 2377
Richard Channing, 1920, 2079
Thomas, 1158, 1796
W. Bedford, 2747-a
Moore's Creek, Albemarle County,
Va., 2919
Moore's Ford, Albemarle County, Va.,
1430, 2907, 2939
Moral Tales for Young People, 2802
Morality, T. J. on, 2868-a
Moran, Mr., 905
Charles E., Jr., 2942
Moravian College for Women Library,
2776-a
Morelli (printer), 2763
Moreman, Mr., 1136
David, 1207
John H., 1207
Morgan, Colonel, 3004
Mrs. Katherine Duane, 3004
Morocco, 794, 2414
Morrir, Colonel, 659
Morris, Mr., 293

Gouverneur, 124–26, 379, 475, 491,
497, 646, 2503
Richard, 1825, 1835, 1845, 1916,
1920, 1927, 1929, 1931, 1932,
2146
Zachariah, 1165, 1171
Morris & Dunnington, 2799-a
Morrison, Colonel, 1944, 3001
William, 1951
Morrison's, Albemarle County, Va.,
2345
Morse, Mr., 648, 803
Sidney, 1981
Mortgages, 575, 2451
see also Bonds, mortgage
Mortimer, Sarah, 3028
Susan, 2831
Morton, Mr., 2820-a, 2868-b
John, 1151, 1153, 1206, 1213, 1232
see also Russell & Morton
Mrs. W. S., 47
William, 1141
Morton & Russell. See Russell &
Morton
Moseby, Mr., 573
Moseley, C. H., Jr., 37
Thomas, 1097, 1136
Moses (slave), 991, 1406, 2778
Moses, Myer, 1125
Mossis, D., 659
*Moste Favourite Minuets with Their
Basses*, 3155
Mott, Richard, 2848-b
Mouldboard plow, 187, 189, 1037
Moulds, 920
Moultrie, Mr., 1053
Mount Air, Va., 1630
Mount Airy College, 2093
Mount Vernon, Fairfax County, Va.,
460, 473, 673, 2475, 2502, 2526
Mountains, 1137
Mousley, Walter, 2428
Muhlenberg, John P. G., 43, 807, 808
Mulberry bushes, 1382, 2918-a
Mules, 566, 590, 603, 2734, 3010-a
Mullins, Mr., 2756
Henry, 321, 393
Mumps, 2526
Munford, William, 1775, 1802, 1814
Munich, Germany, 2161
Munn, Mr., 668

New Jersey (ship), 2715
New London, Conn., 829
New London, Va., 1193, 1551, 1825, 2992
New Olive Branch, . . . an Identity of Interest Between Agriculture, Manufactures, and Commerce . . ., 2974
New Orleans, La., 860, 1344, 2771
  battle of, 1344, 2883, 2888
  Batture controversy, 1092, 2828
  defense of, 982, 2793-a
  Lafayette land grant, 918, 919
  letters from, 1804, 2699
  postal service, 2678
New River, Va., 2355
New Testament, 2702, 2704, 2763, 2962-b
  see also Bible
New York (city)
  clock for, 3076
  defense of, 2793-a
  duties paid at, 2235
  glass production in, 2058
  T. J.'s housing problem, 158
  Jefferson lottery, 3091
  letters from, 78, 89, 123, 130, 132, 144, 154–56, 158–62, 164, 171–79, 183–93, 646, 1016, 1954, 1960, 1964, 1977, 2058, 2233, 2242, 2261, 2265, 2278, 2440–45, 2447–50, 3015-a, 3039-b, 3091
  letters to, 133, 165, 167, 168, 170, 180–82, 194, 382, 517, 540, 600, 1096, 2106, 2135, 2272, 2556, 2660, 2696
  mentioned, 199, 270, 884, 1148, 1426, 2010, 2081, 2133, 2215, 2229, 2248, 2385, 2767, 2828, 3025, 3044-a, 3095
  newspapers, 3058
  possible burning of, 2820-a
  shipping, 2516, 2705
  transferral of stock from, 516
  U. S. auditors at, 2361
  Washington's inauguration, 152
  yellow fever, 951
New York (state)
  climate, 2442
  Ellen Coolidge's trip, 2227
  education, 1821, 2251
  elections, 344

  petitions against Alien and Sedition Acts, 625
  prisoners at, 2377
  ratifies Constitution, 89, 106, 111
  tobacco market, 2587
  travel route, 2479
New York (frigate), 800
New York (ship), 2697
New York Athenaeum, 2278
New York Museum, 2696
Newark, N. J., 1754
Newbern, N. C., 2643
Newgate, Va., 193, 2467
Newport News, Va., 2369
Newspapers, 121, 159, 241, 255, 646, 1096, 2089, 2129, 2524, 2527-a, 2545-b, 2568, 2597, 2652, 2655, 2677, 2736, 2738, 2742, 2848, 2850, 2871, 2957, 2961, 3002, 3050, 3058
  freedom of the press, 2724
  see also names of newspapers
Newton, Colonel, 906
  Major, 1005
  Mr., Jr., 892
  Isaac, 1415
  Thomas, 1468, 2622
Niagara Falls, N. Y., 115
Nice, France, 82, 1647, 2952, 2953
Nicholas, Colonel, 3001, 3002
  Mr., 2079, 2122, 2490
  Mrs., 2417
  George, 1, 282, 2559
  George W., 2009
  John, 624, 2537-a, 2545-a, 2576
  John, Jr.
    clerk of Albemarle County, 11, 13, 577, 752, 784, 785, 798, 799, 838, 843, 870, 897, 907, 914, 915, 970, 977, 1039, 1123
    views academy site, 1306
    witness, 580
  John, Sr., 1, 10, 140, 143, 299
  Philip N., 1882, 2314, 2588-a, 3091-a
  Robert Carter, xvi, 1, 20, 1339, 2364, 2711, 2806, 2871, 2891
  Wilson Cary
    appointment considered, 692
    bond to J. W. Eppes, 1380
    break with Monroe, 1429
    debts of, 1737, 1752, 1798, 1923, 1951, 1968, 1988
    estate of, 1944

Republican Party (*cont.*)
  newspapers, 255
  oration, 1242
  Pennsylvania, 639, 2508
  principles of, 684, 687, 691, 762
  Supreme Court, 1092
  Vermont, 2639, 2641
  victory, 418, 690, 2508
  views on public debt, 420
Republican spirit, 2883-b
Republicanism, 647, 655, 2572, 2711, 2925
Republicans, 994, 2636
Restrictions system, 2866
Retail business, 949, 1151
Reuben (slave), 1336
Revenue laws, 2722
Review of Montesquieu, 1119, 1135, 1270, 1335, 1395, 1404
Revolts. See Insurrections
Revolutionary War. See American Revolution
Rey, Jesse, 1183
Reynolds, Rowland, 1718, 1724, 1732, 1735
Rhenegher's Tavern, McAllister's Town, 2592
Rhetoric, 3039-a
Rhin, Vin du, 2952
Rhode Island
  act concerning, 183
  Constitution, 89, 102, 106, 156
  General Assembly, 706
  T. J.'s visit to, 192
  opposition to federal control of commerce, 68
  U. S. courts in, 180
Rhode Island Resolutions, 2891
Rhubarb, 3082
Rice, 176, 266, 497, 821, 823, 923, 1211, 1215, 1924, 2545-b, 2831
Rice, George, 2377
  Rev. J. H., 1610, 1776, 1779, 1785, 1920
Rich Neck, Va., 442, 2369
Richards, John, 66, 674, 699, 721, 726, 729, 796, 931
  Mark, 805, 2641
Richardson, Mr., 1800
  Dan, 689
  David, 870
  Richard

  mentioned, 638, 656
  overseer at Monticello, 599, 606, 650, 654, 659, 672, 2588
  witness, 2550, 2577
  see also Fox & Richardson
Richardson & Scruggs, 303
Richelieu, Duke de, 271
Richerson, Mr., 1068
Richeson, John D., 3084
Richland, Vt., 2641
Richmond, Va.
  Bank of, 2372, 2833, 2863, 2897, 2951, 2959, 2975, 3095
  Bank of U. S. at, 3061
  books in, 2100, 2727
  bricklayers, 1508
  carriage prices, 3011
  Mr. Cassinove's visit to, 258
  Chickasaw Indians go to, 2578
  college at, 2140
  Common, 2846
  corn prices, 2895
  Court of Appeals, 907
  defense against British in 1814, 1315
  Enquirer, 960, 1520, 1537, 1627, 1633, 1949, 2129, 2156, 2174, 2287, 3033
  flour sales, 1227, 2799-a
  Gazette, 2524
  Governor's House, 2336
  Charles Johnston & Co., 2545-b
  land, 225, 282, 2805, 2806, 2817, 2846
  letters from, 32, 33, 39, 40, 45, 163, 169, 214, 296, 312, 377, 421, 436, 442, 533, 715, 819, 820, 830, 1031, 1045, 1079, 1080, 1084, 1093, 1181, 1186, 1214, 1216, 1262, 1272, 1275, 1322, 1324, 1332, 1377, 1387, 1389, 1390, 1397, 1400, 1402, 1432, 1437, 1438, 1493, 1500, 1504, 1511, 1520, 1528, 1529, 1531, 1533–35, 1537–40, 1543, 1544, 1546, 1569, 1583–86, 1588, 1597, 1600, 1602, 1603, 1608, 1610, 1612, 1614, 1618, 1628, 1633, 1635, 1643, 1644, 1649, 1654, 1656, 1665, 1671, 1681, 1767, 1772, 1774, 1814, 1824, 1833, 1835, 1836, 1840, 1842, 1843, 1845, 1847, 1878, 1889, 1916, 1920, 1922, 1925, 1927, 1929, 1931, 1957,

inoculation of, 268
Monticello, 315, 318, 425, 606, 955,
1054, 1106, 2425, 2748
pecan, 221, 745, 2378
Philadelphia, 337, 445
Poplar Forest, 1137
Prince William County, 2497
silk, 1923
sugar maple, 275, 345, 371
Trent, Mr., 306
Alexander, 1653
Trenton, N. J., 2531
Trepanning operation, 842
Trials, 2728
Trigonometry, 2799, 3165, 3167
Trinity College, 1718, 2063
Tripoli, 794, 800
Trist, Mr., 534, 2559
Mrs., 158, 219, 227, 236, 271, 334,
1729, 2699
Browse, 3038
Elizabeth, 1053
letters from, 1056, 2699
letters to, 2859, 2888
Hore Browse, 351, 603, 612, 766,
2979
Hore Browse, Jr., 2979
Mary, 2699
Nicholas P.
copies and extracts of T. J.'s letters, 68, 78, 86, 87, 97, 98, 102,
103, 105, 106, 108, 111, 113,
117, 119, 156, 166, 177, 188,
231, 263, 266, 320, 343, 360,
561, 614, 615, 622, 623, 625,
637, 639, 647, 649, 661, 690,
691, 694, 708, 730, 757, 760,
761, 769, 862, 1027–30, 1032,
1049, 1101, 1253, 1375, 1395,
1409, 1806, 1811, 1816, 1828,
1875, 1887, 1888, 1904, 2011,
2275, 2319, 2988-a, 3073, 3096,
3100, 3100-a, 3159
introduction for T. J. letter, 2289
T. J.'s executor, 2300
letters to, 2829, 3038
mentioned, 2332
notes by, 3094-a
Trist family, 701
Troast, G., 2123
Troughton, Mrs., 1754
Troup, George M., 2199

Trueheart, George W., 2153
Washington, 1552
Trumbull, John, 95, 101, 104, 114, 115,
120, 125, 126, 2265, 2444, 2590
Trump, Mr., 635
Tryon, William, 26
Tuckahoe, Goochland County, Va.
letters from, 289, 410, 1639
mentioned, 260, 274, 514
Tucker, Mr., 1629, 2378
George, 2119, 2122, 2127, 2154, 2160,
2171, 2241, 2264, 3058-a, 3084
Henry, 2358
Henry St. George, 1470, 1500, 1511,
1614, 2154, 2218, 2269, 3063
James, 2736
John, 1280
St. George, 700, 1957, 2146, 2154,
2358, 2549, 2912
Mrs. St. George, 2087
William, 23
Tudor, Mrs., 725
Tufton, Lady Caroline, 192, 271
Tufton, Albemarle County, Va., 1694,
2289, 2544, 2789-a, 2937, 3109,
3115
Tuggle, Henry, 31
Tullos, Richard, 592, 861, 1131, 1136,
1156–58, 1165, 1171, 1177, 1188
Tunis, 794, 800, 994
Tunis, Bey of, 994
Turin, Italy, 82, 83
Turkey Island, Henrico County, Va.,
2700
Turkeys, 2386, 2751, 2933
Turner, Mr., 3075
Fleming, 1013
N., 1569
Sharon, 3054
Thomas, 2642
Turnips, 366, 675, 2693
Turnpike, 1430
Bill, 1437, 1438
company, 2939
Turnpike, Va., 3147
Turpentine, 1103
Turpin, Dr., 651
Mr., 25, 1136
Philip, 2342, 2385
Thomas, 7, 10, 2342
Tuther, John, 2142
Tutthill vs. Roberts, 2478

"Tweed Side," 3152
Two-penny Act, 2871
Twyman, James, 779
Tyler, John, 1933, 2079, 2122, 2595
Tynes, Rev. John, 2142
Type-founding, 396

Union (ship), 430
Union College, 1754
Union dinner, 661
Unionism, 2888
Unitarians, 1922
United States
  Archives. See United States, public
    papers
  Army, 35, 610, 973, 2742-a, 2793-a
  see also Militia; United States,
    Continental Line
  Attorney General, 3157
  Bank. See Bank of the United States
  Bonds. See Bonds, United States;
    Loan office certificates
  boundary, 1754
  cipher codes, 56, 2390
  citizenship, 2840
  Commissioners of Bankruptcy. See
    Bankruptcy, Commissioners of
  Commissioners to the Indian Treaty,
    2517
  Comptroller, 2563, 2580
  Congress
    acts of, 2439, 2518, 2636-a, 2771
    adjournment, 413, 771, 2502, 2516,
      2559, 2562, 2587, 2678, 2683
    appropriations, 2438
    convening of, 2527, 2591
    debates, 123, 2547
    difficulties with, 2682, 2684
    Hamilton's control over, 360
    Patrick Henry leaves, 2910
    Journals of, 1939, 3002
    mentioned, 59, 113, 371, 385, 476,
      518, 639, 766, 1109, 1253,
      1923, 2375-a, 2416, 2530, 2782-
      a, 2793-a, 2823
    no session, 2677
    petitions to remit tariff, 1905–
      1907, 2239, 2286, 2298, 3000,
      3045, 3092
    at Philadelphia, 171, 176, 186,
      2442, 2444, 2508, 2910
    purchase of T. J.'s library, 1395,
      1405
    qualifications for members of,
      1273
    removal to Lancaster, Penn., 522
    work load, 2493
    see also United States, House
      of Representatives; United
      States, Senate
  Constitution
    amendments to, 177, 2745-a
    compared to British, 231
    division of powers, 706, 1273, 1395
    Hamilton and T. J. on, 360
    T. J.'s views on, 86, 188, 266, 360,
      601, 694, 730, 757, 760, 763,
      989, 1091, 1101, 1253, 2202, 2275,
      2596
    James Madison discusses, 89
    nullification, 1055
    opposition, 156, 2711
    property under, 267
    provisions for ambassadors, 2728
    ratification, 89, 96–98, 102, 103,
      105, 106, 108, 111, 113, 117,
      119
  Constitutional Convention, 78, 87,
    89, 1939
  consular service. See under United
    States, State Department
  Continental Congress, 39, 40, 68,
    2358, 2370, 2385, 2386, 2586,
    2711, 2957
  Continental Line, 2360, 2368, 2373-c,
    2377
    southern regiments, 2369
    Virginia regiments, 2361, 2373,
      2711
    see also Militia
  courts. See United States, judiciary
  currency, 2368, 2602-a, 2833
  Declaration of Independence. See
    Declaration of Independence
  District Court, 2371
  economy, 1489, 2800-a, 2820-a, 2872-a
  elections. See Elections
  executive branch, 89, 385, 730, 1101
  fiscal policy, 231, 2549
  foreign affairs, 1261, 2413, 2464,
    3002
    see also France; Great Britain;

illness of, 277, 283
T. J.'s confidence in, 102
T. J.'s opinion submitted, 438
letters from, 130, 132, 144
letters to, 133, 263, 343, 360, 469,
    494–497
mail for, 2475
mentioned, 89, 344, 354, 355, 406,
    460, 473, 474, 509, 544, 681,
    924, 1055, 1091, 2385, 2482-a,
    2530, 2910
monarchist tendencies, 640
at Mt. Vernon, 2502, 2526
Philadelphia, 478, 518, 534, 2522
portraits of, 2124, 3035
praised by Petersburg citizens, 482
presidency, 343, 584
print of (?), 2666
sailing party with T. J., 171
scheme of crop rotation, 369
southern trip by, 243, 2485
speeches, 311, 2493
statue of, 2582-a
sugar maple seed for, 371
vetoes representation bill, 339
visits Rhode Island, 192
Martha, 311, 673
William, 743, 744
Washington, D. C.
bank, 2647
British attack of 1814, 1307, 1310
commercial center, 1118
commissioners, 230, 2636-a
construction prices, 1762
Court clerk, 3001
embargo report, 2813
flood danger, 1309
housing costs, 2591
T. J.'s stay in, 2599, 2604
letters from, 673, 677, 681, 682, 684,
    685, 688, 690–93, 695, 702, 707,
    708, 712–14, 717–20, 725, 738,
    739, 746–48, 754, 760, 762, 763,
    766, 768, 770, 771, 775, 776, 779,
    781, 804, 812, 813, 816, 818, 821,
    822, 827, 829, 831, 832, 834, 835,
    839, 840, 846, 847, 858, 864, 867,
    869, 876, 892–94, 896, 900, 904,
    906, 912, 913, 918–20, 928, 929,
    935, 938, 952, 955, 957, 960, 973–
    75, 984, 985, 987, 990, 993, 994,

1010, 1017, 1022, 1023, 1026,
    1041, 1048, 1049, 1051, 1054,
    1074, 1081, 1100, 1229, 1547,
    1599, 1651, 1726, 1727, 1757,
    1810, 1820, 1864, 1867, 1938–
    41, 1947, 2063, 2065, 2128, 2141,
    2147, 2298, 2320, 2591, 2595,
    2596, 2604, 2607–10, 2612, 2613-
    a, 2620-a, 2622, 2623, 2626, 2630,
    2632–34, 2636, 2636-a, 2642,
    2643, 2647, 2649, 2650, 2651,
    2654–56, 2658–62, 2665–67,
    2669, 2674, 2678, 2681–84,
    2686-a, 2690, 2692, 2697-a, 2698,
    2700, 2704, 2717–19, 2723, 2730,
    2734-a, 2738, 2744, 2745-a, 2747-
    a, 2749, 2755, 2759, 2766, 2769,
    2773, 2774, 2779, 2781-a, 2782-a,
    2786, 3001
letters to, 669, 672, 674–76, 678, 679,
    686, 697, 703–5, 711, 716, 732,
    741, 745, 749, 750, 756, 764, 774,
    780, 782, 783, 794, 800, 806–8,
    810, 811, 814, 815, 817, 818, 820,
    824, 825, 830, 833, 836, 837, 841,
    842, 844, 845, 859, 860, 863, 865,
    868, 872–75, 877–82, 895, 905,
    910, 916, 922, 925, 927, 931, 932,
    934, 936, 940, 959, 961, 962, 969,
    972, 976, 980, 983, 986, 988, 991,
    998, 999, 1014–16, 1018, 1020,
    1021, 1037, 1038, 1040, 1042–47,
    1050, 1052, 1053, 1065, 1069,
    1119, 1523, 1592, 1893, 1945,
    2016, 2138, 2590, 2603, 2701,
    2771, 3015
James Madison's stay in, 2920
mentioned, 509, 729, 1095, 3004,
    3067, 3076
National Intelligencer. See *National
    Intelligencer*
origins, 290
public buildings, 831, 832, 2336
purchase of, 183
retail business in 1151
sale of lots in, 2636-a
shipping, 2632
slave uprising, 802
society in, 707
trips to, 814, 1052, 2746, 2772,
    2781-a, 2787

mentioned, 72, 79, 314, 415, 941, 993,
1950, 2686-a, 2944, 3027
tariffs on, 856, 2472-b
see also names of wines
Wingfield, Mr., 3101
Charles, 2804
Christopher, 907
William, 907
Winn, John, 1208, 1306, 1988, 2009
Richard, 47
Winn [John] and Davis, 3097
Winston, Edmund, 1470
Horatio G., 2153
John, 2360
Winter, 2788
Wintipock, 22
Wirt, William
attorney for T. J., 985, 1092, 1178,
1179, 1191, 1460
lettercover from, 3157
letters from, 2709, 2911
letters to, 1179, 2710, 2871, 2891,
2908, 2909, 2912, 2914
mentioned, 1111, 1393, 1479, 2065,
2312, 2961
Sketches . . . of Patrick Henry, 2908–
12, 2914
see also Hay, Wirt & Tazewell
Wishaupt, Mr., 648
Wistar, Dr. Caspar
death of, 1530, 1536, 1545
letter for, 1328
mentioned, 1040, 1052, 1138, 1757
teaching methods, 2059
vaccine from, 2774
Witherspoon, Dr., 348
John, 2386
Witkins, I., 709, 2636
Woglome, Abraham, 1664
Wolf, Johann Christian von, 438
see also Martin vs. Wolf
Wolf breeding, 2474
Wollaston, William H., 2868-a
Wood, 323, 2507, 2515, 3007
see also Firewood; Lumber
Wood, Colonel, 19, 2375-a
Mr., 575, 1078, 2923, 2943
Billy, 589
Daniel, 2507
David, 362
Dick, 2544

Henry, 2, 3
James, 19, 592, 2373-a, 2373-b,
2373-c, 2383-a, 2544
Jane, 2544
John, 908, 1493, 1498, 2276
Lucy, 2544
Lucy Henderson. See Lucy Hender-
son
Reuben, 2544
Valentine, 31
William, 750, 907, 1183, 1332, 2544,
2700-a
Wooddeson, Richard, 2988
Woodhouse, Dr., 1040, 1060
Seabrook, 37
Woodlawn, Va., 1140, 1217
Woods, Mr., 1365, 2845-a
Micajah, 1459, 2100
William, 642, 741, 753, 1459, 1761
John, 9, 31
Samuel, 304–6, 316, 553, 643, 669,
2489, 2491
Tucker M., 643, 685, 907–9, 935
Wood's, Albemarle County, Va., 2345
Woodson and Lewis, 316, 553, 2489,
2491
see also Robert Lewis; Samuel
Woodson
Woodson's Ferry, 3132
Woodstock, Va., 2467
Woodward, Rufus, 1795
William W., 2700-b
Wool, 1336, 2779, 2781, 2820-a
Wool-carding machines, 1265
Wool cards, 3056
Woolwich, England, 2208, 2257
Wooton, William, 47
Workman, James, 989
Wormely, Captain, 3055
Wormly (slave), 969, 1729, 2759, 2778,
3012
Worthington, Charles, 2779-a
Wrappers, 3163, 3164
Wray, Major George, 363
Wren, Colonel, 2690
Wren's, Va., 2467
Wright, Joseph, 2530
Writing desks, 545, 2259, 2262, 2465,
2531, 3094
Wyandotte Indians, 35, 2754
Wycombe, Lord, 266

Errata

Item No.	Correction
52	For *John Wayles* Eppes, read *Francis* Eppes.
54–55	For *James* Maury read *Matthew* Maury.
282	For *Edward* Randolph, read *Edmund* Randolph.
323	Delete *Photostat*.
335	For Mar. *14*, read Mar. *4*.
374	For date *1972*, read *1792*.
451	For Aug. *3*, read Aug. *31*.
572	For date *1895*, read *1795*.
595	For date *1797*, read *1791*.
666	For Aug. *23*, read Aug. *28*.
682	For Anne *Jefferson*, read Anne *Randolph*.
750	For Nov. *11*, read Nov. *6*.
875	For date *1804*, read *1805*.
878	For Mar. *10*, read Mar. *12*.
1008	For date *1807*, read *1801*.
1019	Omit this item. Correct date given in item 1042.
1091	For Sept. *10*, read Sept. *20*.
1131	For *Edward* Tate, read *Edmund* Tate.
1191	Letter is from T. J.
1267	Add Sept. 7 to date.
1351	Omit this item. Correct date given in item 1557a.
1420	For *Biddle*, read *Riddle*.
1426	For *Biddle*, read *Riddle*.
1427	For *Biddle*, read *Riddle*.
1447	For *T. M.* Randolph, Jr., read *John* Randolph.
1453	For *Cobbate*, read *Abbott*.
1488	For Oct. *24*, read Oct. *26*.
1501	For *Zaccariah* Collins, read *Zaccheus* Collins.
1601	For Jan. *20*, read Jan. *24*.
1988	For *Branham*, read *Bramham*.
2025	For Sept. *23*, read Sept. *20*.
2100	For *William* Russell, read *Michael* Russell.
2711	For *1805 Aug. 4*, read *1812 Apr. 12*.

Nos. 581, 592, 643, 732, 736, 1054, 1207, 1647, and 2133 are in the McGregor Library; Nos. 702 and 1399 are in the Carr-Cary Papers; Nos. 778 and 1117 were deposited by Robert H. Kean; Nos. 1972 and 2074 are in the Edgehill-Randolph Papers.